NO REGRETS

# No Regrets

## *The Rise and Fall of Sir William Hearst*

BRIAN DOUGLAS TENNYSON

UNIVERSITY OF TORONTO PRESS
Toronto Buffalo London

Toronto Buffalo London
utppublishing.com
Printed in Canada

ISBN 978-1-4875-5009-7 (cloth)
ISBN 978-1-4875-5013-4 (EPUB)
ISBN 978-1-4875-5010-3 (UPDF)

**Library and Archives Canada Cataloguing in Publication**

Title: No regrets : the rise and fall of Sir William Hearst / Brian Douglas Tennyson.
Names: Tennyson, Brian Douglas, author
Description: Includes bibliographical references and index.
Identifiers: Canadiana (print) 20260129577 | Canadiana (ebook) 20260129593 | ISBN 9781487550097 (cloth) | ISBN 9781487550103 (PDF) | ISBN 9781487550134 (EPUB)
Subjects: LCSH: Hearst, William, Sir, 1864-1941. | LCSH: Progressive Conservative Party of Ontario. | LCSH: Premiers (Canada)—Ontario—Biography. | LCSH: Politicians—Ontario—Biography. | LCSH: Ontario—Politics and government—20th century. | CSH: Ontario—Politics and government—1905-1919. | LCGFT: Biographies.
Classification: LCC FC3073.1.H43 T46 2026 | DDC 971.3/03092—dc23

Cover design: Alexa Love
Cover image: Sir William Hearst, Premier of Ontario Date: ca. 1930 (Archives of Ontario)

The manufacturer's authorized representative in the European Union for product safety is Mare Nostrum Group B.V., Doelen 72, 4831 GR Breda, The Netherlands. Email: gpsr@mare-nostrum.co.uk

We wish to acknowledge the land on which the University of Toronto Press operates. This land is the traditional territory of the Wendat, the Anishnaabeg, the Haudenosaunee, the Métis, and the Mississaugas of the Credit First Nation.

University of Toronto Press acknowledges the financial support of the Government of Canada, the Canada Council for the Arts, and the Ontario Arts Council, an agency of the Government of Ontario, for its publishing activities.

Canada Council for the Arts Conseil des Arts du Canada

Funded by the Government of Canada Financé par le gouvernement du Canada

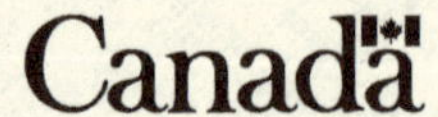

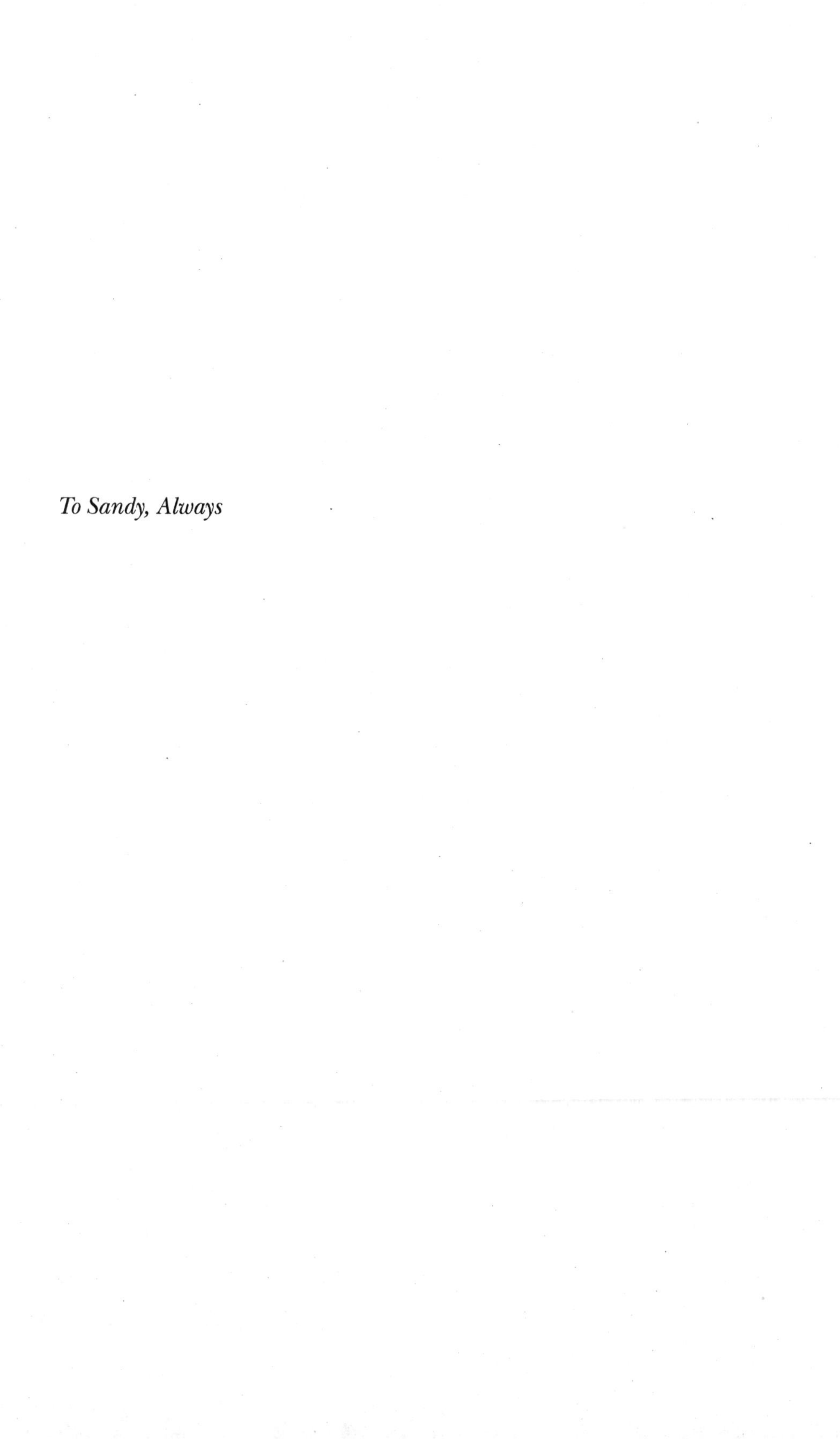

*To Sandy, Always*

# Contents

# Foreword

A hometown can evoke a feeling that is difficult to describe. It's that special place where you feel at ease. It's a place that you know inside and out. For me, Sault Ste. Marie is that place. It's the place I love to talk about to anyone willing to listen. It's why I was surprised, many years ago, to learn that Sault Ste. Marie was home to a Premier of Ontario I had never heard of. As someone interested in both history and politics, it seemed unfathomable that a former Ontario Premier was not being celebrated by my hometown. It became even more unfathomable when I learned of the enormous and lasting impact that Sir William Hearst had on Ontario. From recognizing women's voting rights to enacting prohibition to more than doubling the size of the province to introducing the first worker's compensation system, Sir William H. Hearst undeniably left his mark. Yet, here was Sault Ste. Marie – nearly a century after his time as Premier – letting history get lost in the cracks of time. The more I learned, the more committed I became to ensuring that Premier Hearst got his proper due. I researched and wrote a brief article about him for a magazine about local history called *Townies.* Around the same time, I was a summer student at City Hall, and every so often, I would pass along *Townies* articles to the city councillors I encountered in the hope that they would spur some municipal recognition of Premier Hearst's achievements. Unfortunately, they did not, and this cemented my drive to right this wrong. I was already keenly interested in politics and decided that if I were ever in a position with the capacity to effect change, I would make sure Hearst got his due. The next five to seven years involved researching every piece of history I could find about Hearst – with no specific goal in mind – but knowing in the back of my mind there was enough content to fill a book on his Premiership.

In my research, I kept coming across the same name over and over, that of Brian Douglas Tennyson. It seemed that over forty years earlier, there was another student of Hearst's who did much of the research and was the authoritative figure on his accomplishments. By chance and through my continued research, I stumbled upon a source reference to a thesis Tennyson had written in 1969 about Hearst. I was, at that time, a student at the University of Ottawa, so I went to the Library and Archives Canada building to track down this thesis. I was told it was on microfiche, so to print it would take some time. Finally, I did receive it – I had hit the Hearst jackpot. The next week or so was spent reviewing 200 pages of Hearst information and 700 footnotes for source materials. It was bliss! The microfiche thesis was old and partly illegible, so, where I could, I tried to make sense of otherwise incomprehensible materials.

Despite the difficulty reading it, the material was understandable enough to get a sense of the importance of Hearst's impact on Ontario at the time and the aspects of Ontario today that could trace their roots back to his term in office. On a whim, I decided to look more closely into the thesis's author, Mr. Tennyson. For someone who had written a PhD thesis in 1969, rough math told me he would be of fairly advanced age in the mid-2010s – if he was still alive. I found a Brian Tennyson who was professor emeritus at Cape Breton University, so I reached out to the university to see if it had contact information. A reply back confirmed they had passed my outreach on to a then-retired Professor Tennyson, who subsequently emailed me directly. I was now in personal contact with the authority on Hearst. This would be like a Beatles fan meeting Paul McCartney. Professor Tennyson could not have been more generous. I explained my deep interest in Hearst's Premiership and the fact that, while I had read his thesis, I missed large portions of it because of the poor quality of the microfiche from which it was printed. Being that it was written many years before a "soft copy" was a concept, Professor Tennyson rifled through his attic and sent me an original hard copy, printed on onion-skin paper, which was in mint condition. As all this was happening, I was also elected to the Sault Ste. Marie City Council and was finally in a position to help Hearst get his due. I struck a committee to look at ways to honour him, and it recommended that the City of Sault Ste. Marie rename its municipal holiday from "Civic Holiday" to "Sir William H. Hearst Day." The recommendation was passed unanimously at Council, and since 2015, the first Monday in August is Sir William H. Hearst Day in the City of Sault Ste. Marie.

The next step in the Hearst journey was, I believe, the definitive step that led to this book. My law firm, the Wishart Law Firm, had organized a fundraiser for a local child development centre. A partner of the law firm had gone to law school with Dalton McGuinty, himself a former Ontario Premier, who had, at this time, just released his own memoirs.

In an effort to raise additional funds for the fundraiser, it was decided to invite Premier McGuinty to Sault Ste. Marie to combine his book tour with the fundraiser for the child development centre. I was tasked with what should have been the simple duty of arranging for a gift of gratitude for Premier McGuinty. Armed with a single copy of the onion-skin Hearst thesis, I knew there would be no better gift for an Ontario Premier pitching his own memoirs than the definitive history of a past Ontario Premier. I sat at my kitchen table for the next seven consecutive evenings and typed the thesis, word by word, footnote by footnote. I printed and bound it and gave a copy to Premier McGuinty – a unique gift for his role in a successful fundraiser. I sent the soft copy to Professor Tennyson and asked about pitching it to publishers, which he agreed to and which I did for the next short while. After getting no uptake, I thought the cause was lost.

Until, that is, Professor Tennyson informed me that he intended to rewrite his 1969 thesis with a view to publishing it. He worked at it for what likely ended up being roughly four years, with draft chapters sent to me to review periodically. Draft after redraft, followed by publisher outreach and pestering, finally produced what you are reading: the definitive history of Sir William H. Hearst's Premiership. This book gives Hearst his due. He made mistakes. He got things right. It is all here for you, and history, to judge.

What I hope this book does is help Ontarians realize the impact a single MPP from Sault Ste. Marie was able to have on our province at a critical time in our history and how the decisions of the past continue to inform our present. More than anything else, I encourage anyone who has a passion for something to chase it down the rabbit hole and see it through. For me, that passion is Sault Ste. Marie. Hearst's role in my hometown history is just one of the tools I have used to try to show the greatness of Sault Ste. Marie to the world abroad, and this book serves as a tremendous means to tell an overlooked part of our history.

Matthew Shoemaker

NO REGRETS

The Rise and Fall of Sir William Hearst

# Introduction

WILLIAM Howard Hearst has been a part of my life for a very long time. I first discovered him in 1962 when I was in the MA program in history at the University of Toronto. That program offered two options: two courses and a thesis or four courses and no thesis. I chose the first option because I had discovered during my undergraduate years in the modern history honours program that I enjoyed research and writing. That discovery, greatly reinforced by the experience of spending months in the national and provincial archives while in the master's program led me to change my career plan from teaching high school history to becoming a historian.

The two courses I took were Maurice Careless's seminar on pre-confederation Ontario history and Jack Saywell's seminar on modern Canadian political history. I enjoyed them both, which was hardly surprising because I liked almost every course I had taken in the undergraduate program, but I was particularly keen on political history. So keen that I confess that I joined the campus Progressive Conservative Club – it was 1958, after all – and rose to the dizzy height of president for two years, much to the dismay of my father and grandfather, both of whom were life-long Liberals. As for Jack Saywell, I think he found it amusing to have an apparently otherwise reasonably sensible young man in his seminar. In retrospect, I believe that my extensive exposure to practical politics and many politicians was valuable practical experience for someone who planned to spend his life studying Canadian political history. And to be honest, I had a lot of fun and met many interesting people, including the Liberal, New Democrat, and Communist leaders who visited the campus.

For students who were seriously interested in Canadian political history it was an exciting time. Donald Creighton published his hugely popular two-volume biography of Sir John A. Macdonald in 1955 and 1956, Roger Graham published his first volume on Arthur Meighen in

1960, and MacGregor Dawson published his first volume on W.L. Mackenzie King two years later. On the provincial level, Margaret Prang completed her doctoral dissertation on Newton Rowell in 1959, and Charles Humphries completed his on Sir James Whitney in 1966, and both were eventually published in the Ontario government's ambitious Historical Studies project. Over the years this project published biographies of Mowat, Whitney, Ferguson, Drury, Hepburn, Frost, and Robarts, but not Hearst.

This notable omission clearly reflected the belief that he was an insignificant transitional figure. Margaret Prang's biography of Rowell refers to Hearst occasionally but in a distant way as though he was a minor figure, while Charles Humphries apparently thought Hearst so insignificant that he mentions him only three times in his biography of Whitney, even though Whitney's last act before he died in 1914 was to ensure that Hearst succeeded him as Premier. Charles Johnston only mentions Hearst briefly when discussing the transfer of power to Drury in 1919. Peter Oliver pays more attention to Hearst because Ferguson played a major role in his government, but his focus is obviously elsewhere, and he ignores the political and social environment of 1919 when he argues simplistically that it was Hearst's weak leadership and general incompetence that caused the government's defeat in 1919.[1]

And yet, Hearst was a very significant political figure before and during the First World War. He championed the opening up and development of northern Ontario, provided the leadership that made Ontario the industrial heartland of Canada during the war while providing 40 per cent of the men who enlisted in the Canadian Expeditionary Force, and closely aligned himself and his government with the governments of Robert Borden. Even then, the growing literature on various aspects of Ontario history during the first couple of decades of the twentieth century, including the province's involvement in the war makes very few references to Hearst, although some scholars have begun assessing his government's economic and social policies. Even historians who focus on the province's environmental and Indigenous history rarely mention him. Brittany Luby, for example, manages to discuss Hearst's decision in 1915 to remove jurisdiction over waterways from Indigenous reserves without mentioning his name in her challenging book, *Dammed: The Politics of Loss and Survival in Anishinaabe Territory*.[2] This apparent lack of interest in him is symbolized by the fact that the Ontario Archives, even though they house his papers, possess only one photograph of him, and it was taken in 1929, ten years after he left office.

That was why I decided to write my thesis on Hearst. For obvious reasons I knew virtually nothing about him other than that he was responsible for prohibition and giving women the vote but was thrown out of office after one term. But that was an advantage because he was in effect a blank canvas. Equally important was that the provincial archives, where his papers were housed, was conveniently situated on the edge of the University of Toronto campus, just across the road from Queen's Park, in those days. I completed the thesis in the summer of 1963 and received my degree at fall convocation on the evening of 22 November, a date better remembered by most people as the day that President John F. Kennedy was murdered in Dallas.

I went on to study at the Institute of Commonwealth Studies (ICS) at the University of London and in due course was awarded my PhD. That research and the remarkably stimulating seminars at the ICS attended by not only faculty and graduate students but also visiting scholars from all over the Commonwealth and the United States greatly stimulated my interest in imperial relations in the period that bracketed the First World War, so my two theses actually had something in common because Hearst, like many Canadians during the war, was a committed imperialist. Over the years I taught a variety of courses at Cape Breton University and published some books and several journal articles on aspects of Canada's participation in the war and that, perhaps inevitably, brought me back to Hearst because historians were still ignoring him or dismissing him as an insignificant political figure.

How could that be, given that he had introduced popular social reforms such as bringing under control the very serious social plague of alcohol, enfranchised women, established reconstruction programs for veterans, introduced mothers' allowances (the equivalent of the federal family allowance program established in 1945), subsidized public housing, and reformed the educational system to make it more relevant to an increasingly industrial society? His government had also played a major role in encouraging industrial development by fostering the huge pulp and paper mining industries, including pressuring them to build mills and smelters within the province. But because his government had firmly aligned itself with the Borden government and conscription, many people, most notably rural farmers and urban workers, wanted not only that the post-war world should be a better place but that traditional politics somehow should be replaced with a better system. Hearst was frankly bewildered by the chaos and didn't handle it well, and this book tries to explain why. It should be needless to say that he was not the only politician who struggled with the situation, just one of the first.

There are various ways to explore Canada's experience of the war and biography is one of them. Many books and journal articles have been written about the war period, examining and attempting to explain the military, political, economic, and social aspects, but memoirs and biographies humanize the story because they help us to understand how real people responded to the experience and how it affected them, their families, and their communities. As L.P. Hartley famously wrote in 1953, "the past is a foreign country; they do things differently there."[3] That was a profound observation. Trying more than a century later to understand the values, experiences and behaviour of the men and women who lived during the war years requires us to realize that most middle-aged adults like Hearst were born in the 1860s or 1870s and were the sons and daughters of immigrants, most of them poor people from Britain who arrived with little or nothing but cleared land on which to farm or settled in the country's many small urban centres as labourers or factory workers.

Hearst represents those people. His father emigrated from northern Ireland at the age of fifteen with little or no education but understanding that his choices were to work hard or starve. He worked on farms, married and raised a large family, and eventually got his own farm in Bruce County in western Ontario. He was very typical of the people from the land of his birth and of many if not most Ontarians of his time: a staunch Methodist, Orangeman and Conservative. Of his nine children only the youngest, William, was able to obtain an education but even that only extended to high school, after which he articled with a lawyer because university and law school were far beyond the family's reach. Hearst's ability to obtain a profession despite his humble background because of the support of his family was not unusual; in fact, it was common. To cite just one example, Newton Rowell, who became Hearst's major political rival over the years, had the same background, and yet both men became successful lawyers and prominent politicians.

I didn't realize it at the time, but in retrospect I think I was drawn to Hearst because I felt a very real connection between his family's history and mine. My great-great grandfather emigrated from Yorkshire in 1817 at the age of twelve. His family followed two years later and, like the Hearsts, the Tennysons moved around trying to find good farmland. Hearst's family eventually settled in Bruce County as did my great-great grandfather, albeit some years later. Other Tennysons settled in communities like Paisley and Walkerton, and Port Elgin in Huron County, communities that Hearst would have known well.

A successful biography depends to a considerable extent on the author's ability to gain a thorough knowledge of his subject in order to gain some understanding of his attitudes and behaviour. Unfortunately, Hearst did not leave a diary or a rich collection of letters, but I was able to interview his two sons, Vernon and Irving, and Irving kindly sent me copies of family correspondence that was very helpful in tracing its background in Ireland and immigration to Canada. Many years later he also wrote a lengthy and very personal memoir of his father, based on his own recollections as well as stories that his father shared with him. He also donated to the Ontario Archives a valuable collection of letters that his father wrote to him when he was serving overseas during the war. Vernon's grandson, Chris De Guerre, has also kindly shared information and photographs. I have, of course, consulted extensively the records of other relevant political figures of the period and made extensive use of newspapers. This was more important than it might be today because newspapers were generally owned by individuals, not corporations, and they expressed the views of their proprietors, most of whom took a keen interest in politics.

Fortunately, historians in recent years, while largely ignoring Hearst, have published many scholarly publications on the political, economic, and social history of the times, and I have made much use of them in an effort to understand not just Hearst's decisions, behaviour, successes, and failures but also the context in which he lived and functioned. The reader will, of course, decide if I have been successful, but I have striven to avoid falling into the trap of hagiography.

I make no claim that Hearst was a great man but his almost total neglect and the casual ridicule by writers who didn't – and actually couldn't – know much about him is shocking a century later. What I do claim is that he was a well-intentioned man who, while partisan, genuinely meant it when he said, as he often did, that he would rather be rejected by the voters than do something that he thought was not in the interests of the province. In fact, he may have been the only major Canadian politician in office who suspended partisan politics during the war years and enjoyed the support of his opponents until the summer of 1918. His closest political colleague, Howard Ferguson, thought he was naïve and didn't really understand politics, and perhaps he was right because Ferguson's political career proved to be much more successful than Hearst's.

He entered politics because he was young and ambitious, of course, but also because he was a Macdonald Conservative who believed profoundly in the National Policy and was convinced that Ontario was the "empire province" because of its size, geographic location, and rich resources. He particularly believed deeply in northern Ontario's destiny to become the industrial heartland of Canada, not only because that was where the province's vast resources were located but also because its central location on the transcontinental railways connected east and west and local railways linked them to ports on James Bay and American railways at Sault Ste. Marie. And as it happened, he was in the right place at the right time, because a momentous shift in provincial politics was about to take place, from the era of Liberal domination since Confederation to the era of Conservative domination from 1905 to the 1980s. Hearst contributed to that transition in northern Ontario, entering the legislature in 1908 and becoming Premier in 1914. It was a meteoric rise, especially for a man from a community so far distant from the province's heartland.

And yet, historians have apparently not thought it worthwhile to study the man who led the province during a critical and highly controversial period. Even the growing literature on various aspects of Ontario history during the first couple of decades of the twentieth century, including the province's involvement in the First World War, makes remarkably few references to Hearst. This apparent lack of interest in him is symbolized by the fact that the Ontario Archives, even though they house his papers, possess only one photograph of him that was taken in 1929, ten years after he left office. Clearly, there is a gap to be filled in our knowledge of Hearst and his times.

Hearst was typical of many Canadians, especially in Ontario, whose patriotism combined a love of Canada, which he regarded as a primarily Anglo-Protestant country, with pride in its place in the British Empire, which was different from other nations and empires because of its unique role as a civilizing force in the world. That was why he totally supported Canada's participation in the First World War from the outset and also conscription because he believed from early on that the war was an existential conflict between good and evil. That kind of thinking isn't popular today, although a casual familiarity with international affairs in the more than seventy years since the Second World War makes clear that similar extreme and distorted views of reality remain popular with politicians in Canada and elsewhere. Hearst was also typical of many people in that, while he was conservative, he was moderately progressive and supported and advocated social reforms from the outset of his public career. This likely reflected the fact that he was a devout Methodist when its Social Gospel was a powerful force in English Canada. At the same time, however, like his mentor, Sir James Whitney, he thought governments should reflect public opinion, not lead it.

He was very much Whitney's protégé, but ironically, Whitney's success in ensuring that Hearst succeeded him undermined his legitimacy from the outset, and he was never able to heal that wound. His loss in the 1919 election reflected the sharp divisions within his party as much as the discontent of farmers and workers. And his defeat is still commonly attributed to the Ontario Temperance Act, even though it was only enacted after a massive provincial petition calling for it was presented to the government, it was sustained by a large majority of the voters in the 1919 referendum, and it laid the foundation of Ontario's policy on alcohol for the next eighty years. Hearst was surprised by the outcome of the election and was certainly hurt by it, but he accepted his fate gracefully and left public life with a clear conscience and no regrets, knowing that he had done his best in difficult, indeed unprecedented, circumstances. He also felt vindicated when Howard Ferguson, his closest colleague in the government and his choice to succeed him as leader, returned the party to office just four years later and remained there until 1934.

Many people helped over the years to make this book possible. I have already mentioned Vernon and Irving Hearst. As well, the then Hydro-Electric Power Commission of Ontario allowed me to read its file of correspondence with the Premier's office from 1914 to 1919, and the University of Toronto Library gave me access to the correspondence between the Ontario Department of Education and the Roman Catholic authorities concerning the bilingual schools issue. The Canadian Section of the International Joint Commission in Ottawa allowed me to consult files and correspondence relating to Hearst when he was a member of the commission. The staff of the United Cooperatives of Ontario generously gave me access to UFO archival material in their possession, and Mr. C.A. Morrison kindly allowed me to consult J.J. Morrison's memoirs. The Toronto *Daily Star* generously allowed me to spend weeks in its microfilm room reading its daily issues from 1914 to 1919, a fascinating educational experience. More recently, Matthew Shoemaker, who has actively promoted greater awareness of Hearst in Sault Ste. Marie, cheerfully became an unpaid research assistant, looking up material in issues of the *Sault Daily Star* and patiently finding answers to my inquiries on local issues, hopefully not to the detriment of his law practice. He also read the manuscript and made helpful suggestions. The Sault Ste. Marie Library and Archives kindly gave me permission to use a photograph from its collection and Kevin Meraglia, the Library's archive technician, took the trouble to make sure I obtained a high-resolution copy. Deb Sturdevant, archivist at the Bruce County Museum & Cultural Centre, was very helpful with information and photographs. Susan Peters, the archivist at the Dundas County Archives, promptly provided me with helpful information on the 1914 by-election that followed the death of Sir James Whitney. Mr Bernie Crosby, secretary of the St Joseph Island Historical Society, also assisted me with information on John Hearst, and Laura Syms, Business & Data Services Librarian, Cape Breton University Library, once again found an obscure but important piece of information for me.

I also appreciate the many valuable comments made by the anonymous readers who made several valuable suggestions and raised questions that greatly improved the manuscript. I alone, of course, am responsible for any errors or weaknesses that remain. Profound thanks to Len Husband of the University of Toronto Press, who has accompanied me through this project's seemingly endless life in the age of COVID-19. As always, I am grateful to my wife, Sandra Atwell-Tennyson, for patiently tolerating my obsession and insisting that I come up for air from time to time. I couldn't have done this without her support.

Brian Douglas Tennyson
7 August 2025

# 1 The Young Politician: 1864–1911

*We want to bind this Dominion of Canada together, so that we shall know neither East nor West, neither North nor South, but one united Canada, pulsating with intellectual and industrial life from the Atlantic to the Pacific and from her southern boundary to the shores of the Hudson's* [sic] *Bay.*[1]

WHEN the Napoleonic Wars finally ended, Britain entered a period of profound economic disruption and political instability. This was especially true of Ireland, whose population was growing faster than its overwhelmingly agricultural economy, resulting in shrinking landholdings, declining living standards, and a "depressingly low" life expectancy. "To these factors," as historian Michael Cross once observed, "could be added the evident lack of an economic future, high rents and low wages, frequent famine and disease, a near chronic state of civil war, and political and religious suppression."[2] In Fermanagh, Cavan, and Armagh, where Protestants were a minority, "the favourable leases they had previously enjoyed were being renewed at the same rates as those for Catholics. This had the effect of increasing their isolation amongst a Catholic majority."[3]

Not surprisingly, people began to emigrate, initiating a movement that rose to astonishing numbers from the 1830s to the 1850s. Most went to the United States, but many also went to Canada. In 1832, 28,000 of the 62,000 immigrants who arrived at Québec, the main port of entry to Canada, were Irish.[4] Among those who arrived in August of that year were James McFadden, his wife Frances, and their seven children. They were Protestants from Lough Erne, near Enniskillen in Fermanagh, which was part of Ulster in the north. James McFadden was a farmer, and like most farmers, he had struggled to support his family on a small farm and hoped that life would be better in Canada.

The McFaddens were accompanied by seventeen-year-old William Hearst, about whose early life we know very little, other than that he was born on 14 February 1815, possibly in Magheracross, although the family is thought to have originated at Drumderg, a village situated between Enniskillen and Tempo, and its name was Hurst.[5] His parents were James and Catherine (Peabody) Hurst, but his mother "died when he was quite young," and it was "the rule of a stepmother" that "caused him to leave home at a very early age to make his own way in the world."[6] He left behind two siblings, Thomas and Elizabeth, who also subsequently emigrated and joined William. Whether William knew the McFaddens or got to know them on the ship is unknown, but it seems likely that he already knew them because he lived with them after their arrival in Canada.

They sailed in 1832 from Sligo, a major Atlantic port south of Enniskillen, probably on one of the many ships that brought timber from Canada to Britain and transported poor emigrants as ballast on the return journey for nominal fares. According to Margaret McFadden, James's eldest daughter, the journey from Ireland took two months, during which "much of the time the passengers were confined between decks, where there was no ventilation" and "little light." They "had to provide and prepare their own food," and "all cooking had to be done on deck for fear of fire."[7]

Their timing was unfortunate because immigrant ships were usually overcrowded and grossly unsanitary and often carried the cholera epidemic that was sweeping Europe. The government of Lower Canada responded by establishing a quarantine station at Grosse Ile, an island downstream from Quebec, that processed more than 51,000 of the immigrants who arrived in 1832.[8] The ships carrying the other 11,000 immigrants were allowed to bypass Grosse Ile after inspection. Luckily for the McFaddens, there was no cholera on their ship, even though Sligo was being ravaged by it when they were there in August.[9] After arriving at Quebec City, they made their way upriver to Montreal in early October, where they spent the winter months because the Montreal Emigrant Society provided temporary employment and relief in sheds at the Lachine Canal on the western edge of the city. [10] Their destination was Prescott, a Loyalist community on the St. Lawrence River in Upper Canada, which had been created in 1784 to provide land for Loyalists who had supported Britain in the American revolution.

The Montreal Emigrant Society also covered the cost of their journey to Prescott in the spring of 1833. From there they moved inland and settled in Dummer Township in the Newcastle district, later Peterborough County, on land that had been "ceded" by treaty by the Michi Saagig (Anishinaabe) First Nation to provide land for immigrants.[11]

The term *ceded* is controversial because, as historian Olive Dickason explains, "in the legal terminology of the day, 'Indian title' meant rights of occupancy and use, not ownership in fee simple" and the Crown had the right to acquire Indigenous lands by a treaty negotiated at a public meeting."[12] Between 1781 and 1825 ten such treaties were signed, giving the government almost the entire peninsula between Lakes Ontario, Ontario, Erie, and Huron.[13] Unfortunately, the First Nations believed that they were only sharing their land, not surrendering all their rights to it.[14] Being uneducated immigrants, the McFaddens and Hearst would not have known that, but coming from rural Ireland they might have appreciated the distinction.

Dummer was a small but growing community of nearly 700 people, most of whom were Irish Protestants from Armagh, Fermanagh, and Cavan.[15] Immigrants received free land grants, but they had to clear the land of trees and build primitive houses before they could plant crops. Usually they built crude log shanties with a sloped roof of overlapping wooden slabs or strips of elm bark.[16] Before winter set in "an effort was sometimes made to construct a fireplace at one side of the shanty, though many a pioneer family lived for several years without one."[17] McFadden had the advantage of having two teenaged boys, as well as his wife and younger children, to assist with the work. Even so, the first year must have been hard. While much can be surmised, little is actually known about their experiences in those first few years. We do know that when the 1837 uprising took place the McFaddens and Hearst were among the loyal majority. The instability lasted long after the actual uprising because of continuing unrest at Prescott and sporadic raids organized by the American Sons of Liberty and Hunters Lodges seeking to "liberate" Canada. James's son William served in the Dummer Township militia and was called out twice, but Hearst served for five months (November 1838–March 1839) in the 7th Provisional Battalion, whose members were "organized and uniformed like troops of the line."[18] That meant that they received the pay and allowances of regular troops, which no doubt was welcome. The 7th Battalion saw no action, however, beyond the inevitable clashes between the Irish Protestant and Catholic men.

Hearst was virtually a member of the McFadden family, living and working with them on their farm, and the relationship became more formal when he married Margaret McFadden on 11 October 1844. Shortly afterward they all moved to Manvers Township in nearby Durham County, but they didn't stay there long, moving farther west around 1850 to Mount Pleasant in Holland Township, five kilometres northwest of Markdale in Grey County, on land that had been "ceded" to the Crown in 1836 by the Anishinaabe First Nation. James and two of his sons, Robert and John, each received farmland there, and so too did Hearst, because by now he and Margaret had three children – John (1845), Robert (1847), and Jane (1849) – and needed their own place. It was situated on a hill close to the McFadden farms known locally as "the sink hole swamp,"[19] and the land in Holland Township proved to be too rocky, so around 1857 they all moved yet again, this time slightly north-west to Arran Township in Bruce County.

The McFaddens and Hearst acquired land near Arkwright, a small village that at its height boasted two general stores, two hotels, two blacksmiths, a physician, a post office, a school, a Methodist church, and an Orange hall.[20] Arkwright was close to Tara, the major community in Arran Township, which had saw and grist mills, a foundry producing agricultural implements, a wagon works and a tannery. It also had ambitions of developing into a significant commercial and manufacturing centre, and local promoters were hopeful that a railway would soon link the town to Toronto.

According to Irving Hearst, his grandfather "succeeded in making [his 235 acres of land] into a good farm."[21] Wheat and oats were grown and hauled in the autumn to Port Elgin or Southampton, two ports about sixteen kilometres away on Lake Huron. Buyers stationed themselves at Burgoyne, just west of Arkwright at the intersection of county roads 3 and 17, where the farmers decided which port they should proceed to according to which buyer paid the best price. The buyer would provide a chit for the local general store where William would purchase the family's winter supplies. He also raised cattle during the American civil war "as there was a good market for them in the States."[22] That was a good thing because the family grew to include nine children.

We don't actually know much about either William or Margaret. Irving claimed that his grandfather's life was "one of poverty and ceaseless toil," an observation presumably based on comments by his father because Irving was only four years old when his grandfather died. But it was undoubtedly true, because they had little or no education, had immigrated to a new land, and had struggled to find good land where they could settle permanently. They never achieved real prosperity, although they managed a modest living from their farm at Arkwright. Commenting on a photograph taken when William was an old man, Irving thought he needed "only the addition of an up-side-down clay pipe to make him look like the typical stage Irishman." He "looked rather uncomfortable in a suit with a low collar and a broad four-in-hand tie, and he probably was. His face was shaved down to the line of his jaw, below which the hair grew in a sort of fringe, framing his face, which had a look of stubborn endurance from which all hope had long since fled."[23] Irving remembered his grandmother and described her "as a kindly person, but ... a bit austere." She was "not without a sense of humour," however, and "was noted for her Irish hospitality" and "cheerful spirit, even amid distressing afflictions," about which he does not elaborate.[24] The Hearst home was devoutly Methodist and for many years accommodated the circuit-riding ministers as they passed through the area. Irving recalled visiting his grandmother once as a child, sitting "in her tall-backed rocking chair, with her bible on a small table beside her, singing, in a toneless voice, 'When this poor lisping stammering tongue lies silent in the grave.' It was a Methodist hymn that wasn't warranted to cheer up a child very much."[25]

The youngest of the nine Hearst children was William Howard, known to his family and friends throughout his life as Billy, who was born on 15 February 1864. By then the older children – John (1845), Robert (1847), Jane (1849), James (1850), Margaret (1852), Sarah (1854), Elizabeth (1856), Rebecca (1858), and Mary Ann (1861) – were helping with the farm, so life was becoming somewhat easier. Because he was the youngest, Margaret understandably doted on him, perhaps at least partly because had "an unruly mop of red hair and a face covered with freckles."[26] He also had the advantage of making his appearance when the family farm was established and providing a modest living. For this reason his parents dared to hope that he might achieve more in life. That meant that he was spared to some extent from the daily hard work of the farm in order to get a better education than had been possible for the others. It was – and still is – a common ambition for many immigrant families. Many rural families like the Hearsts, who did not achieve real prosperity in a life of hard labour, recognized that education was the path to greater opportunities and a more comfortable life, in which they might share in their old age. Many if not most of the men young Billy encountered in later years had very similar backgrounds. Even so, he certainly helped on the farm and "was adept at driving oxen." He was also "good with horses and could get the best out of them."[27]

He attended the local school in Arkwright, a log structure built by his older brothers and their friends, until 1876 when his parents passed the farm onto their oldest son, John, and retired to a cottage in Tara. Billy went with them and attended the school there. In 1880, at the age of sixteen, he was sent to Collingwood, eighty-four kilometres away, to attend high school because he, perhaps encouraged by his parents and older brothers, had decided that he wanted to become a lawyer. Law students were not then required to attend university, and his family could not have afforded that anyway, but they could apprentice with a lawyer and then write their exams at Osgoode Hall in Toronto, home of the

Law Society of Upper Canada. In either case he required a provincial matriculation diploma, and the high school in Collingwood was the closest to Tara that offered it.[28] Hearst roomed with Alexander Smith, a boy from Saugeen, a nearby community on Lake Huron. Its proximity to Southampton, the home of A.E. Belcher, a prominent Bruce County Conservative who knew the Hearst family well,[29] suggests that he may have arranged Hearst's accommodation. Hearst and Smith became close friends and enjoyed rowing on the bay in good weather.[30] The move to Collingwood effectively ended Hearst's childhood, for he never lived under his parents' roof again.

After completing high school in 1882, Hearst was sent to Owen Sound, only about twenty-five kilometres from home, to study law in the office of James Masson. We don't know how this was arranged, but Belcher may have arranged that too because Masson was a prominent Conservative lawyer, but it seems more likely that Hearst's brother, John, arranged it through Alexander McNeill, the Conservative MP for Bruce North and a fellow Ulsterman. John was active in the Orange Order and the Conservative Party, serving on the township council and as reeve from 1886 through 1889.[31] According to Irving, Hearst had already established his credentials as a Conservative in a high school debate on John A. Macdonald's National Policy. Among the guest speakers was Donald Sinclair, the Liberal MPP for Bruce North, who later recalled the "young red-haired farm boy" who "pushed his way to the platform where, with gesturing arms, he told in ringing tones of the prosperity that the National Policy was to bring to Canada. Needless to say, the Conservatives won the debate."[32]

It was while studying law in Masson's office that Hearst met John McKay, a boy from Goderich who was also studying law with Masson. Not surprisingly, the two boys, both living away from home on meagre incomes, became close friends. Thus, they agreed that when they were admitted to the bar they would set up a practice together. They wrote their examinations at Osgoode Hall in 1888 and were called to the Bar at the end of the Michaelmas term of that year.[33] The question now was where they would establish their law firm. Like many other young Ontarian men, they naturally thought of moving west, where the opportunities seemed unlimited. Their original plan was to settle in Vancouver, then a small community at the mouth of the Fraser River but one with a bright future because it had been designated the western terminal of the Canadian Pacific Railway. Its population had been only about 1,000 when train service began in May 1887, but it soared to 14,000 by 1891, 26,000 in 1901 and 120,000 by 1911. Clearly, the idea of moving to Vancouver was a shrewd one.[34]

But Vancouver would have to cope without Hearst and McKay because they quickly realized that they could not afford to make such a bold move. Instead, they looked closer to home and decided to try their luck in Sault Ste. Marie, a small town in northern Ontario situated on the St. Mary's River that linked Lake Superior to Lake Huron. Known to the Anishinaabe as Bawating, meaning "place of the rapids," this was the centre of Anishinaabe territory, perhaps because of the spring and fall migrations of fish and fowl, the sugar maple trees, and the wild rice that could be harvested there. The first European to visit the area was Étienne Brûlé in 1623, who named it Sault de Gaston after Louis XIV's brother. As the fur trade spread into the region a trading post was established, and Jesuit missionaries arrived in 1669. Over the years the fur trade moved farther north and west, however, and by the 1840s the trading post had been reduced to little more than a provisioning depot, primarily serving the local community until it closed in 1869.

That might suggest that Sault Ste. Marie was a poor substitute for Vancouver, but in 1888 the two communities were not dissimilar because both were small places with significant growth potential. In the case of the Sault, it was situated in a strategic location at the point where Lakes Huron and Superior met, and there was a growing timber industry in the area. There were also significant mineral resources. Resource development was problematic, however, because it involved encroaching on Anishinaabe territory. When the government issued a lease to the Quebec and Lake Superior Mining Company in 1846 to develop a copper mine near Sault Ste. Marie, Chief Shingwaukonse challenged its legality because the land had not been "ceded" in a treaty. He did not object to the mine, however, but demanded that his people should get a share of the profits. When the government ignored him he led an armed group and shut down the mine. That got the government's attention and, amid unfounded rumours of a massacre, sent Thomas Anderson, the Superintendent of Indian Affairs, accompanied by a magistrate and a rifle brigade, to Sault Ste. Marie. The leaders of the "uprising" were arrested, but instead of charging them, the government wisely appointed William Robinson to negotiate treaties with the Anishinaabe leaders.

The result was the 1850 Robinson-Huron and Robinson-Superior treaties, which "ceded" a vast territory north of Lakes Huron and Lake Superior, an area twice what "had already been given up in all previous treaties combined in Canada West," which meant that the Anishinaabe were agreeing to greater Euro-Canadian penetration of their territory. In return, they achieved "recognition of their title to tracts that would be reserved for their exclusive use in the pursuit of traditional economic activities" and annuities.[35] Meanwhile, loggers who were exploiting the region's vast timber resources were encroaching on Indigenous reserved lands in the Temiskaming and Abitibi regions, as well as the Ottawa Valley. The government also passed legislation in 1850, intended to protect Indigenous peoples' established right to the lands that had been set aside for them, made it an offence for private individuals to negotiate with Indigenous leaders concerning their lands, excluded First Nations land from taxation, freed them from seizure for non-payment of debt, and provided damages from public works activities such as railway construction.[36] These were positive protections, but they were later weakened with a clarification clause stating that Indigenous hunting and fishing rights on "ceded" lands excluded "such portions of the said Territory as may from time to time be sold or leased to individuals or companies of individuals and occupied by them with the consent of the Provincial Government."[37]

Meanwhile, some of the northern chiefs complained to Robinson that their annuities were small compared to those being given in southern Ontario. Robinson's explanation was that the land in the south was more valuable because it was well suited for agriculture, and that meant that the ability of Indigenous people to hunt was being reduced by the influx of settlers, whereas there was little or no land suitable for agriculture in northern Ontario, which meant that there was little if any impact on hunting.[38] There was some logic in that, of course, but it ignored the impact of logging, pulpwood harvesting, mining, and the construction of roads, railways, and townsites on the pollution of air, land, and water in hunting or fishing territory and introduced competition for the game and fish, not to mention creating a higher risk of forest fires.[39]

Ontario had always viewed the northwest as its hinterland and by the 1880s and 1890s its business and political leaders were beginning to recognize that what they had thought was a harsh and barren wilderness blocking access to it, actually possessed a seemingly endless supply of trees as well as minerals and waterpower, the key ingredients for industrialization. In other words, exploitation of the resources of what people were beginning to call New Ontario would create "a new pattern of industrialization linked to the northern resource base."[40] At the same time, clearing its forests would make land available for agricultural settlement, as had been the case in the southern part of the province. The growth of forestry and mining in northern Ontario would also increase commercial prosperity in the south, especially in view of the fact that natural resources came under provincial jurisdiction.[41]

Accordingly, the province's political leaders, both Liberals and Conservatives, were quick to realize the need for infrastructure to support the region's development. The government of Sir George Ross began construction of the Temiskaming and Northern Ontario (TNO) Railway,[42] the province's first public utility, to link Toronto with the Canadian Pacific Railway at North Bay. The TNO almost immediately proved its value when construction work exposed the vast silver deposits at what became Cobalt, 145 kilometres north of North Bay, in 1903. That was followed by the Abitibi gold rush when the huge gold deposits at Timmins and Kirkland Lake were discovered, and the TNO built a spur line to facilitate their development. All of this was done on Indigenous lands without the consent of the First Nations, who complained that the railways, their builders, and prospectors were trespassing on their lands.[43]

Meanwhile, the American community on the Michigan side of the St. Mary's River, also called Sault Ste. Marie, had built a ship canal in 1855, but that didn't help the Canadian community much, and when the vessel carrying troops to the Red River uprising in 1870 was denied passage through it the decision was made to build a Canadian canal. The rapids had considerable value, however, for the generation of electricity. Then the Canadian Pacific Railway built a branch line linking Sudbury with Saulte Ste. Marie and a railway bridge spanning the river in the 1880s, enabling it to connect with an American railway.[44] These projects dramatically stimulated the local economy and the population almost doubled to 4,000 between 1871 and 1887, enabling Sault Ste. Marie to achieve town status. New houses, schools, stores, hotels, and churches were built; new streets were built complete with sidewalks; and more professional people such as lawyers, doctors, and dentists were attracted to the community.

Among them were Hearst and McKay, who found themselves on Plummer Dock in September 1888, ready to start their careers and hoping to grow with the town.[45] The law firm they established was initially known as Masson, Hearst and McKay. James Masson, who had been elected to parliament in the 1887 federal election, never actually participated in it but lent his prestigious name to his former students to help them attract business.[46] Inevitably, the early days were difficult and the two young lawyers had to sleep in their law office.[47] But it prospered, enabling Hearst to rent a room at the Victoria Hotel on the corner of Pim and Queen Streets, then into the new modern Algonquin Hotel, and James Darling joined the firm in 1901. When MacKay was appointed a provincial judge in Port Arthur in 1909, the firm became Hearst and Darling and with the addition of William Eberts Brown, a young lawyer from Owen Sound. Darling left the firm in 1913 and was replaced by Thomas Rowland, a lawyer who had moved to Sault Ste. Marie from Niagara on the Lake in 1899. When Brown went overseas with the 227th Battalion in 1916, Hearst, Rowland and Brown then briefly became Hearst, Rowland and

Atkin with the addition of Welberne Atkin, a lawyer from Elgin County who had moved to Sault Ste. Marie.[48] It became one of its leading law firms and was still functioning under that name during the war years, although Hearst ceased to be involved in it after he moved to Toronto in 1912.[49]

Hearst quickly became active in the community because that's how ambitious young lawyers become known and attracted business in small towns. Not surprisingly, he was especially involved in the Methodist Church, which was then a small mission church on Pim Street that the congregation had outgrown. A larger building was needed, and Hearst served on the building committee, along with Dr. John Shannon, the local dentist, and Charles Farwell, a local lawyer and Algoma's Liberal MPP. They raised the funds to build what became Central Methodist Church on the corner of Albert and Spring Streets. Construction began in 1900, but the building was not completed until 1911, presumably because of the grand scale of the building. Hearst served as Sunday School Superintendent for many years and joined the voluntary fire brigade, even serving for a time as chief. According to Irving, it was not unusual for him to put in a full day's work at the office after spending a night fighting a fire. He was also a high school trustee; president of the Board of Trade; a member of the Keystone (later Algoma) Lodge of the Masonic Order, rising to the rank of district deputy grand master; and was active in the temperance movement.[50]

Hearst was an outgoing young man, slender, moderately athletic, and "hail-fellow-well-met with everyone,"[51] according to the prominent journalist Hector Charlesworth, who first met him in Sault Ste. Marie during the 1902 provincial election campaign."[52] Hearst's son, Irving, agreed with this description, describing his father as "something of a local blade" as a young man, although "he did not drink or smoke and his greatest imprecation was 'My stars alive!'"[53] Like many men at the time, he wore "a luxurious moustache, the ends of which were waxed in the fashion of the day." One day a few years later, however, "he came home with the waxed ends cut off and we hardly recognized him." When his friend William R. Smyth, owner of Sault Ste. Marie's *Weekly Star* newspaper and the Conservative MPP for Algoma from 1902 to 1908, "saw the mutilated moustache, he said that if he [Hearst] did it again he would have him read out of the Conservative party."[54] In fact, Hearst wore a conservative "toothbrush" moustache for the rest of his life.

On 28 July 1891 he married Isabella Jane "Bella" Duncan,[55] a daughter of John and Jane (Graham) Duncan, whom he had met at a dance at the International Hotel when she was visiting her sisters, Annie and Emma. Annie had married John Meir, an Owen Sound merchant, in

1883 and then moved to Sault Ste. Marie in the late 1880s. Similarly, Emma had married William Thompson, a merchant from Hollen, Wellington County, in 1887, and they had moved to the Sault as well. According to Irving, "it was love at first sight."[56] The marriage took place in St James's Methodist Church at Simcoe, Norfolk County, where Bella's parents, John and Edith Duncan, lived.

Irving described his mother as being of medium height with blue eyes and black hair that began greying at an early age. She and her brothers and sisters were "a merry lot," and when they "got together over a teapot, they all talked at once and listened to nobody, and they had a wonderful time."[57] Bella brought her knowledge of bookkeeping to the marriage, handling the family finances, including the purchase, sale and maintenance of properties, leaving William free to focus on his growing law practice and politics. Irving recalled his father as an "indefatigable worker" who "probably made more money when he practiced in the Sault than any other lawyer there."[58]

According to Irving, Bella was also responsible for William being "converted." This is somewhat misleading because he had grown up in a strict Methodist home, but his habits may have become more liberal over the years. He and Bella attended a revival meeting held by Canada's leading touring evangelists, John Edwin Hunter and Hugh Thomas Crossley, when they visited Sault Ste. Marie. Like later evangelists such as Billy Graham, their approach was non-denominational, eschewing doctrine and emphasizing the importance of individual commitment to Christ. They had already converted Sir John A. Macdonald and his wife in 1888, and Hunter's biographer specifically mentions Hearst as one of the prominent men he and Crossley "converted."[59]

The young couple's first home was "the little shingle house" on Bay Street near East Street. Heated by stoves, it "had an outside necessary house" and no water "other than that which was caught from the roof in a rain barrel" or obtained from the river just across the street. "Every few days a man would come with a buckboard and take the barrel that stood by the back and drive his horse up to his belly into the river … and take the barrel back to the house, for the price of ten cents."[60] When their first child, Howard Vernon Hearst, always known as Vernon, was born in July 1892, the little cottage was no longer big enough, and, luckily, they were able to rent Judge Walter McRae's house, as he had died a month earlier. It faced the water and had a boathouse, and they remained there for a decade, during which three more children joined the family: William Irving, always known as Irving, in 1894; Isabelle in 1896; and Evelyn in 1898. When bicycles became popular William bought two for Bella and himself. According to Irving Hearst, "he used to get up early in the morning to ride around what was known as the twelve-mile block with his friend Dr. Shannon." Bella showed less interest, or perhaps need, for such exercise.[61]

As his practice prospered, Hearst bought three lots of land between 1902 and 1904 and built an impressive brick house with a furnace, indoor bathroom, hardwood floors, and electric lights. They named it Eastbourne because it lay on the eastern edge of town at the corner of Queen Street East and Upton Road. One feature of the new house was that it was large enough to allow Bella's mother and sister Gertrude to live with them when they moved to Sault Ste. Marie following John Duncan's death in 1901. Gertrude worked as a stenographer in Hearst's office until she married Dr. Samuel Fleming, a local physician.[62] There was also a hired girl who helped with the cooking and housework. It was a Methodist home. Irving recalls that "before going to bed" his father "would read a chapter of the Bible to my mother, and I have heard the murmur of his voice as he said his prayers with her before retiring."[63]

On 24 May – Queen Victoria's birthday – and in the summers the family went for picnics and even camped at Pointe aux Pins, popularly known as Pine Point, about ten kilometres west of town on the St. Mary's River. It could be reached by road, but it was "a long and tedious journey,"[64] so the family made the trip on the *Camilla*, a small steamer that passed through the canal, a thrilling adventure for the children. One summer, when the family camped at the point, Hearst couldn't resist the temptation to abandon them briefly when he heard that Wilfrid Laurier was visiting the Sault. This involved rowing a skiff back to the locks and then walking a couple of kilometres into town.[65]

Around 1903 the family built Rockwood, a cottage at Richards Landing on St. Joseph Island, about thirty-two kilometres east of town at the mouth of the St. Mary's River.[66] A British fort had existed there in the eighteenth and early nineteenth centuries, and the island had been "ceded" by the Anishinaabe in the Robinson Treaty. There was some agriculture and lumbering on the island, and Hearst's brother, John, had moved there with his family in the 1890s, attracted by the free agricultural land available to homesteaders.[67] But by the turn of the century it was becoming popular as a summer resort community. John's son, Herbert, moved into Sault Ste. Marie, however, and in July 1899 married Elizabeth Baldwin, daughter of Chandler and Emma Baldwin. John and the rest of the family followed because the farm had become too much work for him. It seems likely that they made the move after the 1905 provincial election that elected the province's first Conservative government. That meant that William could use his influence with James Whitney, the new Premier, and Frank Cochrane, the Conservative leader in northern Ontario, to get him hired by the Department of Lands, Forests and Mines as a forestry scaler. That proved to be too physically demanding, however, and a year later he was appointed governor of the county jail in Sault Ste. Marie, a position that included accommodation. He retained it until his death in December 1915, when he was succeeded by his son, Robert Milton Hearst, a foundry worker in Meaford, Grey County, who moved with his family to Sault Ste. Marie in 1916 to take up the position.[68]

Clearly, Hearst and McKay had made a wise decision when they moved to Sault Ste. Marie because the town continued its extraordinary growth during the 1890s. That was partly because of the new ship canal and the rail link being built by the Canadian Pacific Railway (CPR) to connect it with US midwestern lines. It also reflected the recognition by local businessmen of the great potential of the St Mary rapids for generating electricity that could power industrial development based on the vast woodlands and potential mineral wealth of the area. Supported by the town, they incorporated the Sault Ste. Marie Water, Gas and Light Company but ran out of money before the plant was completed. Then F.H. Clergue, "an ebullient, hard-selling American entrepreneur,"[69] arrived on the scene, looking for investment opportunities. He purchased the bankrupt company, renaming it the Lake Superior Power Company, and increased the plant's generating capacity. Then he built the first pulp mill in Ontario to be situated "close to and in association with a hydroelectric project, drawing its raw material, spruce wood, from a huge hinterland of crown land forest. Up until this time lumber and pulp and paper mills had been located in the older, more settled parts of the province, closer to the consumers than to the forests."[70]

Clergue also acquired an iron ore mine at Wawa and began construction of the Algoma Central Railway (ACR) to haul the ore to Sault Ste. Marie, where he began construction of a steel plant to process it. The provincial government, keen on industrial development in northern Ontario, subsidized the ACR by granting Clergue 7,400 acres of land per mile of construction, including the timber and mineral rights. He also established a fleet of steamers to transport the finished products to southern markets. Within five years he pumped as much as $120 million into the local economy and was employing 7,000 workers under the umbrella of the Consolidated Lake Superior Company. Sault Ste. Marie's population, which had been 2,414 in 1891, rose to 7,169 in 1901 and 10,894 in 1911.[71]

Meanwhile, Hearst had not neglected politics. Having grown up in an Irish Protestant family, it was not surprising that he was a Conservative. His father and brother John had been active in both the Conservative Party and the Orange Order in Bruce County,[72] but there were other factors as well. Hearst had grown up admiring Sir John A. Macdonald and supporting his National Policy, undoubtedly influenced by James Masson.[73] But he also became caught up in the wave of imperialist sentiment that swept the British world, including Anglo-Protestant Ontario, in the late nineteenth and early twentieth centuries. The first election in which he participated, albeit informally, was the federal contest of 1878, when he was still a high school student in Collingwood and defended the Conservatives' National Policy in a school debate.[74] He also worked for the Conservatives while a law student in Owen Sound, presumably in the 1886 provincial election and on Masson's behalf in the 1887 federal election. It was natural, therefore, that he became involved with the Conservative Party as soon as he arrived in Sault Ste. Marie. In 1908 he claimed that he had attended "every convention held in Algoma for twenty years" since his arrival in 1888. [75]

The 1890 provincial election was the first in which he took an active part, however, and this may be what Hector Charlesworth had in mind when he later wrote that Hearst had participated as an "active ... speaker in the Conservative interest" in Sault Ste. Marie in that election.[76] Oliver Mowat's Liberal government, first elected in 1872, was seeking another mandate, and William Meredith, who had led the Conservatives since 1878, was trying once again to convince Ontarians that it was time for a change. Robert Lyon, the Manitoulin lumberman who had held Algoma East for the Liberals since 1878, was considered vulnerable because his company had gone bankrupt two years earlier, and the local Conservatives asked Hearst to represent them.[77] He must have been flattered but declined because his law practice was still modest and he needed to build it up further before he could get seriously involved in politics. Alexander Campbell, a former mayor of Brantford and publisher of the Brampton *Conservator* before moving to Sault Ste. Marie in 1889, ran instead and won the seat.

Four years later, however, Campbell abruptly announced that he would not seek re-election in the 1894 election, and Hearst was again approached. This time he reluctantly agreed to represent the Conservatives, even though he still did not think he should do so because he now had a young family to support.[78] But Campbell had proven that a Conservative could win in Algoma East and the 1894 election was unlike previous provincial elections because it wasn't a traditional two-party contest. The Patrons of Industry represented disgruntled farmers and urban workers, while the Protestant Protective Association (PPA) represented Protestants who feared that Roman Catholics, especially francophones, were engaged in a conspiracy to gain control of the province. Both ran their own candidates, but in several ridings the Patrons supported

Liberal candidates and the PPA supported Conservatives. Mowat lost eight seats, but Meredith lost eleven. Sixteen members of the legislature were elected with the support of the Patrons of Industry – twelve Liberals, one Conservative, and three who ran only under the Patron banner, while the PPA helped to elect nine members: six Conservatives, one Liberal, and two as PPA candidates.

In Algoma East the battle was a straight two-way battle between the Liberal candidate, Charles Farwell, and Hearst but it was just as hard fought as any of the other contests in the province and Hearst lost by a mere sixty-six votes out of the 3,898 cast.[79] He must have had mixed feelings about the result because he didn't like to lose but couldn't afford to win. And he learned a practical lesson about politics when Captain John Sullivan, the Liberal organizer in the area, later told him that several of his scrutineers had been "bought."[80]

Meanwhile, the political landscape was beginning to change. When Laurier won the 1896 federal election, defeating the long-entrenched Conservatives, he persuaded Mowat to move to Ottawa as his Minister of Justice. He was succeeded at Queen's Park by Arthur Hardy, his Commissioner of Crown Lands. At the same time, Meredith retired as Conservative leader and was succeeded very briefly by G.F. Marter, then by James Pliny Whitney, who had represented Dundas in the legislature since 1888. The Conservatives had finally found their man.

Hearst was approached to run again in the 1898 election but declined to do so because he still couldn't afford to run or to serve if elected. He and Bella had three children by now, with another (Evelyn) on the way. Meanwhile, his father was seriously ill and died in September, placing some responsibility on Hearst because he was the only member of the family who had a decent income. The Hardy government gained six seats in the election but Whitney gained nineteen because all of the PPA and Patron members elected in 1894 were defeated. The Conservatives were on the rise and Hardy retired a year later. He was succeeded by George Ross, who campaigned in the 1902 election on the government's record, even though it was clearly tired after thirty years in office.

Whitney tried desperately to stir up the latent discontent. The Conservative campaign in northern Ontario was managed by Frank Cochrane, the prosperous hardware merchant and mayor of Sudbury who was also the Conservative candidate in Nipissing West. When Whitney spoke at Sault Ste. Marie on 12 May, Hearst would have been among the local Conservatives who welcomed him to their now booming town. He had again been approached to run in the election but still felt unable to do so, and the Conservatives ran Andrew Miscampbell, who had represented Simcoe in the legislature since 1890 but had recently moved to the Sault to manage the Consolidated Lake Superior Corporation's steamships.[81] Hearst supported Miscampbell, of course, but was also one of Cochrane's "chief aides"[82] in the campaign in northern Ontario, helping to organize the new ridings that had been created in the redistribution following the 1901 census. The government survived the election but with only a precariously thin majority: fifty Liberals to forty-eight Conservatives. Three of the Conservative gains were in the new northern constituencies of Algoma, Manitoulin, and Sault Ste. Marie, a result that Charlesworth attributed to Hearst's "effective methods."[83]

The victories in Sault Ste. Marie and Manitoulin proved to be problematic, however. Miscampbell had defeated the Liberal, Charles Napier Smith, owner of the *Sault Express*, despite intervention on Smith's behalf by the steel company.[84] The Liberals contested the result and Miscampbell was unseated in March 1903. The resulting by-election called for 27 October proved to be an exciting one. The same candidates resumed their battle and the Consolidated Lake Superior Corporation again intervened on Smith's behalf, this time in a much more flagrant manner. On polling day, the *Minnie M*, a company steamship – one wonders if the irony of the situation amused Miscampbell – sailed across to Sault Ste. Marie, Michigan, picked up twenty Americans and brought them back "as pluggers in the election." They were met by a special train of the ACR, which took them up to the Helen Mine at Michipicoten where they all voted under names provided to them. They were then whisked back down to Michipicoten Harbour, where they again voted under names provided to them, after which they were taken back across the river.[85]

The local Conservatives had not been unaware of what was happening. Miscampbell had learned of the Liberal plot some days in advance and had asked Attorney General J.M. Gibson to send up special constables to supervise all polls. When he rejected Miscampbell's claims as improbable,[86] the local Conservatives took action on their own. Hearst delegated two boys to watch the *Minnie M* and report to him when it slipped anchor so that the Conservatives could follow in another steamer loaded with special volunteer scrutineers to see exactly what the *Minnie M* was up to.[87] This failed, however, because the Liberals were able to prevent the Conservative ship from sailing on the technical grounds that it did not have a licence to carry passengers![88]

To no one's surprise, Smith was again elected, this time with a substantial majority, and the Conservatives naturally contested the result. The Liberal government was understandably reluctant to take any action due to its precariously thin majority, but eventually on 13 September 1904, "one of the most sensational election trials in Canadian history" began.[89]

Newton Rowell, the Consolidated Lake Superior Corporation's lawyer, represented the Liberals and Hearst represented the Conservatives, proving that at least thirty-six fraudulent votes had been cast and that a senior official of the company and Smith himself had been at least aware of what was going on.[90] Shortly afterwards, P.J. Galvin, the central figure in the whole affair, issued a statement that directly implicated J.R. Stratton, the Provincial Secretary, and other prominent Liberal officials and organizers.[91] As a result of these revelations, Smith was unseated in September 1904, but the government declined to call another by-election, leaving Sault Ste. Marie unrepresented in the legislature until the next general election.[92]

Meanwhile, another scandal, which has been described as "the greatest scandal until that time" because it "charged provincial cabinet ministers with bribery,"[93] had broken out in February 1903. This one centred on Robert Gamey, the Conservative who had won Manitoulin in the 1902 election. Shortly after his victory he announced that he intended to support the Ross government out of concern for the development of northern Ontario and in particular his own constituency. W.R. Smyth, who had won Algoma – the two Algomas had been merged prior to the 1902 election – no doubt reflected the frustration of local Tories when he expressed the hope in the Sault *Weekly Star* that "the people of Manitoulin will tar & feather him."[94] But then Gamey rose in the legislature on 13 March to make the sensational announcement that he hadn't really switched sides but had led the Liberals to think he had in order to prove their corruption. Now the Tory hero, he flourished $2,000 in Ontario bank bills that Captain Sullivan and his son Frank had promised him in Stratton's Queen's Park office and given him in the legislature's smoking room.[95]

The Conservatives had, of course, been accusing the Ross government of gross corruption for some time – Hector Charlesworth described the Ross years as "an era of ballot-stuffing, ballot-burning, ballot-switching, impersonation, and vote-buying on a very extensive scale"[96] – but had so far been unable to obtain incontrovertible proof. Now, with Gamey gleefully waving the cash in the legislature, there was tremendous public shock and consternation. The government responded by appointing a royal commission to investigate, but it somehow managed to clear Stratton and called Gamey a liar.[97] Whatever the truth was, the government lost considerable prestige from the Gamey revelations, especially coming as they did at almost the same time as the *Minnie M* affair, and J.S. Willison, the editor of Toronto's *Evening News*, was undoubtedly right when he concluded that the government had "outlived its usefulness."[98]

Ross gave up the struggle in December 1904 and called an election for January 1905, perhaps hoping to benefit from Laurier's victory in the

November 1904 federal election but, as he later acknowledged, with "the uncomfortable feeling that the Government did not represent a majority of the electorate."[99] Unwisely, he ran on his record, while Whitney and the Conservatives naturally promised clean, honest government. But this election was not just about the Ross government's fatigue and corruption. It was also about northern Ontario, or New Ontario as many were beginning to call the region. From being regarded as a rugged barren wasteland, it had been emerging in the public consciousness since the 1890s as a vast storehouse of valuable resources such as timber and minerals, but also even possibly agricultural land. That was why ambitious young men like Hearst had been moving there. The development of New Ontario in effect came under the jurisdiction of the Commissioner of Crown Lands, a cabinet-level department responsible for the management of public lands, forestry, mining, and immigration. In 1891 a Bureau of Mines had been created within the department, followed by a Bureau of Forestry in 1895 and a Bureau of Colonization in 1900. Whitney repudiated this gradualist approach and promised that if elected he would create a Department of Mines and the minister would come from New Ontario.

The election of 1905 was hotly contested all over the province but nowhere harder than in Sault Ste. Marie, where the *Minnie M* affair lent particular strength to local Conservative charges of Liberal corruption. It actually appeared for a while that that episode was going to be repeated when the Conservatives discovered that some forty-five men had left for Michipicoten, presumably to cast fraudulent votes for Smith, who was again the Liberal candidate. Moses McFadden, the Conservative candidate,[100] complained to Gibson, who this time acted promptly. Investigation revealed, however, that while the company did again throw its influence behind Smith, the men in question were merely employees on their way to work at the Helen Mine.[101] Hearst had been optimistic about the result, but Smith was re-elected by a narrow majority. In view of the "terrible fight we had here and the influence that worked against us," Hearst told Whitney, "it would have almost been a miracle to have succeeded under the circumstances."[102] The good news was that the Conservatives won seven of the nine constituencies in northern Ontario, including Manitoulin.[103] Better news was that the Conservatives were "swept into power on a wave of public indignation,"[104] capturing sixty-nine seats to the Liberals' twenty-eight. Five cabinet ministers fell, including Gibson. Stratton, the minister directly implicated in both the *Minnie M* and Gamey scandals, did not seek re-election, and his seat was won by a Conservative. Clearly, Ontarians had concluded that the government was both tired and corrupt and it was time for a change.

When Whitney constructed his cabinet, one of his first actions, as promised, was to rename the Department of Crown Lands the Department of Lands and Mines. He wanted the minister to be from northern Ontario and Frank Cochrane was his man, but he hadn't run in the election. It's not clear why but there were likely a couple of reasons. One was that he had run and lost in 1902, but probably more important was the dramatic impact of the recent discovery of the world's largest copper-nickel deposits at Sudbury and silver deposits at Cobalt. A prominent hardware merchant in the area, he invested extensively in mining ventures and had also established a hydroelectric power company that by 1904 was supplying power to Sudbury. He was fully content to remain behind the scenes in politics and therefore almost certainly recommended to Whitney in November 1904, even before the election had been called, that he should approach Hearst, who was emerging as an influential Conservative in Sault Ste. Marie, the major industrial centre in northern Ontario and had assisted Cochrane in the recent elections and by-elections. But he hadn't run in the election, even though, according to Irving Hearst, Whitney had sent "a special messenger to the Sault" to urge him to run and offering him a portfolio. Once again, however, Hearst pleaded that he still could not afford to enter public life, but he also claimed that his health was not good.[105] He had recommended Moses McFadden and when he was defeated recommended Smyth, who had been re-elected in Algoma,[106] pointing out that, while poorly educated, he had sound business ability and unquestionable integrity and was developing into a very effective platform speaker. "He is a man that all New Ontario would have the utmost confidence in."[107] Clearly, Hearst was unaware that Whitney wanted only Cochrane or Hearst, later telling Smyth that he had "made up my mind" before the election to appoint Cochrane "if possible" because he needed "a man from New Ontario at once able and capable and who had also the necessary knowledge and experience for such a position."[108] That was blunt and probably explains why Smyth switched to federal politics and served in parliament from 1908 to 1917.

Meanwhile, Cochrane had apparently changed his mind about entering the legislature, probably because the Conservatives were now going to form the government. Thus, when Sudbury's Conservatives gathered on 2 February 1905, eight days after the election, George Gordon, a Sturgeon Falls lumber merchant who had run unsuccessfully in the 1904 federal election, stated that Charles Lamarche, the provincial Conservative candidate in Nipissing East, had told him before the election that "if he carried the constituency" he would resign and offer the seat to Cochrane, "whom he wished to see a Cabinet Minister."[109] Cochrane, no doubt with tongue firmly in cheek, declared that Gordon's statement "came to him as a great surprise. He was not looking for a seat in the Cabinet, as he thought 90 per cent of those elected to support Mr. Whitney were better qualified than he was."[110] The Liberal *Sudbury Journal* disagreed, expressing its hope that Cochrane would be appointed because there was "a strong feeling" among men from both parties that "the office should be given to a New Ontario man" and there was "none better qualified to fill the position than our townsman."[111] Cochrane did not commit himself but set out for Toronto. While boarding the train, however, he lost his footing, fell, and was badly injured. He was rushed to a hospital in Copper Cliff, where his right leg was amputated below the knee, and it was not until more than a month later, on 9 March, that he was able to travel to Toronto. Three months later he was still recuperating and adjusting to an artificial leg. Meanwhile, Whitney was keeping the position open for him, with J.J. Foy, the Attorney General, acting as Commissioner of Crown Lands.

In June Whitney, likely on Cochrane's recommendation, again sounded out Hearst, promising to find a seat for him if he would join the government.[112] When Hearst remained reluctant, Whitney summoned the two men to his office and, as Hearst recalled several years later,

> told us in his own emphatic way, that one or other of us must come into the government as the representative of northern Ontario and he would give us until the next morning at 11 o'clock, to decide which one it would be. Mr. Cochrane and I spent that night until the early hours of the next morning ... each one trying to persuade the other that it was his duty to accept the position. Mr. Cochrane eventually consented, but not before he had exacted from me a promise that I would seek election at the next general election and in time relieve him as minister for northern Ontario.[113]

Accordingly, Lamarche resigned his seat on 27 May, Cochrane was elected by acclamation in the by-election on 13 June and was promptly appointed minister of the new Department of Lands and Mines.[114]

It is difficult to tell from the available evidence if Whitney wanted Cochrane more than Hearst or just wanted one or the other. Cochrane undoubtedly had more to offer than Hearst in view of his significant business interests, his knowledge of the mining industry in northern Ontario, and his greater political experience. His real value, however, was that he was an effective campaign organizer and backroom manager of party affairs, a role that he preferred over elective office. Although largely unknown today, he was a major political figure in his time on both the provincial and federal levels. In 1908 he headed the group of

Conservatives – A.E. Kemp, the party's chief fundraiser in Ontario, E.B. Osler, the wealthy stockbroker and MP, George Gooderham, a member of the wealthy distillery family and MPP, and J.D. Reid, a surprisingly influential MP from Eastern Ontario whose wife was a member of the Labatt brewery family – who purchased the independent Toronto *Evening News* from J.W. Flavelle and converted it into a party organ.[115]

Hearst was younger and had less experience, but he had impressed Cochrane and was the rising man in the industrial centre of northern Ontario. The fact that Whitney offered this key position – the *Globe* thought it "the most important portfolio in the Government" because it generated a third of its revenues[116] – to Hearst reflected his rising status in northern Ontario, both as a lawyer in its largest and most important industrial community and among the region's Conservatives. The arrangement made it apparent that Cochrane was grooming Hearst to take over when the appropriate time came, and the fact that Hearst began to be seen as Cochrane's protégé must have enhanced his influence in the area as well.

His influence certainly increased when, shortly after the election, he was appointed one of the provincial government's three representatives on the board of directors of the Consolidated Lake Superior Corporation. The presence of government representatives on the board came about when Clergue's empire collapsed in December 1902 because of his free-spending financial mismanagement.[117] The crisis and negotiations with bankers in New York and the provincial government dragged on through 1903 until operations shut down in September 1903, leaving 3,500 workers unpaid and out of work.[118] On the morning of 27 September, supported by other local workers, hundreds of them gathered outside the plant's general office and began throwing bricks and rocks through the windows. Some men got into the general office and destroyed furniture and company records. Mayor W.H. Plummer read the Riot Act, suspended streetcar service, shut down the bars and taverns, and sent the ferry across the river.[119] He also called out the militia, and on 29 September, 362 officers and men from the Queen's Own Rifles, the 48th Highlanders, and the 10th Royal Grenadiers arrived from Toronto to restore order. Fortunately, there was no more violence, and after patrolling the streets for three days the militia returned home.

The company was restructured and the Ross government guaranteed a $2 million bank loan, arguing that the company was too important to northern development to be allowed to fail. As Nelles points out, while "many such organizations had been successfully established in the United States in recent times, this one was the first to locate in Canada and in a sense the reputation of the country, by implication, depended upon it."[120] In return, however, the government took a mortgage on the company's railway properties and claimed the right to appoint or have the approval of three directors on its board as long as the guarantee remained a liability on the province.[121] Ross had appointed two prominent businessmen, C.D. Warren of Toronto and T.J. Drummond of Montreal, and Newton Rowell, a Toronto lawyer and rising figure in the Liberal Party who had been "a key figure" in restructuring the company.[122] Rowell appropriately resigned after the 1905 election and Whitney appointed Hearst in his place.

Hearst was the logical choice for this appointment, not just because he was a Conservative but also because nobody other than the company's officers and possibly Rowell knew more about its affairs than he did because he represented many of the American creditors who had secured the court order in December 1903 to wind up the company's affairs. That order had been rescinded when the Guarantee Act was passed in 1904 on the understanding that the company would arrange a satisfactory settlement with the creditors that Hearst represented. When this did not happen, Hearst had moved in December 1904 to proceed with liquidation proceedings. As expected, the threat proved sufficient and the company settled its affairs with the creditors. Hearst personally blamed Rowell for much of the trouble between the company and its creditors because he had been serving as both company solicitor and government representative on the board of directors, a situation that Hearst considered a conflict of interest.[123]

And so began a relationship between two political rivals who, for several year, found themselves in conflict even though they had much in common. Both were born in the 1860s, the sons of British immigrants who had settled in western Ontario and struggled to make a living as farmers, both had trained as lawyers because they couldn't afford to attend university, both were Methodists and temperance advocates, and both were attracted to provincial politics. Hearst ran first, in 1894, Rowell in 1900, and both were defeated. They became rivals in the 1911 and 1914 elections but came together in 1917 because both were Anglo-Protestant imperialists who fully supported the war effort, conscription, and Union government.[124]

From this point Hearst played a significant role in the Sault, promoting the interests of the Consolidated Lake Superior Corporation and other businesses. He became solicitor – and likely an investor – for the Bruce Mines & Algoma Railway Company, for example, whose president was his law partner, John McKay. Aided by a provincial subsidy, the railway had been chartered in 1899 to connect the Rock Lake copper mine with the CPR so that the ore could be shipped to a smelter in northern

Michigan. Another subsidy in 1902 extended the line to another copper mine at Bruce Mines. The mines closed in 1903, however, creating a major problem for the railway.[125]

Perhaps not surprisingly, the company was reorganized when the Conservatives were elected. Hearst presented a petition to the Whitney government seeking further assistance for the railway's construction. The Calumet and Algoma Mining Company, a Michigan mining company, was planning to revive copper mining and needed to extend the line another 145 kilometres. It was, Hearst explained, prepared to spend $9 million on the project but sought a government subsidy of $2,000 and 6,000 acres, but the government was not persuaded and no aid was forthcoming.[126]

Hearst was also a leading member of a group of 200 prominent citizens representing the Advisory Union of Algoma Municipalities who met with Whitney and Cochrane on 13 February 1907. The Union had been organized by the twenty-eight communities in the Algoma district in December 1906 to promote its interests.[127] Their major complaint was that a very great amount of wealth was being extracted from Algoma but that little, in their opinion, was being spent there by the government. They called for a much more vigorous development and colonization policy and more support for the settlers against the domination of northern lands by lumber interests and speculators.[128] Specifically, they wanted the 1.5 million-acre Mississagi forest reserve opened to settlement, legislation preventing speculators from tying up large blocks of non-revenue producing land, and a time limit within which lumbermen must take off their timber so that the land could be opened to settlement. The delegation also wanted a $300,000 government subsidy for construction of a wagon road from Sault Ste. Marie to Sudbury and a railway linking the Sault to the Canadian Pacific and National Transcontinental Railways. Finally, they wanted more vigorous encouragement of the mining industry, especially smelting and refining, and called on the government to spend 50 per cent of the revenue garnered from Algoma on public works in the district.[129]

Whitney refused to commit the government to spending 50 per cent of the revenue from Algoma in the district but assured the delegation that the amount of revenue from any area would be a factor in determining how much the government would spend there in public works. He also revealed that he and Cochrane had already agreed to subsidize the construction of the desired wagon road. When Cochrane spoke he declared his strong opposition to opening the Mississagi reserve to settlement since it contained much valuable timber which he thought should be preserved for future needs, the reason for its creation.[130] If it seemed that the delegation had not accomplished much, it had made an extremely favourable impression in the provincial capital because of its highly respectable composition and effective presentation.[131] It also returned home in remarkably good humour, perhaps aware that it had made a favourable impression on Whitney. It may not have been coincidental that the government introduced the Mineral Refining Bounty Act just a few days later to encourage smelting and refining in Ontario instead of shipping the ore to American refineries.

A month later Hearst led another delegation Queen's Park to support Francis Clergue's appeal for financial support to enable him to complete construction of the ACR, which had been discontinued when the Consolidated Lake Superior Company entered bankruptcy in 1903. The completion of the ACR was critical to the company's success because its purpose was to link its mills at Sault Ste. Marie with the CPR mainline with a branch line to haul logs and iron ore from Michipicoten.[132] The government had already agreed to a construction subsidy of land, including timber and mineral rights, but Clergue wanted to convert that into a cash subsidy of $25,000 per mile.[133] Despite his reluctance to subsidize railways, Whitney gave in, acknowledging that the Consolidated Lake Superior was the largest company in the region and its mills were now much stronger financially.[134] Although there is no supporting evidence, it is hard to believe that Cochrane and Hearst had not already persuaded Whitney to respond favourably to the request.

Only a year later Hearst found himself in the awkward position of returning with another delegation asking Whitney to restore the land grant to the Algoma Central. The company now had about 112 kilometres of track laid and a further 160 graded, so it was nearly complete but needed $14 million.[135] Hearst tried to justify this application with the usual arguments on the vast wealth and potential wealth of the region north of Lake Superior that, if properly developed, could support a population of millions. But his main argument was that what the region needed was a colonization railway because the two transcontinental lines merely skirted the area, and the Algoma Central would not only serve this purpose but could also eventually be extended to a port on Hudson Bay.[136] Whitney appeared to be impressed by these arguments and in 1909 the government granted the company a subsidy of $3,000 and 400 hectares per mile of construction.[137] When the Algoma Central was completed in 1914 it connected with the CPR, the Canadian Northern, and ultimately the National Transcontinental – at a community named after Hearst – but 240 kilometres short of James Bay.

In May 1908, Whitney decided to test the popularity of Ontario's first Conservative government since 1872 and called an election for 8 June. There was little question in anyone's mind about what the result would be. As one observer wrote, "the Whitney Government was ... too certain of its position, too assured of its success, too flushed with the consciousness of a good record in legislation and work during the previous three years, to allow a prospective contest being exciting."[138] The Liberals, by contrast, were under their third leader in as many years and had not yet recovered from the scandals that had toppled them in 1905. Nor were the Conservatives prepared to let the people forget the scandals or the fact that A.G. MacKay, the Liberal leader, had been a member of the late Ross government. The only real question was how large Whitney's majority would be.

In northern Ontario, there were four new ridings this time, making a total of thirteen, and as polling day approached the Liberals were rumoured to be confident of taking six of them.[139] That was wishful thinking. Cochrane, who was again managing the campaign in northern Ontario, acknowledged that the Liberals were "making great efforts [in] some places" but thought they were having "a hard time to create much enthusiasm" and assured Whitney three weeks before polling day that "everything looks remarkably well."[140] That confidence may have been based, at least in part, on the major revisions that Cochrane had made to the province's mining legislation after holding informal consultations in mining communities and a provincial conference in Toronto attended by 113 industry representatives. Their major demand was that the mining regulations should be uniform throughout the province and should not be manipulated by the government through orders-in-council. Cochrane had accepted this very reasonable demand, and his revisions standardized the mining regulations and offered financial support to encourage the establishment of nickel and silver smelters. He also provided for the appointment of regional mining commissioners, empowered the government to regulate working conditions, and introduced a 3% profits tax in place of the former royalty regime.

Most of this pleased the mining industry, and "despite its protestations to the contrary, the mining industry discovered that it could live quite comfortably with the modest toll"[141] because marginal mines were exempt and legitimate expenses and local taxes could be deducted. Between 1906 and 1916 the value of the output from Ontario's mines grew from $78 million to more than $267 million and generated dividends of more than $111 million. As Nelles says, "in the space of a few short years the province witnessed the rise of a brash, boisterous, and rich mining industry.[142] The Whitney government naturally claimed the credit for this growth and the dramatic increase of revenues that it generated to support public services.

One of the seats the Conservatives hoped to win was Sault Ste. Marie. Charles Napier Smith was seeking re-election and Hearst intended to be the Conservative candidate. This must have been rather awkward because both men were members of the Methodist church. But according to Irving Hearst, Smith was "a suave individual and one the boys" who only attended church during election campaigns when he could "stand outside the church door and shake hands with each of the worshippers as they emerged." Hearst, by comparison, was superintendent of the Sunday School, and he and his family attended church twice every Sunday, the two girls leading the way, followed by the two boys, "with our parents bringing up the rear, a small Christian battalion."[143]

Aside from having promised Cochrane in 1905 that he would run in the next election, Hearst's financial position had improved with the growth of his legal practice and his position on the board of the Consolidated Lake Superior Corporation, and he had been appointed a King's Counsel.[144] Because Smith was considered vulnerable and the general view that Sault Ste. Marie would join the rest of the province in giving Whitney a strong majority, there were eight men seeking the Conservative nomination. One was Hearst's brother-in-law, William Thompson, who was now mayor of Sault Ste. Marie. There were only fifty-seven voting delegates at the nominating meeting held on 3 April, but according to the Sault *Weekly Star*, the hall "was filled to its utmost capacity by enthusiastic workers for Conservatism" and it was "by long odds the most representative and enthusiastic gathering of the kind ever held in the Sault." The voting narrowed down to two candidates, Hearst and William Munro, a bridge inspector and town councillor, and "the hearty cheers" when Hearst was declared the victor "showed the satisfaction of those present." Munro's declaration "that he was as an [*sic*] enthusiastic supporter of Mr Hearst as any man present" was also "greeted with much applause."[145]

In his acceptance speech, Hearst expressed his pride at being the nominee of "such an intelligent, representative and enthusiastic convention." Having in mind the *Minnie M* and Gamey scandals, his comments focused on the issue of electoral corruption, claiming that Whitney's government was "the most business like [and] the most fearlessly honest administration Ontario had ever seen," and it was his "hope and desire that the campaign would be a clean, honest and honourable one on both sides, devoid of the personalities and bitterness that too often characterized fights." In a clear reference to Smith and the 1902 election, he declared that he was "anxious to win if he fairly and honestly could but would rather a thousand times go down to defeat than to win a victory by unfair, corrupt or dishonorable means, and would never accept a seat obtained in this way." He therefore cautioned his supporters "to be scrupulously careful not to say or do anything that might have even the appearance of being unfair or improper, so that no possible ground for criticism could exist as to the manner in which the campaign was conducted."[146]

Scott and Astrid Young report incorrectly that Frank Cochrane attended this convention and spoke on Hearst's behalf. The guest speaker was actually Arthur Boyce, the popular Conservative MP for Algoma West since 1904.[147] The Youngs also claim that, as Cochrane toured northern Ontario during the campaign, he made a point of telling his audiences that Hearst would soon join him in the cabinet.[148] Whether or not that is true, Whitney was following the situation because he immediately – on 4 April – sent a telegram to Hearst for publication in the Sault *Weekly Star* congratulating both him on his nomination and the Sault's voters "on the representative they will have in the Ontario Legislature in the future."[149]

The 1908 election was a massive Conservative victory, the greatest electoral sweep in Ontario history to that time. The Conservatives gained seventeen seats for a total of eighty-six, while the hapless Liberals won only nineteen. In northern Ontario, the Conservatives won all thirteen seats compared to just six out of eight in 1905,[150] and Hearst toppled Smith in Sault Ste. Marie by a majority of 241 out of 2,571 ballots cast.[151] One of the unsuccessful Liberal candidates was his law partner and friend, John McKay, who had run against Albert Grigg in Algoma.[152] This triumph reflected not just the popularity of the Whitney government and the disarray of the provincial Liberals but also the fact that the provincial Conservatives were better organized. It was so well organized, in fact, that Borden had agreed in 1907 to merge the federal and provincial organizations with Whitney's men – primarily Frank Cochrane, J.S. Carstairs, and A.E. Kemp, the wealthy Toronto manufacturer and MP, as fundraiser – managing both provincial and federal campaigns in Ontario.[153] The frosting on the Conservative cake was added a month later when Whitney was knighted while attending the tercentenary celebrations of the founding of Quebec.

Undeterred, Laurier dissolved parliament and called a federal election for 26 October. He faced stronger opposition in Ontario than in previous elections because of the popularity of the Whitney government and the amalgamation of the federal and provincial Conservative organizations. Cochrane managed the campaign in northern Ontario, and as usual, it proved to be interesting.[154] Arthur Boyce was safe in Algoma West, but Cochrane thought A.E. Dyment, a lumberman at Thessalon who had held Algoma and then Algoma East for the Liberals since 1896, was vulnerable. Dyment agreed after Cochrane persuaded W.R. Smyth, who had just been re-elected in Algoma West in the provincial election, to resign and run against him, acknowledging that Smyth would "poll hundreds of votes more than anyone else they could have brought out."[155] Cochrane also persuaded George Gordon to run again against Charles McCool, the Liberal who had held Nipissing since 1900, because he thought McCool was vulnerable.

The Liberals accused Cochrane of improper and even illegal behaviour in trying to influence the vote in northern Ontario. Dyment, for example, claimed that he "was determined to defeat me by fair means or foul, and he simply held a gun at the head of every man, Lumberman, Hotel Keeper and Fisherman, who has any business whatever with the Ontario Government.[156] James Conmee, the Port Arthur lumberman, railway contractor and Liberal MP for Thunder Bay and Rainy River since 1904, similarly complained of Cochrane's tactics, which was rich given Conmee's "well-earned reputation for corrupt political and business practices."[157] Conmee's complaints were probably true, of course, but that was how the system worked, and he had benefited from it for many years. Indeed, Hearst notified Attorney General J.J. Foy on 19 October of widespread irregularities in the compiling of the voters' lists in the two Algomas. Only men resident in the area since 1 August were eligible to vote, but Liberal enumerators had allegedly listed 439 men in lumber camps in Algoma East and 370 more in Algoma West who had come into the area only recently for the winter logging operations. According to both the Conservative Toronto *Mail and Empire* and the Liberal *Globe*, most of them were from Quebec and others were unnaturalized Italian immigrants.[158] Foy promptly sent fourteen special constables to investigate the charges and supervise the polling, and several men were charged with fraudulently registering ineligible men to vote.[159]

Several seats changed hands in the election, but in the end the Conservatives won forty-nine of the Ontario seats compared to the Liberals' thirty-seven, a gain of one. In northern Ontario, where the Conservatives had won only two out of six in 1904, they won five.[160] Dyment, understandably bitterly, proclaimed the contest in Algoma East "the most despicable campaign in Canada" and accused the provincial Conservatives of using "every influence, fair or foul, in their means to defeat him.[161] That was probably true and Dyment wasn't accustomed to being on the receiving end.[162]

When the Ontario legislature met in February 1909, Hearst was among the many new Conservative members who took their seats on the government benches but was immediately singled out by Whitney for the honour of moving adoption of the address in reply to the speech from the throne. He began by asserting that he had been chosen because he represented a northern riding, claiming that this reflected Whitney's keen interest in developing New Ontario. Accordingly, he extolled the vast wealth of the north and its great potential for the benefit of the province and the whole Dominion. He particularly praised Cochrane for his leadership in this development as representative of northern Ontario in the cabinet and as Minister of Lands, Forests and Mines.[163] This appears to have been Hearst's only contribution to the debates in the 1909 session. For the rest of it, he was content to observe and learn.

He was somewhat more active in the 1910 session. When Liberal leader A.G. MacKay commended the government for having established three technical schools and called for many more of them, Hearst agreed and highly praised the one in Sault Ste. Marie but also thought it important not to make the mistake of thinking that technical schools could or should replace traditional on-the-job training.[164] It was a balanced non-partisan response and typical of Hearst's cautiously progressive approach to issues.

More significant was his private member's bill, introduced on 14 February 1910, that sought to strengthen the Public Health Act by empowering municipalities to regulate the slaughter and processing of meat. The federal government had passed such legislation in 1907, but it only applied to plants engaged in interprovincial or international trade. Upton Sinclair's sensational 1905 book, *The Jungle,* had revealed that food-borne illnesses were the major cause of death in the United States and, as one scholar has written, "some Ontario slaughterhouses had been causing problems ... especially in cities like Toronto where waste disposal and land-use issues were problematic."[165] Hearst's bill proposed that municipalities be given the authority "to pass by-laws providing for the inspection of slaughterhouses outside the municipality, the produce of which is offered for sale within the municipality and forbidding the sale of meat within the municipality not slaughtered in slaughter houses approved by the Board of Health.[166] When the bill was debated on second reading, Whitney worried that it might result in jurisdictional clashes between municipalities, while MacKay more vaguely wondered if a better solution to the problem could not be found.[167] Jacob Kohler (Liberal, Haldimand) produced the obviously better solution by proposing that the provincial government simply accept responsibility for inspecting all slaughterhouses.[168] This was going too far, apparently, and Hearst's bill died in committee, but four years later the City of Toronto established a municipal abattoir in a limited effort to protect consumers. Hearst's first political initiative was significant, however, because it was another signal that while he was a conservative, he was more progressive than some.

In fact, his political career would indicate that he was a moderately progressive conservative. He never discussed his political philosophy publicly, other than his pride in being a citizen of the British Empire and a proud Canadian who, like many other Ontarians of his time, believed that the province was the driving force and the heart of the Canadian federation. But he was also a deeply committed Methodist, a fact that would shape his career. While there is no decisive evidence, Hearst appears to have been influenced by the progressive Social Gospel movement. Led primarily by Methodist and Presbyterian clergy, it shifted the focus of Christianity from salvation, as Richard Allen has put it, "to realize the kingdom of God in the very fabric of society."[169] The Fred Victor Mission, founded in Toronto in 1894 by the Massey family, the University of Toronto Settlement (1907), and the creation of a Department of Social Service at the University of Toronto in 1914 all reflected the influence of the Social Gospel movement. So too did the growing calls for social reform legislation.

Hearst tackled another social problem in the 1911 legislative session when he introduced a private member's bill to require undertakers to report all funerals to the Board of Health and require all prospective embalmers to pass examinations, thereby establishing common professional standards throughout the province.[170] The more conservative Whitney initially feared that the bill would create a closed corporation or guild, which he did not think was in the public interest. When Hearst explained how important such legislation was for protecting public health, especially in urban areas, Whitney relented and declared that he would not oppose it.[171] The bill passed second reading and was referred to the "embalming committee," as J.J. Foy, its chairman, somewhat ominously referred to the legal committee. In fact, the committee reported the bill with no amendments, and it was approved by the legislature with only minor amendments.[172] This was a significant advance in public health policy in an era before cremation, but it was also an accomplishment for a young backbencher to succeed in piloting a private bill through the legislature. More significant, perhaps, was the fact that he had succeeded in getting Whitney to change his mind, not a common event. And Hearst had shown that while he was a traditional Conservative, he also understood that governments had a role to play in addressing social issues.

# 2 Minister of Lands, Forests and Mines: 1911–14

*Never before has the north been so well satisfied and never before has there been as little fault finding.*[1]

The year 1911 was the year of the great clash over Laurier's proposed reciprocity agreement with the United States and his plan to build a Canadian navy. Both issues sharply divided Canadians, raising the long-standing struggle between English and French Canadians to a new level. Whitney fully supported Borden's positions on both issues but especially on reciprocity, which he feared would have very serious implications for Ontario. Hearst, like Whitney, was a traditional Anglo-Canadian imperialist and made his first major speech in the legislature when the Premier called on it in March 1911 to condemn reciprocity. Not surprisingly, Hearst focused on its potential impact on northern Ontario, which he was convinced would be negative because the region produced raw materials like minerals and timber that were already too often shipped to the United States to be processed and manufactured into finished products. Instead, Canada's policy should be "Canadian raw materials manufactured in Canada by Canadian workmen, who will receive Canadian money in return,"[2] with northern Ontario the linchpin between east and west because of its strategic location and vast resources.[3] It was a powerful speech, and it did not go unnoticed, with the *Mail and Empire* calling it "careful, painstaking, and well considered."[4] Whitney's resolution passed on a party vote of seventy-four to seventeen, whereupon the Conservatives rose in their places to sing "The Maple Leaf," "Rule Britannia," and "God Save the King."[5]

If the proposed reciprocity agreement threatened to drag Canada into the American empire by drastically altering its trading patterns, the other major issue in 1911 – Laurier's decision to build a Canadian navy – raised concerns about Canada's relationship with the mother country.

Most people, at least in English Canada, were open to the idea of Canada taking more responsibility for its own defence, and Laurier's plan to build a navy for coastal defence that could also collaborate with the Royal Navy made sense and was a step forward in the Dominion's evolution. But it would take years to build a navy, especially since Laurier thought it should be built in Canadian shipyards. That mattered because Borden believed that the naval arms race taking place between Britain and Germany since the turn of the century had become so critical that it made more sense in the short term to contribute financially to the Royal Navy and plan to build a Canadian navy over the longer term. A complicating factor was that most French Canadians weren't convinced that Canada needed a navy at all and feared that having one would inevitably drag Canada into British colonial wars, just as it had been pressured into sending troops to South Africa in 1899.

When Laurier unwisely called an election to resolve both issues, he seriously underestimated the emotional strength that they aroused among Canadians about their identity and Canada's place in the empire. While he pleaded for a rational debate on the issues, Québecois nationalists denounced him for selling out to the English Canadian imperialists while the Conservatives denounced him as disloyal for seeking to weaken the imperial connection while drawing closer to the United States. Clashes between the French and English in Canada had been taking place ever since Confederation and before, but the growth of Anglo-Protestant imperialism in the 1880s had a profound impact on the situation, stimulated by the 1885 Northwest uprising and the fate of Louis Riel, the Jesuit Estates controversy, and the Manitoba schools dispute. Imperialist nationalists like D'Alton McCarthy spoke for many, especially in Ontario, when they argued that to fulfil its destiny and take its rightful place within a united empire, Canada must be English in speech and British in thought. Suggestions by Québecois nationalists like Henri Bourassa that Canada should become a bicultural and bilingual nation moving towards independence were totally unacceptable.

The election campaign in Ontario was especially nasty because many people there, including some Liberals, had been distrustful for years of a francophone prime minister. Part of the "problem," of course, was that francophones were also Catholic and Anglo-Protestants were inclined to regard the Catholic Church as an international conspiracy aimed at total domination. As one scholar of the period has put it, "Protestantism was believed to be synonymous with democracy and liberty, as much as Catholicism was its antithesis."[6]

This feeling in Ontario focused on a specific issue that had emerged in 1910: the province's bilingual schools. These schools had existed in

Ontario since before Confederation and the Mowat government had shown a tolerant attitude, leaving it pretty much to local school boards to determine the question of language. This policy had proven successful in German settlements, where English was unquestionably the language of instruction and communication in the schools by 1889, but not much headway had been made in Franco-Ontarian communities. The Department of Education had issued instructions stating that English must be taught in all schools except where impracticable, but they had not been enforced.[7] Over the next twenty years, while many anglophone Ontarians were moving west, francophone Quebecers were moving into eastern and northern Ontario. The result was that, while the total population of Ontario rose from 1.9 million in 1881 to 2.5 million in 1911, the francophone population rose from 103,000 to 202,000 or possibly as high as 247,000.[8] In other words, it had risen from about 5 per cent to nearly 10 per cent of the provincial population. This alarmed some people and when the Conservatives came into office in 1905, the anti-French and anti-Catholic wing of the party pressed for stronger action.

Whitney tried to resist this pressure and maintain the policy of his predecessors, but times had changed. Conflict between Anglo-Protestantism and French-Catholic nationalism was increasing, as was seen in the uproar over the Laurier government's inclusion of Catholic schools in the autonomy bills when the provinces of Alberta and Saskatchewan were created in 1905, the Manitoba government's repudiation of both official bilingualism and then Catholic schools, the *Ne Temere* controversy in 1907 over a papal declaration invalidating marriages involving a Catholic unless performed by a parish priest or bishop, and Protestant indignation over a six-day international eucharistic conference held in Montreal in 1910.[9]

Then, when a commission appointed to investigate Ontario's bilingual schools reported that same year not only that the amount of English being taught was generally inadequate but that the schools were also inefficient and generally below standard, the government took further action. New regulations were issued, stating that English must be the language of instruction and communication except where the pupils did not understand English, but French could be taught as a subject of study in the curriculum in areas where the French language prevailed.[10] This was Regulation 12, which became Regulation 15 and played a major role in the bilingual schools controversy.

Franco-Ontarians understandably interpreted the government's policy as an attack on their language and culture and founded L'association canadienne-française d'education d'Ontario (ACFE) in January 1910 to ensure that "the French language and religious instruction shall occupy a place of honour" in their schools. This, they proclaimed, would require "primary bi-lingual schools, secondary bi-lingual schools, national bi-lingual schools and as a crown to the whole, a bi-lingual University."[11] This demand shocked most Anglo-Protestants, who thought it was one thing for francophones in Quebec to insist on their rights but quite another when francophones in Ontario claimed rights that they did not have. The Orange Order, which had long thought French Catholics dominated the Laurier government, led the way in denouncing these aspirations, convinced that the ACFE had been founded as another move in what it saw as a French Catholic plot to overrun Ontario.[12] In view of the growing strength of the nationalist movement in Quebec, this was not entirely untrue, as many anglophones realized when a magazine article pointing out that francophones already had "a preponderant voice in about fifteen counties of Ontario" and predicted that within a century the province would "be Gallicized by the logic of events" was translated into English and published in the popular *Canadian Magazine.*[13] The historian W.S. Wallace spoke for most Anglo-Protestant Canadians when he described the article as "a frank and ingenuous account of the aims and aspirations of the Nationalist party in Quebec" that was "all the more valuable" because it stated "freely and without reserve all those things which the nationalist leaders hesitate to say in public, and especially before an English audience."[14]

This was precisely what Anglo-Protestants feared. But the issue was actually larger than that because at least some Anglo-Protestants were becoming concerned not just about the "threat" to their identity and culture posed by the growing numbers of francophones but also the growing numbers of European immigrants under the Laurier government's open-door immigration policy. Religion was not necessarily an issue, except to extremists, because English-speaking Catholics, most of them Irish, were increasingly integrating into "the mainstream, Anglo-Protestant socio-economic milieu of English Canada."[15] According to Kevin Anderson, however, francophone Catholics "were certainly still held to be beyond the pale of true belonging" because they were perceived as refusing to participate in English Canadian society and even stressed their "otherness" through language, culture, traditions, and, of course, religion. This placed them in the same category as other non-British and racialized people, all of whom were perceived as objects to be acted upon and to be fixed while Anglo-Protestant Canadians were subjects to be protected, cultivated and included.[16]

A major complicating factor in the dispute was that Catholic separate schools in Ontario had been guaranteed by the British North America Act but not French-language schools. Inevitably, Catholic schools in predominantly francophone communities had in effect become bilingual schools, technically violating Ontario school policy. The government had accepted that children might need instruction in French at first but required them to learn English as well, for their own benefit if they were going to live in Ontario. English-speaking Catholics agreed with this policy, so the bilingual schools dispute was not simply between Protestants and Catholics; it was also between English-speaking and French-speaking Catholics.[17]

This being the case, English-speaking Catholics feared that the Franco-Ontarian agitation would arouse greater hostility to the separate school system. This fear was justified when the Anglo-Protestant reaction to the founding of the association caused Whitney to cancel plans he had been preparing to increase the provincial grants to separate schools.[18] This reaction was what alarmed Ontario's Catholic bishops. Bishop Michael Fallon of London, the most outspoken of them, strongly opposed the demands of the francophones, as did Archbishop Charles Gauthier (an anglophone despite his name) of Kingston and Bishop David Scollard of Sault Ste. Marie. They were supported by British Archbishop Francis Bourne, who was brave enough to declare at the eucharistic congress in September 1910 that the Catholic Church in Canada should identify itself with the English language. In an unexpected alliance, the Orange Order, which opposed Catholic schools on principle, found itself siding with English-speaking Catholics because it "saw the tragic history of the Eastern Townships being re-enacted in the eastern counties of Ontario."[19]

Whitney recognized by late 1910 that something had to be done. He therefore appointed Dr. F.W. Merchant, a senior official in the department of education, to investigate and report upon conditions in the bilingual schools. Merchant had already conducted studies of the schools in the Ottawa Valley, reporting in January 1909 that Catholic religious instruction was being given in bilingual schools during school hours and that the teaching and general use of English was wholly inadequate.[20] This was now followed by the release in December 1910 of reports from school inspectors from all over the province indicating that the same conditions were prevalent in bilingual schools throughout the province.[21]

In the spring of 1911 Howard Ferguson, the Conservative MPP from Grenville, began making extremist speeches at Orange gatherings around the province, establishing himself as a leader of the extreme Protestant wing of the Ontario Conservative Party. This did not please Whitney who, according to David Jamieson, the Conservative MPP for Grey South, openly "lashed out viciously at Ferguson" at a caucus meeting over his "too-free tongue at Orange picnics. I had never seen any man get such a dressing down as Whitney gave Ferguson," who "had tears in his eyes when he emerged from caucus."[22]

Undeterred, however, Ferguson introduced a motion in the legislature declaring that "no language other than English should be used as a medium of instruction" in any school in the province.[23] This enraged Whitney because Ferguson did it without first discussing it with him or even giving him advance notice that he was going to do it. As he would demonstrate more than once, Ferguson was not only very ambitious, but he was also never reluctant to act independently if he thought it would promote his career. Laurier was at least partly right when he concluded that Ferguson "had calculatingly grasped for himself the leadership of the extreme Orange element and was opposing bilingual schools for the sake of party advantage."[24] That was not quite true; Ferguson was promoting himself, and "for the first time he became a figure of provincial importance, his name blazoned in headlines alongside that of Bishop Fallon as a leader in one of the great questions of the day."[25] Whitney sensibly concluded that Ferguson was not a team player and never took him into the cabinet, although, as Ferguson's biographer points out, he was fully prepared to use him as the party's hatchet man.

Ferguson's unanticipated intervention was awkward because it came just as Robert Borden was flirting with Quebec's Nationalists with a view to ganging up on Laurier in the next federal election. Ferguson was persuaded to withdraw his resolution, replacing it with one that stated only that English should be "the language of instruction and communication in the public and separate schools of the Province, except where in the opinion of the Department of Education it is impracticable by reason of the pupils not understanding English."[26] This, as Whitney blandly pointed out, merely reiterated the existing law, that is, Regulation 15. The legislature accepted this assurance, and the resolution was adopted without debate.[27]

This kept a lid on the situation although the issue had a major impact in Ontario during the 1911 federal election, which proved to be one of the nastiest in Canadian history. Laurier found himself being denounced as disloyal while Bourassa's Nationalists, even though loosely allied with the Conservatives, were condemning him for selling out to the Anglo-Protestant imperialists. In Ontario the Orange Order inevitably claimed that bilingual schools were the supreme political issue and called on its members to support only candidates, regardless of party, who pledged their abolition.[28]

Whitney, who by 1911 had a firm grip on Ontario, regarded it as the patriotic duty of all loyal British subjects to oppose both the reciprocity agreement and the proposed navy and therefore did "all we could" to assist the Conservative campaign.[29] As in 1908, the federal and provincial Conservative organizations worked together.[30] Frank Cochrane again played a major role as well and, according to J.D. Reid, Ferguson "was the first man Cochrane asked for,"[31] his chief value being his willingness to campaign throughout the province stirring up ethnic and religious prejudice. The Conservatives were assisted by Clifford Sifton, Laurier's former Minister of the Interior, who did much to link disaffected Liberal businessmen with the Conservative campaign.[32]

Whitney not only advised Borden on campaign strategy and tactics in Ontario; he also allowed eight of his MPPs to contest federal ridings. He also personally campaigned extensively, as did most of his ministers and members. That included Hearst, who worked hard not only in the two Algomas but also throughout northern Ontario.[33] The result was never in doubt. The Conservatives won a comfortable majority nationally, including seventy-two seats in Ontario against only thirteen for the Liberals.[34] Charles Napier Smith, the former Liberal MPP whom Hearst had defeated in 1908, ran in Algoma West and was initially optimistic,[35] but both Algomas stayed Conservative. Indeed, the Conservatives retained the five constituencies they had won in 1908 and took Thunder Bay-Rainy River as well for a clean sweep of the north. The result in Ontario was due to both the reciprocity and naval issues and the poor state of the Liberal organization.[36] There was much truth too in Laurier's belief that he had been rejected in Ontario because he was a francophone Catholic.

Borden promptly summoned Whitney to Ottawa, hoping that the popular Premier would join his cabinet. Whitney declined to do so but had considerable influence in determining Ontario's representation,[37] and he wanted Cochrane in the cabinet as the unofficial representative of the Whitney government. Once again George Gordon, who had been re-election, in Nipissing, resigned to enable Cochrane to win the seat in a by-election and he moved to Ottawa as Minister of Railways and Canals.[38] That meant that Whitney needed a new Minister of Lands, Forests and Mines and representative of northern Ontario, and there was little doubt as to whom it would be.[39]

Hearst was, of course, expecting the call and returned to Toronto almost immediately, taking Vernon and Irving with him because Vernon was entering his third year and Irving was going into his first at the University of Toronto, where classes began on 28 September. Bella and the girls remained in Sault Ste. Marie because Bella had to sell Eastbourne and organize the move to Toronto. At the same time, her mother was seriously ill and could not be moved. Eastbourne was purchased by George

Mead, the new manager of the Spanish River Pulp and Paper Company, while Bella auctioned off unneeded furniture and other household goods.[40] When her mother died in May 1912, Bella and the girls joined William, Vernon, and Irving in Toronto. As Irving recalled, they "left the town the way my father had come to it twenty-four years earlier, down the river on a steamer."[41]

It must have been exciting for the family to move from a small industrial city in northern Ontario to the far-distant capital of the province where they knew nobody. But Hearst had found a new home for them on Glen Road in Toronto's exclusive Rosedale neighbourhood, considered "one of the healthiest and most desirable residential districts in the city."[42] It was conveniently close to Branksome Hall, a private girls' school, and the University of Toronto and wasn't far from Queen's Park. Because ministerial stipends were very modest and legislative sessions only took place in the spring, Hearst initially intended to carry on with his law practice in the Sault. He soon came to realize, however, that his responsibilities as a minister made this impossible, so he gave up the law, although his law firm continued to list him as senior partner.

Although not officially sworn into office as Minister of Lands, Forests, and Mines until 12 October, Hearst attended his first cabinet meeting on 3 October. There was no time to get a grip on his department, however, because Whitney had called on 11 October for an election to take place on 11 December. This seemed an unnecessarily long campaign in view of the fact that Ontario had just voted overwhelmingly for Borden's federal Conservatives and the provincial government clearly was very popular, but Whitney believed in holding elections every three years, and there were eleven vacancies in the legislature waiting to be filled.[43] In addition, the Conservative campaign organization had just performed brilliantly and was ready to go. The fact that Whitney didn't even wait until Borden was comfortably settled in at Ottawa came as no surprise to observers.[44]

No one – not even the Liberals – doubted that the Conservatives would be re-elected; the only question was how large their majority would be.[45] In the hope of at least minimizing their losses, the Liberals persuaded the hapless A.G. MacKay, who had led the party since 1907, to resign. He was replaced by the more high-powered Newton Rowell after W.L. Mackenzie King, who had served briefly as Laurier's Minister of Labour, refused the position.[46] It was a dubious honour, at least in the short term. How dubious was suggested by the fact that sixteen Conservative MPPs, including Hearst, were elected by acclamation.

As Charles Napier Smith acknowledged, the Liberals in Sault Ste. Marie could "scarcely hope to redeem the riding" because Hearst was popular, even with many Liberals.[47] Besides, given that the government was clearly going to be re-elected, "it might not be wise in the interests of the town" to oppose the minister who held "the most important portfolio that affects the Soo."[48] F.H. Clergue reinforced this idea by publicly praising Hearst when he addressed a public banquet held in his honour on 7 November, in the midst of the campaign. Clergue's speech on that occasion complained about "governmental indifference in the past" to his industrial enterprises at the Sault that had changed since Hearst's election in 1908. His appointment to the cabinet as Minister of Lands, Forests and Mines "showed [that] the government was realizing more than ever the importance of New Ontario." In fact, Hearst's appointment was "the wisest step from a New Ontario standpoint ... since I came to Canada."[49] Many prominent local Liberals expressed their support for Hearst at the banquet as well, and this was likely the occasion at which he was presented with a chest of silverware "in token of the esteem in which he was held."[50] When Alex McIntyre, a "popular contractor," showed interest in running for the Liberals he was, according to the Sault *Weekly Star*, "persuaded" not to do so.[51]

This enabled Hearst to support other candidates throughout northern Ontario, and he did so by talking about how the forest and mining industries were thriving, as were Clergue's steel and pulp mills in Sault Ste. Marie, which he attributed to the fact that the Whitney government was investing heavily in the region. Indeed, according to Arthur Matheson, the Provincial Treasurer, more than $20 million of the province's $24.5 million debt had been incurred in expenditures in New Ontario on the construction of the TNO Railway, colonization roads, land surveys, and other public works.[52]

As strong as the government was, Rowell proved to be a more effective leader than MacKay, not just attacking Whitney's record but also offering a progressive platform. He wisely promised a royal commission to study the problem of rural depopulation, supported public ownership of electric power – MacKay had opposed it – and proposed to extend the Hydro-Electric Power Commission's mandate to include telephones. He also promised workmen's compensation and anti-trust legislation.[53] But he was leading a dispirited party, still in shock from losing the recent federal election and struggling to offer a meaningful alternative to the respected Whitney and his popular policies.

Whitney understandably ran on his record, secure in the knowledge that it was an excellent one. The government's "progressive and vigorous" agricultural policies were defended and statistics were quoted to show that the decline in the rural population had actually levelled off since 1909.[54] Mainly, however, he ran on his own personal prestige and the fact that he was giving Ontario the "clean, progressive and efficient

Government" that he had promised.[55] By implied contrast, the Conservatives pointed out that the seemingly progressive Rowell was actually a corporation lawyer who represented large American companies such as United States Steel and the Great Northern Railway, the major rival of the CPR and National Transcontinental railways, and had recently supported Laurier's unpopular reciprocity agreement.[56] Ontarians could presumably draw their own conclusions.

This election was significant, however, because it was the first time, but certainly not the last, that two controversial issues – temperance and bilingual schools – played a major part. While this reflected the times, it also reflected the fact that Rowell was a prominent member of the Methodist Church and a vice-president of the Dominion Alliance, the nation's main prohibition movement.[57] On that issue he was more radical than Whitney and most Conservatives; on bilingual schools he tried to give the impression that he was less extreme, although the truth was that he supported the government's policy, as did most Liberals.

Temperance had been a political issue in Ontario for many years. The first legislation on the subject was the Crooks Act, which had established the local option system in 1876.[58] Support for stronger temperance legislation had grown steadily since then and three plebiscites – two provincial and one federal – had been held on the question. All had registered majorities in favour of stronger legislation or even prohibition, but only a minority of the population had voted, so nothing much had been done before Whitney came into office in 1905.

The no-nonsense Whitney had no sympathy for temperance. As Joseph Schull has put it, he faced it "with a cold and steady eye. Detesting windy eloquence and sanctimonious pretensions, he saw both in many supporters of the movement."[59] As a pragmatic politician – and a man who had enjoyed alcohol in his younger years – he "was contemptuous of the cant surrounding prohibition and equally so of attempts to make it law."[60] He was a realistic politician, however, and recognized that he had to keep pace with public opinion but thought restrictions on the availability of alcohol should only be introduced when strong public support was evident. For this reason he had passed legislation in 1906 requiring a three-fifths majority in all local option contests while also approving the sale of alcohol on ships and trains within the province. These changes naturally prompted temperance advocates to charge that he was a tool of the liquor industry, ignoring the fact that he had also tightened up the licensing and inspection service and reduced liquor profits by increasing provincial fees. The result was that the number of "dry" municipalities had risen from 187 compared to 607 "wet" in 1905 to 440 "dry" and only 380 "wet" in 1911.[61] The number of tavern and shop licences had also declined from 2,516 to 1,630 and from 298 to 226, respectively, in the same period.[62]

MacKay had tried to avoid the temperance question, recognizing how divisive it was, but that changed when Rowell became leader. He promised to repeal the three-fifths clause[63] but couldn't go any further because he had not yet had time to consult his colleagues to work out a party policy.[64] Whitney was content to point out the progress that had been made since 1905 and defended the three-fifths rule as "the best, the wisest and the most common sense enactment with relation to the subject which has been adopted within my recollection."[65] That was probably true, but many temperance advocates agreed with Rowell that the government should go further and some were thought to be switching their support to the Liberals on this issue.[66] This infuriated Whitney, who condemned men who would desert a government that they generally supported except on one issue to support a party whose policies they generally opposed except on that one issue.[67] Hearst fully supported Whitney's approach to the issue because it reflected the state of public opinion.

As for bilingual schools, even though ethnic and religious animosities had been greatly stirred up in the recent federal election Whitney tried to avoid the issue pending Merchant's report, which he made sure was not submitted until after the election. The extremist Protestant wing of his party wasn't having that, however, and the Orange *Sentinel* was calling for the complete abolition of French in the schools.[68] Howard Ferguson, having been re-elected by acclamation in Grenville, toured the province stirring the pot with fire-breathing speeches at Orange gatherings, supported by Toronto's *Evening Telegram* and even by the only two Catholics in the cabinet, J.J. Foy, the Attorney General, and J.O. Reaume, the Minister of Public Works and Ontario's first Franco-Ontarian cabinet minister.[69]

Hearst appears not to have taken a public position on the issue, but there is little doubt that he fully supported Whitney's policy, which focused on language and had nothing to do with religion, well aware that Sault Ste. Marie's Catholic bishop, David Scollard, thought that the government's policy was "pre-eminently fair, just and equitable, and should satisfy all fair-minded men."[70] Liberal newspapers such as the Toronto *Daily Star* and the *Globe* fanned the flames of prejudice by running articles describing the rapid growth of the French-speaking population in northern Ontario and warning that French Catholics would soon dominate that part of the province.[71] Rowell was cautious on this issue, stating only that while English must be taught in all schools, the children of French-speaking parents were entitled to instruction in their mother tongue as well.[72]

Whitney was not worried about the outcome of the election because he knew that the public generally supported the government's position on both temperance and bilingual schools. As he told Cochrane on 15 November, while "our opponents are trying to make considerable noise ... so far I do not see much sign of any effect."[73] It was true, and W.L. Mackenzie King, now president of the General Reform Association of Ontario and chairman of the committee that wrote the Liberal Party's platform, explained why: "we had no money, no anything, the outlook was hopeless and there was little to criticize in the Government save inaction, and indifference."[74] Or, as historian Robert Cuff put it, the Whitney government's willingness "to advance progressive policies" had "left little room for Liberal alternatives."[75] That may explain why the Liberals didn't even contest twenty-eight constituencies.[76]

The government's confidence was vindicated on election day, when the Conservatives swept back into office with 83 of the 106 seats, compared to the Liberals' 22.[77] This was a decline of four for the Conservatives and a gain of three for the Liberals, but the Conservatives could hardly complain. In northern Ontario, Hearst had done his job well: the Conservatives held on to twelve of its thirteen ridings.[78] As for the bilingual schools issue, six Franco-Ontarians were elected, compared to four in 1908, but in both elections the two parties split them evenly, so it is difficult to assign any significance to the results. Reaume retained Essex North, but he had had to fight "a bruising" battle for the Conservative nomination with "Orange Order insurgents" who then ran an independent candidate against him. The result was that, even though he and the Liberal candidate had agreed that francophone children should be educated in French "provided they received adequate English instruction," Reaume won by only fifty-six votes.[79] The Conservatives also retained Nipissing and, rather surprisingly, added Ottawa East, the centre of the bilingual schools controversy, by running a francophone against the anglophone Liberal incumbent. However, the Liberals retained Russell and added Sturgeon Falls and Prescott.[80]

Hearst was now able to get down to work in his department. It was a major portfolio that focused largely on the development of northern Ontario, in which he was keenly interested. The Ross government had recognized the potential importance of the region since a federal scientific study had reported at the turn of the century that the so-called Great Clay Belt, more than 40,000 square kilometres of land – equivalent to four-fifths of the province's existing agricultural land – extending from the Quebec boundary to the District of Thunder Bay in the territory north of the height of land dividing the Great Lakes and Hudson Bay watersheds.[81] The Ross government had understandably begun encouraging young men seeking land to move north instead of west, a policy continued more vigorously by the Whitney government. Ownership of the territory had been disputed by the federal and Ontario governments for several years because it had been part of the Hudson's Bay lease until 1884 when the Judicial Committee of the Privy Council awarded it to Ontario. But it had not yet been "ceded" by the Anishinaabe and Mushkegowuk peoples, and that needed to be done and the Canadian Transcontinental and TNO railways were already being built through it. The result was that the federal government negotiated Treaty 9, by which the Anishinaabe and Mushkegowuk "ceded" the territory in 1905 in return for a reserve, annuities, and the right to continue hunting and fishing. As has been noted earlier, however, Indigenous peoples interpreted "ceding" lands to mean sharing it, not selling it. Four years later Frank Oliver, the Minister of the Interior and Superintendent-General of Indian Affairs in the Laurier government, amended the Indian Act to allow portions of reserves to be expropriated by municipalities or companies for roads, railways, or other purposes in violation of treaties.[82]

What was unusual about the negotiations was that the government negotiators included a representative of the provincial government: George MacMartin, a prosperous businessman in Perth and close friend of A.J. Matheson, the Provincial Treasurer in the new Whitney government.[83] That was because Whitney's goal was to develop a diversified economy in the northland based on forestry, mining and agriculture, and that the area would soon be "thickly settled" with a million people.[84] This was why one of his first actions in 1905 had been to convert the Department of Crown Lands into the Department of Lands, to which he added responsibility for mines, signalling the department's new focus on northern Ontario. At the same time, he moved the Bureau of Forestry – renamed the Bureau of Colonization and Forestry – from the Department of Lands to the Department of Agriculture, from which the Ross government had moved it, with the new mandate of "promoting the settlement of new farmlands" in northern Ontario.[85] The idea of linking agriculture and forestry in the north was not a novel idea. The Quebec government's northern policy gave agriculture "complete primacy" over forestry.[86] And the experience of Dryden, north-west of Port Arthur, appeared to support the idea. Founded as an agricultural community in 1895, a sawmill had been built there two years later, followed by two more, and the community had grown to 600 farms within a decade. In 1907 Cochrane and Nelson Monteith, the Minister of Agriculture, explored the clay belt and chose a site near Iroquois Falls for a northern experimental and demonstration farm, and two years later forestry was returned to the Department of Lands and Mines, which became the Department of Lands, Forests and Mines.

Historian Barry Boothman has claimed that the politicians misled people into thinking that the northern wilderness could be transformed into "into gardens of plenty," while Mark Kuhlberg, the pre-eminent historian of Ontario's forestry history, more subtly argues that the government continued to make such claims even when "almost immediately it became clear that this dream would never materialize."[87] S.J.R. Noel has suggested that many people in southern Ontario believed these claims because of "ignorance ... on the part of an agrarian people" with "no direct experience" of a "hard Laurentian land."[88] But the Ross government cautioned prospective settlers in 1902 that farming in the north "involves much hard, rough work for comparatively slight returns at the outset" and that "for some time to come" settlers must "be prepared to dispense with many conveniences and luxuries easily obtainable even by the poor in an older community, but unprocurable in a bush settlement."[89] Similarly, the Whitney government pointed out to potential settlers in 1907 that they would need to supplement their incomes with employment in "lumber, mining or railway construction camps" or in nearby villages and towns that also provided markets for their produce.[90]

But there is no denying that when Hearst became minister and then Premier his enthusiastic claims about northern Ontario's ability to support agriculture were extreme. Speaking to the Canadian Club in Toronto in November 1912, for example, he pointed out that "much of what we call northern Ontario lies south of the International boundary," meaning presumably that it was no farther north than the western provinces. That was true but profoundly misleading. But then he reported that J.F. Whitson, a North Bay surveyor who had just returned from the area, "can tell you of the beautiful weather they are having in the country around Cochrane now." Indeed, they were enjoying summer weather in "the great banana belt" and Whitson had "found snow and cold only when he came [south] to North Bay."[91] Whitson was not an unbiased witness. He had joined the department in 1890 and, according to his obituary, was "one of the first to realize the possibilities of the Great Clay Belt ... as an agricultural asset to the Province."[92]

One would like to think that Hearst was deliberately exaggerating to make his point that agriculture was feasible in the north, but when Bernhard Fernow, the University of Toronto's first dean of forestry, concluded after touring the area that "too sanguine expectations are being entertained and should be guarded against,"[93] Hearst foolishly responded, "I know a great deal more about northern Ontario than any professor in the country" and that "there are millions and millions of acres of the very best agricultural land in the world."[94] That was a gross exaggeration. There were pockets of rich soil where root crops and short-season varieties of other crops were feasible, but the average frost-free growing season was only eighty days in a total growing season of one hundred days. And this was only an average: in 1918 there were only eleven days from the last spring frost to the first autumn frost.[95]

Kerry Abel has flatly charged that Hearst's claims "bordered on the criminally misleading." That would be true if Hearst was knowingly making false claims, but he wasn't. He believed what he was saying and Abel concedes that New Ontario, having "sustained an Aboriginal people for thousands of years … seemed to promise endless opportunity for Canadians at the beginning of the twentieth century."[96] The problem was that Hearst, who was a generally modest and cautious man, got carried away in his enthusiasm for the part of Canada he had embraced and genuinely loved and believed was destined for greatness while denying its very real limitations. As he told the Ottawa Canadian Club in November 1913, New Ontario was destined to become "one of the great manufacturing centres of the American Continent" because of its vast natural resources and central location and would not only support a population of millions but would also help tounify Canada because its wealth would benefit both east and west by means of Canada's transcontinental railway network. "We want to bind this Dominion of Canada together," he declared,

> so that we shall know neither East nor West, neither North nor South, but one united Canada, pulsating with intellectual and industrial life from the Atlantic to the Pacific and from her southern boundary to the shores of the Hudson's [*sic*] Bay. This is the object that I have before me as a public man. This is the ideal that I have in my view."[97]

It was a noble vision that placed Hearst squarely in the Macdonald tradition of Canadian Conservatism: a belief in national development that would unite Canadians, with each region contributing its own strengths and benefiting from the strengths of the other regions, all bound together by the east–west transportation network, centred on northern Ontario, "a domain that could bring substance to the visions of a provincial Manifest Destiny." This was, of course, only a modified version of what Ontario's political leaders had sought since at least the 1850s: the creation of a transcontinental economic and political empire that the so-called empire province would dominate because of its large population and strategic location, which was why it had been the driving force behind Confederation.

Meanwhile, the forestry industry was going through a dramatic transformation, shifting increasingly from the production of lumber to pulpwood to supply the seemingly insatiable American market for newsprint. But pulp mills required vast amounts of fibre because the complex and very expensive chemical process of converting trees into paper involved a high ratio between raw material and final product. According to Mark Kuhlberg, every 100 tons of mill capacity required approximately 2.225 million cords of pulpwood. That meant that pulp mills required a much larger investment and much larger long-term timber leases than lumber mills. Pulp mills also required a lot of power: 10,000 horsepower of electrical power for every 100 tons of mill capacity.[98] Happily, northern Ontario had an abundance of trees and rivers on which hydroelectric plants could be built.

Liberal governments had supported the growth of the pulpwood industry, beginning with the St. Anthony Lumber Company at what became the village of Whitney in Nipissing District, Clergue's mill at Sault Ste. Marie in 1895, and the Dryden Board Mills Company in 1903. The Whitney government took a different approach to forestry, however, favouring lumber companies because they harvested on a smaller scale and provided essential seasonal employment for the settlers. Thus, one of its first actions in 1905 was to retender the timber lease of the Dryden Board Mills Company that was building a lumber mill on the Wabigoon River[99] and supported the Wisconsin-based Pigeon River Lumber Company, which had built a large sawmill at Port Arthur in 1901. It also denied pulpwood leases to the Fort Frances and Port Arthur Pulp and Paper Companies, forcing them to obtain pulpwood from settlers in the area.[100] At the same time, however, it did grant small pulpwood leases to lumber companies that were subsidizing their declining supplies of quality pine by harvesting pulpwood as well.[101]

And yet Aubrey White, the department's deputy minister, told the Canadian Forestry Association in 1908 that the province's "greatest timber asset" in the "not distant future" would be pulpwood.[102] Four years later the government granted a pulpwood lease to the Montreal-based Abitibi Pulp and Paper Company to cut pulpwood but not prime timber and was authorized to build a mill at Iroquois Falls on the Abitibi River 300 kilometres north-west of North Bay and hydro-electric power plants at the Iroquois Falls and Couchiching Falls. Abel claims that Abitibi was "an instant political darling, courted devotedly by the Ontario government and promoted as a sign of the success of its policies." The Whitney government boasted in 1914 that Abitibi would employ between 1,500 and 1,800 men and was proof of the success of its northern development policy. In fact, however, J.A. McAndrew, the company's secretary, privately told Hearst that Abitibi would only employ 250 to 300 men in the near future.[103] In 1916 Frank Anson, the company president, promised Howard Ferguson, then Minister of Lands, Forests and Mines, that it would enlarge its mill to double production if the government gave it additional cutting rights. Ferguson, who keenly supported the pulp and paper industry, took no action until 1919, however, when he provoked a major scandal that helped to bring down the government.[104]

Politics had played a major role in the forestry industry for many years. James Conmee, a Port Arthur railway builder, lumberman and the most influential Liberal politician in north-western Ontario had controlled the granting of timber leases and other forms of patronage, along with his businessman son-in-law James Whalen and Walter Russell, a lumberman. After the 1905 election they were replaced by Frank Cochrane and a group of Port Arthur Conservative businessmen such as J.J. Carrick, J.A. Little, and D.M. Hogarth. Carrick was a real estate developer, owner of the Port Arthur *News-Chronicle*, mayor, MPP from 1908 to 1911 and MP for Rainy River from 1911 to 1917. J.A. Little was manager of Molson's Bank in Port Arthur until 1917 when he resigned, as the *News-Chronicle* put it, to "give his whole attention to private business affairs which have been increasing in volume to a considerable extent during the past few years."[105] According to H.V. Nelles, "no one cut anything in the northwestern part of the province" between 1911 and 1920 "without first doing business" with them and "all government appointments, including those in the Department of Lands, Forests and Mines whose regulations they were flouting passed through their offices."[106]

The fact that Cochrane continued the Liberal practice of managing timber leases politically was understandable, but the tracts were rarely surveyed and no effort was made to determine their actual value. Cochrane also decentralized management of the department, increasing the importance of the cullers, who were part-time employees paid directly by the companies whose cut they were scaling. According to Aubrey White's biographer, when Cochrane introduced new cutting regulations in 1907 based on volumes cut, they depended on numbers declared by the lumbermen themselves and verified by the cullers. "No bureaucratic reform accompanied this system, a failure that left much control in the hands of the lumberers [*sic*] and placemen who traditionally ruled field operations."[107] "The situation was," as forestry historians Gillis and Roach conclude, "made to order for pork barrelling and boondoggling"[108] and Carrick and his associates fully exploited the situation for their own benefit. J.A. Little, for example, formed the New Ontario Contracting Company, which illegally harvested pulpwood along the National Transcontinental Railway line near Sioux Lookout and on crown lands in the Thunder Bay district on which it had staked much cheaper mining claims. All this pulpwood was shipped across the border, "thus turning a handsome profit for nominal expenditure."[109]

The lumberman who almost certainly benefited the most from his political connections was James Mathieu, who had moved from Minnesota to Fort Frances to manage the Rainy River Lumber Company's sawmill and rose to become vice-president of the Shevlin-Clarke Company, reputedly the largest pine sawmill for thirty years.[110] He not only received timber leases without having to tender for them but got them "at well under one-third their market value" and harvested them "practically unimpeded" by the Crown Timber Act regulations.[111] Not coincidentally, he was also the Conservative MPP for Rainy River from 1911 to 1923.

How much Hearst knew about corruption in his department when he was minister isn't really known. It seems inconceivable that he was not aware of it and perhaps just tolerated it as being a necessary part of politics. The only defence of his management of the department, if it can be called that, has been offered by Gillis and Roach, who claim that he was "less interested in the day-to-day details of resource administration" than Cochrane had been. This may just have reflected his personality, of course, or his belief that ministers should not get too involved in the workings of their department, and to be fair, he had total confidence in his deputy minister, the very able and experienced Aubrey White.[112] Peter Oliver, Howard Ferguson's biographer, speculates that Hearst deliberately "maintained a degree of detachment from what he may have considered the seamier side of the political process," leaving it to "the Fergusons and McGarrys to tend to such matters."[113] That had been Whitney's policy too, and he had enjoyed a reputation for honesty and integrity, while others did what seemed to be necessary in politics.

Having said that, we do know of one instance in 1913 when Hearst intervened when Edward Backus, president of the Minnesota and Ontario Paper Company, sought a 3,000 square-kilometre timber concession at Lake of the Woods to supply a pulp mill that he proposed to build at Kenora. Town council and Harold Machin, the local Conservative MPP, supported the proposal and Hearst initially approved it. When the local lumbermen complained that the lease should include a provision allowing them to continue to harvest sawlogs in the area, Hearst allegedly retorted in frustration that the people of Kenora apparently did "not want a pulp mill, as no mill could operate under the terms you propose." Within days, however, perhaps having consulted White, he reversed his position and rejected Backus's proposal. Negotiations continued for several months until Backus got his lease after agreeing that the local lumbermen could not only harvest the pine at no cost but also any pulpwood they encountered in their operations. The contract also reserved all the poplar for a local barrel-making company. What this meant, according to Mark Kuhlberg, was that "in no uncertain terms, the lumbermen enjoyed much greater privileges on the Lake of the Woods pulpwood concession than Backus, who was the concessionaire."[114] The result was that when Backus's newsprint mill at Fort Frances became operational in 1914 he had to import timber from Minnesota. It was not until after the 1919 election that he acquired several pulpwood leases from the new Drury government to supply the two newsprint mills he planned to build at Kenora and Fort William.

Hearst's greatest achievement as minister undoubtedly was the role he played in settling the long-standing Keewatin territorial dispute. The District of Keewatin was a large region between north-western Ontario and north-eastern Manitoba that both provinces had been squabbling over since 1872, partly because its timber and mineral resources were important but also because Ontarians had regarded the north-west as a logical extension of their territory since at least the 1850s. The federal government's acquisition of the Hudson's Bay Company's empire and the creation of Manitoba raised concerns in Ontario because of the vague boundaries, and by the 1880s its territorial ambitions in the region "were vast," its government "unyielding," and its people "in no mood to accept anything less than what they believed to be their full entitlement."[115] The Mowat government had gained 285,000 square kilometres of territory in an arbitration ratified by the Judicial Committee of the Privy Council in 1884, but the extension of Keewatin territory to the coast of Hudson Bay in 1895 made it potentially more valuable. The creation in 1905 of the provinces of Alberta and Saskatchewan further complicated the issue because their northern boundaries were set at the sixtieth parallel, naturally prompting the government of Manitoba to claim that its territory should do so as well.

The Laurier government had refused to address the issue, but shortly after the 1911 election, Manitoba's Conservative Premier Rodmond Roblin raised the question with the new federal government that he had helped to elect. But if Manitoba deserved to be rewarded for electing eight Conservatives, Ontario deserved more because it had elected seventy-two – more than half of Borden's 136 seats – and Whitney fully expected Ontario to be rewarded as well. Behind-the-scenes negotiations began in November 1911 and continued until February 1912.[116] That was when Robert Rogers, formerly Roblin's right-hand man but now Minister of the Interior in the Borden government, cheekily introduced a bill in parliament to annex Keewatin to Manitoba. Needless to say, Whitney was outraged. Having contributed so much to Borden's victory, his position would be impossible if he could not now get what Ontarians expected from a Conservative government. Cochrane assured him that Ontario would get most of what Whitney wanted in the negotiations for the simple reason that Ontario had more influence than Manitoba, and Cochrane was reliable.[117] Rogers had played his first card, but he knew a compromise would be necessary. As J.W. Dafoe, the editor of the *Manitoba Free Press* and a strong Liberal, once said of him, "Mr. Rogers played the game hard."[118] But so did Frank Cochrane.

What did Whitney want? He had suggested in 1906 that the existing Manitoba–Ontario boundary should run straight north to the Churchill River and then proceed down its middle channel to Hudson Bay with both provinces sharing Port Churchill, the only usable port on the western shore.[119] This was a rather extreme proposal but not as extreme as what the provincial Liberals were demanding, which was their unrealistic 1905 proposal to extend the existing boundary northward to the sixtieth parallel, which would cut Manitoba off from Hudson Bay. That suggestion was just partisan politicking, of course, although Whitney did fear that Roblin and Rogers were out to cut Ontario off from the western shore of the bay, which would be a "manifest and savage injustice."[120] Whitney was convinced that a reasonable compromise could be negotiated and had already proposed in 1909 that the Nelson River, about 161 kilometres south of the Churchill River, be the boundary because this would still give Ontario access to the harbour at York Factory. Manitoba had rejected that proposal.

Whitney called Cochrane down to Toronto to discuss the problem and Hearst was, of course, present. When Cochrane made an offer that called for certain concessions by Ontario, Hearst refused to surrender any territory that he regarded as rightfully Ontario's, largely because of the potential mineral resources.[121] The final settlement does appear to have been agreed upon at this conference, at least in outline, and Hearst subsequently went to Ottawa to work out the details.[122] The only question now was whether Roblin would accept the arrangement; Whitney desperately hoped he would, and quickly, for he knew he was going to be faced with embarrassing questions in the 1912 session of the legislature, which was about to begin.[123] Inevitably, Rowell did raise the issue in the legislature but to no avail because Roblin accepted the arrangement "in the form arranged with Mr Hearst."[124]

Whitney and Borden jointly announced the terms of the settlement on 27 February. Manitoba's northern boundary was extended northward to the sixtieth parallel on the western side but north-eastward to Hudson Bay to a point due north of the junction of the Ohio and Mississippi Rivers. This added 290,000 square kilometres to Manitoba, including 1,295 kilometres of coastline on Hudson Bay, and the province's federal grant was raised as well, so Roblin could claim that the province had achieved equality with Alberta and Saskatchewan. Ontario's territory was extended due north from the Lake of the Woods, then northeast to Hudson Bay, adding 80,000 square kilometres of territory, and it was granted a railway right-of-way to either York Factory or Port Churchill.[125] It was less than Whitney and Hearst had hoped for, but it was equitable because Ontario would benefit significantly from the additional resource revenues while Manitoba, like the other prairie provinces, would not. And the federal government sweetened the deal by agreeing to pay a subsidy of $2.1 million to the provincially owned Temiskaming and Northern Ontario (TNO) Railway, something the Laurier government had refused even to consider.[126]

The evidence suggests that Hearst's role in the negotiations was critical because the final agreement was based on his recommendations. This made sense because he was not only the minister responsible for northern Ontario and the development of its resources, he also lived in the area and knew it better than anyone else in the government and both Whitney and Cochrane trusted his judgment. The provincial Liberals naturally criticized the settlement, cynically overlooking the fact that it was much more favourable than what the Laurier government had offered.

Hearst wasted no time after the judgment before sponsoring legislation regarding jurisdiction over rivers and streams, a subject of dispute between Ontario and the federal government since Confederation. He was responding to a conflict between the Keewatin Power Company and the town of Kenora over jurisdiction on the Winnipeg River, which flows from Lake of the Woods to Lake Winnipeg and then drained via the Nelson River into Hudson Bay. The company had been granted land on the western bank but claimed to own the western half of the riverbed as well, on the grounds that the river was not "navigable." The Hudson's Bay Company owned the eastern bank of the river in the same area and similarly claimed to own the eastern half of the riverbed. The question was whether or not the Winnipeg River was a "navigable" or an "inland waterway." If deemed to be navigable, the crown owned the riverbed, but if deemed to be an "inland waterway," it belonged to the adjacent landowner, although the right to surface navigation was preserved. Because of the importance of the timber industry in the area, the dispute had major implications. The company claimed that the Winnipeg River was an inland waterway, but Kenora claimed that it was navigable because it ultimately drained into Hudson Bay. When the dispute went to court in 1906, Rowell represented Kenora, presumably in the interests of the timber companies, and Hearst represented the Crown with a watching brief.[127] The lower court ruled in favour of Kenora, but the Ontario Supreme Court reversed this decision, and Kenora did not carry the issue any higher.[128]

The government passed legislation in 1911, however, declaring that the riverbeds of inland waterways did not automatically belong to the adjacent landowners. Hearst now intervened because Kenora had built a power plant at the rapids on the river and a log slide with a charter granted by the provincial government.[129] He followed up in 1913 with two more bills. The first prevented the Provincial Secretary from allowing any company to build dams or slides for the transmission of lumber down rivers without the approval of the Minister of Lands, Forests and Mines.[130] The second stipulated that "where a dam is now or shall hereafter be erected on or across any river down which timber is usually brought, such dam shall at all times be provided with a slide or apron for the passage of timber, rafts and crafts of such description and dimensions as shall be prescribed in the regulations."[131][132]

This seemed a reasonable compromise except for the fact that the 1873 Treaty 3 with the Anishinaabe First Nation had acknowledged its rights over local fisheries, not just on reserve land but also throughout the vast tract of land surrendered, and that included compensation for the construction of dams, canals, and other public works that infringed on those rights and the acquisition of a large part of Keewatin Territory required Ontario to collaborate with the Department of Indian Affairs in determining the location and size of Indigenous reserves in the area, a process that continued until August 1914.[133] Aubrey White handled the negotiations with Duncan Scott, his federal counterpart, but Hearst was fully briefed on these negotiations. Despite Treaty 3, both men agreed, as White put it, that "it surely was never intended that lands under a river should belong to the Indians."[134] They also discussed whether boundaries should be along the shorelines, as they had been surveyed, or along a line between the projecting headlands. White's view was that the headland-to-headland option "left the door open for all kinds of disputes and misunderstandings hereafter."[135] Scott agreed, as did W.J. Roche, the Minister of the Interior and Superintendent-General of Indian Affairs. The Ontario legislation, titled An Act to confirm the title of the Government of Canada to certain lands and Indian lands, was passed on 8 April 1915 "after an all-night sitting."[136] It declared, contrary to Treaty 3, that waterways did not "form part" of reserves, a dubious decision that is currently being litigated more than a century later.[137]

This reflected the Whitney government's commitment to developing New Ontario, which it announced in April 1912 with a multi-year $5 million Northern Development Plan. This was an extraordinary commitment when it is remembered that the government's total annual budget was only about $12 million. Most of the money would be spent on the construction of roads extending north and south of the National Transcontinental and west for more than 321 kilometres from the Quebec boundary in order to open up 304,000 hectares for settlement and provide land for some 5,000 farms.[138] to be managed within his department under the direction of J.F. Whitson.

While Whitney and Cochrane had strongly believed in northern Ontario's potential as an agricultural region, Hearst was almost evangelical. His enthusiastic promotion of the northland was frequently commented on in the press, and on one occasion the members of the Toronto Press Club actually serenaded him with a song, asking,

> What's the matter with William,
> William Howard Hearst?
> What's the matter with William?
> There's nothing but his thirst.
> William thirsts to sally forth
> And rave and rave of the wonderful north.
> What's the matter with William?
> There's nothing but his thirst.[139]

Perhaps recalling his own family's experience back in the 1840s, 1850s, and 1860s, Hearst thought the ideal settlers for the northland were "people from Old Ontario who were accustomed to the hard life of frontier farming." As for immigrants, British, Germans, and Scandinavians would be appropriate, although even they would be "much better fitted for settlement in northern Ontario by spending two or three years in Older Ontario and adapting themselves."[140] Apparently confusing southern Europe with eastern Europe, he thought that "many of the people" who had been encouraged to settle on the prairies were not "adapted for a country like Northern Ontario" because they weren't hardy enough for the conditions.[141] Hearst was, of course, merely reflecting the commonly held racial views of his time, but his recommendation that farmers wishing to settle in northern Ontario should gain some experience in southern Ontario did appear to conflict with his claim that northern Ontario was the banana belt of Canada. In fact, many of the people who did settle there turned out to be eastern Europeans or francophone Catholic Quebecers, not quite what Whitney and Hearst had in mind.

The Liberals didn't oppose the Northern Development Plan in principle but they didn't think Hearst should be granted such a large amount of money to be spent over a prolonged period. Rather, the legislature should grant smaller amounts annually as required. Rowell suggested that the government create a separate Department of Northern Affairs.[142] These suggestions were not unreasonable as legislatures were not yet in the habit of approving large multi-year program funding. Hearst dismissed their concerns, however, accusing the Liberals of not really wanting to develop the northland, and the bill passed on a party vote.

Meanwhile, Whitney was seeking a major change in the province's federal subsidy. Because of the growth of provincial responsibilities since Confederation, that subsidy, which had contributed 75 per cent of Ontario's revenues in 1868, now contributed only 25 per cent. During the same period the provincial subsidies had declined from 35 per cent to only 10 per cent of the federal government's revenues. All of the provinces were struggling with the same problem, of course, but the situation was even worse from Ontario's point of view because the provincial subsidy was not calculated on a per capita basis. Thus, for example, Ontario's subsidy amounted to ninety-seven cents per capita, while Alberta's was $3.37.[143] Whitney sensibly did not mention that during the same period Ontario had received significant – and growing – revenues from the development of its natural resources, a source of income denied to the prairie provinces.

Whitney had proposed in 1913 not only that the subsidy be determined on a per capita basis but that the provinces should receive a percentage of federal tariff revenues as well because tariffs had contributed significantly to the rise in federal revenues over the years. This was received coolly by Borden and coldly by Thomas White, his Minister of Finance, both in principle but also perhaps because the country was sliding into a recession which was having an impact on federal revenues as well. They did agree, however, to assist the provinces with the cost of agricultural education and highway construction, matters that came under provincial jurisdiction. This was a significant precedent although the funding was not substantial: $10 million over a decade for agricultural education and $1 million for highways, $350,000 of which went to Ontario. The Liberals – led in the Senate by former Ontario Premier Sir George Ross – allowed the agricultural education program but blocked the highways program, describing it as "a permanent corruption fund."[144] The outbreak of war in August 1914 quickly ended any further discussion of a more generous sharing of revenues, creating a problem that Hearst would have to deal with as Premier.

Issues related to New Ontario occupied much of the legislature's time during the 1913 session. Hearst introduced no fewer than sixteen bills, fifteen of which became law. Perhaps the most important made extensive amendments to the Mines Act, which reflected the concern for public health he had shown as a private member. No children under fourteen years of age were to be employed in or around a mine, no boys under seventeen years of age were to be employed underground, and women were to be employed only in office work. Hoists were to be operated only by persons over eighteen years of age, twenty in the case of hoists carrying people. There were several clauses regarding sanitary conditions in mines and precise safety regulations regarding the use and storage of explosives. Finally, there were elaborate regulations regarding the use of electricity for lighting or to operate machinery.[145]

Legislation was also passed establishing the eight-hour day for underground miners. This had been discussed in the 1912 session when Hearst supported it in principle, but he had reservations. He didn't think hours of labour should be regulated in only one industry and also feared there was a risk of infringing on the rights of workers. "How far are you going with the man who wants to work?" he asked. "The State is interested in protecting the health of the men, but if their employment does not affect their health, how far is this House prepared to go … in preventing a man from working ten hours a day if he wants to?"[146] No doubt this response caused some to wonder if Hearst accepted the principle of the eight-hour day. In fact, his concern reflected the fact that in many mines the men worked on a piecework basis rather than an hourly or daily rate, and many of them had no desire to be limited to eight hours per day.[147] But while Hearst thought the legislation was necessary because of the unhealthy and dangerous nature of mining generally, it did not apply to iron mines because the government did not think the need was as great there. Also, the iron and steel industry required careful fostering and many related industries were "dependent" on it.[148] The government was wrong about this, of course, because iron mining and processing mills were very unsafe and unhealthy workplaces. Even so, some 4,000 workers benefited from this legislation.[149]

The fact that Hearst was minister of the most important department in the government meant that he was under constant fire from the Liberals during the 1913 session. On three occasions, they introduced motions attacking his northern development program. Despite the government's claim in the throne speech that 563 kilometres of new roads had been built in 1912 and a further 1,159 kilometres improved under the program, the Liberals called for "a more comprehensive and adequate policy to promote the construction of good roads."[150] This was defeated on a party vote and the legislature instead adopted a resolution moved by Reaume and seconded by Hearst stating its approval of the government's policy.[151]

The amount of progress achieved on road building wasn't really the issue. The real target of the Liberals was the northern development program itself, and once again they charged that giving the minister such a large amount of money to be spent over several years was subversive of the principle of responsible government. There was no denying that it was unusual at the time. William Proudfoot (Liberal, Centre Huron), who has been described as "stubborn and wily" and "the closest friend and associate" of Newton Rowell,[152] moved the resolution, claiming that the money was being spent where most useful politically. This brought Hearst to his feet to denounce the insinuation, which he promised would be resented by the people of northern Ontario who supported the program. This resolution also fell on a party vote.[153] Undeterred, Rowell resumed the offensive a day later, introducing yet another resolution condemning the program. Hearst again defended it and, in his usual manner, ignored the actual accusations and accused the Liberals of actually being opposed to the development of New Ontario. Amid loud Conservative applause, he assured government members that they had no reason to blush when voting down the resolution, which they proceeded to do.[154]

Hearst wasn't Proudfoot's only target in the 1913 session. He also attacked W.J. Hanna, during a meeting of the legislature's public accounts committee, accusing him of corruption for accepting a campaign donation from a government contractor. Accusations of corruption are always dangerous to a government, but this one was particularly so because the government's popularity was largely based on Whitney's reputation for honesty and integrity. Hanna was a popular target for such attacks, however, because he was one of the most effective ministers in the government but also a wealthy corporation lawyer.

The so-called Proudfoot charges were referred to the legislature's public accounts committee, which was chaired by Howard Ferguson, one of the most aggressively partisan members of the legislature. Hearst later told his son Irving that it was he who had persuaded Whitney that Ferguson was "the best man" to chair the committee, presumably because of his fierce partisanship. Because Whitney and Ferguson "were not then on speaking terms," Whitney asked Hearst to offer Ferguson the chairmanship.[155] Ferguson cheerfully agreed and refused to allow Proudfoot's charges to be discussed by the committee, forcing the issue to be debated in the legislature where it would get more publicity. That enabled the highly respected Whitney to defend Hanna in the debate, acknowledging that the contractor had contributed to Hanna's campaign but claiming that he had received no benefit in return. Then he used his majority not only to declare Hanna innocent but to also censor Proudfoot for making a false accusation.[156] Public opinion was tested a couple of months later in a by-election caused by A.G. MacKay's resignation, during which Hanna and Proudfoot publicly debated the issue. The Conservative candidate, Colin Cameron, not only won but was re-elected in the 1914 general election as well.

Hanna's troubles may explain why Hearst was the government spokesman on issues unrelated to his department during the 1913 session. On 31 March, for example, he introduced a bill requiring mandatory retirement of provincial civil servants at sixty-five years of age but establishing a contributory pension plan for them. This was a progressive measure in 1913, but neither Hearst nor the government actually claimed credit for it. As Hearst explained, he was only introducing the bill on behalf of the Civil Service Association and the government was not proposing that it become law at this time. Indeed, the government didn't even necessarily accept either the principle or the details of the bill. It did, however, hope to attract attention to the issue and invited public comment.[157] Accordingly, when the bill appeared for second reading, he withdrew it.

Hearst was also the government's main speaker in a debate on the cost of living, occasioned by a double-barrelled Liberal resolution that blamed the government for the rising cost of living while complaining that farmers were not benefiting adequately from rising consumer food prices. The government, the Liberals declared, should launch a full investigation into the problem.[158] Again, one would have thought that Hanna would have led the government's response but Whitney assigned the task to Hearst. His remarks are interesting because they reflected some of his thinking on social questions and probably contributed to the belief that gradually developed among farmers and workers that he was not as progressive as he sometimes seemed.

Hearst acknowledged that the cost of living had increased in recent years but urged – as Whitney and he often did – that partisan politics should not be dragged into the situation. Inflation was a national problem and he reminded members that the government had asked the Laurier government in 1910 to undertake a full investigation into it but nothing had been done. Nevertheless, he thought that governments should intervene when combines raised prices without apparent justification, although he did not explain what authority they had to do so. Then, referring to rising food prices, he declared somewhat fatuously but to Conservative applause, "[I]f I am not satisfied to stay in the city and pay the high prices demanded for foodstuffs there is lots of farmland I can go to and till."[159]

This rather odd response was presumably meant to reassure farmers that he for one did not object to paying just prices for farm produce so that they could share in the prosperity of the Whitney era. He was also indirectly recognizing the importance of a healthy agricultural economy and making clear that he was not one of those who looked down on farmers or welcomed rural depopulation. Whether these implications were fully recognized or satisfying is questionable. Certainly, his suggestion that people living in urban centres had the option of becoming farmers and growing their own food was supercilious and impractical. Then he amended the Liberal resolution – which was carried by a party vote – to put the blame for the whole problem on the federal government.[160]

Inevitably, however, Hearst was focused on issues related to northern Ontario. One awkward one was the Bruce Mines and Algoma Railway. Hearst, as the company's solicitor, had petitioned the Whitney government in 1905 for government assistance, and despite Whitney's reluctance to subsidize railway construction, legislation had eventually been passed in 1909 granting the company a subsidy of $3,000 and 1,000 acres per mile of construction.[161] The project had not gone ahead, however, and Albert Grigg, the Conservative MPP for Algoma, again sought assistance in 1912. Whitney reiterated his opposition to railway subsidies[162] but Hearst supported it. He was no longer involved with the company, but he continued to believe that it would stimulate economic development and settlement in the area. Accordingly, Grigg sponsored a bill that changed the company's name to the Lake Huron and Northern Ontario Railway Company and greatly increased its authorized capitalization.[163] The new company promised to build a 325-mile line within the next four years linking Rock Lake with the National Transcontinental, and in recognition of the government's focus on getting settlers to move to New Ontario, also promised to bring in 3,750 settlers within the next ten years to erect lumber mills and build local improvements such as roads, bridges and schools.

Hearst massaged the bill to permit the government to sell up to 4,000 acres per mile of construction to the company at twenty-five cents per acre for the first 3,000 acres and fifty cents per acre for the final 1,000 acres per mile but reserving mineral and waterpower rights to the Crown.[164] More importantly, his bill allowed the railway to run through the Mississagi Forest Reserve, which Cochrane had established in 1904. Forest reserves were large tracts of forest set aside for future exploitation and not open to settlement.[165] Even so, because of its overriding commitment to northern development, the government excluded ore-rich townships from the reserves and even sometimes allowed very limited harvesting of trees in them. Hearst justified the project on the grounds that the railway would attract as many as 30,000 settlers and pour $20 million in investment into the area if it ran through the Mississagi Reserve.[166]

When the Liberals strongly opposed the bill, arguing that no more land should be turned over to private companies and that if a railway was needed in the area, the government-owned TNO Railway Commission should build it, Hearst pointed out that the Bruce Mines and Algoma Railway were paying almost the same price for the land as settlers generally paid and had to make extensive local improvements as well.[167] At the same time, because the land was in a forest reserve, the government reserved the right to determine which lands the company could select and promised that alternate townships along the line would not be sold. The government also reserved the rights to red and white pine, plus the right to place all of it under crown timber licence.[168] All of this was consistent with the government's colonization policy but Hearst concluded his argument with the usual patriotic plea – so exasperating to the Liberals – for all to join in developing Ontario's great natural heritage in the northland,[169] and the bill passed on a party vote. In the end it didn't matter because the outbreak of the First World War meant that the company couldn't raise the necessary private-sector investment.

This episode was perhaps more significant than it appears at first glance. The discovery of iron ore at Atikokan and Wawa had been followed by the discovery of copper and nickel at Sudbury, silver at Cobalt, and similar mineral discoveries in other areas in northern Ontario, culminating in the stunning discovery of gold at Timmins in 1909. The result in every case was, of course, a flood of prospectors and speculators into those areas. What these discoveries had in common, aside from the initial one at Cobalt, was that most were within or on the edge of forest reserves. Because the government had eliminated the ore-rich townships from the forest reserves, it appeared to be placing a higher value on economic development than conservation, but it was more a matter of timing because the forest reserves were set aside for future development, not to be conservation areas.

That is not to say that there was no interest in conservation. Algonquin Park had been created in 1893, the first provincial park not only in Ontario but also in Canada. Provincial parks were intended to preserve forested areas for recreational purposes but also to encourage the regeneration of the pine forest in areas that had been clear-cut or burned out. Conservation was an emerging public issue by this time because of the extraordinary rate at which Ontario's southern forest had been cleared and the northern forest was now being harvested. Algonquin Park encompassed nearly 4,000 square kilometres in the District of Nipissing. Loggers had already been cutting in the area for many years, however, and the government had no intention of terminating their licences because the local communities depended on the jobs and the government wanted the revenue, so the challenge was to find an acceptable compromise. None had been found by January 1910 when J.B. Tudhope, an Orillia lumberman, carriage and automobile manufacturer and Liberal MPP, joined with A.E. Munn to form the Munn Lumber Company. It then purchased the St. Anthony Lumber Company's timber rights in and adjacent to the park.

Two years later Hearst announced that the government would buy up as many of the timber licences in the park as possible. He was responding to Munn's aggressive clearcutting at Cache Lake, the site of the Department of Lands, Forests and Mines district headquarters and the popular Highland Inn, which had shocked the district superintendent and outraged the public. The government did buy back the Munn lease at a cost of $290,000 and closed down its operations.[170] This strong response was presumably easier than it might have been if the St. Anthony Lumber Company, which was managed and partially owned by Sir James Whitney's brother, Edwin, still owned the timber rights adjacent to the park. The outbreak of the war "brought commercial logging in Algonquin to a virtual standstill, however, because of labour shortages and a depressed building industry."[171]

The discovery of clear-cutting in Algonquin Park should not have surprised anyone because it was common in the north, just as it had been in the southern forest in the nineteenth century. Traditional lumbering practices, being unregulated, were bad enough but when the forest industry shifted into harvesting softwood to produce pulp and paper, the scale of clear-cutting rose exponentially. Rather than opening up fertile agricultural land for settlers, clear-cutting created barren wastelands in the absence of reforestation policies. The impact – erosion and the desertification of once arable land – was beginning to be recognized in southern Ontario but not in the north, perhaps because its forest seemed endless. Another serious problem was the damage being done to the forest and soil in northern Ontario and the very real danger to people living there from the frequent fires caused by slash (debris) from lumbering, farmers burning trees to clear their land, and trains running through the region.

One major fire occurred at Porcupine, a community near Timmins, in July 1911, when high winds whipped bush fires into an inferno that swept through mining camps, razing the towns of South Porcupine and Pottsville and partially destroying Golden City (Porcupine) and Porquis Junction, consuming some 200,000 hectares of forest and killing at least seventy-one people.[172] Hearst was not yet Minister of Lands, Forests and Mines at that point, but in 1912 he hired Dr. E.J. Zavitz, a professional forester teaching at the Ontario Agricultural College who had established a very successful reforestation program in southern Ontario, to serve as Ontario's provincial forester.[173] That seemed encouraging except for the fact that Hearst was only responding to federal legislation requiring provincial governments to appoint foresters to regulate the railways, which were a major cause of forest fires. Hearst actually opposed that legislation because he thought the management of public lands should remain with the province's 1,400 crown timber agents, presumably because, while they were employed by the government, they were paid by the companies, which meant that they were part of the problem. Foresters took a very different view of forest management and worked for the government, not the companies. Historian John Bacher claims that it was White who, recognizing the seriousness of the forest fire problem, persuaded Hearst to comply, but Hearst may also have been influenced by Frank Cochrane, who was by then Minister of Railways and Canals and had also been one of the founders of Zavitz's reforestation centre.[174]

It took the largest and most deadly forest fire in Canadian history in July 1916 to force the government to get serious about the problem. The so-called Matheson fire consumed more than two million hectares of forest and destroyed not only the Hollinger and Dome gold mines, the largest in Canada, but also the communities of Iroquois Falls, Porquis Junction, Kelso, Nushka, Matheson and Ramore, and partially razed Homer and Monteith. More appalling, it killed 223 people and left 3,000 others homeless. By now Howard Ferguson was Minister of Lands, Forests and Mines and he responded by creating a Forest Protection Branch in his department with Zavitz as its director. He also passed the Forest Fires Prevention Act, which imposed regulations on railways and regulated – but did not ban – burning by settlers or require logging companies to clean up their slash, a dangerous concession to the companies. But with his support Zavitz created a fire protection program that included a network of fire towers, fire protection roads and trails, the acquisition of portable fire pumps and trucks, and hired 1,000 rangers to patrol the forests.[175] This response would have been more impressive if Hearst hadn't excluded provincially owned railways from the regulations. The TNO Railway was the only provincial railway in Ontario, it was owned by the government, and it ran through the northern clay belt.[176]

Fires weren't the only problem caused by the forest industry. It was totally unregulated with respect to its massive environmental impact. Lumber mills had always dumped their sludge into adjacent waterways, reducing their flow and polluting them and the fish that lived in them, but the problem became much more serious when pulp and paper mills came to dominate the northern forest industry during the Whitney and Hearst years. These mills required vast supplies of trees and consumed large amounts of fresh water, but they also used toxic chemicals such as sulphur and chlorine which they discharged into the waterways and atmosphere.[177] This not only poisoned the waterways; it also made the fish that lived in them toxic, with disastrous repercussions for the Indigenous people for whom fish were a major part of their diet. And because pulp and paper mills required a lot of electrical power, they or the provincial government took advantage of the region's many rivers and lakes to build hydro-electric power plants on them. Electricity generated by regional hydro plants seemed infinitely preferable to coal-fired plants because waterpower was a readably available, seemingly clean, source of energy. But hydroelectric plants manipulated the natural flow of rivers with dams that sometimes seriously harmed the local habitat, reduced water levels, and altered water temperatures. This had a negative impact not only on the rivers but also on their surrounding territory when animal and fish migration paths changed. And sometimes local communities – usually Indigenous – were displaced by their construction despite their treaty rights. None of these issues were addressed at the time because industrial development was seen as progress, and yet the manufacture of pulp and paper wasn't even efficient because the kraft pulping process only utilized 50 per cent of the tree, the rest becoming sludge that was burned, spread on land or dumped in landfills.[178]

Environmental devastation was not confined to the forest industry. It was just as serious, if not more serious, in mining communities like Sudbury, the largest producer of nickel in the world whose smelters were the largest source of sulphur dioxide in the world. The result was that 20,000 hectares of land were "denuded … of any kind of vegetation, leaving blackened rocks," 80,000 hectares of semi-barren land, and the acidification of 7,000 lakes to the point that no fish could survive in them. [179] This was an extreme example, but all industrial communities suffered serious environmental degradation with the inevitable impact on those who lived and worked in them. Sault Ste. Marie's steel plant emitted large amounts of highly toxic pollutants into both the air and the water. Most politicians didn't understand the price of industrial development or accepted it as the cost of "progress," and governments collaborated with them. As Mark Kuhlberg has pointed out, referring to the forest industry, a landlord–tenant relationship developed because highly technical industries involving huge investments naturally sought partnerships with governments and political success was largely dependent on governments' ability to deliver prosperity.[180] Perhaps unlike many politicians, Hearst was personally affected by the environmental degradation caused by industrialization because when he and his family lived in a house facing the St. Mary's River in the 1890s they obtained their drinking water directly from it. His son Irving later recalled his father boasting that he "was drinking the purest water in the world that flowed from nature's reservoir."[181] He couldn't do that after the steel mill was built.

Some politicians, such as Sir Wilfrid Laurier and Sir Clifford Sifton had reservations about the situation and in 1909 created the Commission of Conservation to advise governments on the most up-to-date scientific advice on the conservation of human and natural resources, with a focus on the wastefulness of resource exploitation. The members of the commission included provincial ministers responsible for resources, which included Hearst between 1911 and 1914. One would like to think that this was why he hired Edward Zavitz as Ontario's chief forester, in 1912, but Bacher thinks he was responding to pressure from the Borden government.[182] Even so, this represented a significant reversal of policy in the department because Zavitz was a keen and determined advocate of conservation, one of whose first actions was to take the management of public lands out of the hands of the crown timber agents.[183] He then proceeded over the years to "alter the entire pattern of the Department of Lands and Forests [*sic*] to become an effective instrument of conservationist, scientific forest management."[184] This must have been a struggle because Zavitz totally disagreed with Hearst's belief in the agricultural potential of northern Ontario, with the exception of a few isolated pockets of good soil. In his opinion, the most suitable crop in the northland was trees, and the forest needed to be managed with a view to reforestation, the protection of areas for recreation and future needs, and fire protection. That included regenerating the white pine forest in Algonquin Park and elsewhere.[185]

The 1913 session was a busy one for Hearst, and he was no doubt relieved when it ended. He and Cochrane then travelled extensively in northern Ontario, inspecting the lands available for settlement and the progress of construction on the National Transcontinental. Hearst was immensely pleased with what he saw and heard, reporting to Whitney that "never before has the north been so well satisfied and never before has there been as little fault finding."[186]

# 3 Whitney's Successor: 1914

*Let us hold together in this day of trial, knowing that out of this night of darkness must evolve a greater, better and nobler Empire even than that of the past.*[1]

THE 1914 session was unusual because it took place in the absence of Whitney, whose health had seriously deteriorated in 1913. He was struggling with heart failure and went to New York to consult medical specialists during the Christmas break. Because public concern was high, the doctors treating him issued daily bulletins. One hopeful sign was that he was expressing his "hatred of hotel life and his desire to get home."[2] Robert Pyne, who was not only his Minister of Education but also his closest friend in the cabinet and his personal physician, was there with him, collaborating with the specialists. J.J. Foy filled in as Acting Premier in Whitney's absence and was expected to lead the government in the legislature when it opened in February. "It is generally understood, however," the *Sault Daily Star* assured its readers, that Foy would not succeed to the premiership if Whitney died or retired because "the Acting Premier is a Roman Catholic."[3] Whitney returned to Toronto on 19 February and was taken immediately to the newly completed Toronto General Hospital, where he remained until late February before being allowed to return home.

When the legislature opened on 18 February, it was actually Pyne who served as Acting Premier because Foy, who was in very poor health as well, had also gone to New York for what was described as a brief vacation. Given the circumstances, the throne speech "was a mere recital of the year's progress, neither recalling any notable issues nor hinting at anything sensational to come,"[4] with the notable exceptions of the proposed Workmen's Compensation bill and the required adjustments to constituencies as a result of the 1911 census. While Whitney tried to provide general direction from home, his senior ministers had to manage the session and advance the government's agenda largely on their own. As in the 1913 session, Hearst played a prominent role, sponsoring several pieces of legislation and participating actively in debates on matters not directly related to his own department. There was no indication in the press that anyone thought this unusual.

Perhaps the most important piece of legislation relating to his department that Hearst sponsored in 1914 dealt with radium. Discovered in the 1890s, radium had quickly become important for its use in X-ray technology, which had been invented in the 1890s. Radium was found in uranium, a rare mineral that had not yet been found in Canada. It was first discovered in Saskatchewan and the Northwest Territories and the Ontario government understandably hoped that it would be found in Ontario as well. It did more than hope, however, offering a reward of up to $25,000 to the first person who discovered it while stipulating that any uranium discovered on crown lands could be sold only to the government and setting the price that it would pay for uranium produced by privately owned mines. Hearst's radium bill also authorized the government to purchase any uranium-bearing property not already in its possession or the mineral rights on such property. Finally, the government was authorized to establish plants to process uranium ore.[5] This was a far-sighted piece of legislation, so both government and industry were ready when uranium was discovered in Ontario – at Bancroft, Espanola, and Elliot Lake – in the 1940s.

No doubt because of the so-called Proudfoot scandal, Hearst also introduced two bills dealing with political contributions in election campaigns. The first declared that contributions could only be made through a candidate's official agent and that a detailed statement of all financial contributions and all expenses, including invoices, receipts, and vouchers, must be made within two months of an election. The second bill made it illegal for corporations, liquor licence holders, and public contractors to contribute in any way in an election either to support or oppose any candidate or for any candidate to accept support from such persons or corporations.[6] Hearst explained, perhaps with tongue in cheek, that he did not really think there was much political corruption in the province, but it was well to provide for future contingencies. Not surprisingly, the Liberals did not entirely agree in this regard, although Rowell did concede that there was probably little gross or flagrant corruption although he thought there was widespread corruption on a lesser level. He, of course, was focused on the alleged evils of the liquor trade and believed that Hearst's bills did not go nearly far enough to ban contributions from persons involved in it.

When the Liberals introduced two bills of their own, similar to Hearst's but somewhat stronger, Hearst sensibly responded by recommending that the legislature approve all four bills in principle so that they could all be considered together in committee.[7] This was done and when Hearst introduced his two amended bills for final consideration it was clear that some concessions had been made to the Liberals. These bills made it illegal for corporations and their officers, licensees, members of liquor associations and public contractors to contribute to the election or defeat of any candidate. A licensee was defined as "the holder of a license issued for the manufacture, sale or warehousing of liquor under the Liquor License Act," and liquor associations were defined as "every association, society or body of persons promoting or assisting or furthering or protecting the trade in intoxicating liquor, or any branch or part of such trade."[8] A significant new clause required all employers to give their workers a half-holiday or for polling hours to be extended to enable workers to vote. The bills also generally improved the organization of elections.[9] This was progressive legislation for its time, and Hearst had shown sound leadership in his bipartisan approach to a controversial subject.

He proved to be less progressive when the Liberals introduced a motion calling for the creation of an independent civil service commission to recruit provincial civil servants by competitive examination. He was, in fact, the government's chief speaker in this debate rather than Hanna, the Provincial Secretary. Whatever the reason, Hearst's attitude reflected the quaintly reactionary feelings of many politicians that persisted for many more years. An independent civil service commission was not practicable, he thought, because there were too few civil servants on the provincial payroll and they were spread among too many different branches throughout the province. Besides, political patronage was not a serious problem, pointing out that his own two deputy ministers and the northern roads commissioner – the three top officials in his department – had been appointed by the previous Liberal government more than thirteen years earlier. "I have yet to find a better system," he said, "than that of appointments recommended by the local member for the constituency where the appointment is to be made, who appreciates the situation better than anyone else, who knows the qualifications of the man for the position and who is responsible to the Government, which in turn is responsible to the Legislature and the people."[10] There is no reason to think that he was being disingenuous in expressing these views, and many, if not most, other politicians thought the same way. Accordingly, he moved an amendment to the motion, eviscerating it by declaring that because "it would be wholly unwise and practically impossible to bring under such a system the various officials in the service of the Province," the legislature "recognizes the wisdom and fairness [with] which the Government has dealt with appointments and promotions in the Government service."[11] The motion as amended was, of course, approved.

If the government's response to civil service reform was reactionary, its major piece of legislation during the 1914 session – the workmen's compensation act – was decidedly not. The 1889 Royal Commission on the Relations of Labour and Capital in Canada had noted the high rate of injuries among industrial workers and made recommendations on improving working conditions but the federal government had sidestepped the issue by asserting that this type of social legislation came under provincial jurisdiction.[12] The Mowat government had passed legislation in 1886 making employers liable for workplace injuries, but it required workers to sue their employers for compensation. Labour leaders considered this inadequate, and Whitney, who enjoyed widespread political support in Ontario's growing urban communities, had appointed a royal commission in 1910 chaired by Sir William Meredith, the Chief Justice of Ontario and former leader of the Ontario Conservative Party, to study workmen's compensation programs in other countries and make recommendations. Meredith submitted his lengthy report in 1913, and the government passed the legislation in 1914.[13]

It was the first legislation of its kind in Canada and was damned by businessmen as socialism of the worst sort but hailed by the labour newspaper *Industrial Banner* as "the most far-reaching legislation that has ever been enacted by any Government in Canada in the interests of labour."[14] What made it so important was that it legislated compensation without regard to responsibility. On this occasion Hanna introduced the bill, but Hearst supported it, and because he soon became Premier it was he who implemented it, so he was generally given credit or blame for it. Other provinces soon followed Ontario's lead, starting with Nova Scotia in 1915, British Columbia in 1916, and Alberta and New Brunswick in 1918.

When the 1914 session prorogued on 1 May, it was generally expected that an election would be called within eight weeks.[15] The present legislature had lasted three years, and Whitney had never allowed more than three years to pass without an appeal to the people. But Whitney was a very sick man, and because he had not appeared in the legislature or at Queen's Park throughout the session there was speculation that he would have to retire in the near future. He was determined to carry on, however, and no one in the party was about to question his judgment, at least not publicly. They may have understood, as he probably did, that they would fare better in an election under their popular and respected leader than under anyone else.

The *Globe* reported on 7 May that it had been told by "one in the confidence of the party leaders" that the cabinet was divided on the issue with Hearst, Hanna, I.B. Lucas (Provincial Treasurer), James Duff (Minister of Agriculture) and Reaume favouring an early election and Pyne and Beck, a minister without portfolio, arguing that they should wait. But how could they seek re-election if Whitney was too ill to lead the party or even to appear in public? The fact was that the old man still hoped that his health would improve over the next few months and enable him to lead the party one more time. He therefore attended a cabinet meeting on 6 May to try to persuade them to hold off the election, but remarkably, they stood their ground and in the end he yielded to their views.[16]

One major factor in the decision was the availability of Ontario's many Conservative MPs to participate in the campaign because the provincial and federal organizations had functioned as one since 1908. Borden had written to Hanna, Foy, and Hearst on 5 May, and on 10 May, Hearst and Lucas went to Ottawa to discuss the matter with him.[17] Hearst and Lucas didn't just discuss the date of the election with Borden. They also discussed "the singular attitude of Beck" who was "recalcitrant" and threatening to resign from the cabinet if an election was called. Borden subsequently "discussed [the] same situation with Rogers and arranged to bring all possible influence on Beck," who was going to Ottawa two days later. When Borden met with him on 13 May he "endeavoured to dissuade him from retiring."[18]

It is noteworthy that Cochrane didn't participate in these meetings. In fact, Borden deliberately scheduled the meetings to take place just days after Cochrane had left for Europe in hopes of restoring his failing health. That doesn't mean that Borden and Cochrane hadn't discussed the situation, but if they did Borden didn't mention it in his diary. But Cochrane's position as the senior Ontario minister in the Borden government in 1914 was not what it had been. Aside from his serious health issues, Borden "was beginning to think" that he had "not [been] a great success as an administrator,"[19] and within months he and Cochrane were discussing possible patronage appointments, including the lieutenant governorship of Ontario. In any case, the decision was made to call an election. The legislature was dissolved on 29 May, the federal parliamentary session ended on 12 June, and the election was called for 29 June. Clearly, Whitney's senior ministers were convinced that it should take place before Whitney's health deteriorated any further, and Beck did not resign.

It cannot be said that the campaign got off to a good start because the newspapers on 29 May were full of reports of the greatest marine disaster in Canadian history, the sinking early that morning of the Canadian Pacific liner *Empress of Ireland* in the Gulf of St. Lawrence. It was en route from Quebec City to Liverpool, carrying 1,477 passengers and crew when it collided in heavy fog with the *Storstad*, a Dominion Coal Company collier. It sank within minutes, causing the deaths of 1,012 people, more than the number who had died in the *Titanic* disaster two years earlier.[20] Some 200 of them were from Ontario, mostly from Toronto.

Whitney again ran on his record, still a strong one, and again, the Conservatives relied primarily on his personal prestige and integrity and the moderately progressive leadership he had given the province since 1905. As in 1911, the two main issues were temperance and bilingual schools, and this time both were fought on a considerably more hysterical level than in 1911. Newton Rowell, the Liberal leader, was a prominent Methodist and an ardent prohibitionist. He had challenged the Conservatives on the temperance issue in 1911, and this time he led what he considered was a moral crusade against the demon liquor that he – and many other social reformers – believed was responsible for other major social issues such as poverty, public health, and the welfare of women and children. Many pro-temperance clergymen of various Protestant denominations and other progressives favoured temperance reform for this reason.[21] The *Globe* portrayed Rowell as St. George setting out on his white charger to slay the liquor interests, depicted as a fire-breathing dragon.[22] Specifically, his policy was to "abolish the bar," that is, to close bars and taverns and restrict the sale of alcohol to licensed shops.[23] In his final statement to the voters at the end of the campaign, Rowell actually summed up the options for voters not as a choice between Liberals and Conservatives but between "on the one hand organized Christianity, and on the other hand the organized liquor interests."[24] This said much about Rowell; within two years he would be using similar language about the meaning of the First World War.

Whitney understood that there was strong support for temperance but defended his record, convinced that a majority of people supported his gradualist approach to the problem.[25] Incensed at the Liberals' outrageous efforts to link him with the liquor interests, he reminded voters that the number of licences in the province had been cut in half since 1905.[26] He realized, of course, that some Conservatives – and Liberals for that matter – didn't actually share the rising temperance tide and so followed Rowell's example in appealing to people to keep the temperance issue out of politics.[27] But while Rowell thought voters should ignore all other issues and join the temperance crusade, Whitney thought that people who supported his government on all or most other issues should not switch to a party with which they disagreed on one issue.[28]

The other major issue in this election was the government's policy on bilingual schools and, like temperance, it was much more highly charged than it had been in 1911. The 1912 Merchant report had concluded that English was not being used or taught adequately in the province's bilingual schools but that this was part of a larger general problem of low standards. The result was that "a large proportion of the children in the communities concerned leave school to meet the demands of life with an inadequate equipment in education."[29] This was attributed to inadequately trained teachers, most of whom were members of religious orders who could not themselves speak English or did so only with difficulty.[30] As a result of this report, Whitney had assured the legislature that the government would carry out the policy enunciated in the Ferguson resolution of 1911, which had actually just confirmed the Department of Education's long-standing policy. In other words, the problem was "simply one of administration" because the government was only correcting a situation that should not have been allowed to develop. As Whitney explained to Bishop W.A. Macdonell of Alexandria,

> the main point is that through negligence, and carelessness, and want of proper inspection many of these schools were allowed to drift, so to speak, until they became in reality French Schools instead of Public or Separate Schools under the provisions of our school laws. Consequently, a great many of the parents to-day think that the condition of things mentioned in Dr Merchant's Report is the normal condition of affairs, and that they are entitled to have such schools ... instead of such schools being a direct infringement of the law.[31]

In other words, two school systems – public and separate (Catholic) – were legal but a third system – French or ethnic – was not and would not be tolerated. Conservatives, well aware of the feelings of the powerful Orange Order and its chief spokesman in caucus, Howard Ferguson, were convinced that this was what the Franco-Ontarian extremists wanted, and they were determined not to allow it.[32]

The result was that the Department of Education issued Regulation 17 in June 1912, which ordered all public schools to use English as the language of instruction but allowed the use of French in Form 1 if students did not know English well enough to function in that language, but French could be taught as a subject of study in the upper forms for one hour a day if the parents requested it.[33] Clause 4, the most controversial section, stated that "for the school year of 1912–13, in schools where French has hitherto been a subject of study, the ... School Board ... may provide ... for instruction in French Reading, Grammar and

Composition in Forms I to IV." This instruction in French was to be "subject to the approval and direction of the Supervising Inspector and shall not in any day exceed one hour in each classroom."[34]

Regulation 18 followed a few months later. It declared that any school board that failed to comply with Regulation 17 or hired unqualified teachers would forfeit its annual provincial grant and would therefore be legally unable to pay such teachers from taxes collected for the support of schools under its jurisdiction. Teachers who refused to comply with Regulation 17 risked having their certificates suspended or cancelled and were ordered to sign a statement pledging that they would comply with the department's regulations.[35]

In August 1913, however, the Department of Education issued an amended, permanent, version of Regulation 17 that offered a modest compromise to the Franco-Ontarian community. The main difference was that authority regarding language in the bilingual schools was shifted from the local school boards to the department. Each year the minister would designate which schools were to be classified as "English-French" to operate under Regulation 17 and which were to continue under Regulation 15. At the same time, a daily hour of French instruction beyond Form 1 was permitted, subject to the approval of the chief inspector, "in the case of pupils ... who are unable to speak and understand the English language."[36]

This was a significant concession but it was rejected by the Association canadienne-français d'education d'Ontario (ACFEO), perhaps because it thought it wasn't enough, but more likely because Franco-Ontarian leaders, generally supported by Québecois nationalists, believed – wrongly – that "Le Canada est un pays bilingue, soumis à la couronne d'Angleterre ... Les franco-canadiens ont un droit historique incontestable à l'enseignement et à la conservation de leur langue maternelle dans toutes les provinces du Canada."[37] These rights they believed had been guaranteed in old treaties and legislation, including the British North America (BNA) Act. "Les plus anciens traités ... assurent aux Canadiens-français l'usage de tous leur droits civils parmi lesquels, de toute evidence, il faut placer au Premier rang la langue."[38]

They were wrong, of course, because the BNA Act guaranteed Catholic separate schools at the primary level in Ontario but said nothing about French language rights, whether in schools or elsewhere.[39] The Whitney government never indicated any intention of interfering with separate school rights, but having said that, it was understandable that Franco-Ontarians saw Regulation 17 as an attack on their rights because it was virtually impossible in practice to separate religious and language rights in communities with a significant francophone population. As

Rev. J.O. Routhier, vicar general of Ottawa, explained to Whitney, "Il faut aux catholiques des écoles où l'on enseigne la religion. Il faut aux Canadiens français des écoles françaises, ils veulent garder la Langue et la Foi. Il faut defender les écoles bilingues."[40] Thus, many Franco-Ontarians feared that the Whitney government was attempting to separate them from the Catholic church, as can be seen from this statement by Philippe Landry, the Conservative speaker of the Senate and now president of the ACFEO: "[the dispute is] après tout, qu'un incident, bien fâcheux sans doute, mais qui disparait ou doit nécessairement disparaître devant la question primordiale de l'éxistence des écoles séparées dans votre province."[41]

While Anglo-Protestant Ontarians did generally object to Catholic separate schools, they hadn't really created the crisis. What they saw was that in some communities, primarily in and around Ottawa, separate schools had also become French schools, and this aggravated a larger concern about the fact that francophones were moving into eastern and northern Ontario in significant numbers and naturally bringing not only their religion with them but also their nationality. Anglo-Protestant Ontarians, regardless of party, were almost all agreed that Ontario was and should remain an English-speaking British community, and they saw French schools as a direct threat to its identity and values.

A major complicating factor in the dispute was that the bilingual schools dispute was not simply between Protestants and Catholics; it divided Catholics as well because Catholic separate schools were attended by both anglophone and francophone students and many anglophones – mostly Irish – feared that the Franco-Ontarian agitation would arouse greater hostility to the separate school system itself.[42] This fear was justified when the Anglo-Protestant reaction to the founding of the ACFEO caused Whitney to cancel plans he had been preparing in 1910 to increase the provincial grants to separate schools.[43] Conflict over language in the separate school system was, however, only part of the larger conflict taking place in parishes and dioceses over power and control. Franco-Ontarians thought there should be more francophone bishops, for example, while anglophones generally thought that the hierarchy, like most of the Catholic population, should mostly be anglophones. In fact, they were, and they supported the government's position on bilingual schools. Bishop Michael Fallon of London, the most outspoken of them, strongly opposed the demands of the francophones, as did Archbishop Charles Gauthier (an anglophone despite his name) of Kingston and Bishop David Scollard of Sault Ste. Marie. They were supported by British Archbishop Francis Bourne, who was brave enough to declare at the eucharistic congress in September 1910 that the Catholic Church in Canada should identify itself with the English language. In an unexpected alliance, the Orange Order, which opposed Catholic schools on principle, found itself siding with English-speaking Catholics because it "saw the tragic history of the Eastern Townships being re-enacted in the eastern counties of Ontario."[44]

The struggle of the Franco-Ontarians soon focused on Ottawa's separate schools, no doubt because the headquarters of the ACFEO was there. It fully supported the Ottawa separate school board, which had a Franco-Ontarian majority under the chairmanship of Sam Genest, and totally rejected the government's policy. The conflict in Ottawa was largely local and indeed, internal between the English-speaking and French-speaking factions within the separate school board. The complicating factor was that English-speaking Catholics agreed with the government's policy on language but shared the fear of French-speaking Catholics that the very survival of separate schools was being endangered by the controversy. Another complicating factor was that the French-speaking element was numerically larger and steadily growing but the English-speaking element was wealthier and therefore paid the bulk of the separate school taxes.[45]

Although the Ottawa separate school board passed a resolution declaring it would not enforce Regulation 17, its bilingual schools opened without incident in September 1912.[46] It then offered to negotiate with the government, with the result that representatives of nearly all the bilingual school boards in the province met with Whitney at Queen's Park in December 1912. Nothing was achieved, however, because Whitney refused to withdraw Regulation 17 and urged the boards to give it a fair trial, emphasizing that ethnic schools would not be tolerated.[47] When the permanent form of Regulation 17 was issued in August 1913, the Ottawa board declared that the time for compromise had passed and it would fight for total victory.[48] And it now had a newspaper, *Le Droit*, which had been established in March 1913 by the Missionary Oblates of Mary Immaculate for the express purpose of defending Franco-Ontarian rights.[49] Meanwhile, Quebec was becoming increasingly aroused over the dispute as well.

So too was Anglo-Protestant Ontario. There was a widespread feeling that Whitney had made concessions to the Franco-Ontarians in revising Regulation 17, and several newspapers demanded that French should be abolished altogether from the province's schools.[50] The *Globe* reported that extremists believed that these alleged concessions were the result of a deal that Frank Cochrane had made with the Quebec Nationalists when they supported Borden in the 1911 federal election,[51] but there is no evidence to support this assertion. The dispute came to a climax during the 1913–4 school year when the Ottawa board reiterated that it would not enforce Regulation 17. This time the government reacted by cutting off its annual grant, and soon afterwards, both the children and several teachers walked out, and the schools closed for the remainder of the year.[52]

Thus, the government and the Franco-Ontarians were completely at loggerheads when the 1914 election took place. Whitney made clear during the campaign that his policy was "that English shall be the language of instruction in the schools of Ontario. Upon that we shall stand or fall."[53] Anglo-Protestant extremists went further by claiming that Ontario's British Protestant identity was under attack, inflaming anti-French and anti-Catholic sentiment. Many of these extremists, though certainly not all, were Conservatives, especially those who were members of the Orange Order. But some Conservatives welcomed the bilingual schools issue because they thought it diverted attention from the temperance issue.[54] Meanwhile, Whitney, always the moderate, had sent a subtle signal in February 1914 that he didn't agree with the extremists when he appointed Richard Preston, the Conservative MPP for Lanark North, rather than Ferguson, to represent Eastern Ontario in the government.

As for the Liberals, they were divided. While some were assuring Franco-Ontarians that they would protect French-language rights, others were flatly declaring for English only.[55] This was true of both Anglo-Protestant Liberals and English-speaking Catholic Liberals. Rowell basically agreed with Whitney's policy but tried to distance himself somewhat by accusing the Department of Education of gross mismanagement and excessive harshness to Franco-Ontarians.[56] Meanwhile, the Liberal *Globe* hopefully declared that bilingual schools were not an issue at all.[57]

There was no doubt that the government would be re-elected. It had won all nine by-elections held since the 1911 election, taking two seats from the Liberals, and the Liberals didn't even run candidates in fourteen constituencies.[58] But Whitney, its greatest asset, was in no condition to actually participate in the campaign. He did bravely manage to hold one large meeting at Massey Hall in Toronto on 23 June, when he thanked the voters for supporting him over the years. Declaring himself "an unreconstructed Conservative and an unrepentant one to boot," his only promise was that he would continue to serve the people "as long as my renewed health and strength are vouchsafed to me" and would "endeavour to give them the same service I have in the past."[59] It was an emotional appeal from a man who probably knew he was dying, offered to a large gathering of devoted followers who hoped it wasn't so. It probably rallied them, but the more detached must have wondered who was actually going to lead the government after the election.

The Liberals, understandably but probably unwisely, went about the province accurately but indelicately accusing the Conservatives of fraud because they were seeking re-election under Whitney's leadership when he clearly could not long continue as Premier, a charge that Whitney denounced as "impertinent and utterly untruthful."[60] The Liberals also suggested that when Whitney was forced to retire, he would be succeeded by Hanna, whom they accused of being allied with the liquor interests. They made a mistake, however, when they predicted that Hanna, as the heir apparent, would introduce the Premier at his Massey Hall rally.[61] Whitney easily squelched that assertion by having Beck introduce him.

Hanna did not attend the Massey Hall rally, nor did Hearst. He was touring northern Ontario, defending his northern development policies and repeating his charge that the Liberals were not really interested in developing the northland.[62] Cochrane accompanied him on this tour, but he did not play as important role in this election as usual because of his serious health issues. On the temperance issue, Hearst defended the government's local option policy as the surest path to ultimate prohibition if that was what the people wanted. Hearst personally believed in temperance and had participated in a number of local option contests in Sault Ste. Marie.[63] Like Whitney, however, he feared that Rowell was actually harming the cause by making it a partisan issue because that forced people to take sides, to make a choice that might conflict with their political allegiance.[64] He must have winced when the Methodist Young Men's Association of Toronto passed a resolution endorsing Rowell's policy, urging all its members to vote Liberal, and approving a special censure on Conservatives who believed in temperance but defended their party's position for political reasons.[65]

And there were signs of trouble within the party. Only one Conservative member was re-elected by acclamation compared to sixteen in 1911, and several Conservative members, some of them prominent, had to fight for their nominations. Two of them – Joseph Reaume in Essex North and W.K. McNaught in Toronto North – were defeated. W.R. Plewman, the editor of the Orange *Sentinel*, later rather bizarrely claimed that Adam Beck engineered their defeats because they did not support his leadership aspirations,[66] but there is no evidence to support this. Both men had to compete for their nominations because of the redistribution of constituencies, which forced McNaught to compete with W.D. McPherson and Thomas Crawford for one of the two seats in Toronto Northeast A. There is no apparent reason why Beck would have objected to McNaught because he was a long-time advocate of public power and was very supportive of the Hydro Commission.[67]

As for Reaume, he was in serious trouble because of his loyal support of the government's bilingual schools policy. He had faced a challenge for the nomination and barely survived the 1911 election and now, according to the *Windsor Evening Record*, many francophones in Essex were "ready to place race above politics in the fight for bilingual schools."[68] Despite Whitney's public support of Reaume, the local Conservatives chose Dr. Paul Poisson, a twenty-six-year-old physician with two years' experience as a councillor in Sandwich East Township. The Liberals ran Severin Ducharme, who had nearly won the seat in 1911, and he won it this time.

Reaume then ran as an independent "Whitney choice" candidate in the newly created riding of Windsor that had been carved out of Essex North, even though the Windsor Conservatives had already nominated Oscar Fleming, a prominent lawyer, former mayor and Orangeman. According to historian Jack Cecillon, Whitney "stayed away from Windsor for the entire campaign" because he was "unwilling to face either faction."[69] That was not the case. Whitney did not visit any constituencies because of his failing health. With the Conservative vote divided, the Liberal candidate, James Craig Tolmie, a Presbyterian minister, easily won the seat.[70] Reaume's loss was significant because he was the only Franco-Ontarian in the cabinet and in fact had been the first Franco-Ontarian to be included with a portfolio in any provincial cabinet.

In Sault Ste. Marie, Hearst was nominated at a meeting of local Conservatives, held on the evening of 8 June in Columbia Hall. Mayor T.E Simpson chaired the meeting and Cochrane, Boyce and Grigg were in attendance. The *Sault Daily Star* described the event as "a really remarkable" evening and "a real tribute" to Hearst because those in the packed hall endured several speeches, including a seventy-five-minute one by Hearst, in a "sweltering" ninety degrees (thirty-two Celsius). "Fancy a hall full of people holding the fort till eleven o'clock," the *Sault Daily Star* writer observed, "to hear political speeches while collars wilted and clothes grew clammy!" Their patience was, he thought, "a real tribute to the minister who "never appeared to such good advantage. He has gained in poise, power and the ability to drive home his argument. Always a tactful man on the platform his speech … was both an effective call to friends and a reasonable call to Liberals to not sacrifice the present good of the district to mere politics."[71]

Hearst's opponent was Francis Crawford, a real estate and insurance agent who was also a city alderman. Fred Denman, a local millwright, had announced that he was going to run as a labour candidate but in the end he didn't. Hearst stood on his record and the record of the Whitney government, while Crawford ran largely on Rowell's temperance policy. The *Sault Daily Star*, pointing out that the Whitney government was obviously going to be re-elected, cynically suggested that the people of Sault Ste. Marie would be foolish not to re-elect a senior minister who had done much for northern Ontario. It went further than that, however, suggesting that in view of Whitney's failing health, Hearst might well be the next Premier. "Do we want," it asked, "a Minister of the Crown and who will be in all probability Premier of the Province, or do we want plain Mr. Crawford in opposition?"[72] What inspired this speculation is not known, but Crawford couldn't have inspired Liberals when he assured the audience that he "had nothing against" Hearst personally and had only agreed to run because local Liberals wanted to give the voters "a chance to express their views" on Rowell's temperance policy.[73]

The real difference between the Liberals and Conservatives on temperance was actually one of degree, not of principle. Rowell was a moral crusader, while Whitney and Hearst believed that government should take a gradualist approach, only interfering in such a controversial issue as public opinion dictated. Indeed, in what was one of Hearst's common themes in politics, he called Rowell's temperance policy "the most retrograde movement in connection with temperance in many years" because he had made it a political issue. "Formerly, all had worked together for temperance, but this move had divided the forces in honest disagreement as to the method to adopt." He also pointed out that Rowell wanted to abolish bars while leaving the abolition of shops to local option. In Hearst's view, local option "was the proper method to adopt in the abolition of both bar and shop at the same time" and "so long as I remain a member of the government, every measure which we are convinced will advance the cause of temperance and in which we have the support of public opinion, will be placed upon the statutes."[74]

On 25 June – four days before the election – Plewman complicated the situation by resigning as editor of *The Sentinel*, accusing the government of trying to sidetrack the temperance issue by raising the bilingual schools question.[75] His defection was significant because, like many other Conservatives, he was not only a staunch Orangeman but also "a straight-laced and hardrock Methodist" deeply committed to the temperance cause.[76] H.C. Hocken, who owned the *Sentinel* and in fact was Plewman's father-in-law, remained loyal to Whitney, however, and that counted for a lot, at least in Toronto, because he was also the very popular Conservative but progressive mayor of the city. Indeed, he wasn't just popular; he was unbeatable. After two terms as mayor, he was elected to parliament in 1917 and remained there until 1930 when he moved into the Senate. Plewman returned to the Conservative fold after Hearst became Premier a few months later, presumably satisfied with his commitment to temperance.

Plewman's desertion wasn't the only last-minute surprise in the election. Having been told that Hearst was on the "wrong" side of the liquor issue, the Rev. G.S. Faircloth, who had been the minister of Hearst's church before moving to Toronto, sent a telegram to John Shannon, appealing to Sault Ste. Marie's Methodists to support Rowell in the election. The letter was read during a joint church service at the Presbyterian church that Hearst and his family attended on 28 June. "I could hardly believe my ears," Hearst later told Irving. "It was despicable to think that anyone would employ such tactics,"[77] especially on Sunday when polling would be taking place on Monday. Hearst did not respond, but he was both offended and outraged, but in the end it didn't matter. He was popular and everyone in town knew that he was a temperance man. And most voters clearly agreed with the *Sault Daily Star* that Rowell's temperance policy had little bearing on the city's future and what really mattered was government support for the town's growth, which "must come from government favor."[78] Hearst was re-elected with a majority of more than 1,200, 61 percent of the vote, the largest that any candidate had ever received in the constituency.

In the end the Conservatives coasted back into office with eighty-six seats, compared to the Liberals' twenty-four.[79] The Conservative victory was generally – and rightly – regarded as a personal tribute to Whitney.[80] No doubt with a twinkle in his eye, Whitney described it as an "unmistakable shewing by the people of Ontario of the common-sense which they possess in such a marked degree."[81] Whitney believed that the temperance issue had affected the outcome in only one or two ridings.[82] Indeed, he was convinced that the Liberal efforts to exploit the temperance and bilingual issues had both failed.[83] But Reaume's defeat left the cabinet without a Franco-Ontarian representative, there now being only one Conservative Franco-Ontarian member left in the legislature. This undoubtedly removed a modifying influence from cabinet discussions of the bilingual schools issue, although how much influence Reaume had actually had is open to question.

In northern Ontario, Hearst could also take satisfaction from the fact that twelve of the fourteen northern ridings had elected Conservatives, and one of them, Nipissing, was the only predominantly francophone riding in the province to elect a Conservative. The party's success in northern Ontario was at least partially attributable to Hearst, the region's influential representative in the cabinet, and his northern development program. With Whitney very likely to retire in the near future and the question of his successor foremost in the minds of many people,

Cochrane's protégé had established himself as a capable administrator, an effective performer in the legislature, and a successful organizer and campaigner. Perhaps more importantly, he had emerged as one of Whitney's closest cabinet colleagues without alienating his rivals.[84]

Three months later, at about noon on Friday, 25 September 1914, Sir James Whitney died of a cerebral haemorrhage in his home at 113 St. George Street. Even though he had been seriously ill for a year, his condition had been reported on 24 September as improving,[85] so his death came as a distinct shock to everyone. This included the members of his cabinet, who had just gathered at Queen's Park when Horace Wallis, Whitney's private secretary, arrived with the news. The meeting immediately adjourned while Pyne left hurriedly for Whitney's house. The problem was that Whitney was the first – and remains the only – Premier to die in office, so there was no protocol for how his successor should be chosen. The ministers agreed, however, as Pyne said when asked by a reporter from the *Globe*, that "we are still holding office and will continue to do business."[86] Perhaps significantly, Hearst appears to have been one of the few ministers who made a public statement, describing Whitney's death as "a staggering blow" that left him "without words to adequately express the profound sorrow" that he "felt ... at the loss of a dearly loved personal friend and a leader so greatly honoured."[87]

As the senior minister, J.J. Foy would normally have served as Acting Premier but he was sixty-seven years old and too ill to accept the responsibility. That meant that Pyne, next in line, took his place, so he was the man who would advise the lieutenant governor on Whitney's successor. That was fortuitous because, aside from having been Whitney's closest personal friend in the cabinet, Pyne had no desire to become Premier. He knew he was not a leader, and he also believed that the Premier should be a lawyer or businessman.[88]

Whitney's body lay in state in the legislative chamber at Queen's Park on 28 September to allow the general public to pay their respects, then was taken to St. James Cathedral for the funeral on 29 September. A "vast crowd ... thronged the streets and cathedral grounds" that afternoon, the church was packed, and the members of his cabinet served as honorary pallbearers.[89] Following the service, his remains were taken home to Morrisburg by private train for interment, accompanied by many friends, colleagues and Conservative politicians. Among them, inevitably, was Frank Cochrane who, as Minister of Railways and Canals, enjoyed a private car at the rear of the train. According to the *Globe*, Pyne "mingled little with the members" and "no attempt was made to hold any sort of a caucus,"[90] but it did not go unnoticed that there was a steady stream of politicians to the back of the train.

The three leading candidates for the leadership were Hearst, Hanna and Lucas, and according to the well-informed *Globe* correspondent, Hearst was Cochrane's choice; Hanna was "his own choice, if that term can be used"; and Lucas was "looked upon as a compromise man" who "is without doubt thoroughly popular among the members" and "would be favoured openly by Sir Adam Beck and his friends."[91] Both the *Globe* and the *World* thought it "altogether likely" that Pyne would summon a meeting of the Conservative caucus to choose Whitney's successor, the *World* pointing out that "the rank and file of the membership of the legislative assembly" had been "very outspoken in their demand for it."[92] But that didn't happen. On the morning of 30 September, having spoken to several of the Conservative MPPs at Queen's Park, the *Globe* correspondent reported that "the holding of a caucus is not now likely."[93] Why?

What the members of the caucus didn't know was that on 13 May Whitney had written a "memo" intended for the cabinet on who should succeed him, and his private secretary, Horace Wallis, had handed it to Pyne when he went to Whitney's home on 25 September.[94] There is no evidence to suggest that Pyne revealed the existence of the memo or its contents to anyone before the cabinet met on 30 September, the day after Whitney's funeral, and it remained secret for many years. Cochrane certainly knew about it, however, because he was with Whitney at his home on 13 May when he wrote it.[95]

When cabinet met on 30 September the only item on its agenda was to decide who Pyne should recommend to the lieutenant governor to assume the premiership. The ministers must have been surprised, if not astonished, to learn of Whitney's memo and to hear its contents:

> In the event of my death I desire to say to my colleagues that, in my opinion, Mr. Foy should succeed me as Prime Minister. In the event of his declining, an effort should be made to get Mr. Cochrane to accept the position.
>
> If this cannot be brought about then, in my opinion, Mr. Hearst or Mr. Lucas should be chosen. This is all merely my opinion which I give for what it is worth, but the reasons behind my opinion will at once occur to those who give consideration to the matter. Among them are [*sic*] the geographical position of Mr. Hearst which gives him a great advantage over others. Mr. Foy deserves anything that our party can give him, and there is no stronger man in the province than Mr. Cochrane.[96]

Whitney's memo was carefully written. Only four names were mentioned, and Whitney knew that two of them, Foy and Cochrane, would not accept the leadership if offered to them. Aside from the fact that

Foy was anxious to retire, he was also a Catholic and Ontario's Conservative Party was certainly not yet ready for a Catholic leader. Cochrane was not as old as Foy but he too was ill and was already discussing his retirement with Borden. In fact, Borden had just offered him the lieutenant governorship of Ontario.[97] Hanna and Beck, two of the best-known and respected members of the government, were not even mentioned.

Hanna was only two years older than Hearst, but he had been in the legislature since 1902 and a member of Whitney's cabinet since 1905. Charlesworth surely exaggerated when he claimed that Hanna was "probably the most popular man in Canadian politics,"[98] a popular gregarious politician and a loyal, hard-working minister whom the *Globe* described as "unquestionably the strongest man" in Whitney's cabinet.[99] But he was also controversial. A highly successful corporation lawyer who represented the Imperial Oil Company and sat on the boards of the Imperial Bank of Canada and other companies, he represented the conservative wing of the party and opposed Adam Beck's public utility policy.[100] The fact that Whitney made no mention of him in his memo must have been a humiliating shock but Hanna attempted to conceal his disappointment by declaring publicly, after Hearst was chosen, that he would not have accepted the premiership "under any circumstances."[101] His disappointment simmered, however, probably fuelled by the conviction that he would have been a more effective leader than Hearst, until 1916 when he left the government.

Neither was Adam Beck, the Conservative MPP for London, mentioned in Whitney's memo, even though he was one of the most powerful and popular political figures in Ontario by 1914.[102] Beck was a wealthy businessman who had emerged over the years as leader of the progressive wing of the party by leading the battle against the private utilities for publicly owned electricity. This was an increasingly important public issue because industrialization and the growth of urban communities required power for factories, offices, street railways, and lighting for homes and streets. So far power had been generated from American coal, but the ability of Niagara Falls to generate hydroelectric power had long been realized and the technical problem of long-distance transmission of electricity had recently been solved. That made hydroelectric power available wherever there were communities large enough to justify building the transmission lines to them. The construction of power plants and transmission lines stimulated a debate over whether power generated from a natural resource should be privately or publicly owned, especially when there was dissatisfaction with the high cost and level of service provided by private companies. The Ross government supported the privately owned utilities, but Whitney boldly embraced the idea of public power, and after winning the 1905 election he created the Hydro-Electric Power Commission and appointed Beck its chairman. Its mandate was to work with the municipalities to develop a provincial transmission system but soon began producing its own power by buying existing generating plants and building new ones. Although he was a member of the cabinet because the HPEC was funded by the legislature, he managed the HEPC as a quasi-independent agency, but Whitney was never able to bring him under control, and Beck would have had no support in cabinet.[103]

That was a real political problem because Beck was enormously popular. The Toronto *Evening Telegram* went so far as to claim that Beck "represented "whatever is most progressive, most far-sighted and most courageous in the work of the Conservative party" and had "done more for the good of this province than any of his colleagues – one might almost say than all his colleagues put together."[104] But there is no evidence that Beck wanted to be Premier. He had found his mission in life, enjoyed more freedom of action leading his public power crusade than he would have had as a regular politician, and was well aware that, as one historian has said, he was "the Prometheus of Canadian politics," at "the height of his power" with "a more ardent following than the government itself."[105] He was no doubt being truthful when he said that he would not accept the premiership if it were offered to him.[106]

The choice facing the cabinet, therefore, was between Hearst and Lucas. They had much in common. Both were Irish Protestants, both were lawyers who had articled in Owen Sound where they first met as teenagers, and they were the youngest members of both the legislature and the cabinet. While Lucas was three years younger than Hearst, he had been elected to the legislature a decade before Hearst, but Hearst had entered the cabinet in 1911, a year before Lucas. What distinguished them was that Whitney had shown interest in Hearst as early as 1904 but left Lucas on the back benches for fourteen years. An attractive, personable, very competent minister and an effective speaker, Lucas would have been the choice of the party caucus,[107] but Hearst was Whitney's choice. The only reason he gave in his memo was that Hearst's "geographical position" gave him "a great advantage over others." This presumably reflected Whitney's belief in the growing importance of northern Ontario, but Sault Ste. Marie was a long way from southern Ontario, where most people lived and had only 14 seats in a legislature of 111 seats.

The cabinet meeting was brief, all apparently accepting Whitney's advice, and Pyne drove to Pendarves, the mansion then serving as Government House, to advise Lieutenant Governor Gibson to invite Hearst to form a government.[108] Gibson subsequently met with Hearst, then met again with Pyne. Upon his return to Queen's Park, Pyne "was closeted for some time in the council chamber" with Hearst and Lucas but Hanna quietly left the building "early in the afternoon."[109] "After a while Mr. Hearst came out, and in a few minutes entered a motor car and was whisked away to Government House," returning about six o'clock. Clearly, Pyne had advised Gibson to call on Hearst to form a government, he had done so, and Hearst had accepted the responsibility.[110]

In retrospect, it is surprising that the press did not more fully realize the strength of Hearst's position. But considering that the party caucus might have chosen Hanna, "the only man whose grip and ability ever impressed either the Legislature or the public," or Beck, who "could ... have organized a Government in sympathy with progressive social and industrial legislation," the *Globe* concluded that Hearst's appointment could only be explained as the choice of "the party organization." That meant Cochrane, because in the view of the *Globe* Hearst was "a junior member, an inferior in politics, and one rather unhopeful in leadership" even if he had administered his department "with much vigor."[111] That statement could be dismissed as partisan except that the Conservative *World* agreed. Hearst's appointment, it declared, was "a great day for the Liberal party" because the Conservatives had "deliberately thrown away their advantage, disgusted their members, and flown in the face of all Conservative Party principles by submitting to the dictation of outside agencies, and failing to insist upon a caucus for the choice of a new leader."[112]

The press was not aware of Whitney's memo, of course, nor did it know that Whitney had encouraged Hearst to seek election and offered him a position in cabinet as early as 1905. But it should have noticed that on more than one occasion since 1911 Hearst was one of only two or three ministers who met alone with Whitney. Nor, apparently, did it see any significance in the fact that at Christmas 1913, when Whitney was seriously ill in New York and all the other ministers – except Pyne, who was in New York with Whitney – were scattered for the holidays, only Foy and Hearst remained at Queen's Park.[113] Similarly, the announcement of the 1914 election had come after an inner cabinet meeting attended only by Whitney, Foy, Pyne and Hearst.[114] Clearly, Whitney had developed a healthy respect for his young colleague's common sense and political skills, his role in settling the Keewatin territorial dispute, his dedication to the development of northern Ontario and its resources, and the results of the 1911 and 1914 campaigns in the region. Upon reflection, the *Globe* did acknowledge that Hearst had been "close to the Premier" as an "able, loyal subordinate" with "much of Cochrane's force" and "few public enemies," but then it added that he had also become "aggressive" and "brusque," his youthful joviality having waned."[115] Historian Joseph Schull claimed, without offering any evidence, that "his habitual manner reminded his critics and even some friends of the abrasive, self-righteous assurance of a Sunday School superintendent."[116] Whether or not that was true, Whitney and Cochrane did neither Hearst nor the party a favour in manipulating his appointment as they did because it undermined his legitimacy from the outset. In retrospect, Hearst should have insisted on being elected or at least confirmed by the caucus. His failure to do so was a serious misjudgment, for which he paid a high price.

The *World*, an independent Conservative newspaper owned by the outspoken William "Billy" Maclean who was also a Conservative MP from 1892 to 1926, began undermining Hearst from the outset, predicting "the decadence and ultimate break-up" of the provincial party because "government by junta or by clique or by any form of kaiserism is utterly foreign to the spirit and principle of the Conservative party and the Conservative voters of Ontario."[117] Its point, of course, was that Hearst had not been chosen by the party caucus but Frank Cochrane, acting on behalf of Borden and the federal Conservatives. Maclean wasn't the only one who thought Hearst's appointment was an undemocratic backroom deal, and he warned Hearst that "the idea that Ottawa may have too much to say in the direction of Ontario politics will not die out until Premier Hearst shows that there is nothing to warrant it, and he had best make that demonstration by going ahead on the work that Ontario needs and avoiding entanglements of any kind elsewhere."[118] That might not have been an unreasonable suggestion except for the fact that Canada had been at war for two months and close collaboration between the federal and provincial governments was almost certainly going to be greater than normal.

Hearst's appointment was well received in Sault Ste. Marie, however. As the *Sault Daily Star* rightly observed, "every man in Algoma takes Mr. Hearst's election [*sic*] as a personal compliment." Arthur Boyce, noting that Hearst was taking office "in turbulent times," expressed his confidence that he was "endued with the genius to deal with the situation bravely in a broad Canadian spirit." Alexander Smith, a former Liberal Party organizer who had known Hearst since they were teenagers in Collingwood, thought his "rapid rise" to the leadership was "just what was expected except by Mr. Hearst himself who was always a willing worker in the ranks of his party." Similarly, James McLurg, the president of the Algoma West Liberal Association, thought the Conservatives had "made a good choice" and was "pleased that the new Prime Minister is a man from Northern Ontario."[119] As for most Ontarians, if their response was not overly enthusiastic, neither was it unfavourable because most people outside of northern Ontario didn't really know much about him.

At ten o'clock the next morning, 2 October, Sir John Gibson performed his last official act, swearing Hearst into office. He also swore in Finlay MacDiarmid, who was replacing Reaume as Minister of Public Works. Two hours later, Sir William Meredith, the chief justice, swore in John Hendrie, a wealthy businessman, Conservative member of the legislature since 1902 and minister without portfolio since 1905, as the new lieutenant governor. Hearst and the members of his cabinet were in attendance, as were Frank Cochrane, Charles H. Ritchie, a prominent Toronto Conservative lawyer, and A.E. Ames, the Toronto financier.[120] Also in attendance were Bella Hearst, Mary Pyne, and two of J.J. Foy's daughters. A brief reception followed, hosted by Hendrie, in which "the health of the new Premier was drunk in mineral water, for Mr. Hearst is a temperance man."[121]

Because the government had just been re-elected in June, it had virtually a full term of office ahead of it, which would give Hearst ample opportunity to make his mark before another election was necessary. Having said that, however, the government had been in office since 1905 and, despite its re-election in 1914 some thought it had been drifting since 1913, perhaps due to Whitney's poor health. Would that change under Hearst's leadership? He did not have Whitney's strong personality, nor did he share Whitney's high reputation for common-sense probity or perhaps even his well-honed political skills, but he was younger, clearly well intentioned, and honest. In his first public statement he assured the province that he would continue Whitney's moderately progressive policies and maintain the reputation he had established for clean, honest government.[122]

Hearst was not going to have the luxury of merely carrying on Whitney's policies, however, because just two months earlier the world had changed dramatically. Britain had declared war on Germany and Austria-Hungary on 4 August, and no one could possibly predict what lay ahead. One thing was certain: Canada would be involved. Borden had promptly committed Canada to fully supporting the mother country in its hour of need, and public support for this commitment was virtually unanimous. This meant that Canada would be sending troops overseas to fight in a general European war for the first time. How long would this war last, and how great was Canada's contribution going to be? And what impact would this have on Canadian society? It was an uncertain time for those who had to play a role in guiding the country through uncertain times with so much unknown and unpredictable.

# 4 Taking Charge: 1914–16

*Let us hold together in this day of trial, knowing that out of this night of darkness must evolve a greater, better and nobler Empire even than that of the past.*[1]

HEARST'S first task was to form a government. He knew better than to attempt too many changes too soon, because Whitney had built up a winning team and extensive changes hardly seemed necessary. Hanna, whom many had thought would refuse to serve under Hearst, did not resign and, although "openly bitter,"[2] served loyally for the next two years before leaving for Ottawa to serve as national food controller. Foy, who was ill and had only stayed in office this long at Whitney's request, was anxious to retire but agreed to carry on for a couple of more months.[3] But the Department of Public Works was vacant as a result of Reaume's defeat in the election and Hendrie's elevation to the office of lieutenant governor. In the first indication of his innate caution, Hearst retained the Department of Lands, Forests and Mines for the present and appointed Finlay MacDiarmid, a farmer from Elgin West, as Minister of Public Works. He didn't replace Hendrie as minister without portfolio, and for the first time since 1905 that there was no Franco-Ontarian in the cabinet. There was, in fact, only one Franco-Ontarian Conservative in the legislature – Henri Morel, who had held Nipissing since 1908 – and for whatever reason Hearst chose not to include him.[4]

The most significant change was not an appointment to the cabinet but Adam Beck's resignation. The reason he gave was to loosen his link with the government, but the real reason likely was that Beck "simply refused to serve under the younger and less experienced Hearst."[5] Hearst had never publicly expressed his views on public power, but Cochrane was known to be less than enthusiastic about it, and one of Whitney's last acts had been to arrange the appointment of John Hendrie to lieutenant governor. This was significant because he was a prominent engineer and a minister without portfolio who had represented the government on the Hydro-Electric Power Commission (HPEC) with a mandate to "keep a firm hand" on Beck.[6] Clearly, this was not only a conciliatory gesture to Beck but also to his thousands of supporters, including the strongly pro-hydro Conservative *Evening Telegram*, which pointedly warned that "the people will not tolerate back-sliding" on the HEPC's continuing development.[7] Hearst replaced Hendrie as the government representative on the HEPC with the hydro-friendly I.B. Lucas. He also extended the appointment to the commission of W.K. McNaught, a Toronto manufacturer, Conservative MPP, and strong supporter of public power since 1907, even though he had lost his seat in the 1914 election.[8] These gestures did not improve Beck's attitude to the government and may even have strengthened his suspicion that Hearst was a weak leader. That made Beck more dangerous, which may have been what the *World*'s Maclean had in mind when speculating that the "most notable thing" about the Hearst government was that Beck was no longer a member of it.[9]

Two months later, Hearst handed over the Department of Lands, Forests and Mines to Howard Ferguson. It is not entirely clear why he made this appointment. Lands, Forests and Mines was the most important department in the government because the resources it managed accounted for a third of its revenues. Hearst knew, perhaps better than most, that the department needed a strong minister and Ferguson would certainly be that, but it was also probably the most politically sensitive department aside from education because Ferguson approached all issues and policies through a thick partisan filter. Whitney would never have included Ferguson in his government, although he had allowed him to stir up ethnic and religious controversy when it seemed necessary. But Hearst knew that he needed a strong colleague who could serve virtually as deputy Premier while he concentrated on the war effort. The surprising thing is that Ferguson was not only loyal to Hearst, the two men somewhat improbably became close friends even after Hearst's retirement from politics.

As expected, it wasn't long before long he ended the Whitney–Hearst policy of favouring lumber mills over pulp and paper mills, declaring that his goal was "to see the largest paper industry in the world established in the Province."[10] He was in the right place at the right time, because the department was now "more thoroughly dominated by lumbermen and promoters than at any time in its history." Then, when Aubrey White, the deputy minister, died in 1915, Hearst appointed Albert Grigg, the Conservative MPP for Algoma, to replace him, signalling to Ferguson – whether intentionally or not – that he would have a free hand in running the department. Nobody has ever accused Grigg of either incompetence or corruption, but as Nelles has claimed, he was a small merchant from Bruce Mines who "could not see what was going on around him." Gillis and Roach are closer to the mark when they describe Grigg as "an ineffectual figure" who "became a cipher for the wishes of Ferguson and his overbearing private secretary," Carroll Hele, who largely ignored him and ran the department themselves.[11] John Bacher, the most recent scholar writing on the subject, agrees that Grigg's honesty "was never doubted despite his being in the midst of timber scandals,"[12] and when E..C. Drury, who despised Ferguson and his corruption, became Premier he retained Grigg as deputy minister. Indeed, the Drury government continued the Whitney–Hearst policy that "aimed primarily to export pulpwood from both private and Crown lands."[13]

Because the government had just been re-elected in June, it had virtually a full term of office ahead of it, which gave Hearst ample opportunity to make his mark before another election was necessary. Having said that, however, the government had been in office since 1905 and, despite its re-election in 1914, some people felt that it had been drifting since 1913, perhaps because of Whitney's deteriorating health. Hearst naturally promised to carry on Whitney's policies, but it did not take long to become obvious that the world had changed dramatically since August 1914 when Britain declared war on Germany.

Borden had promptly committed Canada to fully supporting the mother country in its hour of need, a decision that most Canadians supported. This meant that Canada would be sending troops overseas to fight in a European war for the first time. Sam Hughes, the Minister of Militia and Defence, quickly mobilized more than 30,000 men for basic training at Camp Valcartier and when they sailed for England in late October, a second contingent was already being planned, and there was no knowing how many more men might be needed. While many thought, or perhaps hoped, that the war might be a short one, more knowledgeable people knew that it would likely be a long one because all of Europe was involved. And despite Canada's distance from Europe, the war's impact would almost certainly be profound in ways that it was impossible to foresee. But no one who knew Hearst doubted that he would support the war effort in every possible way.

As an Anglo-Protestant imperialist, Hearst was representative of most Ontarians, who fully supported the decision to support Britain in the war. They had welcomed the resurgence in imperialism in recent years, seeing no conflict between being proud Canadians but also members of the British Empire. Whitney had reflected this kind of thinking when he declared on 5 August that Canadians would respond to Borden's call to support Britain "with cheerfulness and courage" because "we are part of the Empire in the fullest sense and we share in its obligations as well as its privileges."[14] Hearst similarly expressed his confidence that Ontario would "hold together in this day of trial, knowing that out of this night of darkness must evolve a greater, better and nobler Empire than that of the past."[15] The *Sault Daily Star* was representative of most of Ontario's newspapers when it proclaimed that Canada's duty was "clear" and "not a day should be lost in showing to the world that that duty will be discharged." Being a Conservative paper, it couldn't resist reminding its readers that Canada had "shirked too long her responsibilities as an integral portion of the British Empire," so contingents "should be promptly and eagerly sent to prove again that Canada is willing to share the perils as well as the profits of the Empire."[16]

Hearst set the tone in his very first speech after becoming Premier, delivered on 16 October, when he proclaimed that

> the growl of the Canadian whelp of the old lion has become a roar. Canada is in it to the end. She will not stop until "Rule Britannia" and "The Maple Leaf" sound on the streets of Berlin. One contingent has gone, another is in preparation, and I am given to understand now that, if the necessity arises they will be followed by another and another and another. And they will all go gladly with the same spirit of patriotic determination. It is Britain's war, and it is Canada's war.[17]

As quaint as Hearst's views on the empire and Canada's place in it were, they represented the attitudes of most British Canadians. In the first place, Hearst thought it was "a good and grand and glorious thing ... to be a Briton" because the empire was "the greatest secular influence for good that the world has ever seen."[18] To suggestions that it was in decline, he responded that, "great as she is today, great as she has been in the past, mighty as her power has been for good, she is but on the threshold of her power and influence for good, and she will go on as long as time shall last, the great dominating influence for righteousness and truth and goodness the wide world over."[19]

Like Borden, he thought the empire was "destined to grow into one great confederation,"[20] and when the imperial war cabinet was created in 1917, he saw it as a major step in that direction. "What has long been looked upon as a fantastic dream of an Imperial Visionary is, in a qualified sense at least, an accomplished fact."[21] A more unified empire would benefit all humankind and liberty. As for practical details, again like Borden he did not hesitate to say that he personally favoured sharing the burden of imperial defence with a voice in imperial defence policy.[22] Indeed, this would become inevitable because Canada was destined to become "the dominating influence" in the empire.[23] Within the next century, its population would equal or exceed that of Britain and Canada would therefore have to bear an equal or greater share of imperial defence than the mother country.[24] And if Canada's future was virtually unlimited growth and prosperity, Ontario was the "the keystone of the great arch of Confederation," destined to be "the greatest and most important territory on the face of the earth; no longer the backbone, but it will be the head and lungs and heart and vitals of the Dominion of Canada, breathing power and life and energy north and south and east and west."[25]

Patriotism and pride in the values that Hearst and many others believed the empire represented were, of course, standard rhetorical fare at the time. But the Rev. H.J. Cody, rector of St. Paul's Anglican church in Toronto and a man widely recognized as one of the city's leading intellectuals, gave a foretaste of how public opinion was going to be radicalized when he claimed in a widely publicized speech in November 1914 that "hatred of the English had been carefully and persistently instilled into the very souls of the German people for the past forty years" and that Germany's goal in the war was "to wipe forever from the face of the earth the British people as an empire."[26] Cody's view that Britain and its empire were not engaged in a traditional European war but an existential struggle between right and wrong, good and evil, quickly became the main thrust of British propaganda and was widely accepted.

That included Hearst, who believed as early as January 1915 that Great Britain was defending the liberty of the world and was confident that Canada would stand by her "as long as there is one man left to hold a rifle or one dollar left with which to buy ammunition." Nor did he hesitate to go to New York to tell the neutral Americans that this was their war too, because "if Prussian ideals are to prevail, if the law that might is right is to be supreme, then there is no place on earth for democratic nations, or for countries cherishing the ideals which the British Empire and the United States hold dear."[27] Towards the end of the war, by which time many Ontarians were seriously questioning the wisdom of Canada's total commitment to victory at all costs, Hearst would bring Cody into the government as Minister of Education.

This extreme emotional view of the war inevitably prompted some people to question the loyalty of Germans and Austrians (terms used for anyone who lived in the eastern portion of the German and Austro-Hungarian Empires, most of whom were actually Slavs) living in Canada. In Ontario many were Loyalists and Mennonites who had arrived after the American Revolution. The largest concentration was in Waterloo County, whose shire town was the now unfortunately named Berlin. Not surprisingly, the wave of anti-German sentiment that swept through the province after the outbreak of war was especially strong in that area, although it was by no means confined to it. In fact, the first incident took place as early as 5 August in Toronto when a mob of 500 people surrounded the Liederkranz Club, a German cultural society, demanding that it take down the German flag and fly the Union Jack. The police arrived in time to avoid possible violence and the club did raise the Union Jack two days later.[28] That opened the floodgates and on the weekend of 23/24 August some overheated patriotic teenagers pulled down a bust of Kaiser Wilhelm's grandfather in Berlin's Victoria Park and dumped it into the lake. In February 1916 intoxicated soldiers from the Berlin-based 118th Battalion attacked and trashed the Concordia Society, which had been celebrating German culture since 1873, and then paraded through the city singing patriotic songs. Three months later the citizens voted by a narrow majority to change the name of their city to Kitchener, about as patriotic a name as anyone could think of because Lord Kitchener, the British Secretary of State for War, had just died when the ship on which he was travelling to Russia was struck by a German mine in the North Sea.[29]

Meanwhile, xenophobic patriots were demanding that enemy aliens be watched carefully or, even better, dismissed from their jobs on the grounds that they were probably sympathetic to Germany and might even be spies. When they demanded that the University of Toronto dismiss three German professors, President Robert Falconer responded reasonably that none of them had done anything to justify their dismissal. That prompted the Toronto Board of Education, backed by a petition signed by more than 100 people, to demand that the provincial government intervene. Hearst "wanted nothing to do with the whole affair," stalled for several days, and then wrote to Falconer but only to observe that the issue was one "for the Board of Governors, not for the Government." When Falconer responded that the board saw no need for action, Hearst concluded that "no further discussion was needed."[30]

But the university's board of governors was actually divided on the matter. Some, like Reuben Leonard, J.S. Campbell, E.B. Osler and D.R. Wilkie fanned the flames while others like J.W. Flavelle, B.E. Walker and Zebulon Lash urged moderation. The moderates were supported by the vast majority of the students but in the end the three professors were given extended leaves of absence during which they eventually resigned and found positions elsewhere.[31] That didn't end the matter, of course, because the press had reported the situation and many Conservatives thought Hearst should have intervened. Richard Preston, Hearst's obscure minister without portfolio from Carleton Place, actually told

Falconer that the government would not prevent an employer from firing a German, even without cause, and Tory backbencher Thomas Hook, an Ulster Orangeman, told the North Toronto Conservative Club that "if we can't get university professors of British blood then let us close the universities," a suggestion that was "applauded ... enthusiastically" by the audience. The *Globe*'s report of this meeting included the claim that rural MPPs, "always suspicious of the 'rich man's university,' were at the forefront of these legislative protests."[32]

Hearst avoided public comment until 15 December when a delegation including MPPs from both parties, although most were Conservatives, and others including representatives of Toronto's Board of Education, "laid siege to his office" demanding that the government tighten its control over the university.[33] Whitney had passed legislation in 1905 making the university autonomous, however, and Hearst had no intention of reopening that debate. Instead, he sought to reassure the delegates that no one was "more British" than his government and he would "look into" the matter and launch a formal inquiry if necessary. When one man in the crowd shouted "Dismiss them!" – referring to the professors – the *Globe* reporter noted that Hearst "smiled but made no comment."[34] Nor did he take any action. Was that why Falconer awarded him an honorary degree in the spring of 1915?

Meanwhile, the federal government had responded to the perceived enemy alien problem by requiring more than 80,000 people to register and report to police on a regular basis because they were deemed to be a risk to the war effort. Of that number, 8,579 (including more than eighty children) were arrested and sent to internment camps, 3,138 of them classified as prisoners of war.[35] Twenty-four internment camps were established throughout the country, six of them in Ontario.[36] As misguided as that was, most of these men were not even Germans or Austrians. According to Watson Kirkconnell – later a distinguished Slavic scholar and president of Acadia University – who served at the internment camp established at Kapuskasing, the "great majority" of them "were Slovaks, Ruthenians, and Poles," plus "a hundred Turks, a few Bulgars, a Magyar or two, and a handful of genuine Austrians."[37] In other words, they were subject peoples who had immigrated to Canada and felt no loyalty to their former rulers. It was a vital distinction that the Borden government and Canadians generally failed to grasp or chose to ignore, thus doing an irrational injustice to these unfortunate people. This seemingly wilful ignorance was, of course, part of the general attitude of Canadians, especially Anglo-Protestants, who tended to regard everyone else, whatever their culture, language, and religion, as alien, inferior, and potentially dangerous.

The camp established at Kapuskasing was actually Hearst's idea because it was situated on the edge of the clay belt in north-eastern Ontario, where the men could clear land and build roads, particularly at the site of the government's proposed experimental farm. Instead of being "an unproductive charge upon the state," therefore, the internees would do work desired by the province at no cost because the federal government paid them a nominal daily wage of twenty-five cents, equivalent to what soldiers received for non-military duties. At the same time, by advancing the government's northern settlement program, this project would "give employment ... to Canadians and increase the productiveness [*sic*] of this country."[38] That was true, at least in theory, but these recent immigrants, through no fault of their own, found themselves separated from their families and communities and forced to perform hard manual labour in a harsh climate while being guarded by 256 soldiers.[39] Another camp was established at Sault Ste. Marie in January 1915 because of the large immigrant population that had been attracted to the thriving industrial centre in the years before the war. Some were housed in the city's armoury, while others were housed on nearby Whitefish Island, initially in a railway boxcar and then in bunkhouses, before being sent to Kapuskasing. In both instances they were guarded by the 51st (Soo Rifles) Regiment. The internment of these so-called enemy aliens created a couple of unanticipated problems: no provision was made for the support of their families, and their internment created a labour shortage. By 1916 the government recognized that the Slavic internees were harmless and paroled them to return to their industrial jobs. Even though they were now contributing to the war effort, however, they only received the equivalent of a soldier's pay, not what the other workers were paid, so they were cheap labour.[40]

When the camp at Kingston was closed in November 1917, its inmates were also transferred to Kapuskasing and the camp was surrounded by two tall, barbed-wire fences because most of them were Germans. These men initially refused to work but soon changed their minds when they realized that their primary task was to cut firewood to heat their accommodations during the winter. The German government also instructed them to work, and the Canadian government doubled their wages.[41] In the summer of 1919 the Canadian government decided to repatriate all of the internees to Europe, but it took until February 1920 to do so because of the shortage of shipping.[42] Kapuskasing was the last camp to close and was converted into an agricultural settlement for returned soldiers.

One of the first problems Hearst faced as Premier was unemployment. The country had slid into a recession in 1913, the *Globe* reporting 15,000 unemployed in Toronto alone in January 1914.[43] The outbreak of war and the call for volunteers in August provided an outlet for many unemployed men, but the situation apparently did not improve. The *Daily Star* reported in December 1914 that 351 applicants sought one position advertised for a hotel waiter.[44] As one speaker at a meeting of unemployed men declared in January 1915, "single men are going to war, not because they love their country, but because conditions force them to join the army or starve."[45] This caused some to suspect that the federal and provincial governments were deliberately not trying to alleviate the situation in order to force men to join the army, but the real problem was instability in financial markets and a disruption in trade with European markets. The Toronto Stock Exchange closed during the July 1914 crisis that led to the outbreak of war in August and did not reopen until early in 1915.[46]

Hearst took the situation seriously, introducing an extensive public works program and announcing in November 1914 the creation of the Ontario Unemployment Commission, chaired by Sir John Willison, publisher of Toronto's *Evening News.* Its purpose, as Willison explained, was to investigate the causes of unemployment and to recommend ways of reducing it and its members were a solid mixture of businessmen, labour representatives, clergy, and social activists.[47] The commission undertook its work at a difficult time. The labour market was very fluid as a result of dislocation occasioned by the war, and the *Daily Star* declared unemployment to be the number one social problem.[48] Members of the Canadian Manufacturers' Association were somewhat uncooperative, however: only 651 of the 1,637 questionnaires sent out to factories and plants were returned. Even so, this information showed that employment in those establishments alone had fallen by 20,000 between January 1913 and June 1914.[49]

The commission's interim report, issued in July 1915, proposed the establishment of a provincial Department of Labour, a system of government employment bureaus throughout the province, increased training in primary schools in domestic science, manual and agricultural skills, and raising the school leaving age from fourteen to fifteen. It also proposed a form of unemployment insurance, whereby the government would pay 20 per cent of the amounts at present paid out in unemployment relief by the various mutual benefit societies serving workers.[50] These were helpful progressive recommendations, but by the summer of 1915 unemployment was actually declining because of enlistments in the army and the economic revival stimulated by the war. The *Daily Star* noted the changing conditions as early as June, and it was not long before they were apparent to all observers.[51] Indeed, when the enlistment rate began to decline later in 1915 some blamed the falling unemployment rate.[52] Hearst noted the changed conditions in a speech in the legislature during the 1916 session. "Never in the history of this country," he declared, "were there so many avenues open for workers of all classes and conditions to find employment as there are today."[53] It was true, but that did not mean that he was not prepared to take action on the recommendations of the Unemployment Commission. On the contrary, over the next five years, all of its recommendations except unemployment insurance were put into effect.

The war created a tremendous demand for all kinds of war material, and when the Imperial Munitions Board was created in November 1915 to manage the purchasing of war supplies, factories were "deluged with orders."[54] Ontario, being highly industrialized, inevitably benefited from this demand and the rash of government contracts. Of the $1.1 billion in contracts that the IMB issued during the war, about $649 million went to companies in Ontario.[55] To cite just a few examples, Sault Ste. Marie's Algoma Steel Company converted its entire production from rails to shell casings, the Steel Company of Canada at Hamilton produced shell casings and steel panels for ships and railcars, and Brantford's Harris farm machinery company produced high-explosive shells, time and percussion fuses, and airplane engines for the British government, as well as naval gun mounts, fuses, and shells for the American government.[56] Two companies at nearby Welland, Canada Forge and Canadian Billings and Spencer, produced shell casings and gun barrels, and Canadian Billings and Spencer also manufactured Ross rifles. Page-Hersey and the Electro Metals Company, also in Welland, manufactured shrapnel shell casings, and Electro Metals also produced ferrosilicon for armaments and hydrogen for barrage and observation balloons. The British American Shipbuilding Company at Welland built the hulls for five government-funded cargo vessels.[57] The Canadian Car and Foundry plant at Fort William built railway boxcars and six minesweepers for the French government. Canadian Explosives built a plant that produced vast quantities of cordite at Nobel, near Parry Sound,

The IMB also created subsidiaries of its own, mostly in Ontario. It leased the O'Brien Munitions Company at Renfrew that packed cordite into every twenty-five-pound shell made in Canada.[58] It also leased the O'Brien Company's Energite Explosives Company, renamed British Explosives, and employed 3,000 workers in plants at Haileybury, Widdifield (near North Bay) and Renfrew.[59] The British Cordite Company at Nobel, near Parry Sound, was producing 1.5 million pounds of cordite per month by 1918.[60] Canada's largest explosive plant, and "one of the largest of its kind in existence,"[61] was the British Chemical Company at

Trenton that manufactured artillery, rifle and small arms ammunition. It employed 3,000 workers and allegedly produced almost half of the sulphur-based TNT used by the Allies in the war until it caught fire and was destroyed by several explosions.[62]

There were three IMB plants in Toronto: Canadian Aeroplanes, British Acetones and British Forgings. Canadian Aeroplanes was the former Curtiss airplane factory founded by aviation pioneer Glenn Curtiss, which now produced almost 3,000 aircraft for the Royal Flying Corps and has been described as "a model of highly mechanized, tightly organized mass production" and "probably the most successful of the IMB's national factories."[63] British Acetones leased the Gooderham and Worts distillery building in Toronto, which became the largest producer of acetone, an essential ingredient in the production of munitions, in the British Empire. British Forgings built the world's largest electrically powered steel plant on Toronto's waterfront and employed 1,600 workers who by the end of the war had produced ingots that were then fabricated into more than three million shell casings.[64] In fact, by 1916 Ontario was producing one-quarter to one-third of the ammunition and half of the shrapnel used by British forces overseas.[65]

Meanwhile, the mining industry was thriving, especially at Sudbury, where the American-based International Nickel Company and the British-based Mond Nickel Company produced 90 per cent of the world's nickel, vital in the production of war materiel ranging from bullet and shell casings to armoured plating for tanks and battleships. Inevitably, production and employment soared in their mines as well. Because these were not Canadian or British companies, allegations were raised that Friedrich Krupp AG, the enormous German steel and armaments company, owned shares in International Nickel, but it did not. Similarly, overzealous patriots in Britain believed that Mond was a German company because its president was Ludwig Mond, who was born in Germany. In fact, Mond had lived in England since the 1860s and was a British citizen.

Given that there were no nickel smelters in Ontario, a more legitimate question was where the nickel matte was shipped for processing and where did the processed nickel go after that. In Mond's case, that was clear: it was shipped to Wales and after processing was sold to British armament companies. And, as Lucas informed the legislature, Mond had offered the Canadian government full control over all its nickel output for the duration of the war.[66] International Nickel, however, was an American company that shipped its matte to its smelter in Bayonne, New Jersey, but was it selling nickel to Germany? The United States was, of course, a neutral country until April 1917. The Borden government – Frank Cochrane, in fact – had been monitoring the company's sales since

October 1914, however, with the full cooperation of the company, which had agreed on 1 January 1915 that all nickel exports would only be made with the approval of the British government. And the sale of war materiel to Germany hadn't seemed to be a practical problem because the Royal Navy's blockade of Germany included warships patrolling off the American coast that inspected the cargoes of all ships going to Europe.

That changed dramatically in July 1916 when the *Deutschland*, a large unarmed German cargo submarine, arrived at Baltimore and loaded cargo that included 341 tons of refined nickel and then returned to Germany. A few months later it returned and picked up another load. When it set out on a third trip the German government recalled it because German–American relations were by then rapidly deteriorating.[67] In other words, a small amount of Ontario nickel had in fact reached Germany in 1916 because, as an investigation by the federal government revealed, International Nickel had sold some nickel to another American company that must have resold it to Germany and no one had foreseen cargo submarines, which could evade the naval blockade by staying submerged while in coastal waters.

The best guarantee that no Ontario nickel could get to Germany was to have it refined in Ontario, and as Ferguson told Borden in January 1916, the issue had "been a live one with the Government for a number of years."[68] In fact, the Hearst government had created a royal commission in February 1915 to examine the issue.[69] Chaired by George Holloway, vice president of the Institute of Mining and Metallurgy in London (England), the commission included Thomas Gibson, the deputy minister of mines, Willet Miller, the provincial geologist, and McGregor Young, the province's solicitor. A few months later the federal Munitions Resources Commission chaired by Thomas Cantley recommended that the federal government "insist" that International Nickel build a refinery in Canada, and in January 1916 it agreed to do so.[70] When Ferguson met personally with Ambrose Monell, the president of International Nickel, to make clear the government's determination to have a nickel refinery in the province, he gave in and agreed to build it.[71]

The shipment to Germany of two very small quantities of nickel was not a serious breach in the blockade, but it was embarrassing and offered critics of both the Borden and Hearst governments a golden opportunity to denounce their apparent incompetence. The provincial government bore no responsibility for the failure of the federal government's monitoring of International Nickel's sales but Hartley Dewart, a Liberal firebrand who relished sensational scandals, naturally exploited the situation. Indeed, he kept talking about it from the summer of 1916 to the autumn of 1919, wildly claiming that the "Cochrane-Hearst-Ferguson nickel plated policy" had allowed "thousands, and possibly millions, of tons of Ontario nickel" to be shipped to Germany "and ... finally ended in the flesh of many a British soldier."[72]

Hearst's initially tepid response was that the government had no control over a privately owned American company, which was obviously inadequate in the circumstances. But the government was not, as H.V. Nelles claims, guilty of "an apparent lack of interest."[73] In fact, it was moving towards a confrontation with International Nickel. Hearst's first move was to announce in July 1916 that the government had secured patents for at least two new nickel refining methods. That significantly weakened International Nickel's negotiating strength that was based on its hitherto exclusive refining technology. Even better, one of the processes could be powered by electricity, which would greatly reduce production costs. Eight months later, the nickel commission issued its massive report – more than 950 pages – recommending that International Nickel be required to refine its ore in Ontario. The government immediately accepted that recommendation and revised the Mining Tax Act to require all minerals to be refined in Ontario and established "a progressive but far from onerous" tax rate graduated according to profit level."[74] It also demanded $1.3 million in back taxes. International Nickel accepted the inevitable and the refinery was built, not at Sudbury, as expected, but at Port Colborne, a village on the Lake Erie entrance to the Welland Canal.[75] No doubt one reason for building the refinery there was that Port Colborne was close to Niagara Falls and could access hydroelectric power rather than the more expensive coal-fired Orford process for separating nickel and copper.[76] The impact of this development at Port Colborne was profound because it became an industrial community employing thousands of men over the years but at a cost because the refinery polluted surface water and contaminated the soil that contributed to serious environmental health issues.[77]

Meanwhile, the government was spending large amounts of money in support of the war effort. In August 1914 it had donated 250,000 bags of flour to the British government and 100,000 evaporated apples to the Belgian Relief Fund. In July 1915 it contributed $500,000 to the federal government to purchase machine guns and $2.2 million to the Canadian Patriotic Fund. Spending on various war-related projects and activities throughout the war amounted to $51 million by 1918. This money obviously had to be found somewhere, and the government introduced new amusement taxes, a special war tax on all property, and a death tax on large estates. Meanwhile, when the federal government discovered that it could raise a lot of money through Victory Bonds, Ontario residents invested more than $800 million of the total $1,710 million.[78]

The government's most significant contribution was the Ontario Military Hospital at Orpington, a "peaceful little Kent village among the fields and hop gardens of the Weald" south-east of London, England.[79] It was Pyne's idea and reflected his discovery in the spring of 1915 that there were only two small hospitals for Canadian soldiers in England: the Queen's Canadian Military Hospital near Folkestone and the Duchess of Connaught Hospital at Cliveden. The Queen's Canadian Hospital could only accommodate sixty-five patients, and the Duchess of Connaught Hospital only 100.[80] Canadian troops had only gone into action early in February so the number of wounded or ill Canadians was still relatively small, but even so they were scattered among British hospitals throughout the country and their numbers would increase. Accordingly, Pyne, who was then serving as Acting Premier because Hearst was ill, offered in May to build and maintain a 1,040-bed hospital and to contribute six ambulances for use at the Front. Both offers were promptly accepted and Pyne left for England in June to manage the hospital project. Officially opened in February 1916, the hospital's medical staff included thirty-six doctors and eighty-one nurses, all of whom were Ontarians.

Hearst had proposed that A.E. Ross, the Conservative MPP for Kingston, a physician who had gone overseas with the First Division in October 1914, command the hospital but Ross thought he was more useful serving with the troops.[81] Dr. D.W. McPherson, a prominent Toronto physician, accepted the position with the rank of lieutenant colonel, and Margaret Heggie Smith, an experienced military nurse from Ottawa, served as chief matron.[82] Both had been active in the militia for several years and Smith had served in the South African War in 1902, and both had gone overseas with the first contingent in October 1914. McPherson had served as commanding officer of No. 2 Canadian Field Ambulance at the Front before being given command of the Canadian Convalescent Hospital at Woodcote Park, Epsom, in September 1915, and then was transferred to Orpington in November. Smith had served with No 2 Canadian Stationary Hospital at Le Touquet, the first Canadian military unit to go to France in November 1914.[83] The hospital was doubled in size at Ontario's expense in September 1917 before being taken over by the Canadian Army Medical Corps and renamed No. 16 Canadian General Hospital. By the end of the war it had treated more than 30,000 patients, not all of them Ontarians or even Canadians, at a total cost of $1.3 million to the provincial government.[84]

The government also transferred three hospitals in Ontario to the Military Hospital Commission, created in 1915 to establish and operate convalescent hospitals for wounded soldiers requiring further treatment after returning home. One was a psychiatric hospital housed in the former Victoria College building in Cobourg, another was a new building in Whitby originally intended to be a psychiatric hospital, and the newly built Guelph reformatory, which included a farm, was converted into the Speedwell Military Convalescent Hospital.[85]

When Rowell proposed during the 1916 legislative session the creation of a provincial committee to mobilize Ontario's resources for the war effort. Hearst welcomed the idea, with the qualification that "there is no thought or criticism of the Dominion Government, or no criticism in any way of what they have done," and invited Rowell to draft the bill establishing the committee, which he did.[86] This was significant not only for its own sake but because it marked a change in Hearst's relationship with Rowell. As much as they had disagreed on various issues before the war, Rowell fully shared Hearst's views on the war and became one of the most prominent Liberals in Canada who supported conscription and became a major figure in the Union government in 1917. When the Organization of Resources Committee (ORC) was established, it consisted of Lieutenant Governor Hendrie as chairman, Hearst and Rowell as vice-chairmen, and seven other members of the legislature, four Conservatives and three Liberals.[87] Representatives of the public were to be added later. The ORC's mandate was to "to enquire into and report" on ways in which Ontario could support the war effort through the "organization of our resources, particularly in assisting the work of recruiting men for the Canadian Expeditionary Force (CEF), ensuring a sufficient supply of labour for the agricultural interest and the necessary industrial operations of the Province," and to promote "thrift and economy among the people, thereby strengthening our financial position during the War and preparing for the period of Reconstruction after the War.[88]

So far so good, but Rowell had difficulty adjusting to bipartisan cooperation. When Hearst was unable to attend the committee's first meeting because of urgent business in his distant constituency, Rowell accused him of not giving the committee's business the priority it deserved. One is inclined to wonder if this petty and unworthy accusation reflected the fact that Rowell had never held public office and perhaps didn't appreciate the many demands made on a Premier. Or perhaps he just felt embarrassed because he had arranged for Lionel Curtis, the influential British imperialist who was visiting Toronto, to describe the work being done by the British resources organization. Then when Hearst suggested that the appointment of the public representatives on the committee might wait until the committee was functional, Rowell complained that the public representatives should be appointed immediately and accused him of not being serious about the whole project.[89] Frustrated, Hearst bluntly told Rowell that his comments seemed to show "a desire to criticize and complain rather than a disposition to help and co-operate in a common object."[90] The public representatives were appointed a month later.[91]

When Rowell complained a few months later that the committee wasn't meeting often enough, suggesting sarcastically that the committee was not necessary because "the governments at Ottawa and here had all matters so well in hand," Hearst had had enough. After reminding Rowell that he was not the chairman of the committee, he pointedly reminded him that they were serving on the committee as concerned citizens, not politicians, so its members should regard it as a non-partisan body. This caused Rowell to back down, claiming that this had not been his understanding but admitting that there was much to be said for this view of the committee and he was sure they would get along splendidly now that they understood each other.[92]

Whether or not Hearst and Rowell got along splendidly, the committee didn't actually accomplish a great deal, although by the end of 1917 it had established 525 branches in communities throughout the province that worked in cooperation with the Departments of Agriculture and Education and the Labour Bureau, reporting on Ontario's war record and suggesting what the province should do in the immediate future, especially to stimulate greater farm production.[93] If this didn't seem like much, it reflected the fact that it was not at all clear what a provincial body of this kind could do. There was also the very real problem of getting men – and they were all men – to work collaboratively in a non-partisan way, even in wartime. Hearst was also very concerned that the creation of the committee and its activities not imply criticism of the federal government's war effort. Still, the committee's activities involved many well-intentioned people and its publications may have contributed to Ontario's very significant contribution to the war effort. That was all that Hearst had expected of it. Rowell, however, being a very ambitious and able man but an increasingly frustrated one as a politician in opposition, had hoped for more. He wanted to play a meaningful role in the role and his opportunity soon came.

Rowell was not the only prominent politician who did his best to make Hearst's life difficult. Adam Beck, who has been described as "a scrapper and sometimes a bully" who had "regarded the government and the legislature with disdain"[94] even when Whitney was alive, was positioning himself as an independent political leader committed solely to the Hydro Commission and guarding its independence from political oversight. H.V. Nelles's claim that Beck exercised "near complete control over the Hearst government"[95] is an exaggeration, but Beck did press more forcefully his claim that as chairman of the commission he was not answerable to the cabinet. That was delusional, of course, in view of the fact that it was the government that appointed the chairman and funded the commission and Hearst recognized that Beck's resignation from the cabinet in 1914 had been the opening shot in his direct challenge to his authority.

The government began its effort to bring him under control somewhat indirectly by amending the Hydro-Electric Railway Act. This act had been passed in 1914 to support Beck's scheme, conceived in 1912, to build a network of electric or radial railways in southern Ontario by repealing the requirement that municipalities bear all costs of their construction. When Beck had first proposed the idea, the commission had surplus power that could be used for the trains, but by now there was a growing shortage of power. The very idea of electric railways was highly controversial as well because steam-powered railways had been overbuilt and were struggling financially – the Borden government nationalized most of them in 1917 – and the Hearst government had committed itself in 1916 to developing a provincial highway system. Thus, when Beck created a municipally based lobby group, the Radial Union, to pressure the provincial government to support his scheme, there were many who questioned both the need for such railways and their cost. Among them was James Mavor, the outspoken and somewhat eccentric professor of political economy at the University of Toronto, who derided the idea as "not only untimely, it was ridiculous."[96]

Hearst did not actually oppose the idea of electric railways, but he did have reservations because of their significant cost in the midst of a global war when money for infrastructure was tight, there was already a network of regional railways in the province, and motor vehicles were growing rapidly in popularity and they needed roads linking the province's communities. In 1904 there had been only 535 motor vehicles registered in Ontario, but by 1913 there were 17,300 motor vehicles in the province, a figure that tripled to more than 54,000 by 1916. The first Ford assembly plant, built at Windsor in 1906, was by 1914 the largest industrial establishment in the British Empire, and there were other smaller companies such as the Russell Motor Car Company in Toronto, the McLaughlin Motor Car Company in Oshawa, and the Tudhope-McIntyre Company in Orillia.[97]

But there were no paved highways. Ontario's road system consisted of 50,000 kilometres of gravel roads and 40,000 kilometres of macadamized roads, that is, dirt roads covered by compacted crushed granite. The Ontario Good Roads Association had been advocating since 1894 for better and safer roads, and a Commissioner of Public Highways had been appointed in 1900. Five years later he was transferred to the Department of Public Works as deputy minister. In 1913 Whitney had appointed a three-man Public Roads and Highways Commission chaired by Charles A. Magrath, an Ontario-born businessman and Conservative politician from Lethbridge, to develop a working strategy for provincial roads. Magrath's commission issued its report in March 1914, recommending the creation of a Department of Highways to build and maintain good roads with a budget of $30 million over fifteen years, primarily because of the "economic importance" of good roads to farmers, enabling them to "increase" their output, which would benefit "the entire community."[98]

Perhaps symbolically, that was when the members of the Conservative caucus purchased a Wolseley touring car with a convertible top for Whitney, who regularly rode a bicycle from his home on St. George Street to Queen's Park. When they presented it to him in front of the legislature he was very reluctant to make an appearance, and when he eventually did he refused to get into the car so that the press photographers could take a picture. Whitney was a modest man, notoriously gruff, but also politically astute. He knew that his image would be damaged if a picture circulated throughout the province showing him being driven in an expensive chauffeured car. The result was that he rarely used it and continued riding his bicycle to work, which must have been an entertaining sight. When he died, his widow didn't want the car either, so the government purchased it, making it the first one owned by the province. It was placed under the authority of Finlay MacDiarmid, the Minister of Public Works, and could only be used by ministers with his permission. Hearst, less politically sensitive than Whitney, did use the car. Every morning it picked him up at his home to take him to Queen's Park, then drove him back again at the end of the day. How he had got to and from work before that is unknown, but somehow one cannot envision Hearst riding a bicycle in downtown Toronto. He never used the car for personal or family purposes, however, and his son Irving later recalled that his father refused even to take him to the University of Toronto campus, which was just across the street from Queen's Park, because people would think he was using it for family purposes.[99]

Whitney did not take any action on the Public Roads and Highways Commission, nor did Hearst until January 1916. No doubt with Beck in mind, he created a Department of Public Highways with the very able Finlay MacDiarmid, who was already Minister of Public Works, as its first minister. His mandate was to plan, build and maintain a network of smooth and safe paved highways that would connect communities throughout the province. MacDiarmid quickly developed a plan and began construction of the province's first inter-urban paved highway. Not coincidentally, it ran from Toronto to Hamilton through south-western Ontario, the focus of Beck's radial railway ambitions. When completed in November 1917, the Toronto-Hamilton highway was the first concrete road in Ontario and one of the longest inter-urban concrete roads in the world. Hearst attended the official opening ceremony at Mimico, just south-west of Toronto on Lake Ontario, where George Gooderham, who chaired the commission that built it, smoothed the last slab with a silver trowel before a bronze tablet was inserted into it.[100] Unfortunately, the engineers who built the road had not understood that expansion joints were needed in a concrete road, and it heaved and cracked badly even before it went into service. Hearst was appalled, saying, "I don't know what the people of Ontario are going to say when they see what they got for their money in that road." A solution was found, however, when the ridges were smoothed off, but "the uneven cracks filled with tar were visible for many years until covered with asphalt."[101]

The creation of a Department of Public Highways was just Hearst's first move in the government's attempt to bring Beck under control. The timing may have seemed fortuitous because a scandal had broken out over the federal government's purchase of horses for the CEF, and Beck appeared vulnerable because he was a member of the Remount Commission that advised the Militia Department on the purchases. The other commissioners were Clifford Sifton, J.B. Hall, and J.W. Allison. The government subsequently reversed the centralization of horse purchasing and divided the country into two zones and Beck, now one of Sam Hughes's honorary colonels, was placed in charge of the eastern zone, that included the area from Port Arthur to Nova Scotia. More importantly, his position was changed from an advisory one to active management, and when A.D. McRae, a wealthy Vancouver Conservative businessman appointed to manage the western zone went overseas in 1916 to become Director of Supplies and Transport in the Canadian Army's Service Corps, Beck was placed in charge of the western zone as well.

One might have thought that Beck had more than enough on his plate already, but he clearly was a very energetic man and no doubt wanted to feel that he was doing his bit for the war effort, and he did know a lot about horses. But now he was being asked to manage the purchase of between 8,000 and 10,000 horses as quickly as possible, as well as 436 horses for the British army.[102] Beck dispatched fifteen purchasing committees that consisted of only a purchasing agent and a veterinarian to acquire them and between October 1914 and July 1915 bought 17,320 horses.[103] Because the system was all very informal and ad hoc, it was probably inevitable that the purchase of horses got caught up in the wave of war supply purchasing scandals and there were allegations that in some cases the Remount Commission paid too much for horses or purchased horses that were unfit for military service at any price. The government appointed Sir Charles Davidson, former chief justice of the Quebec Superior Court, to investigate and he identified two situations in Ontario and Nova Scotia in which the allegations proved to be correct. Not surprisingly, both involved Conservative politicians, James R. Fallis, the Ontario Conservative MPP for Peel, and Arthur DeWitt Foster, the Conservative MP for Kings County in Nova Scotia. Fallis was a livestock dealer who had purchased good horses but bought them privately and resold them to the government at a profit, while Foster had purchased many aged and/or unhealthy horses because he was a teacher and unqualified for the job.

Fallis didn't think that he had done anything improper but donated his profit to the 126th Battalion then being recruited in Peel County and resigned his seat in the legislature so that the voters could pass judgment on his behaviour in a by-election, which he lost.[104] Foster, who claimed that he had only accepted the position on the clear understanding that he would receive no remuneration, promptly resigned his seat in parliament. When the Davidson commission issued its report in 1917, it agreed that there had been corruption in the purchasing of horses, describing Fallis's profits as "the questionable fruits of jobbery" but finding Foster only "weak in administration and grievously so in financial supervision and methods."[105] Meanwhile, the Militia Department had learned that British remount officers were complaining that too many of the Canadian horses, most of which were purchased in Ontario and Western Canada, were "weedy, long-backed, poorly ribbed up horses" and "not suitable either for riding or draft."[106] Given the apparent difficulty in finding enough suitable horses and the considerable expense in buying and shipping them overseas, Davidson recommended ending the program and allowing the CEF to obtain its horses from British remount depots, a recommendation that Hughes wisely accepted.

Davidson's report contained no comments directly critical of Beck's management of the remount commission, although as its director he had to assume a certain level of responsibility for its activities, especially in Ontario. In fact, the report didn't even mention Beck although he had been questioned by the commission. H.V. Nelles is undoubtedly right when he describes Beck as "honest and incorruptible personally,"[107] and there was no reason to think that he was responsible for the minor amount of corruption that was revealed, but he would have been embarrassed by the negative publicity because he was a proud man. Hearst knew that, of course, and one cannot help wondering if the government thought the time was propitious to cut him down to size.

James Clancy, the provincial auditor, provided the opportunity when, as Nelles puts it, he finally "threw up his hands at Hydro's accounting practices."[108] Lucas then launched the government's attack by amending the Hydro-Electric Railway Act to halt bond issues and construction until after the war, Ferguson followed up by undercutting Beck's strategy of competing with private power companies until their leases expired, and McGarry attempted to strengthen the legislature's oversight of the Hydro Commission's finances. That was highly desirable but also highly risky because anyone – including the Premier or his ministers – who questioned Beck's budgets and expenses had always been "battered into submission and put on his list of enemies."[109] McGarry countered that by hiring E.R.C. Clarkson, a prominent Toronto chartered accountant, to conduct an independent audit of the commission's finances. This, not surprisingly, revealed that between 1911 and 1915 it had spent $4.2 million more than the legislature had approved.[110]

The dispute dominated the proceedings of the legislature's public accounts committee in the 1916 session when Joseph Atkinson, owner of the usually Liberal *Daily Star*, opposed Beck's radial scheme as "grandiose" and thought Beck was "playing an effective role in pulling down the Cabinet with which he has been in more or less rivalry since the beginning."[111] It seems that Atkinson was right, because the end result was a "compromise" in which the HEPC's financial accountability to the government was strengthened but it was given "corporate-like financial freedom." What that meant in practice was that the commission was required to submit annual reports including financial statements and the government appointed a comptroller to supervise them.[112] Needless to say, even though he accepted these changes, Beck continued to be uncooperative.

At this point James Mavor joined the fray, publishing a series of articles in Toronto's *Financial Post* between 15 July and 23 December denouncing not only the very idea of public ownership of electric power but also Beck for his irresponsible extravagance and the Hearst government for its apparent inability to get a grip on the situation. Such outspoken criticism from a respected economist must have been very annoying but Hearst came perilously close to worsening the situation when he wrote privately to Robert Falconer, the president of the University of Toronto, asking if it was "wise" to employ in a "very important position" a man who was "reckless in his statements and as illogical in his arguments as this gentleman shows by his writings." Because Mavor had earlier publicly criticized the Workmen's Compensation Act, Hearst charged that he appeared "anxious to injure the Government whenever he [can] and to attack everything in the nature of progressive legislation for the benefit and comfort of the people."[113]

In case his meaning was not clear, Hearst went further by suggesting that Mavor was "bringing condemnation upon the University" that might have an adverse impact on the government's support for the institution, concluding with the suggestion that perhaps "the proper authorities" should give the matter some "attention."[114] This was clearly a threat that government funding of the university might be reduced if Falconer did not do something about Mavor. That was shocking and totally out of character for Hearst, who had never attempted to interfere in the affairs of the University of Toronto or any other educational institution before. It will be recalled that when xenophobic patriots had demanded in 1914 that he pressure the university to dismiss three German professors he ignored them. His reasoning then was simple: the Whitney government had given the university a new constitution in 1906 that made it essentially autonomous, so the provincial government would not get involved.[115]

But now, two years later, he had got involved. Falconer deftly sidestepped the issue by passing Hearst's letter on to Mavor, who, not surprisingly, provided a vigorous and lengthy defence of his published comments and then naturally shifted the debate to academic freedom and the university's autonomy. Hearst's letter was out of order, Mavor argued, because "a university is fundamentally a group of scholars who meet for free discussion. If the Members of the University are to be subjected to the dictation of the Government as to what they may or may not discuss, the University may as well at once strike its name from the roll of Universities." Then, unable to resist the temptation but perhaps to Falconer's delight, Mavor went on to compare the government's performance unfavourably with that of the university.[116]

Falconer forwarded Mavor's response to Hearst, discreetly omitting the comment on the government's performance, at which point Hearst appears to have realized that he had disturbed a hornet's nest because Mavor wasn't an obscure academic; he was actually a prominent figure in Toronto whose friends included prominent business leaders like Sir Edmund Walker and Zebulon Lash. They also included Sir William Mackenzie, who owned the Electric Power Development Company that operated the large hydroelectric power plant at Niagara Falls. Hearst therefore drafted a response to Mavor but sent it to Falconer, asking him to comment on it before he sent it.

It's not clear what advice if any Falconer may have offered, but when Hearst did send his response he sent it to Falconer, not Mavor, and backpedalled furiously, denying that he had ever, "directly or indirectly, by hint, insinuation or otherwise," intimated that the university might suffer as a result of Mavor's articles. All he had intended, he claimed, was to "point out the unwisdom ... of a Professor ... of the Provincial University largely aided by public funds, carrying on a newspaper campaign of the kind in which Professor Mavor has been engaged" because that could "create distrust as to the ability and judgment of its Staff" and might cause some people to think "that the University is the friend and ally of the rich and the corporations, as against the labouring man."[117] Whether or not he really believed that cannot be determined, but Hearst did always regret that he had been too poor to attend university. Falconer wisely closed the file, probably much to Hearst's relief, and nothing more was said on the matter, except by Mavor, who had his articles reprinted in book form.[118]

The government also bypassed Beck and the Hydro Commission in 1916 when it purchased the Seymour Power and Electric Company, which operated generating plants stretching from Oshawa to Kingston in Eastern Ontario, serving about 250,000 people. This initiative was driven by Howard Ferguson, who had long objected to the fact that the commission's focus was on south-western Ontario, so that people in the central and eastern parts of the province weren't getting the benefit of low-cost public power. Walter Plewman, Beck's biographer, claimed that Ferguson "rammed the purchase" through the legislature, obviously with Hearst's support but against Beck's threat that he would not include the new system in the commission's network. "That blankety blank of a blankety blank Ferguson bought the system," Beck declared, so "let the blankety blank operate it."[119] Beck's ire stemmed not from the fact that he was against expansion but because he deeply resented outsiders interfering with the Hydro Commission's affairs.

Just a few months later, however, whether because the war situation had become so worrisome or perhaps because Hearst still sought to improve the government's relationship with Beck, he made a significant concession to him when the government created the Bureau of Municipal Affairs. The first step towards creating a Department of Municipal Affairs, the bureau replaced the Ontario Railway and Municipal Board that Whitney had established in 1906 to oversee municipal finances and supervise the then rapidly growing railway system between and within municipalities and explicitly excluded both the Hydro Commission and municipally owned public utilities that "developed or distributed electrical power" from its jurisdiction.[120] This was a major retreat from the ORMB's mandate, which had included them. But there was more. The government also abandoned its proposed amendments to the Power Commission Act to allow the commission to nominate the comptroller and to limit his powers to making recommendations to the Hydro Commission. In fact no comptroller was appointed, and in 1918 further amendments to the act recognized that the commission was the trustee of a municipal cooperative, as Beck had always claimed it was.

As political scientist Neil Freeman rightly observes, Beck "had won the corporate autonomy struggles with the Hearst government."[121] Hearst and his ministers, especially Ferguson, McGarry and Lucas, had caved in. Did this reflect weakness on the part of the government? Perhaps, but its more urgent priority at the time was to maximize the production of war materiel, which meant that more power was needed and "only Beck was capable of delivering power quickly."[122] And he was: the Hydro Commission doubled its production between 1916 and 1917 from 167,000 horsepower to 333,000 horsepower to meet the needs of munitions factories and other war-related industries. Even so, the blackouts that had been taking place since 1916 increased in both frequency and severity and by October 1917 street lighting was prohibited between five and eight in the evening, and every second street light in Toronto was turned off entirely.[123] J.B. Maclean, the publisher of the *Financial Post* and *Maclean's Magazine*, blamed the shortage on the fact that Beck had "thoughtlessly or for some unexplained reason" signed "a gigantic contract" to fuel the new steel plant on Toronto's waterfront "when he had not the power available."[124] He may have been right.

Given the seriousness of the situation, the power issue became a major political issue. Beck had a short-term solution for the problem, of course, which was for the federal government to simply halt the sale of Ontario electricity to the United States until the shortage was eliminated. This suggestion was aimed at the privately owned Toronto Power Company and the American-owned Canadian Niagara Power Company, which were selling power to New York state. Beck portrayed this as unpatriotic, but the reality was that much if not all of that power was being used by factories in the Buffalo area that were producing war supplies for the British government, so Hearst could not cut it off. When the US government expressed its concern, Borden appointed a royal commission chaired by Sir Henry Drayton – a prominent Toronto Conservative lawyer who was also chairman of the Board of Railway Commissioners – to examine the problem. Drayton sided with the Ontario government, very quickly concluding that the American contracts must be honoured. More controversially, he also recommended the appointment of a power controller to coordinate supply and demand.[125] Borden, perhaps mischievously, established a cabinet committee chaired by Frank Cochrane to follow up on Drayton's report. Needless to say, Beck was not amused and after a "stormy" meeting that "broke up in anger"[126] he let it be known that he might run Hydro candidates against Unionists in the forthcoming 1917 federal election. Borden responded to that threat by appointing Drayton the national power controller.

Meanwhile, the provincial government approved the continued expansion of the Hydro Commission's generating capacity. It began by acquiring the American-owned Ontario Power Company in August 1917 at a cost of $22 million, then negotiating the purchase of 50,000 horsepower from the Canadian Niagara Power Company and 11,000 horsepower from the Toronto Power Company.[127] This was only a short-term solution to the power shortage, however. The long-term solution was for the commission to build new generating stations, primarily at Niagara Falls but elsewhere as well. Accordingly, it began to plan the construction of a massive power plant near Queenston and its first hydroelectric plant in northern Ontario at Port Arthur.

If all this was not stressful enough, the war was not going well and Hearst increasingly focused his energies on supporting the war effort, with a focus on promoting enlistments. By the end of the war he had made some 200 patriotic and recruitment speeches in communities throughout the province. In the words of one contemporary observer, "the War was a theme which stirred him to eloquent effectiveness and he did much to educate and maintain the high ideals of popular action to which the Province rose during this period."[128] When he attended the presentation of its colours to the 160th (Bruce) Battalion on 3 June 1916 his speech was described as "a forceful one" in which he described the volunteers as "worthy sons of pioneer fathers," adding "with a glow of pride" that the 160th "had been formed more rapidly than any other rural Battalion in Ontario."[129]

He might have spoken at even more patriotic meetings but his health, always somewhat fragile, prevented him from doing so. McGarry publicly acknowledged in the spring of 1916 that Hearst had been "unable to do much in that way" in recent months because he had "overtaxed his strength before full recovery from an earlier illness."[130] He had been seriously ill during the winter of 1915, and photographs of him show that he had put on a lot of weight by then, perhaps because his heavy workload left no time for exercise. That may explain why he travelled to London in August and remained there until early October. This wasn't just a vacation, however; he wanted to get a better understanding of how Ontario might be able to support the overseas soldiers. His itinerary was arranged and guided by Richard Reid, Ontario's agent general in London and must have been an exciting if not awe-inspiring experience for a country boy from Bruce County making his first visit to the heart of the empire.[131] One minor highlight was a dinner party whose guests included Winston Churchill. Then out of power as a result of the failure of the Gallipoli disaster, he reportedly spent the evening "with a bottle of whisky before him, drinking alone."[132]

Hearst visited the Ontario hospital at Orpington, of course, but also discovered the Maple Leaf Club, an organization that Lady Julia Drummond had established in London to provide accommodation and social facilities for Canadian enlisted men on leave from the war zone.[133] The widow of Sir George Drummond, a prominent Montreal businessman, banker and Conservative senator, Lady Drummond was a remarkable woman. She was the first president of the Montreal branch of the National Council of Women, a founder of the Montreal branch of the Victorian Order of Nurses, president of the city's Charity Organization Society, and a suffragist. She was also the mother of Lieutenant Guy Drummond, who was killed in the notorious Second Battle of Ypres in April 1915.[134] She had moved to London to head the Canadian Red Cross Information Bureau, which provided information to families of missing and wounded soldiers, an experience that made her realize the need for facilities in the city for Canadian servicemen on leave. Her particular concern was the enlisted men because officers were welcomed by London's exclusive men's clubs.

Even though the value of the Maple Leaf Club's services quickly became apparent, the federal government declined to provide any financial support and Lady Drummond relied on contributions. Hearst quickly recognized the club's importance because many if not most enlisted men on leave from the front could not afford respectable accommodations or a place just to relax other than public houses, and about 40 per cent of them were Ontarians. Hearst took a keen interest in the Maple Leaf Club, with the result that Ontario funded the rental and equipment of five additional houses, enabling it to provide additional accommodation for between 350 and 400 men.[135] Another five buildings were opened in March 1918, and by the end of the war the club had eighteen buildings in London that had provided accommodation for 565,830 soldiers and served more than a million meals.[136] Ontario was its largest sponsor, having contributed more than $81,000 for rent, equipment, and furnishings.[137]

Although this trip was useful and no doubt refreshing, Hearst's health did not improve. In fact, his health was a recurring problem throughout his career because he had had a mild heart condition since his youth, and he admitted privately early in 1917 that "the burden of work I am carrying now taxes my strength to the utmost."[138] In fact, Vernon later claimed that his father was bluntly warned that year that his heart would probably give way under the strain if he did not retire.[139] Hearst had taken a short vacation in Barbados in May 1916, accompanied by Forbes Godfrey, the Conservative MPP from York West who was also a physician, and went to Puerto Rico in April 1918. Meanwhile, Bella, who had never participated in public affairs, joined the prominent women who addressed a women's conference in Toronto in 1917 to discuss problems of the war such as conservation of resources, food supplies, and thrift.[140] The stress on both Hearst and Bella must have been greatly enhanced by the fact that both of their sons had joined the 74th Battalion in 1915 and gone overseas in the spring of 1916.[141]

Meanwhile, the bilingual schools controversy was becoming more serious, inflamed by the war and the growing divisions between English and French Canadians. Hearst had fully supported Whitney's policy on this issue and maintained it unchanged.[142] He may have been influenced by Sault Ste. Marie's Catholic Bishop David Scollard, who, like the other anglophone bishops in Ontario, regarded Whitney's policy as "not only just but generous to the French-Canadian people" and hoped that Hearst would "be firm also on this question."[143] He was. When the separate school board of Rockland, a town just east of Ottawa, appealed to him to consider "the unswerving loyalty of the French Canadian to the British Crown" and to reverse his policy because it "divided energies which should be concentrated on the triumph of a cause dear to all classes irrespective of race and creed," it got a cold response. While the government "appreciates the unity of sentiment" towards the war, Hearst reminded the board that the legislature had "unanimously" endorsed Regulation 17, so the government was "merely doing its duty in carrying out the school law."[144]

The attitude of Ontario's bishops reflected their fear that the controversy over bilingual schools threatened the Catholic separate school system and their ambition to expand it. The clause in the British North America (BNA) Act that guaranteed Catholic separate schools in Ontario only applied to elementary-level schools, but the hierarchy was already extending it by means of "continuation" classes at the upper level of the elementary schools and was pressuring the government to give it a larger share of tax revenue to fund secondary schools. This was problematic for the government for two reasons. It feared that a fully developed Catholic school system would threaten the common school system but, more importantly, it knew that allowing an expanded separate school system would produce a fierce Protestant backlash. And part of the problem was that provincial governments had allowed the hierarchy to establish these "continuation" classes without grasping until 1914 that the goal of the bishops was to establish a separate secondary school system. The government had therefore prohibited further extensions beyond the fifth form, a serious setback to the hierarchy.

Unfortunately for the bishops, they were no longer dealing with the flexible Robert Pyne but Howard Ferguson, who was serving as Acting Minister of Education because Pyne was fully absorbed in establishing the Ontario Military Hospital. Actually, Hearst had wisely appointed the moderate Lucas in January 1915, but the additional responsibility had proven to be too much for him, and Hearst turned to Ferguson in April. Hearst knew that Ferguson was a fiercely partisan Anglo-Protestant extremist and prominent spokesman for the Orange Order[145] and would take a hard line on the issue, so we have to conclude that this was what Hearst intended, and Ferguson bluntly told the bishops that the government accepted the terms of the BNA Act but Catholic secondary schools would never be allowed in Ontario.[146]

The controversy had not eased up in recent months. In fact it got worse because feelings on both sides were aggravated by the war. Extremists in Quebec were referring to the Franco-Ontarians as "les blessés d'Ontario," comparing them to war casualties, and Henri Bourassa and his Nationalist followers were regularly comparing Hearst and his colleagues with the Prussians, "tout en faveur des Prussiens."[147] Even such a moderate as Quebec's Cardinal Archbishop Louis-Nazaire Bégin was urging all Québecois Catholics to assist their brethren in Ontario, while Quebec's long-time Liberal Premier, Sir Lomer Gouin, led the Quebec legislature in appealing to Hearst to show justice and generosity to the minority.[148] Shortly afterward, Liberal Senator L.O. David, a former president of the Association Saint-Jean-Baptiste de Montréal and a close friend of Laurier, attempted to cool things off by introducing a resolution calling upon both sides to settle the question "on fair and patriotic lines and ... in such a way as to preserve peace and harmony between the different national and religious sections of this country."[149] The debate continued until parliament prorogued in April 1915 but accomplished nothing more than to show that Quebec Liberals generally lined up against a combination of Conservatives and English-speaking Catholics, regardless of party.

In fact, the division was even worse than that. Québecois Nationalists like Bourassa believed that Regulation 17 was unconstitutional because Canada was officially a bilingual country. Somewhat surprisingly, they were supported in this misconception by J.S. Ewart, the prominent Toronto lawyer widely recognized as a constitutional authority, who declared that French had equal status with English in Ontario.[150] Bourassa and Ewart were both wrong. What was guaranteed by the BNA Act was separate Catholic primary schools. The language problem arose from the fact that these schools were shared by anglophone (usually Irish) and francophone Catholics. This worked in terms of religion but not language. The two groups had already fought a nasty battle over the University of Ottawa, then a Catholic institution, and now, led by their hierarchy, they were fighting over the schools. Thus, the Quebec hierarchy led by Montreal's Bishop Bruchési were insisting on their "rights" while the Ontario hierarchy led by London's Bishop Michael Fallon totally shared the view of Anglo-Protestants that Ontario was and must remain an English-speaking province. Fallon has been described as "an ardent imperialist" who "believed that the British institutions of crown, parliament, and common law were the best guarantees of corporate and individual freedom in a world beset by aggressive nationalism."[151] As he put it in one of his many outspoken tirades, "the whole purpose of this agitation is to gradually establish a system of French schools in Ontario, with the ultimate object of making this a French Province, and part of a French Republic on the banks of the St Lawrence."[152] The leaders of the Orange Order could not have agreed more.

Hearst had no intention of allowing the government's policy to be influenced by either the Quebec legislature or the Senate[153] but he was trying to navigate between the extremists on both sides. While Quebec was demanding that bilingual schools be allowed in Ontario, anglophone extremists – not all of them Conservatives – were becoming more extreme in their utterances. Many Ontario newspapers began referring to Bourassa as Von Bourassa, and the *Ottawa Journal* actually called him a traitor. J.W. Edwards, a Conservative member of parliament and prominent Orangeman from Eastern Ontario, went further, suggesting that Bourassa should be hanged as a public enemy.[154] Shortly after that Landry tried appealing to Hearst to compromise in the interest of national unity during wartime, asking, "[S]hould not the entente cordiale which today united the English and French on the battlefields of Europe be able to bring together in our own country the descendants of those two great nations?"[155] He got no answer.

During the 1915 session of the legislature, the government passed a bill empowering it to establish a commission to assume the duties of the Ottawa separate school board pending a final settlement of the controversy if that board continued to refuse to comply with the Department of Education's regulations. Hearst assured the legislature that the government would not invoke the powers granted in the bill unless that proved to be absolutely necessary. Significantly, the Liberals did not oppose the bill, Rowell stating that while the government was responsible for the legislation, "if you are seeking to find a solution of the problem I will put nothing in your way."[156]

At this point Montreal Archbishop Paul Bruchési attempted to mediate the dispute. He met with John Waugh, Ontario's Chief Inspector of Public and Separate schools, and James McGregor Young, a prominent Toronto lawyer representing the provincial government. According to Young, Hearst was "well disposed" and Ferguson was taking a more liberal view of the matter now that he was a member of the cabinet.[157] Young was not delusional. Ferguson was presenting a more moderate face, at least publicly, since joining the cabinet. Indeed, claiming that the government's position was not "an unreasonable one or an ungenerous one," Ferguson pointed out that the government was taking steps "to give the Franco-Ontarians teachers of their own race" and "to encourage the training of teachers of the French tongue." While the government would never concede that the French language had equal rights in Ontario, it did recognize that the situation of the bilingual schools was "exceptional" and that the purpose of Regulation 17, rather than seeking to "restrict the use of the French language in the Province, was really a privilege" being extended to Franco-Ontarians.[158] In other words, the government was not trying to assimilate francophones in Ontario; it was trying to improve the efficiency of the schools to ensure that francophone children received an education that would prepare them for life in an English-speaking province.[159]

The Franco-Ontarians of Ottawa weren't buying that, however, provoking Bruchési to warn them that if they didn't agree to a compromise they would be accused "de vouloir continuer la lutte pour la lutte." He followed that up by telling the priests of the francophone parishes "que s'ils s'obstinent à refuser les propositions du gouvernement, ils perdront toutes les sympathies qu'ils ont dans Québec."[160] In other words, if a compromise solution was not reached the Ontario government could reasonably claim that it had tried. This episode may have been the basis of rumours that Genest and Murphy had worked out a compromise settlement, a claim that was denied by all concerned, including Hearst.[161]

When the Ontario Supreme Court ruled in July that Regulation 17 was constitutional, the government promptly transferred control over Ottawa's separate schools to the commission.[162] Its members were Dennis Murphy, chairman; Thomas D'Arcy McGee; and Arthur Charbonneau, two anglophones and one Franco-Ontarian. Samuel Genest, the school board's chairman, reluctantly handed the board's books over to the commission but stated that the board would not recognize the authority of the commission and immediately took steps to appeal the court's ruling to the Judicial Committee of the Privy Council, the ultimate court of appeal in the empire.[163]

The schools opened peacefully in September 1915, however, with Genest insisting that the board was operating the schools and the teachers insisting that they still recognized its authority. Murphy responded blandly that the commission "are quite satisfied with the situation, now that the schools are open and the children accommodated ... If the members of the old board care to assume that they are in possession, they are at liberty to do so."[164] When French-speaking teachers in Ottawa refused to accept their salaries from the commission because that would mean they were acknowledging its authority, a committee began collecting twenty-five cents per week from Franco-Ontarian parents in Ottawa.[165]

Not surprisingly, the rhetoric continued to heat up. Senator Landry urged Franco-Ontarian parents everywhere to continue the struggle, comparing their position with that of the Christians in the time of Nero![166] In October, the students of all the Ottawa bilingual separate schools walked out of their classes in protest against the government's policy and a few months later, 122 teachers followed suit, with the result that the schools closed and did not reopen during the 1915–6 school year.[167] The Rev. Elie Latulipe, the newly appointed Bishop of Haileybury, declared that he was "plus convainçu que jamais que notre résistance est un devoir sacré."[168]

In early March 1916, Laurier told Rowell that he had been approached by a friend whom he believed to be acting as an unofficial emissary of Hearst and Borden. He was probably referring to Liberal Senator Napoléon Belcourt, a likely candidate for such a delicate task because, while he had grown up in Quebec, he had been born in Toronto and lived in Ottawa. He had served for seven years in the House of Commons before being appointed to the Senate, during which time he had taken it upon himself to represent Franco-Ontarian interests. He was trusted by Franco-Ontarians because he had chaired the 1910 meeting of the ACFEO, served as its attorney, and founded Ottawa's *Le Temps* newspaper. At the same time, he understood the Ontario political environment better than Québecois leaders like Bourassa and Lavergne or even Laurier.[169] According to Laurier, "this person" – presumably Belcourt – claimed that Hearst wanted to work out a compromise with the Ottawa separate school board based on the Landry proposal. If the separate school board would cooperate in reopening the schools, the government would pay the teachers and Regulation 17 would be held in abeyance until its legality was finally determined by the Judicial Committee of the Privy Council, the imperial supreme judicial authority.[170]

Belcourt did in fact approach Hearst proposing a compromise, but nothing came of it, perhaps because Hearst feared that Rowell's Liberals would attack him for giving in to the French, although more likely because "Howard Ferguson and the extreme Orange element feel that there is Party advantage for them in insisting upon greater restrictions in the teaching of French" and Hearst saw no need to compromise.[171] Mahlon Cowan, a Windsor lawyer and former Liberal MP, told Laurier that public opinion overwhelmingly supported the government's policy and would "oppose and slaughter any man or any party who talks of granting greater privileges to the French."[172] I.B. Lucas confirmed that when he declared in June that "all the compromise had been made that is going to be made,"[173] Zotigue Mageau, the Liberal MPP for Sturgeon Falls, responded on behalf of Franco-Ontarians when he told a St. Jean Baptiste gathering on 24 June that "there is neither rouge nor blue. It is French-Canadian and Catholic before all. It shall ever be so till they give us our language."[174] Robert Rumilly did not exaggerate, therefore, when he claimed that "le fossé entre les deux races n'avait jamais paru si profond."[175]

At this point, Landry tried his hand at finding a compromise. Negotiating through Conservative Senator Thomas Chase Casgrain, Postmaster General in the Borden government, he proposed that the provincial government abolish both the Ottawa separate school board and its own commission and administer the bilingual schools directly through the Department of Education without changing existing personnel, pending final settlement of the dispute in the courts.[176] It may also have been Landry who prompted Sir John Hendrie, the Conservative lieutenant governor, to contact A.H.U. Colquhoun, the Deputy Minister of Education, and Borden, wondering if a compromise could not be found.[177] On 8 March, C.J. Doherty, Borden's (Catholic) Minister of Justice, brought Senator Casgrain and Sir Charles Fitzpatrick – who had been Louis Riel's chief counsel in 1885, then Laurier's Minister of Justice before being appointed Chief Justice of the Supreme Court – to try to impress on Borden how serious the situation was. They were "very much alarmed over [the] situation" and appealed to Borden to discuss the situation with Hearst because they feared that his government was on track to "bring about absolute hostility between English and French."[178]

Borden did raise the question with Hearst that same day, but his position had hardened: he would not compromise as long as Quebec was comparing Ontario to Prussia and accusing him of bigotry.[179] Doherty was so distraught by this time that when he met privately with Borden on 11 March, he "nearly wept in reciting [the] injustice to Catholics and [spoke of] retiring from [the] Govt."[180] Borden's diary notes suggest, rather disturbingly, that he thought the issue was religious rather than linguistic. Hearst sent Ferguson to Ottawa on 13 March to explain the political reality to Borden: the government's bilingual schools policy had the full support of not only Ontario's Conservatives but its anglophone Liberals as well.[181]

Borden really didn't want to get involved in a controversial issue that clearly came under provincial jurisdiction anyway, but when Laurier gave notice that he intended to raise the issue in the House of Commons, Borden feared that all his Québecois members might desert the government, possibly bringing it down. With Doherty predicting "a national crisis," Borden told Reid to "send for Ferguson."[182] When they met the next day, Ferguson repeated that public opinion in Ontario was "intense," that the provincial Liberals fully supported the government's policy, and that the government "would not live an hour if it made [the] slightest concession."[183] On 11 April, Borden met with Casgrain, then with Charbonneau of the Separate Schools Commission, who explained that the "French people have been deliberately misled as to Regulation 17."[184] By now the demand was for the federal government to disallow it, which Borden refused – and actually couldn't – do.

That triggered a crisis in the government. Casgrain, P.E. Blondin, and E.L. Patenaude, the three Québecois representatives in the cabinet, informed Borden that they would not participate in cabinet until the federal government took action of some kind.[185] Two days later they proposed that the "king in council" be asked to inquire into and advise on the status of the French language in Canada. This was a non-starter because the phrase "king in council," as they surely knew, was the constitutional term for the federal cabinet, unless they were actually suggesting that all privy councillors be included or meant the British cabinet. In vain, they tried to convince Borden that "the destiny of the Conservative Party" was threatened by the controversy and that the failure of the government to intervene made their positions in the government "absolutely untenable in their Province."[186] Borden somehow persuaded the ministers not to resign and the cabinet crisis passed as quickly as it had arisen. The fact that the Quebec ministers backed off no doubt sent a clear message to Franco-Ontarians and Bourassa's Nationalists alike.

On 8 May, Laurier gave Borden a copy of the Lapointe resolution, which requested the Ontario legislature not to interfere with "the privilege of the children of French parentage of being taught in their mother tongue." When Borden "told him it could do no good and might do much harm," Laurier "said he was alarmed at conditions in Quebec and that he must have "some sheet anchor with which to fight nationalists."[187] The debate took place on 10 and 11 May, with Borden dismissing the resolution as a mere political manoeuvre aimed at defeating the government.[188] The motion was defeated handily, but eight francophone Conservatives voted with the Liberals and twelve anglophone Liberals voted with the Conservatives.[189] More significantly, all of Ontario's Liberal MPs, with the notable exception of Newton Rowell, supported the motion out of loyalty to Laurier, albeit only after he threatened to resign as leader. "The result ... was greeted with loud cheers from our side," Borden wrote, and "the Grits [were] correspondingly depressed."[190]

Laurier wasn't just depressed; he was also angry and deeply disappointed. As he told Stewart Lyon, editor of the *Globe*, it had been agreed forty years ago "that every child in Ontario should receive an English education but that parents of French origin should also have the right … to have their children taught in their own language. Who can object to this?" For his part, he refused to yield to "the extremists of Toryism" just as he opposed "the extremists of Nationalism." He was even harsher with Rowell, telling him that the "Orange doctrine" he had supported was "absolutely tyrannical" and their relationship was now "final and beyond redemption."[191] Hearst was undoubtedly pleased with the outcome and also the Roblin government's provocative decision to rescind the clause in Manitoba's provincial school act giving parents of ten or more children in a school the right to bilingual instruction. Meanwhile, Landry resigned from the speakership of the Senate and severed his ties with the Conservative Party and Montreal's city council donated $1,000 to the Separate Schools Commission.[192] This was not the end of the matter, of course. With the two sides deadlocked like the armies on the Western Front, all they could do was wait for the ruling by the Judicial Committee of the Privy Council. That removed the issue from Canadian politics, at least temporarily, although the highly divisive school issue continued to do enormous harm to English–French relations at a time of national crisis.

# 5 Progressive Conservative: 1916–19

*I would ten thousand times rather go down to political oblivion and disappear forever from view as a public man than to fail in what I believe to be my duty at the present time.*[1]

HEARST'S honeymoon with the people of Ontario began to crack in 1916 when he addressed the two major controversial issues that defined his term in office. The first was temperance and the second was female suffrage, and they were closely related. Hearst showed real leadership on both issues even if he was somewhat hesitant on female suffrage. A committed Methodist, Hearst appears to have been influenced by its Social Gospel movement, which called on Christians "to realize the kingdom of God in the very fabric of society." The impact of the war strengthened this movement, to the point that the Methodist Church called in 1918 for "complete social reconstruction by a transfer of the basis of society from competition to cooperation."[2] Major steps in this direction included temperance reform and granting women the franchise.

The temperance movement had already made significant progress in recent years. By 1915, 333 of the province's 847 municipalities were under local option, 305 were under the Ontario License Act, and forty-six were under the Canada Temperance Act, leaving only 163 unlicensed.[3] The outbreak of the war greatly strengthened the temperance movement, enabling it to add patriotism to the traditional social reform impetus. Thus, grain was needed for food and should not be wasted in the production of liquor, and surely it was not asking too much of the men at home to surrender their alcohol during the war when other men were risking their lives overseas. Toronto's *Daily Star* led the temperance forces, pointing out that the king had pledged in April 1915 not to consume alcohol during the war. But Canadian soldiers serving overseas were excepted because of the appalling conditions in which they fought. Like the British troops in the trenches, they received two ounces of 186 proof Jamaican rum to each man twice daily.[4]

The temperance movement had been greatly encouraged when Hearst became Premier because he was known to be a Methodist teetotaller who was more sympathetic to the issue than Whitney had been. His Liberal opponent, Rowell, was also a Methodist and a fervid crusader for prohibition. Referring to his "insistent righteousness," the journalist Augustus Bridle once described Rowell as having "the bearing of a man who long ago felt that he was called to do something for a cause or a country and has never got over it."[5] At this point in his career, his cause was not just a stronger temperance policy but full prohibition. Rowell challenged Hearst shortly after he became Premier to support a bipartisan measure that would close shops, clubs, and bars for the duration of the war, but Hearst feared that was going too far too quickly. Instead, he announced that shops would be required to close at 8:00 p.m. rather than 11:00 and added Labour Day to Christmas Day and Good Friday as holidays on which they could not open at all.[6]

This left the bars untouched, reflecting Hearst's belief that the shops were a larger problem than bars. Even so, he assured a mass delegation from the Ontario branch of the Dominion Alliance in March 1916 that "your desires can be no stronger than my own, or than the desires of the Government," and promised that "everything which we can do [we] purpose [*sic*] to do." Inherently cautious, Hearst said, "[W]e have tried to give great thought to the liquor question," meaning that he was monitoring public opinion, "and I assure you that before long liquor legislation will be brought down in the House."[7]

Three weeks later Hanna introduced legislation to establish the Board of License Commissioners to administer the province's licence laws, including suspending licences for infractions and regulating hours of operation in accordance with local sentiment. This was a significant step forward because it meant that local licensing commissions and locally appointed inspectors were being replaced by a provincial commission and provincial inspectors, ensuring uniformity of policy. The government's hope was that this would reduce the influence of local pressure on the administration and enforcement of the liquor license laws. It also distanced the problem from the Provincial Secretary's department and, ideally, would take it out of active politics. Hanna was not exaggerating when he claimed that this legislation was "probably more radical and more far-reaching ... than any ever introduced in the history of the province."[8]

If that wasn't immediately obvious, it quickly became so when the members of the commission were appointed in April. All were temperance advocates, at least three were Conservatives, two were from or involved in northern Ontario, one was an Orangeman, and another was a Catholic. The chairman, J.D. Flavelle, was a Methodist businessman in Lindsay, Ontario, and the brother of J.W. Flavelle, the prominent Toronto businessman. William S. Dingman, the vice chairman of the commission, was the son of a Methodist clergyman, publisher of the Stratford *Herald*, and a former mayor of Stratford. John Ayearst was a Methodist minister from Thamesville and an active member of the temperance movement. At some point he had reportedly been a member of a delegation that met with Hanna to complain about the lax enforcement of the liquor regulations. Hanna had responded by challenging him to take on the job of liquor inspector to see if he could do better. Ayearst had accepted the challenge and, according to the *Globe*, "illicit liquor traffickers had reason to quake when John A. Ayearst got on their trail."[9] The temperance views of Frederick Dane and George T. Smith are less obvious, and one wonders if they were political appointments. Dane had emigrated from Belfast and was a tea merchant in Toronto. More importantly, he was also a fire-breathing Orangeman who had served two terms as Grand Master of the Orange Order of Ontario.[10] For some reason, presumably his Conservative Party connections, he had also been appointed to the Temiskaming and Northern Ontario Railway Commission. George T. Smith of Mattawa was the first mining recorder at Haileybury in Temiskaming.[11]

The commission proved very quickly that it meant to take a strict temperance attitude on the administration of the laws and it was not long before the *Daily Star* was praising its work and its chairman in particular.[12] That didn't satisfy Rowell, who continued to denounce the government, claiming that it was under the influence of the liquor interests.[13] The truth was that Hearst thought Rowell's "Abolish the Bar" policy was deeply flawed because it would close the bars but leave "the liquor shops to ply their trade in both large and small quantities without interference of any kind."[14] He must have taken great satisfaction from knowing that the Rev. Dr. Samuel Chown, superintendent of the Methodist Church, agreed with Hearst, declaring, "[W]e will have nothing to do with license ... We are out to annihilate the trade, and nothing else will do."[15]

In fact, the government was sharply divided on what to do. According to the *Globe*, the cabinet was divided between those like "the masterful" McGarry, who thought it was unnecessary to restrict the operating hours of bars, and those like "the worldly wise" Ferguson, who "fears the effect of early closing when the Government goes to the country." Hearst was in the middle and "should he take the wrong road the eloquence of McGarry and the political cunning of Ferguson will not avail."[16] The temperance forces grasped the situation and wisely shifted ground to attract more Conservative support by making prohibition a non-partisan issue. The non-sectarian and non-partisan Citizens' Committee of One Hundred was founded in May 1915 for the sole purpose of securing prohibition. Its president was the highly respected and remarkably energetic G.A. Warburton, general secretary of the Toronto YMCA, who had organized the first Patriotic Fund in Toronto and ten other cities. Among the Citizens' Committee's prominent members were J.W. Flavelle, Sir Clifford Sifton, and, of course, Newton Rowell. The *Daily Star* claimed that one of Hearst's brothers was a member.[17] The committee immediately began setting up branches all over the province and collecting names on a mass petition.

Hearst welcomed this development, seeing the creation of the committee as a public repudiation of Rowell's "Abolish the Bar" policy. "Success can only come," Hearst believed, "in the manner contended by the Conservative Party, namely – by the voice and with the desire of the people of the Province expressed with reference to the subject itself, unbiased and uninfluenced by political motives or aspirations." Equally important was that the committee recognized that "if anything can be accomplished by a Province-wide measure the bottle trade must be included in the prohibition."[18] Meanwhile, Hearst continued Whitney's policy, claiming that when the time seemed right he would "go ahead irrespective of what course the Committee of One Hundred, the liquor trade, or any other interests may say."[19] In fact, according to Warburton, Hearst "helped us by encouraging his followers to act on county committees" and by "using his influence with the Conservative press." He also "faced the party in caucus and lined the party up."[20]

When Rev. Ben Spence, secretary of the Ontario Branch of the Dominion Alliance for the Total Suppression of the Liquor Traffic and representatives of "practically every social reform society and association interested in temperance reform" met with Hearst on 24 September 1915, asking for legislation to suppress the retail sale of liquor for the duration of the war, he told them that the liquor question had been before cabinet constantly for the previous six months and that the Liquor License Commission was expected to make recommendations shortly. Although he promised nothing definite, Spence and the other temperance leaders seem to have been impressed.[21]

Only a couple of weeks later, it was rumoured that Hearst and Flavelle had agreed that bars should also be closed at 7:00 p.m. instead of 11:00 p.m.[22] This provoked immediate opposition from labour spokesmen, who pointed out that this would hit hardest at working men for whom bars were important evening social clubs. They also pointed out that such a move would almost certainly force many breweries out of business and create serious unemployment among their workers, bartenders, and waiters.[23] James Cosgrave, president of the Cosgrave Brewing Company, told the government that his plant was already operating on a four-day week and this change would force a further cutback to a two-day week.[24]

The cabinet remained sharply divided. When it met two days later in a daylong session to discuss the issue, "a right royal battle" took place between those favouring early closing of the bars – Hearst, Lucas, and MacDiarmid – and those opposed, Hanna, Ferguson and McGarry.[25] Beck, although not a member of cabinet but an influential Conservative, told Mackenzie King that Hearst "had put through the Prohibition measure off his own bat with[out] consulting his colleagues. That he had opposed him bitterly."[26] Not surprisingly, the result was a compromise, requiring bars to close at 8:00 p.m. for the duration of the war. As with most compromises, no one was satisfied. Businessmen engaged in the production and sale of alcohol claimed that this would cost them $9.1 million per year, while prohibitionist leaders and the *Daily Star* inevitably denounced the government for giving in to the "liquor interests."[27] Speaking to the annual meeting of the Ontario General Reform Association in November, Rowell claimed that the public wanted "not regulation, but abolition," claiming that the money spent each year on liquor in Canada was enough to equip and maintain 100,000 soldiers.[28]

It is debatable if most people supported abolition, but it certainly seemed by 1916 that they did indeed want further restrictive legislation. Two-thirds of the province's municipalities had enacted local prohibition, and four-fifths had voted majorities in favour of it if not the required three-fifths majority needed to carry it.[29] The Citizens' Committee of One Hundred claimed in January 1916 to have seventy-seven county or city organizations, 700 municipal organizations, and 35,000 volunteers, all working to collect signatures on a giant petition,[30] and Warburton had no doubt that Hearst would respond favourably when it was presented. This statement was interpreted as having considerable weight, for it was known that he had been in touch with Hearst when the committee was being organized and that the Premier had assured him that the government would take action if the committee could produce evidence that public sentiment favoured prohibition.[31] By now, most Conservative newspapers were at least not critical of it, a fact that Warburton attributed to Hearst as well.[32]

It was no real surprise, therefore, when the throne speech at the opening of the 1916 session of the legislature on 28 February included the announcement that legislation would be introduced "for the prohibition of the sale of intoxicating liquor within the Province and for the submission of the same to the electors." Warburton was undoubtedly correct in concluding that Hearst and his followers were finally yielding to public opinion.[33] They were in good company. Prince Edward Island and Saskatchewan had already enacted similar legislation, a referendum had recently carried favourably in Alberta, and British Columbia, Manitoba, New Brunswick and Nova Scotia would all enact strict temperance legislation before the end of the year. Clearly, prohibitionist sentiment was sweeping the country.

The decisive factor, without question, was the fact that the Citizens' Committee of One Hundred would be delivering its petition to the government a week later. Hearst knew that and he probably had a good idea of how many signatures were on it. On 8 March, 15,000 people marched to Queen's Park to deliver the petition, which had been signed by 825,572 people, approximately one third of the province's total population. Perhaps more significantly, 348,166 of them were eligible voters, equivalent to 71.5 per cent of the total number of ballots cast in the 1914 general election.[34] Hearst needed no further convincing. He had always personally favoured strict temperance legislation but had maintained Whitney's cautiously progressive policy of responding to public demand but not getting ahead of it. Whitney had established the three-fifths rule for local option contests, and the petition had comfortably exceeded that threshold for the province. "The evils flowing from the liquor traffic are very great," he told Willison, "and it surely seems to me that it is our duty to make a strong effort to limit these evils as much as possible. I would rather try and fail than not try at all."[35]

Speaking in the throne speech debate, Hearst explained that the government had not held back because it did not support strict temperance legislation. In fact, the liquor question had occupied the government's attention more than any other issue in the past six months, and he bitterly attacked prohibitionist leaders who accused anyone who had not agreed with their methods of being in league with the liquor interests. The government's concern was to ensure that a significant majority of the population supported such an important social change, and he believed that the work of the license commission had done much to build that support. The government, therefore, was now ready to act, but even so, the voters would be given the opportunity to confirm, modify, or rescind the legislation in a provincial referendum. He gave no date for the referendum but talked as though it would take place in the near future.[36] He did not explain what he meant by "near future," but he may have been thinking, as Arthur Belcher suggested, that the referendum should take place "in a year or so, after the War ... (when the soldiers who are away will have a chance to vote) whether they wanted this condition to continue or be changed."[37] What could be more democratic? At the conclusion of his speech, the members of the legislature – on both sides – rose and sang "God Save the King," so Hearst had achieved the bipartisan support which he had sought for such a major piece of legislation.

Not everyone supported prohibition, of course. The Personal Liberty League had been established to fight the Citizens' Committee of One Hundred and carried on an extensive advertising campaign opposed to prohibition, rejecting it both in principle and as a solution for intemperance.[38] Such strict legislation was, the league argued, an undemocratic infringement of individual rights that was even more unacceptable in view of the fact that about 100,000 Ontario voters were serving overseas in the war. It also argued, correctly, that the Ontario Temperance Act (OTA) was in effect class legislation because it discriminated against workers. Because the province had no jurisdiction over interprovincial trade, wealthier people could order alcohol from Quebec and have it shipped to their home while workers would no longer be able to drink at public houses. At the same time, workers in the industry would lose $5.7 million in wages. Just as unacceptable was that the government was shutting down a legal industry with no offer of compensation. That was wrong in principle, but it also constituted an annual loss to brewers and distillers of $8 million, not to mention the provincial government's loss of $1.3 million in tax revenue.[39] The economic and social impact would be enormous. Meanwhile, breweries were desperately advertising the medicinal value of beer and the fact that it was made in Canada.

And, despite the unanimity in the legislature, there were men in both political parties who opposed the OTA. The greater threat was to the Conservative Party because Social Gospel reformers were more likely to be Liberals. Many Conservatives had gone along with local option but were not ready to accept such a drastic province-wide policy as Hearst was now proposing. It was little short of prohibition and, as Hearst acknowledged, went as far as the provincial government could legally go. The Conservative caucus had debated the issue several times, and as the *Globe* said, "there is good reason for believing that the cabinet was not unanimous" and "the temperance legislation … comes from the Prime Minister."[40] Rowell correctly claimed that Ferguson, Lucas, and McGarry opposed the bill in cabinet and the *Daily Star* included MacDiarmid as well, although years later Hearst claimed that Ferguson had played a major role in drafting the OTA. [41] It seems likely that Hanna had grave reservations about it as well, although as Provincial Secretary he introduced the bill.

There was much dissent in the party caucus, so much that the opening of the legislature had to be delayed for two hours on 22 March. Mark Irish and George Gooderham, two prominent backbenchers, led the

Conservative opposition to the bill. Neither of them openly opposed strict temperance legislation, but both thought the government should compensate businessmen who had invested in a legal industry. Gooderham had a personal interest, of course, because his family owned the Gooderham and Worts distillery, one of the largest in the country. Harold Machin, the outspoken Conservative MPP from Kenora, agreed with that but was also concerned about the impact on the many people who worked in the industry.[42] Machin did not participate in the caucus debate, however, because he had been appointed lieutenant colonel of the 94th Battalion and had to join his unit on 22 March, but he had a heated private meeting with Hearst on the previous evening. Hearst seems not to have been deterred or influenced by these arguments and never explained why he didn't offer compensation to the business interests. The reason probably was that Rowell almost certainly would have argued that this was further proof that the Conservatives were still tools of the liquor industry.[43] But perhaps Hearst, like Rowell, just didn't see any legitimate reason to compensate men who had engaged in an industry that had inflicted so much social harm over the years.

"Never before," Hearst told his followers in caucus on 22 March, "was Temperance sentiment as strong and as solidified throughout the Province as it is today," and he and Whitney had always promised to go as far as public opinion demanded. Confronted with the mammoth petition, the government could not "stand still or attempt to stem this tide even if it wanted to." Its responsibility was to respond to the clear wishes of the voters even if doing so would result in the defections of some Conservative voters, but "to retain the question in politics will drive a wedge into the Conservative party that very soon will split it in two."[44] The OTA was a temporary wartime piece of legislation that he hoped would remove the temperance issue from party politics until the post-war referendum took place, giving voters the opportunity to decide if it should be maintained, amended, or rescinded. That hope proved to be a naïve assessment of how events would unfold.

After the stormy caucus session, Hanna introduced Bill 100, which Hearst later said was based on the prohibition act passed in 1900 by Hugh John Macdonald's government in Manitoba.[45] It was a sweeping piece of legislation that banned drinking in bars, clubs, hotels, offices, businesses, and boarding-houses but allowed private consumption at home. All retail stores were closed and no new licences would be issued after 1 May, although alcohol could still be sold for medicinal, mechanical, scientific and sacramental purposes. Rather oddly, perhaps because it was so unpalatable, local wineries were allowed to continue selling their product. The OTA would be regulated by the Liquor License

Commission, which would be reorganized for the purpose.[46] Finally, the government promised to hold a referendum to ratify, modify or rescind the act after the soldiers returned home and would only require a simple majority.[47]

Hearst made his appeal to members of the legislature on the second reading of the bill on the evening of 4 April. He rose amid loud applause and in a speech described by the *Mail and Empire* as "splendid … powerful and sustained"[48] and by J. Castell Hopkins as "eloquent, earnest and forcible – possibly the best he had ever delivered in the House,"[49] laid his political life on the line. As Hearst fully realized, there was no significant opposition from Rowell's Liberals, so he focused entirely on trying to convince his own members, many of whom formed the real opposition on this issue. Inevitably, he tried to win them over by claiming that the legislation was fully in line with Whitney's approach to the issue:

> The policy has been clear and distinct that we would legislate to minimize the evil effect of the liquor traffic as fast as circumstances and public opinion would warrant. Those who sat year after year in this House with the late Prime Minister know how often he affirmed and re-affirmed that position … And knowing Sir James Whitney's views intimately on this subject as I do, I have no manner of doubt that if he were living to-day he would be taking such action as we are taking.

That was questionable, but his main appeal was patriotic. The war had changed everything and, in view of what was at stake,

> surely those of us who are too old or too infirm or not courageous enough to enlist … should at least give up the pleasure of our beer and our whiskey, give up even what we may consider our personal liberties and personal rights, so that we can save every dollar and conserve every ounce of energy for a cause in which our sons, our brothers and the best men of our land are freely shedding their blood.

In other words, even if the legislation "would bring no benefit to the province from a moral standpoint, if the results that follow its implementation would add nothing to the health and happiness of our people – as a war measure, for the purpose of aiding economy, thrift and efficiency, it is justified – it is made possible – yea, it is demanded – by public opinion."

To those who claimed that his government had no mandate to pass such far-reaching legislation, an argument he had himself made on previous occasions, he challenged any man to declare his belief that a referendum held now would not overwhelmingly endorse the bill. Even so, he recognized that he was placing his political career in jeopardy:

> Some have said that by this measure I have sealed the political doom of my Government and signed my death warrant as a public man. My answer to such is that I would ten thousand times rather go down to political oblivion and disappear forever from view as a public man than to fail in what I believe to be my duty at the present time [Applause].

Turning directly to his own followers, he declared that "the man who chooses the path of political expediency as against the path of duty" is "not worthy of the support of the splendid body of men that sit to the right of the Speaker in this House, or of the great body of citizens that belong to the grand old Conservative Party, and above all is not worthy to stand in the shoes of the great Whitney who was ever bold enough to be honest and honest enough to be bold. [Loud Applause]." Finally,

> it matters little to me whether my career as Prime Minister of this Province is long or short, but it does matter that I discharge my duty to the best of my ability while I retain that high position ... I have, personally, however, faith without a doubt that not only the public of today, but the public of tomorrow, and the public of years to come, will say that the Government did what was right under conditions as they existed at the time. I fear not the verdict of this day or of future generations; I am content to await, and will await with confidence, the verdict of the people when the right time comes for them to render their verdict – and I am satisfied that the Conservative, who in years to come reads the record of his party we are writing today, will have no cause to blush as he reads that record. [Applause]
>
> And whatever comes, approval or condemnation, I will always have the witness of a clear conscience that in the hour of my country's greatest peril I hesitated not to do what to me seemed right and waited nor to count the cost.[50]

It was a powerful, honest declaration of a kind not commonly heard in legislatures, at least not from those in office, and it was received with applause and cheers, after which all of the members rose and sang "God Save the King." This included the many Conservatives who disagreed with Hearst but weren't prepared to say so, at least not publicly. As Rowell observed, "the only reason the Government's forces remained intact in support of the Bill was because there was nowhere for them to turn. They could not come to us."[51] This was true, but the time was not far off when widespread dissent on this and other issues would emerge as large numbers of people began to lose faith in both political parties.

The OTA passed unanimously. All bars, clubs and liquor stores would be closed on Sunday, 17 September 1916. The OTA did allow bars and hotels to serve light (2.5 per cent) beer – previously the alcohol content of beer was 9 per cent – but only if they also provided meals, clear and cold drinking water, and modern bath and toilet facilities for both sexes. The rationale, of course, was that light beer was not intoxicating. Breweries and distilleries could still manufacture alcohol for sale outside the province because the provincial government had no jurisdiction over that.[52] This meant that those who could afford it could order regular beer and liquor from Quebec or elsewhere, an option not available to the majority of people who could not afford it.

Six months later, in October 1916, Hearst "was glad to say" that the OTA was "succeeding beyond my fondest dream, from every standpoint." As he told Irving, "arrests for drunkenness and crimes arising out of drunkenness for the last month in Toronto under prohibition were about 1/7 what they were for [the] corresponding month last year" and "this is typical of conditions all over [the] Province." Businesses were "delighted" with the greater efficiency of their workers and "grocers, butchers & merchants generally find improved conditions of trade." At the same time, the breweries were producing low-alcohol beer and non-alcoholic beverages "& will not be as heavy losers as they expected," while the distillers were now "engaged ... in producing acetone and other products for war purposes."[53] Irving later recalled that his father was hopeful "that the liquor question had been settled for a long time in a manner that would leave Ontario a province of enviable sobriety."[54] Sobriety was not in itself the goal, of course. The assumption of the Women's Christian Temperance Union (WCTU), a major force in the temperance movement, was that prohibition was "the chief panacea for a multitude of social ills."[55] That remained to be seen.

The number of breweries in Ontario declined from forty-nine in 1915 to twenty-three in 1917, and the number of men jailed for drunkenness declined from 5,968 in 1916 to 3,907 in 1917 and 2,595 in 1918.[56] At the same time, however, the number of prescriptions being written by pharmacists for "medicinal" alcohol rose significantly, as did the number of illegal stills, although their operators naturally kept a low profile.[57] But then the situation changed dramatically when the federal government issued an order in council in December 1917 banning the importation of alcoholic beverages and another in March 1918 banning their interprovincial transport and if necessary even their manufacture.[58] This meant that strict temperance had become prohibition.

Charlesworth later claimed that Hearst thought the federal government had gone too far but, "having nailed his colours to the mast, was obliged to accept."[59] In fact, he welcomed the federal action, hoping that it might "perhaps to some extent relieve the hostility of anti-temperance people to my Government." At the same time, however, he worried that "people may more readily forget the pioneer work I did, without which the Dominion Government would I know not have taken the stand it has."[60] The truth probably was that those who supported strict temperance were pleased that the Borden government was backing up the provincial government, while anti-temperance people saw yet another example of Hearst's too close relationship with the Union government.

Until the spring of 1919, when he recognized the strength of anger among workers and veterans towards 2.5 per cent beer, Hearst never considered modifying the OTA, convinced that he had done the right thing at the right time and that it was not unfair to the minority who opposed it.[61] He did regret the fact that the act cost him the friendship – and political support – of many people but always insisted, "I now have the only satisfaction that is worth while to a public man, the knowledge that I have helped my fellow man."[62] Remarkably, even Newton Rowell conceded that the act was "a great measure of social reform,"[63] for which he not unreasonably claimed some credit. Sir Wilfrid Laurier claimed in 1916 that "prohibition for the last forty years has been ... a football which the Tories managed more cleverly than the Grits."[64]

He was wrong. Despite the obviously popular support for strong temperance legislation and the unanimous bipartisan approval of the OTA by the legislature, there were many who thought it went too far. Even though the entire Conservative caucus – except Machin, who was not there – had voted for the OTA, many had done so with fingers firmly crossed, too timid to challenge what appeared to be the will of both party leaders and most Ontarians. The politicians were very quickly about to learn a hard lesson in interpreting public opinion and the cost to those who got it wrong.

When the 1916 session of the legislature ended, Hearst called by-elections to fill vacancies in three constituencies that had been held by Conservatives. James Torrance had retired in North Perth, and Samuel Armstrong (Muskoka) and J.J. Foy (Toronto Southwest A) had died. The Conservatives had won six of the seven by-elections that had taken place since Hearst became Premier in 1914, the one exception being Peel, which was a special situation that did not reflect dissatisfaction with the government. The Muskoka by-election, which took place in June 1916, continued this trend, with the Conservative candidate being elected by acclamation.[65]

The by-elections in North Perth and Toronto Southwest were another story because they took place in July and August after the passage of the OTA. Both parties, apparently already aware that there was significant hostility to the act, cynically ran candidates who favoured modifications in it while denouncing their opponents for doing so. In North Perth the Liberals accused James Makins, the Conservative candidate, of being "shaky" on temperance, while the Conservatives countered that the Liberal candidate, Wellington Hay, had the support of "the hotel people."[66] Hearst sent almost his entire cabinet into North Perth to campaign on Makins's behalf and Lucas and Ferguson openly hinted that the OTA might be modified in the near future.[67] Somewhat surprisingly, G.A. Warburton, a prominent social reformer and leading member of the Committee of One Hundred, spoke on Makins's behalf.[68] Similarly, in Toronto Southwest A, the Conservatives ran J.A. Norris, a local businessman who favoured beer and wine sales, while the Liberals ran Hartley Dewart, a popular lawyer who openly condemned the OTA on the ground that it was class legislation that discriminated against working men. The Methodist *Christian Guardian* newspaper, that had been so supportive of Rowell, described Dewart as the "chief representative of the liquor interests,"[69] as did the *Daily Star*, although its moral indignation may have been somewhat weakened in this case by the fact that Dewart had recently successfully sued it for libel.[70] Ferguson tried to divert people's attention from the OTA by arguing that the "greatest of the issues before us" was not prohibition but bilingual schools, which he clumsily tried to blame on Dewart and the Liberals.[71] Dewart took a similar diversionary approach, accusing the Hearst government of allowing Ontario nickel ore to be sold to Germany to be used in the manufacture of munitions that were killing Canadian soldiers.

The Conservatives lost both North Perth and Toronto Southwest. Dewart's victory in Toronto Southwest was especially shocking because the Conservatives had held all the Toronto seats since the 1870s. But Toronto Southwest was a working-class district, and Dewart had established a reputation for supporting workers. Joseph Atkinson accused the Conservatives of "almost inconceivable weakness and duplicity" in both constituencies, which had earned both "the contempt of the liquor people … and … the distrust of the temperance people."[72] That was true, but it was also true of the Liberals who were now becoming divided between the Rowell and Dewart factions. As O.D. Skelton, a prominent scholar at Queen's University and a strong Liberal, righty observed, Dewart would enhance the Liberals' "hitting force" but "not their reputation for godliness."[73] Within a year Rowell would leave provincial politics to join Borden's Union government and Dewart would replace him as provincial leader, aligning the party with Laurier in opposition to conscription, the Union government and Hearst's alliance with it. Hearst couldn't have been happier because he had little respect for Dewart and did not regard him as a serious threat.

Historian Peter Oliver has argued that the by-election results signified that Hearst "had failed dismally in his first major test as party leader" because "he had split his party unnecessarily and shaken the confidence of many in his political judgment."[74] Whitney, he argues, would have found a less divisive temperance policy. It is, however, impossible to know what Whitney would have done in 1916 because, while he had never concealed his contempt for moral crusaders, he had responded during his nine years in office to the growing strength of the temperance movement by steadily reducing the number of liquor licences in the province and strengthening the legitimacy of local option by requiring a three-fifths majority vote. That had seemed to satisfy most people before the war, although Whitney had lost seats in the 1914 election when temperance was a major issue. And it is difficult to believe that he would have ignored a petition signed by 71.5 per cent of all those who had voted in that election, especially in the middle of a global war when stricter temperance legislation seemed to many a reasonable temporary patriotic sacrifice. He might, however, have brought in somewhat less stringent legislation, such as what the Conservatives were hinting at in the by-elections.

The losses in North Perth and Toronto Southwest alarmed many Conservatives. A week after the North Perth by-election Hearst publicly acknowledged the existence of widespread dissatisfaction within the government, and according to the *Globe*, Lucas, Ferguson and McGarry were threatening to depose Hearst.[75] Whether or not that was true, it was conceivable because, as Atkinson said, a break-up of the cabinet was "almost wished for by the supporters of prohibition who see no security for their movement so long as it is in the hands of men like Lucas."[76]

Borden was particularly rattled by Dewart's victory, describing it as "a severe blow to [the] Hearst Gov't" and when he and Willison discussed the situation on 31 August they actually discussed who might replace Hearst as leader. Willison thought Ferguson and Beck were the "only available" candidates.[77] Meanwhile, W.F. Nickle, the influential Conservative MP for Kingston, wisely explained that the situation was more complicated than hostility to the OTA. Ontario was "in a bad way" because "Hearst [was] ill, Hanna [was] taking no interest, [and] Pyne [was] pottering around England in connection with [the Ontario] hospital."[78]

His reference to Hanna was perceptive because Hanna had lost whatever confidence he ever had in Hearst's leadership. Still the team player, however, he waited until December to submit his resignation and even then agreed to stay on as a minister without portfolio. The reason he gave for stepping down was the pressure of his business interests, but the truth was that he had been shocked and humiliated when he was not chosen to succeed Whitney as Premier and by late 1916 he had had enough. This was not only a significant blow to the government because of Hanna's stature, it was a turning point. Hector Charlesworth, the well-informed journalist, later wrote that from that point Hearst was "politically doomed," adding brutally that "ten years from now, when his name is mentioned most people will think that the illusion is to William Randolph Hearst, the yellow journalist."[79]

The wave of support for strict temperance legislation was followed by another wave, this time demanding the enfranchisement of women. The two issues were not unrelated, of course, because women's organizations like the WCTU understood that the enfranchisement of women was critical to temperance and other social reforms. There had been agitation on the franchise question since at least 1881 when the first delegation seeking it had waited upon the provincial government.[80] Nothing had been accomplished, however, except that unmarried women and widows were granted the municipal franchise. Whitney had supported that but thought it irrelevant to the issue of the provincial franchise, which he refused to consider. Even when the Canadian Suffrage Association, supported by thirteen other women's organizations and reform groups, presented him in 1909 with a petition signed by 100,000 women, Whitney impatiently "brushed [it] aside" "with a dismissive 'Not Now.'"[81] Clearly, however, the movement was assuming serious proportions and a private member's bill introduced in 1911 was the first to be seriously debated. Whitney was still not persuaded and his Conservative majority voted down the bill. He never changed his mind, declaring in 1913 that the issue was "dull, torpid and dead."[82]

He was wrong and they had one prominent advocate in Newton Rowell, the leader of the Liberal Party since 1908, although he did not attempt to impose his views on the party.[83] As with so many other issues, the outbreak of the war dramatically changed the political environment. The extraordinary contribution that individual women and women's organizations were making in the war effort proved to all but the most stubborn that women were as capable as men in creating local, regional, and national organizations and managing them. And as the manpower shortage developed, women took the place of men in offices, factories, and mills, proving that they could handle physically demanding tasks as well. Employers, often initially reluctant to hire them, were soon delighted because they paid women less than the men they replaced. This, of course, soon sparked another campaign led by women, demanding equal pay for equal work. That made getting the franchise – and the right to hold public office – even more relevant and important.

Hearst struggled with the issue. Whereas Whitney had simply dismissed the idea as nonsense, Hearst insisted that he didn't oppose enfranchising women in principle. Nor did he dispute the idea that men and women were equal, but as a conservative male, he believed that the roles of men and women in society were different. He had expressed that view publicly in his first speech after becoming Premier in October 1914 when he told a Conservative women's club that "if every woman had a dozen votes she could never equal the influences which a Christian woman exercises in the community."[84] That presumably meant that the role that women played in managing the home, supporting a husband, raising children, and contributing to society through churches, women's institutes, and other organizations should not be considered inferior to the role played by men, just different and complementary. Besides, "up to the present there has been no great interest exhibited on this subject throughout the Province, either by men or women."[85]

These comments reflected his cautious attitude to change. Like Whitney, he was moderately progressive but didn't think it was the role of government to lead on social issues. Rather, government should seek to represent public opinion, which meant that government should not address an issue unless there was a pressing need or widespread consensus on it. In the case of enfranchising women, that consensus was emerging. Thirty-three municipal plebiscites held between 1914 and 1916 supported extending the municipal suffrage to married women.[86] Even so, when he met with representatives of the Canadian Suffrage Association on 15 February 1915 he reiterated his belief that the roles of men and women in society were inherently different. "Having regard to all the circumstances, *the constitution of women*, the especial duties, responsibilities and incidents of wifehood, motherhood and guardianship of the home," was it, he asked, "in the best interests of the state as a whole that women should have added to their burdens and responsibilities the burdens and responsibilities of the franchise?" "To what greater extent, if any," he wondered, would women "be able to exercise an influence for good upon the community and upon the legislation of the Country, if endowed with the franchise than they do now?"[87] Indeed, he said that "the Government was not yet satisfied that the majority of women desired any extension of the franchise."[88] And when Rev. J.C. Tolmie, the Liberal MPP for Windsor, introduced a bill to give the municipal franchise to married women, Lucas spoke for the government in opposing it, even though widows and unmarried women already had that right. Claiming that "the great mass of women" were "indifferent to the exercise of the franchise," he cited the example of California, where only 27 per cent of women eligible to vote did so compared to 93 per cent of eligible men. The government used its majority to vote down the bill.[89]

A year later, when Hearst met with a labour delegation that raised the question, he was reported to have been "was sympathetic but definite in the statement that the present was not the time to introduce such a measure."[90] Accordingly, when that same day William McDonald (Liberal, Bruce North) introduced a private member's bill, as he had done in previous years, the government voted it down, "the chief Conservative objection being that it was inopportune."[91] What made it inopportune was the fact that the government intended to pass the OTA in that session.

By this time women's suffrage had become a major public issue, however, partly because of the role women's organizations were playing in the temperance movement. Hearst now argued that "it would be a great mistake to introduce any measure that would have the slightest tendency" to divide "women of the liberal and conservative persuasion [who] are working side by side in splendid patriotic work." He even cited Emmeline Pankhurst, the prominent British suffragist who was then touring Canada encouraging women to set aside the franchise issue and dedicate their energies to the war effort.[92] The response to that was a monster petition – stimulated no doubt by 1916's temperance petition – that circulated throughout the province demanding the provincial franchise for women. Both party caucuses discussed the issue before the opening of the 1917 legislative session. The Liberals endorsed female enfranchisement,[93] and the Conservative caucus was rumoured to have decided either to support it or to hold a referendum on the subject, with the *Mail and Empire* claiming that "most of the members were in favour of having the legislation adopted without further delay."[94]

What had changed since 1916? Margaret Prang, Rowell's biographer, claiming that "there was much puzzlement over the government's sudden conversion," speculates that the federal Conservatives may have pressured Hearst to take action because they "were already considering ways of allowing women to vote in the next federal election on the assumption that most of them would support conscription if it were presented to them."[95] That seems unlikely, however, because the Borden government had not yet decided on conscription in February 1917. And when it did adopt conscription in April, subsequently formed the Union government, and called an election, it was very careful to enfranchise only carefully selected women, that is, military nurses and close female relatives of men already serving in the armed forces. Prang also wonders if the Ontario Conservatives "simply acquiesced in the trend of the times" because Manitoba, British Columbia, Saskatchewan, and Alberta enfranchised women in 1916 or 1917.[96] Carol Bacchi similarly suggests that Hearst, "like most politicians at the time, realized that the reform could no longer be resisted and that he might as well take the opportunity to feather the Conservative Party's political nest with thankful female voters."[97] The reality was that he was a progressive, albeit a conservative one, who believed that government should keep pace with public opinion, and he had come to recognize that the time had come, even if he personally still had reservations. But it would be naïve not to acknowledge that he assumed that most women would support the government that had passed the OTA.

Another critical factor in changing Hearst's mind on women's suffrage was the impact of the war, which he recognized was changing social values and attitudes on this and other issues. He was well aware that women were making a significant contribution to the war effort and had "earned a greater place in the councils of the Country than they have occupied in the past." This did not mean that they were now entitled "to something in the nature of a reward for the work they have done, but [that] they have shown by their capacity for organization, by their energy, and by their work ... their qualifications to assist and their ability to advise in the work of the nation." In other words, they had proven that they were just as intelligent, knowledgeable, and energetic as men, so they were entitled to participate in the political process as well.

At the same time, he believed that "a large body of women in this Province, particularly mothers ... feel they have ample scope under present conditions to exercise their influence" and "feel that the franchise is a responsibility and burden that they are not called upon to undertake and that they have not the opportunities to freely perform, in view of their responsibilities as wives, mothers, and guardians of the home."[98] That statement appears obviously condescending today, but Hearst seems to have thought that it was only a militant minority of women who were demanded the franchise. And, bizarre as it may seem, there were women who didn't want the franchise and had established an Association Opposed to Woman Suffrage in Canada that had been sponsoring public meetings and issuing pamphlets for several years.[99] He wondered too if it was wise to distract public attention from the essential task of winning the war and arousing disunity and controversy at such a time and if more than doubling the electorate was too large a step to take all at once.[100] He even questioned the wisdom of making such a radical change in the electoral system without a mandate from the people, an odd suggestion given that the only "people" who could vote in a referendum would be men.

Having said all this, however, Hearst insisted that he was not opposed to female suffrage, pointing out that he had never at any time expressed any objection to the idea in principle. The simple truth was that he was honestly struggling with his very traditional view of the appropriate role of women in society while also recognizing not just that women had made an extraordinary contribution to the war effort but had also proven their ability to organize and manage a wide range of organizations such as the Imperial Order Daughters of the Empire (IODE), the Canadian Red Cross, and the Canadian Patriotic Fund.[101] Not only had more than 3,000 women served as military nurses with the rank of lieutenant, their matron in chief was a woman, Margaret Macdonald, who was given the military rank of major. The contributions of these organizations and their leaders is a story that is just beginning to be told, but their enormous contribution to the war effort rightly made a profound impression at the time.

The second factor was that Manitoba, Saskatchewan, British Columbia, and Alberta had enfranchised women, but only Saskatchewan and Alberta had done so before their provincial elections in 1917 and both governments were re-elected, so there didn't appear to be any strong difference between the voting patterns of men and women. In other words, giving women the franchise would neither accomplish all that suffragist leaders hoped for nor destabilize the political system as some men feared. And finally, perhaps, there may have been a political calculation. Having allowed the Liberals to get much of the credit for the OTA, Hearst may have seized the opportunity on female franchise when the Liberal Party was showing signs of serious division on the temperance issue. What he told his son Irving, however, in March 1917 was, "I think it is right. The main thing in politics as in every other walk of life is to do what we think is right and then we can only trust the good Lord that it will work out all right."[102] Perhaps he also took some comfort from knowing that his political hero, Sir John A. Macdonald, "was of opinion that women ought to have votes," at least according to his son, Hugh John Macdonald.[103]

When the 1917 session opened on 20 February, however, there was no mention of the question in the throne speech, so Rowell introduced an amendment calling for the municipal and provincial enfranchisement of women. Hearst responded by criticizing him for trying to make political capital on this issue, given that William McDonald had again given notice of his intention to introduce a private member's bill, as did J.W. Johnson, the Conservative MPP for Hastings West, who had been advocating the enfranchisement of women for years.[104] Hearst took that opportunity to announce that the government would state its policy when their bills came before the legislature "and my honourable friend will find that this Government is always abreast of public opinion on every great question, and that we do the right thing and do it at the right time."[105]

When the McDonald and Johnson bills came up for second reading a week later, the women's suffrage leaders were in the galleries, which were packed for the debate. Significantly, Bella Hearst and "several other Conservative spouses" were among them.[106] The suffragists had distributed yellow daffodils – their symbol – with a card to all members asking them to support the bills and most members, including most of the cabinet, were wearing them in their lapel. Hearst was not wearing his, however, and as he rose to speak he made some suffragists nervous when he moved the flower to one side of his desk. What did this mean?

In his speech, Hearst acknowledged that he still thought many women did not want the franchise and were even opposed to it. At the same time, there was no question that there had been a marked increase in sentiment favouring it since the outbreak of the war. In fact, support for it had "advanced more ... in the last twelve months than ... in a quarter-century before" and that was because of "the splendid part the women of this country and the women throughout the whole British Empire have played in this war." And, "having taken our women into partnership with us in our tremendous task I ask, can we justly deny them a share in the government of the country, the right to have a say about the making of the laws they have been so heroically trying to defend? My answer is, I think not." The government therefore "endorses the principle of the bill now before the House and assumes full responsibility for it, and I call upon my supporters to vote in its favour."[107] As he sat down amid loud applause from both sides of the legislature, Hearst pinned the yellow daffodil to his lapel. Rowell supported the bills, and both were approved unanimously.

It was a curious performance but typical of Hearst. Having decided that it was time to extend the franchise to women, he did so but with some reluctance. One cannot help wondering why, having made that decision, he did not project himself as a progressive political leader at the forefront of an obviously popular cause. It was almost as though he was trying to evade total responsibility if there was a backlash, thinking of those by-elections that followed passage of the OTA. Ambivalent timidity on a major political issue did not inspire confidence in a time of social turbulence, but there were no more by-elections until the summer of 1918.

Meanwhile, women were still not eligible to hold either municipal or provincial elective offices. Not surprisingly, Rowell introduced a bill later in the session to address this anomaly, pointing out that it was only logical if women could vote that they should be able to serve as well. Hearst claimed that he did not oppose the idea in principle and the government would consider the matter. But there had been no demand for this right, he thought, so the legislature should wait until public opinion had formed on the question and women had adjusted to exercising the franchise.[108] It was a typically cautious response and less than inspiring in the circumstances, but the government did in fact pass legislation in the 1919 session giving women full political equality with men. They could now seek election to the legislature, municipal offices, and school boards. All three bills passed unanimously.

What impact would granting women full political equality have on Ontario politics? Some thought it would strengthen public support for social reform, while others thought that women would approach political issues in much the same way as men, particularly their husbands if they were married. Only time would tell, but Hearst believed that many women would support the Conservative Party in the next provincial election because it had brought in the OTA and was moving forward with other progressive legislation. And yet, one cannot help thinking, as Joseph Schull put it, that he "had fudged too much" and his cautious, seemingly even reluctant, approach to the franchise issue may not have benefited him politically as much as it might have done if he had shown more enthusiasm.[109]

Not only did 1916 and the first few months of 1917 mark the high point of Hearst's term in office, but they also marked the turning point. Two major pieces of progressive social legislation had been passed with the support of the Liberal opposition, and the long-simmering bilingual schools controversy had been more or less resolved, also with the support of most Liberals. At the same time he was also leading Ontario's significant contribution in men, resources, and money to the war effort. The 1916 edition of the *Canadian Annual Review* concluded that he had "continued … to prove himself an energetic public man who succeeded in doing important things and impressing the people with his earnestness and honesty of principle." That was true, but he had not, as the *Canadian Annual Review* thought, "improved his position as a new leader,"[110] at least not within his party. But he had the satisfaction of knowing that his work was appreciated by the federal government and was recognized by his king, George V, who conferred on him a knighthood in February 1917.

# 6 Conscription

*No person with a human heart could desire to continue the grim tragedy of destruction, sadness, sorrow and tears now being waged but we owe it to the cause that the task to which we have set our hands should bour hands should be completed.*[1]

ENLISTMENTS continued to be strong in 1915 but the pattern established in August and September 1914 – that only one-third of Ontario's volunteers were Canadian-born – continued. The *Globe* also noted in January 1915 that the enlistment rate was lower in rural areas than in urban areas, concluding that "it would almost seem that outside of the larger centres of population the war is regarded as something remote and uninteresting, only as a drama, the action of which may be followed in the daily press."[2]

Military authorities were aware of the situation and staged an impressive parade in Toronto on 19 January 1915 in which 4,000 recruits marched from the training camp at Exhibition Park to Queen's Park. It was the largest parade in Toronto's history, so long in fact that when those at the front reached the legislature those at the rear were still at Bloor Street. The government cooperated by closing schools for the day so that children, and hopefully young men, could enjoy the spectacle and be inspired. According to historian Charlotte Gray, "crowds lined the route, cheering fathers, brothers, sons and friends who would soon leave homes and family far behind in Canada, in order to fight against a brutal enemy."[3]

When the First Division went into action in a month later in the second Battle of Ypres and sustained more than 5,000 casualties, patriotism met reality. As Leslie Frost – then a young man – later recalled, this was when "the war came with its full impact to Orillia" and "a great change came over the ... community. The war was no longer an adventure. It had become something which affected everyone, a personal responsibility, particularly for the men of military age."[4] The First Division was joined in September 1915 by the Second Division, forming the Canadian Corps. Because the Corps grew to four divisions and participated in all the major battles over the next three years, the need for enlistments was constant, not only to fill the many new battalions and other units being authorized but also to supply reinforcements for those in the field.[5] On the whole, enlistments remained strong through 1915, although they continued to remain lower in rural areas.[6] To some extent this reflected the fact that the federal and provincial governments were urging farmers to produce as much food as possible because the German navy was blockading Britain, and industry was booming with war contracts.

The result was that recruiting became more aggressive. Another enormous parade took place in Toronto in November 1915 to stimulate enlistments and "practically the whole city" turned out to watch it, with citizens "crowding six or seven deep over the entire route." Businesses and schools closed for the event and buildings and homes along the parade route were decorated with flags. This time more than 10,000 troops in full battle gear, plus field kitchens, ambulances and gun carriages, accompanied by sixteen military bands marched from Exhibition Park to Queen's Park and back. Buses "filled with young volunteers waving to the cheering crowd" were decorated with signs calling for more volunteers. Sam Hughes was on the reviewing stand in front of the legislature, as were Hearst, Toronto Mayor Tommy Church, and other dignitaries.[7]

This event was repeated on an even larger scale in March 1916 after Borden astonished the country – and his own cabinet – by announcing in January that Canada would double its commitment to the war effort from 250,000 to 500,000 men. Hearst fully supported this announcement and participated in this event, well aware as he was that there was an enlistment problem even in Anglo-Protestant Ontario.[8] The result was that the emphasis in recruiting efforts began to shift from trying to persuade men to enlist not just to support Britain but to also protect their own wives and children. An alarmist American film, *Battle Cry of Peace*, that "showed scenes of German brutality in Belgium and France, emphasizing the brutality to civilians, including the rape of women and killing of children," played at Toronto's Massey Hall for two weeks in March and again in May.[9] The 204th Battalion then being recruited, not only urged men to see it to learn "what might happen to Canada if men do not rise to the defence of their homes"[10] and even sponsored a free showing. Not surprisingly, the Borden government published and distributed recruiting posters with the same message.[11] The 204th, whose commanding officer was W.H. Price, the Conservative MPP for Parkdale, proved to be the most successful recruiting unit in Toronto in 1916.

The "greatest military parade in the history of Canada," consisting of 18,000 soldiers accompanied by thirty-one bands led by Hughes on horseback marched from Exhibition Park to Queen's Park on 1 March. This time, pointedly, new recruits still in civilian clothes marched along with the troops. Upon arrival, Hughes dismounted to take his place on the reviewing stand alongside Hearst and other dignitaries. Again, virtually the entire business community shut down for the event, and tens of thousands of men, women, and children lined the route and showered the soldiers with cigarettes, chewing gum, and candy whenever the parade paused.[12] That was followed by an Easter Sunday religious service held at Queen's Park on 23 April that was attended by the Governor General and 18,000 troops from "every unit in the city" and more than 100,000 people who filled "every space in Queen's Park … from Avenue Road to University Avenue." The *World* observed that "the Easter sun, shining brilliantly on deep ranks of men trained and clad to kill, struck one at first as incongruous," but "it was fitting" because Easter "celebrates the triumph of sacrifice, even unto death. The tranquillity of the day was prophetic of the peace that shall follow war when the menace of Europe shall have ceased." Major Cecil Williams, then the senior chaplain of Military District 2, gave the sermon, telling the troops that "theirs was a holy call, a call of empire, a sacred crusade" because Britain was fighting "on the side of Christianity and humanity." When the service concluded, "the National Anthem received such a rendering as is seldom given to a man to hear twice in a lifetime."[13]

These events certainly stimulated enlistments in Toronto, at least briefly, but enlistments in rural areas continued to lag behind those in urban centres.[14] The explanation seemed clear. While the Department of Militia and Defence was doing its best to raise more men, both the federal and provincial governments were urging farmers to produce more food. There was a shortage of farm workers by the spring of 1916, which the provincial Department of Agriculture sought to overcome by publishing advertisements in urban newspapers calling on boys between fifteen and nineteen years of age who would be paid between $12 and $30 per month plus room and board to work on farms during the summer as "Soldiers of the Soil."[15] That attracted some boys but not enough, and of course, teenaged urban boys were of limited usefulness. Many of them found the work and living conditions too difficult, and at least some also found the farmers unreliable when it came to paying them.

And yet, as Hearst acknowledged when speaking at a recruiting rally in Toronto in October 1916, "for some reason difficult to explain, interest in the war … does not seem to be as intense as it was six months or a year ago." There did "not … seem to be the same spirit of sacrifice and service among our people that existed at an earlier stage of the war."[16] Perhaps that was why he singled out the 204th Battalion, popularly known as the Toronto Beavers, in January 1917 for special recognition for having carried out the most successful recruiting campaign in Toronto in 1916.[17] Two months later, on 16 March 1917, the 204th marched from Exhibition Park to Queen's Park where Lieutenant Colonel Price and a contingent of forty men were met by Hearst and escorted into the legislative building to deposit its colours, while the rest of the battalion, along with relatives and friends, waited outside. One wonders how the commanding officers and men of the other Toronto battalions, indeed the other Ontario battalions, felt about the 204th being singled out for this honour.

Whether or not the event stimulated recruiting in Toronto, its effect didn't last long, and the explanation was not all that difficult to grasp: three weeks later the Canadian Corps lost 10,000 men at Vimy Ridge and that was after incurring more than 24,000 casualties on the Somme in 1916. These numbers went far beyond what Canadians had been expecting in August 1914, and not everyone agreed that the war was an existential crusade justifying whatever sacrifice seemed to be necessary. As the *World* observed, a major victory like that at Vimy Ridge "would have been hailed in 1914 with such demonstrations, probably, as would have rivalled Mafeking night," referring to the patriotic celebrations throughout the country following a major victory in the South African War. "Yet in Toronto, where thousands of her sons have gone to battle, and where the news of the capture of Vimy Ridge is the greatest event in local history, there has not been a flag raised to signalize the occasion."[18]

In fact, instead of patriotic celebrations, there was a riot in Toronto on 15 April by more than 100 soldiers angered at reports that a disabled soldier had been insulted by an Austrian waiter in Child's Restaurant on Yonge Street. They began by attacking the restaurant and only stopped when the manager stood on a table waving the Union Jack and pleading with them to stop. Two employees, neither of whom was Austrian or even an enemy alien, were identified and escorted to a nearby police station for no apparent reason. Meanwhile, the large crowd that had gathered accompanied the soldiers as they proceeded to other restaurants, seizing men thought to be enemy aliens. Major General W.A. Logie, the commanding officer of Military District 2, had to dispatch troops from Exhibition Park to restore order. In the aftermath, he blamed the police for not handling the problem properly, to which police inspector Samuel

Dickman responded that there had been no need for the police to take any action against civilians.[19]

Mayor Church, being a politician, blamed the restaurant owners for employing enemy aliens during the war because it was provocative. That might have been a fair comment except that none of the waiters at Child's Restaurant were enemy aliens. Nevertheless, a few days later city council unanimously approved a motion calling on the federal government to deport "all natives of alien enemy countries now domiciled in Canada who are known to be or might in future be found to be guilty of using seditious language, or of sympathy with the German cause … at the close of the war … and that legislation be enacted to debar subjects of alien enemy countries entering Canada in future."[20]

The changing mood might also explain the service "to offer thanksgiving for the victory" at Vimy Ridge held at St. Paul's Anglican Church on 16 April. It was led by Rev. Henry Cody but organized by the Great War Veterans' Association with Logie's support and was attended by Lieutenant Governor Hendrie, Hearst, Rowell, and Mayor Tommy Church and the members of the city council. More than 900 veterans led by Lieutenant Colonel J.A. Currie, the former commanding officer of Toronto's 15th Battalion (48th Highlanders), were also in attendance, along with representatives of the local militia regiments.[21] Rather oddly, the only seating available to the public was in the aisles, but that seemed to suffice.

Meanwhile, Hearst had resumed his demanding speaking tour, warning people that if declining enlistments reflected a belief that the war was won, they were seriously mistaken.[22] As one observer noted, the war "was a theme which stirred him to eloquent effectiveness" and his speeches "rang with assured conviction."[23] Speaking to the Women's Canadian Club of Brockville in December 1916, he had asked if people understood the urgency of the situation. "No person with a human heart," he acknowledged, "could desire to continue the grim tragedy of destruction, sadness, sorrow and tears now being waged but we owe it to the cause that the task to which we have set our hands should be completed."[24]

There could be no doubt about the strength of his convictions and his sincerity but his speeches weren't always very logical. Speaking in the legislature in 1917 on a bipartisan war resolution, for example, he declared first that Germany's goal was "the domination of the world," then warned that "it is her life or ours," apparently meaning that it was an existential struggle. Shifting ground again, he claimed that "the essence of the conflict … is the difference between right and wrong. There is no room for compromise, either right is going to prevail or wrong is going to prevail."

Germany was guilty of unprovoked aggression and "crimes and practices unbelievable before the outbreak of this war. She has violated and set at naught every rule and principle supposed to govern civilized nations in warfare." Even worse, Germany was "unrepentant, unregenerate and blasphemous." Finally, Britain and its allies were "fighting that our children and our children's children shall not in the days that are to come endure the agony through which we are now passing. This generation is suffering that future generations may be free."[25]

With enlistments continuing to decline in 1917, Borden decided that conscription was necessary. Recognizing that his government, elected in 1911, did not have a mandate to make such a drastic decision, he formed a Union government committed to winning the war, as British politicians had done in 1915. His goal, no doubt, was to unite the country behind the war effort, and most prominent Liberals in English Canada agreed to participate despite their belief that the Borden government had been incompetent and corrupt. As the journalist H.F. Gadsby optimistically observed, "all loyal Canadians will agree that it is a sweet and becoming thing that old discontents and quarrels should be buried so long as the Hun is thundering at the gate."[26] But neither the politicians nor Canadians generally were united. Many people throughout the country thought that Canada had already done more than its share in the war effort, while others were prepared to accept conscription but couldn't bring themselves to support the Borden government even when several prominent Liberals joined it. As late as August 1917 Sir George Foster was writing in his diary that "the war spirit appears weak."[27]

Hearst fully supported conscription and Union government. He agreed that compelling young men to go to war against their will was repellant in principle but if, as he believed, the government had no choice but to do whatever needed to be done to achieve victory it was surely right that partisan politics should be set aside. The fact that the Union government would not be representative of Quebec did not concern him because he believed that it was the root cause of the manpower shortage. Ignoring the fact that enlistments were declining in Ontario and elsewhere, that was because it did not share Canada's Anglo-Protestant values.

And so began the most tumultuous period in Canadian history when the country divided not just on conscription but more fundamentally on what it meant to be Canadian. Men like Hearst believed that Canada was an Anglo-Protestant English-speaking country that shared British values while Germany and its allies represented autocracy, repression, and barbarism. Clearly, there could be no compromise between good and evil, right and wrong, civilization and barbarism. This explains why the Protestant churches in Ontario, having embraced the war as virtually a

Christian crusade, passed motions at their annual conferences endorsing conscription as a sacred duty and social responsibility. It was not coincidental that Lieutenant Colonel Cecil Williams, who had been appointed the recruiting officer for Military District 2 (Toronto), was a British-born Methodist clergyman.[28] In fact, Hearst told a gathering of Methodist ministers at Carlton Street Methodist Church in Toronto that it was "the solemn duty" of "preachers and leaders in public thought" to "stir the very best that is in our citizens, old and young; surely we must by our exertions in the pulpit, in the legislature and in every walk of life, do our best to maintain a country, a civilization and a citizenship worthy of the noble men that are fighting and dying for us at the front."[29]

He did more than just talk. His government had already issued two orders in council in January 1917 providing that preference would be given to veterans when making appointments to the provincial civil service and no men eligible for military service would be appointed except in exceptional circumstances. Speaking in the debate on a war resolution in the legislature in 1917, Hearst declared: "We criticize without mercy the eligible young man that fails without proper excuse, to respond to the call for recruits ... There is no excuse for such a one. He hasn't learned aright the duty of citizenship or the obligations that rest upon him. There is something wrong in his moral make up."[30]

And yet, when Williams pointed out that conscription was "doubly necessary" because voluntary enlistment in Ontario had failed, Hearst took offence, claiming that Ontario had done more than its share in terms of enlistments and that the shortage of manpower was a Quebec problem. He was right: with 31 per cent of the Canadian population, Ontario provided 43 per cent of Canadian enlistments up to October 1917.[31] That raised the question of why he was travelling around the province encouraging men to enlist, but as the debate became increasingly heated in 1917 his speeches did shift to blaming the manpower crisis on Quebec. Like most Ontarians, including Rowell, he agreed when the Orange *Sentinel* attacked French Canadians for their "conspicuous unreadiness to enlist in the Dominion forces," which it attributed to the "fact" that they weren't loyal British subjects.[32]

Unfortunately, this debate was taking place as the long festering bilingual schools issue reached its climax. Howard Ferguson had spent the summer of 1916 doing his best to keep the issue alive, accusing Laurier and the federal Liberals of exploiting the issue for political reasons. "No man in public life today," he declared, "was ever guilty of a greater crime against the well-being of Canada" than Laurier because he had "connived and planned to make the Ontario school question an issue in Dominion politics so as to solidify the province of Quebec, and to do that in the midst of this awful war for no other purpose than party advantage." He got even nastier at an Orange gathering when he "revealed" to his avid listeners that the bilingual schools controversy was actually a conspiracy. The French Canadians weren't actually the cause of the problem, he claimed; it was priests who had been expelled from France and had infiltrated the bilingual schools where they were "instilling ... the idea of a new France – of segregating themselves in this new continent and building up a greater France than ever existed in Europe."[33] Ferguson's biographer, acknowledging that his subject had reverted to "the extremist of 1911," suggests charitably that he "may have believed [that] the equally abusive language to which the province ... was being subjected" but was "not a justification."[34] Sam Genest may have been closer to the mark when he said that Ferguson was "a fool, ignoramus and malicious scoundrel."[35]

Two events took place in the autumn of 1916 that effectively settled the dispute. The first was the appearance in October of a papal encyclical letter, *Commisso Divinitus*, in which Pope Benedict XV granted that Franco-Ontarians had a right "to claim, in a suitable way ... that French be taught in schools attended by a certain number of their children" but reminded them that ... the one thing of supreme importance above all others is to have Catholic schools and not to imperil their existence."[36] This was, of course, the position that Ontario's Catholic hierarchy had been taking all along. The pope therefore urged moderation and obedience to the civil authorities and most Franco-Ontarians obeyed him.[37] Shortly afterwards, the Judicial Committee of the Privy Council (JCPC) issued its rulings in the two cases appealed to it by the Ottawa separate school board and the Association canadienne-française d'education d'Ontario.

In *Ottawa Separate School Board v. R., Mackell et al*, the JCPC ruled that Regulation 17 was within the constitutional jurisdiction of the provincial government and did not violate the British North America Act because its educational guarantees applied only to religious minorities.[38] At the same time, however, the JCPC ruled in *Ottawa Separate School Board v. Ottawa City Corporation, the Quebec Bank et al* that the government's creation of a commission to manage the schools in place of the separate school board was unconstitutional because it violated the Separate Schools Act of 1863.[39]

The appearance of two JCPC decisions hard on the heels of *Commisso Divinitus* had a marked impact on the controversy. Most people, even in French Canada, accepted the decisions as impartial and – more importantly – final. Newspapers that had been most vociferous in the struggle commented moderately on them and then largely abandoned the issue.[40] Genest capitulated on 3 November and proposed that Regulation 17 be given a fair trial without further opposition, after which the government might re-examine the whole question.[41] The school commission returned the administration of Ottawa's separate schools to Genest's board on 7 December, and Hearst made a conciliatory gesture by arranging for the government to pay two-thirds of the total litigation expenses despite his earlier announcement that it would not.[42] The changed atmosphere was probably most notable in the Quebec legislature, where Premier Gouin observed that provincial assistance to the Franco-Ontarians no longer seemed appropriate.[43]

But when the government learned in the spring of 1917 that Regulation 17 was still not being enforced in Ottawa's bilingual schools, Hearst passed another bill empowering the government to establish another school commission if necessary.[44] How could he do this if the previous legislation had been unconstitutional? His explanation was that the previous act had been declared unconstitutional because it gave the Minister of Education arbitrary power to withdraw the rights and powers of a local school board for an indefinite period. This bill only authorized the government to appoint a commission subject to appeal to the Ontario Supreme Court, which would determine whether or not the government was justified in the circumstances and when the local school board should be reinstated.[45]

Rowell, as usual, offered no opposition to the bill, and it passed unanimously with only the five Franco-Ontarian Liberal MPPs opposing it. Distrustful as always, Rowell feared that the bill had been "deliberately introduced with a view of laying a trap for us, and that if we opposed it they [i.e., the Conservatives] would go all through the country in their campaign to link us up with the opposition of the Ottawa School Board to the regulation. We cannot permit them to put us in this position."[46] Senator Belcourt agreed, concluding that the government "did not want the question to be settled, that it looked upon the difficulties caused by Regulation 17 as its best ground for retaining power."[47] This conclusion may have been reinforced by the government's decision to require Franco-Ontarians applying for land grants in northern Ontario to sign a pledge that they would obey the school laws.[48]

When the Ottawa separate school board went to court to recover the money spent by the first commission while administering the schools, Hearst put another bill through the legislature in April 1917, indemnifying the late school commission for the expenses it had incurred.[49] This proved unnecessary, however, when the JCPC rejected the board's case on the ground that the commission had only spent the money for legitimate purposes.[50] Thus, while feelings were still running high in 1917, the issue had been pretty well settled. It did not prove necessary to establish the second school commission, as the bilingual school boards across the province, including Ottawa, generally accepted the inevitable and made varying attempts to obey the regulations.

The bilingual schools dispute must stand in Ontario's history as a profoundly regrettable episode and one that is difficult to understand more than a century later. But it was virtually inevitable in the context of the times when Canadians were sharply divided over religion and language as they struggled to define what it meant to be Canadian. The war increased the stress because it raised the question of how much authority the state had over people's lives, including life and death in the case of young men. The Conservative Party in English Canada, having embraced the idea that the emerging nation was at the same time an integral part of the empire, alienated French Canadians – and others – and still struggles to attract francophone support a century later. In predominantly Anglo-Protestant Ontario, however, where its policies represented the views of most people, it dominated the political scene until 1985.

And yet, while the Franco-Ontarians claimed to be fighting against the proscription of their language, "their intention," as historian Marilyn Barber correctly pointed out half a century ago, "was not to defend their rights but to extend their rights, not only to protect existing rights but also to secure additional ones."[51] And the government had in fact extended francophone rights when Regulation 17 allowed French instruction in the first form and an hour per day to teach French as a subject. But the government had no intention of allowing French-language or ethnic schools in Ontario and was only attempting to ensure that Franco-Ontarian children became proficient in English, as moderate Franco-Ontarians like J.O. Reaume understood. Rightly or wrongly from our perspective, the concept of bilingualism was totally unacceptable to most Ontarians, who identified it with Henri Bourassa and radical Quebecois nationalists who wanted Canada to become a bilingual and bicultural nation. Unfortunately, most people of British descent in Ontario and other provinces believed that Canada was and should be an Anglo-British country and no Ontario government could have accepted the francophone Catholic minority's demand for equal rights in the school system. It could, however, have focused on the constitutional and social aspects of the issue and discouraged the ethnic extremism that it fostered.

The irony of the whole controversy, considered in the light of its repercussions on the national fabric and the political life of the nation, is that when Howard Ferguson became Premier he commissioned Dr. Merchant to re-examine conditions in the bilingual schools, and he found that they were almost exactly what they had been in 1912.[52] In the view of historian

Françoise Noël, it had been "simply impossible to enforce" Regulation 17, but the struggle had "helped to strengthen both the boundaries of the Franco-Ontarian community and the power and influence of the French-Canadian Catholic Church in matters of schooling."[53] Ferguson quietly shelved the regulation.[54]

Meanwhile, the conscription crisis brought Hearst and Rowell closer together because of their shared attitudes to the war, conscription, Canada's place in the empire and Ontario's role as Canada's "empire province." Hearst's passage of the Ontario Temperance Act despite divisions within his party impressed Rowell and now, following two by-elections in Simcoe West and Toronto Northeast B in January 1917, both of which the Conservatives won, he proposed that the informal political truce they had established should include by-elections and no provincial election until after another session.[55] Typically, Rowell made clear that he believed he was making this offer from a position of strength because, "as matters stand, I believe we could carry Ontario" in an election.[56] Whether or not that was true, Hearst welcomed the political truce because it offered the benefits of union government without having to share power with the Liberals, a point that Hartley Dewart pointed out repeatedly in his attacks on Rowell. A truce also served Rowell because it meant that he would not have to fight a wartime election in which the Conservatives would very likely stir up ethnic and religious divisions at a time when the Liberal Party was already sharply divided. Rowell also expected to be offered a senior position in the Union government, so he would finally, after ten years in opposition, get his chance to make a difference.

Hearst and Rowell first appeared together at a large recruiting rally at Toronto's Massey Hall on the evening of 11 June, the same day that Borden tabled the Military Service Act in parliament.[57] Negotiations had already begun on the composition of the union cabinet and Hanna had participated in them, consulting prominent Ontario Liberals on Borden's behalf.[58] Because the Conservatives had won a huge majority in Ontario in 1911, however, Borden clearly saw no need to be generous and Ontario's Liberal Unionists got only two of the province's seven seats in the new government. Thus, Rowell and Sydney Mewburn joined the five Conservatives – Cochrane, Crothers, Kemp, Reid, and White – who were already in the government. Hanna, however, who had met with Borden on 7 June and thought he had been promised a position in the cabinet as Dominion Food Controller with a seat in the Senate, was appointed food controller but not included in the cabinet or given a seat in the Senate. Whether he had misunderstood Borden's intentions or was betrayed, he had been humiliated for a second time in his career and served for only a few months before resigning and being appointed president of the Imperial Oil Company.[59]

The absence of a senior representative of the Ontario Conservative government in the Union cabinet seems odd at first glance. It's true that Cochrane was still there but his health was so poor by this time that he could only serve as a minister without portfolio.[60] Hearst was not invited to join the government, although he had been mentioned as a replacement for Cochrane in 1914, but by 1916 Borden had developed reservations about Hearst's leadership skills. Nor does Hearst appear even to have been consulted during the union negotiations.[61] But there is no evidence to suggest that Hearst wanted to leave the provincial scene, and he likely thought that being Premier of the most important province in the country trumped being a minister in a short-term war cabinet.

The new government proceeded to pass the Military Service Act and prepared for an election. The campaign began unofficially in Ontario at a "Win-the-War Convention" of Conservative and Liberal Unionists in Toronto on 2 August, at which Hearst and Rowell shared the platform for the first time. When Hearst spoke, he toned down his rhetoric, presumably reaching out to the many Ontarians who had reservations about conscription, declaring only that "whether we like it or not," conscription would "fulfil our pledge to the men at the front" and "there is no other way to save us from disgrace."[62] A week later, when the federal Liberals met in Winnipeg and expressed their support for Laurier, Hearst told Irving that "the honest fair minded Grit" was "humiliated & ashamed" and he hoped that God would "grant that right may yet prevail and Canada be saved from the humiliation of a Laurier anti-war Government."[63]

It wasn't long, however, before it became clear that Ontarians' support for Union government and conscription was not as overwhelming as it had first appeared. It was true that the Conservative press fully supported the cause, as did every Liberal daily newspaper with the exceptions of the London *Advertiser* and the Brockville *Recorder*. But the truth was, as the astute Willison observed, that most Ontarians supported conscription but not of Ontarian men.[64] But most of the Liberal newspapers that supported conscription had mixed feelings about the Union government because of the dubious record of the Borden government. That was why, when representatives of twenty Liberal papers met in Toronto in July 1917 and agreed to "stand squarely for compulsory military service" and to support only candidates who supported it in the impending election, they also made it clear that they were supporting Union government only in order to win the war because the Borden government had "proved themselves unequal to the task."[65]

More ominously, all of the province's rural weeklies, including the *Weekly Sun* and *Farm and Dairy*, opposed conscription because many if not most farmers saw conscription as unnecessary and unwise, at least in Ontario. The government had been urging them since 1914 to produce as much food as possible because it was vital to the war effort, but the farmers could hardly maintain, let alone expand, production if their workers – many of whom were their own sons – were taken away. The summer and autumn of 1917 proved their point: the farmers produced a good crop but the shortage of workers to harvest it was even greater than it had been in 1916. Hearst, who was still Minister of Agriculture as well as Premier, responded by publicly appealing for 10,000 men from urban areas to help out, and more than 6,000 responded, 2,000 of them from Toronto. That wasn't enough but many urban workers were not prepared to "volunteer" for the wages that farmers could afford to pay.[66] The government then encouraged urban students and women not otherwise employed to help out if they could.

There was a labour shortage in the industrial economy as well. That was partly offset when women took jobs in factories to replace the men who had enlisted, but that created problems too. Factory owners were prepared to hire women, even if they initially had doubts about their ability to handle the work, but they usually paid them less than men, presumably because they were women. That kind of discrimination was obviously unfair, although not unexpected at the time, but it also worried male factory workers who feared that their wages would be reduced to match them. More problematic was the fact that many in the labour movement were beginning to see the conscription issue from an emerging sense of class consciousness. Why should workers be forced to risk their lives – to invest their only "capital" as it were – while businessmen were safely making record profits in the production of war supplies? And while workers who enlisted were away, the government was doing nothing to support their families, aside from cooperating with the Canadian Patriotic Fund, a private initiative that assisted needy families.[67]

With the election set for 17 December, Borden officially launched his Ontario campaign on 21 November with a large rally at Massey Hall in Toronto. As in every election since 1908, Ontario's provincial Conservatives put their organization fully behind him and Hearst was on the platform with Borden that evening. His speech essentially reiterated what he had been saying for months, that without conscription, Canada's war effort would be weakened and that would lead not only to "Prussian militarism in Canada" but also to "having the light of freedom extinguished throughout the world." If that seemed an overheated exaggeration of the reality, he added that "with all the earnestness I possess, with a full realization of all that the words mean – we must face either failure or conscription." But then he got to his real point, which he knew would resonate with the audience: the problem wasn't that Ontario men had not enlisted in large numbers. The problem was that Quebec was not contributing its share of enlistments, and that was because Quebec didn't share "Canadian" values.[68]

Speaking at Georgetown on 12 December, he went further, declaring that the real issue in the election was, "[S]hall Canada have Union Government of all Provinces and parties outside Quebec, or shall a solid Quebec control the destiny of a divided Canada?" To Hearst the answer was clear: "Ontario must stand by the Union of the Eight Provinces and must do so in a manner so emphatic and conclusive that Quebec domination will never again be attempted."[69] This was, of course, the main theme of the Unionist campaign. Frank Cochrane, speaking two days later, said that "the country realizes that it must face and settle once and for all the question of Quebec domination. That province has to be put in its place."[70]

It was one thing for political leaders to join together in a Union government, but the practicalities of getting local politicians and party activists to cooperate was quite another. J.D. Reid, the very partisan Conservative/Unionist Party manager who was in charge of the Ontario campaign, had to collaborate with Rowell and, not surprisingly, it was an "uneasy alliance."[71] Having generated long-term partisan animosities and distrust during past electoral conflicts, Conservatives and Liberal Unionists now had to agree on who was going to run in the various constituencies. That would be difficult at any time, but it was more so in 1917 because both were confident of sweeping the province. When Rowell demanded that the Liberal Unionists be allocated twenty-four constituencies, Reid, perhaps not unreasonably, refused, given that the Conservatives had won a large majority in 1911 and at dissolution held seventy seats compared to the Liberals' twelve. The situation was further complicated by the fact that the decennial redistribution of constituencies took effect in this election. That raised the number of seats in the House of Commons from 221 to 235, but Ontario's representation declined from eighty-six to eighty-two. That meant that some constituencies were abolished, new ones were created, and others had their boundaries changed. In the end, the Conservatives claimed seventy-two of the nominations and the Liberal Unionists were reduced to ten.

This inevitably created some awkward situations and some downright nasty battles. Rowell himself found it difficult to find a seat. He had hoped to run in Toronto, but every Conservative riding association in the city warned that it would run a candidate against him if he did. Eventually

Jonas Thornton, the Conservative incumbent in Durham stepped aside to enable Rowell to run there. Both the journalist Augustus Bridle, writing in 1921, and the historians Patrice Dutil and David Mackenzie, writing in 2017, infer that Thornton was rewarded a seat in the Senate. In fact, he neither asked for nor received any reward.[72] In return, Rowell had to grit his teeth and endorse Frank Cochrane in Temiskaming instead of Arthur Roebuck, a young progressive lawyer who supported conscription but not the Union government and ran as a Liberal-Labour candidate.

In Oxford North the Liberal incumbent, Edward Nesbitt, supported conscription and Union government and was endorsed by Borden but the constituency's Conservatives and the local branch of the Great War Veterans Association (GWVA) strongly supported Lieutenant Colonel Donald Sutherland, a Norwich physician who had joined the Canadian Expeditionary Force (CEF) in 1914, was serving in France, commanded the 52nd Battalion and was twice wounded, who ran as a Laurier Liberal. Nesbitt won, no doubt partly because Oxford North had only elected Liberals since 1867 but also perhaps because he was allocated most of the overseas soldiers' votes for the constituency.[73] In Oxford South, the Conservative incumbent – also called Donald Sutherland – ran as a Unionist against Malcolm Schell, the former Liberal MP, who promised to support the Union government but remained very critical of the Borden government and would not support the conscription of farmers. Sutherland won and held the seat until 1926. In Brant, Borden appointed John Fisher, the Conservative incumbent, to the Senate to enable John Harold to run as a Liberal Unionist. The Laurier Liberals ran a candidate but more significantly, Henry Cockshutt, president of the farm implement company, ran as an Independent Conservative, but Harold won by a slim majority.[74]

The situation was more messy in Algoma West, where the Conservative incumbent, A.C. Boyce, had been appointed to the Board of Railway Commissioners, so the seat was vacant. When the local Conservatives met on 24 October they invited the Liberals and the local branch of the Canadian Labour Party to join with them in selecting the Unionist candidate. The Liberal Unionists agreed but only when they couldn't find a candidate and T.E. Simpson, a Conservative and former mayor of Sault Ste. Marie, was chosen. The Laurier Liberals, however, nominated Charles Napier Smith, the former Liberal MPP and publisher of the *Sault Express* newspaper, who ran officially as an independent candidate. There was a good reason for that.

Smith had always been a controversial figure, but he had risen to new heights in June 1916 when he ran a lengthy front-page editorial in his newspaper declaring that Canada "should not send any more of her sons overseas to engage in this frightful cataclysm" because "there has already been too much Canadian bloodletting and the cost of [the] British connection has been away and beyond what our people counted on." That was fair comment but he crossed a line when he charged that those who "sleep in a foreign land" had died "for a foreign cause" and suggested that Canada would "contribute more to the future greatness of the Anglo-Saxon race by pursuing her own ideals and minding her own business on this side of the Atlantic."[75]

That was more radical than anything Laurier would have endorsed, and it shocked not only Conservatives but many Liberals as well. Boyce complained to Pierre Blondin, the Secretary of State, whose responsibilities included press censorship, arguing that the editorial would make recruitment even more difficult than it already was. Blondin agreed and not only ordered all copies of the 23 June edition seized and destroyed but also shut down the *Express*. That was pretty extreme too and was in fact the only instance during the war of the government shutting down a newspaper except for Kitchener's *Ontario Journal*, formerly called the *Berliner Journal*, which was banned in September 1918 because it published in German. [76] When Sault Ste. Marie's legal community, apparently not thinking the *Sault Daily Star*'s punishment sufficient, pointed out that local newspapers were essential for publishing legal notices, Blondin agreed to allow Smith to publish such notices in a serial flysheet.[77]

The demise of the *Express* was a serious loss to the people of Sault Ste. Marie, and its closure was a sad end to Smith's colourful career as journalist and politician. As John Irving, a prominent local lawyer who supported conscription and the Union government, observed, Smith "had always been known as a hard shell Grit, and the shell was just as hard as ever."[78] Toronto's *Evening Telegram* offered backhanded sympathy for Smith when it suggested that "an editor who has written himself down as an ass ... should not be written up as a martyr in legal proceedings for high treason, petty treason, or any other sort of treason ... Mr. Smith belongs not in a jail for traitors, but in an asylum for fools."[79] Hearst, who knew Smith well, commented that he had committed political suicide because only "the French and Foreign vote, the anti-conscriptionists and disgruntled Tories" would vote for him while "decent Liberals" would vote for Simpson. In fact, Simpson "should win hands down," Hearst thought, but having said that, he told Irving that he "would be surprised at some of the men I am told are backing Smith."[80]

As Hearst intimated in his reference to "the Foreign vote," Sault Ste. Marie was an industrial community whose population was largely made up of millworkers, many of them recent immigrants. The local branch of the Canadian Labour Party ran James Lockwood, an engineer at the paper mill. This meant that Simpson was running against two anti-conscription candidates, although it is possible that, like many labour candidates, Lockwood might have supported conscription if it included the conscription of wealth as well. Hearst expected for some reason that Lockwood would withdraw from the campaign, but he didn't[81] and Simpson won handily.

Not surprisingly, Ontario Liberals were sharply divided on more than conscription. According to Hearst, some were "bitter on Rowell" because "it appears that he never consulted the Liberal members in [the] Legislature before going into [the] Ottawa Government and all the die-hard Grits & Laurier supporters of every kind are down on him,"[82] It was certainly true that the Laurier Liberals were upset with him, and their unofficial leader, Hartley Dewart, had a field day attacking Unionists of both stripes. Reporting on one of Dewart's campaign meetings in the middle of November, Hearst claimed that he "abused bitterly ... the Liberals that had gone into [the] Borden Government, likened Rowell to Judas, and was so vile and abusive that the papers did not report much of what he said." The reason, according to Hearst, was that Dewart was "drinking heavily lately."[83]

By the middle of November Hearst was confident that "the elections are all over now but for the shouting" because he had "never addressed so large enthusiastic and interested audiences before" and "do not think there is any doubt of the result."[84] Given that the Ontario campaign hadn't even been officially launched yet, he was seriously out of touch. Main Johnson, Rowell's private secretary, thought that "never in Canadian politics was there greater chaos than in the Ontario situation during these critical weeks" and it was having a negative impact on the Unionist cause. "Public opinion," he warned, "seemed to be strongly against us, and getting worse all the time."[85] Clifford Sifton, an astute political observer, admitted to being "very uneasy," especially because he detected "a very decided reaction ... amongst the poorer class of voters in favour of Laurier."[86]

Sifton was even more worried by the end of the month, telling Borden on 30 November – just two weeks before polling day – that the situation was "very dangerous," not least because there was "no effective headquarters organization" in Ontario.[87] Borden immediately met with Sifton, Rowell and Cochrane – but not Reid – that same day and placed Sifton in charge of the campaign "with special responsibility to resolve the constituency conflicts."[88] Rowell supported this move but advised Sifton "to remain behind the scenes" and keep independent of Cochrane.[89] When Sir George Foster, Borden's Minister of Trade and Commerce and a Toronto MP, protested against involving the controversial Sifton in the campaign, Borden responded bluntly that the government "would be defeated unless active steps [were] taken."[90]

Sifton quickly "began to bring some order out of the organizational chaos."[91] According to Main Johnson, "he had his hand on the throttle, and although it was shaken hither and thither in the commotion, it never loosened its grasp, and gradually, relentlessly, it began to get control."[92] John Godfrey, a prominent Liberal Toronto lawyer, later said that he "never saw such a rapid change in public opinion."[93] The explanation for that was that General Mewburn – on Sifton's advice – announced first that agrarian representatives would be included in the conscription tribunals in rural areas, then exempted the sons of farmers from conscription, a cynical concession that guaranteed a majority in Ontario and probably in the rest of English Canada as well.[94] Rowell had been advocating for months that conscription should exempt "any men now in agriculture who cannot be replaced" because "we must keep up our agricultural production and there was already a shortage of farm labour," but he had been ignored. In any case, the farmers were, as Godfrey put it, "placated."[95]

It was at this point that Hearst and Rowell toured northern Ontario, starting at Sault Ste. Marie on 5 December. It was a much anticipated affair because, as the *Sault Daily Star* rightly observed, "it will be an interesting sight to have these old political opponents speaking from the same platform for the same cause."[96] Rowell went up by train, arriving in Sault Ste. Marie at 1:45 p.m., and spoke in the afternoon to "a large audience of ladies" at the recently opened Duchess Theatre. The event was chaired by John Irving who, to give him credit, openly wondered why the organizers had chosen him instead of a woman. Rowell sensibly directed his speech to the female audience, declaring that it was "the policy of the Prussians to so terrorize the women of the country they invade, so as to break the national spirit," and that "the Hun barbarities ... are not simply the acts of a drunken soldier, but ... part of the German organized barbarity."[97] According to the *Sault Daily Star*, "it was not a difficult matter to see which way the sympathies of the ladies was going, and that their hearts are set on doing everything in their power to stand behind the boys in the trenches."[98]

Hearst arrived at 5:15, and then both men proceeded to the curling rink for the evening meeting. It was chaired by Mayor Francis Crawford, a Liberal, and "never in the history of the Sault," the *Sault Daily Star* declared, had there been "such a large ... political meeting" in the community. The more than 3,000 men and women in attendance "taxed the capacity of the curling rink ... filling every nook and corner of the building, even to the platform." Seating at the front was reserved for "at least one thousand ladies and their escorts"[99]

Simpson, the Unionist candidate, set the tone by pointing out that Laurier had been invited to join the government but "was not big enough to measure up to the needs of the country." Fortunately, however, many of his followers had shown themselves to be "big enough and patriotic enough to sink party differences." And "what better evidence do you want of Union Government," he asked, than to see Hearst and Rowell on the platform supporting "the same cause?" Acknowledging that the Independent Labour Party was running a candidate, Simpson claimed that he agreed with "many things" in the labour platform "but did not think that the country should be divided on economic issues in wartime because "they sink into insignificance before the question of reinforcements." He also acknowledged that there had been "a lot of grafting and profiteering under the last Government" but assured the audience that the Union government "would eliminate that to a very large extent." Simpson also addressed the enemy alien issue, suggesting that the many "Austrians" working at the steel mill and elsewhere should only be paid a living wage, with the balance of their pay going into a fund to support veterans or their dependents or "to help carry on the war."[100]

When Crawford called on Hearst to speak, "it was some minutes before the Premier could get started as the great crowd rose to their feet and made the building resound with cheers while the band played 'The Maple Leaf Forever.'" When it settled down, Hearst declared that "it is a great thing to come home" and thanked Algoma's Liberal Unionists "for the magnificent spirit they have displayed in this campaign. In the hour of their country's need, they have shown they can lay aside their political differences and have put their country before party." It reminded him, he said, of a cartoon in *Punch* that showed John Redmond and Sir Edward Carson, bitter rivals over the status of Ireland, shaking hands and Redmond saying, "No one but the Kaiser could have brought this about." It was an apt comparison.

Getting down to business, Hearst claimed that the fundamental issue in the election was whether Canadians were "going to fight or are you going to quit" and, "looking into the faces of the mothers of boys in the trenches I say it would be treason to forsake them" because the Western Front was "the only thing between the Hun and Canada." As for Laurier's call for a referendum on conscription, he noted that there hadn't been a referendum in 1914 when the first troops were sent overseas. He also reminded his audience that when Quebec was the only province to vote no in the 1893 federal referendum on prohibition, Laurier said that it wasn't fair for the other provinces to force their opinion on it and that would almost certainly be the result again now. He concluded with a special appeal to women, many of whom now had the franchise under the Wartime Elections Act. It was "a sacred obligation," he reminded them. "See that you protect your loved ones with your ballot, as they are protecting you with bullets in the firing line. You are given an opportunity to serve your country and opportunity means responsibility." But, he assured the gathering, "I have no misgivings about the women, whatever I have about the men."[101]

Rowell focused his speech on rallying Liberals to support the Union government, emphasizing that it was a new government and should neither be blamed for the mistakes nor credited for the achievements of the previous Conservative government. The new government, he claimed, had already abolished patronage, placed the purchasing of government supplies under one central purchasing commission, and limited the profits of "the pork packers and millers." Reaching out to both industrial workers and farmers, he also argued that the Military Service Act was better than a ballot draft because it took into consideration whether a man was more value at home than overseas. Referring to the local tribunals that dealt with exemption claims, he allowed that "some had made mistakes in taking men away who should have been left to continue in the production of food" but thought "on the whole" that they were showing good judgment. Unable to resist taking a shot at Quebec, however, he charged – incorrectly – that there "had been wholesale exemptions" in that province.[102]

It was a successful evening with Hearst and Rowell working effectively, combining Hearst's rather simplistic patriotism with Rowell's more lawyerly approach in what both genuinely believed was a noble cause. But the Sault rally was just the first in a series of campaign stops in northern Ontario. The two men left the next day for North Bay, where they found themselves in the unusual situation of urging voters to vote for Charles Harrison, the Unionist candidate in Nipissing, whose opponent was a francophone Laurier Liberal. This had been Frank Cochrane's riding since 1911, but he was running in Temiskiming this time.

Given that Nipissing was sharply divided between anglophones and francophones, it is not surprising that the battle there was "acrimonious," with Harrison's supporters accusing the Laurier Liberals and their local candidate, Edmond Lapierre, of "stabbing Canada's soldiers in the back by refusing to endorse conscription."[103] Hearst and Rowell stoked that fire. Rowell ranted about the negative influence that he believed Quebec's Catholic hierarchy held over the country, claiming that "a Nationalist, clerical and reactionary movement [was] at work in the Province of Quebec that to-day dominates the political situation in that

Province, and is using this hour of grave national peril to dominate the political situation throughout the Dominion." That wasn't acceptable, but even worse was the "fact" that it was being driven by disloyal members of French religious orders who had found asylum in Canada but were working to weaken its war effort.[104]

Hearst was equally extreme. Expanding on his charge at Sault Ste. Marie that "it would be treason to desert the men at the front" and that the Western Front was the only thing keeping the Huns from Canada, he now actually suggested that Germany might attack Canada. Referring to the massive Halifax explosion that had occurred the day before, he asked "what would happen to Canada if the Western line was broken because of lack of reinforcements, and the Germans were able to bombard Canada with their naval guns and other coastal cities were damaged as Halifax has been by the explosion?"[105] This was scaremongering at its worst. While he didn't attack Quebec, having left that to Rowell, he agreed with Rowell's comments. Writing to Irving on 23 December, he attempted to explain the problem. The "average French-Canadian habitant is not educated," he said, and "does not read even his own newspaper, and takes his politics like his religion from his Priest and Laurier."[106] That was why Union government was the only alternative to a government dominated by Québecois nationalists and Catholic priests. In other words, the traditional party system had broken down and Anglo-Protestants needed to recognize that Laurier and his followers had become the tools of an insidious clerical force that overruled partyism.[107]

Hearst and Rowell presumably were sincere in their extreme views but they must also have known that they were playing a very dangerous game when they fanned the flames of Anglo-Protestant fear of the French Catholic "threat." A dramatic example of what this xenophobic fear could lead to had already occurred in June when military police raided St. Stanislaus Novitiate, a Jesuit seminary on the outskirts of Guelph, in the belief that it was sheltering young men who had not reported when conscripted. When news of the raid became public, Anglo-Protestants naturally jumped to the conclusion that the Jesuits were guilty and ipso facto disloyal, especially in view of the fact that the director of the seminary was a French Canadian Catholic. However, Catholics, including anglophones, were offended by the accusation and the heavy-handed manner of the officer who led the raid. Any possibility that this affair might have been dealt with quietly was impossible because, as it happened, Rev. William Power, the head of the Jesuit Order in Canada, was visiting the seminary at the time of the raid and one of the novitiates was the son of C.J. Doherty, the Minister of Justice in the Union government.

The technical root of the problem was that the Military Service Act specifically exempted clergymen from conscription. What most Protestants probably didn't know was that, while Protestant theology students do not become clergymen until their ordination, the Catholic Church considers novitiates to be priests even before their ordination. This distinction was essentially irrelevant, however, because all thirty-six of the young men at St. Stanislaus had exemption certificates so none of them were guilty of evading conscription. Eight of them were exempt even without exemption certificates because they were not Canadians (six were Americans, one was British, and another was Polish), and Doherty's son had been exempted for medical reasons. It has never been explained why Captain A.C. Macauley, the Assistant Deputy Provost Marshal who led the raid, did not ask if the students had exemption documents or why the priest in charge of the seminary did not tell him. More bizarre was the fact that the raid had taken place in a very aggressive manner late at night by men not in uniform who were unable to identify themselves as military police officers.[108]

In the end, Mewburn apologized on behalf of the government. That might have put the matter to rest except that Harold Machin, the outspoken Conservative MPP from Kenora who had been appointed Director of the Military Services Branch – the conscription enforcement branch of the Militia Department – publicly denounced those responsible for the raid for being "worse than the Huns." He also, rather unnecessarily but no doubt to the delight of Catholics, took the opportunity to claim that there was "a powerful cabal" against Doherty in Ottawa, adding for good measure the gratuitous remark that "the greatest menace in the province of Ontario at this time is the Methodist Church, which seeks to make us the most hypocritical province in Canada."[109] That seemingly irrelevant comment was, of course, a reference to the fact that the Methodist Church – the largest religious denomination in Ontario – had led the campaign that brought about the Ontario Temperance Act in 1916. To his credit, Rev. William Power expressed his confidence that the Anglo-Protestant "clerical firebrands ... do not represent the best elements of the Protestant community of Guelph."[110]

Borden quickly appointed a royal commission headed by two prominent judges to investigate the affair, who concluded that there had been no justification for the raid and severely criticized Macauley's behaviour. What really mattered, however, was that Macauley's attitude and behaviour clearly reflected the general atmosphere of religious intolerance that had been aggravated by irresponsible Anglo-Protestant extremists. It can't be said that Hearst helped to calm the waters because a frequent theme in his speeches during the election campaign was that he would "see that Sir Robert Borden and Mr. Rowell keep their promises to Ontario and that the people of Quebec are compelled to do their share before further sacrifices are demanded from Ontario."[111] What that actually meant is impossible to say, but it seemed to mean that conscription would somehow really only apply to Quebec, which was what Ontarians wanted to hear. That was not possible, of course, but Mewburn's exemption of farmers' sons sealed the deal and, as Borden blandly observed, the people of Ontario "realized the country's need and nobly discharged their duty."[112]

On the surface, the election result was a great triumph for Borden and the Union government. Nationally, they won 153 seats against eighty-two seats for the Laurier Liberals. Hearst rejoiced because "we won everywhere except where French and German votes were strong" and he felt gratified that Quebec, which "has heretofore held the balance of power" with the result that "both political parties catered too much" to it while other provinces divided on party lines, had been firmly rebuked. "Now under Union Government Quebec has isolated herself" and "may now as never before see the folly of the policy she has pursued." The result of the election, he hoped, "will be to make them stop and think, and if wise counsel prevails at Ottawa I believe conditions will soon commence to improve." Perhaps in an attempt to display some moderation, he clarified that Quebec "should not be treated harshly or unjustly but she should certainly be treated firmly."[113] This simplistic analysis expressed the view of many Anglo-Protestants, but it was a serious misreading of what actually happened in the election. It was true that the Union government's 153 seats were more than the 135 seats the Conservatives had won in 1911, but the eighty-two seats won by the Laurier Liberals were only three less than they had won in 1911. The unfortunate difference was that most of them were in Quebec.

In Ontario, the Unionists elected seventy-two members, exactly the same number the Conservatives had won in 1911, but now ten of them were Liberal Unionists, one of whom was the only Unionist to win by acclamation.[114] In Hearst's home territory, northern Ontario, all twelve constituencies elected Unionists. Even Laurier, who had won Ottawa in 1908, was defeated by Dr. J.L. Chabot, a prominent physician who was commanding officer of the Ottawa General Military Base Hospital during the war. He now became one of only three French Canadian supporters of the new government and the only Franco-Ontarian.[115] Laurier's loss in Ottawa was not as significant as it might appear at first glance because he was re-elected in Quebec East, the seat he had held since 1877.[116]

But while the Liberal Unionists won only ten seats in Ontario, the Laurier Liberals won eight, a decline of only five.[117] All eight – Bruce South,

Essex North, Kent, Middlesex West, Prescott, Renfrew South, Russell, and Waterloo North – had significant French and/or German populations. They might not have won four of them except for the fact that their candidates in Bruce South, Essex North, Kent and Middlesex North actually supported conscription. Ruben Truax (Bruce South) and Archibald McCoig (Kent) opposed the Union government because of the alleged mismanagement and corruption of the Borden government.[118] William Kennedy (Essex North) agreed that conscription was necessary but was "consistently critical of the government's application of the Military Service Act, especially to farmers."[119] In Middlesex South the Liberal incumbent, Duncan Ross, a son of Sir George Ross, was being challenged by George Elliott, formerly the MP for Middlesex North, a constituency that had been abolished in 1914. The choice was, therefore, between a popular Liberal who supported conscription and a well-known Conservative Unionist. The voters re-elected Ross. Anti-conscription labour candidates ran in fifteen constituencies, but none were elected.[120]

In four constituencies the overseas soldiers' ballots were used to ensure Unionist victories. In Essex South the Liberals initially nominated G.P. Graham, a former leader of the party who supported conscription, but when this caused a split in the local party he withdrew and Robert Atkin ran as a Laurier Liberal. He won narrowly on the civilian vote but lost to John Brien, a Windsor physician who had briefly served overseas in the Canadian Army Medical Corps, when the military vote was counted. In Nipissing, the Laurier Liberal, Edmond Lapierre, won the civilian vote but lost when the military votes were counted, as did William Forrester in Perth South.[121] In Parkdale, Herbert Mowat, a long-time militia officer who had not gone overseas because of his age, was the Liberal Unionist candidate. His opponent was Major Carson McCormack, who had served overseas as an officer in the 3rd Battalion until being granted home leave in October 1917, presumably to run in the election. He ran as an independent, representing the soldiers. The Laurier Liberals ran Gordon Waldron, "a well-known and rather dyspeptic" Toronto Liberal lawyer.[122] McCormack won the civilian vote but was narrowly defeated because virtually all of the nearly 4,000 overseas soldiers' votes assigned to Parkdale went to Mowat.[123] McCormack returned overseas in January 1918, having been promoted to major, and rose to lieutenant colonel of the 3rd Battalion.

The manipulation of the overseas soldiers' vote in Parkdale was not an isolated event. The 1917 election was the most corrupt federal election in Canadian history because of how the rules were changed: enfranchising women related to overseas soldiers, disenfranchising large numbers of immigrants from the countries with which Canada was at war, allowing

Unionist officers to pressure their men to support the government, and distributing thousands of overseas soldiers' votes to constituencies where they were needed to ensure victory. This travesty of democracy reflected the belief of Borden and the Unionists that the maintenance of Canada's war effort had to be assured at whatever cost. They achieved their goal but at an appalling cost in terms of national unity, not to mention the price paid by the Conservative Party in Quebec for the next half century and the political imbalance that resulted. In Ontario, what appeared to be a huge victory quickly proved to have been a political disaster because of the post-war backlash against any politician identified with conscription.

On 7 February 1918 William Proudfoot, who had succeeded Rowell as interim leader of the provincial Liberals in January, proposed that the life of the legislature be extended "until a year had elapsed and a [legislative] Session [had] been held after the return of the soldiers."[124] Hearst and Rowell had already agreed during the 1917 session to suspend the requirement that by-elections caused by the death of a sitting member take place within three months.[125] While there is no proof that Hearst and Proudfoot had agreed on this in advance, there can be little doubt that they had because, "amid loud applause from both sides of the House," Hearst accepted the offer, which he interpreted to mean that the next election would not take place "until all our men are home again from Overseas, and a reasonable time thereafter to allow conditions to become normal."[126]

This was almost certainly a serious political misjudgment, and he knew it but not for the right reason. It was "not the best political move for [the] Govt," he thought, because "we are very strong in [the] country, Grits very weak. The opposition wouldn't have a corporal's guard left" if he called an election. "But there is a strong feeling against stirring up strife and discord in a party election at the present time" because "the one thing that matters is to win [the war] now, and to this end my whole energies should be directed." He also thought it was "about [the] greatest tribute a Prime Minister and Government ever received. An admission by [the] Opposition that there was no issue before the public. Practically that they had no criticism to offer."[127] He did ask Proudfoot to extend the political truce to include by-elections as well and Proudfoot agreed.[128]

Hearst was well aware of how fortunate he was to be dealing with Proudfoot, not only because he was a Liberal Unionist who supported conscription and the Union government but because he also agreed with Hearst that all other issues were secondary to winning the war. Indeed, he told the *Goderich Signal Star* that he was "strongly in favour of the Provincial Government, during the term of the war and afterwards, doing everything that will prove of beneficial assistance to the soldiers."[129] Clearly, he posed no threat to Hearst, who described him as "an honest, decent chap" but a man who would "never inspire much enthusiasm anywhere."[130] That included the Liberal Party, and because Proudfoot was only the interim leader of the party, a leadership convention was imminent. Hartley Dewart had already broken with Rowell's strong temperance policy and now he staked his claim to the leadership by being the only member of the legislature who opposed the political truce.[131]

Hearst knew, of course, that the Liberal Party was "broken up and discouraged,"[132] but he didn't know how serious the problem really was. Proudfoot's political truce and broad support for Hearst's policies not only didn't have the general support of the provincial Liberal Party, but they didn't even have the support of his own constituency association. When it met in May and expressed its "entire disapproval" of his policy, he responded that "every elector who did not support" Union government was "a rebel."[133] A month later the provincial party held a leadership convention and unceremoniously dumped him in favour of the more combative Dewart.[134]

Hearst didn't realize it but this marked a significant change in the political environment because the Liberals under Dewart's aggressive leadership were determined to bring down the government. If Hearst had continued Whitney's practice of going to the voters every three years, he would have called an election in the summer of 1917 and very likely would have won it. He hadn't done that, however, claiming that he didn't think political divisions should be stirred up during wartime. He almost certainly meant that, and there really was no apparent need for an election as long as Rowell and then Proudfoot led the Liberal Party. By 1918 social and political unrest was rising in Ontario for a variety of reasons that included the OTA, conscription, and the Hearst government's close relationship with the Union government. Dewart claimed in July 1919 that Hearst seriously considered calling an election in 1918, citing as evidence that James Hartt, the Conservative MPP for Simcoe East who was serving overseas in the Canadian Forestry Corps, returned home from France in January and didn't return until May. Because Hartt was grand master of the Orange Order in Ontario, Dewart believed that he had been summoned home "to organize ... the Orange lodges" for an election campaign. Hearst dismissed the charge as "ridiculous,"[135] which it may have been for three reasons: Hartt's CEF service file states that he was given leave to return home to attend the 1918 session of the legislature, Dewart had a tendency to focus on scandals, and Hearst believed in the spring of 1918 that his government was popular. He told Irving on 24 March that the Conservatives were "all ... loyal and enthusiastic."[136]

Three months later, however, he appeared less confident when he told the Toronto Northeast Conservative Association that "the fortunes of political parties or political leaders are but dust and ashes in the balance when the liberty of the world is at stake" and he thought people would respect leadership that didn't always place party interest first.[137]

That belief was tested when Hearst called four by-elections in August and September. Toronto Northeast A, York East, and Lennox were all safe Conservative seats and Oxford North had been Liberal since Confederation. Somewhat surprisingly, Dewart honoured the political truce and two of the by-elections (Lennox and Oxford North) were Conservative acclamations. Independent candidates prevented acclamations in Toronto Northeast A and York East, however, an indication that the political environment was changing because of the growing level of social unrest and the dissatisfaction of many veterans with how governments were handling their reintegration into society. Women also voted for the first time in these two by-elections. In fact, the *Globe* noted that the voting lists included more women than men and many of the poll officials were women as well. In an attempt to accommodate workers, the government adjusted the regulations so that polling stations opened at six in the morning, enabling people to vote on their way to work.[138]

The two contested by-elections took place on 19 August. Toronto Northeast A had been held by Robert Pyne since 1898, but he had retired, making a safe seat available for Henry Cody, who also succeeded him as Minister of Education. Cody was the rector of St. Paul's Anglican Church, reputed to be the largest congregation in Canada, and Archdeacon of Toronto. He was also a fire-breathing imperialist who fully supported conscription and the Union government. His appointment came as "a great surprise," according to J.B. Maclean, who claimed that it raised a cry from the old party politicians and Bolshevik journalists."[139] Castell Hopkins more moderately described it as "new and interesting" because Cody had never been involved in politics, but he was a highly respected educator and educational administrator. Howard Ferguson may have proposed Cody because they had been close friends since attending the University of Toronto, but Hearst chose him because he wanted him to modernize the province's school system. Despite his somewhat aristocratic public image, Cody was, in Castell Hopkins's words, "a democratic Anglican parson."[140]

Both Hearst and Cody probably expected an acclamation but there were many in the constituency who thought there should be a contest, given the growing unrest among workers and returned soldiers. Accordingly, William Varley, a union secretary, labour activist and returned soldier ran, offering a clear alternative to Cody. Charlesworth reflected the general view when he described Varley as "a popular soldier who had distinguished himself overseas on active service."[141] Having returned to Canada in November 1917, he soon became active in labour politics in Toronto and during the 1917 federal election had publicly criticized what he regarded as the poor treatment being received by returned soldiers. According to historian James Naylor, this led to his being confined for a time in a psychiatric hospital at Whitby, clearly implying that Varley was incarcerated in a psychiatric facility against his will for political reasons.[142] It's a shocking allegation for which Naylor offers no supporting evidence or even a reference, perhaps because there is none. It is true that the provincial government had built a psychiatric hospital at Whitby between 1913 and 1916 but upon completion the facility was immediately turned over to the Military Hospitals Commission (MHC) to serve as a convalescent hospital for soldiers wounded in the war. It wasn't actually until 1919, when the MHC returned the building to the provincial government that it began functioning as a psychiatric hospital.[143] In any case, there is no reference in his service file to his having been sent to the Whitby hospital, only a brief notation that he spent an unspecified period immediately after his arrival home in a convalescent home in Kingston.[144] Varley was an active member of the Independent Labour Party and ran against Cody as a soldier-labour candidate with the support of the Toronto District Labour Council and the Great War Veterans' Association (GWVA), despite the GWVA's prohibition on political endorsements. Allan Studholme, Walter Rollo, M.M. McBride, and a Reverend Archer Robinson all spoke on his behalf.[145]

The symbolism of a contest between a working-class wounded war veteran and a scholarly High Church Anglican priest, albeit a well-known, highly respected, and intelligent one, was not lost on many observers and the contest was a bitter one. Naylor claims that the Conservatives attacked Varley for his low social status and lack of education, to which Varley allegedly retorted that nobody in the trenches had "ask[ed] what your calling in life was or what church you belong to."[146] It was an effective response and was no doubt true as well, but Cody never made disparaging remarks about Varley, and a more sympathetic interpretation might be that many Conservatives and perhaps others simply thought that rejecting a highly respected educator who was Minister of Education in favour of an uneducated iron worker made little sense. In any case, to no one's great surprise, Cody won comfortably, but Varley did receive 32 per cent of the popular vote, which was a moral victory for those who were becoming increasingly dissatisfied with the political situation. It was also a warning to both parties because that was 32 per cent of the 29 per cent of the eligible voters who bothered to vote.[147]

The York East by-election came about because Hearst had appointed George S. Henry Minister of Agriculture. York East had been held by the Conservatives since 1905 and Henry had held it since a 1913 by-election. A successful dairy farmer, Henry was popular in York East and it was expected that he would be re-elected by acclamation. That didn't happen, however, because John Stupart Galbraith, a returned soldier, decided to run against him as an Independent Conservative. Galbraith was a civil engineer who had served overseas as an officer in the 123rd (Royal Grenadiers) Battalion and been awarded the Military Cross for "conspicuous gallantry and devotion to duty" during the Battle of Cambrai in December 1917.[148] He had no organization behind him and didn't campaign, however, so it was hardly surprising when Henry won with a large majority.[149] The voter turnout was even worse than in Toronto Northeast, with only 13 per cent of the voters casting ballots.[150]

Hearst naturally declared the results of both by-elections as "most satisfactory" and a recognition of "the esteem" in which Cody and Henry were held by the electors." That was no doubt true, but he went further, attributing the poor turnout in both cases to the fact that "the temper of the people is distinctly against election contests at a time when our energy and resources are so urgently required for the winning of the war."[151] That was questionable and ignored the fact that both ministers had been challenged by veterans, and Varley had won more votes than any previous labour candidate in Toronto.

# 7 The Gathering Storm

*Government by the people is a myth. The real rulers of Canada are the knighted heads of combines.*[1]

UNREST among the province's farmers and workers was clearly serious by 1918, but the emerging crisis did not reflect just the social and political divisions created by the war. It was the climax of their long struggle to get the politicians to take seriously their concerns and grievances that had been building since Confederation and the National Policy began shaping an economic empire centred on Toronto and Montreal, protective tariffs, and an east–west transportation system. The Dominion Grange movement had brought farmers together to discuss common interests but largely avoided politics, but the arrival in Ontario in 1889 of the Patrons of Industry, a more politically active organization, changed that. Within five years the Patrons had 50,000 members[2] and ran several candidates in the 1894 provincial election who called for reciprocal free trade with the United States and tariffs only for revenue purposes. They also reached out to workers, demanding legislation to protect them from combinations and monopolies and calling on governments to stop subsidizing railways with construction bonuses.

More generally, they sought strict economy and the elimination of corruption in the administration of government, abolition of the Senate, and the reservation of public lands for actual settlers. They also sought greater local autonomy, meaning that all county officials should be appointed or elected by the county rather than the provincial or federal governments and electoral districts that conformed more closely to the principle of representation by population.[3]

As can be seen, many of the Patrons' policies related to federal issues, but their emphasis on local autonomy resonated in rural communities, and they elected seventeen members in the 1894 provincial election, most of them former Liberals. They also ran twenty-seven candidates in the federal election of 1896 but elected only three, after which the movement declined steadily in popularity because the interests and circumstances of farmers varied according to the type and scale of agriculture they practised and conflict between those who believed in commercial marketing and those who favoured cooperatives. Even so, the initial success of the Patrons movement displayed at least a willingness on the part of farmers to bond together for united action, and it continued to be an important organization in rural communities throughout the province that would soon influence a more successful agricultural movement, the United Farmers of Ontario.[4]

The election of the Liberals in 1896 after sixteen years of Conservative rule in Ottawa was welcomed by many farmers because the Liberal Party had opposed the National Policy tariffs. But part of the reason that Wilfrid Laurier won the election was that he had embraced protective tariffs but promised to modify them in the interests of farmers. What he actually did was to reduce the tariffs on British goods, because Britain had no protective tariffs, and to offer to extend a similar reduction to the United States if it reciprocated. The likelihood of that happening was remote and Laurier's gesture didn't impress farmers. As E.C. Drury, who was emerging as a prominent figure in Ontario's farm movement, later wrote that "by the middle of the first decade of the century, it was plain that Mr. Laurier ... had forsaken his Free Trade principles and had gone over to protectionism."[5]

The farmers began to organize again, founding the Farmers' Association of Ontario, which was organized along constituency lines and took definite stands on public issues, advocating lower tariffs, government ownership of utilities, reduced railway rates, and introduction of the initiative and referendum. Meanwhile, Goldwin Smith, a former Oxford professor who had somewhat improbably moved to Toronto, acquired *The Farmers' Sun*, which had supported the Patrons. Renamed *The Weekly Sun*, it became the most important rural newspaper in the province.[6] In 1910 the Canadian Council of Agriculture was founded, and one of its first efforts was to organize a mass delegation that went to Ottawa to urge Laurier to adopt complete free trade with Great Britain. After replying that this was impossible, Laurier revealed that he was working on a reciprocity agreement with the United States.[7] When the government announced that an agreement had been reached, the farmers were understandably delighted, "not for what it was," as E.C. Drury later recalled, "but for what it might lead to. We regarded it as the 'entering edge of the wedge' that could topple the whole structure of tariff protection."[8]

Many in the business community agreed with that but in alarm, fearing it would lead to complete free trade. Many, including prominent Liberals, rallied around the Conservative Party, which forced Laurier to call an election on the issue. The resounding Conservative victory had a profound negative effect on the farm movement, especially in Ontario. According to Drury, "more than half the local Granges had folded up, and the annual conventions of 1911 and 1912 were poor affairs – a few dozen delegates where before there had been hundreds."[9] The defeat of reciprocity "so shook our faith in the old parties," he later recalled, that "we turned, slowly and unwillingly, toward direct political action."[10] In 1913, Drury, J.J. Morrison, W.C. Good, and J.Z. Frazer met in Toronto and decided to form yet another new farm organization. Following several regional meetings, a provincial meeting took place in Toronto in March 1914, at which the United Farmers of Ontario (UFO) organization was founded, and Drury was elected president.

Unlike previous farmers' organizations, the UFO did not focus so much on specific issues such as protective tariffs as trying to identify the real causes of the problems being experienced by farmers. The most important, it concluded, was rural depopulation.[11] Since at least the 1880s young people had been leaving rural communities to seek employment in urban centres because John A. Macdonald had introduced his so-called National Policy – protective tariffs – in 1878. And as Drury argued in 1909, that was when Ontario's rural population began declining and was by then "decreasing at the rate of six thousand a year ... and I think the coincidence clearly indicates the cause of the decline."[12]

It was true: the percentage of Ontario's rural population had declined from 48 per cent in 1881 to 31 per cent in 1911, while its urban population had grown from 31.5 per cent to 52.6 per cent,[13] and both trends continued through the war years. While many were moving into towns and cities, attracted by cash wages, shorter working hours, and the usual attractions of urban centres, others were moving west to secure inexpensive land, and some were going to the United States for various reasons. The rural birth rate in Ontario was declining steadily as well, from 6.2 per cent in 1851 to 5.1 per cent in 1891, and 2.9 per cent in 1921.[14] As Toronto's *Daily Star* observed, "the farmer's grievance is [that] ... he sees the skyscrapers and marble palaces which big business rears in the cities, and is doubtful whether the cost to the country is not greater than the service ... He thinks there has been an overgrowth of cities at the expense of the rural districts."[15] This mattered because, as Drury explained, rural people "saw a very serious menace to our national life in the decrease of rural population and the lowering of rural standards."[16]

Farmers also noted that parliament and the provincial legislature were dominated by urban business and professional men while farmers were grossly underrepresented. In the pre-election 1919 Ontario legislature, for example, only 18 of the 111 members were farmers even though seventy constituencies were predominantly agricultural. Similarly, only six of Ontario's eighty-two members of the House of Commons listed themselves as farmers. This presumably explained why James Duff, the long-serving and popular Minister of Agriculture under Whitney and Hearst, had little influence in cabinet. On one occasion, the *Daily Star* suggested that he "walk into the Premier's office, with his hat on the back of his head, bang his strong right fist on his leader's desk, and announce that he is not the good-natured joker that his lawyer colleagues take him for and that he is either going to have a little bit of his own way as Minister of Agriculture or he will pack his bag and quit the job."[17] Duff didn't do that, and when he died in November 1916 Hearst made the remarkable decision to take over the department himself, at least temporarily.[18]

The reason he gave was that it would enable him to better understand the needs of farmers so that the government could serve them more effectively. They didn't believe him, for two good reasons: the Department of Agriculture was too important to have only a part-time minister, and Hearst was a lawyer, although he had grown up on a farm.[19] Some thought he should have appointed George Henry, the Conservative MPP for York East, but Dan Spanner, Henry's biographer, claims that Hearst was "unsure of Henry's strength in East York," meaning that he wasn't confident that Henry could win the by-election required when a member of the legislature was appointed to cabinet. This seems unlikely because Henry had served on York Township Council from 1903 to 1919, was township reeve from 1906 to 1910 and warden of York County in 1909, then won York East in a by-election in 1913, and was easily re-elected in the 1914 general election.

More likely was that Hearst had reservations about Henry because he came from a wealthy family; attended Upper Canada College, an elite private school; was a graduate of the University of Toronto; and became a lawyer. While he qualified as a farmer because he owned a dairy farm on the edge of Toronto, he was primarily a businessman who owned a dairy. And as Henry's biographer acknowledges, Henry was not a good party man. "There were clear limits to what George Henry would do for his party; for throughout his long career the concerns of his constituency would always come first, the economic welfare of his province a very close second, and the well-being of the Tory party a distant third."[20] And although a Methodist, he did not think it was the role of government to legislate on moral issues such as temperance.[21] "In truth," according to Spanner, Henry "found the whole temperance issue extremely bothersome" because "social and moral issues could not be allowed to stand in the way of tangible economic progress."[22] Nor does Spanner explain why he thinks that Hearst was insensitive to rural concerns. His government provided enormous support to farmers during the war, so Spanner presumably is referring only to the fact that Hearst didn't appoint a new Minister of Agriculture in 1916, although one wonders why Hearst declined to address the UFO's annual convention in 1917.[23]

Hearst's decision to take charge of the Department of Agriculture "brought serious criticism from the province's farmers" because "their interests required greater consideration than that offered by the Premier, whose own duties were challenging enough."[24] That was true, and one wonders why Hearst did not appoint Finlay MacDiarmid, a popular farmer from Elgin West. Hearst had appointed him Minister of Public Works in 1914 and he proved to be a reliable, hard-working, and versatile minister who took on other responsibilities as well, but he might have been more valuable as Minister of Agriculture. Why Hearst decided finally in 1918 to appoint a Minister of Agriculture is unclear, but exhaustion must have been the major factor because he declined to address the UFO's annual convention in 1917.[25]

And Henry was the obvious choice not only because he was a farmer but also because he had the support of senior members of the UFO such as R.W.E. Burnaby, a cattle breeder who was also president of the UFO, and Manning Doherty, the UFO's vice-president and director of the United Farmers' Co-operative Company. Indeed, Doherty told Henry when he was appointed, "[Y]ou may be assured that you will enjoy the support of all the old OAC [Ontario Agricultural College] boys."[26] What they liked about Henry was that he operated a large dairy farm, but had attended the OAC as well as the University of Toronto, became a lawyer, and was one of the founders in 1910 of Farmers' Dairy, a successful business that supported many other Ontario dairy farmers. In other words, he understood the need for farmers to use modern methods and to integrate with the food and dairy industries.

That was also his problem because there was a growing cleavage between traditional farmers who had learned their trade on the family farm and the "book-smart" graduates of the OAC. As historian Charles Johnston said of Frank Biggs, a graduate of OAC and a prominent farmer in Wentworth County who became Minister of Public Works in the Drury government, he "seemed to be an early prototype of the agricultural businessman; besides his successes as a herdsman, breeder, and dairyman, he was profitably involved in commercial and real estate operations" and "seemed to be a striking example of what would later be called an assimilationist, the farmer who recognized current trends for what they were – in this case urban tastes, technology, and business techniques – adapted to them, and in the process made farming an economically attractive occupation."[27] It may not have helped that York East, the constituency Henry represented, while predominantly rural, also included the outskirts of Toronto.[28]

Men who thought this way were actually engaged in a cultural war. Profoundly convinced that agriculture was the backbone of the nation and the bulwark of democracy, farmers were slipping into second rank socially while urban communities, which they regarded as unproductive and parasitical, were gathering all the wealth and power. This was signified by the condescending attitude of urban people towards them, an attitude perhaps encouraged by the very fact of rural depopulation. In other words, there was a growing sense that people who lived in urban centres thought it was the more intelligent and/or more ambitious people in rural areas who moved into the cities, leaving the dullards on the farms.[29] In 1925 the UFO actually published a pamphlet that it thought "demonstrated the fact that the farmer *is not* a person of low intelligence and high credulity but an individual to be seriously reckoned with in the world of affairs."[30]

At the same time, many religious leaders, particularly those in the Methodist, Presbyterian, and Anglican churches, were recognizing that churches could no longer focus entirely on the traditional theology of salvation when so many people were living in poverty, ill fed and ill housed with no social safety nets such as minimum wages, public health and sanitation programs, compensation if injured at work (until 1914), protection for women and children, and old age pensions, that had not seemed necessary in the past. This was especially true in the growing urban centres, but it was also true of rural communities.

In 1912 church leaders and others who shared these concerns established the Social Service Council of Canada to coordinate and promote their efforts to address these problems. Two years later its first Conference on Charities and Corrections focused on the rural problem. The two key speakers were OAC President George Creelman and Rev. John MacDougall, author of *Rural Life in Canada* (1913), who spoke on rural depopulation.[31] By 1918 the Social Service Council had founded *Social Welfare*, a journal that came to have a major influence in educating people to the prevalence of social problems and the ability of governments to address them. That same year the Social Service Council of Ontario embraced the Rural Community Life Movement, an American initiative that focused on farm economics and labour practices, the disabilities of farm women in isolated communities, and the weakness of rural churches that were inevitably declining along with the rural depopulation. Ministers of "all the mainline Protestant denominations" formed "the "backbone" of the movement, with the result, according to historians Nancy Christie and Michael Gauvreau, that rural issues "achieved equal stature with such causes as mothers' pensions, minimum wage laws, and temperance."[32]

Meanwhile, the Commission of Conservation, established by the Laurier government in 1909 and chaired by Sir Clifford Sifton until 1918, frequently reported in its publication, *Conservation*, on suggestions for modernizing the farm economy. After surveying rural conditions in 1916, the commission concluded, perhaps somewhat surprisingly, that "along with improvements in such basic amenities as plumbing, electrification, and better telephone and mail service, the greatest incentive to keeping women on the farm would be the introduction of the automobile."[33] The Commission of Conservation published several progressive books and reports of this kind, but according to historian Peter J. Smith, "achievements in public policy were not as great" because "governments were slow to accept the commission's advice."[34]

Not surprisingly, the farmers' grievances became much more urgent during the war but not immediately because, according to historian Jonathan Vance, "interest in the outside world was neither broad nor deep"[35] and there was a tendency in rural communities to suspect that business and military people wanted wars for their own selfish interests. The Grange had agitated against military training in the schools and demanded Canadian immunity from imperial military and naval burdens.[36] Vance claims that the people of East Flamborough in Wentworth County were probably typical of rural communities when they "accepted news of the war [in 1914] and went about their business."[37] But the war expanded the industrial economy, further accelerating the growth of urban communities and rural depopulation, while many young men in rural communities enlisted in the army, albeit at a lower rate than young men in urban areas.

Farmers especially resented the drain on their manpower during the war because feeding urban Canadians and the troops, not to mention Britain, was surely just as important and patriotic as having their young men join the army. Indeed, the federal and provincial governments repeatedly told them so. As early as the autumn of 1914 the Borden government had begun urging farmers to increase production as much as possible, and Major General Sir William Otter, Canada's most distinguished soldier, presumably spoke for the army and the government when he urged farmers to regard the production of food for Britain as "one of the greatest services which the Canadian people can render to the Empire."[38] At the outset of the war, the Hearst government donated 250,000 pounds of flour to Britain[39] and Duff launched a "Patriotism and

Production" campaign to encourage farmers to produce as much food as possible because of its importance to the war effort.

From this point on, as the Department of Agriculture's 1915 annual report acknowledged that "the need of the largest possible production from the land was emphasized at every opportunity ... with the result that farmers everywhere put forth their very best efforts, not only utilizing more land but also in adopting better methods."[40] The result was that they produced 28 million bushels of wheat in 1915, compared with 16 million in 1914.[41] Ontario also exported large quantities of butter, cheese, eggs, beef, and bacon to feed the Canadian Corps and the Allied countries.[42]

The Hearst government didn't just urge the farmers to produce more food. It offered practical assistance. It encouraged urban people to plant vegetable gardens, organized a program that enabled between 18,000 and 19,000 high school students – roughly 70 per cent of those enrolled province-wide – to help with seeding and harvesting crops. It also recruited about 2,400 female teachers, university students and married women, known as "farmerettes," to pick fruit and vegetables on the farms in the Niagara Peninsula.[43] It asked manufacturers to release as many workers as possible to help with the harvest and purchased and distributed 130 tractors at a cost of $503,758 and seed grain at a cost of $168,765.[44] When a harsh winter depleted the acreage of fall wheat, the Department of Agriculture purchased 40,000 bushels of wheat from western Canada and encouraged the planting of spring wheat, the acreage of which rose from 182,957 in 1917 to 351,423 in 1918, raising the yield from 3.7 million to 8.3 million bushels. When global demand for wheat reached an all-time high in 1918, the Department of Agriculture purchased 50,000 bushels of spring wheat seed from the federal government and sold it to individual farmers and farmers' clubs. As historian Kerry Badgley has noted, this "achieved three main goals: the province had surplus wheat available for export at harvest time; by and large it was a standard type of wheat; and farmers believed that the state was working in their interests," although "some farmers ... protested that this scheme deliberately undercut the UFCC's seed prices."[45] Similarly, when it was discovered that there was a shortage of livestock feed during the winter of 1917–8, the government purchased stock feed in the United States at a cost of $750,000.[46]

Meanwhile, the Department of Agriculture had established a Cooperation and Markets Branch in 1914 to encourage and facilitate cooperative marketing and assisted in organizing more than 400 Farmers' Clubs in the province, "giving full information as to the organization and business, but leaving the conduct of the business affairs to the farmers themselves."[47] James Simpson Gould, the Conservative candidate in

Lanark South in the 1919 election, went so far as to claim that "seventy-five percent of the cooperative effort of the farmers" was "due to the foundation educational work ... carried out by the Department of Agriculture."[48]

Hearst certainly seemed to understand the importance of the contribution that farmers were making to the war effort. He described farming as a "sacred duty" that "represented a form of national service integral to the successful prosecution of the war and the support of Britain," and if that was not clear enough, declared that "the farmer in the field" was "doing as much in this crisis as the man who goes to the front."[49] In 1917, when the food crisis was much more serious than it had been earlier in the war because of the German submarine blockade, Martin Burrell, the Minister of Agriculture in Borden's government, published an advertisement in daily and weekly newspapers throughout the country declaring that it was "the supreme duty of every man on the land ... to use every thought and every energy in the direction of producing more – and still more" because widespread famine in the Allied countries "would be a worse disaster to the Empire and the Allies than reverses in the Field."[50] But farmers could not expand or even maintain production without the necessary workers, and there was already a shortage of farm workers by 1916.[51]

Meanwhile, there was a shortage of coal, which was essential not only for the war industries but also for home heating and to run some electrical power plants. The federal government appointed food, fuel, and power controllers in an effort to manage the situation, but farmers found themselves being accused of profiteering while nothing was being done about manufacturers and food processing plants. This, as J.J. Morrison pointed out, "created an acute cleavage between the producer and consumer who each fancied that the other was the exploiter and did not realize it was the exploiting middle man who got the profits."[52] That cleavage was also aggravated by reports that farmers did not contribute as generously as urban people to the Canadian Patriotic Fund or the Victory Loan campaigns.[53] Some urban observers jumped to the conclusion that this reflected less enthusiasm for the war effort in rural areas but the more likely explanation was that farmers generally tended not to have much ready cash available except at harvest time, aside from the surely obvious fact that there was a much greater concentration of capital in urban areas. The size of the urban contributions was also skewed by the fact that many companies, especially those engaged in the production of war materiel, made large donations.

The flashpoint in the growing tension between urban and rural values and attitudes was conscription. In 1916, before the issue became critical, the UFO stated unequivocally that "the conscription of men for battle" was "a manifest and glaring injustice while plutocrats, fattening on special privileges and war business, are left in undisturbed possession of their riches.[54] Underlying the debate, however, was the fact that there seemed to be less enthusiasm for the war in rural communities than in urban communities, but the UFO took no part in the 1917 federal election campaign and issued no statements. At least two of its leading figures, however – E.C. Drury and George Burgess – ran as independent candidates in Simcoe South and Lanark. But when the Union government realized how strongly farmers objected to the conscription of their sons, it promised late in the campaign to exempt them if they were needed on the family farm. The result was that Unionist candidates won a resounding victory in Ontario, including the rural areas, because farmers didn't object to the conscription of other people's sons, especially French Canadians. But this cynical decision aggravated the growing rift between urban and rural communities because the idea of exemptions for farm boys was bound to be resented by urban families whose sons were being conscripted. Judging from the hostility expressed in some of the newspapers, they were. This naturally frustrated farmers because, as E.C. Drury explained, "we are not seeking to escape military duty ... We were told that food production was of paramount importance, and now we are called food profiteers."[55]

The need for farm labour was even greater in 1918 than it had been in 1917, a fact acknowledged on 20 March by provincial politicians when the legislature voted unanimously in favour of a resolution moved by Hearst and Proudfoot praising "the strenuous and patriotic efforts which the farmers of Ontario have made and are making to produce more crops." No doubt the farmers appreciated this gesture but perhaps not the resolution's call on them to make "unprecedented efforts" to produce even more, even though the supply of farm labour had "become seriously insufficient ... and many of those left on the farms, both men and women, are working to the limit of human endurance."[56]

In an attempt to help the farmers, the Organization of Resources Committee joined the new Canada Food Board in an effort to recruit people, "particularly those living in urban centres," to volunteer as Soldiers of the Soil. This initiative was supported unanimously by the members of the legislature, who declared that "every man, woman, boy, or girl who labours this year to help the farmers to produce more food is a veritable soldier of the soil" and was "playing a most worthy and essential part ... in ensuring that the sacrifices hitherto made by our soldiers and our heroic dead shall not have been made in vain, and in hastening the hour of final Victory."[57]

The initial quota was 15,000, but some 16,700 volunteered in the first two days. On 24 April the local Soldiers of the Soil and "farmerettes" paraded through the streets of Toronto led by five tractors and three bands.[58] The timing of this event proved to be unfortunate, however, because the federal government had just cancelled the exemptions for farmers' sons and conscientious objectors, totally alienating the farmers and understandably dampening the enthusiasm of the urban volunteers. A well-meaning but insensitive suggestion in the urban press that city women might go out and cook meals on the farms to release farm women to work in the fields was not well received by farmers either.[59]

When George Henry became Minister of Agriculture in May 1918, he tried to be helpful by travelling around the province praising the farmers "for their patriotic perseverance in helping to win the War."[60] Less helpful – even if true – was his comment on the hot-button issue of rural depopulation when he pointed out that not all of the young people who were leaving the province's rural communities were moving into its urban centres; Ontario was also "sending the best of our sons and daughters to the west," where they were continuing to live on farms in rural communities.[61] Equally insensitive was his claim that the amount of land being farmed in Ontario had grown by 560,000 acres during the war because mechanization had improved efficiency and productivity and many farmers were shifting to dairy and livestock operations that were less labour-intensive. His point, of course, was that farmers' sons could be spared for military service.

Frank Carvell, the Minister of Public Works in the Union government, threw gasoline on the flames when he foolishly claimed that "thousands and tens of thousands, yes, hundreds of thousands among the farming classes … have tried assiduously to evade military service," resorting to "every device … to which the ingenuity of men could think of [*sic*]."[62] If he was referring to the fact that the vast majority of young farmers applied for exemption when they were called up, that was true, but so did the vast majority of men in urban areas.[63] Then, when the federal government panicked because of the German army's shocking breakthrough on the Western Front in March and cancelled the exemption of farmers' sons, the response was an explosion of outrage from the farmers, who thought they "had been duped."[64] About 3,000 farmers from Ontario and 2,000 from "disloyal" Quebec descended on Ottawa, seeking to present their case to Borden. But when they paraded to the Victoria Memorial Museum, the building temporarily housing parliament since the fire in the Centre Block in 1916, they were blocked at the entrance and Borden initially refused to meet with them.[65]

This was the turning point in the evolution of the UFO into a political movement. Peter McArthur, the prominent rural affairs journalist, spoke for many when he suggested that, "instead of being the end of a futile protest, it may be the beginning of a movement that will shape the destiny of Canada."[66] M.H. Staples, the UFO's educational director, agreed, saying that "this literal shutting of the door in their faces did more than any one thing to cause the political upheaval," which subsequently took place.[67] In 1915, the executive had agreed not to take stands on public issues, and the 1917 convention had only gone so far as to authorize the appointment of a committee to report annually on legislation affecting agricultural interests.[68] That, clearly, had not been enough. The UFO now organized protest meetings throughout the province, and Morrison summoned a mass protest meeting at Toronto's Massey Hall that was attended by more than 3,000 farmers, who decided on direct political action. At the same time, frustrated by the fact that all of Toronto's newspapers had supported the government against the farmers on conscription, the meeting decided that farmers needed a newspaper that would represent their interests. The result was that the UFO acquired the *Weekly Sun*, which had already been serving as its unofficial organ, renaming it the *Farmers' Sun*.

But there would not likely be another federal election for three years. There would, however, be a provincial election before that, probably in 1919, and Hearst and his colleagues had stood foursquare behind the Union government and conscription. They had, it was felt, not only not done much for farmers but had declared a political truce at Queen's Park. Federal and provincial, Conservative or Liberal, they all represented the same interests and shared the same values even though 63 per cent of Ontario's provincial constituencies were predominantly rural. The real problem, of course, was not conscription. It was, as R.H. Halbert said, that "government by the people is a myth. The real rulers of Canada are the knighted heads of combines."[69] If this was true, and many thought it was, it followed logically that only farmers, coming from the clean air and pure soil of the country, should organize and mobilize their power to create a government that actually represented the people. Their goal, as Drury said, was "to sweep the two old parties into a single organization, which they really are," and "form the nucleus of a new party ... that will stand for wisdom, justice and honesty in public affairs; a party untainted by campaign funds contributed by selfish interests, and that will cleanse the whole public life of Canada."[70] Not all militant farmers shared Drury's vision of creating a new political party, however. Many believed that the party system itself was the problem and sought to replace it with one in which representatives of the various economic interests would meet to promote "the general welfare of the community."[71]

The UFO started out by "stealing" the farmers' clubs that the Ontario Department of Agriculture had established to replace the Grange clubs. There were some 250 of them throughout the province, and their primary purpose was to promote advanced methods of agriculture and introduce new equipment. But because they also provided some of the few occasions when local farmers got together, Morrison conceived the idea of making them the nucleus of the new movement.[72] In March 1917 the UFO had 200 clubs and 8,000 members, a number that rose to 350 clubs and 12,000 members by December. By December 1918, when the end of the war had proven that the cancellation of the farmers' exemption from conscription had been unnecessary, there were 615 clubs and 25,000 members. Their growth did not end with the war either. During 1919 the numbers almost doubled again to 1,130 clubs and 48,000 members.[73] Meanwhile, women's and youth organizations had also been established and were flourishing and the circulation of the *Farmers' Sun* was growing rapidly. At the same time, sales by the United Farmers' Cooperative EC: Company, which had been established in 1914, soared from $1.8 million in 1918 to $8.5 million by the end of 1919.[74] What made this dramatic growth so impressive was the fact that it was taking place in a genuine grass-roots movement to which the central executive responded more than it led.

It was in this environment that Hearst called a by-election for 24 October 1918 to fill the vacancy in Manitoulin created by the death of Robert Gamey in March 1917. When the Liberals again honoured the political truce, Hearst expected either an acclamation or an easy contest, as in Toronto Northeast and York East, but the local farmers weren't having that and what he got was a humiliating wake-up call. Aside from their general dissatisfaction, conscription, the cancellation of the exemption of farmers' sons and the federal government's hard line on public dissent were the major issues. While the local tribunals set up to deal with the many thousands of claims for exemption had been generous in their decisions, there had been some harsh court rulings that were widely reported in the press. The most significant one involved George Gray, an unmarried young farmer who had homesteaded in Nipissing and was cultivating thirty-six acres with no one to help him. When the local tribunal rejected his claim for exemption, Gray challenged the constitutionality of the order in council cancelling the exemption of farmers from conscription, on the grounds that the Alberta Appellate Division had just declared that the government did not have the power under the Military Service Act to override decisions of military tribunals. What Gray only learned in court was that the cabinet had passed secret orders in council overturning the Alberta decision, establishing regulations applicable only to the Gray case, and expressly prohibiting challenges to the Supreme Court on his habeas corpus application. When the case reached the Supreme Court, it not only upheld the validity of the order in council but sentenced Gray to life imprisonment.[75] This was when, following a 1918 conscription riot in Quebec City, the government passed an order-in-council permitting the military to prosecute individuals by court martial.

That understandably shocked the farmers, but the government was even more heavy-handed when it charged a number of farmers with sedition for criticizing it. According to historian Jonathan Swinger, prosecutions for sedition between 1914 and 1918 took place throughout Canada, but the number of them in Ontario (25) was exceeded only by Alberta (48).[76] J.A. Cross of Brant, for example, was convicted and fined $500 for comparing the government to the Prussian government by a judge who had declared that "a lot of farmers need to be jailed" and that he "was going to put the agitation of the farmers down." On appeal, Ontario's Chief Justice, Sir William Meredith – a former leader of the Conservative Party – bizarrely ruled that these comments were not evidence of bias.[77] Isaac Bainbridge, a leading member of the Social Democratic Party and editor of the *Canadian Forward* newspaper, was charged three times with seditious libel and once for possession of seditious material for opposing conscription, and twice served more than four months in prison (November 1917 to February 1918 and May to June 1918). His experiences with the law were well reported and he had strong support from the labour movement, the UFO, and even mainstream newspapers such as Toronto's *Daily Star*.[78]

Both the Military Service Act and the War Measures Act were, of course, federal measures, but Hearst had not merely supported conscription but had been one of the Union government's most prominent campaigners in Ontario in the 1917 federal election. And he had certainly made perfectly clear his views about those who did not enlist or did not show total support for the war effort. By now, however, he was trying to distance himself from Ottawa, pointing out that "everything pertaining to Military Affairs belongs to the Federal Government and the Ontario government has nothing to do with it."[79] But conscription was not the only issue in Manitoulin. As historian Foster Griezic has shown, the farmers there – reputedly among the poorest in the province – had not been impressed by Hearst's management of the Department of Agriculture, and his belated appointment of George Henry to the ministry didn't help much. Like many farmers across the province, they had come to the conclusion that it was time "for the assumption of the duties of leadership by an organization that has something clear-cut to offer a mass of disorganized electors looking for real leadership."[80]

It cannot be said that Hearst offered leadership in the Manitoulin by-election. The Conservatives unwisely ran Byron Turner, a merchant, former mayor of Little Current and long-time president of the local Conservative Association, who had run unsuccessfully in the 1904 federal election. Even so, J.D. McColeman, a former Conservative who was now the secretary of the Manitoulin UFO Club, which had only been organized in the spring of 1918, initially reached out to Hearst, asking if he would support a UFO candidate if one were nominated. "We know there is one candidate already, but we don't know whether he will meet the approval of the majority of the farmers here," and if not the UFO would offer a candidate. This obviously placed Hearst in an awkward position, and he responded by pointing out that the local Conservatives who had chosen Turner included farmers. He also assured McColeman that Turner would represent the farmers and urged the UFO not to force a contest. He was out of touch. McColeman then approached the Liberals, who refused to run a candidate.[81]

That forced the UFO to make a bold decision: to support Turner and hope that he would adequately represent the interests of farmers or to run a candidate of their own who would definitely represent their interests. The UFO held a nominating convention on 29 August and nine men were nominated. Among them were McColeman and John Learmont, a prominent former Liberal. The man selected, however, was Beniah Bowman, a farmer and Mennonite minister whom Morrison described as a "fairly good speaker, good looking, robust and honest."[82] It was a momentous decision, one that would be watched with much interest not only by both the Conservatives and Liberals but also by those in the UFO movement who thought it should become politically active.

Hearst understood the significance of this by-election. Not only was the record of his government on trial, but so too was his own political power in northern Ontario, if not throughout the province. He therefore personally visited the constituency, something he had not done in any of the previous by-elections. He even brought Bella with him to host an afternoon tea for the women of Gore Bay, who would be voting for the first time. As things turned out, it would have been better if he had stayed in Toronto because his performance certainly didn't help either Turner or his own reputation. Instead of reaching out to the farmers, he attacked Bowman for forcing an election "when the very foundations of liberty are tottering." This was an odd comment in late October 1918, but the suggestion that voters had no right to choose who should represent them during wartime was foolish in the extreme. Some in Manitoulin may not have been surprised by it, however, because Hearst had denied them representation in the legislature for the past seventeen months since Gamey's death.

But that was just the beginning. Hearst then attacked Bowman on religious grounds, asking "[B]y what right should this man seek to make the laws of the land and leave it to you and your sons to fight and perchance to die to defend these laws?"[83] His not-very-subtle point was that Bowman was a Mennonite, a religious sect some of whose members had sought exemption from conscription because they were pacifists. Hearst's outbursts were not accidental; they set the stage for the Conservative campaign. Because there were several Orange lodges in Manitoulin, H.C. Hocken, the Grand Master of the Orange Order and former mayor of Toronto and MP since 1917, campaigned for Turner, denouncing Mennonites as a "menace" to Canada and "not worthy to enjoy those priceless privileges of freedom which are the heritage of the Anglo-Saxon race." The Orange *Sentinel* – which Hocken personally owned and edited – went further, declaring that Mennonites should not even be allowed to vote, let alone serve in legislatures or parliament. The *Weekly Sun* responded to that by listing the names of hundreds of Mennonite ministers and their sons who had volunteered for military service.[84]

Hearst's performance was not just offensive; it was also very weak. And unfortunately for him, J.J. Morrison had had gone up to Manitoulin – on the same train as Hearst – and followed him around the constituency, speaking in the same places a day later and responding to Hearst's statements. To Hearst's ill-considered attack on Bowman, Morrison declared that the farmers of Manitoulin gladly accepted the responsibility for wanting to vote on who was going to represent them. Besides, he suggested, sarcastically but to the delight of many, the women of Gore Bay would never have been treated to afternoon tea with Lady Hearst if her husband had not called the by-election. In fact, Hearst would not have bothered to visit the riding himself if there hadn't been a by-election.[85] That was a bit of an exaggeration but not entirely unjustified because Hearst's visits to Sault Ste. Marie and the surrounding area had become rare since the outbreak of the war.

Morrison later believed that the by-election was won at his first campaign meeting, but Hearst "proceeded to give new ammunition at every meeting throughout the campaign. He was honest in his remarks but did not understand the new psychology he was facing in the farmers' movement. From meeting to meeting he left himself open to similar damaging thrusts and before the campaign was over the farmers had unknowingly formed themselves into a solid fighting force gaining strength every day."[86] When Hearst realized that old friends in Manitoulin didn't want to be seen speaking to him for fear of arousing the wrath of farmers, he wisely retreated to Toronto and sent in MacDiarmid, McGarry, and Henry to campaign on Turner's behalf.[87]

It was in vain. The farmers and their wives turned out in large numbers on polling day and elected the first UFO member of the legislature, albeit with a narrow majority of 240 votes.[88] The Toronto *Daily Star* concluded, simplistically, that the result reflected the dissatisfaction of the farmers, but the reality was more complicated than that. Morrison claimed that Bowman was actually elected by "the Orange Tory vote,"[89] a surprising interpretation but one that was shared by the *Globe* and the *Sault Daily Star*, a Conservative paper. It was certainly true that Bowman had won almost twice as many votes as Turner in the traditionally rural Conservative communities, but Turner did much better in the towns. In fact, as Griezic points out, "the polling centres that supported Bowman were almost identical to Gamey's areas of strength in 1914."[90] As for Hearst, fixated as he seemed to be on the Mennonite threat to Canadian values, he attributed Bowman's victory to the large number of Mennonites that he thought lived in Manitoulin, who had voted against conscription. In fact there were only about a dozen Mennonite families in the area. They doubtless did vote for Bowman, not least because of Hearst's attacks on them, but there weren't enough of them to make a significant difference.

It's not at all clear if Hearst really appreciated the significance of this loss. Losing Manitoulin, a Conservative riding since 1902, was unfortunate but would not necessarily be considered significant except for the fact that it had been lost to a candidate who didn't even have a party organization behind him other than the UFO clubs in the area. But Hearst had put his own personal prestige on the line; Manitoulin was in northern Ontario adjacent to Algoma, he had personally campaigned there, and there was no denying that he and what he represented had been rejected. More important was the fact that he had not effectively responded to a local populist uprising because he didn't understand it.

But others did. Morrison believed that the victory in Manitoulin launched "organized agriculture into active politics and [gave] a new impetus to the United Farmer Movement."[91] The UFO's provincial leaders responded by producing a platform-style document that included direct legislation, proportional representation, a provincial reforestation policy, equal educational opportunities for all children, abolition of patronage, and a reduction in public spending, including reducing the cost but not the expansion of the Hydro Commission. The public power issue was more important among farmers than is usually acknowledged. They could see its benefits, but the cost of power in rural areas was much higher than in urban areas, which is why only 2,900 rural residences in the province had received power through short-line extensions from existing urban and suburban systems.[92] According to the *Farmers' Sun*, however, the UFO's two top priorities were to eliminate government waste and abolish party patronage.[93] Because the UFO leaders, like Hearst, thought the temperance issue should be taken out of politics, their document only promised to support whatever decision the voters made in the promised referendum.

Undeterred, Hearst called another by-election, in Huron North, to take place in December 1918. It was caused by the retirement of the Conservative incumbent, Armstrong Musgrove, who had held the seat since its creation in 1908. Hearst expected an acclamation because Proudfoot was still honouring the political truce and the UFO was not thought to be strong in the constituency. But when the local Conservatives met to nominate Musgrove's successor, the result was a disaster. Two men, Dr. Thomas Case, a physician at Wawanosh and George Spotton, a Wingham businessman, sought the nomination, and when the voting resulted in a tie, the chairman cast the deciding ballot in favour of Spotton. Case and his supporters walked out in protest, and he ran as an independent. That provided an opportunity for dissident Liberals, and they, possibly supported by local UFO members, nominated William Henry Fraser, a local farmer, who ran as an independent. When he won, Hearst understandably claimed that the loss had been expected because of the Conservative division and that the combined votes of Case and Spotton exceeded Fraser's vote. That, he concluded, while regrettable, "would not indicate a lack of popularity on the part of the government in the riding,"[94] and he was probably right because John Joynt took the seat back for the Conservatives in 1919 and held it until 1926.

Two months later the Conservatives lost another by-election in Ontario North, a formerly safe seat held since 1898 by William Hoyle until his death in October 1918. Encouraged by the results in Manitoulin and Huron North, the local farmers, "without consulting the leadership of the UFO,"[95] nominated J.W. Widdifield, an Uxbridge farmer and former Liberal who ran as a non-partisan candidate, focusing on issues of importance to farmers and rural society and emphasizing the inherent corruption and inefficiency of the traditional political system. Hearst sent Henry, McGarry, and Lucas to campaign in this predominantly rural constituency, and they defended the government's general record with an emphasis on its war effort. The Liberals not only did not run a candidate but, according to the *World*, Proudfoot was seen "visiting and dining with Mr. Henry" during the campaign.[96]

The *World* reported as early as 7 February that "the farmers expect to win,"[97] which Widdifield did with a comfortable majority, although Harry Cameron, the Conservative candidate, carried the towns and villages.

Hearst did not comment publicly on the result, but Henry insensitively dismissed the loss as "just one of those temporary waves which are seen periodically in the politics of every country" and did not reflect dissatisfaction with the government.[98] That seemed a remarkably obtuse statement, and it was also dishonest because, as the *World* pointed out early in the campaign, the government had been "determined to prevent the farmers from taking a third consecutive fall out of them"[99] and it had failed. Indeed, it had lost three by-elections in a row, two of them to a "party," that didn't formally exist.

Farmers weren't the only people upset with the government. So too were many working men and women in urban communities. Like the farmers, many workers had been trying for years to create organizations that would speak on their behalf and represent their interests. Their situation was different from that of farmers, of course, because farmers were in effect small businessmen, while workers were employees. It had been illegal for them to form unions to represent them until 1872 when the Macdonald government legalized them. That gave them the right to strike, but picketing remained illegal until 1934. In the 1880s the Knights of Labour, an American fraternal organization, established branches in Ontario and elsewhere but failed to become a significant force.[100] More importantly, the Canadian Trades and Labour Congress (TLC) was founded in 1886 to represent workers and encourage direct labour representation in local councils, provincial legislatures, and the federal parliament.

The Laurier government recognized early on the growing need to accept some responsibility for managing problems related to industrialization and created a Department of Labour in 1900. It only had a part-time minister, who was already Postmaster General, but he was William Mulock, a major force in the Ontario party, and he wisely hired the young, progressive, and very ambitious William Lyon Mackenzie King to be his deputy minister. That same year the TLC decided to form an independent labour party, and six years later it authorized provincial organizations to do the same.[101] Thus, in contrast to the various farmers' associations, organized labour sought almost from the outset to take direct political action.

The results of the two different approaches were about the same initially: neither accomplished very much. Both faced the same problem: that most of their members supported one of the established political parties and weren't convinced of the need for or wisdom of independent interest-based parties. Growing industrial unrest in the years before 1914 and the strains brought on by the war soon changed that. As Toronto's *Daily Star* concluded in 1915, it was pointless for delegations to wait upon the governments at Ottawa and Queen's Park demanding various reforms when they controlled few if any votes. Governments would only pay attention and be responsive when they knew that the delegations' demands were backed by thousands of votes.[102]

The reality was that industrialization provided jobs but life for many if not most workers was a constant struggle because of low wages, unsafe and unhealthy working conditions, crowded and unhealthy living conditions because of the cost of urban housing, and the absence of a social support system such as unemployment insurance, workmen's compensation (until 1914), and pensions. But social reformers and some politicians were beginning to recognize that the very serious problems created by having large numbers of people crowded into inner-city slums lacking essential services such as public health regulations, clean water, inside toilets, and garbage collection needed to be addressed. The population of Toronto, for example, more than doubled in the first two decades of the century, stimulated by industrialization that accelerated during the war. At the same time, the influx of workers flattened wages, at least until enlistments created a shortage of workers during the war.

Many labour leaders in Canada and elsewhere opposed war in principle on the ground that it only benefited businessmen and financiers at the expense of workers, and there is no denying that the war did have a serious negative impact on them. They inevitably supplied most of the men who filled the ranks serving overseas, leaving their families to cope without a wage earner. It was true that soldiers could assign a portion of their pay to a family member, but an enlisted man's pay was very modest, and the government didn't provide any support for dependent families, although both the federal and provincial governments contributed to the Canadian Patriotic Fund, a private organization that raised millions of dollars to assist thousands of families. At the same time, working-class families lived with the very reasonable fear that their husband, father, or son might not be coming home, or if he did, his injuries – whether physical or psychological – might make him unemployable and there were no pensions for soldiers or their dependents when Canada went to war. Accordingly, while most workers shared the general view that German imperialism was a threat to all freedom-loving people and had to be defeated, they also had good reason to be worried about the cost, and some of them understandably became radicalized.

Life on the home front became increasingly difficult as the war dragged on. In addition to food shortages, there was also a shortage of coal, which heated virtually all urban homes, and inflation in its price because Ontario imported its coal from the United States. The federal government gradually realized that it had to intervene and appointed food and fuel controllers to try to manage what was available and encourage efficient consumption. Even so, there was such a shortage of coal in January 1918 that R.C. Harris, Toronto's long-time Commissioner of Public Works who had been appointed provincial fuel controller, limited householders to a two months' supply, restricted lighting in shops, theatres, offices, homes, and on the streets, encouraged churches to combine services, closed some schools for weeks, and required others to organize classes on a shift basis. In February the federal fuel controller closed all manufacturing plants for three days with the exception of war plants, newspapers, and businesses producing perishable goods. No heat was provided for offices, shops, and warehouses, and food shops were only allowed heat during the morning hours. Between 18 February and 25 March Mondays were "heatless" in all places of amusement. The crisis was relieved only by the arrival of spring.[103]

Meanwhile, many workers were becoming disillusioned by the war. The overblown patriotic propaganda with which the country had been flooded, with its grossly distorted depictions of Germans as Hun barbarians, was wearing thin. Mark Irish, who was now Director of Labour at the Imperial Munitions Board, noted in the spring of 1918 that productivity in war plants had declined by 30 per cent, which he attributed to the fact that "all the enthusiasm and all the idea that munitions are vitally essential had gone out of the minds of the workpeople and ... today they take the War, and the work related to it, as they take the sunrise – an incident of the day."[104] That may have been just war weariness or it may have reflected labour's failure to win what it regarded as fair contracts in the IMB's war supply contracts, a factor that historian David Bercuson has described as being "of singular importance in the development of trade union apathy towards the hoopla and bunting of the government's campaign of organized patriotism."[105]

There was no denying that the attitude of many workers towards the war had changed over time. In 1914 recruiters had been able to turn away more than half of the "keenest volunteers" because they did not meet the army's modest standards, and many more were rejected when they failed the Canadian Expeditionary Force's (CEF's) "stringent medical exams that demanded good teeth, high arches, and healthy lungs." By 1916, however, the CEF was so desperate for volunteers that it "routinely embraced" the "malformed, maladjusted, and miniscule [*sic*]," and even then it wasn't getting enough men.[106] Of the 261,695 men examined under the Military Service Act in 1917–8, 181,225 – almost 70 per cent – were found physically unfit to serve in the army.[107] Meanwhile, workers saw businessmen growing wealthier on war contracts, so when in July 1917 the federal government called on all men to register so that it could ascertain the nation's manpower reserves, district labour councils in Ontario responded by calling for the conscription of wealth as well.

Not coincidentally, this was when the Independent Labour Party (ILP) was founded in Hamilton, an industrial community and hotbed of labour radicalism that was already represented in the legislature by Allan Studholme, Ontario's first Labour MPP.[108] The ILP represented the coming together of local labour parties that had been organized in several industrial communities as early as November 1916.[109] Declaring grandly that "we stand for the industrial freedom of those who toil, and the political liberation of those who have long been denied justice,"[110] the ILP's platform was similar to that of the Canadian Labour Party, which was founded a few months later at the instigation of the TLC, to which were added demands that Canada complete the steps necessary to achieve independence from Great Britain and that the banking and credit systems be eliminated along with all unearned increment through progressive income tax. It also sought pensions for mothers with dependent children and old age pensions. ILP members were forbidden to belong to any other party, although they were free to support the candidates of farmers' and other non-capitalistic parties.[111] There was much traditional British working-class idealism here.

The last straw for labour was the formation of the Union government in 1917, in which politicians of both parties joined together to more effectively support the war effort. From the labour point of view, what this really meant was that they were joining together to force working men to go overseas to fight while leaving wealthy businessmen to profit from manufacturing and selling war supplies. Not coincidentally, the provincial Conservatives and Liberals in Ontario agreed to a wartime political truce. That meant in effect that there were no politicians in Ontario – with the notable exception of Allan Studholme and Hartley Dewart – speaking for the workers. The result was that the ILP, under the leadership of Walter Rollo, secretary of the Hamilton TLC, ran nineteen candidates in the 1917 federal election.[112]

None were elected and T.W. Crothers, a sixty-seven-year-old lawyer from St. Thomas who had been appointed Minister of Labour in 1911, remained in that position in the Union government. Borden had, however, appointed Gideon Robertson, a former telegrapher from Hamilton, to the Senate in January 1917 and included him in the cabinet as a minister without portfolio, and he succeeded Crothers as minister in November 1918. He seems to have had little influence, because the politicians in the Union government reflected the views of most businessmen who believed that the labour movement was infected by alien influences and/or that the good men had enlisted, leaving the rabble to make trouble at home.[113] It was an odd attitude in view of the fact that most labour leaders were Canadian-born or British immigrants.

The real concern of the business community was that the labour movement had grown dramatically during the war, with union membership rising from 140,000 in 1915 to 250,000 in 1918, at least 40 per cent of them in Ontario.[114] It also grew more militant: the number of working days lost in Ontario because of strikes rose from 25,000 in 1915 to more than 120,000 in 1918,[115] and according to labour historian Greg Kealey, the spring of 1919 was "the greatest period of industrial unrest in Canadian history."[116] Ontario led the country with 158 of the 428 strikes that took place in Canada that year in industrial communities such as Toronto, Brampton, Hamilton, Kingston, Ottawa, London, St. Catharines, Windsor, Welland, Midland, Peterborough, Collingwood, Cobalt, Kirkland Lake, Fort William, and Port Arthur.[117]

The reasons were not hard to identify. Companies that had employed so many men – and women – during the war no longer had contracts, so they were laying off large numbers of workers. Sudbury was especially hard hit by the greatly reduced demand for nickel, and 4,000 men had lost their jobs by May 1919.[118] So alarmed was the federal government that it appointed a royal commission to "enquire into Industrial Relations in Canada." When it travelled across Canada from late April to June, it not only heard workers' grievances but was told repeatedly and emphatically on many occasions that capitalism was beyond reform and must be transformed.[119] Frederick Eldridge, the secretary of the Sudbury TLC, told the commission that "the workers do not get enough of that which they produce," that the government should own all means of production, and that "hundreds of workmen in Sudbury ... think the same thing."[120] Many others made similar comments. In other words, as was obvious from the Winnipeg general strike, many in the labour movement had moved on from seeking improved labour legislation to demanding systemic change.

This rising labour unrest reflected the impact of the war on "the problems created by the government's wartime policies, particularly the failure to deal with inflation," which "intensified the sense of exploitation felt by workers."[121] As Mourad Djebabla notes, inflation had been a problem since before the war; but "it reached record levels" during the war, rising by 71.7 per cent between 1915 and 1920; and it was "felt particularly in the towns, the main area of consumption, affecting first the poorest working classes."[122] There was little a provincial government could do to mitigate this problem, however, other than the reconstruction programs and services that it had been developing since 1917 for both the veterans who were returning home and others having to adjust to the changing conditions.

The ILP's unsuccessful participation (nineteen unsuccessful candidates) in the 1917 federal election had not discouraged it, and workers were now even more angry and frustrated. The ILP directly challenged the government for the first time in a by-election held in St. Catharines during the same week as the Ontario North by-election. The Conservatives had held the constituency (Lincoln, reorganized in 1914 as St. Catharines) since Elisha Jessop, a popular physician, won it in 1898 and held it until his death in October 1918. The Conservatives nominated Fred Parnell, a businessman, Orangeman, and Mason who was also president of the St. Catharines Conservative Association. Once again the Liberals did not run a candidate and quietly supported Parnell. But the ILP nominated W.E. Longden, an unemployed mechanic and returned soldier who was virtually unknown in the community.[123] According to the *World*, his nomination was initially "regarded as a joke," but in the course of his campaign he gained "more and more support."[124] Prominent labour leaders such as Allan Studholme, Tom Moore, Walter Rollo, M.M. MacBride, and Harry Halford campaigned on his behalf. So too did Rose Henderson, the fiery Montreal social activist, who spent two weeks campaigning for Longden and mobilizing women on his behalf.[125]

Longden focused his campaign on the government's reconstruction program, declaring that "the soldiers and their wives ... had not suffered for four long years to be reduced to poverty in peacetime" and accusing Hearst of "having no practical plan for bridging the war to peace gap with its prospect of widespread unemployment."[126] Hearst sent in McGarry, normally one of the government's best campaigners, but he seemed insensitive to the very real and understandable concerns of veterans. He certainly didn't help Parnell's cause when he foolishly took a cheap shot at Henderson at a campaign rally, asking why people in St. Catharines should take advice from a woman from Quebec, "the province that has sent a miserable 25,000 men to the front." It was, he declared, "an insult to the intelligence of the people of Ontario – an insult to the loyal ladies of this gloriously loyal province."[127] That kind of attack represented an old-fashioned approach to politics for which many people, especially workers and veterans, had no patience after four years of war. According to Joseph Marks, the ILP's provincial secretary, McGarry's remarks were not well received by "the bulk of the audience" who were "in favor of the Labour candidate, every reference to his name being received with applause."[128]

Much to Hearst's relief, Parnell retained the seat but only by 174 votes. The closeness of the vote in a traditionally Conservative constituency even with Liberal support indicated not only the seriousness of labour unrest and the growing strength of the ILP but also the emergence of women and veterans as political factors as well. As the *Daily Star* acknowledged, the result reflected "something … intangible," a political awakening, "a feeling justified or unjustified that power hitherto has been exercised by a comparatively few men to their own advantage, and that the common people have been making a mistake not only in the class of representatives they have been sending, but in bowing the knee to inflexible idols of partisan party politics."[129] Or as the *World* more simply put it, "the Labor party has arrived in Ontario politics."[130]

Fig 1: The Hearst Farm, Arkwright, Bruce County LAC, Mikan No. 3301114.

Fig 2: Tara, 1905. Courtesy of Bruce County Museum & Cultural Centre, A2014.008.1097, Valentine & Sons Publishing Co. Ltd.

Fig 3: Sault Ste. Marie, 1910. Toronto Reference Library, Baldwin Collection, Call Number/Accession Number PC-ON 1899.

Fig 4: Hearst c1910. Sault Ste. Marie Library and Archives.

Fig 5: Lake Superior Corporation Industries, Sault Ste. Marie, 1910. Toronto Reference Library, Baldwin Collection, Call Number/Accession Number PC-ON 1895.

Fig 6: Sir James Whitney. Wikimedia Commons.

Fig 7: Photo of Hearst at the presentation of colours to the 160th Battalion at Chesley 3 June 1916, presided over by Lieutenant Colonel Robert Johnston. Mayor M.A. Halliday donated the colours and his wife presented them. Johnston was a local businessman, politician, and officer in the militia, but Adam Weir was the commanding officer of the battalion. Bruce County Museum & Cultural Centre. A958.075.001.

Fig 8: Prohibition, Toronto Daily Star, 16 September 1916 (Toronto Star).

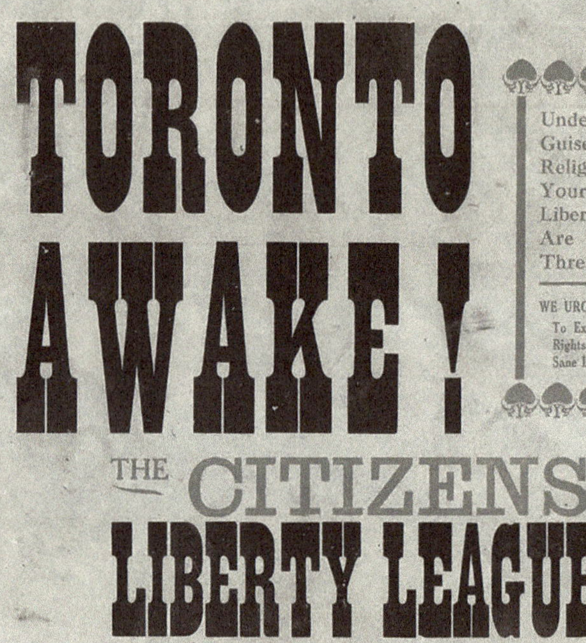

Fig 9: Toronto Awake Poster, c 1919. (Vintage Toronto Photos).

Fig 10: Opening of Toronto-Hamilton Highway, 24 November 1917. City of Toronto Archives, Fonds 1548; Alan Howard fonds; Series 393, Item 20.

# Ontario Emergency Volunteer Health Auxiliary

# Wanted, Volunters!!

The Provincial Board of Health, with the authority of the Government of Ontario, has organized an "Ontario Emergency Volunteer Health Auxiliary" for the purpose of training and supplying nursing help to be utilized wherever needed in combatting the Influenza outbreak. A Strong executive has been formed in Toronto. It is strongly recommended that each municipal council and local Board of Health, working in co-operation, take immediate steps to form a local branch of this organization. The Volunteer Nurses will wear the officially authorized badge, "ONTARIO S.O.S." (Sisters of Service. This "S.O.S." call may be urgent. Classes taking lectures are already opened in the Parliament Buildings, Toronto "Private Bills' Committee Room, ground floor", where they will be carried on every day at 10 a.m. and 3 p.m. until further notice. Young women of education are urged to avail themselves of this unique opportunity to be of real service to the community. If they are not needed, so much the better. If they are needed, we hope to have them ready. All towns and cities are urged to organzie and prepare in a similar manner.

A Syllabus of lectures is being sent to the Medicial Officer of Health of all cities and towns. Further information may be had on application to John W. S. McCullough, M.D., Chairman of Executive, Parliament Buildings, Toronto, Telephone Main 5800.

C. S. NEWTON, Secretary-Treasurer.
W. D. McPHERSON, President.
J. W. S. McCULLOUGH, Chairman of Executive Committee.

Fig 11: "Wanted, Volunteers" poster. Belleville Intelligencer, 16 October 1918; (Firstworldwarbelleville.ca).

Fig 12: Adam Beck. Wikimedia Commons.

Fig 13: Howard Ferguson. Wikimedia Commons.

Fig 14: I.B. Lucas, 1919. Wikimedia Commons.

Fig 15: T.W. McGarry; Wikimedia Commons.

Fig 16: H.J. Cody; Wikimedia Commons.

Fig 17: Hartley Dewart, 1912 Wikipedia Commons. HH Dewart 1912.jpg

Fig 18: E.C. Drury, 1920. Wikimedia Commons (HS85-10-36997).

Fig 19: Walter Rollo; Wikimedia Commons.

Fig 20: Sir John Willison. Wikimedia Commons.

Fig 21: Hearst, 1930. Wikipedia Commons. https://en.wikipedia.org/wiki/William_Howard_Hearst

Fig 22: C.A. Magrath; Wikipedia Commons; https://lop.parl.ca/sites/ParlInfo/default/en_CA/People/Profile?personId=5061/

# 8 Reconstruction

*What was being done for the wives and dependents of soldiers was no more than what was right and proper, and, in the absence of the men, the women and children were only receiving their just rights.*[1]

MEANWHILE, the war had finally come to an end on 11 November 1918. The first to know were those who worked in telegraph or newspaper offices, but the news quickly spread as church bells rang, factory whistles blew, and fire trucks drove through the streets with their sirens blaring. People rushed out of their houses in communities large and small and gathered in the streets and town centres to celebrate the long-awaited victory. As it happened, a Victory Loan parade had been organized for 11 November in Toronto and, with factories and shops closed for the day, 200 thousand people turned out to enjoy it. The parade included female munitions workers and veterans marching – or being transported in automobiles if they were unable to march – from lower University Avenue to Queen's Park, accompanied by nine brass and pipe bands and the US Navy Band led by John Philip Souza. The highlight of the parade undoubtedly was the flypast in battle formation of fifteen airplanes that performed stunts, including "swooping around the steeples of St James Cathedral."[2]

At Queen's Park, where 100,000 people gathered for a service of thanksgiving, Hearst and other dignitaries made the appropriate speeches, the crowd sang patriotic songs and hymns thanking God for supporting the righteous cause, and the service ended with a minute of silence to remember those who had lost their lives. Then the celebrations resumed and continued all day and well into the night.[3] According to the *Daily Star*, "the city was awake for the full 24 hours. Awake and letting the world know it. There was almost enough noise for Berlin to hear the roar of triumph."[4] But many thousands of households understandably accepted the news more quietly, having lost fathers, sons, and brothers and, in some cases, even sisters and daughters.

But the Allied governments had discovered a new enemy, the Bolshevik revolutionary government in Russia, which they decided had to be overthrown, so fighting continued, albeit it on a smaller scale. The initial justification for the Allied intervention in Russia had been to reopen the Eastern Front and Borden, badly misreading public opinion, had agreed that Canada would participate. That made no sense after 11 November, especially when it became clear to all but the most naïve that the real goal was to overthrow Bolshevism, which Allied leaders feared was contributing to the social and political unrest in their own countries.

Hearst never spoke publicly about the Russian intervention, but it is reasonable to assume that he supported it if for no other reason than that the Union government did. As it happened, Hearst had a personal stake in the intervention. His son Vernon was a lieutenant in the 259th Battalion which sailed for Vladivostok on Boxing Day 1918. There was little fighting on the Siberian front, however, and Borden and his colleagues soon came to their senses and withdrew the Canadian troops from this ill-conceived venture. Hearst and his family were no doubt relieved when Vernon was demobilized in June 1919. Irving had arrived home from England in April.[5]

They were among the thousands of soldiers who returned home in the spring and summer of 1919, no doubt happy and relieved to have survived but at the same time rightly concerned about what awaited them. Aside from the often difficult readjustment to civilian life, they needed jobs and other forms of support because many found that the jobs they had left were occupied while others required retraining because they were no longer physically able to return to their former jobs. Governments, both federal and provincial, had promised to take care of them and had indeed been developing policies and programs but it was an enormous task and no one had any experience in resettling large numbers of veterans. It didn't help that the soldiers were returning home at the same time that wartime production was being slashed, creating unemployment when jobs were so desperately needed.

Governments had very little experience in managing the economy other than with tariffs and subsidies, although they had begun creating and managing some social services before the war. But they had dramatically intervened in the economy during the war, responding to a growing demand for social services, and the federal and provincial governments had even begun collaborating in joint programs. While some thought – or perhaps hoped – that life could just revert to the way it was before the war, many, if not most, thought that if governments could take on new responsibilities in wartime they surely could also do so in peacetime. The politicians and other public figures had promised that the most destructive war in global history with its appalling cost in human lives would result in a better world. This mattered, because how else could it be justified? As Stephen Leacock, the popular humourist who was also a professor of economics at McGill University, recognized in the autumn of 1919, the role of government and the meaning of citizenship changed because of the war. "If every [male] citizen owes it to society that he must fight for it in case of need," he wrote, "then society owes to every citizen the opportunity of a livelihood." Unemployment, "in the case of the willing and able," had become "a social crime."[6]

The Borden government accepted this responsibility in 1915 when it created the Military Hospitals Commission (MHC) to provide convalescent medical and retraining facilities for the 150,000 wounded soldiers – almost half of them Ontarians – who began returning home in 1915. In October 1915 the government convened a federal–provincial conference to address the problem.

Hearst agreed with this decision, declaring that when political leaders urged men to "go and fight for us" they were also making "a most solemn" compact that governments would "take care of [them] to the best of our ability."[7] He played a major role in the conference, meeting separately with the other provincial Premiers and presenting their "unanimous agreement to establish provincial commissions to cope with the problems of returned men and to help find them work." The federal government, for its part, accepted full responsibility for restoring and training the disabled. As Desmond Morton and Glenn Wright have written, "with their constitutional sensibilities at least partially anaesthetized by the war emergency, the provinces could congratulate themselves on avoiding a costly and potentially touchy problem." The Premiers also debated their "more urgent concern" that returned soldiers "might well swell the flight from the countryside," leaving Ottawa "with the task of planning for a soldiers' agricultural settlement program."[8]

In addition to transferring three hospitals and other facilities to the MHC, Hearst also established the Soldiers' Aid Commission (SAC), which supported veterans' families and cooperated with the MHC in providing vocational training. W.D. McPherson, the Provincial Secretary, chaired SAC, and John Baird Laidlaw, the Canadian manager of the Norwich Union Fire Insurance Society, was vice-chairman.[9] SAC's official historian, James Onusko, claims that more than 1,000 men had received vocational training by August 1918 and another 399 began similar training in mid-October, although Morton and Wright claim that only nineteen veterans applied for SAC's vocational training program and McPherson blamed the hospitals for not cooperating and "almost deliberately" discouraged the men.[10] J. Castell Hopkins claimed in 1919, however, that SAC provided financial support and vocational training to more than 24,000 men and, in some cases, their dependents.[11] An unexpected issue that SAC found itself having to deal with was motherless children whose fathers were serving overseas. In October 1918 McPherson reported that the commission had found homes for 321 such children in Toronto.[12] SAC's work had a significant impact not only on those who benefited from its services but also in changing public attitudes. As the *Globe* declared in December 1917, soldiers' aid was not charity. "What was being done for the wives and dependents of soldiers was no more than what was right and proper, and, in the absence of the men, the women and children were only receiving their just rights."[13]

Meanwhile, Hearst had also commissioned Lieutenant Colonel Cecil Williams to determine what Ontario men expected upon their return from the war. Not surprisingly, Williams concluded that their major concern was jobs and "warned Hearst that these men would not just "seek reward for [their] sacrifice" but would also "aggressively demand what they esteem their right to support, maintenance and betterment at the hands of those in authority."[14] Hearst agreed and had been stating publicly since at least the summer of 1916 that "our first duty to Ontario is to look after the boys at the front, their families at home, and the returned heroes."[15] Borden was more specific during the 1917 election campaign, declaring that "duty and decency demand that those who are saving democracy shall not find democracy a house of privilege, or a school of poverty and hardship." The returning solders "would be re-educated where necessary and re-established on the land or in such pursuits or vocations as they may desire to follow … the maimed and the broken will be protected, [and] the widow and the orphan will be helped and cherished."[16]

In February 1918 the Department of Civil Re-establishment was created to focus on the rehabilitation of veterans. It took over responsibility for the Military Hospitals Commission, medical treatment for veterans and vocational training for disabled men and those who had enlisted as minors. It also established an artificial limb and surgical appliance factory and paid disability allowances. Recognizing that health and education came under provincial jurisdiction, Borden subsequently summoned a federal–provincial conference, at which Hearst led the Premiers in fully supporting the federal government's initiatives. The war was "a national undertaking," he declared, and Ontario had "no desire" to fight over jurisdiction. The result was that the federal government paid the costs of medical treatment and rehabilitation and the provinces agreed to help veterans find jobs, including the establishment of employment offices.[17]

Hearst had already created a network of provincial employment offices to help veterans and men and women who had worked in war industries to find post-war jobs, one of the major recommendations of the Commission on Unemployment that he had appointed in 1915. The Trades and Labour Congress (TLC) had opposed the idea at that time, fearing that the role of such offices would be to bring in cheap labour from Britain. But Allan Studholme, the labour MPP from Hamilton, had warmly endorsed the idea, and the TLC's attitude changed when it realized that thousands of soldiers would be returning home at the same time that thousands of men and women working in war industries were losing their jobs. Ontario and the other provinces now joined the federal government in creating the Employment Service of Canada, a national network of labour exchanges jointly financed and administered by both levels of government. The system was administered by the Department of Soldiers' Civil Re-establishment, but the provinces had complete authority over its creation and operations. The first offices in Ontario were opened in the autumn of 1917 and by 31 October 1919 more than 50,000 job applications had been processed and positions had been found for about 45,000 people.[18] Historian Jeff Keshen describes the program as "a start but a far cry from the unemployment insurance that Canadians were demanding," but, as James Struthers has pointed out, it was significant because it was not just a short-term effort to find jobs for veterans and laid-off munitions workers; it was actually "a necessary response ... to the consequences of an industrial society as well" by men like Borden and Hearst, moderately progressive conservatives in the pre-war years who had been convinced by 1918 of the need for greater state involvement in the economy.[19]

A century later these reconstruction policies for returning soldiers may seem modest and there is no denying that veterans had to fight for pensions in the 1920s, but historian Peter Neary is right when he claims that they were "ground breaking" at the time.[20] Until the First World War the only compensation or assistance offered to veterans had taken the form of land grants or a cash settlement. Even in the case of the thousands of veterans of the relatively recent South African War, neither the Canadian nor the provincial governments had accepted any additional responsibility for the welfare of veterans or their families, not even those with disabilities.[21]

Hearst's reconstruction policies and close cooperation with the federal government broke new ground but reflected his response before the war to some of the problems being created by industrialization and urbanization.

Poverty had always existed, of course, especially in urban areas, but it had become more apparent when large numbers of volunteers were found to be physically unfit for military service.[22] Similarly, home visits by Canadian Patriotic Fund case workers had revealed the shocking poverty and living conditions of many of the families left behind by the men serving overseas. But mothers' allowances were being advocated as part of the war effort, as a supplement to soldiers' pensions and were even referred to as "widow's pensions." That meant that the only women who would benefit from the program would be wives or widows of soldiers. But concern for the welfare of women and children had been a major reason why Hearst supported strict temperance legislation, and he was inclined to think that all mothers needing support should be helped, not just the wives of soldiers, without having to turn to local charitable relief.

In the spring of 1917 he asked Walter Riddell, who had been appointed Superintendent of Trades and Labour in Ontario's Department of Public Works in 1916, to look into the matter and make recommendations. Riddell was a Methodist clergyman who had studied sociology and economics at Columbia University and had practical experience working on social issues in Manitoba for the Methodist and Presbyterian churches.[23] He was also the son of a widowed mother. After extensive study, Riddell recommended "a generous, rights-based scheme which marked a decisive and radical break with the philosophy of needs-based private charity and public municipal relief" and included all single mothers, widowed, deserted, deserted or unmarried.[24] Unfortunately, he had not yet submitted his report when the provincial election took place, and so the legislation was passed by the Drury government in 1920 but, as historian James Struthers points out, "the decision … to launch such a scheme" was made by Hearst.[25]

Hearst also responded positively to the growing demand for legislation guaranteeing a minimum wage for women employed in the workplace. The need for such legislation had emerged during the war because large numbers of women were working in factories and other industrial enterprises, but they were paid less than men and male-dominated unions didn't want to include them. Hearst's Commission on Unemployment had addressed the issue but stopped short of recommending it in its report. Support for the idea grew, however, and the Women's War Conference, held in the spring of 1919, called for a minimum wage for women, as did the Trades and Labour Congress.[26] Even the Canadian Manufacturers' Association, which had formerly opposed the idea of minimum wages, was advocating "fair" wages by the end of 1918, no doubt because of the growing social and industrial unrest and its fear of Bolshevism.[27]

The federal government responded by appointing Manitoba Judge Thomas Mathers to chair a royal commission to investigate the causes of industrial unrest. When he submitted his report, the government organized a National Industrial Conference that brought together representatives of business, labour, and government in September 1919. It focused on Mathers's report, which had concluded that the industrial unrest reflected economic conditions rather than agitation by foreign aliens and recommended reforms such as minimum wage legislation, an eight-hour day, unemployment and health insurance, the recognition of unions, and free collective bargaining. The Canadian Manufacturers' Association's members rejected the eight-hour day, minimum wage legislation for all workers, and compulsory collective bargaining but did agree to minimum wages for women if they were determined by quasi-judicial provincial boards.[28]

Such boards had already been established in the three western provinces, and Hearst supported the idea. Inevitably, this proved to be controversial because, while minimum wage legislation had the support of organized labour and workers generally, the rural press opposed it. The *Farmers' Sun* called it "class legislation" and accused Hearst of "preparing huge concessions to socialism."[29] Hearst pacified the farmers by excluding farm workers from the legislation[30] but he was still denounced by pro-business Conservatives who saw minimum wage legislation as further evidence that their party had been "captured by Methodist do-gooders."[31] It was too late in September 1919 for Hearst to be able to pass the legislation, but a watered-down version was one of the first pieces of legislation passed by the Drury government – with the support of virtually all members of the legislature, including the farmers and the surviving Conservatives.[32]

Hearst also tackled the very serious problem of affordable housing for workers and veterans. The problem was that there was a shortage of it and much of what there was lacked clean water and proper sewerage, a major problem in crowded urban communities. In fact, the number of habitable houses in Toronto had actually declined by 5 per cent since 1914, and it was estimated that more than 5,000 families required sanitary dwellings that simply did not exist.[33] When the Toronto chapter of the Canadian Manufacturers' Association (CMA) declared the situation a "menace" not just to Toronto but to the "industrial, social and political welfare of the whole country,"[34] it was clear that something had to be done. Hearst was aware of the problem, telling Willison in May 1918 that the situation was "acute" not only in Toronto but also "in almost every industrial centre in the Province."[35] He summoned a meeting with representatives of the CMA, the Board of Trade, the Great War Veterans'

Association (GWVA), and organized labour to discuss the situation and then created the Ontario Housing Committee (OHC) to examine the problem. Willison, who had chaired Hearst's Commission on Unemployment, chaired the committee and its members were, for the most part, surprisingly well chosen for their relevant experience and interests.[36]

To no one's surprise, the OHC found compelling evidence of housing shortages throughout Ontario. Its survey of Toronto, which didn't even include what historian John Bacher describes as "the notorious 'ward' or central Jewish ghetto," found that 54.9 per cent of dwellings were occupied by more than one family because low-income families could not afford the rent on their own. The situation was similar in other urban centres, sixty of which were appealing for provincial housing assistance. Meanwhile, employers reported that the housing shortage was making it difficult to obtain workers. Hearst did not think the provincial government should get directly involved in building or financing housing but the government established a $2 million loan fund to enable the municipalities to do so.[37] The houses were not to exceed $2,500 in price, or, if rented, the rent was not to exceed $25 per month.[38] Hearst stressed, however, that this plan was "only intended as a temporary one to assist in meeting the pressing emergency with which we are confronted."[39]

Hearst's housing program has been criticized for being too modest in scale and restrictive in its terms. It was not large enough to meet the actual need and the war had inflated building costs, which meant that acceptable houses could not realistically be built for $2,500 or less. Historian John Bacher claims that the OHC knew the $2,500 ceiling was unrealistic and had not been determined by builders but had been based on the patronizing fear expressed by Frank Beer, a member of the OHC, that providing housing for workers that was better than what they had enjoyed before the war might "encourage a standard of living that may not be justified by subsequent events" and might actually "add to labour unrest." Instead, he thought the government housing program should actually be designed to teach workers to face "a lower level of living comforts."[40] That was surprising coming from Beer, because he was an active member of the urban reform movement and had spearheaded the development of Toronto's first experiment in social housing, Sumach Street Terraces, a housing development for lower-income families. C.B. Sissons, a progressive Methodist University of Toronto professor and secretary of the OHC, was enthusiastic, however, predicting that there would now be "no reasons for denying to the humblest city workers of the future the charms of Rosedale without its inconveniences."[41]

More than sixty municipalities participated in the program and by 1922, 2,771 houses had been built, 830 by local commissions and housing companies, and 1,941 by builders hired by individual loan recipients.[42] But these numbers represented at most only 15 per cent of the estimated need for new houses,[43] and the provincial program has generally been regarded as a failure. The explanation for that, according to Bacher, was that the $2,500 ceiling was unrealistically low, with the result that many homes were poorly built or were incomplete when occupied and subsequently required upgrading at significant additional cost.[44] Those critical of the program inevitably compared its low ceiling with the government's astonishing extravagance in the construction of a new official residence for the lieutenant governor.

Ontario's original Government House had been built in 1870 in the southwestern part of the city that had become an industrial community, so the Whitney government sold the property to the CPR, which tore it down and converted the space into a railyard. Fourteen acres of land were then purchased in upscale Rosedale and construction of Chorley Park, an enormous mansion designed in the then popular French chateau style began in 1912.[45] By the time Sir John Hendrie was able to move in in 1915, the cost of the mansion had more than quadrupled from $215,000 to more than a million dollars, the equivalent of about $5.3 million today. Not surprisingly, opposition politicians and representatives of the farmer and labour movements found this extravagance outrageous. Hearst could reasonably argue that he had not authorized the construction of such a luxurious residence and its construction had been managed by the Minister of Public Works, J.O. Reaume, until 1914, then Finlay MacDiarmid. Still, Hearst was a member of the government when the project was authorized, much of the work had been done while he was Premier, and there is no evidence that he ever tried to rein in the extravagance.[46] To be fair, he probably couldn't have stopped it or had it reduced in scale, but his image wasn't improved when the legislature raised his salary as Premier by $3,000 during the 1918 session. He had not requested that, but neither did he decline to accept it. Meanwhile, he had also received a knighthood in March 1917. None of this could have helped his image with workers and farmers.[47]

The reality was that the magnitude of the government's housing problem was too great for the province to handle on its own. The OHC recognized this when it recommended in September 1918 that housing should become a federal responsibility because of the disruption to the residential construction industry caused by the war. At the very least, it thought the federal government should lend the provinces $10 million for housing, to be administered by a board that would "distribute responsibility and ensure speedy action" by "provinces, municipalities and employers of labour." The newly formed Canadian Construction Association, representing industries involved in the building trades, supported this proposal, as did Hearst. He raised the issue at the 1918 dominion-provincial conference, arguing that the problem of insufficient affordable housing was a "war" problem and a "national" problem because decent affordable housing was a "necessity for the returned soldier." He also pointed out that increased residential construction would create jobs for veterans at a time when job creation was critically important because, as the federal Department of Labour was warning, the returning soldiers would be far more militant than the pre-war unemployed.[48] The Union government, by now very concerned about rising political and social instability, therefore supported Hearst's proposal. In fact, to Hearst's surprise, Sir Thomas White, who was serving as acting prime minister because Borden was in England, agreed "without consultation with his colleagues other than those who surrounded him at the table."[49]

Hearst therefore seized the opportunity to get the federal government to agree as well to make the loans available at 5 per cent, which was below the prevailing market rate, to compensate for the abnormally high post-war construction costs. Accordingly, the federal government established a national loan fund of $25 million for workers' housing, of which $8.5 million was allotted to Ontario.[50] Housing was to be made available for any worker, but the federal government would determine the kind and quality of houses to be built, the province would administer the loans, and the price ceiling was set at a higher, more realistic, level than the ceiling in Ontario's program. The program went into effect almost immediately by order in council and the provincial government passed the Ontario Housing Act in the 1919 legislative session. As the OHC had been dissolved by now, implementation of the act was handled by a Housing Branch created within the Provincial Secretary's department.

There were still problems, however, because the cost of land and construction was limited under the scheme. Indeed, municipal leaders in Toronto claimed the financial limits were impossible, a view that Hearst and Willison attributed to the real estate and construction interests. They may have been right because Toronto's leaders opted out of the federal–provincial scheme and the city established its own housing commission, chaired by H.H. Williams, head of the largest real estate firm in Canada. He soon abandoned the project as unviable because of post-war inflation. That left the city with a significant financial liability that took years to discharge. The federal–provincial program also proved to be unviable for financial reasons.[51]

Bacher claims that builders "frequently" skimped on materials or actually omitted foundations, verandas, or even windows, and governments, both municipal and federal, incurred significant additional expenses as a result.[52] Other scholars, however, have disagreed, claiming that Bacher "unfairly" based his evaluation of the program on its admittedly "spectacular failings at Ottawa, while ignoring its quiet successes elsewhere" and that it was "more successful in reaching working-class borrowers than is generally thought." An analysis by historians Matt Sendbueuhler and Jason Gilliland of the people who took advantage of the program shows that less than half of them were industrial workers, so it "certainly ... did not reach the unemployed and casually employed working-class families most in need of better housing," "nor was it intended to, and nor did it leave out the working class entirely."[53] The primary goal of the federal program was to create jobs and decent housing at minimal risk to government, which meant placing "as much of the risk as possible onto the borrowers, but also targeting a class of borrowers thought likely to be able to handle the risk easily."[54]

Another major initiative that proved to be unsuccessful was the government's Soldiers Settlement program. Launched in April 1918, it was aimed specifically at returned soldiers and continued a long tradition of offering free land grants to veterans. This program no doubt had particular appeal to Hearst because it fit in with the government's commitment to promote agricultural settlement in northern Ontario's vast clay belt. That policy had been moderately successful because the government backed up its rhetoric on the economic potential of the northland with a dedicated development program that included support for agriculture and mining, the construction of new roads and improvements to existing roads, and a focused approach to the forestry industry that favoured settlers. It was not surprising, therefore, that Ontario was the first provincial government to offer land to Great War veterans. The area selected was on the National Transcontinental Railway where it crossed the Kapuskasing River west of Cochrane. Some land had already been cleared there by the unfortunate inmates of an internment camp for enemy aliens, and a primitive road had been built. The government had also built a training school and was developing a demonstration farm at nearby Monteith. The scheme also anticipated the construction of a pulp mill, which would purchase logs cut by the settlers in the winter months. Veterans who were interested in becoming farmers received free land plus a loan to purchase equipment and training at the experimental farm if necessary.[55]

By the middle of September 1917 forty-five settlers and their families had built a small village of frame cottages fronting on the graded road. Meanwhile, 700 acres had been cleared for the federal experimental farm, of which 250 acres were ready for cultivation. During the period when Hearst was Minister of Agriculture as well as Premier, the government contributed $1 million to this project.[56] Ferguson, the Minister of Lands, Forests and Mines, was enthusiastic as well and Borden was so impressed that he created a similar program for the western provinces.[57] Writing in 1919, Hopkins described the project as "a bold effort" that was "carefully-contrived and attractive ... with promising prospects,"[58] a statement made before the realization that it was a costly failure. This was primarily because the soil was fertile but shallow and the climate was harsh and unpredictable, with long cold winters and short summers often punctuated by killing frosts.

That wasn't the only problem. Many of the more than 100 veterans who participated in the scheme proved to be unsuitable for such a challenge. According to Watson Kirkconnell, who served as an officer with the troops guarding the nearby internment camp, the settlement was "almost volcanic with grievances" by the autumn of 1919 "as many families faced an alternative of starvation or hopeless debt; and complaints were rife against officials of the supervising Department."[59] That was the Militia Department, which chose the men who managed the project because they commanded the internment camp and were selected for political reasons. This could not be blamed on Hearst or Ferguson, although they could have insisted that the colony be managed separately from the camp.

The first superintendent, Major T.L. Kennedy, was actually a good choice because, while he was a Conservative, he was a successful farmer from Streetsville in Peel County who had served overseas for two years before being repatriated for medical treatment.[60] When he was unable to get the support he needed to do the job he resigned in the spring of 1918 and was succeeded by Robert Innes, a young man from a prominent Conservative family in Nova Scotia who, astonishingly had been appointed lieutenant colonel of an overseas battalion at the age of twenty-four. That didn't last long, and he subsequently moved to Ottawa where his connections resulted in this appointment, for which he was also unqualified. Not only that, but he was also given the higher title of director, which gave him the greater authority denied to Kennedy. Innes was not a farmer although he had grown up on a farm but had never managed anything. He was also determined to assert his newfound authority. When some of the settlers attempted to organize a branch of the GWVA he not only ordered it disbanded but had the "ringleaders" rounded up, placed in a boxcar, and removed from the settlement.[61]

That effectively ended the project. When E.C. Drury became Premier in the autumn of 1919, he met with a delegation from the settlement. Drury was, of course, a successful farmer and had had reservations about the project from the outset. What he heard from the delegation confirmed his suspicion that the scheme had been "ill conceived, ill executed, [and] founded on a mistaken appraisal of the agricultural possibilities" of the region. He appointed a Commission of Enquiry chaired by W.F. Nickle – a Conservative – that vindicated the settlers' complaints and recommended that the handful of settlers still there be brought home. The government agreed and wrote the scheme off "as a total loss."[62] Hearst was certainly primarily responsible for promoting the idea of an agricultural settlement at Kapuskasing and Ferguson had been in charge of the project, but neither of them was responsible for appointing Robert Innes to manage it.

Meanwhile, the government was actively supporting an ambitious public health program and reforming the province's school system. As with some of Hearst's other initiatives, these actually predated the war but now assumed greater importance as the government recognized the essential role that it must play in the related fields of health and education. Contagious diseases like typhoid fever, tuberculosis, diphtheria, and polio took a heavy toll on society a century ago, but all were caused by problems like contaminated water and milk, inadequate garbage collection, and unsanitary toilet facilities that could and should be addressed. Ontario actually had a relatively good record in the emergence of public hygiene going as far back as 1882 when it was the first province to establish a provincial Board of Health to educate the public and provide advice to the network of local boards of health that the legislation also required. When an outbreak of smallpox in 1884 caused only twenty-one deaths in Ontario compared to more than 7,000 in Quebec, the local boards of health were given authority to conduct compulsory vaccination and to expropriate land for isolation hospitals when necessary, and by 1890 there were 576 local boards with 356 medical health officers.[63] Subsequent amendments to the act enabled the board to deal more efficiently with contagious diseases, to establish isolation hospitals, to control communicable diseases, and to inspect dairies, dairy farms, and abattoirs.

Meanwhile, following several outbreaks of typhoid in 1882 that were traced to the milk supply, the Public Health Act was amended to allow local boards of health to inspect dairies and meat supplies originating within or outside a municipality. In 1895 authority was given to the provincial board to require that all plans for water supplies and sewerage works be submitted for approval. In the same year legislation was passed relating to the tuberculin testing of milk cows, the inspection of bake shops, and meat inspection.[64] These were progressive acts, but they only applied locally, not provincially.

In 1912, after Dr. John McCullough became medical health officer, the province's public health laws were consolidated into the Public

Health Act in an effort to address epidemics caused by poverty, particularly in the province's growing urban centres, because of overcrowding, inadequate garbage collection, the prevalence of outdoor privies and contaminated water. The act divided the province into ten health districts and gave their medical officers of health and boards more power, authorizing them in the event of an outbreak of communicable disease to "use all possible care to prevent the spread of infection or contagion by such means as in their judgment is most effective for public safety."[65] Ontario's Public Health Act became the model for similar legislation throughout Canada.

Hearst had supported the public hygiene movement for years. In 1910, before he became a member of cabinet, he had introduced a private member's bill enabling the province to regulate abbatoirs, and in 1911 he had succeeded in passing legislation establishing provincial regulations for embalmers. In his first year as Minister of Lands, Forests and Mines he had legislated the eight-hour day for some underground miners. In 1916, when he was still Minister of Agriculture as well as Premier, he boldly tackled a much larger and more controversial problem, the pasteurization of milk. For at least a decade Canadian physicians had been explaining that pure milk was essential to the eradication of tuberculosis and intestinal diseases among children. The Whitney government had passed legislation enabling municipalities to regulate and inspect facilities where milk was produced, handled, or sold, but no provincial standard had been established. That was the purpose of Hearst's legislation, and the Dairy Standards Act was a significant advance because it "tightened inspection regulations and provided for the selling of 'certified milk' that met certain bacteriological standards." Although it stopped short of actually requiring the pasteurization of milk because of the strong opposition of dairy farmers,[66] the *Public Health Journal* expressed its relief that the province had "at last realized the importance of prompt action in State prophylaxis."[67] Progress came at a cost, however, because the dairy farmers now had another grievance against the government. Hearst responded by agreeing to postpone proclamation of the act until March 1918 and appointing a prominent dairy farmer, George Henry, as Minister of Agriculture.[68]

Meanwhile, despite the 1912 Public Health Act, the provincial Board of Health could not effectively deal with a disease that rapidly spread to virtually every locality in Ontario because its mandate was to provide leadership and support to the local health boards. But the government could and did cooperate with the federal government when a polio epidemic struck the northeastern United States and Canada in 1916. Federal border services required children entering the country from the

United States to have medical certificates, and the Ontario government blocked people from entering the province from Quebec. That may have seemed drastic to many but there was no cure for this terrible disease, although eventually "iron lung" machines were devised to help victims to breathe while imprisoned in them.

This was the situation when the Spanish influenza pandemic swept the world in 1918 and 1919. It appears to have entered Canada at Sydney, Nova Scotia, in September 1918 when an American troopship came into the port with 150 infected men on board. Within two days their number had risen to 500, and it was spreading throughout the province. By the end of the month the epidemic had reached Ontario.[69] Dr. McCullough initially expressed no concern because influenza was a common illness in the autumn and winter, declaring in his first official statement that there was "no evidence that the disease is as dangerous as measles, scarlet fever or many other of the communicable diseases."[70] That meant that cases didn't have to be reported or require quarantine, and because he lacked the authority to impose measures on the municipalities he could only recommend courses of action in any case.[71] He did have an advisory role, however, and because he didn't initially realize the seriousness of the situation, he recommended that local health officers not do anything that might dislocate business or daily life but assured them that the board would not overrule them if they thought it necessary to take such measures.[72]

The reality, of course, as McCullough quickly realized, was that this was not the usual influenza and thousands of people, including doctors and nurses, became seriously ill and hospitals were soon overwhelmed. He then encouraged the local public health officers to close public gathering places such as schools, churches and theatres and advised the public to avoid crowds, wear gauze face masks, wash their hands frequently, and avoid eating in restaurants unless they were confident that stringent sanitizing procedures were in place.[73]

A health crisis of this magnitude was catastrophic because most people couldn't afford medical treatment, especially if the family wage earner was afflicted, and the social support systems taken for granted a century later did not exist. Various community organizations like the IODE, fraternal societies, and churches provided a range of services, ranging from preparing and delivering meals to setting up makeshift hospitals in church halls and other facilities.

The provincial government responded in two ways: by creating the Emergency Volunteer Health Auxiliary (EVHA) and expanding the mandate of the Ontario employment bureaus created to help find jobs for veterans or wartime industrial workers who were being laid off. The EVHA organized women throughout the province who had completed the emergency nursing assistant training courses of the St. John Ambulance and Voluntary Aid Detachment (VAD), which had provided nursing assistants in military hospitals in Canada during the war but had not actually joined the VAD. Designated Sisters of Service, these women assisted people with basic care in their own homes.[74]

Because public health came under the jurisdiction of the Provincial Secretary, the auxiliary was chaired by W.D. McPherson, giving it direct access to the government, but it was managed by Dr. McCullough. This was obviously helpful to afflicted families and also lessened the strain on hospitals. The fact that they received only "three days of intensive training"[75] caused the professional nurses' association to raise questions about their usefulness, repeating a concern it had expressed about VADS during the war. But nobody was claiming that these women were nurses; their task was to do whatever they could to help sick people and their families in their own homes, whether that was cleaning, cooking, caring for children, or whatever. As nursing historian Linda Quiney has rightly observed, "in the midst of the crisis, the [nursing association] leadership was in no position to object to the assistance of volunteers who had a reasonable level of training, experience, and education." What level that might be, given what was expected of them, is hard to say but as Quiney adds, "under the circumstances, any training was better than none"[76] and the work of the Sisters of Service was greatly appreciated by thousands of people.

The network of Ontario employment bureaus throughout the province played a role as well. According to the *World*, the one in Toronto was "one of the busiest places" in the city. People seeking help were "received constantly all day," which Laura Duff, who was in charge, thought was "a natural course of events from the very start, as it had always been open as an employment bureau." But then "city nurses started phoning there for assistance, or referring people to them, and soon the work was more than could be handled by the girls in charge," so a special department was "set aside for flu, with an adequate staff of workers."[77] This was in fact a logical linkage because, aside from the appalling impact the epidemic had on individuals and their families, it also inevitably had a major impact on the economy because thousands of men and women were not able to work, and that affected production in factories and businesses of all kinds. Its impact in coal mining communities in both Canada and the United States contributed to the coal shortage during the winter of 1918–9.

Eventually, some 55,000 Canadians, about 10,000 of them Ontarians, died.[78] That was the third-lowest rate among the nine provinces, a result which medical historian Allan Marble has attributed to "the quick action by public health officials in closing public places and isolating people from those who were infected with the virus."[79] Most of them were young adults including veterans, and some were war widows. They left behind hundreds of orphans, some of whom were able to live with relatives, but SAC stepped in to accept nearly 600 who were raised in hostels operated by the commission or in foster homes or were boarded with farm families.[80] The stress caused by this unprecedented crisis, coming as it did during the final days of the war and continued into 1919 must have had a significant impact on public morale, the political environment, and attitudes towards the role of government.

At least some politicians recognized the logic that if governments could intervene dramatically in the economy in wartime it could surely do the same in peacetime, and the growing social and political unrest in 1918 and 1919 suggested that many people wanted them to do it because the appalling cost of the war could surely only be justified if the post-war world was a better place. Accordingly, Newton Rowell was appointed the first federal Minister of Health in July 1919, with responsibility for "the promotion of the health and social welfare of the people of Canada."[81] To be effective, of course, the federal role in public health had to cooperate closely with the provincial governments, and Hearst was planning to appoint a provincial minister.

Happily, he had an outstanding candidate in mind: Arthur Ross, a physician who had served overseas with the Canadian Army Medical Corps, rising through the ranks to become the Canadian Corps' director of medical services with the rank of brigadier general. He was also the popular and respected Conservative MPP from Kingston. Ross joined the government in September 1919 as a minister without portfolio and advised the government on issues relating to not only public health policy but also veterans' affairs while awaiting the creation of the department. That hadn't been done when Hearst lost the 1919 provincial election. Somewhat surprisingly, the Drury government didn't follow through, even though Ross was re-elected in 1919 and likely would have served in the UFO government, so Ontario did not get a Minister of Health until 1924.

Looking to the future, the government also committed itself to a major reform of the province's school system to make it more relevant to the changing needs of society. Pyne had actually begun the process before the war, recognizing that it was not keeping pace with industrialization and the shift of population from rural to urban areas seeking employment. Toronto, to cite the most dramatic example, had seen its population rise from 181,000 in 1891 to 377,000 in 1911 and 522,000 in 1921.[82]

The province's industrial economy had also grown dramatically during the war and factories were becoming larger and using increasingly complex machinery powered by electricity. Industrial workers needed to be trained in the new skills, and that meant not only that children needed to remain in school beyond the mandated age of fourteen but that technical education was necessary alongside the traditional liberal education offered in secondary schools.

The trend towards technical education at the secondary level had begun at the turn of the century and, as Kathleen Yolande Sharman and Larry Glassford have pointed out, it "enjoyed broad-based public support" because "the interests of working-class parents who desired employment opportunities for their children coincided with the interests of capitalists seeking a qualified work force."[83] The Canadian Manufacturers' Association had been advocating federal support for technical education since 1904, not so much because of the benefits it would provide for individual workers but because industry needed skilled labour. The Laurier government had taken no action, however, because education came under provincial jurisdiction, even though supporters of the change argued that federal financial support did not constitute a violation of the British North America Act. The Whitney government had sought federal support for technical education from the time it took office in 1905, Robert Pyne telling the annual meeting of the Ontario Educational Association in 1906 that federal support for technical education "would be money better spent ... than building transcontinental railways or dealing in tariffs."[84]

The situation began to change somewhat in 1909 when W.L. Mackenzie King became the first full-time federal Minister of Labour and the *Globe* began proclaiming that Canada's economic future depended on the improvement of technical education.[85] Two years later Whitney passed the Industrial Education Act (1911), which has been described as "a landmark piece of legislation" because it authorized the creation of vocationally oriented industrial schools, technical high schools, and even technical departments in existing collegiate secondary schools. It also required that each school have a community advisory committee representing business, labour, and other local interests.[86] King followed up by appointing a royal commission chaired by James Robertson, the principal of Macdonald College in Montreal, to look into industrial training and technical education. His interim report, submitted to the Borden government in 1913, strongly recommended the introduction of technical education in secondary schools because it would benefit industry, the national economy, and workers. Robertson also recommended that the federal government establish a $3 million fund to assist the provinces in achieving this goal over a ten-year period. Although the CMA and the TLC both praised the report, the government took no action before the war broke out but Hearst and Pyne went ahead anyway, establishing the Central Technical School in 1915 and the Central High School of Commerce in 1916, both in Toronto.

By 1919 the Robertson commission's recommendations were exceptionally relevant to the collaborative reconstruction programs of the federal and provincial governments. That was why, in the midst of that spring's widespread social and industrial unrest, Gideon Robertson, the new Minister of Labour, introduced the Technical Education Act, and parliament promptly approved it. It legislated Robertson's 1913 recommendations except that the cost-shared budget was dramatically increased from $3 million to $10 million over a ten-year period.

Hearst and his progressive new Minister of Education, Henry Cody, welcomed this legislation "with open arms"[87] because children needed to be prepared "for their walks in life" in the post-war world, especially "in the north and all the urban municipalities."[88] F.W. Merchant was appointed Director of Technical Education, and industrial and technical education quickly joined commerce and agricultural and domestic science as growth areas among the courses being offered in Ontario's secondary schools. The number of technical and vocational secondary schools rose to sixteen by 1921 and sixty-five by 1935.[89] The Hearst government also passed the Adolescent School Attendance Act in 1919, raising the age of mandatory attendance from fourteen to sixteen. That meant that the thousands of young Ontarians who had traditionally entered the workforce after elementary school would now attend high school for at least a couple of years and had industrial and technical courses available to them as well as the usual liberal arts. In another important move, the government ended the practice of allowing public secondary schools to charge tuition fees for any of their programs.

Cody's educational reform program included rural Ontario as well. Cody believed that rural depopulation could be "very largely stayed" by replacing small community schools, 40 per cent of which were "not fit to raise swine in" according to Dr. W.H. Hattie of the Dominion Council of Health,[90] with consolidated regional schools that included agricultural and household science in their curricula. The government also sought to strengthen rural education by adding "an extra quarter of a million dollars" to the budget to improve the salaries of rural teachers and called on school boards to respond "with equal generosity." These changes, combined with the declining cost of electrical power in rural areas, the province's rural roads program, and the growing popularity of motor vehicles, Cody believed, would "very largely" reduce the exodus of rural youth into urban communities.[91] They didn't, but they did improve the rural education system.

The government also welcomed the Union government's decision in 1919 to help the provinces with the cost of building and improving roads, an effort that had been attempted in 1913 but was blocked by the Senate. One of the first cost-sharing programs in dominion-provincial relations, the Canada Highways Bill was a $20 million five-year program that would meet a need because the number of cars in Canada had risen from 74,000 in 1914 to 350,000 in 1918.[92] The government's objectives were to create jobs in the post-war recession and to develop a system of interprovincial highways that would in effect constitute a trans-Canada highway, including a road through northern Ontario to link Quebec with Manitoba.[93] The program came under the jurisdiction of the Department of Railways and Canals and was administered by A.W. Campbell. A civil engineer from St. Thomas and long-time advocate of good roads. Campbell was well qualified because he had been deputy minister in Ontario's Department of Public Works from 1900 to 1910, then deputy minister in the Department of Railways and Canals until his appointment as Dominion Highways Commissioner in 1919. He soon became known as "Good Roads" Campbell, an international expert on highway construction and maintenance.[94] Ontario benefited significantly from this project, receiving about 30 per cent of the total funding. It did not apply any of that money to road building in the north because the Hearst government's Northern Development Plan was part of the Department of Lands, Forests and Mines and its mandate was to build colonization roads. The result was that anyone wanting to drive across Canada had to detour south of the Great Lakes and "much of northern Ontario remained impenetrable by car in 1928 when the act expired."[95]

Meanwhile, Ontario's post war reconstruction depended on resolving its electrical power shortage to meet the rapidly rising needs of industry, farms, homes, and local public utilities. Not surprisingly, Beck had the solution: to build a massive plant at Niagara Falls that would generate between 175,000 and 200,000 additional horsepower of electrical power. That would cost, he claimed, an estimated $20 million because its construction would involve diverting water from the Niagara River above the falls, carrying it by an overland canal to the escarpment near Brock's Monument at Queenston, and there turning it back into the river below the falls, a distance of about twenty-one kilometres.[96]

Aside from the enormous cost, the decision to build the plant would mark a decisive and irreversible change in the Hydro Commission's mandate. Until now, it owned only small plants and purchased much of its power from private companies, but building this plant would make it the dominant producer and distributor. Needless to say, the business and public power communities took a profound interest in the matter because Sir Henry Pellatt's Toronto Power Company already had a generating plant at Niagara and wanted to expand its capacity. What did the people want? Hearst believed that they wanted public power and supported this project, although he worried about finding the money to pay for it.[97] Ever cautious, however, he also thought that the voters should be consulted before the government made such a critical irreversible decision, and therefore called a referendum. This, of course, was consistent with the practice when regional hydroelectric projects were proposed. When the referendum took place on 1 January 1917, every municipality except Goderich and Waterford returned a favourable majority. Accordingly, the government promptly passed the enabling legislation during the 1917 session, guaranteeing the Hydro Commission's bonds, and construction began in May.[98]

It soon became obvious that the cost of the project was going to be much higher than $20 million. This could not have been a surprise because Beck regularly low-balled his estimates. But this was different because the Niagara project was massive, involving the excavation of seventeen million cubic yards of material, the pouring of 450,000 cubic yards of concrete, and the laying of more than 132 kilometres of railway track. Special construction equipment even had to be designed and built especially for the project. At the peak of work, about 100,000 men were employed with a semi-monthly payroll of $750,000,[99] making it a huge public contribution to the creation of jobs. The final cost proved to be $76 million, almost four times the original estimate. That reflected the complexity of the project, and the fact that Beck decided during construction to more than double the plant's generating capacity, initially to 425,000 horsepower and then to 525,000 horsepower. While not appreciated at the time, that proved to be a wise decision.

The sky-rocketing costs and Beck's refusal to consult or even keep the government informed greatly strained his relationship with Hearst and the government. The *Canadian Annual Review*, always sympathetic to the Hearst government, pointed out that a plant of this size would reduce Ontario's soft coal imports by half, for a saving of some $100 million.[100] But Drury was sceptical, and when he took office he appointed a royal commission to re-examine the costs. No doubt to Beck's delight and certainly Hearst's relief, it concluded that the Queenston-Chippawa project was "a magnificent piece of engineering" and there was "not a breath of suspicion of any personal wrong-doing ... concerning the management."[101] Not surprisingly, however, it did chastise the government for failing to maintain control over the Hydro Commission. What the commissioners apparently didn't realize or simply didn't accept was that the government had tried to control Beck, as had the no-nonsense Whitney, and it couldn't be done because Beck's popular support exceeded that of any other politician. It was true that Hearst, because of his management style, had not kept a close watch on commission affairs, leaving that largely to McGarry and Ferguson.[102] Having said that, however, and in fairness to both Beck and Hearst, the original cost estimate of the project had been based on $105 per horsepower, calculated in 1914–5 dollars. The final cost was $138 per horsepower in 1918–21 dollars that were only equivalent to about $70 in 1914–5 terms of purchasing power.[103] In other words, the cost of the project had escalated along with the size of the project but had actually been completed well under budget on the basis of generating capacity.

When it opened in December 1921, the Queenston-Chippawa plant was the largest hydroelectric plant in the world, and Hearst was justly proud of it. It was, to be sure, a Hydro Commission project and Beck was the driving force behind it, but the government was ultimately responsible for it and had had to finance it. More significantly, the government had made the critical decision that the Hydro Commission should be the primary producer of electrical power in Ontario, a policy that endured until 1998. And that involved the government having to fight the private power interests over the rights involved and face the results at the polls. As John R. Robinson, editor of *The Evening Telegram*, wrote in 1925, "Sir William Hearst was never given the credit that [he] earned by the wisdom and courage of his final decision to cut loose from Conservatives who tried to throttle the policy of starting work on the Chippewa [*sic*]."[104] Nor did he get any credit from Beck. Even so, he Hearst later declared that his authorization of the scheme had given him greater satisfaction than anything else he had done during his term in office.[105]

Less controversial was the Hydro Commission's construction of its first generating plant in northern Ontario. Its purpose was to provide power to the twin cities of Port Arthur and Fort William – now combined as Thunder Bay – that were growing rapidly because of the thriving forestry and mining industries, their strategic position on the transcontinental railway, and their shared harbour on the western edge of Lake Superior. The commission had been purchasing power for Port Arthur from the Kaministiquia Power Company since 1910, but the 10,000 horsepower it provided was becoming inadequate, and the contract was due to expire at the end of 1920. Construction of a Hydro Commission generating plant began in June 1919 was a challenging construction project because it involved building a channel in "one of the most rugged terrains and climates on earth" to funnel water from Lake Nipigon through generators at Cameron Falls on the Nipigon River and transmitting the power to Port Arthur 129 kilometres away.[106] It was the first of ten major generating sites that Hydro built in north-western Ontario that fuelled an economic development. "The bad news," as Howard Hampton has pointed out, was "that these and other northern Ontario power developments often trod on the ancestral homelands of First Nations peoples, with the tacit consent of the government.[107]

Meanwhile, despite Hearst's efforts to address their needs, many of the thousands of soldiers returning home thought them inadequate. Their major grievance was the difficulty that they encountered in finding jobs, and some of them quickly identified what they thought was the problem. It was immigrants, some of whom they believed had come from the countries they had been fighting against. The reality was that many of the immigrants they thought were Germans or Austrians were actually from the large regions in eastern Europe that were part of the German and Austrian Empires and had been able to emigrate to Canada during the Laurier years. That distinction didn't matter much, really, because some veterans and civilians were really complaining about all immigrants.[108] Why, they asked, should "real" Canadians be struggling to find jobs while immigrants who had remained safely in Canada were employed?

The GWVA, the largest veterans' organization in the country, launched a national anti-immigrant campaign in February 1918 with a mass rally in Toronto. Not surprisingly, the xenophobic Lieutenant Colonel Cecil Williams pandered to the crowd by declaring that "we cannot allow Canada to drift into the hands of aliens." Williams was himself an immigrant but from England, which was, of course, was not regarded as the same thing. Hearst, the son of immigrants, spoke at the rally as well, albeit more moderately, assuring the veterans only that he opposed a federal proposal to allow the immigration after the war of enemy aliens, people from neutral countries, and Asians.[109] Proudfoot was also on the platform and agreed with them, as did many labour leaders.

Five days later "representatives of Guelph's merchants and manufacturers, members of city council, private citizens and hundreds of returned soldiers" packed the town's Opera House to discuss the problem. Anglican Archdeacon A.C. Macintosh, who had served in the war as a chaplain and was now president of the GWVA's Guelph branch, charged that while Canadian soldiers were fighting and dying overseas, aliens at home had "without sacrifice" made more money than they ever could have earned in their home countries. "They are not British subjects" but they had made "big money," while Canadians were "dodging shot and shell for $1.10 a day" only to return home to find the aliens holding all the jobs. "What we want, in plain speech and without hedging, is a white Canada," he announced. "We want the alien fired from his present position as long as there is a returned soldier in Canada who is able to work." Even William Turley, the GWVA's provincial secretary, who was considered a moderate, claimed that the country was overrun by immigrants who "came to this country to get all they could" and were "drawing down big envelopes" while "our boys are walking around the streets looking for work." He went further, however, declaring that it was "time we made this a white man's country" by deporting the immigrants as soon as transportation could be arranged.[110] The meeting concluded by unanimously supporting a resolution calling on employers in Guelph to fire all enemy aliens and replace them with returned soldiers. The Guelph *Mercury*'s reporter, reporting on the event, declared it "the most wonderful meeting held in Guelph since the war started."[111]

The situation deteriorated two weeks later at the GWVA's national convention in Toronto when reports circulated that foreign-born waiters (probably Greeks) at the White City Café had assaulted a disabled veteran. Enraged veterans descended on the café and after destroying the interior went on to attack a dozen other restaurants and engage in street battles with the police. The next day, "having found automobiles to transport them to different sites across the city, they began destroying more foreign-owned restaurants." Toronto's chief constable, G.J. Grasett, who "spoke out vigorously against Toronto's foreign element" during the war,[112] cleared the streets and made fifteen arrests while a crowd of "tens of thousands" watched and some "actively supported" the veterans. The rioting resumed the next night because the veterans were angry about alleged police brutality against "innocent and disabled veterans" on the previous evening. When they gathered at police stations throwing rocks at the police and charging the stations' doors demanding that these men be released, the police responded by charging the veterans with batons, supported by mounted constables who "used whips" to disperse them. That ended the violence, but for the next few days the police were reinforced by troops from the Royal Canadian Dragoons wielding axe handles.[113] The police response to the rioting resulted in an investigation that "exonerated the department as a whole, but led to the dismissal of two inspectors, a sergeant, and a constable."[114]

The hostility to immigrants did not end with the war, partly because conditions didn't improve and some Conservative politicians continued to fan the flames. In January 1919, Howard Ferguson denounced "the alien in our midst," suggesting that he "should be eliminated and deported to whence he came."[115] In the days leading up to 19 July, which had been designated Peace Day throughout the empire to celebrate the signing of the Treaty of Versailles and the official end of the war, leaders of the GWVA and the Grand Army of Canada, a veterans' organization that was more broadly based and somewhat more radical than the GWVA, expressed the fear that "the foreign element" would treat it as a normal workday, and the *Daily Star* warned that "for them to attempt to make profit by it would be an insufferable sacrilege."[116] Toronto's Mayor Church agreed, as did Grasett, who urged "alien shopkeepers" to recognize the holiday.[117] On 19 July, thanksgiving services were held in communities throughout Ontario, businesses and houses were decorated with flags and other patriotic paraphernalia, and veterans paraded in uniform alongside floats from local businesses and organizations and children. Effigies of former Kaiser Wilhelm were burned, and there were concerts, picnics, sporting competitions, fireworks, and the inevitable patriotic speeches.

The main event took place in Toronto where 25,000 people gathered at Queen's Park to hear a band concert and participate in a sing-along of patriotic songs and hymns led by local choirs and schoolchildren. "Occasionally," according to the *World*, "a cheer and a round of applause greeted a company of war veterans."[118] Despite the threats of violence, it was a fairly peaceful day, although a mob of about 200 "youths led by two veterans with criminal records" threw bricks at a Jewish peddler and set his stable and wagons on fire. Rioters broke into and vandalized several restaurants, two streetcars were damaged by fire, and a crowd broke into a Chinese-owned store that was closed but had left its lights on.[119] In Hamilton, Mayor Charles Booker pandered to a gathering by declaring that "the only good German is a dead one" and "anyone who buys German-made goods in Canada within the space of twenty years is a traitor to his country." Veterans in the crowd reportedly interrupted his speech with demands for beer, which must have chagrined Hearst if he knew about it because, in response to an appeal from the Grand Army of Canada, he had released veterans in custody for breaches of the Ontario Temperance Act so that they could participate in the peace celebrations.[120]

The "patriotic" xenophobic prejudice against foreigners reflected the rising level of discontent over the high rate of unemployment and the failure of wages to keep pace with inflation. The average price of farm products had risen by 80 per cent during the war and that of industrial products by 170 per cent.[121] There was also a strong sense among veterans that their sacrifices were not being recognized in a meaningful way. Whether or not that was true, there was strong public support for the veterans, most of whom were workers. This was demonstrated three weeks later when a cheering crowd of 100,000 people gathered in Toronto to see the Prince of Wales – in uniform – officially open the Canadian

National Exhibition. Two days later, when he reviewed "a spectacular parade of veterans" and awarded military decorations, the scene was "so big, so picturesque and so charged with emotion that even a cynic would have been stirred" by the sight of cots with injured soldiers, blind soldiers, amputees, thousands of veterans, and shouting Boy Scouts.[122]

The situation became more serious when radical labour leaders inspired by the Bolshevik revolution in Russia began demanding not just reforms but also revolutionary change. The Union government, clearly rattled and sharing the public prejudice against aliens, responded by making the Immigration Act more restrictive. Immigrants from formerly enemy countries were specifically prohibited, as were anarchists or political extremists of any kind and immigrants of any nationality, race, occupation, and class if they were deemed unsuitable to the "climatic, industrial, social and educational, labour or other conditions or requirements of Canada."[123] Few seemed to realize or care that many if not most of the political extremists were Canadian-born or had emigrated from Britain.

The historian Donald Creighton once referred to the atmosphere in 1919 as "a bewildered sense of social injustice,"[124] but many, if not most, farmers and workers were not bewildered. They felt pretty sure that the problem was the traditional party system, because both parties had long supported economic policies that encouraged the industrialization that encouraged young people to leave the farms for jobs in urban communities. This had had a profoundly damaging impact on rural communities, which urban people did not appreciate because increasing mechanization meant that production could be maintained or even increased while rural communities continued to decline. That meant that rural values, which farmers believed were vital to a healthy, balanced society, were increasingly being viewed as old-fashioned and irrelevant. Meanwhile, urban workers were struggling with unemployment, unacceptable living and working conditions, limited public health programs, exploitation of women and children in factory work, and related social problems.

William Proudfoot's proposal on 7 February 1918 that the political truce agreed upon by Hearst and Rowell in 1917 be extended "until a year had elapsed and a [legislative] Session [had] been held after the return of the soldiers"[125] confirmed the growing belief that there was no real difference between the two parties. Proudfoot's suggestion meant that there would not only not be an election until sometime in 1919 but the two parties wouldn't even contest by-elections.[126] While there is no evidence that Hearst and Proudfoot had agreed on this in advance and Proudfoot claimed that he had made the offer "without previous consultation with Premier Hearst,"[127] cynics like Dewart had no doubt that they had. And it did seem more than coincidental when it was revealed that Proudfoot had just become the first opposition leader to be given a stipend to cover his office expenses. In any case, Hearst accepted the offer "amid loud applause from both sides of the House," saying that he understood it to mean that the next election would not only be delayed "until all our men are home again from Overseas" but also allowed "a reasonable time thereafter to allow conditions to become normal."[128] This seemed like a good idea because it allowed both the government and the Liberal opposition to set politics aside and focus on the war effort but didn't go as far as forming a provincial union government, but it delegitimized both parties in the minds of many people and contributed to the social and political unrest.

It was in this political climate that the 1919 session of the legislature took place. It was the sixth session under a government that had now been in office longer than any provincial administration since Confederation, and clearly, it would be the last. The government naturally used it to lay the groundwork for an election to take place in the summer or autumn, outlining its achievements, its undeniably impressive record on the war effort and its sound financial management. Although spending had risen during the four war years from $12.7 million to $17.5 million, about $10 million of that had been spent on war initiatives ranging from the Ontario hospital at Orpington to contributions to the Canadian Patriotic Fund and other worthwhile activities that benefited Ontario – and Canadian – soldiers and their families.[129] And this was achieved with annual surpluses that totalled $4.9 million despite the loss of nearly a million dollars a year as a result of the OTA. The government had also negotiated the first increase in the federal subsidy since Confederation, raising it from $1.4 million to $2.4 million, and raised $22 million from the sale of provincial bonds. It did not directly address the call from agricultural and labour leaders to conscript wealth, but it did introduce a wartime property tax and tightened up its administration of succession duties, raising its revenue from that source to $13 million while exempting the estates of soldiers killed in the war.[130] It was true, as UFO leaders liked to point out, that the province's debt had risen to $75 million, which they attributed to extravagance and wastefulness, but $44 million of the debt had been spent on Hydro Commission expansion – which was needed and had strong public support in both rural and urban areas – and $22 million had been spent building the Temiskaming & Northern Ontario Railway, which had proven its value in opening up north-eastern Ontario for the development of its resources.[131]

The government was well aware that there was widespread dissatisfaction in rural Ontario and relied on McGarry, normally a popular and entertaining public speaker, to make the government's case for re-election, and he in effect prepared the way in his annual financial statement in the legislature. McGarry flatly rejected the claim that farmers were under-represented in the legislature, insisting that they "never were so well represented." This made no obvious sense because only a handful of MPPs were farmers even though seventy of the 111 constituencies were predominantly rural, but what McGarry actually meant was that the existing MPPs had effectively represented farmers and "taken a prominent part in the debates … dealing with agricultural questions every year" even if they themselves weren't farmers.[132] That was simply foolish when the government could simply have acknowledged the problem and promised to increase the number of farmer candidates in rural constituencies. As for Hearst's controversial decision to serve as Minister of Agriculture for two and a half years, McGarry boldly claimed, presumably with a straight face, that it had been "absolutely essential" for the Premier "to study at first hand all the problems which the war had produced for Departmental action." That was very much in the interest of farmers because "in future legislation the knowledge which he acquired during those months will be exceedingly valuable."[133]

The idea that the agricultural community would benefit in future by having had a part-time minister who was a lawyer because he wanted to learn more about the industry was more unacceptable in 1919 than it had been in 1916. Hearst made the situation even worse when he rejected the complaint of rural spokesmen that his government was made up mostly of lawyers and businessmen, boasting that his ten-member cabinet was the first to include two farmers.[134] But that wasn't true until May 1918 when Henry joined MacDiarmid in the government and many farmers did not consider Henry representative of their interests. That didn't faze McGarry, who declared, "I do not know of any class of people who get more actual benefit from the expenditure of money in their interest than the farmer."[135] That may have been true in fact, but it quickly became clear that the government's strategy in the election was to fight the militant farmers and their organization.

# 9 The Election of 1919

*No Government in this or any other Province has ever been able to present a better or cleaner record, a record of more progressive and helpful legislation and measures for the development of our resources and the benefit of our people.*[1]

The year 1919 was not a good year for an incumbent government to seek re-election, and Hearst knew it. The social and political unrest that had emerged in 1918 continued to grow, and by July four of the five Conservative provincial governments in office when the war broke had been toppled. In Ontario, the government had managed to retain only one of the three Conservative seats in which by-elections were held, and that was very close. What should the government do? Just two days after the Ontario North and St. Catharines by-elections, I.B. Lucas frankly explained its dilemma to the *World*:

> If the government should hold an election and leave the prohibition act as it is, they fear the anti-prohibition vote. If they hold a temperance plebiscite with an election to follow, as has been practically agreed upon, they fear the temperance vote, because the prohibition leaders do not wish present conditions interfered with until the soldiers have all been repatriated.

That being the case, "the government's intention [was] to go to the country soon,"[2] but that was improbable because Hearst had promised that neither the election nor the referendum would take place until the soldiers had arrived home. He spent the summer touring the province, hoping to get a better feel for the situation. That convinced him that the popularity of the UFO was growing and would likely be greater by the spring of 1920.[3] One positive development, he believed, was that the Ontario Liberals had unceremoniously dumped Proudfoot in June and chosen Hartley Dewart to lead them. Hearst had no respect for Dewart personally or fear of him politically because he had opposed the Ontario Temperance Act (OTA), conscription and Union government and led a sharply divided party.

But Hearst also had to decide if the temperance referendum should take place before or after the election or on the same day. When Lucas had said in February that the government had "practically agreed upon" holding the referendum before the election, he was reflecting Hearst's thinking at the time because he was confident that the OTA would be ratified and that surely would be helpful to the government. Just in case, however, he made two major announcements in the closing days of the legislative session. The first was that the OTA would be amended to raise the alcohol content of beer from 1 per cent to 2.51 per cent. This was a concession to what he believed "the Labour Congress, and others desiring light beer, ask for" and was "the same definition of light beer" that was in Quebec's temperance legislation act.[4] The second was that, because "many good and conscientious citizens ... do not approve of the Act as it stands to-day but are absolutely opposed to a return to the old license system," the government intended to create a provincial commission to manage the sale of alcohol through its own stores, while policy would remain in the hands of the government. This laid the foundation of the system still in effect a century later. It's doubtful if these changes satisfied many people because 2.51 per cent beer was still very light beer, not in fact what the workers and veterans wanted, and bars remained closed. What Hearst was trying to do, of course, was to take the liquor issue out of politics, something that Whitney and he had always advocated.

On 9 September, Hearst announced that the referendum would take place on 20 October. It would consist of four questions and the responses of the voters would be binding on the government:

1. Are you in favour of the repeal of the Ontario Temperance Act? Are you in favour of the sale of light beer containing not more than two and fifty-one hundredths per cent alcohol weight measure [i.e. 2.5 per cent alcohol content] through government agencies and amendments to the Ontario Temperance Act to permit such sale?
2. Are you in favour of the sale of light beer containing not more than two and fifty-one hundredths per cent alcohol weight measure in standard hotels in local municipalities that by a majority vote [to] favour such sale and amendments to the Ontario Temperance Act to permit such sale?
3. Are you in favour of the sale of spirituous and malt liquors through government agencies and amendments to the Ontario Temperance Act to permit such sale?

In other words, voters could choose to repeal the OTA or to allow light beer to be sold in government outlets and hotels where it had been approved by local option and/or to allow the sale of liquor through government outlets. Hearst pledged that the government would fully honour the wishes of the electorate, as did the other political leaders with the exception of Dewart.

At first glance, the referendum seemed satisfactory, but closer examination caused concern among prohibitionists because voters were required to respond to all four questions or their ballot would be discarded. Inevitably, some saw a conspiracy. Proudfoot thought this demonstrated that the government had been "influenced, not by the temperance people of the province, but by the liquor elements in the Government Party and also a desire on the part of the Government to cater to the liquor interests."[5] The reality was that the government wanted to obtain the clearest understanding of precisely what the voters wanted because it recognized that many people supported temperance but thought that the OTA had gone too far. Surely, offering options was a reasonable and responsible action, especially as it went against Hearst's personal preferences.

But when would the election take place? The government claimed that "no consideration" had yet been given to that, but according to the *World*, it was "almost an open secret that the members of the cabinet are unanimous in the matter of bringing off the double event on the same day."[6] The problem was that "the temperance people ... have made strong representations to the government, asking for a separate day on which the vote shall be taken" because they "are extremely anxious to keep the question of prohibition altogether outside of politics." That reportedly had strong support in Toronto, Hamilton, and other "large centres" and the *World* thought it "not unlikely" that those favouring two separate dates would prevail.[7] But there was strong support "from the rural parts of the province" where "people have a natural objection to going long distances on separate occasions to record their votes."[8]

The advice that Hearst received from Conservatives wasn't much help. Alex Ferguson, the Conservative MPP for Simcoe South, and Gordon Wilson, the Unionist MP for Wentworth, thought the referendum should take place first because if the voters wanted changes in the OTA the government could make them before the election.[9] Robert Davison, a Conservative businessman in rural Picton, reported that several farmers had told him that having the two votes on the same day would be a "very bad" idea because "a great number" of women would come out to vote on the referendum "and would therefore also vote in the election" but "would not come out if it were only an ordinary election," and "as there is quite a following here of the United Farmers of Ontario (UFO) of course, the majority of women would vote for that candidate."[10] T.E. Simpson, the Unionist MP for Algoma West, perhaps more realistically, thought it mattered little if the two votes took place on the same day or not because a lot of people were angry about the OTA and would vent that anger on the government.[11]

In fact, Hearst had already decided to hold both votes on the same day, although he waited another two weeks before making the election announcement on 23 September. The announcement was not unexpected. George Ramsden, a Toronto Liberal alderman, had publicly declared on 9 September that even "if the Premier does not desire to announce the date we already know what is going to happen," and the *World*, although a Conservative paper, accused Hearst of misusing his position to give the Conservatives an unfair advantage in the campaign.[12] Hearst said only that having both votes on the same day would be more convenient for voters and would save on expense to the province. That was true, of course, but Horace Wallis told Davison that Hearst's summer speaking tour of the province had convinced him of the growing strength of the UFO and Independent Labour Party (ILP) and 90 per cent of the Conservative MPPs and constituency leaders thought the government would benefit from holding the election on the same day as the referendum.[13]

It has been said that Hearst was "complacent and unruffled" in 1919,[14] but in fact he was well aware of how unstable the political situation was. In December 1918 he had told Willison that he had given "the best service I was capable of ... during four very trying years," and while "undoubtedly mistakes have been made and opportunities for service lost ... there was little I would do differently if I had an opportunity of living those four years over again."[15] He was optimistic, however, because he believed his government had a strong record and that the OTA was popular. While the greatest threat was in the rural areas, they were also where support for the OTA was strongest. And even though he and his ministers were highly critical of the UFO, he felt confident that its members would support his government if he did not win a majority rather than Dewart's Liberals. He also hoped that the Conservative Party's traditional strength in urban areas would hold because of its social legislation, and women would surely support the government that had not only passed the OTA but also given them the vote. It never occurred to him that the UFO would win as many seats as it did, and he underrated dissatisfaction with the government for other reasons among many people who supported the OTA.

One of those reasons was the government's close alignment with the Union government, which was unpopular. Perhaps this explains why the federal Conservatives kept a low profile during the campaign. Cochrane had been seriously ill for some time and died on 22 September, the day before Hearst called the election; Borden had gone south for a badly needed vacation; and J.D. Reid, who had managed the 1917 federal election in Ontario, sat this one out, perhaps because he was in ill health and had wanted to retire in June 1919.[16] Even Sir George Foster, a diehard prohibitionist, was unable to help because he was serving as Acting Prime Minister in Borden's absence and his wife had just died. That essentially meant that Hearst had to rely primarily on Ferguson, McGarry, Lucas, and W.G. Clysdale, the party's provincial organizer since 1914.[17]

He did get some backhanded support from Newton Rowell, who, apparently unaware of how unpopular the Union government was, urged Liberals "to support the Union Government in Ontario," adding that when Hearst and Proudfoot extended the provincial political truce in 1918 he had suggested "that if Mr. Hearst wanted to be consistent with his Unionist professions he should form a union government and take Liberals into the cabinet."[18] Hearst had "spurned" that suggestion, but Rowell ploughed on, claiming that Lucas had agreed with him that "the realignment of party lines in Ontario" would prove to be "permanent" because the Liberal Unionists and Conservatives would "virtually coalesce" as those on the federal scene had done.[19] Whether or not that was meant to be helpful to Hearst is hard to say, but it must have confirmed the view of many farmers and workers that there was no meaningful distinction between the two old parties.

The 1919 election was the most democratic election ever held in Ontario to that time. No fewer than 289 persons – including two women – sought election in the province's 111 constituencies, even though no party ran a full slate. The Conservatives ran only 105 candidates, not bothering with Essex South, Glengarry, Hamilton East, Huron Centre, London, and Russell because they were considered hopeless.[20] On a more positive note, four Conservative MPPs – George Black (Addington), Henry Cody (Toronto Northeast A), J.R. Cooke (Hastings North) and A.E. Ross (Kingston) – were re-elected by acclamation, so, effectively, the Conservatives only had to contest 101 constituencies. The Liberals ran only sixty-seven candidates, the UFO sixty-four, and the ILP twenty-one. There were also fourteen independent candidates: six Labour-UFO candidates, three Independent Conservatives, three Socialists, two Soldier-Labour candidates, two Soldier candidates, one Liberal-UFO, and one Independent Liberal. Clearly, the two-party system had broken down at least temporarily, but the situation wasn't quite as chaotic as it appeared, because the UFO and ILP were allied in this election, something that, as historian Charles Johnston has rightly observed, "would have been dismissed as pure fantasy in prewar years."[21] Even so, the fact that 57 of the 111 seats being contested had three or more candidates might work in the government's favour.[22]

Dewart, with the support of William Lyon Mackenzie King, the newly elected and Ontario-based federal Liberal leader, attacked the government's record and its close ties to the Union government, conscription, and post-war efforts to suppress labour unrest. Dewart also reached out to farmers, trying – as King would do in 1921 – to avoid contests between Liberal and UFO candidates so as not to divide the progressive vote but also trying to get Liberal farmers nominated in rural ridings before the local UFO clubs chose a candidate.[23] That strategy largely failed because the Liberals still competed against UFO candidates in forty of the sixty-seven constituencies they contested.[24] But Dewart knew that some UFO candidates were former Liberals and hoped that if elected they would support a minority Liberal government.

Inevitably, the most significant single issue in the election was the OTA because it was so divisive. Many supported it, many opposed it, many others thought it was good in principle but was too extreme, and some thought it outrageous that a legal industry had been arbitrarily shut down with no compensation to the men who had invested in it and also showed no concern for the men who lost their jobs. Among those who held this view were several of Hearst's own MPPs. Arthur Pratt and Harold Machin were the most vocal, but Pratt publicly claimed in September 1919 that at least twenty-seven of the Conservative MPPs opposed the OTA.[25] This was probably true because twenty-one of those who had voted for it in 1916 either did not seek re-election or lost their nominations, and four others ran as independents.[26] Conservative incumbents who sought re-election despite opposing the OTA included McGarry, MacDiarmid, and Ferguson,[27] three of the strongest men in the cabinet, as well as George Gooderham, Mark Irish, and Adam Beck, although Beck ran as an independent. Gooderham, Irish, and Machin did not object to the OTA in principle but thought it went too far and should have offered compensation to those whose legal business had been summarily shut down.[28] Gooderham also thought the government was being blamed for total prohibition, which was actually the result of the federal government's orders in council.[29]

Machin had privately warned Hearst in 1916 on the day before he introduced the OTA that he was making a serious mistake. After returning from war service, he publicly denounced the OTA in the legislature on 4 March 1919 and became a prominent member of the newly formed Citizens' Liberty League, which opposed the act on the ground that it constituted an unacceptable assault on individual rights. Always a refreshingly outspoken man, Machin thought the OTA reflected "fanatical puritanism" on the part of people "who no doubt mean well" but in fact had "the narrowest vision and most intolerant attitude" and "by continuously shrieking in season and out of season" had "convinced this Government, or at least the Prime Minister, that they form a great majority of the people of the Province."[30] He also denounced "the savagery, brutality and offensiveness with which this Government and its officers have persecuted the people of this Province for breaches" of the act.[31]

That was a distortion of the facts, of course, in view of the massive petition that had been presented to the government in 1916 and the fact that the act was supported by every member of the legislature. Even so, Machin's view was widely supported by the labour movement and the returning soldiers who, as historian Craig Heron has put it, saw prohibition as an attack on "the rights they thought they had been fighting for."[32] As the Parkdale branch of the Great War Veterans Association (GWVA) put it, "having resisted the tyranny of Wilhelm, [we do not] propose to submit to ... the petty tyranny of petticoat government."[33] That left them with a problem in the election because there were only two candidates in Parkdale: William Price, the Conservative incumbent who had served overseas "and was a strong advocate of temperance," and Dr. John Hunter, a Liberal and long-time member of the Toronto Board of Education, who described himself as "a Hearst Independent prohibitionist."[34]

They were joined by public figures as diverse as Stephen Leacock, the respected academic and popular humourist, and Catholic Bishop Michael Fallon, both of whom worried about how far the state should go in trying to regulate human behaviour.[35] It didn't help that there were frequent newspaper reports of liquor inspectors displaying excessive zeal in enforcing the act. Toronto's *Daily Star*, a progressive Liberal newspaper that strongly supported the OTA, tried to rally temperance supporters behind Hearst, denouncing the "considerable effort" that was being made "to punish Sir William Hearst for the service he has given the cause of temperance in Ontario." In its view, having failed to prevent prohibition, it charged that opponents of the OTA were hoping to achieve "the next best thing" by punishing the man responsible for it. If they succeeded, it warned, "the lesson that all politicians and public men" would learn "will be this, that people will only support Prohibition if it does not interfere with their politics," and called on all those who believe in prohibition to "not abet this purpose" and "see the thing through to a finish."[36] Although the *Daily Star*'s editor couldn't quite bring himself to utter the words, he was calling upon Ontarians, and particularly Liberals, to vote for Hearst.

The division over the OTA in the Conservative Party was more a symptom of a problem than the actual problem, however. The real problem was that many MPPs and party activists had never accepted Hearst's legitimacy because they had had no say in his appointment as party leader and Premier. Because Whitney's letter recommending Hearst had been kept secret, only Cochrane and the members of Whitney's cabinet knew about it, which left the impression that Cochrane, whom many regarded as an unprincipled old-school politician more concerned with power than policy, had used his very considerable influence to ensure that Hearst was chosen, then was the power behind the throne. The *World* was undoubtedly right when it claimed that the manner of Hearst's selection had been "bitterly resented" and had "fatally undermined him within the party from the outset."[37] His appointment might have been more acceptable if the members of caucus been told that he was Whitney's personal choice, but they weren't.

As late as 1923 Pratt was still referring to "men who thought themselves leaders" and had "forced themselves into leadership without the formality of selection by the rank and file."[38] By then his primary target was Howard Ferguson, but now he was blaming Hearst for making it possible for Ferguson to rise to the leadership of the party. According to Pratt, Ferguson had been "a continual thorn in the flesh" of Whitney, who had "threatened to read [him] out of the party and debar him from caucus," but Hearst had brought him into the cabinet and he had become Hearst's "chief confidante [*sic*] and advisor."[39] That was undeniably true and the fact that Ferguson, who succeeded Hearst as Minister of Lands, Forests and Mines, had boldly and unapologetically raised the level of corruption in the forestry industry to a point that it had become a major scandal that did not help the government's image in 1919. Irving Hearst, presumably repeating what his father later told him, attributed Pratt's hostility to the fact that he wanted to be appointed Ontario's agent general in London when Robert Reid died in October 1916. When he didn't get it, "he was my father's enemy thereafter and sought every opportunity to embarrass him."[40] The *World*, referring to Cochrane, Ferguson, and McGarry, also criticized Hearst for "not being strong enough to restrain the predatory instincts of some of those around him."[41]

In fact, Hearst's leadership style was similar to Whitney's, namely, to determine the government's priorities, allow his ministers wide latitude in managing their departments, and not get personally involved in what Oliver has called "the seamier side of the political process."[42] When the *World* claimed that "the Fergusons and McGarrys" had "cancelled all the favor which Whitney's policies had gained for the Conservative party,"[43] it was ignoring the fact that Cochrane had been Whitney's closest political advisor and Whitney had been very willing to use Ferguson as the party's attack dog while keeping his distance from him. But the political environment became much uglier during the war, and Hearst lacked Whitney's strong personality and long-established reputation for common-sense probity. Hearst needed Ferguson and McGarry for their political skills, just as he needed Lucas and MacDiarmid for their managerial skills.

The idea that Hearst was a weak leader took hold, however, perhaps because of his management style but also perhaps it was in sharp contrast with Whitney's style. Nobody had ever doubted that Whitney was fully in control of his government even when he tolerated Ferguson's extremism on the bilingual schools issue. And yet Hearst's critics denounced him as a Methodist do-gooder when he overrode the objections of some Conservative MPPs to pass the OTA and a socialist when he introduced other progressive social legislation. There were two fundamental problems. A modest man lacking the strong personality necessary to lead a political party, he also didn't have a mandate. The voters had re-elected Whitney in 1914, not Hearst, and party members hadn't chosen him to lead them either. He might have earned that mandate if he had called an election in 1916 or 1917 because he likely would have won it. He later acknowledged that he had considered doing that but had thought it unwise to have an election during the war, even though the federal government and every other provincial government did so.[44] This decision was typical of Hearst, in that he was prepared to subordinate party interests to the more important goal of winning the war. No doubt this was what Ferguson had in mind when he said that Hearst "never really understood the party game."[45]

What the dissidents needed was someone who could challenge Hearst's leadership, and Pratt knew who that was. In January 1919 he approached Adam Beck, proposing that he lead the uprising against Hearst "and his following of lawyers" who had "lost touch with the rank and file" of the party," with the result that the party was "drifting towards shipwreck."[46] If Hearst refused "to abdicate gracefully," Pratt assured Beck, "we will defeat him on a want of confidence motion" because "many other members have expressed similar views."[47] Beck presumably passed this on to the *London Free Press*, which duly reported the situation, agreeing that Hearst was "not ... measuring up to the standards set by Sir James Whitney" and should resign and allow Beck to form a non-partisan pro-Hydro government.[48] As bizarre as this may seem today, the situation was not unlike Brian Mulroney's winning the leadership of the Progressive Conservative Party in 1983 when his predecessor, Joe Clark, proved not to be a strong enough or skillful leader.

It is difficult to know if Beck really wanted to become the leader of the party or just to destroy Hearst. What made him dangerous was that he was one of the most popular and influential – some say *the* most popular and influential – figures in Ontario politics because of his undeniable achievements as the chief promoter and builder of the province's publicly owned power utility. His success reflected his vision and determination – some thought it megalomania – but it also depended on the support of the Whitney and Hearst governments, which he resented but effectively exploited. The financing of the massive Queenston-Chippawa project placed a good deal of strain on the government, but even before it was completed Beck was promoting his next ambitious scheme: to build a network of electric railways throughout southern Ontario. Hearst had serious reservations about the scheme, partly because of the cost and the actual need but more because the government was developing a provincial highway system. That seemed to make sense in view of the rapidly growing numbers of motor vehicles and offered better service in rural communities at less cost at a time when the federal government was nationalizing the Grand Trunk and National Transcontinental railways and some local railways were being closed.

Even so, Hearst did not object when Beck led the required municipal referendum campaigns to win endorsement of the necessary municipal by-laws. But when the government did not immediately issue the order in council authorizing construction of the railway that would link Toronto with St. Catharines, Hamilton, and London after the referendum endorsed it in the spring of 1919, Beck exploded and triggered his final break with Hearst, denouncing him for not supporting the Hydro Commission over the years.[49] This was, of course, absurd, and Hearst declared himself "dumb-founded" and "totally at a loss" to comprehend how Beck could say that, given that the government had borrowed $44 million to fund the Queenston-Chippawa project and other power projects.[50] He then rather pathetically complained that Beck had never taken him – the Premier – into his confidence, had displayed a cavalier attitude towards both the government and legislature, and even denied responsibility for the Hydro Commission's mounting debt. Beck's response was to declare that he no longer supported the government and would run in the election as an independent.[51]

Hearst was aware that some party members wanted to replace him and that Beck was flirting with the idea of challenging his leadership. He later told his son Irving that when the Conservative MPPs assembled for the opening of the 1919 session of the legislature, Herb Lennox, the MPP for York North, spoke to Hearst. "Indicating Sir Adam Beck, who could be seen moving from one member of the party to another, he said, in the forceful English that he was sometimes known to employ:

> 'Do you see what that – – is doing to you over there, Bill?'
>
> 'Yes, Herb, he wants my place as leader.'
>
> 'I don't like your liquor policy, Billy, but at least I am no – – traitor.'"[52]

Hearst ignored Beck because he didn't believe there were more than a handful of dissidents in caucus and when Pratt called in March for the confidence vote that he had promised Beck, the Conservative caucus unanimously supported Hearst's leadership.[53] Many of them apparently did so with their fingers crossed behind their back. J.D. Reid warned Hearst in May that Beck was "working up public opinion" against the government "to such a position [that] we must all take a hand in and let the public know what the correct situation is."[54] That was good advice but neither Hearst nor Reid actually did anything.

Pratt and Machin spent the summer of 1919 calling for a party convention to address the leadership issue and draw up a platform for the coming election. They were supported by a number of Conservative newspapers, including the *World*, the *London Free Press*, the *Stratford Beacon,* and the *Glengarry News.* As the *Stratford Beacon* put it in August 1919, "the grand old Conservative party ... was virile healthy and sane when handed over in 1914 ... to the present leader" and if it hoped "to retain public confidence and save itself from merited defeat ... an early provincial party convention must be called to lay down a platform to meet changed conditions and to take such action as may be necessary to restore the party to the confidence of the people." By "action" they meant electing a new leader. The *Glengarry News* agreed, warning that the number of people "opposed to the Government ... will probably increase if something is not done by it to stop the tide that is rising against it."[55]

At this point Pratt demanded a leadership convention, claiming that twenty-seven Conservative MPPs wanted a new leader. Hearst didn't believe him, nor did Lucas, who insisted, somewhat incredibly, as late as 22 September that the only dissidents he knew of were Pratt and Machin and "if there were [more] they were keeping it very quiet."[56] It seems inconceivable that Hearst and Lucas could not have known that the number was much higher, because by the time the nominating conventions were completed a week later twenty-two Conservative incumbents – including Beck, Pratt, and Machin – had not stood for re-election or failed to win their nominations.[57]

Beck therefore ran as an independent, although Thomas Crerar, the president of the Manitoba Grain Growers Association who had served in the Union government as Minister of Agriculture, was convinced by July that Beck, while running as an independent, "would probably" lead the UFO "in the next house."[58] Similarly, the *Daily Star* claimed in September that the UFO was considering asking Beck to lead its candidates in the election.[59] Many years later a *Daily Star* writer, Fergus Cronin, claimed that Beck had been receptive to the idea and visited UFO headquarters "on more than one occasion to indicate his attitude."[60] Whether or not that was true, J.J. Morrison – one of the founders of the UFO and its first secretary – later acknowledged that Pratt met with him in early September and told him Beck had sent him to let the UFO know that he was prepared to lead it in the election and told him that many leading Conservatives would follow him because they could see that the UFO was going to win a large number of seats.[61] There is no reason to doubt Morrison's recollection, but other UFO leaders like E.C. Drury, W.C. Good, R.W.E. Burnaby, W.A. Amos, and H.C. Nixon all later disclaimed knowledge of Morrison's meeting with Beck.[62] That may just mean that he chose not to tell them about it.

Having been denied the nomination by the Norfolk South Conservatives, Pratt ran as an independent Conservative supporting Beck for the leadership of the party,[63] but no other Conservative incumbents followed his lead. And Hearst publicly praised Beck's achievements as chairman of the Hydro Commission during the election campaign, and Beck somewhat weakly endorsed the Hearst government because it "contains everything that is good." Even so, he claimed that it was "only as an Independent" that he could "look after the interests of Hydro for the people of the Province in the most efficient manner"[64] and limited his public statements in the campaign to speaking on commission affairs.[65]

If the Conservatives were seriously divided in 1918 and 1919, so too were the Liberals. Out of office since 1905, they had never really posed a serious threat even under Rowell's leadership. Their divisions had begun with the bilingual schools dispute, when Rowell was unable to hold together the Irish Catholic and Franco-Ontarian factions but became more serious because of his almost fanatical crusade for strict temperance legislation. But the most divisive issue was conscription. When Rowell supported it and joined the Union cabinet in 1917, he left many Liberals behind. While many could accept conscription, especially if the sons of Ontario farmers were exempted, abandoning Laurier and joining forces with the hated Tories was a step too far. They rallied around Dewart, who opposed conscription, denounced the corruption and imperial extremism of the Unionists and thought the OTA went too far. When Proudfoot proposed extending the life of the legislature in March 1918, Dewart had not only been the only member to vote against it, he had pointed out that Proudfoot did this just after the government had generously decided that the leader of the opposition should start receiving an annual $5,000 grant to cover his expenses.[66] This was when the party called a leadership convention that dumped Proudfoot and chose Dewart to lead it in the election. Because of the sharp divisions between the Rowell/Proudfoot and Dewart factions, ten of the Liberal incumbent MPPs retired or were rejected, a higher percentage of its caucus than that of the Conservatives.[67] That must have been somewhat encouraging to Hearst.

In fact, Hearst was delighted with the selection of Dewart to lead the Liberal Party because he couldn't believe that Ontarians would vote for anyone who supported Laurier, whom he regarded as disloyal for opposing conscription and the Union government. He also couldn't believe that Ontarians would vote for a man who was known to enjoy alcohol and was considered "the Champion of the Liquor Interests,"[68] although he did not oppose the OTA, like many Ontarians, thought it had gone too far and was being enforced with excessive zeal. He was also a maverick and irresponsible scandalmonger. Even so, he was a successful Toronto lawyer, intelligent, politically shrewd, and more in tune with the political climate than Hearst was[69] and had developed a reputation as a defender of working people. And as a Laurier Liberal, he was allied with Mackenzie King, the most progressive and very ambitious rising Liberal in the province who succeeded Laurier as leader of the federal party in August 1919.

Hearst had laid out the defence of his government in the speeches he made during his summer tour of the province. Speaking at Eugenia Falls in Grey County on 26 June, for example, he claimed that his government had "maintained unsullied the good reputation established by Sir James Whitney for clean honest administration of public affairs." Reminding voters of the Whitney connection was important, but he also claimed that "no Government in this or any other Province has ever been able to present a better or cleaner record, a record of more progressive and helpful legislation and measures for the development of our resources and the benefit of our people than we are now able to do," and "I challenge comparison with any Government in Canada or elsewhere."[70]

What worried him, and he acknowledged it, was that having more than two political parties or groups running in the impending election would divide the votes and possibly weaken support for both the government and the OTA. Hearst therefore sought to persuade rural voters that the politicization of farmers' organizations was unwise, pointing out that the province's history was "full of wrecks of Farmers' organizations which attained some success in a business way, but were disrupted by political controversy." The Patrons of Industry, for example, had done good work when promoting rural interests until the 1890s when they turned political. The result was "the total disruption of the organization as a force in the Province and putting back for a quarter of a century the organization of farmers on proper co-operative lines." There was truth in that, and Hearst urged members of the UFO to stay focused on the main purpose for which their organization was formed, "seeking for and demanding proper assistance and [the] co-operation of the Government and exercising your political inclinations and influence in the usual way."[71]

That was not an unreasonable point of view, even if obviously self-serving, but Hearst foolishly didn't stop there. He went on to blame the farmers themselves if the government had not been sufficiently responsive to their needs. "Was that not actually the fault of the farmers themselves," he asked? "Was it not the duty of the UFO's leaders and paid organizers to point out to the government where action was desired?" During his term as Premier, when he had also served as Minister of Agriculture for seventeen months, "not one demand" had "been made ... in the interests of Agriculture that I can recall that has not been met. Not one single reform of any merit suggested that has not been adopted." As for the two UFO members who had served in the legislature in the 1919 session, they had been "unable to make and did not make a single constructive suggestion or criticism." Whether or not these assertions were valid, telling people who saw themselves as victims that they were responsible for their situation hardly seems like a good political strategy. Remarkably, all he offered farmers was "the greatest possible" assistance to agriculture, the enforcement of the people's verdict on the OTA, continued vigorous support of the Hydro Commission, including further expansion of public power in rural areas, and continued development of the provincial highways program so that good roads would soon extend into every part of the province.[72]

Recognizing that the OTA would be a major issue in the election despite its popularity, Hearst didn't see any need to defend it in his campaign speeches. Instead, he addressed the complaint of some that it should not have been passed without first obtaining a mandate. But the 1914 election had been fought very largely on the temperance issue, and 71.5 per cent of eligible voters had signed a petition two years later demanding that the government shut down the bars and liquor stores. And when the OTA was passed, it had the unanimous support of the members of the legislature. Even so, it had been passed "as a War measure" with the clear commitment that there would be a referendum after the war to enable the voters, who now included women, to determine if they wanted to maintain, modify, or even terminate it, and he was confident that "practically no person advocates that the old order of things should be restored."[73]

Well aware of how unpopular the Union government was, Hearst also pleaded with voters not to condemn him for the actions of the federal government. It was Borden's Union government that had introduced conscription, promised and then cancelled exemptions to farmers' sons, turned temperance into prohibition, and was taking a hard line on labour unrest. "In the name of fair play and all that is decent in public life, do not condemn my Government for something with which we have nothing to do."[74] That too might have been a reasonable plea except for the fact that he had fully endorsed conscription and the cancellation of exemptions and had welcomed the federal government's orders in council prohibiting the manufacture or importation of liquor. He was also ignoring the fact that the federal and provincial Conservative parties in Ontario had functioned as one organization since at least 1908 and that some had believed since 1914 that Hearst had been foisted on the provincial party by the federal party's leaders. And Hearst had received a knighthood for his war services while eleven of his MPPs had actually taken leaves of absence to serve overseas but retaining their sessional stipends thanks to Hearst, leaving their constituents unrepresented in the legislature.[75] To charge the government with insensitivity would be a massive understatement.

Much worse, and madly provocative, the government had actually passed a punitive bill during the 1919 session disqualifying for ten years anyone who had failed to perform any duty required under the Military Service Act or was convicted of any treasonable or seditious offences during the war, from holding any provincial, municipal or educational office or from being able to vote in elections for such offices.[76] This legislation didn't affect just defaulters, many of whom were farm workers, but anyone who had been convicted of criticizing the government. To give him credit, Proudfoot had asked, no doubt with tongue in cheek, if the act would apply to profiteers, well aware as were many others that neither the federal nor the provincial governments had ever charged anyone with profiteering.[77]

At the same time, however, the Hearst government had proven to be surprisingly progressive and was proposing to do more in response to the new demands of the post-war world. It had already established an affordable housing program for workers and returned soldiers, employment bureaus, and financial assistance to veterans interested in farming in northern Ontario. A Department of Labour had been established and a Department of Health would be established after the election, and their ministers would represent veterans and workers.[78] Legislation had already been drafted for a mothers' pension program and would be introduced at the next session. Minimum wage legislation for women and girls was also being prepared,[79] and action would be taken to modernize the province's labour laws and to coordinate them with those of the other provinces as much as possible.[80]

It was a moderately progressive program, seemingly somewhat more focused on urban voters than rural, presumably because Hearst was more worried about labour unrest than rural unrest. He was, of course, thinking strategically, fully aware that hostility among urban workers to working conditions, inflation, and the OTA was much stronger than in the rural areas. He also knew that many of the UFO candidates – the *Daily Star* said two-thirds[81] – were former Conservatives. Still optimistically hopeful that he would be returned to office but with a smaller majority or even in a minority situation, he thought at least some of them would support a government led by him than one led by Dewart.[82] The Conservative but always outspoken *World* was not impressed, however, concluding that Hearst apparently "hopes to continue doing business at the old stand in the same old way … We look in vain … for any bold forward-stepping policy such as distinguished the platform of the Whitney party in 1904."[83] That seems unfair in view of the government's record and its definite commitments on social and labour issues but did represent the attitudes of many people in 1919.

Meanwhile, even though Hearst had known since at least the spring of 1919 that he would be calling an election within months, it wasn't until 25 September that he asked Howard Ferguson, who was responsible for the party organization, "[I]f we could get a little Committee capable of turning out good campaign material that would be used by the press," adding that "you know better than I do whether we could get material of this kind."[84] One would have thought that the party leader and his campaign manager would have had this organized and in operation before this. Whether or not Ferguson was "better equipped than any other Tory" to manage the provincial campaign, as his biographer suggests, the formerly well organized and well-funded Tory machine "did not function smoothly." Oliver attributes this to the fact that in the past Ferguson had worked closely with Cochrane, but he had been in very poor health since 1917 and died on 22 September. Oliver does not exaggerate when he acknowledges that "his guidance was missed."[85] At least equally significant was the fact that the Hearst government had suspended all "partisan activities" and "devoted itself unreservedly to the organization and leadership" of the war effort because "the fate of the Empire [had] hung in the balance."[86]

Hearst returned to Sault Ste. Marie on 29 September for his nomination meeting and to launch his local campaign. He received a warm welcome at the Conservative nominating convention at the Grand Opera House, which "was filled to the doors from floor to gallery … with an audience that would prove an inspiration to any public speaker."[87] The meeting was chaired by Howard Barnes, a local merchant, and Hearst was nominated by Frank Davey and Florence Whitehouse, who had obviously been carefully selected for the honour. Davey was an alderman and president of the local Conservative Association, but more significantly, he was a railway engineer who had formerly worked at the paper mill and in 1914 had founded the House of Refuge, a home for seniors and destitute people who would otherwise have been housed in the local jail.[88] Florence Whitehouse was the twenty-eight-year-old wife of Fred Whitehouse, a steelworker. There were no other nominations, so Hearst was the unanimous choice.

In his acceptance speech, he emphasized the government's record. "I don't ask your support on promises of what we will do if we are returned," he said, "but on the record of what we have done." One achievement of which he was proud was that, while half the money spent by the federal government on the war effort had been contributed by Ontario, the revenue of "nearly every department" had also nearly tripled since 1914, most of it coming from succession duties and the taxation of large corporations "who were well able to meet the demands." The province had spent $10 million on war purposes, including the Ontario hospital at Orpington; spending on education had doubled, and spending on agriculture had risen by a million dollars. Sault Ste. Marie alone had received more than $386,000 in provincial grants since he was first elected in 1908, and he now announced that approval had already been given to build "one of the finest technical institutions in the province" there. He didn't make a lot of promises, however, saying only that the government intended to modify the income tax on workers' salaries "so that men with families will not be taxed the same as those without children," a minimum wage would be established for women and children, and a Department of Labour would be established. He defended the controversial extension of the legislature, claiming, "[W]e did not want to put on a khaki campaign," even though he knew that he "was throwing away an opportunity to sweep the country." Acknowledging that the OTA "had been much criticized," he declared, "I believed when I took that step that it was right, and if I had it to do over again I would do the same thing." Having said that, however, it was a war measure, and now the voters could decide on its future in the referendum and "whatever verdict you give we will carry it out."[89]

Hearst spent a couple of days speaking in the area and took advantage of his position to distribute some patronage, especially to the farmers of the area. Knowing that the Central Algoma Agricultural Society was planning to enlarge its grounds and improve its buildings, he announced that the government "had a nice little nest egg stowed away for you" because "nothing gives such good returns as farming." Indeed, he claimed, "northern Ontario was the best seed potato growing section in the Dominion." Edwin Keyes, the society's president, naturally thanked the Premier and declared, "[W]e wish you every prosperity in your work as head of the government ... and hope you may long be spared to fill this important office and to lead this great province on to greater development."[90]

The Sault's Conservatives thought it quite likely that Hearst would be re-elected by acclamation because, as T.E. Simpson liked to point out, having the Premier as the community's representative had distinct advantages.[91] But Sault Ste. Marie was an industrial community and the members of the local ILP weren't going to allow that to happen. They met on 1 October and nominated James Cunningham, who worked at the paper mill. He had helped to organize the Carpenters' Association in 1915 and was its first president, then became president of the Trades and Labour Council of Sault Ste. Marie in 1918, and in 1919 was president of the local ILP as well.[92]

The local UFO club chose not to nominate a candidate because, as William Lethbridge explained, "it's hard to pull the farmers away from a man who has done so much for them and in fact given them everything they have asked for."[93] But six farmers attended the ILP's nomination meeting, making clear that they were there as "independent farmers," not representatives of the UFO. To his credit, Cunningham said he "had no quarrel with the Premier but with the system" and believed that he would be "backed up by all the labor men in the city and some outside the city."[94] When the Liberals met on 9 October, they couldn't find anyone prepared to challenge Hearst, so they followed Dewart's advice "that there not be a three cornered fight" and did not nominate a candidate. But they unofficially threw their support behind Cunningham because he was a former Liberal.[95]

Cunningham didn't issue his manifesto in the *Sault Daily Star* until 18 October. An idealist, his goal was to "repeal and amend laws which enable a privileged class without labor to live upon the produce of our toil; and also to frame laws which will stimulate production and reduce the cost of living, and tend towards placing the idle poor, the idle rich and those who wait upon the idle rich, in some useful occupation." He also promised that if elected he would be independent, "free to support any measure, by whoever introduced, that is deemed to be in the interest of labor and industry." In fact, he advocated corporatism, a political system that achieved some popularity in the early 1920s because it advocated representation by economic interest groups instead of political parties. "As a substitute for partyism," Cunningham declared, "I would strive to obtain a fair and equable representation of all the great interests of the Province, meeting in the Legislature, not to struggle against each other ... but to unite in their efforts to [undecipherable] the general welfare of the community."[96]

Hearst could only spend a few days in his own constituency because he had to campaign throughout the province. This may have reinforced the feeling held by at least some that they didn't see their MPP very often since he became Premier. In fact, whenever he did show up, he was literally just visiting because he had sold the family home in 1912 and lived in Toronto, which was a long way from Sault Ste. Marie. This was a difficult situation that all MPPs from distant constituencies faced, of course, but as party leader and Premier his general absence was especially harmful in view of the fact that his government had alienated a lot of people, including immigrants and francophones – of whom there were many in Sault Ste. Marie – as well as many workers and veterans with its strong support for conscription and total commitment to the war effort. Even so, he did not return to Sault Ste. Marie until 17 October.

It is clear from the reports of his speeches that Hearst was convinced that the OTA was the critical issue in the election. Speaking at the Russell Theatre in Ottawa on 14 October, for example, he said "in an eloquent outburst ... before the large crowd" that "many old friends, both political and personal," had told him that his government "had been good and its acts progressive but they could not and would not" support him because of the OTA. His response, as usual, was that he was "sorry to lose the friendship of those men but I would not be worthy of the position of Prime Minister of this great province if I deflected from the course which I believe to be the right one." At the same time, he reminded his critics that the OTA had been a wartime measure that could now be modified or terminated.[97] This was true of course, but those who opposed the OTA knew as well as Hearst did that the majority of people would vote to retain it.

While Hearst focused his campaign on defending the OTA, reaching out to farmers and labour while attacking the UFO, there were other issues. One major one was corruption in the forestry industry, a long-standing issue that was now focused on the lease in 1917 of three timber limits in Quetico Provincial Park in north-western Ontario. It had been created in 1909 as a forest reserve adjoining the Superior National Forest established by the US government earlier that year. When Hearst followed up in 1913 by passing the Provincial Parks Act, empowering the government to set aside for recreation lands not suitable for agriculture or settlement, Quetico Forest Reserve became a provincial park, alongside Algonquin Park in Nipissing and Rondeau Park, near Chatham on Lake Erie, both of which had been created in the 1890s.

Limited cutting was allowed in forest reserves and provincial parks but the issue in 1917 was that Ferguson sold the cutting rights in Quetico Provincial Park to the Shevlin-Clarke Company for $9.50 per thousand board feet when the going rate was closer to $20. That should have been cause for concern, but when he added two more timber limits in the summer of 1919, just two months before the election, the press and politicians reacted.[98] Shevlin-Clarke was a Minnesota company that already operated the largest pine sawmill in Canada at Fort Frances.[99] More significantly, its general manager and vice president was James Mathieu, who not coincidentally was also the Conservative MPP for Rainy River, the least populous constituency by population in the entire province. Even worse, Mathieu was helping Ferguson to manage the Conservative campaign, distributing election funds that presumably had come from Shevlin-Clarke.

This seemingly obvious corruption in the province's major industry convinced many people that Howard Ferguson "exquisitely personified" the Hearst government's "waste and corruption."[100] Dewart openly called him "the most corrupt influence in the Government,"[101] which, unusually for Dewart, may not have been an exaggeration. E.C. Drury was not only saying the same thing but also made a point during the campaign of promising that Ferguson's department would be investigated if the UFO formed the next government.[102] Hearst's inadequate response was that "there is nothing for which I need to apologize, nothing to take back."[103]

As the campaign drew to a close, he kept reaching out to farmers, explaining to an audience at Strathroy on 15 October how Cody's new consolidated school system would benefit rural students and rural communities, as would the province's provincial highway construction program.[104] At the same time, however, recognizing that his government might be returned with only a minority, he boldly defied his critics, declaring that he "did not care to be elected unless at the head of a strong majority" because "reconstruction problems have to be faced and dealt with effectively" and "only a stable government could do them justice." In fact, he actually declared that he no longer hoped that many UFO candidates if elected would support his government because having to rely on independent MPPs would make it "more difficult to achieve results." Recognizing that many voters were likely to vote for farmer or labour candidates, however, he promised to "give careful consideration to the claims of proportional representation."[105] Clearly, he was desperate.

While attacking the UFO, the government reached out to labour in an effort to hold on to its long-standing popularity in urban centres by publishing a full-page advertisement in the *Sault Daily Star* and other newspapers on 15 October, promising "recognition of labor needs" through "broad and sound labour legislation and an efficiently administered Department of Labor," including "cooperation with the accredited representatives of organized labor," "recognition of the eight hour day for the building trades on Government contracts," and "vigorous support" of the government's public employment service, which would be expanded, but there would be "strict regulation and restriction of private employment agencies" and "improved educational opportunities and specially for technical education." The Workmen's Compensation Act would be strengthened by imposing "increased responsibility upon employers," introducing stricter regulations regarding the operation of dangerous machinery, "minimum wage legislation based on the cost of living," the creation of part-time training courses and time given from employment to attend such courses, and investigation of hygienic conditions in industrial plants.[106]

Hearst's final campaign event before returning to Sault Ste. Marie took place on 15 October in Guelph's Griffin Theatre, which was packed for the occasion. Hearst appears to have selected Guelph for his final event because the Conservatives had held Wellington South from 1902 to 1914, when it was narrowly won by Liberal Sam Carter, a local businessman, former mayor, strong supporter of hydroelectric power and cooperative movements, and a prohibitionist. The Conservatives were hopeful that they could take it back in 1919 because their candidate, Caleb Buckland, was a popular Anglican clergyman, Orangeman, and prominent militiaman who had served overseas as a chaplain while his two sons served overseas in the army. Carter was a strong candidate but, unfortunately, he supported Dewart's claim that the government had knowingly allowed nickel to get to Germany to be used against Canadian soldiers, a claim that he repeated throughout the election campaign.[107] Perhaps understandably, Hearst took the opportunity to declare in his remarks that "no more unfair, cruel statement was ever made by any public man in public life"[108] because Dewart's charges had been debunked long before October 1919."[109] Meanwhile, the local ILP and UFO were running a joint candidate, John Cockburn, a prominent farmer and cattle breeder who had long been active in in church, agricultural, and educational affairs and also had lengthy experience on the municipal council of Puslinch Township.

The fact that Hearst spent the last three days of the campaign in Sault Ste. Marie reflected his awareness of how dangerous the situation was, and he reportedly spent much of his time moving around the constituency accompanied by T.E. Simpson.[110] On the evening of 17 October the man who, as the *Sault Daily Star* put it, "has put Northern Ontario on the map, including Sault Ste. Marie, while at the same time giving clean, honest administration to the whole Province,"[111] made his final appeal to the voters of Sault Ste. Marie at a political rally in the Columbia Hall.

The meeting drew an overflow crowd that filled "every inch of space from platform to the sidewalk all the way down the stairs," no doubt because political rallies in Sault Ste. Marie gave all election candidates the opportunity to speak. The *Sault Daily Star* optimistically thought that most of the people who attended "were "enthusiastic admirers" of Hearst, "evidence enough" that he "was popular in his old home town," but this proved to be not quite the case.

The evening began with Rev. H.J. Pritchard, the Presbyterian minister of St. Andrew's church and a keen prohibitionist who "was received with thunderous applause," explaining how to mark the referendum ballot without spoiling it. T.E. Simpson then introduced Hearst, reminding people that during the thirty years he had lived in Sault Ste. Marie "there was nothing of a public nature which he did not heartily endorse that was for the improvement of local conditions." As for his record as Premier, he had not been given the opportunity to lead the province in "normal conditions" but had done everything in his power to support the war effort "and I challenge any man to say he has not been true to that promise."[112]

That seemed a somewhat muted endorsement, but then Fred Davey, the chairman of the Conservative Association who was chairing the meeting, invited Arthur Roebuck to speak on behalf of James Cunningham, the ILP candidate. Roebuck was a young progressive lawyer who had lived for a decade in New Liskeard and knew northern Ontario well. He had been owner/editor of the *Temiskaming Herald* and the Cobalt *Citizen* and had run in the 1911 and 1914 provincial elections and as a Liberal in Temiskaming in the 1917 federal election ran against Frank Cochrane as a Laurier Liberal. Roebuck was a powerful speaker and, according to the *World*, "made a wonderfully telling address" that was "most effective" on the nickel issue, and "when he left the platform the crowd cheered and demanded that he continue speaking." Hearst, according to the *World*'s report, "did not even attempt" to rebut Roebuck's charges,"[113] but he was, in fact, rattled and responded by asking if the audience seriously preferred to have a millworker represent them instead of him, reminding the audience that "there are only two leaders" leading parties in the election and "Dewart cannot possibly win and Mr. Cunningham cannot be Premier." In other words, the Conservatives were most likely going to win the election, even if with a minority, so the people of Sault Ste. Marie would be foolish not to want the Premier as their representative. That was hardly an inspiring appeal for public support and in fact seemed to justify the widespread public dissatisfaction with the party system. He ended by asking how he had failed them. "During eleven years, wherein have I failed as your representative? What request has been made that I have not complied with? What demand has not been filled?" He ended with a plea and a risky challenge: "If I have been faithful, fair play and common justice entitles me to continuation of your support. If I have failed, then drive me from public life."[114]

The *World*, although a Conservative newspaper, may have exaggerated when it claimed that Roebuck's performance and Hearst's response "contributed more than anything else" to Hearst's defeat in Sault Ste. Marie, but there was no denying that it had made a strong impact.[115] The *Sault Daily Star* apparently agreed because its report on the meeting made no reference to the incident.

Meanwhile, Dewart had begun unofficially campaigning during the summer as well, but he was controversial even among Liberals because of his opposition to conscription and prohibition. But like Hearst and Drury, he promised that if elected he would carry out the wishes expressed by the voters in the referendum. Not unexpectedly, he waged a nasty campaign, spending nearly as much time attacking Rowell and Unionist Liberals as he devoted to Hearst and his government. Indeed, he lumped them together, arguing that when Hearst, Rowell and Proudfoot agreed on a political truce and even extended the legislature Hearst, they had in effect formed a provincial Union government.[116] But Dewart also ramped up his attacks on the nickel issue, insisting that the government had knowingly allowed Ontario nickel to be shipped to Germany during the war, making Hearst and Cochrane responsible for the deaths of thousands of Canadian soldiers. There wasn't much that the government could say except to repeat that only a very small amount of Ontario nickel had reached Germany in 1916, that was because the German cargo submarine carrying it had slipped through Britain's naval blockade in 1916, and that was not the provincial government's fault. Dewart also denounced the government for not forcing International Nickel to build a smelter in Ontario. In this case he was either badly uninformed or simply dishonest because he must have known that the government had in fact forced International Nickel to build a smelter at Port Colborne. Indeed, the government had also raised the tax on nickel mining and demanded $1.3 million in back taxes from International Nickel as well.[117] The political reality, however, was that Dewart was a nuisance but not a serious threat to the government. As Toronto journalist Ross Harkness later wrote, the Liberal Party under Dewart's leadership was "ineptly led, badly divided, and devoid of any program."[118]

The real threat to the Hearst government came from the UFO and, because it was a populist movement rather than a political party, it was difficult for traditional politicians like Hearst – or Dewart, for that matter – to respond effectively to it. That was because many rural people had come to the conclusion that Hearst wasn't really the problem; he was just the latest incarnation of a system committed to industrialization and urbanization, with little knowledge, interest, in or appreciation of the importance of agriculture and rural values to a healthy society. Rural depopulation wasn't just a political issue; it was also an existential threat that had been ignored for too long. Both parties were guilty in this respect. As a UFO committee had reported as early as 1916, "neither political party appears to have any true conception of the situation. Both parties are struggling for party advantage. They are seeking for pallatives [*sic*] rather than for true, fundamental reforms. The farmers of Ontario must rise to and deal with the situation themselves."[119] That surely became obvious when a debate on rural depopulation took place in the 1919 session and barely a quorum of members stayed in the legislature to participate or even listen. Even worse, when the debate concluded with a request to establish a commission to study the problem, the government insensitively rejected it.[120]

That, of course, was remarkably foolish in view of the surely obvious groundswell of frustration and anger that had been emerging in the rural areas of the province since 1918. But none of the chief UFO leaders – Drury, Morrison, Good, and Burnaby – sought election in 1919. The local UFO clubs acted independently, and their nominating conventions were enthusiastic affairs, reflecting the farmers' determination to create a new world in which they would have their rightful place. Most of the sixty candidates nominated during the summer of 1919 were seeking representation, not to form a government. As J.J. Morrison later recalled, "had any person hinted at such a thing it would have been received with ridicule."[121] Their goal, as the *Farmers' Sun* put it, was "to put in parliament a set of men organized to champion the farmers' cause and for that purpose to be free of the party restraints which now render farmers in parliament incapable of affording the championship desired."[122] Hearst's response to this was to remind voters that "every vote cast against a recognized supporter of the Government is a vote against the Government and its policies" and "a Government can be sustained only by the election of men who have confidence in it."[123]

What might seem like a modest change was in fact revolutionary because what many of these farmers sought was a whole new, nonpartisan, approach to politics. This was what confused and worried both Conservatives and Liberals because it was difficult to cope with a populist uprising that had no leader or political organization. The UFO's central office did, however, support the local clubs by sending out speakers and creating a committee that drafted a provincial platform.[124] Released in August 1919, that platform contained nothing new or startling; it repeated demands that farmers had been making for years: lower tariffs, reciprocity with the United States, legislation favouring cooperatives, and political reforms such as proportional representation, introduction of the initiative and referendum, and abolition of party patronage. Other demands were for a more equitable system of taxation that would make urban property owners bear their fair share of the tax burden resulting from the war, equal education facilities throughout the province, good township roads, and an expanded conservation program. It also endorsed prohibition and the continued expansion of the Hydro Commission and called for a publicly owned provincial telephone system – something that Beck had attempted to establish before the war – and the nationalization of privately owned railways. At the same time, they also called for retrenchment in government expenditures.[125]

Although the provincial government couldn't do anything about lower tariffs, Hearst's close associate Sir John Willison was strongly urging him in February 1919 to make them the main issue in the forthcoming election. Willison was president of the Canadian Reconstruction Association, an organization established in 1918 to promote business interests, and it feared that a reduction in tariffs would cause "prostration of industries, much unemployment, exodus of Canadians to American industrial centres, summary stoppage of the establishment of American factories in Canada and a great check to industrial and national development … How long," he asked Hearst, "can you keep the issue out of Ontario politics since hostility to the tariff is the chief bond of union among the organized farmers [?]"[126] Hearst sensibly ignored that issue and also the suggestion that he should oppose the nationalization of privately owned railways. Instead he focused on provincial issues on which he believed the government had a good record: supporting cooperatives, conservation, reforming the educational system to make it more relevant to farmers and workers, developing a provincial highway system intended to benefit farmers and rural communities generally, and building the largest hydroelectric generating plant in the world, as well as smaller regional ones. The government had, however, built a publicly owned provincial railway to open up the northland and could have introduced proportional representation and the initiative and referendum, but there wasn't actually widespread demand for such changes, and a century later no government in Canada has embraced them.

Who should control telephone service was a more serious issue, however, because telephones were becoming increasingly common, including in small communities and rural areas. The industry was, not surprisingly, dominated by Bell Telephone but there were hundreds of private companies as well, 450 of them small companies in rural Ontario.

Adam Beck had sought to include telephones – and telegraph services – in the Hydro-Electric Power Commission's mandate since at least 1910 and was supported by Newton Rowell when he became leader of the Liberal Party.[127] The government balked, presumably because of the cost but also perhaps because of pressure from business interests. Meanwhile, the UFO also called for retrenchment in government expenditures.[128]

The UFO did have specific demands, therefore, but it fought the election more on general reform principles and as representatives of the rural countryside versus the big interests and the political machines they controlled. When E.C. Drury campaigned against such things as the protective tariff and rural depopulation, for example, he declared, "[W]e are determined – and we are going to get it – to have economic freedom, and we are going to get rid of the Tariff that has allowed one class of exploiters to plunder the public."[129] Similarly, J.J. Morrison asked dramatically: "Where are the girls and boys who should be here? Gone to the city!" And the reason was clear: "Under the policy pursued by the old parties the concession lines and side-roads have been bled white, and the smaller urban centres have lost ground, while the larger centres have been made greater." This meant that only 30 per cent of the province's population were food producers who had to feed not only themselves but also the other 70 per cent, which explained the high cost of living. It was "a direct result of this upsetting of the balance in population."[130]

The UFO's strategy was very simple. Seventy of the province's 111 constituencies should be represented by a farmer because they were predominantly agricultural, and ideally the UFO candidates should be men who had formerly supported the party that had been most successful in the riding if there was one. "It was not to be expected," as Morrison explained, that a life-long Liberal would leave his party to support a Conservative principle that he may have favoured. Neither was it expected that a Conservative would leave his party and align himself with the Liberal for a similar purpose, but there were likely many people who would leave their party to vote for principle if they could do so without aligning themselves with their former enemy party. Thus the UFO "formed 'A No Man's Land' where these defecting partisans could meet on common ground and support principles that appealed to them as being in the interests of their industry and the state."[131]

This strategy proved to be effective, partly because there were three or more candidates in more than half (59) of the province's constituencies. Morrison claimed, no doubt honestly, that the UFO clubs were "absolutely impartial as between the old parties,"[132] but the government stood to suffer most from this strategy because it enabled rural Conservatives who had opposed conscription (at least after the exemption of their sons was cancelled) to abandon their party without having to vote Liberal. In the pre-election legislature the Conservatives held forty-six of the seventy predominantly agricultural constituencies and a large number of the UFO candidates – Morrison said two-thirds – in those constituencies were former Conservatives.[133] This was why Hearst initially felt confident that many of them would support him if he came out of the election with a minority government.[134]

In fact, Conservative strategy was to try to nominate rural candidates who were members of the UFO. That seemed to make sense but showed that the Conservatives didn't grasp the fact that the goal of the farmers' movement, as the *Farmers' Sun* explained, was "not merely to elect farmers but to put in parliament a set of men organized to champion the farmers' cause and for that purpose to be free of the party restraints which now render farmers in parliament incapable of affording the championship desired."[135] In case this wasn't clear enough, the UFO leaders declared early in the campaign that no member of the movement who accepted a Conservative or Liberal nomination would be allowed to carry the local club with him. And only one candidate, Nelson Parliament, who had been elected in Prince Edward County as a Liberal in 1914, did manage to carry the local UFO organization with him, but only after two UFO candidates had been nominated and withdrew from the contest.[136]

The other major element of UFO strategy was its working alliance with the Independent Labour Party. Unlike the UFO, the ILP was a political party but "not a mere party of reform, but as the party of a newly reconstructed social order" created by a loose alliance of local labour parties, trade union leaders, and socialists.[137] The war had stimulated labour radicalism in industrial communities and there were many such communities, large and small, in the province, ranging from Toronto in the south to London in the west and Welland in the south, Belleville and Renfrew in the east, and Fort William, Port Arthur, Sudbury and Sault Ste. Marie in the north. Not a cohesive party, its components shared a determination to obtain direct labour representation in the legislature. The ILP platform called for public ownership of all utilities, natural resources, banks and the credit system, the gradual elimination of unearned increment through taxation, pensions for mothers with dependent children, old age pensions, unemployment insurance, minimum wage legislation, and an eight-hour day. They also wanted to make the Canadian parliament and legislatures supreme and to abolish the Senate.[138] The ILP platform had nothing to say on the temperance question, however, because the labour movement was seriously divided on the subject. While many Labour men and their wives favoured temperance, many others, especially veterans, thought the Ontario Temperance Act had gone too far when it closed bars and taverns and drastically reduced the alcohol content of beer.[139]

Unlike the UFO, several prominent labour leaders ran in the election on behalf of the ILP: Morrison McBride in Brantford, John Vanier in Cochrane, Henry Mills in Fort William, George Halcrow and Walter Rollo in Hamilton, Peter Heenan in Kenora, Thomas Tooms in Peterborough, Frank Greenlaw in St. Catharines, James Cunningham in Sault Ste. Marie, and John Macdonald and James Simpson in Toronto.[140] The UFO's W.C. Good met several times with the ILP executive, with the result that the two movements worked together in several mixed rural–urban constituencies. In some cases joint nomination meetings agreed on a candidate or sometimes agreed to nominate a member of the one movement for the provincial election and a member of the other movement in the next federal election. In the end, there were six Farmer-Labour candidates and two Soldier-Labour candidates.

As polling day drew near, most observers thought that Hearst would be returned to office, albeit with a reduced majority. The *Daily Star* took this view, noting on 16 October that four Conservatives (in Addington, Hastings North, Kingston, and Toronto Northeast) had already won by acclamation. Two of them – Henry Cody, the Minister of Education, and A.E. Ross, whom Hearst intended to appoint Minister of Health – were considered almost non-partisan.[141] The Liberals were not even running candidates against forty-one other Conservatives. The *Daily Star* also expected that, if elected, Beck and Pratt would support the Conservatives. More importantly, "as two-thirds of the UFO candidates are former Tories and as the farmers are strong for total prohibition, the outlook is promising for both the OTA and the Government which enacted it." The *Daily Star* also believed that the UFO would elect more members than the Liberals, a view shared by I.B. Lucas and E.C. Drury. [142] The next day the *Daily Star* reported that Conservative Party organizers were more optimistic, expecting to win seventy seats, the Liberals expected to win at least forty, and UFO organizers thought they would win thirty. This pleased the *Daily Star*, which had generally supported the Whitney government since 1905 and endorsed Hearst because "he was … honest, puritanical, a prohibitionist, and a friend of public ownership."[143] The *World* somewhat more accurately predicted on 17 October that the Conservatives and Liberals would each elect forty-two members and the UFO would hold the balance of power with twenty-two seats.[144]

Election Day, Monday, 20 October, was "a bright fall morning, and the roadside maples were dressed in autumn glory."[145] Because the harvesting was completed, the rural roads were in good shape, people would be voting in the referendum as well as the election, and women were voting for the first time, "a bumper crop of votes" was expected.[146] E.C. Drury later recalled how he and his wife "walked together to the polling place in the old Temperance Hall, some half a mile [800 metres] down the road from their farm. He "found it a very pleasant experience, going with my wife beside me to cast our votes."[147]

The enfranchisement of women naturally had more or less doubled the number of eligible voters compared to the previous election in 1914, but the turnout in 1919 was more than double. Indeed, the 1.2 million people who voted constituted an astonishing 94.8 per cent of those eligible.[148] An exceptionally high turnout in an election normally reflects a high level of dissatisfaction with a government, and that was certainly the case in 1919. In Toronto that evening, "the downtown district began to fill with people as early as seven o'clock, and by nine o'clock it was impossible to move even an automobile in front of the newspaper offices, where bulletins were being flashed on the screen. Not a street car moved … in the newspaper district … so dense was the mass of people." The *World* thought it "peculiar" that "there was an absence of cheering," except from the crowd in front of its building, which "alone sustained old-time election night traditions." Its perhaps egotistical explanation was that it was the only Toronto newspaper that had "given expression in recent days to the insurgency in the ranks" and the crowd that gathered in front of its offices constituted "a liberal representation of those who had heard the call to a new order of things."[149] If that was indeed the explanation, the crowd would not have been disappointed with the result.

The Conservatives were crushed on all sides, dropping from eighty seats to twenty-six and a collapse in their popular vote from 54.6 per cent to 34.1 per cent.[150] The Liberals gained four seats, from twenty-four to twenty-eight, although their share of the popular vote dropped from 37.36 per cent to 25.43 per cent. Most dramatically, the UFO won forty-two seats, with 20.9 per cent of the popular vote, and the ILP won eleven seats, with 9.5 per cent of the popular vote. In other words, if the UFO and the ILP are treated as a single group, the Conservatives won the most votes but the fewest seats.[151] In terms of seats, allowing for the results of the twelve by-elections that had taken place since the 1914 provincial election, the Conservatives lost twenty-seven of the forty predominantly agricultural constituencies that it had held before the election, tying them with the Liberals at thirteen each, while the UFO jumped from two to forty-four seats. Even constituencies with long Conservative histories like Carleton, Dufferin, and Dundas elected UFO members. In the thirty-seven predominantly urban constituencies, the Conservatives dropped from thirty-one seats to twelve, the Liberals rose from six to thirteen and a mix of Labour,

Labour/UFO, and Soldier candidates won twelve. In northern Ontario's fourteen constituencies, the Conservatives dropped sharply from eleven to five while the Liberals rose from only two to five. The ILP rose from zero to three (Fort William, Kenora, and Sault Ste. Marie) and the UFO held onto Manitoulin. Clearly, the UFO had won a stunning victory. As "Spectator" declared in the *World*, "never was there such a wreckage of political orthodoxy ... The people have demanded a new deal; and if they don't get it there will be a ghastly failure on somebody's part."[152]

Because it had never anticipated being that successful, however, the UFO found itself in unexpected and uncharted territory because it didn't think of itself as a political party and didn't even have a leader. In fact, none of its most prominent spokesmen had even sought election, except for Manning Doherty, who came a poor third in Peel. That naturally encouraged Dewart, who had tried to avoid running Liberal candidates against UFO candidates, to think that he might be able to form a minority government with the support of the UFO members. That wasn't going to happen, however, because the UFO had no more use for the Liberals than the Conservatives, although J.W. Widdifeld had shifted from the UFO to the Liberals and been re-elected. J.W. Curry, who had won Toronto Southeast B for the Liberals, astutely recognized that his victory was less an endorsement of him or the Liberal Party than a desire by "many conservatives ... to send into oblivion the Hearst government."[153] W.D. Gregory and W.K. Murphy, prominent Liberals in Toronto, essentially agreed. Gregory told Mackenzie King that the result reflected widespread "disgust with the Hearst government and its works, or its lack of works," while Murphy said "it was a case of vote for any person but defeat the Government."[154] King, self-centred as always, naturally concluded that the results represented "the overthrow of Toryism. It means as sure as I am writing that I shall be called on to form a government at [the] next election if no serious mistakes [are] made in [the] interval."[155]

The Conservative *Sault Daily Star* conceded only that it "was one of the most remarkable elections that Ontario has ever experienced."[156] That was a gross understatement: the Hearst government hadn't just been defeated; it had been humiliated. Hearst and five of his nine cabinet ministers – Lucas, MacDiarmid, McGarry, McPherson, and Preston – were defeated. Only four – Cody and Ross, who had been re-elected by acclamation, and Ferguson and Henry had survived. The survivors were an odd lot: Cody and Ross were highly respected men widely regarded as virtually non-partisan, while Ferguson and Henry were the ministers of the two most criticized departments.

Part of the explanation for the remarkable success of the UFO was the fact that so many constituencies had multiple candidates, with the result that many won their seats with only a plurality of the votes, while the Conservatives won only twenty-six seats but placed second in sixty-two others. In effect, a farmer's vote had been worth almost twice that of an urban resident. The result was a phenomenal turnover of MPPs: only 33 of the 111 pre-election members would be returning to the legislature.

The disaster was made worse, or at least more painful to Hearst by his personal defeat in Sault Ste. Marie. At the outset of the campaign had felt quite secure in the riding he had represented since 1908. The *Sault Daily Star* had shared his optimism, even suggesting that he should be returned by acclamation in view of the fact that the community's prosperity depended largely on government support.[157] Surely, it argued, it would be irresponsible to elect a millworker to represent Sault Ste. Marie when it could have the Premier. But many people weren't thinking that way in 1919, especially as it became increasingly likely that the government was in real danger of being defeated. Hearst's brief comments on election night revealed his shock and disappointment. "No man has ever carried a greater strain in public life," he said. "I had to contend with many obstacles but I will show a record of which I will not be ashamed. Evidently," he concluded rather pathetically, "the people don't want me to represent the Sault any more."[158]

The 1919 election is generally interpreted as a victory by disgruntled farmers and workers over the two traditional parties. It was that but the reality was much more complex. In what might be described as a perfect storm, anger and frustration among both farmers and workers had reached the point, unthinkable before the war, that they not only sought direct political action. Their goal was not just to elect more MPPs who actually represented their interests but also, in many cases, to change the political system. We can only speculate, but it is reasonable to assume that their mothers, wives, and daughters, who were voting for the first time in 1919, agreed with them.

Another factor in the election was that almost all of Ontario's soldiers were home by the summer of 1919, and James Eayrs was undoubtedly right when he wrote that "those returning knew they were lucky to have returned at all, but the frame of mind of the homecoming Canadian soldier was not exactly placid."[159] Many of them also came home injured in body or mind, and while the federal and provincial governments had established convalescent hospitals and retraining programs, many veterans found them inadequate. Perhaps most seriously, many of them found it very difficult to reintegrate into civilian society after spending up to four years in dangerous and appalling conditions under a level of stress that no one who had not been there could possibly understand. They also came home to discover that they could not legally buy alcohol or enjoy a beer in a tavern with their friends.

Most of them were, inevitably, farmers or workers. Farmers felt betrayed by the Union government when it conscripted their sons after assuring them that it would not do so, and it had been fully supported by the Hearst government. Many workers were also angry because the politicians had promised that they would be taken care of when they returned home but what they often experienced was that their former jobs had been given to others who had not gone overseas or, in some cases, were now held by women who wanted to stay in the workforce and were favoured by employers because they were paid less than the men they had replaced. In other cases their jobs were held by immigrants, sometimes men from the countries that the veterans had been fighting. Some, perhaps unreasonably, were also angry to discover that the gross inequality of pay, privileges, and conditions between officers and men while overseas continued as former officers received higher pensions than enlisted men, and only former officers were appointed to the "lucrative positions" in the "overloaded" bureaucracy created to deal with veterans' affairs.[160] By 1919 many veterans were demanding that the federal government give them a cash gratuity, a proposal that the GWVA had endorsed in February, as did the Liberal Party convention in August. When Borden rejected the idea of a gratuity, "disaffected veterans" staged a demonstration at Queen's Park and formed the United Veterans' League. Their grievance was with the Union government, of course, but they were clearly and understandably making no distinction between the Borden and Hearst governments. The goal of the United Veterans' League, according to its president, John Henry Flynn, was to unite all veterans "into one grand body for political purposes, not necessarily a political party, but to use our political power to dictate the platform of one political party, and put that political party forth to represent us."[161] That prompted the federal government to create a parliamentary committee which was holding hearings on the matter of gratuities at the time of the provincial election. Although its report was not tabled until 31 October, nobody had seriously expected it to recommend gratuities, which must have further angered veterans during the election campaign.[162]

Thirty-five MPP veterans ran in the election. Fifteen were Conservatives, eight of them (incumbent MPPs: James Hartt [Simcoe East], Donald Hogarth [Port Arthur], Herbert Lennox [York North], Thomas Magladery [Temiskaming], Alfred Nixon [Halton], William Price [Parkdale], Arthur Ross [Kingston], and Donald Sharpe [Welland].[163] All but Sharpe were re-elected, Ross by acclamation. The other seven – Andrew

Gray (Leeds), Thomas Kennedy (Peel), William McBrien (Toronto Southwest B), James Mowbray (Kent), Paul Poisson (Essex North), Robert Soden (Peterborough West), and Joseph Thompson (Toronto Northeast B) – were new candidates, and only three of them (Gray, Kennedy, and Thompson) were successful. In other words, ten of the fifteen Conservative MPP veterans were elected. Three Independent Conservative veterans also ran in the election. Two of them – Harold Machin (Kenora) and Arthur Pratt (Norfolk South) – were incumbent Conservative MPPs who had broken with Hearst; the third was Arthur Kelly Evans (Toronto Northeast B), a prominent businessman who was a Conservative but thought the OTA was too extreme.[164] Only Kelly Evans was successful.

Seven Liberal veterans – Malcolm Lang (Cochrane), James Tolmie (Windsor), Kenneth Stover (Algoma), James Cane (Toronto Northwest A), Ashton Fife (Kenora) and Robert Arthur (Sudbury) – ran in the election. Lang and Tolmie were incumbent MPPs and both were re-elected. Of the five new candidates, only Stover and Fife were successful. Thus, Liberal veteran candidates won only four of seven seats. In a sense, the UFO did better because only two veterans – Dougald Carmichael (Grey South) and William Fenton (Bruce North) – ran for it and both won. Three veteran candidates ran for the ILP, two of them competing with George Halcrow, the prominent labour leader in Hamilton East, the constituency formerly held by Allan Studholme, the only Labour member of the legislature, from 1906 to 1919. Maurice Fitzgerald ran as a Soldier candidate, while Samuel Landers ran as a Soldier-Labour candidate.[165] Halcrow won comfortably. Samuel Wilkinson, who was only twenty years old, ran as a Soldier-Labour candidate in a four-man race in Wentworth South that was won by the UFO candidate.[166] He came in fourth.

As shocking as the overall election results were, Hearst was more surprised by the success of ILP candidates than the UFO candidates, telling Arthur Meighen that he had "never dreampt [*sic*] that labour would sweep the urban areas as they did."[167] This seems an odd observation, given that the ILP only elected eleven of its twenty-one candidates (Brant South, Fort William, Hamilton East, Hamilton West, Huron Centre, Kenora, London, Niagara Falls, Peterborough West, St. Catharines, and Sault Ste. Marie), but that did constitute a high success rate for a new party even if it was insignificant in a legislature of 111 seats. What is surprising, however, is that ILP didn't win any of Toronto's thirteen seats, although Joseph McNamara won Riverdale as a pro-labour Soldier candidate. John Vick, a labour leader, and George Lockhart, a socialist, were both defeated in Riverdale, John Buckley was defeated in Toronto Northeast B and John MacDonald lost in Toronto Southwest B. The real gains in Toronto were made by the Liberals. The city had been solidly

Conservative for many years until Hartley Dewart won Toronto Southwest A in 1916, but the battle in 1919 was intense because the two old parties were now competing with disgruntled veterans and an aroused labour movement. That meant that the twenty-five candidates seeking the thirteen seats included not just Conservatives and Liberals but Independent Conservatives and Liberals, soldier candidates, representatives of labour, one socialist, and combinations of these labels as well.

Indeed, the results of the election suggest strongly that many voters were more influenced by the background and values of candidates than the party or group that they represented. Dougall Carmichael, for example, who defeated Isaac Lucas in Grey South, had commanded the 116th Battalion in 1918, was twice wounded, and returned home with the Military Cross and bar and the Distinguished Service Order and bar, but the evidence suggests that it was his personal character and dedication to farming that earned him the respect of his community. According to the Ontario correspondent of the *Western Independent* newspaper, "two days after being demobilized he was into his overalls and hard at work again on his farm."[168]

But he was also one of the founders of the Grand Army of Canada,[169] although Margaret Haile, a socialist, had run in the 1902 election. That didn't change when the Hearst government enfranchised women but legislation allowing women to serve in the legislature was passed in the 1919 session. Only two women ran in the election: Henrietta Thompson Bundy in Toronto Northeast B and Justinia Sears in Ottawa West. The first woman to represent one of the two political parties in an election, Bundy was president of the Toronto Women's Liberal Association. Little is known about Sears, but she was a widow and for several years a bookkeeper at Ottawa's city hall until she took over the management of her son's business after he was killed in the war. She ran as an Independent, although her inclinations were Conservative and she subsequently became a founding member of Ottawa's Women's Conservative Association. Both women supported the OTA and were progressive on social issues. Bundy certainly received a very respectable 8,685 votes in a battle between two Conservative veterans, Joseph Thompson and Arthur Kelly Evans, in Toronto Northeast B. Sears came a weak fourth in Ottawa West.[170] But if the Conservative Party did not run a female candidate in 1919 it nearly did. Dr. Caroline Brown, an obstetrician at Women's College Hospital, member of the Toronto Board of Education and the Orange Order, contemplated challenging W.D. McPherson for the Conservative nomination in Northwest B, but in the end changed her mind. That may have been a mistake because she might have been a stronger candidate than McPherson, who was defeated in a close two-way race.

If there was any good news for Hearst in the election results, it was that Adam Beck was defeated in London. Both the Conservatives and the Liberals had kept out of the contest, making it a straight two-way race between Beck and Dr. Hugh Stevenson, a popular physician and former mayor who was well known and respected in the city. As popular as Beck was for his leadership of the public power movement, his box factory paid very low wages and he was known to be anti-union. According to the *World*, he was not only "repudiated" by the labour unions; the campaign against him "was financed by funds from the Montreal corporations and such interests as are represented by The Financial Post of Toronto."[171]

The results in northern Ontario, like the rest of the province, were a disaster for the Conservatives because they lost eight of the eleven seats they had won in 1914, not only the three (Fort William, Kenora and Sault Ste. Marie) won by Labour candidates but five to the Liberals, a gain of three (Algoma, Nipissing and Parry Sound). The Conservatives, who had dominated the region for years, retained only Muskoka, Port Arthur, Rainy River, Sudbury, and Temiskaming. Manitoulin re-elected its UFO member. All of the losses in the region except for Muskoka were in industrial communities. The party's collapse in northern Ontario no doubt reflected the Hearst government's identification with the Borden government and conscription, but there were other factors as well.

Some people in northern Ontario thought, despite the significant efforts of the Whitney and Hearst governments to develop the region, that it might be better off if it separated from Ontario. Northerners could hardly complain about the amount of money spent on roads and other policies designed to support forestry, mining and agriculture, but some felt that their voices were not being heard in Toronto. Whether this reflected the fact that 14 constituencies out of 111 did not give them much leverage or because they thought the government didn't recognize that policies that were popular in southern Ontario did not necessarily serve the north. James Hylands, a mining engineer in Cobalt, linked the OTA to growing alienation in northern Ontario when he denounced "the Uplifters of the South, who have everything," apparently unaware that "in this country there are very few pleasures, few diversions." Hylands, who was actually writing to E.C. Drury just after he took office, went on to warn him that just as King George III had lost the American colonies, "it is possible that you will be the man who will go down to posterity as the man who lost Northern Ontario."[172] That seemed a bit extreme but when Howard Ferguson became Premier in 1923 he acknowledged the problem by appointing a legislative secretary for northern Ontario and later established a regional headquarters of the Department of Lands and Forests in Port Arthur.

Another prominent factor must have been the Franco-Ontarian vote. There were some 248,275 Franco-Ontarians in the province, and it has been calculated that they formed a majority of the population in two constituencies, comprised 10 per cent or more in fourteen others, and were sufficiently numerous to be possibly decisive in close contests in six more.[173] In other words, they were a political factor in twenty-two constituencies, and this was a close election in most constituencies. In every constituency in which Franco-Ontarians formed a significant portion of the population, except for Rainy River, Sudbury, and Temiskaming, the Conservatives failed either to retain or recover the seat. They didn't even contest Essex South, Glengarry, Ottawa East, or Russell.[174] The problem wasn't just Hearst's bilingual schools policy; it also appears that Franco-Ontarians voted heavily against him in opposition to the OTA. Ottawa East, the only predominantly Franco-Ontarian constituency for which referendum figures are available, was also the only constituency to vote against retaining the Act. But Joseph Pinard, a Liberal, had won Ottawa East in 1914 and held it until 1929 and then was elected to the House of Commons from 1936 to 1945, so his popularity must have been a factor. In Essex North, Conservative Dr. Paul Poisson, a Franco-Ontarian veteran who had been wounded at Courcelette, was defeated by a Franco-Ontarian UFO candidate with support from the Liberals, so it is not clear how important the OTA was compared to the desire to elect a farmer.[175] Poisson had been defeated in the 1914 election as well.[176]

The province's substantial Irish Catholic population also probably played an important role in the result. The size of the Irish Catholic population cannot be determined with any certainty, but there were approximately 365,700 non-French Catholics listed in the 1921 census, compared with an Irish population of 590,500. Traditionally Liberal, some Irish Catholics had switched to the Conservatives in recent years because of the bilingual schools dispute. At the same, however, some thought the OTA was too extreme.

Meanwhile, resentment among the province's large immigrant population against the discrimination and internment many had faced during the war and the xenophobic attacks by Conservatives in 1918 and 1919 presumably meant that they did not support the Conservatives, if they ever had. Henry Scholfield, who was chairman of the Soldiers Settlement Board and was running in Toronto Southeast B, may have had this in mind when he told a campaign meeting that immigrants who had been disfranchised in 1917 should never again be allowed to vote because, "having once been disfranchised, they can never be got to vote for the Conservative party again."[177] There is no evidence that Hearst agreed with this suggestion and Scholfield was easily defeated in a two-way race by James Curry, a Liberal.[178]

There is also reason to believe that at least some in the business community deserted Hearst. People engaged in the liquor industry in any way were understandably very angry, although the distilleries had actually done well with war contracts for chemical products. But Hearst had also alienated private power interests when he supported the Hydro Commission's expansion into the generation of electricity as well as its distribution, and he alienated many supporters of the commission because of his reservations about radial railways. Even his moderately progressive legislation over the years establishing the eight-hour day for some miners, the wartime moratorium on mortgages, government employment bureaus and his subsidized housing program had been strongly opposed by financial interests and some builders and contractors. As if that weren't enough, he had gone even further during the election campaign, promising minimum wage legislation and the appointment of ministers of health and labour. How serious a factor the business and financial community's hostility to Hearst was in the election result cannot be determined, but that there was hostility cannot be doubted.

There is a tendency to believe that the outcomes of elections are usually pretty straightforward, and in 1919 Hearst was convinced that the Ontario Temperance Act was the major issue. It had, he acknowledged, "turned many warm personal and political friends of my own into enemies. It has brought upon me more abuse and criticism ten times over than all other political questions combined since I entered public life."[179] That was true, but he was downplaying or even ignoring other issues that were also important. Indeed, he thought it inconceivable that "the people of this Province could turn out of power a Government against which no criticism could be brought."[180] And he was encouraged by the fact that he had had "excellent meetings in every section of the Province" during the campaign "and the feeling for the Government appeared to be good," so he had "expected to have a clear majority over all."[181] Clearly, he was out of touch with public opinion and he certainly had not had an excellent meeting in Sault Ste. Marie. Even so, he believed that "many of the United Farmers were friendly to the Government" and "would give the Government independent support" if it didn't win a majority. What did surprise him was the success of the ILP.[182]

This analysis made little sense, however, because Labour candidates won only 11 seats in urban areas – 13 if we include Labour-Independent and Labour/UFO winners – out of 111 seats, while the UFO won 42 rural seats and the Liberals won 28 seats in a mixture of rural and urban constituencies. And the Conservative popular vote had fallen from

54.6 per cent in the 1914 election to 34.1 per cent and that was in an electorate that had more than doubled from 498,091 to 1,170,831. Having said that, however, the Conservatives had won a plurality of the popular vote. The Liberals had come second, with 26.5 per cent; the UFO third, with 20.9 per cent; and the ILP last, with 9.5 per cent.[183] These results were inevitable in a first-past-the-post electoral system when there were more than two candidates in so many constituencies.

Still, the results did broadly represent the attitudes of the province's voters in 1919, and Hearst had seriously misread the situation. He had believed that his government would "sweep the country" because he had assumed that people who supported the OTA would also support the government that had passed it.[184] So too did Sir George Foster, who denounced the "rank ingratitude" of "the temperance people for whom [Hearst] imperilled his political future."[185] What both men failed to recognize was that, while most people did support the OTA, they were not otherwise satisfied with the Hearst government, which explains why two-thirds of them voted to retain the OTA unchanged but only slightly more than one-third of them voted to re-elect the government.

The problem was that the 1914 election had taken place before the war and Sir James Whitney, who had led the Conservatives into power in 1905, had been both popular and respected. Hearst's succession came as a surprise because he hadn't appeared to be the obvious candidate, and he led a divided party because he hadn't been chosen by his caucus. But the government had been in office for fourteen years by 1919, and its close identification with the Borden government, which had been an asset until 1914, had become a handicap because times had changed dramatically during the war.

Throughout his term in office Hearst had tried to continue Whitney's strategy of identifying the Conservative Party with the rapidly growing urban industrial areas while maintaining its rural base as well.[186] It was a shrewd strategy and might have succeeded if the war hadn't changed the political environment. Hearst's government did, as he believed, have a good record on supporting the farmers during the war while advancing social legislation to assist workers, women, and veterans, but it had also unreservedly supported conscription and Union government even when Ontario was contributing 40 per cent of the volunteers.

The 1917 federal election, which had seemed a great victory, was in reality a disastrous failure of leadership because it involved abandoning the fundamental responsibility of all national governments to preserve and promote national unity. Wilfully blind to the reasonable view of their opponents that there surely was a limit to Canada's responsibility in what was, after all, a European war, they denounced their opponents as disloyal, rewrote the electoral laws to deprive many people of their right to vote, and flagrantly cheated in the distribution and counting of ballots. They had also, in the view of many people, lied to the voters and especially to the farmers when they exempted farmers' sons from conscription only when they thought they were going to lose the election, then cynically cancelled the exemption three months later. Hearst had supported all of this.

Many people would probably have acknowledged that the Borden government had had to deal with an immensely difficult situation since 1914 and might be forgiven for some errors and misjudgments. What many people could not forgive was a government that got into office by fostering ethnic and religious division and shameless flag-waving and then clung to power by manipulating the political system, apparently unaware that imperialism, which had been a mainstream attitude in Ontario before the war, became divisive because of conscription and Union government, and a real political liability after the cancellation of the exemption of farmers' sons.

Hearst could hardly deny – indeed was proud – that he had fully supported the Borden government, even as it became increasingly unpopular in 1918 and 1919. The cost of the so-called Great War, which the politicians had turned into an existential crusade, had been high, and some, especially farmers and workers, thought it had been too high. They had opposed conscription and profiteering during the war, and many of them, reinforced by the returning veterans, thought the OTA was too strict and was being enforced too harshly. They also thought Hearst's multifaceted reconstruction program and proposed modifications to the OTA were not enough. The 1919 election provided the first opportunity to those who believed that, after the most terrible war in history, it was surely time for change, perhaps even systemic change.

J.W. Dafoe, the wise and well-informed editor of the *Manitoba Free Press* and no friend of Conservatives anywhere, warned in July 1919 that the wartime governments in Canada – federal and provincial – would not only have to "bear the sins and blunders of the past four years" but would also have to pay the price of "an unpopularity which all governments in reconstruction have to bear, that of not being able to accomplish miracles." Anyone "who holds office now or at any time during the next five years" was "entitled to a measure of sympathy" because "it is going to be demanded of him that he do things that cannot be done; things that are mutually contradictory and destructive; and whatever he does he will have more critics than friends."[187] Sir John Willison said much the same thing when he told the historian G.M. Wrong that "there could not have been a worse time for a general election" because of the wave of anti-imperialism sweeping the country in 1919, and "every anti-Imperialist voted against the Hearst Government."[188]

As usual, they were right, and Hearst was only the first incumbent to offer voters the chance to express their frustration and anger. As Conservative journalist J.K. Munro observed, "constituted authority is more or less in contempt at the present time," and Ontario's voters "showed that they were tired of things as they are and were prepared to try something, or anything else." The "Ontario earthquake was a protest not only against the Hearst Government, but against other Governments of a like kind," specifically the Union government.[189] Arthur Meighen essentially agreed, telling Hearst that he had "suffered no doubt for the acts of the Dominion administration," placing the blame of course on the "wholly irrational state of the public mind at present" voters."[190] The *Daily Star* agreed more temperately that "the feeling of dissatisfaction was so general that neither Sir William Hearst nor any other man in his place could have stood up against it."[191] Even Peter Oliver, who has little good to say of Hearst, concedes that "certainly there was much evidence that the times were out of joint and that Hearst had succumbed to the abnormal conditions of the day."[192]

The collapse of the Ontario government in 1919 tends to be referred to as if it were unique, but the Unionists knew, to quote Munro, that "if we went to the country to-morrow not a corporal's guard would return."[193] In fact, the Hearst government's ignominious defeat was just the first in what became a wave of populist repudiations of the old political parties throughout Canada. Manitoba's Liberal government lost its majority in a 1920 election and was replaced by the Progressive Party two years later. Alberta's Liberal government, in office since 1905, was defeated by the United Farmers of Alberta in 1921. Farmer-labour movements also won seats in the Nova Scotia and New Brunswick legislatures in 1920 and in Saskatchewan in 1923. When the Union government, now under Meighen's leadership, called a federal election in 1921, it mirrored the Ontario result, with the Unionists coming in only a pathetic third with forty-nine seats. King's Liberals won a plurality but were dependent for their survival on the Progressive Party. But the significance of the farmer-labour uprising between 1919 and 1923 wasn't that it toppled a number of governments; it was that it ended the old two-party system.

Hearst contributed to his government's defeat by totally neglecting the party organization during the war and agreeing to a political truce during the war. He also kept aloof from the seamier side of politics, leaving that to Ferguson, McGarry, and Lucas. That was a well-intentioned and honourable attitude of a man who, as Peter Oliver acknowledges, "was dominated by a sense of public duty,"[194] but it was a serious political error that Whitney would not have made and reinforced the view of many Conservatives that Hearst lacked the qualities required of a political leader. Howard Ferguson once claimed that "the most important" task of a political leader was "the creation of an atmosphere," to "give a leadership and trend to public opinion that will secure the support of the press and gradually strengthen his position."[195] Hearst didn't achieve that because he was a modest, diffident man who did not naturally dominate a room as Whitney had done. He didn't even dominate his cabinet, allowing his ministers to manage their departments with minimal direction. He might be described as earnest, a term that Robert Borden often used – perhaps with himself in mind – to describe men who worked hard but lacked brilliance.

But if Hearst lacked Whitney's strong personality, he was more progressive and receptive to the growing demand for social reform even if he approached it cautiously. The reform that he regarded as his most significant achievement was the OTA, which had virtually universal support when it passed. And yet it proved to be the most politically damaging thing he ever did because many of his own caucus members thought it was too extreme and voted for it against their better judgment. When it became politically divisive, many blamed the Methodist "do-gooder" from northern Ontario who had no mandate from either the party or the voters.

And when he welcomed Rowell's offer, extended by Proudfoot, of a political truce until the war was won, he made another serious error because as the war dragged on and the cost in terms of lives and social and economic dislocation mounted, no one in the political system – other than Dewart – was representing those who were increasingly thinking that the cost was becoming too high and nobody was holding the government to account. That forced dissident farmers, workers, and veterans, regardless of their pre-war party loyalties, to question the validity of the system. This bewildered Hearst, whose government did introduce significant reforms to the educational system, collaborated closely with the federal government in reconstruction programs for veterans, introduced several social support programs, and was modernizing its structure to include ministries of health and labour.

Hearst might have been more successful if his party caucus had been allowed to determine Whitney's successor, but it almost certainly would have chosen Lucas or possibly Hanna, but not Hearst. He was chosen by a dying leader who respected his abilities and was strongly influenced by Frank Cochrane, his closest long-time political colleague and advisor. Whether or not Hearst was the best choice is almost irrelevant because many, if not most, members of the party caucus resented having no say in the matter, and Hearst never succeeded in obtaining their full support. Whoever succeeded Whitney would have struggled to fill his shoes, but Whitney and Cochrane had unwittingly undermined him. Hearst might have earned the support of his caucus if he had called and won an election in 1917, and he considered doing that but thought it improper to arouse partisan divisions in wartime even though the federal Conservatives and every other province did, and Whitney likely would have done so.[196] Worse, Hearst also totally neglected the party organization during the war.

Internal party dissent was inevitable, and it wasn't long before at least two dissident MPPs – Arthur Pratt and Harold Machin – began working openly to depose him, encouraged by Adam Beck. The party was so sharply divided by 1919 that twenty-one Conservative MPPs declined to seek re-election or lost their nominations and Pratt, Machin, and Beck ran as independents. A deeply divided party cannot win an election, especially in the stormy political environment of 1919, but the seeds for its destruction had been sown in October 1914.

# 10 The Final Chapter

*Ten years from now, when his name is mentioned most people will think that the allusion is to William Randolph Hearst, the yellow journalist.*[1]

NOT surprisingly, the immediate result of the election was confusion. As Henry Cody observed, "things certainly seem to be somewhat involved."[2] One thing was clear: Hearst had been rejected, both locally and provincially, and he had no intention of staying on as party leader. He immediately announced that he would resign from office as soon as possible and from politics as well. But who would he advise the lieutenant governor to call upon to form the new government? When Hendrie rather foolishly declared that, given the situation, he had the right to call on a member of any party to form a government, the London *Advertiser*, a Liberal newspaper, equally foolishly said that meant that he should call on Dewart because he was the only party leader who had been elected.[3] The reality was that it would have to be the leader of the United Farmers of Ontario (UFO) because it held the largest bloc of seats in the legislature, but the UFO did not have a leader. Even so, Hearst immediately returned to Toronto and met with Drury, the UFO's first president and the only UFO leader with any political background. He had served as reeve of Oro Township in Simcoe County and his father had served in the legislature for thirteen years as a Liberal and from 1882 to 1890 was the province's first Minister of Agriculture. E.C. Drury had run unsuccessfully as an independent Liberal in the 1917 federal election, denouncing the Union government as "merely the old Government with a bit of window dressing" but supporting conscription as a necessary evil while calling for the conscription of wealth as well.[4]

According to Drury, his meeting with Hearst was cordial. Hearst did not conceal the fact that he "felt his defeat rather keenly," believing that "the temperance people of the province had betrayed him" and, to his credit, Drury replied that he "could understand his feelings in the matter and sympathized with them."[5] Drury asked Hearst to remain in office until the UFO leaders and newly elected members met, which they did later that day. After deciding that they would form a government in cooperation with the labour members, they had to choose a leader. One would have thought that Drury would have been their first choice, but he wasn't. It would have been Manning Doherty, except that he was a former Conservative and a Catholic and had been defeated in the election.[6] They also considered Peter Smith, a prosperous farmer from Stratford who had been elected in Perth South, but some had reservations about him.[7] They then approached Adam Beck, who had shown interest in leading the UFO before the election but he had lost his seat in the election.

Drury, who was a member of the committee formed to meet with him, recalled many years later that Beck "received us in a very friendly manner" and gave "a very nice little speech in which he promised full cooperation with any government that might be formed, but – he declined the leadership."[8] Morrison, who was also there, had a quite different recollection. He claimed that Beck addressed the meeting of the UFO members, not just the committee, because he was interested. Morrison was determined to prevent "such a dangerous leadership," however, and he and Drury agreed that, while Beck was "then easily the most powerful political figure in Ontario," he was also "a most peculiar man, and a very hard man to get along with."[9] In Drury's words, Beck "had the instincts of an eighteenth-century European aristocrat and the character of a tyrant."[10] Hearst would have agreed with that.

Beck's refusal left only Morrison and Drury as probable candidates, although neither had run in the election. When the UFO members asked Morrison on 23 October to lead the new government, it is hard not to conclude that they wanted almost anybody but Drury. But Morrison too declined, forcing them to approach Drury.[11] He wisely took a week to think about it before concluding that he "could not refuse and accepted the challenge."[12] A few days later, the Independent Labour Party (ILP), meeting in Hamilton, decided that it would cooperate with the UFO in forming a government if invited to do so.[13]

Hearst now advised Hendrie that he should call on Drury to form a government, which he did, and Drury agreed but asked Hearst to continue in office while he interviewed potential ministers and that was problematic because there were gaps in the expertise of the UFO members. This was, as W.C. Good acknowledged, an "embarrassing situation" for both Hearst and Drury, but it reflected two facts: the election results were "quite unexpected"[14] and the UFO was seriously divided between those like Morrison and Good, who saw it as a non-partisan movement, and those like Drury, who saw it as a new people's party. Hearst had no desire to remain in office after the election, but he understood the situation and agreed to remain in office until Drury was ready to take over.[15] Thus, it was not until 14 November, a full twenty-four days after the election, that the new government took office and Hearst's political career formally came to an end.

Hearst did more than resign from office in November 1919. He gave up the party leadership as well and took no further part in politics in any way for the rest of his life. Nor did he attend the party's leadership convention in 1920 – the one that his critics had wanted to hold in the summer of 1919 – because he knew that the "love feast" as one newspaper described it wasn't for him. The organizers of the event made that clear when they displayed enormous portraits of Sir John A. Macdonald and Sir James Whitney in Toronto's Masonic Hall, presumably because they had been popular winners. No tribute was paid to Hearst for his years of service or even acknowledgment of his government's achievements. The delegates were thinking about him, however, because one speaker's reference to him provoked "excited booing from the floor."[16] They also adopted a resolution declaring that "the leadership of the Conservative party ... is not in the gift of any coterie ... but must emanate from an organic body of the party, constituted for [that] purpose."[17] In other words, leaders would henceforth be selected by party conventions summoned specifically for that purpose. It was the final rebuke of Hearst for the manner of his selection.

The love feast was for Howard Ferguson, who had served as Conservative house leader in the 1920 session of the legislature and was recognized as Hearst's logical successor, presumably because he was so different from Hearst but also because he was one of the four ministers who had survived the election and the most skilful politician among them. He had also been Hearst's closest colleague in cabinet and Hearst had strongly urged him to seek the leadership.[18] There were other nominal candidates, however. The *Globe* claimed on the eve of the convention that George Henry, W.F. Nickle, A.E. Ross, and even Adam Beck would seek the leadership,[19] but only Henry allowed his name to go forward. He did not expect to win, nor did Earl Lawson, an ambitious Toronto lawyer who also joined the contest. As expected, Ferguson won on the first ballot.[20]

If Hearst was a political pariah to many in the Conservative Party, he was not shunned by the former colleagues with whom he had worked most closely. Henry Cody's biographer refers to "dinners back and forth between the Hearsts, the Fergusons, and the Codys" over the years.[21]

Lucas remained a close friend and Hearst included him and one of his sons in a business venture. Hearst scrupulously avoided politics for the rest of his life but not before taking the opportunity, when invited "not long" after his defeat to address the annual conference of the Methodist Church of Canada, to condemn it for not supporting him in 1919. "Still smarting under a sense of injustice from the way the election and the plebiscite [*sic*] had gone," Irving later recalled, he took the opportunity to "point out to the reverend gentlemen that it was not much encouragement for a Christian man to go into politics when he not only could not count on the support of his church, but felt that it abandoned him when he had made great sacrifices to provide the very kind of legislation that they themselves advocated." That was a distortion of the facts, of course, but according to Irving, "the occasion gave him no little satisfaction."[22]

Hearst also made public statements on a couple of occasions. During the 1923 provincial election campaign he spoke on the temperance issue at Sherbourne Street Methodist Church, his own congregation,[23] and during the 1929 election he publicly repudiated Liberal charges that Ferguson had led the anti-temperance Conservative revolt against his leadership in 1919 as "unwarrantable and baseless." Indeed, he claimed that it was Ferguson – not Hanna – who had actually drafted the Ontario Temperance Act.[24] Ferguson and Henry frequently consulted Hearst privately during their administrations.[25] When Ferguson wanted to appoint Charles Magrath to the chairmanship of Ontario Hydro in 1925, for example, he asked Hearst to encourage him to accept the appointment.[26] He did and Magrath took on the position.

The major question was what lay ahead for Hearst. There seemed to be no reason to return to Sault Ste. Marie, since the family had not actually lived there since 1912. He and Bella had an attractive home in Toronto and the family had built their lives there over the past seven years. But Hearst needed an income. He had some investments but he was not a wealthy man. He had always paid his own personal campaign expenses, accepting assistance from no one, and there was no pension plan or even separation allowance for members of the legislature, including ministers. Hearst naturally hoped that his Unionist friends in Ottawa would offer him an appropriate appointment, especially since his strong support of conscription and Union government had played a significant role in the defeat of his government. Hendrie's term as lieutenant governor was drawing to a close, but that would not have been an appropriate appointment in the circumstances, and it was only a short-term position in any case. There was a vacancy in the Senate, but in November 1919 Borden – presumably at Rowell's request – gave that to William Proudfoot, who had lost his seat in the provincial election. One might have thought that Hearst's claim would have been stronger than Proudfoot's, but there is no evidence to suggest that Borden even considered him, and it seems unlikely that Hearst would have accepted it if he had. He was done with politics.

What he hoped for was a judicial appointment. The *Daily Star* thought he might be appointed to the Ontario Supreme Court, whose members are appointed by the federal government.[27] As it happened, a vacancy was imminent because Justice Byron Moffatt Britton – a former Liberal MP – was eighty-six years old and in poor health. Hearst approached Arthur Meighen, the Minister of the Interior in the Borden government, just days after the election and was assured that "you may absolutely depend upon my attitude being favourable."[28] But when Britton died in November 1920, Meighen – who had become Prime Minister in July – appointed John Fosbery Orde, whom Irving Hearst bitterly described as "an unknown lawyer."[29] In fact Orde was a prominent lawyer in Ottawa, a founder of the Canadian Bar Association, and a Conservative. Both of Hearst's sons, refusing to accept that Orde was more qualified than their father, concluded that Meighen had been influenced by J.D. Reid, his influential cabinet colleague from Ontario who was thought to have opposed the Ontario Temperance Act.[30] The more likely explanation for Hearst's failure to obtain a judicial appointment, however, was that Borden had offered Hearst a position on the International Joint Commission (IJC) in December 1919, and he had accepted it.[31]

The IJC is a quasi-judicial Canadian–American joint body that was established in 1909 to prevent and resolve disputes over waters shared by the two countries and for settling other transboundary issues.[32] Hearst had dealt with such issues when he was Minister of Lands, Forests and Mines and Premier and enjoyed the work.[33] Because that work was highly technical and legal, however, and not directly relevant to his political career, it is not discussed here.[34]

But there were two problems. One was that the salary was only $7,500, compared to the approximately $10,000 Hearst had earned as Premier or what he would have earned as a Supreme Court judge.[35] More important was the fact that judicial appointments were tenured and appointments to the IJC were not. Still, the IJC, as Irving put it, offered "at least a dignified meal ticket," and he accepted the appointment "on condition it would not prejudice any changes when a position opened on the Bench."[36] That caveat was meaningless, however, because any future federal government could replace him, but Hearst likely realized that his former friends in Ottawa weren't going to offer him anything better.

He therefore decided that he must also return to the law, and when Irving was called to the bar in 1920, they established the Hearst & Hearst law firm in the Excelsior Life Insurance building on the corner of Toronto and Adelaide Streets in Toronto. According to Vernon, their net fees during the first year averaged only about twenty-five dollars a week, and Sir John Willison, who had worked closely with Hearst on unemployment and housing issues during the war year and was "a good friend," took up a collection among his friends to help him out.[37] One cannot help suspecting that that the situation wasn't as bad as it sounds, however, because when Lorne Campbell Webster, a wealthy Montreal businessman, offered Hearst a position on the board of directors of the Imperial Trust Company in December 1919, Hearst declined it.[38] And it wasn't long before the attorneys general in the Drury and Ferguson governments hired Hearst to prosecute criminal cases for the crown or sought legal opinions from him, and the Ontario Hydro-Electric Power Commission "frequently retained" him "in outstanding negotiations."[39]

More importantly, Willison appointed Hearst vice president and chairman of the executive committee of the Municipal Bankers' Corporation, a mortgage and loan company that he established in 1921, and when he created another company, Canadian Rail and Harbour Terminals, a commercial real estate company, he appointed Hearst vice president of it as well. Hearst also ventured into business on his own. In 1923 he and Irving purchased the Durham Furniture Company in Durham, a town south of Owen Sound, from David Jamieson, the Conservative MPP for Grey South from 1898 to 1919, speaker of the legislature when Hearst was Premier, and a long-time friend. This company had been manufacturing quality furniture since 1889 that was sold nationally through the T. Eaton Company's annual catalogues. It was – and remains – a successful company. Hearst and Irving financed the purchase by incorporating the company and issuing 10 thousand preferred shares of $25 each and 10,000 common shares. This venture was a family affair because the board of directors included not only Hearst and Irving but also Evelyn Hearst and Royden Gilley, whom Evelyn was to marry in May 1924. I.B. Lucas's son, George Kendall Lucas, was company solicitor.[40] Hearst was also president of Professional Offices Limited, a commercial real estate leasing operation that operated out of his law firm's offices.[41] He was also included in a committee of prominent citizens in 1927 that included Sir Joseph Flavelle, Sir James Wood, and Henry Cody to support the creation of a large public square on the land in front of Toronto's newly completed Union Station proposed by E.W. Beatty, the president of the Canadian Pacific Railway.[42]

So, after a difficult year or so, the Hearsts were doing very well in the 1920s. They continued to live in Rosedale, they had at least one maid, they acquired a summer cottage at Lake Simcoe, and they frequently travelled to Atlantic City at Easter and Florida in the winters.[43] And despite the claims of Vernon and Irving that there was strong hostility to their father among Toronto's elite and that he had "few ... real friends,"[44] the evidence certainly suggests that they were part of Toronto "society," if not at the highest level. Vernon later claimed that when Willison sponsored Hearst for membership in the exclusive Toronto Club he was told to drop it or be "blackballed."[45] If that was true, the explanation may be that the Toronto Club was – and still is – the most exclusive private club in Canada and Hearst would have been in good company if he was rejected for membership. But the Hearsts were listed in the Torontonian Society's *Blue Book,* and Hearst belonged to the exclusive Toronto Hunt Club and the Albany Club, the Conservative businessmen's club, as well as the less exclusive Scarborough Golf and Country Club, the Royal Canadian Institute, the Masonic Order, and the Empire Club, of which he was president in 1922. Bella belonged to the Toronto Ladies Club and the National Chorus, a society headed by Sir Henry Pellatt that produced concerts of choral works by British composers. She was also included in a 1930 book titled *Women of Canada* that profiled prominent women, such as Lady Eaton, Lady Beck, and the wives of J.E. Atkinson of the *Daily Star* and J.R. Christie of the Christie Biscuit Company.[46] The Hearsts' two daughters had attended a private school and were now attending the University of Toronto, as both Vernon and Irving had done. One of them, Isabel, was a member of Delta Gamma, an expensive American sorority, and the exclusive Toronto Lawn Tennis Club. In June 1922 she married Sherman Dana Archbold, a wealthy American whose father was secretary treasurer of the Imperial Oil Company. Howard, Irving, and Evelyn also married well, if not as impressively as Isabel.

When Vernon and Irving recalled financial stresses they may have been thinking more of the 1930s when Hearst's income dropped significantly. The global depression proved to be "fatal" to "nearly all" of the Municipal Bankers' Corporation's businesses,[47] requiring the family to manage on Hearst's IJC salary and whatever he earned from his law practice. What that amounted to is unknown but he continued to provide legal advice to the provincial government, for example in 1932 drafting a bill authorizing it to provide a subsidy to the near-bankrupt Abitibi Paper Company.[48] And Hearst still owned part of the Barnes Block, a commercial property in Sault Ste. Marie that he had acquired in 1916. He sold that in January 1932 but held a $3,000 mortgage on the property until it was paid off in May 1934.[49] And he still belonged to the expensive Toronto Hunt Club and the Albany Club, along with less expensive clubs, such as the Canadian Club, Empire Club and Royal Canadian Institute, while Bella belonged to the Toronto Ladies' Club and the IODE.[50]

Little did they know that an old investment, largely forgotten, was about to pay off. Early in the century Hearst had done some legal work for Alois Goetz, a well-known prospector in Algoma. Unable to pay his bill, Goetz conveyed half of his interest in an iron ore claim. Hearst shared it equally with his then law partner, John McKay, and signed his own share over to Bella, who liked to joke over the years about how they would spend their great wealth when the claim was developed. The Josephine mine, as Goetz had named it, was acquired in the 1930s by Thayer Lindsley, who has been described as "the greatest mine finder of all time" and "the father" of Falconbridge Ltd, one of the largest mining companies in the world.[51] He didn't develop the Josephine mine until the early 1940s, too late to help William or Bella, both of whom had died by then, so the money was divided among their four children.[52]

Meanwhile, Hearst enjoyed his work at the IJC.[53] It consisted of six members, three each from Canada and the United States. At the time of his appointment, the other two Canadian members were Charles Magrath and Henry Powell. Born in Ontario, Magrath had moved to Alberta as a young man and prospered, becoming the first mayor of Lethbridge, a member of the Northwest Territories legislature from 1891 to 1898 and MP for Medicine Hat in the House of Commons from 1908 to 1911. He was appointed to the IJC in 1911 and became chairman of the Canadian section in 1915. Hearst had known him since 1913 when Magrath chaired Ontario's Provincial Highways Commission. Powell was a lawyer from Saint John and former Conservative member of the New Brunswick legislature and the House of Commons. The third position had been vacant since December 1918 when P.G. Mignault, a prominent legal scholar, was appointed to the Supreme Court of Canada.

Hearst enjoyed the work of the IJC because it was a quasi-judicial body and dealt with resource issues, but his initial concern about the lack of tenure quickly proved to be justified after the Liberals won the 1921 federal election and King began looking about for offices with which to reward Liberal stalwarts. Within a month he sent for Magrath and made it "very clear" that the government wanted the resignations of the three Canadian members of the IJC.[54] Typically, King assured Magrath that his resignation would not be accepted and it was only Hearst and Powell whom he wanted to replace. Magrath's principled reaction was to tell Hearst and Powell what King had said and to immediately submit his own resignation.[55] This prompted King to meet with the three commissioners on 6 February. According to Magrath, King was "very agreeable," explaining that the government "regarded the Commission not in the same light as the Civil Service Commission" and "felt that we should hand in our resignations. It did not follow that the Government would accept our resignations, though he wished to make it clear that we should not take it for granted that they would not be accepted." When Hearst asked if he might have a little time to think the matter over, King "at once acceded," adding, however, that "if any men were to be appointed, they should be appointed at a reasonably early date, leaving us to understand that more or less prompt action was necessary."[56] The urgency presumably reflected the fact that King was leading a minority government and couldn't be sure how long he would be in office, and he very much wanted to appoint Aimé Geoffrion, a prominent Quebec Liberal whom Laurier had nominated just before the 1911 election. Borden had withdrawn the nomination and appointed Thomas Chase Casgrain, a prominent lawyer and Conservative MP, and when he died in 1916 replaced him with Mignault.

This placed Hearst in a difficult situation because, while he acknowledged that the government had the right to remove members of the commission at will, he needed the job but also believed that he was uniquely qualified for it because as Minister of Lands, Forests and Mines and as Premier he had extensive experience dealing with issues related to resources and Canadian–American shared waterways. Also, he regarded the IJC's work as being "in the very highest sense Judicial and in no sense diplomatic," which meant there was no need for the commissioners to have the political confidence of the government of the day. Indeed, the rationale for the creation of the IJC had been to depoliticize the issues it dealt with. In other words, commissioners, like judges, were expected to be independent of the government of the day.[57] Hearst suspected that King was being pressured by Quebec Liberals to punish him because of the Regulation 17 affair and feared that "if the view spreads that prevails now in some quarters, that I am being sacrificed at the dictation of Quebec … excitement and prejudice will be stirred up and much bitterness strife and hatred engendered."[58]

King claimed, however, that the three Canadian members of the IJC were selected to represent three regions: the Maritimes, Central Canada, and the west. That was true but the representatives of Central Canada since 1911 had been from Quebec and King argued that the commission "cannot be expected to function properly or to carry the weight it should" without a Quebec representative.[59] That meant that there could never be a member from Ontario even though the border and waterways that it shared with the United States were probably ten times those of Quebec, a concern that Hearst had raised with the government in October 1918.[60] King's specious response to that was that Ontario now had two representatives on the commission because Magrath was also from

Ontario. The reality was that, while Magrath had been born in Ontario, he had moved to Alberta at the age of eighteen, became a prominent business figure there, served in the legislature and even represented Alberta in the House of Commons.[61]

Hearst wisely rejected a suggestion that he get the Conservative Toronto *Mail and Empire* to take up the issue, but the Liberal *Daily Star* rallied to his defence with an editorial demanding that King leave the commission alone.[62] Hearst did appeal to Newton Rowell, who had left the Union government in July 1921, and Sir William Mulock, both of whom he regarded as personal friends who had influence with King, to intercede on his behalf. It seems unlikely that Rowell had much influence with King after having led the Liberal Unionists in Ontario, and there is no evidence that he took any action. Mulock did, however, and did have influence with King who had been his deputy minister. To his credit, he wrote "a strong letter" to King, suggesting that he leave Hearst on the commission because he was "poor & out of everything."[63] This was surprisingly generous, given Mulock's intense partisanship and hostility to the Ontario Temperance Act. Likely more important, however, was the fact that King's "chief organizer and the man who is understood to have the patronage in Ontario in his hand told me personally that he would guarantee that I would not be moved."[64] Hearst did not actually name this man, but he appears to have been referring to Andrew Haydon, an Ottawa lawyer who was general secretary of the National Liberal Organization Committee from 1920 to 1922 and King's "most trusted political adviser."[65]

King now claimed that he was "inclined to be generous in this regard if my colleagues can be brought to share my views,"[66] and Hearst thought – or perhaps hoped – that "if King's hands were not tied I think he would give way to pressure that has been put forth on my behalf."[67] There is no record of whom he may have consulted, but the combined influence of Haydon, Magrath, and Mulock prevailed, at least temporarily.[68]

He returned to the issue a year later. While acknowledging that Hearst had "shown real ability and has attended faithfully to his duties … it is natural," he explained, "that many of our own friends should feel that within the Liberal ranks are members of the legal profession as eminently qualified to serve on the Commission as the former Conservative Premier from Ontario."[69] He again consulted Mulock, proposing an arrangement that he thought would achieve his goal but satisfy Hearst as well. Professing to believe that "there should be consideration in regard – even by opponents – for men who have so sacrificed their professional opportunities in an endeavour to serve the public," King made the astonishing suggestion that Hearst could be appointed to the Ontario

Supreme Court if he "could secure the immediate resignation of one of the Merediths."[70] He was referring to the two Meredith brothers, Richard and Sir Ralph, both of whom were Conservatives then serving on the court.[71] The suggestion was clearly outrageous, and King cannot seriously have believed that Hearst would do as he suggested. It was also an insincere offer because he didn't appoint Hearst to the court when Ralph Meredith died a few months later.

For whatever reason Mulock did not support Hearst this time, telling King that Hearst was "not regarded as a strong lawyer, and his appointment to the Supreme Court of this province could not be defended on the merits." Whether or not that was a fair assessment, Mulock's real argument was political. Liberal lawyers would resent the appointment, he thought, and King should not do anything to weaken his political support in Ontario when he was leading a minority government and held only twenty-one of the province's sixty-five seats. Besides, Mulock cruelly added, there was no need to do anything for Hearst. He should simply be given the choice between retiring gracefully or being dismissed, and he volunteered to deliver that message to Hearst![72]

Even King wasn't quite that ruthless, although he did again request Hearst's resignation and, when Hearst again declined, threatened to obtain authority from the British government for the Canadian government to appoint and remove members of the commission. This was a technical matter because the IJC had been created by the Boundary Waters Treaty of 1909, which the British government had signed on behalf of Canada, meaning that to dismiss a member of the commission the Canadian government had to ask the British government to do it on its behalf. This was not an idle threat. While attending the imperial conference in October 1923 King did raise the question with the Colonial Secretary, the Duke of Devonshire, who promised that the British government would cooperate if asked to do so.[73]

Again, however, King let the matter rest, perhaps because he was preoccupied with more pressing political matters. Having managed to survive for four years while leading a minority government, he called an election for October 1925. This must have encouraged Hearst because the likely outcome was far from certain. It was even rumoured during the campaign that Hearst would become chairman of the Canadian section if Meighen toppled King because Magrath had recently accepted – on Hearst's recommendation – Howard Ferguson's offer to succeed Adam Beck as chairman of Ontario Hydro.[74] The Conservatives did win the most seats in the House of Commons, but King didn't resign because he still had a razor-thin majority with the support of the Progressives. The government survived only to June 1926, however, when King resigned and Meighen formed a government that survived only three days. In the 1926 election, King regained power, still dependent on the Progressives, and remained in office until 1930. Meanwhile, despite having become chairman of Ontario Hydro, Magrath continued to serve as chairman of the IJC's Canadian section as well.

In February 1928 King again asked Mulock to talk to Hearst on his behalf. Mulock did so, telling Hearst that King felt he had been very generous in letting him remain on the commission this long, that Powell had indicated his willingness to retire and he should do the same. Mulock also warned Hearst that if he did not retire voluntarily King would dismiss him, pointing out the fact, which Hearst already knew, that he had been given full authority by the British government in 1924.[75] Hearst naturally turned to Magrath, who proposed to King through Charles Bowman, the editor of the Liberal Ottawa *Citizen*, that he appoint a Quebec representative in Powell's place and he would serve under him with Hearst.[76] Magrath's leverage was that he knew King wanted him to leave Ontario Hydro and devote full time to his duties on the commission. King not only rejected the offer;[77] he also didn't take the opportunity when Powell resigned in July 1928 to replace him with someone from Quebec. Instead, he appointed George W. Kyte, a long-time Liberal MP from Nova Scotia. King wasn't interested in a compromise.

But he didn't pursue the matter again before the 1930 election that elected R.B. Bennett's Conservatives with a large majority. That meant that for the first time in ten years Hearst enjoyed a respite, but when Bennett lost the 1935 election, King, now leading his first majority government, resumed his efforts to get rid of Hearst. He was more aggressive this time because, aside from wanting a Quebec representative on the IJC, he was also looking for a suitable position for Charles Stewart, his former Minister of the Interior who had lost his seat in the election. Hearst was seventy-one years old by now but still felt unable financially to give up the post and expressed an almost pathetic wish that he be left alone for just a few more years, when he would retire gracefully.[78] King met with Magrath on 14 November 1935 and told him that "the time had now come when it would be proper to let Hearst know that we felt some change in the personnel of the Commission should be made." Magrath responded that "it would be a pity if we found it necessary to change Hearst; that he was a very useful man on the Commission, having a wide knowledge of conditions, particularly in Ontario, also, that he was a poor man, and would be in great distress" if he was dismissed. Instead, he proposed that he retire because he was seventy-six years old and that would enable King to appoint Stewart as the western representative on the commission.[79] This worked well because Stewart, like Magrath, was from Alberta and could represent the western region. King accepted the offer, conveniently ignoring his earlier claim that Magrath hadn't really represented the west because he was born in Ontario because that was true of Stewart as well. That apparently didn't matter now.

This effectively ended King's long campaign to remove Hearst from the IJC. Hearst was seventy-one years old, and King accepted his promise that he would retire within the near future because his health, never robust, was failing. He had been seriously ill in the spring of 1935 and missed a commission meeting for the first time since his appointment.[80] He retired from his law practice in 1939 but clung to his position on the IJC until in the spring of 1940, when he was diagnosed with Parkinson's disease. He knew he could not carry on and in April submitted his resignation, to take effect on 1 October. It was promptly accepted.[81]

Hearst lived less than a year past his retirement. The Parkinson's disease advanced quickly, and seventeen months later, on 27 September 1941, he lapsed into a coma and died at home two days later. His funeral took place on 31 September at Sherbourne United Church, formerly Sherbourne Street Methodist Church, which he and his family had attended since moving to Toronto in 1912.[82] Its new young minister, Rev. Wilfred Lockhart, conducted the service, assisted by Hearst's old friend Henry Cody, now the president of the University of Toronto. He was buried in Mount Pleasant Cemetery in Toronto, "a place of little valleys and gently rolling hills" among "a great company of men who [had] made their mark in the world of business and public affairs."[83] His immediate neighbours include politicians he had known well during his career: George Ross, Clifford Sifton, Newton Rowell, Howard Ferguson, George S. Henry and W.L. Mackenzie King.[84] When Bella died less than a year later, on 9 April 1942, she was buried alongside him. Vernon, Irvin, and their sister Evelyn are also buried there with their spouses.[85]

Hearst's death went largely unnoticed. The *Sault Daily Star* limited its obituary to a brief factual summary of his career. Toronto's *Evening Telegram*, although a Conservative newspaper, actually ignored his death, perhaps because of its unreserved loyalty to Adam Beck in his battles with Hearst. The unpredictable *Globe and Mail*, which the brash young millionaire George McCullagh had created in 1936 by merging the two former newspapers, praised Hearst as a "staunch supporter of progressive legislation" and a "brilliant lawyer" whose "keen, analytical mind … gained him prominence in the field of law."[86] Like McCullagh, that was somewhat extreme, but at least it was positive. The lengthiest and most thoughtful obituary appeared in the *Daily Star*, which, despite being a firmly Liberal newspaper, had often supported Hearst during his years in office. After reminding its readers that he was "entitled to be remembered for his social reforms" and also for the further reforms that he was preparing when his government fell and were introduced by his successors, it concluded that he was a "good citizen" and "a man whose influence was for good, whose ideals were high, and whose native province was the better for his piloting hand."[87]

If Hearst's death went largely unnoticed in 1941, he remains virtually unknown today. Hector Charlesworth had rather brutally predicted in 1919 that this would be his fate. "Ten years from now," he said, "when his name is mentioned most people will think that the allusion is to William Randolph Hearst, the yellow journalist."[88] That has proven to be true. There is an historic plaque in Tara reminding people that he was born nearby; also a street in northern Toronto, an office tower at Queen's Park, and, some what ironically, a predominantly francophone town in northern Ontario are named after him. He remained largely forgotten in Sault Ste. Marie until recent years when his home was designated a provincial historic site, the city's civic leaders named a street after him and honoured him with a plaque on the city's Walk of Fame. More significantly, they voted in 2015 to celebrate Ontario's traditional August holiday as Sir William Hearst Day.

And yet, more than a century after he governed the largest and wealthiest province in the country, the industrial heartland and the source of nearly half of the Canadians who served in the First World War, most scholarly books and journal articles on the period make only passing references to him, usually negative. Given that no one has ever published a biography of him, one cannot help suspecting that their authors are somewhat lazily playing follow-the-leader. The defining fact about him appears to be that he and his government were thrown out of office after the war. But so too was the Borden government and other provincial governments and the governments of Britain and the United States. In other words, he was the first political casualty, but certainly not the only one, of the widespread social and political unrest that swept the country after the war.

And yet, his legacy was significant. As a young backbencher, he had advocated advocated for health measures, including improved working conditions for miners in northern Ontario. As Minister of Lands, Forests and Mines he played a major role in securing for Ontario the vast Keewatin territory that enlarged the province's territory by half and vigorously promoted the forestry and mining industries and agricultural settlement in northern Ontario. He was a prominent member of the government that passed the first workers compensation act in Canada and was responsible for implementing and improving it. He established Ontario's first government employment agencies and first government assisted public housing scheme, initiated a major modernization of the province's educational system by introducing technical and vocational education and raising the school leaving age. He enfranchised women, including the right to hold public office, and prepared the legislation establishing mothers' allowances and minimum wage legislation for women. He supported Ontario Hydro's transformation from distributor to producer and raised the enormous financing that made it the largest publicly owned power utility in North America. He began the modernization of the provincial government by creating the agencies that became the Departments of Municipal Affairs and Highways, initiating the development of Ontario's provincial highway system, and was about to appoint the province's first Ministers of Labour and Health when he left office.

A century later, however, Hearst is remembered if at all as the politician who imposed prohibition on Ontario, the implication being that he was a narrow-minded puritan who forced his views on the province. In fact, he was a moderate social reformer, and the Ontario Temperance Act was highly popular because it addressed the undeniable social damage that alcohol was inflicting on society. A strong majority of the eligible voters had demanded it in a provincial petition, both political parties supported it, and it was subsequently strongly endorsed in a referendum. And when public opinion chose in subsequent years to modify it, later governments continued to regulate the sale of alcohol, the policy still in place a century later.

At the same time, Hearst led the province's contribution to the war effort, which was enormous, in terms of enlistments and industrial and agricultural production. There is no denying, however, that the war created profound social stress and Hearst's unwavering belief that victory was necessary at all costs while gradually separating him and those who thought like him from the growing number of people who believed by 1917–8 that the cost had become too high. He was well aware that the war was becoming increasingly divisive but, like many others, he was convinced that compromise was not an option in what he regarded as an existential crisis. He could have called an election in the spring of 1917, as Whitney would have done, and probably would have won it because conscription and the frustration and anger among farmers and workers were still in the future. Instead, he established a wartime political truce with his Liberal opponents and, with their approval, delayed the election until the war was over and virtually all of the soldiers were home. By then, the political and social environment had changed radically.

One blot rests on his political career. This was the bilingual schools dispute, which badly damaged relations between English and French Canadians and negatively impacted the war effort. Hearst did not create the problem but he agreed with Whitney that Ontario should not have bilingual or French-language schools. A century later most Canadians have embraced bilingualism and even multiculturalism, but Hearst lived in a very different time when the vast majority of English-speaking Canadians believed that Canada was – and should be – an English-speaking "British" country. This was already problematic before 1914, but it became much worse during the war, fuelled by Anglo-Protestant bigotry and Franco-Catholic nationalism. To some extent the crisis was artificial in that Franco-Ontarians believed incorrectly that the British North America Act guaranteed their constitutional right to bilingual schools, while virtually all anglophones feared that French Catholics were actually challenging Anglo-Protestant supremacy in Ontario. And it was not coincidental that Anglo-Protestants expanded their fear of "others" to include xenophobic hostility to people of enemy descent and virtually all immigrants, a pot that many Conservatives, including Hearst, vigorously stirred.

He has been criticized for ignoring party interests and not maintaining the party organization during the war. In fact, he thought partisan conflict was inappropriate in wartime and welcomed the offer from the opposition Liberals of a political truce. But the alignment of the Conservatives and many English-speaking Liberals in support of the war had the effect of encouraging those who doubted that the war was an existential conflict and objected to conscription, at least in English Canada, causing them to reject both parties and even in some cases the party system. Hearst thought this too radical, unnecessary, and likely doomed to failure, a view shared by many others that, on the whole, proved to be true. The era of the two-party system came to an end, but the two old parties made adjustments and continued to dominate the political scene.

He has even been criticized for not having a magnetic personality. It is true that he was no John A. Macdonald or Wilfrid Laurier, but neither were Robert Borden, W.L. Mackenzie King or Louis St. Laurent, and one can readily think of other politicians who lacked magnetic personalities but were very successful. But there is no denying that he did not have a strong personality. The journalist Augustus Bridle might well have been referring to Hearst when he said of Newton Rowell that "by no exercise of imagination could one conceive such a man as a Canadian political leader. If there is anything in an aura he has it not."[89]

A major criticism of Hearst, especially among the dissidents in his party, was that he was a Methodist "do-gooder" who ignored the views of those who disagreed with him. When Augustus Bridle referred to Newton Rowell's "insistent righteousness," adding that "a halo would have suited him,"[90] he was expressing the view of many of Hearst's Conservative critics. But that was unfair, even if just focused on the temperance issue because, while Hearst certainly believed in strict temperance or even prohibition, he only agreed to pass the OTA when it was clear that there was overwhelming support for it and even then promised to hold a referendum after the soldiers came home. He kept that promise and the act was endorsed by a comfortable majority.

Accusations of insufficient forcefulness and a tendency to "do-goodism" miss his real problem as a political leader. That was that many in his own party never really accepted his leadership because he had not been chosen by the party caucus or a party convention. Instead, he had been chosen by Whitney, influenced by his closest advisor, Frank Cochrane, in a secret letter he sent to his cabinet. Not unreasonably, many if not most Conservative MPPs resented their exclusion from the process, especially those who thought Hearst was not the best choice, not least because it was well known that he was Cochrane's protégé.

This situation was not Hearst's fault, of course, and there is no evidence to suggest that he knew about Whitney's memo recommending him before it was presented to the cabinet. But he doesn't seem to have made any serious effort to reach out to the disgruntled MPPs either. He might have sought confirmation from the caucus, but that would have seemed disrespectful to Whitney and would also have been risky because the most popular members in caucus were Hanna, Beck, and Lucas. Both of them were problematic, however, and the real choice was between Hearst and Lucas, the two youngest men in the cabinet. But Whitney had been grooming Hearst since 1905 while allowing Lucas to languish on the back benches since 1898 before taking him into his cabinet in 1913.

The Toronto *Star Weekly* once commented that Hearst was "an excellent citizen who ... had greatness thrust upon him" but "you never receive from him ... the impression of great reserves of repose on which he never fails to draw."[91] It's not clear what the writer specifically had in mind in that statement but he may have meant that Hearst was not a deep thinker or a politician who had the ability to distinguish between politics and the underlying values of Ontarians. Whitney had had that ability and so too, for better or worse, did Howard Ferguson, and both men proved to be successful Premiers. An unidentified observer probably summed up what the *Star Weekly* was trying to convey when he said of Hearst, "that's a good man, but he isn't quite big enough for his job."[92]

But he was a man of unquestioned integrity who served his province well during a period of unprecedented instability during the greatest global war in history to that time. A traditional turn-of-the-century Conservative, he was also a moderate progressive but struggled to comprehend the social and political turmoil aroused by the war. He undoubtedly made mistakes, but his tenure was fatally flawed by the unfortunate manner of his selection made him the leader of a divided party, a handicap he failed to overcome. He accepted his rejection with serenity – after the initial shock – and genuinely believed, as he predicted in the legislature in 1916, that "the Conservative who in years to come reads the record which his party is writing today will have no cause to blush as he reads that record."[93] He retired from public life with "the witness of a clear conscience that in the hour of my country's greatest peril, I hesitated not to do what to me seemed right and waited not to count the cost."[94]

# Appendices

**Members of the Hearst Government**

*Prime Minister and President of the Council*
William H. Hearst, 2 October 1914–14 November 1919
*Minister of Agriculture*
James Stoddart Duff, 2 October 1914–17 November 1916
William H. Hearst, 19 December 1916–23 May 1918
George S. Henry, 23 May 1918–14 November 1919
*Attorney General*
James Joseph Foy, 2 October 1914–22 December 1914
Isaac Benson Lucas, 22 December 1914–14 November 1919
*Minister of Education*
Robert Allan Pyne, 2 October 1914–23 May 1918ch
Henry John Cody, 23 May 1918–14 November 1919
*Minister of Labour*
Finlay George MacDiarmid, 28 February 1919–14 November 1919
*Minister of Lands, Forests and Mines*
William H. Hearst, 2 October 1914–22 December 1914
G. Howard Ferguson, 22 December 1914–14 November 1919
*Minister of Public Highways*
Finlay George MacDiarmid, 17 January 1916–14 November 1919
*Minister of Public Works*
Finlay George MacDiarmid, 2 October 1914–14 November 1919
*Provincial Secretary and Registrar*
William John Hanna, 2 October 1914–19 December 1916
William David McPherson, 19 December 1916–14 November 1919
*Provincial Treasurer*
Isaac Brock Lucas, 2 October 1914–22 December 1914
Thomas William McGarry, 22 December 1914–14 November 1919

*Ministers Without Portfolio*
Richard Franklin Preston, 2 October 1914–14 November 1919
James Joseph Foy, 22 December 1914–13 June 1916
William James Hanna, 19 December 1916–21 June 1917
A.E. Ross, 22 September 1919–14 November 1919

**Temperance Referendum Results***

1. Are you in favour of the repeal of the Ontario Temperance Act?

| Total Votes | Yes Votes | % | No Votes | % |
|---|---|---|---|---|
| 1,141,595 | 369,434 | 32.4 | 772,161 | 67.6 |

2. Are you in favour of the sale of light beer containing not more than two and fifty-one hundredths per cent alcohol weight measure through Government agencies and amendments to the Ontario Temperance Act to permit such sale?

| Total Votes | Yes Votes | % | No Votes | % |
|---|---|---|---|---|
| 1,142,900 | 401,893 | 35.2 | 741,007 | 64.8 |

3. Are you in favour of the sale of light beer containing not more than two and fifty-one hundredths per cent alcohol weight measure in standard hotels in local municipalities that by a majority vote favour such sale and amendments to the Ontario Temperance Act to permit such sale?

| Total Votes | Yes Votes | % | No Votes | % |
|---|---|---|---|---|
| 1,142,613 | 386,680 | 33.8 | 755,933 | 66.2 |

4. Are you in favour of the sale of spirituous and malt liquors through Government agencies and amendments to the Ontario Temperance Act to permit such sale?

| Total Votes | Yes Votes | % | No Votes | % |
|---|---|---|---|---|
| 1,142,894 | 449,370 | 39.3 | 693,524 | 60.7 |

* *Ontario Gazette*, 52:49 (6 December 1919) 2932–4; reprinted in Larry Johnston and Rick Sage, *Referendums in Ontario: An Historical Summary* (Toronto: Legislative Assembly of Ontario, 2007), 9.

# Notes

### Introduction

1 See Margaret E. Prang, *N.W. Rowell: Ontario Nationalist* (Toronto, 1975); C.W. Humphries, *"Honest Enough to be Bold": The Life and Times of James Pliny Whitney* (Toronto, 1985); Charles M. Johnston, *E.C. Drury: Agrarian Idealist* (Toronto, 1986); and Peter Oliver, *G. Howard Ferguson: Ontario Tory* (Toronto, 1977).

2 Brittany Luby, *Dammed: The Politics of Loss and Survival in Anishinaabe Territory* (Winnipeg, 2020), 18.

3 L.P. Hartley, *The Go-Between* (1953; rpt, New York, 2002), 25.

### Chapter 1

1 Archives of Ontario (AO), Sir William Hearst fonds. Ms of speech to Ottawa Canadian Club, 8 November 1913; cf. ms of speech to Toronto Empire Club, 28 November 1912.

2 Michael S. Cross, "The Shiners' War: Social Violence in the Ottawa Valley in the 1830s," *Canadian Historical Review* 54, no. 1 (March 1973): 4.

3 Dennis Carter-Edwards, "Promoting a 'Unity of Feeling': The Rebellions of 1837/1838 and the Peterborough Region," *Ontario History* 101, no. 2 (Autumn 2009): 169.

4 Rainer Baehre, "Pauper Emigration to Upper Canada in the 1830s," *Histoire sociale/Social History* 14, no. 28 (November 1981): 345.

5 B. Leslie Winslow letter to Irving Hearst, 6 July 1932. Copy shared with the author. Winslow was a solicitor in Enniskillen.

6 W.N. Hurst letter to Irving Hearst, 26 January 1951. Hurst was also an Irish immigrant who had settled in Belleville, Ontario, and was registrar of Hastings County in 1951. Copy shared with the author. Many years later, Elizabeth Hearst, William's daughter, reported "a dreamy recollection of

a family conference at the time of his death, and nothing more definite being arrived at" regarding his birthplace than that "it must have been near Enniskillen as that is the town I remember hearing him speak of." Elizabeth Hearst letter to Irving Hearst, 2 April 1931. Copy shared with the author.

7 W.I. Hearst, *The Red-Haired Boy* (Toronto: Unpublished manuscript, 1982), 4.

8 Don Cummings, Serge Occhietti, and Maude-Emmanuelle Lambert, "Grosse Île and the Irish Memorial National Historic Site," *The Canadian Encyclopedia*, accessed 12 June 2021, www.thecanadianencyclopedia.ca/en/article/la-grosse-ile/.

9 Charlotte Blake Thornley, the mother of Bram Stoker, who lived in Sligo at the time but whose family fled during the epidemic, wrote that when they returned, "we found the streets grass-grown and five-eighths of the population dead." Billy Finn, "Bram Stoker's Donegal Roots," *Donegal Annual: Journal of the Donegal Historical Society* 57 (2005): 66, accessed 13 June 2021, https://donegalhistory.ie/donegal-annual-2005/.

10 The McFaddens were listed in the records of the Montreal Emigrant Society, which supported immigrants upon their arrival and organized their onward journey, on 12 October 1832. Accessed 4 January 2020, www.bac-lac.gc.ca/eng/discover/immigration/immigration-records/immigrants-montreal-emigrant-society/Pages/item.aspx?IdNumber=1339&/. Irving Hearst says that they "spent some time" in the "eastern townships." Hearst, *The Red-Haired Boy*, 5. W.I. Hearst's first name was William, but he was always known as Irving. Similarly, his brother's first name was Howard, but he was always known as Vernon. Irving Hearst says that they "spent some time" in the "eastern townships." Hearst, *The Red-Haired Boy*, 5.

11 Peterborough County First Nations, accessed 4 May 2022, www.ptbocounty.ca/en/growing/first-nations.aspx#:~:text=We%20respectfully%20acknowledge%20that%20Peterborough,Lake%2C%20Georgina%20Island%2C%20Hiawatha%2C. For a useful albeit brief history of the Anishinaabe see Alan D. McMillan and Eldon Yellowhorn, *First Peoples in Canada* (Vancouver, 2004), 108–15.

12 Olive Patricia Dickason, *Canada's First Nations: A History of Founding Peoples from Earliest Times* (Don Mills, 2002), 163.

13 Ibid, 164.

14 Karl S. Hele, "Land Cession," *The Canadian Encyclopedia*," 23 October 2021, accessed 30 June 2022, www.thecanadianencyclopedia.ca/en/article/land-cession/.

15 Carter-Edwards, "Promoting a 'Unity of Feeling,'" 168.

16 Edwin C. Guillet, *Pioneer Days in Upper Canada* (Toronto, 1933), 3.

17 Ibid, 5.

18 Hearst's grandson, Vernon, recalled many years later that the family had always believed that his grandfather fought for the Queen in the 1837 Rebellion. Vernon Hearst interview. Neither William McFadden nor any of the other Dummer Township militia ever received their pay. It's not clear if Hearst did. Carter-Edwards, "Promoting a 'Unity of Feeling,'" 182–6. Cf. Thomas W. Poole, *A Sketch of the Early Settlement and Subsequent Progress of the Town of Peterborough, and of Each Township in the County of Peterborough* (Peterborough, 1867), 176. Cf. Edwin C. Guillet, *The Lives and Times of the Patriots: An Account of the Rebellion in Upper Canada 1837–1838, and the Patriot Agitation in the United States, 1837–1842* (Toronto, 1963).

19 Irving says the hill rose from what was known locally as "the sink hole swamp." Hearst, "Red-Haired Boy," 10.

20 "Arkwright," accessed 4 January 2021, www.ghosttownpix.com/ontario/intros/arkwright.html/.

21 Hearst, "Red-Haired Boy," 12.

22 Ibid, 14.

23 Ibid, 3, 11, 12.

24 Ibid, Foreword, 3.

25 Hearst, "Red-Haired Boy," 2. The actual title of this eighteenth-century Methodist hymn was "There Is a Fountain Filled with Blood."

26 Hearst, "Red-Haired Boy," 2.

27 Ibid, 13.

28 Ibid, 21.

29 AO, Belcher fonds. Undated memo re Hearst by A.E. Belcher. Writing in October 1914, Hearst described Belcher affectionately as "an old Bruce political warrior." Ibid, Hearst to Belcher, 5 October 1914.

30 "Warm Tribute to New Premier by Ex-Liberal Organizer," *The Globe*, 2 October 1914. After attending Collingwood Collegiate, Alexander Smith attended the University of Toronto and became a lawyer but focused on politics. He succeeded W.T.R. Preston as secretary of the Ontario Liberal Association and party organizer for both federal and provincial elections in the province until 1903. A. Margaret Evans, *Sir Oliver Mowat* (Toronto, 1992), 4. Not a modest man, he claimed to have won the federal elections of 1896, 1900 and 1904 for his party "by a technique known as 'Ontario management.'" Henry Ferns and Bernard Ostry, *The Age of Mackenzie King* (Toronto, 1976), 348.

31 Norman Robertson, *History of the County of Bruce, Ontario, Canada* (Toronto, 1906), 270.

32 Hearst, "Red-Haired Boy," 24. W.I. Hearst interview. Hearst fonds. Ms of speech at Sault Ste Marie, n.d. [1920].

33 *The Star Weekly*, 17 October 1914; H.V. Hearst interview.

34 It has been claimed that Hearst initially went to Winnipeg with a view to establishing his practice "but saw no promise there." Shirley McClure, "Sir William Hearst," in *The Bruce County Historical Society Yearbook 1999*, ed. Shirley McClure (Southampton, 1999), 24. I have found no evidence to support this claim.

35 Dickason, *Canada's First Nations*, 233; J.R. Miller, *Skyscrapers Hide the Heavens: A History of Indian-White Relations in Canada* (Toronto, 1989), 137.

36 Dickason, *Canada's First Nations*, 228; J.R. Miller, *Skyscrapers*, 137–8.

37 Quoted in David MacMartin, "D.G. MacMartin's 1905 Diary, Intergovernmental Conflict and Ontario's Treaty 9 Role" (unpublished MA thesis, University of Calgary, 2015), 68. Cf. Dickason, *Canada's First Nations*, 232–3.

38 Ibid, 233.

39 Cf. Peter W. Sinclair, "The North and the North-West: Forestry and Agriculture," in *Progress Without Planning: The Economic History of Ontario from Confederation to the Second World War*, ed. Ian Drummond et al. (Toronto, 1987), 88.

40 H.V. Nelles, *The Politics of Development: Forests, Mines & Hydro-Electric Power in Ontario, 1849–1941* (Montreal/Kingston, 2005), 51.

41 Ibid, 51–2.

42 Temiskaming is now spelled "Timiskaming," but I have used the contemporary spelling.

43 Kerry Abel, *Changing Places: History, Community and Identity in Northeastern Ontario* (Montreal/Kingston, 2006), 45.

44 Anon, "The Sault Ste Marie Bridge," *Engineering News* 24, no. 42 (18 October 1890): 334.

45 Speaking in 1911, Hearst told an audience in Sault Ste. Marie that he had moved there with R.H. Knight in 1887. *Sault Weekly Star*, 9 November 1911. Robert Knight was a merchant in Markdale, so Hearst would have known him, and he moved to Sault Ste. Marie around the same time as Hearst and established a dry goods store there. Hearst may not have meant in his speech that he and Knight literally moved to the Sault together, merely that they moved there at about the same time.

46 H.V. Hearst interview. Masson had been elected to parliament in 1887.

47 Hearst, "Red-Haired Boy," 37.

48 Brown joined the 327th Sault Ste. Marie Battalion but served as a lieutenant in the 75th Battalion. He died in action on 28 September 1918.

49 This information is based on *Vernon's Directories of Sault Ste Marie and Steelton* in the war years.

50 Edward H. Capp, *The Story of Baw-a-ting, Being the Annals of Sault Sainte Marie* (Sault Ste. Marie, 1904), 234. H.J. Morgan, ed., *The Canadian Men and Women of the Time* (Toronto, 1912), 518. Anon, "Remember This? The Saultite Who Became Premier," *Sootoday.com*, 13 March 2016, accessed 28 November 2018, www.sootoday.com/columns/remember-this/remember-this-the-saultite-who-became-premiere-265098/. H.V. Hearst interview. W.I. Hearst, *Red-Haired Boy*, 51. When a new Masonic temple was built in 1928, Hearst laid the foundation stone on 24 November. "Keystone Lodge No 412 History," accessed 10 May 2020, https://algomaeastmasons.com/keystone-lodge-history/.

51 Hector Charlesworth, *More Candid Chronicles: Further Leaves from the Note Book of a Canadian Journalist* (Toronto, 1928), 136.

52 Ibid.

53 Hearst, "Red-Haired Boy," 39, 157.

54 Ibid, 85.

55 The name was sometimes spelled "Dunkin," but the family spelled it "Duncan."

56 Hearst, "Red-Haired Boy," 38.

57 Ibid, 39.

58 Ibid, 156.

59 John Webster Grant, "Hunter, John Edwin," in *Dictionary of Canadian Biography*, vol. 14 (University of Toronto/Université Laval, 2003–), accessed 11 January 2020, www.biographi.ca/en/bio/hunter_john_edwin_14E.html/. Kevin Kee, "John Hunter (1856–1919)," *Online Encyclopedia of Canadian Christian Leaders*, accessed 29 October 2021, www.canadianchristianleaders.org/portraits-collection/john-hunter-1856-1919/.

60 Hearst, "Red-Haired Boy," 40.

61 Ibid, 52–3.

62 *Foster's Sault Ste Marie, Ont. Directory 1901–1902* (Toronto, 1901), 59.

63 Hearst, "Red-Haired Boy," 157.

64 Anon, "Remember This? Pointe aux Pins," *Sootoday*, 27 November 2016, accessed 7 January 2020, www.sootoday.com/columns/remember-this/remember-this-pointe-aux-pins-474834/.

65 Hearst, "Red-Haired Boy," 42. Irving may be referring to Laurier's visit to Sault Ste. Marie in September 1894, before he became prime minister. Invited by friends to attend the evening service at the Methodist church, he did so, arousing a controversy because he was, of course, Catholic. He had also attended the morning service at Sacred Heart Catholic church. *Remember This*, "Wilfrid Laurier Goes to Church in the Sault: Controversy Ensues," *Sootoday*, 9 June 2019, accessed 14 October 2021, www.sootoday.com/columns/remember-this/wilfrid-laurier-goes-to-church-in-the-sault-controversy-ensues-1495954/.

66 Hearst, "Red-Haired Boy," 51.

67 Ibid, 17.

68 Irving Hearst claims incorrectly that Milton did not immediately succeed John but was appointed by the Drury government. Hearst, "Red-Haired Boy," 49. The 1917 city directory makes clear that he had been appointed and was living in Sault Ste. Marie in 1916. *Vernon's 1917 Sault Ste Marie and Steelton Directory* (Hamilton, 1917), 102.

69 Duncan McDowell, *Steel at the Sault: Francis H. Clergue, Sir James Dunn, and the Algoma Steel Corporation 1901–1956* (Toronto, 1984), 28. Alan Sullivan's 1920 novel, *The Rapids,* is a fictionalized account of Sault Ste. Marie's industrial development with the character Robert Fisher Clark representing Clergue.

70 Nelles, *Politics of Development,* 82.

71 For the development of the Lake Superior Corporation, see *Return of Documents in Connection with the Bill Respecting Aid to the Algoma Central and Hudson Bay Railway* (Toronto, 1904); W.J.A. Donald, *The Canadian Iron and Steel Industry* (New York, 1915), 212–9; E.S. Moore, *American Influence in Canadian Mining* (Toronto, 1941), 49–50; Lord Beaverbrook, *Courage: The Story of Sir James Dunn* (Fredericton, 1961), 75ff; Duncan McDowell, *Steel at the Sault: Francis H. Clergue, Sir James Dunn, and the Algoma Steel Corporation 1901–1956* (Toronto, 1984); Margaret Van Every, "Francis Hector Clergue and the Rise of Sault Ste Marie as an Industrial Centre," *Ontario History* 56, no. 3 (September 1964): 191–202; Nelles, *Politics of Development,* 57–60.

72 AO, Belcher fonds. Undated memo re Hearst by A.E. Belcher. Belcher was a prominent Orange Conservative in the Southampton area and knew the Hearst family well.

73 Morgan, *Canadian Men and Women,* 611.

74 Irving Hearst interview. Hearst fonds. Ms of speech at Sault Ste. Marie, n.d. [1920].

75 Quoted in the *Sault Weekly Star,* 9 April 1908.

76 Hector Charlesworth, *A Cyclopaedia of Canadian Biography* (Toronto, 1919), 7.

77 For more on Lyon, see Matt Bray, "Lyon, Robert Adam," in *Dictionary of Canadian Biography,* vol. 13 (University of Toronto/Université Laval, 2003–), accessed 3 December 2018, www.biographi.ca/en/bio/lyon_robert_adam_13E.html/.

78 H.V. Hearst interview; Belcher fonds. Alex F. Campbell to Belcher, 17 January 1922.

79 Roderick Lewis, *A Statistical History of All the Electoral Districts of the Province of Ontario Since 1867* (Toronto, n.d.), 10.

80 H.V. Hearst interview.

81 Andrew Miscampbell was the godfather of Leslie Miscampbell Frost, who served as Premier of Ontario from 1949 to 1961.

82 Charlesworth, *More Candid Chronicles*, 136.
83 Charlesworth, *Cyclopedia*, 7.
84 AO. Whitney fonds. Edgar Brown to Whitney, 30 June 1905.
85 Ibid. Sworn statement of P.J. Galvin, copy. It was Galvin who had rounded up the Americans in question.
86 *The Globe*, 27 October 1903.
87 Irving Hearst interview.
88 *Canadian Annual Review* (1904): 282.
89 Ibid, 281.
90 Ibid, 282–3.
91 Whitney fonds. Galvin statement. Patrick Jeremiah Galvin was born in 1865 in Ennismore, Ontario, and moved to the United States in 1898. He settled in Sault Ste. Marie, Michigan, where he was described as a bartender in the 1900 census, as an electrician in 1910, and as a real estate agent in 1920. At the time of the *Minnie M* affair, he was described in the local newspaper as an employment agent. Sault Ste. Marie (Michigan) *Evening News*, 26 January 1905.
92 Miscampbell did not run in the 1905 election but served as a Conservative organizer and, according to Humphries, "was a diligent worker." Charles W. Humphries, *"Honest Enough to be Bold": The Life and Times of James Pliny Whitney* (Toronto, 1985), 238.
93 Ross Harkness, *J.E. Atkinson of the Star* (Toronto, 1963), 59.
94 W.R. Smyth to Whitney, 5 February 1903, quoted in Humphries, *Honest Enough*, 82. *Cf Canadian Annual Review* (1903): 126. The *Weekly Star* was Sault Ste. Marie's Conservative newspaper. Hearst was a member of its board of directors in 1901–2. *Foster's Sault Ste Marie, Ont. Directory 1901–1901* (Toronto, 1901), 144.
95 *The Mail and Empire*, 12 March 1903. For contemporary accounts of the affair, see Charlesworth, *More Candid Chronicles*, 136–43; and Hearst, "Red-Haired Boy," 75–81.
96 Hector Charlesworth, *Candid Chronicles: Leaves from the Note Book of a Canadian Journalist* (Toronto, 1925), 180.
97 *Cf Report of the Royal Commission re Gamey Charges* (Toronto, 1903). The commissioners were Sir John Boyd, Chancellor of Ontario's High Court of Justice (now the Superior Court of Justice), and Chief Justice William Falconbridge.
98 Willison to Laurier, 11 July 1903, quoted in Humphries, *Honest Enough*, 84. For a fuller account of the Gamey scandal, see Charles W. Humphries, "The Gamey Affair," *Ontario History* 59, no. 2 (June 1967): 101–9.
99 Sir George W. Ross, *Getting into Parliament and After* (Toronto, 1913), 219.
100 Moses McFadden and his brother Uriah McFadden practised law in Sault Ste. Marie from 1900 until 1913 when Moses was appointed a judge. The

brothers also established the *Sault Courier* in 1895 but sold it in 1901 to James Curran, who renamed it the *Sault Weekly Star.* Uriah also became a judge in 1931. These McFaddens were not related to Hearst.

101 *Canadian Annual Review* (1905): 208. Cf. Whitney fonds. Edgar Brown to Whitney, 30 June 1905.

102 Whitney fonds. Hearst to Whitney, 27 January 1905.

103 The Liberals won only Port Arthur and Sault Ste. Marie.

104 Charlesworth, *Candid Chronicles,* 180.

105 Hearst, "Red-Haired Boy," 65. Whitney fonds. Hearst to Whitney, 5 November 1904. Vernon and Irving Hearst interviews. Hearst fonds. Ms of speech at Sault Ste Marie, n.d. [1920]. It's not clear what Hearst's health issues were but he did contract typhoid fever around this time. Hearst suffered bouts of nervous exhaustion throughout his life and in the spring of 1915 was "dangerously ill with pneumonia. Hearst, "Red-Haired Boy," 41, 120.

106 Whitney fonds. Hearst to Whitney, 5 November 1904; Hearst to Whitney, 27 January 1905.

107 Ibid. Hearst to Whitney, 27 January 1905.

108 Whitney to Smyth, undated, quoted in Scott Young and Astrid Young, *Silent Frank Cochrane: The North's First Great Politician* (Toronto, 1973), 17. Whitney fonds. Whitney to W.R. Smyth, 3 June 1905.

109 George Gordon (1865–1942) was a lumber merchant at Sturgeon Falls who ran unsuccessfully as the Conservative candidate in the 1904 federal election, then was elected in 1908 and 1911. He later resigned to make the seat available for Frank Cochrane when he joined the Borden government and was rewarded with a seat in the Senate.

110 Quoted in Young and Young, *Cochrane,* 18.

111 *Sudbury Journal,* 2 February 1905.

112 Whitney fonds. Whitney to W.R. Smyth, 3 June 1905.

113 Hearst fonds. Ms of speech at Sault Ste Marie, n.d. [1920]. Hearst, "Red-Haired Boy," 65.

114 Whitney fonds. Whitney to Cochrane, 30 May 1905; Whitney to Smyth, 3 June 1905. Lamarche was rewarded by being appointed registrar of deeds for the District of Nipissing. He died four years later. The Department of Lands and Mines was expanded in 1906 to become the Department of Lands, Forests and Mines.

115 Richard T. Clippingdale, *The Power of the Pen: The Politics, Nationalism and Influence of Sir John Willison* (Toronto, 2012), 306. Cf. Clippingdale, "Willison, Sir John Stephen," in *Dictionary of Canadian Biography,* vol. 15 (University of Toronto/Université Laval, 2003–), accessed 25 April 2024, www.biographi.ca/en/bio/willison_john_stephen_15E.html/; Minko Sotiron, *From Politics to Profit: The Commercialization of Canadian Daily Newspapers, 1890–1920* (Montreal/Kingston, 1997), 109.

116 *The Globe*, undated, quoted in Young and Young, *Cochrane*, 24. Hodgins et al. give the figure as "more than a quarter" of the government's public revenue. Bruce W. Hodgins, Jamie Benedickson and Peter Gillis, "The Ontario and Quebec Experiments in Forest Reserves 1883–1930," *Journal of Forest History* 26, no. 1 (January 1982): 20.
117 Donald, *Iron and Steel Industry*, 215; *Cf* LAC, Laurier fonds 77492; John McKay to Laurier, 5 October 1903.
118 *Canadian Annual Review* (1903): 514–15.
119 On Plummer, see George Sheppard, "Plummer, William Henry," in *Dictionary of Canadian Biography*, vol. 14 (University of Toronto/ Université Laval, 2003), accessed 3 December 2018, www.biographi.ca/en/bio/plummer_william_henry_14E.html/.
120 Nelles, *Politics of Development*, 136.
121 The Laurier government also helped by promising to buy rails for the Intercolonial Railway.
122 Margaret E. Prang, "Rowell, Newton Wesley," in *Dictionary of Canadian Biography*, vol. 17 (University of Toronto/Université Laval, 2003–), accessed 11 May 2020, www.biographi.ca/en/bio/rowell_newton_wesley_17E.html/.
123 Whitney fonds. Hearst to Whitney, 21 February 1905.
124 Rowell's political career ended with the destruction of the Meighen government in 1921, but his legal practice flourished, and in 1936 he became Chief Justice of Ontario.
125 Whitney fonds. Albert Grigg to Whitney, 13 January 1912.
126 Whitney made the right decision. The Bruce Mines & Algoma Railway was reorganized in 1913 as the Lake Huron and Northern Ontario Railway, with the ambitious goal of linking with the CPR near Chapleau and extending all the way to James Bay. The war made that impossible, and it stopped operations in 1916.
127 *The Globe*, 13 February 1907.
128 Ibid.
129 Ibid, 14 February 1907.
130 Ibid.
131 Ibid.
132 The name of the railway had actually been changed to Algoma Central and Hudson Bay Railway in 1901 when Clergue acquired the charter of the Ontario, Hudson Bay, and Western Railway. The implication was that he was planning to extend the railway to a harbour on James Bay or Hudson Bay.
133 *The Globe*, 26 March 1907.
134 Ibid, 26 March 1907, 21 March 1908. *Canadian Annual Review* (1907): 501. As Whitney feared, the investment proved not to be a sound one. The railway was unable to earn even enough revenue to cover its expenses

and became a serious financial drain on the Consolidated Lake Superior Company. McDowell, *Steel at the Sault*, 53.

135 *The Globe*, 21 March 1908.

136 Ibid.

137 Ibid, 12 April 1913.

138 *Canadian Annual Review* (1908): 322.

139 Ibid, 347.

140 Whitney fonds. Cochrane to Whitney, 16 May 1908.

141 Nelles, *Politics of Development*, 159, 179. On the controversy over the Mines Act, see Young and Young, *Cochrane*, 33–63, and Nelles, *Politics of Development*, 113.

142 Nelles, *Politics of Development*, 180.

143 Hearst, "Red-Haired Boy," 73, 57.

144 He resigned from the board just before seeking the Conservative nomination.

145 *Sault Weekly Star*, 9 April 1908.

146 Quoted in ibid.

147 He held the seat until 1917. His sister was the wife of Harold Machin, the Kenora lawyer and mining promoter who was also a candidate in the election and went on to become a leader of those in the Conservative Party who attacked Hearst and prohibition in 1919.

148 Young and Young, *Cochrane*, 83, 85.

149 Whitney fonds. Whitney to Hearst, 4 April 1908, telegram; *Sault Weekly Star*, 9 April 1908.

150 The number of seats in the legislature rose from 97 to 102 between 1905 and 1908 because of the decennial redistribution.

151 Lewis, *Statistical History*, 236.

152 In 1909 McKay was appointed junior judge of the district court of Thunder Bay.

153 George Emery, *Provincial and Federal Redistribution of Ridings in Ontario, 1840–1954* (Montreal/Kingston, 2016), 186.

154 Curiously, Cuff's account of the Conservative campaign in Ontario omits any reference to northern Ontario.

155 Laurier fonds. 145435. Dyment to Laurier, 30 September 1908.

156 Dyment to Laurier, undated, quoted in Young and Young, *Cochrane*, 89.

157 Young and Young, *Cochrane*, 90–1. McDowell describes Conmee as an "extraordinary politician-cum-promoter." McDowell, *Steel at the Sault*, 28. *Cf* F. Brent Scollie, "Conmee, James," in *Dictionary of Canadian Biography*, vol. 14 (University of Toronto/Université 2003–), accessed 25 April 2024, accessed 3 December 1918, www.biographi.ca/en/bio/conmee_james_14E.html/.

158 *The Mail and Empire*, *The Globe*, 20 October 1908.

159 Ibid, 21 October 1908.

160 Algoma East, Algoma West, Muskoka, Nipissing, and Parry Sound. Only Conmee survived in Thunder Bay-Rainy River.
161 Laurier fonds 146711. A.E. Dyment to Laurier, 29 October 1908; Cf. ibid 145435; same to same, 30 September 1908.
162 Smyth's victory in the federal election created a vacancy in Algoma. In the by-election held in December 1908, Albert Grigg, the mayor of Bruce Mines, retained the seat for the Conservatives.
163 *The Mail and Empire*, 18 February 1909.
164 Ibid, 17 March 1910.
165 Hillary C. Barter, "Slaughterhouse Rules: Declining Abattoirs and the Politics of Food Safety Regulation in Ontario" (unpublished MA diss., University of Toronto, 2014), 49.
166 *Bills Presented to the Legislative Assembly of the Province of Ontario* (Toronto, 1910), #98.
167 *The Mail and Empire*, 24 February 1910.
168 *The Globe*, 24 February 1910.
169 Richard Allen, "The Social Gospel and the Reform Tradition in Canada, 1890–1928," *Canadian Historical Review* 49, no. 4 (December 1968): 382.
170 *Bills Presented to the Legislative Assembly of the Province of Ontario* (Toronto, 1911), #184; *The Mail and Empire*, 25 February 1911.
171 Ibid, 7 March 1911; *The Globe*, 7 March 1911.
172 *The Mail and Empire*, 7 March 1911.

## Chapter 2

1 Whitney fonds. Hearst to Whitney, 4 September 1913; *The Globe*, 13 September 1913.
2 *The Globe*, 11 March 1911; *The Mail and Empire*, 11 March 1911.
3 In October 1910 Hanna had told a banquet in Sault Ste. Marie attended by Frank Cochrane, W.L Mackenzie King, representing the federal government, and almost certainly Hearst that the financial support of both levels of government had made the town an industrial centre and "prophesized unbounded growth for its hinterland, 'a reservoir of untold wealth.'" Quoted in McDowell, *Steel at the Sault*, 58.
4 *The Mail and Empire*, 11 March 1911.
5 *Canadian Annual Review* (1911): 100.
6 Kevin Anderson, "'This Typical Old Canadian Form of Racial and Religious Hate': Anti-Catholicism and English Canadian Nationalism, 1905–1965" (unpublished PhD diss., McMaster University, 2013), 46.
7 C.B. Sissons, *Bi-lingual Schools in Canada* (London, 1917), 30–5. Cf. Marilyn Barber, "The Ontario Bilingual Schools Issue: Sources of Conflict," *Canadian Historical Review* 47, no. 3 (September 1966): 227–9.

8 I have rounded off these numbers. Barber notes that the ecclesiastical census of the province in 1909 reported 247,000 and that the round figure of 250,000 was routinely cited in the press. Barber, "Bilingual Schools," 230.

9 Margaret E. Prang, *N.W. Rowell: Ontario Nationalist* (Toronto, 1975), 93–4; Robert Rumilly, *Histoire de Québec* (Montreal, 1940–60), XVII, 39–80; *Canadian Annual Review* (1910): 355–8.

10 C.B. Sissons, *Church and State in Canadian Education* (Toronto, 1959), 76; O.D. Skelton, *Life and Letters of Sir Wilfrid Laurier* (Toronto, 1921), II, 449.

11 *Le Moniteur* (Hawkesbury), quoted in *Canadian Annual Review* (1909): 243.

12 *The Sentinel*, 9 December 1909, 16 June 1910; *Cf Canadian Annual Review* (1910): 322–3.

13 First published as "L'avenir de la Race Canadienne-française" in *La Revue Canadienne* in April 1910, the article was reprinted as "The Future of the French-Canadian Race" in the popular *Canadian Magazine* (May 1911): 11–7.

14 W.S. Wallace made this comment in the *Review of Historical Publications Relating to Canada* 15, no. 1 (January 1911): 100, after reading Lemay's original article in French.

15 Mark McGowan, "'To Share in the Burdens of Empire': Toronto's Catholics and the Great War, 1914–1918," in *Catholics at the "Gathering Place": Historical Essays on the Archdiocese of Toronto, 1841–1991*, ed. Mark McGowan and Brian Clarke (Toronto, 1993), quoted in Anderson, "Anti-Catholicism," 47.

16 Anderson, "Anti-Catholicism," 47.

17 *The Catholic Record*, 15 November 1913; *The Daily Star*, 30 August 1915.

18 University of Toronto Library. *Correspondence Between the Ontario Department of Education and the Roman Catholic Authorities Concerning the Bi-lingual Schools Issue in Ontario*; John Seath to Sir William Meredith, 17 February 1910; Whitney to the Ontario archbishops, 9 March 1910; Memorandum of Bishop M.F. Fallon to the Ontario bishops, 24 January 1917.

19 Barber, "Bilingual Schools," 236. Cf. Robert Sellar, *The Tragedy of Quebec* (1907).

20 F.W. Merchant, *Report on English-French Schools* (Toronto, 1909).

21 *Canadian Annual Review* (1910): 423–4.

22 Quoted in Oliver, *Ferguson*, 44.

23 *The Globe*, 26 January 1911.

24 Quoted in Oliver, *Ferguson*, 39, 40.

25 Oliver, *Ferguson*, 46.

26 *The Globe*, 23 March 1911.

27 Ibid.

28 *The Sentinel*, 9 November 1911, 29 November 1911.

29 Whitney fonds. Whitney to James McLean, 21 February 1911; Whitney to Borden, 22 September 1911, telegram; Whitney to F.W. Thompson, 22 September 1911, telegram; Whitney to M. Wilson, 23 September 1911.

30 George Emery, *Principles and Gerrymanders: Parliamentary Redistribution of Ridings in Ontario, 1840–1954* (Montreal/Kingston, 2016), 186. Whitney fonds. Borden to Whitney, 31 July 1911; Whitney to Borden, 1 August 1911; Borden to Whitney, 2 August 1911; Whitney to Borden, 3 August 1911; Borden to Whitney, 7 August 1911; Whitney to Borden, 8 August 1911.

31 *Kemptville Advance*, 2 November 1911, quoted in Oliver, *Ferguson*, 46.

32 David J. Hall, "Sifton, Sir Clifford," in *Dictionary of Canadian Biography*, vol. 15 (University of Toronto/Université Laval, 2003–), accessed 15 April 2020, www.biographi.ca/en/bio/sifton_clifford_15E.html/.

33 Irving Hearst interview.

34 Different sources list the number of seats won by the Conservatives as seventy-one, seventy-two or seventy-three. The explanation is that seventy Conservatives were elected, plus one independent Conservative and one Liberal Conservative.

35 LAC, Graham fonds 18671. Smith to W.L.M. King, 26 July 1911, copy.

36 LAC, Lapointe fonds. Charles Murphy to Sir Joseph Pope, 24 October 1919, copy; Skelton, *Laurier*, II, 382; Sir John Willison, *Sir Wilfrid Laurier* (London, 1926), 408; *Canadian Annual Review* (1912): 270. *Cf* Robert Cuff, "The Conservative Party Machine and the Election of 1911 in Ontario," *Ontario History* 57, no. 3 (September 1965): 149–56; and Richard Johnston and Michael B. Percy, "Reciprocity, Imperial Sentiment, and Party Politics in the 1911 Election," *Canadian Journal of Political Science* 13, no. 4 (December 1980): 711–29. The most recent and thorough examination of the 1911 federal election is Patrice Dutil and David MacKenzie, *Canada 1911: The Decisive Election That Shaped the Country* (Toronto, 2011).

37 Whitney fonds. Borden to Whitney, 25 September 1911; Whitney to Borden, 27 September 1911; Sam Hughes to Whitney, 8 October 1911; Whitney to Irwin Hilliard, 11 October 1911; *Cf The Globe*, 29, 30 September 1911; W.S. Wallace, *The Memoirs of the Rt Hon Sir George Foster* (Toronto, 1933), 158–9.

38 Gordon was compensated with a seat in the Senate.

39 *The Globe*, 4, 10 October 1911.

40 A year later Mead sold the house to the Consolidated Lake Superior Paper Company. Anon, "Remember This? Home Is Where the Hearst Is," *Sootoday.com*, 27 March 2016, www.sootoday.com/columns/remember-this/remember-this-home-is-where-the-hearst-is-270513/. Ontario Registry of Deeds, Sault Ste. Marie. Deed of Land transfer from W.H. Hearst to George D. Mead, 25 May 1912. I am indebted to Matthew Shoemaker for obtaining a copy of this document.

41 Hearst, "Red-Haired Boy," 84.
42 Promotional brochure for St. Andrew's College, then situated in Rosedale, quoted in Claude Bissell, *The Young Vincent Massey* (Toronto, 1981), 24.
43 *The Globe*, 12 October 1911.
44 Ibid, 29 September 1911, 5 October 1911.
45 Rowell fonds 8362. A.G. MacKay to Rowell, 3 November 1911; ibid, 8429; H.D. Cowan to Rowell, 3 December 1911; Cf. F.A. McGregor, *The Fall and Rise of Mackenzie King* (Toronto, 1962), 76.
46 MacKay was re-elected in the 1911 election but then moved to Alberta in 1913 and won election to the Alberta legislature. He was appointed Minister of Municipal Affairs in 1918 and then the province's first Minister of Health as well but died of pneumonia in April 1920.
47 Rowell fonds 8360; Charles Napier Smith to Rowell, 3 November 1911.
48 *Sault Weekly Star*, 16 November 1911. Cf. ibid, 23 November 1911, 7 December 1911.
49 Ibid, 9 November 1911.
50 Hearst, "Red-Haired Boy," 82.
51 *Sault Weekly Star*, 7 December 1911.
52 Hearst fonds. A.J. Matheson to Hearst, 3 November 1911.
53 *Address to the Electors of N.W. Rowell* and *New Measures and A New Leader*, both issued by the General Reform Association for Ontario, 1911.
54 Liberal-Conservative Association of Ontario, *Seven Years of the Square Deal* (Toronto, 1911).
55 *The Evening News*, 25 September 1911.
56 *Stratford Daily Herald*, 2 November 1911.
57 R.E. Spence, *Prohibition in Canada* (Toronto, 1919), 388.
58 It was named after Adam Crooks, who as Provincial Treasurer in the Mowat government was responsible for the 1876 liquor licence act.
59 Schull, *Ontario*, 125.
60 Hector Charlesworth, *More Candid Chronicles*, 180, 192.
61 Spence, *Prohibition*, 388.
62 Ibid, 587–8.
63 *Address to the Electors.*
64 Rowell fonds 8425; Rowell to Rev W.W. Anglin, 6 December 1911. *Address to the Electors.*
65 Whitney fonds. Whitney to J.R. Johnston, 10 November 1911.
66 Ibid. Miles Vokes to Whitney, 3 November 1911; J.R. Johnston to Whitney, 9 November 1911.
67 Ibid. Whitney to Miles Vokes, 6 November 1911.
68 Whitney fonds. A.J. Russell Snow to Whitney, 16 November 1911; *Cf The Evening News*, 20, 21, 24 November 1911; *The Evening Telegram*, 1 December 1911.

69 *The Globe,* 21 November 1911, 30 November 1911. This was a distortion of Reaume's views. He supported French-language instruction in Catholic schools but also believed that it was essential for francophone children living in Ontario to be fluent in English. Regulation 17 allowed a daily hour of French instruction, which actually enhanced francophone rights because Section 93 of the British North America Act offered no such protection. Jack Cecillon, "Reaume, Joseph Octave (Baptized Joseph-Octave) (Joseph O., J.O.)," in *Dictionary of Canadian Biography,* vol 16 (Toronto/Quebec City, 2020), accessed 12 September 2021, www.biographi.ca/en/bio/reaume_joseph_octave_16E.html/.

70 D.J. Scollard to Whitney, 21 October 1912, quoted in Humphries, *Honest Enough,* 202. Adam Crerar suggests that "in northern Ontario French Canadians were so much a part of the region's social fabric and sufficiently removed from provincial opinion leaders in the south that Regulation 17 was ignored in practice." Crerar, "Ontario and the Great War," 721.

71 *The Daily Star,* 20 November, 8 December 1911; *The Globe,* 20 November 1911.

72 *The Globe,* 1 December 1911. *Canadian Annual Review* (1911): 466, 468.

73 Whitney fonds. Whitney to Cochrane, 15 November 1911.

74 King to Violet Markham, 15 December 1911, quoted in Humphries, *Honest Enough,* 196. *Cf* Humphries, "Mackenzie King Looks at Two Elections," *Ontario History* 56, no. 3 (September 1964): 203–6.

75 Robert Cuff, "The Conservative Party Machine," 149.

76 The acclamations were in Addington, Durham East, Grenville, Hastings East, Hastings North, Hastings West, Kingston, Lanark North, Lanark South, Lincoln, London, Renfrew North, Renfrew South, Sault Ste. Marie, Simcoe West, and Victoria East.

77 Hamilton East was retained by Allan Studholme, the labour MPP.

78 The exception was Sturgeon Falls, a largely Franco-Ontarian constituency.

79 The *Windsor Evening Record* suggested that Severin Ducharme, the Liberal candidate, might have won if not for the inclement weather and muddy roads in the rural districts. Jack D. Cecillon, "Language, Schools and Religious Conflict in the Windsor Borden Region: A Case Study of Francophone Resistance to the Ontario Government's Imposition of Regulation XVII, 1910–1928" (unpublished PhD diss., York University, 2007), 113–6. Cf. Cecillon, *Prayers, Petitions and Protests: The Catholic Church and the Ontario Schools Crisis in the Windsor Border Region, 1910–1928* (Montreal/Kingston, 2013).

80 It might appear at first glance that J.A. Mathieu, who won Rainy River for the Conservatives, was a francophone, but he was actually a prominent lumberman from Minnesota who had settled in Fort Frances.

81 Morris Zaslow, *The Opening of the Canadian North 1870–1914* (Toronto, 1971), 179.

82 Dickason, *Canada's First Nations*, 303.

83 On Treaty 9, see John S. Long, *Treaty No 9: Making the Agreement to Share the Land in Far Northern Ontario in 1905* (Montreal/Kingston, 2010).

84 Quoted in *Canadian Annual Review* (1911): 427.

85 Gillis and Roach, *Lost Initiatives*, 97.

86 Zaslow, *Opening*, 160.

87 Barry E.C. Boothman, *Corporate Capitalism: Abitibi Power & Paper and the Collapse of the Newsprint Industry, 1912–1946* (Toronto, 2020), 11; Mark Kuhlberg, *From Resource to Revenue: Dryden Mill Lessons for the Ring of Fire* (Thunder Bay, 2016), 6.

88 S.J.R. Noel, *Patrons, Clients, Brokers: Ontario Society and Politics 1791–1896* (Toronto, 1990), 264.

89 Ontario Department of Crown Lands, *Land Settlement in New Ontario* (Toronto, 1902), 18; cited in Benoît-Beaudry Gourd, "La colonisation des Clay Belts du Nord-Ouest québécois et du Nord-Est ontarien: Étude de la propagande des gouvernements du Québec et de l'Ontario à travers leurs publications officielles (1900–1930)," *Revue d'histoire de l'Amérique français* 27, no. 2 (September 1973): 252, www.erudit.org/fr/revues/haf/1973-v27-n2-haf2015/303265ar/.

90 Ontario Department of Agriculture, *Handbook of the Province of Ontario, Canada: Products, Resources, Development* (Toronto, 1907), 134; cited in Benoît-Beaudry Gourd, "La colonisation des Clay Belts," 251–2.

91 *Canadian Annual Review* (1912), quoted in Abel, *Changing Places*, 50.

92 Association of Ontario Land Surveyors, "Reports of Committees,"166, accessed 31 May 2019, www.aols.org/sites/default/files/Whitson-J.F.pdf/.

93 Quoted in Abel, *Changing Places*, 52. Judson Clark, the province's professional forester until he resigned in disgust in 1917, thought that the only crop that could grow reliably in Northern Ontario was trees.

94 Quoted in *Canadian Annual Review* (1914): 359.

95 Abel, *Changing Places*, 12.

96 Ibid, xii, 13.

97 Hearst fonds. Ms of speech to Ottawa Canadian Club, 8 November 1913; Cf. ms of speech to Toronto Empire Club, 28 November 1912.

98 Mark Kuhlberg, *In the Power of the Government: The Rise and Fall of Newsprint in Ontario, 1894–1932* (Toronto, 2015), 50.

99 Mark Kuhlberg, "Natural Potential, Artificial Restraint: The Dryden Paper Company and the Fetters on Adopting Technological Innovation in a Canadian Pulp and Paper Sector, 1900–1950," in *Technological Transformation in the Global Pulp and Paper Industry 1800–2018: Comparative Perspectives*, ed. Timo Sarkka, Miquel Gutierrez-Poch, and Mark Kuhlberg (Cham, 2018), 139.

100 Kuhlberg, “Eyes Wide Open,” 206–9. Kuhlberg, “Backus.”

101 Kuhlberg, “Eyes Wide Open,” 209–10. For a detailed account of the evolution of pulp mills in Ontario, see Barry E.C. Boothman, *Corporate Cataclysm: Abitibi Power & Paper and the Collapse of the Newsprint Industry, 1912–1946* (Toronto, 2020).

102 Quoted in Abel, *Changing Places*, 62.

103 J.A. McAndrew to Hearst, 11 October 1913, cited in Abel, *Changing Places*, 63.

104 Abel, *Changing Places*, 63.

105 Port Arthur *News-Chronicle*, 13 July 1917, accessed 20 November 2019, https://tbayworldwarone.com/wp-content/uploads/2018/01/little-articles.pdf/.

106 Nelles, *Politics of Development*, 377. Little and two partners formed the New Ontario Contracting Company, which illegally harvested pulpwood along the National Transcontinental Railway line near Sioux Lookout and on crown lands in the Thunder Bay district on which it had staked much cheaper mining claims. All this pulpwood was shipped across the border, “thus turning a handsome profit for nominal expenditure.” Then the department granted Little virtually exclusive fishing privileges on Lake Nipigon and he allegedly sold sturgeon commercially, ignoring the quota regulations. No doubt the fact that D.M. Hogarth, an associate of Carrick and Little who took over Carrick’s seat in the legislature in 1911 and served on the legislature’s Standing Committee on Game and Fish between 1911 and 1914, was helpful in this regard. Mark Kuhlberg, “Little, James Arthur,” in *Dictionary of Canadian Biography*, vol 16 (Toronto/Quebec, 2017), accessed 21 September 2021, www.biographi.ca/en/bio/little_james_arthur_16E.html/. When the war broke out Sam Hughes appointed Carrick an honorary lieutenant colonel and proposed to send him overseas as an “intelligence officer.” Sir George Perley, whose judgment was usually sound, made clear to Borden that he thought “badly of Carrick.” In the event, Hughes attached him to the First Division in March 1915 as “Official Recorder.” This appointment was unacceptable to Max Aitken, whom Borden had already designated Canada’s official recorder, and their squabble soon reached Borden. The frequent references to him in Robert Borden’s diary indicate that he was an intimate, at least until 1915. When Carrick was included in a luncheon with Borden in London on 12 July 1915, “he came early and talked rather wildly as to his grievances.” A week later he annoyed Borden by insisting that he should be included in the prime minister’s impending visit to France. When that didn’t happen he asked Borden to appoint him to the Senate. That didn’t happen either, and Borden sent him home to serve at the Department of Militia and Defence headquarters, but he was sacked in May 1917. A.F.

Duguid, *Official History of the Canadian Forces in the Great War 1914–1919*, vol. 1 (Ottawa, 1938), Appendix 229, p 162. After the war Carrick retired to Montreal. He sought his revenge on Aitken in his memoirs when he described Aitken's work as "products of hearsay and collaboration" and "spurious masterpieces of an incompetent absentee." Quoted in Tim Cook, "Documenting War and Forging Reputations: Sir Max Aitken and the Canadian War Records Office in the First World War 1," *War in History* 10, no. 3 (2003): 293. Carrick's memoirs were never published.

Carrick was succeeded in the legislature by his associate, Donald Hogarth, who held the seat from 1911 to 1923, then won it back in 1926. Hogarth was absent during the war years because he joined the army service corps, rising spectacularly from lieutenant in 1914 to major general and acting brigadier general in 1918, a remarkable achievement that suggests either that he was a very effective manager or had the right political connections, possibly both. When Carrick decided not to reoffer in the 1917 federal election, he proposed Hogarth as the Unionist candidate, but the Port Arthur Liberal Association wouldn't have him. Carrick substituted Frank Keefer, a local Conservative lawyer who was acceptable to the Liberals, presumably because he had been associated with Conmee, Whalen, and Russell, and he won the seat. After being defeated in the 1921 federal election, he won Carrick's former seat in the legislature in 1923. When Hogarth defeated him in the contest for the Conservative nomination for the 1926 provincial election, Howard Ferguson created the ideal position for Keefer, legislative secretary for Northern Ontario, and he eventually succeeded in having Port Arthur made the north-west headquarters of the Department of Lands and Forests. Hogarth went on to become a successful mining promoter.

107 S. Barry Cottam, "White, Aubrey," in *Dictionary of Canadian Biography*, vol. 14 (Toronto/Quebec, 1998), accessed 17 May 2019, www.biographi.ca/en/bio/white_aubrey_14E/.

108 Gillis and Roach, *Lost Initiatives*, 100.

109 The department also granted Little virtually exclusive fishing privileges on Lake Nipigon, and he allegedly sold sturgeon commercially, ignoring the quota regulations. No doubt the fact that Hogarth, who took over Carrick's seat in the legislature in 1911 and served on its Standing Committee on Game and Fish between 1911 and 1914, was helpful in this regard. Mark Kuhlberg, "Little, James Arthur."

110 *Fort Frances Times and Rainy Lake Herald*, 23 April 1942, accessed 21 January 2021 www.fftimes.com/100-years-100-stories/SCENDS.html/.

111 Kuhlburg, "Eyes Wide Open," 215.

112 Ibid. Cf. R. Newell Searle, *Saving Quetico-Superior: A Land Set Apart* (St. Paul, 1977), 11–12.

113 Oliver, *Ferguson*, 85.

114 Kuhlberg, *In the Power*, 100. Kuhlberg has examined Backus' long-term difficult relationship with the Whitney-Hearst governments in "'Eyes Wide Open': E.W. Backus and the Pitfalls of Investing in Ontario's Pulp and Paper Industry, 1902–1932," *Journal of the Canadian Historical Association* 16 (2005): 201–33.

115 S.J.R. Noel, *Patrons*, 251.

116 Whitney fonds. Whitney to Cochrane, 20 November 1911; Cochrane to Whitney, 20 November 1911; Whitney to Cochrane, 14 December 1911, private; Whitney to Borden, 18 January 1912, private.

117 Ibid. Whitney to Cochrane, 2 January 1912.

118 Quoted in Karen Nicholson, "Rogers, Robert," in *Dictionary of Canadian Biography*, vol. 16 (University of Toronto/Université Laval, 2003–), accessed 25 February 2019, www.biographi.ca/en/bio/rogers_robert_16E.html/.

119 *Canadian Annual Review* (1912): 329.

120 Whitney fonds. Whitney to Cochrane, 19 January 1912, Confidential; *Canadian Annual Review* (1912): 329.

121 Ibid. Whitney to Cochrane, 26 January 1912, Confidential.

122 Ibid. Borden to Whitney, 5 February 1912, Private.

123 Ibid. Whitney to Cochrane, 6, 19 February 1912; Cochrane to Whitney, 21 February 1912.

124 Ibid. *Borden* to Whitney, 22 February 1912. *The Globe*, 9, 22, 24 February 1912.

125 Ontario subsequently began construction of a railway extension to connect with a railway that the Canadian Northern was building from The Pas to Port Nelson, thus assuring the province access to a port on Hudson Bay. When it was decided that Port Nelson was unsuitable as a port, the railway was built to Churchill.

126 Whitney's biographer claims that the Ontario government was "jubilant" because it "undoubtedly had received its reward for faithful service in the 1911 federal election." But so too had Manitoba. Humphries, *Honest Enough*, 201. Quebec was not ignored, of course: its territory was expanded northward to the eastern coast of Hudson Bay and filling the mainland except for Labrador.

127 Ibid. J.R. Cartwright to Hearst, 4 July 1906; Hearst to Cartwright, 6 July 1906. John Robison Cartwright, a cousin of Sir Richard Cartwright, was Deputy Attorney General of Ontario from 1889 to 1919.

128 Ibid. Allan McLennan to J.J. Foy, 5 April 1908.

129 OA, "Return of Documents re Keewatin Power Company Case," *Ontario Sessional Papers* (1912): #70, unpublished manuscript.

130 *Statutes of Ontario*, 1913, 3 Geo. V. c.34.

131 *The Globe*, December 1917, quoted in James A. Onusko, *Ontario's Soldiers' Aid Commission: 100 Years of Assistance to Veterans in Need 1915–2015* (Toronto, 2015), 16.

132 Ibid, 3 Geo. V. c.26.

133 Brittany Luby, *Damned: The Politics of Loss and Survival in Anishinaabe Territory* (Winnipeg, 2020), 25.

134 White to Scott, cited in David T. McNab, "The Administration of Treaty 3: The Location of the Boundaries of Treaty 3 Indian Reserves in Ontario, 1873–1916," *As Long as the Sun Shines and the Water Flows: A Reader in Canadian Native Studies*, eds. Ian A.L. Getty and Antoine S. Lussier (Vancouver, 1983), 153.

135 White to Scott, cited in David T. McNab, "The Administration of Treaty 3," 153.

136 Ibid.

137 Sean Fine, "Crown Broke 1850 Land Treaties with First Nations, Ontario Court of Appeals Rules," *The Globe and Mail*, 8 November 2021, accessed 25 May 2022, www.theglobeandmail.com/canada/article-crown-broke-1850-land-treaties-with-first-nations-ontario-court-of/#:~:text=Ontario's%20highest%20court%20has%20ruled,northern%20part%20of%20the%20province/; cf. Sean Fine, "First Nations Seek Billions for Broken Treaty, But Ontario Says It Owes No Money," *The Globe and Mail*, 2 February 2023, accessed 15 May 2023, www.theglobeandmail.com/canada/article-ontario-judge-weighs-how-many-billions-governments-owe-over-173-year/. The Ontario Superior Court of Justice disagreed, declaring that the Saugeen First Nation was the rightful owner of Sauble Beach. According to CTV, "a further court proceeding will determine potential damages owed to the Saugeen First Nation for breaking the 1854 Treaty that was supposed to keep Sauble Beach's shoreline under their stewardship." CTV London News, "First Nations Wins Ownership of Sauble Beach Waterfront," accessed 22 May 2023, https://london.ctvnews.ca/first-nation-wins-ownership-of-sauble-beach-waterfront-1.6342060/.

138 *The Globe*, 12 April 1912; *The Mail and Empire*, 12 April 1912.

139 *Sault Daily Star*, 17 December 1917. The event took place in 1914 when Hearst was still Minister of Lands, Forests and Mines.

140 Hearst fonds F6MU1311. Notes of an address by Hearst, 16 April 1914.

141 It's not clear if Hearst had a particular region in mind, but in today's Northern Ontario, the term *banana belt* generally refers to the area around Blind River

142 *The Mail and Empire*, 12 April 1912. The Ontario government did create this department in 1977.

143 Christopher Armstrong, *The Politics of Federalism: Ontario's Relations with the Federal Government, 1867–1942* (Toronto, 1981), 126.

144 Sir Richard Cartwright, quoted in Armstrong, *Politics of Federalism*, 125.

145 *The Globe*, 23 March, 2 April 1912.

146 Ibid.

147 Ibid. *The Mail and Empire*, 23 March 1912.

148 Ibid, 10 April 1913.

149 *Canadian Annual Review* (1913): 378.

150 *Journals of the Legislative Assembly* (1913): 76.

151 Ibid, 77.

152 J. Patrick Boyer, *A Passion for Justice: The Legacy of James Chalmers McRuer* (Toronto, 1994), 28.

153 *The Mail and Empire*, 2 April 1913.

154 Ibid, 3 April 1913.

155 Hearst, "Red-Haired Boy," 92–3.

156 "Minutes and Evidence before the Committee on Privileges and Election in the matter of certain charges made by William Proudfoot, Esquire, Member for the Centre Riding of Huron," *Journals of the Legislative Assembly* (1913): Appendix 2; *Cf The Mail and Empire*, 24, 25, 30 April 1913; 1, 2, 7, 8 May 1913; *Canadian Annual Review* (1913): 401–5. *Cf* Oliver, *Ferguson*, 53–6.

157 *The Globe*, 1 April 1913; *The Mail and Empire*, 1 April 1913.

158 *The Globe*, 27 March 1913.

159 Ibid. Cf. Hearst fonds. Ms of speech.

160 *The Globe*, 27 March 1913.

161 Ibid, 12 April 1913.

162 Whitney fonds. Grigg to Whitney, 13 January 1912; Whitney to Grigg, 15 January 1912.

163 *Statutes of Ontario*, 1913, 3 Geo. V. c.128.

164 Ibid, 3 Geo V. c.134.

165 The Forest Reserves Act was passed in 1898, when the first two forest reserves were created: the Eastern Forest Reserve in Eastern Ontario and the Sibley Forest Reserve on the north shore of Lake Superior. In 1909 Cochrane created the huge – 4,760 square kilometres – Quetico Forest Reserve, which adjoined the Superior National Forest established earlier that year on the Minnesota side of the border.

166 *The Mail and Empire*, 22 April 1913.

167 Ibid, 16 April 1913, 22 April 1913.

168 Ibid, 12 April 1913.

169 Ibid, 22 April 1913.

170 One author has claimed that Munn and Tudhope were quite willing to sell the lease and only began logging ostentatiously when the price offered by the province to buy back the lease was too low. Dave Lang, "The Log Export Question in British Columbia, 1865–1930" (unpublished Hons BA diss., University of Victoria, 2019), 40.

171 Gerald Killan, *Protected Places: A History of Ontario's Provincial Parks System* (Toronto, 1993), 40.

172 "Great Porcupine Fire," in *Wikipedia*, accessed 21 September 2021, https://en.wikipedia.org/wiki/Great_Porcupine_Fire/.

173 Cf. John Bacher, *Two Billion Trees and Counting: The Legacy of Edmund Zavitz* (Toronto, 2011).

174 Ibid, 90–1; Bruce M. Pearce, "A Built-to-Order Forest," *Maclean's* (1 April 1929): 13.

175 Mike Commito, "The Deadliest Fire in Canada's History Was in Northern Ontario," 28 July 2017, www.sudbury.com/columns/canada150/canada150-the-deadliest-fire-in-canadas-history-was-in-northern-ontario-683018/.

176 Bacher, *Two Billion Trees*, 93.

177 Energysage, "Hydro Power Pros and Cons," accessed 21 September 2021, www.energysage.com/about-clean-energy/hydropower/pros-cons-hydropower/. Cf. Kiwi Energy, "Pros and Cons of Hydroelectric Energy," accessed 21 September 2021, https://kiwienergy.us/pros-and-cons-of-hydroelectric-energy/. Toxic pulp and paper mill emissions continued long after the Whitney and Hearst years. In the 1960s and 1970s, the Dryden Chemical Company dumped ten tonnes of mercury into the English-Wabigoon River upstream of the Grassy Narrows First Nation, with horrendous results for the Anishinaabe people living there.

178 Cf. Delores Broten and Jan Ritchlin, "The Pulp Pollution Primer," *Watershed Sentinel*, 15 October 2012, accessed 22 September 2021, https://watershedsentinel.ca/articles/the-pulp-pollution-primer/.

179 Krista McCracken, "Sudbury: The Journey from Moonscape to Sustainably Green," *Active History*, 10 June 2013, accessed 18 September 2021, https://activehistory.ca/2013/06/11360/; Sara Miller Llana, "The Sudbury Model," *Christian Science Monitor*, 24 September 2020, accessed 21 September 2021, www.csmonitor.com/Environment/2020/0924/The-Sudbury-model-How-one-of-the-world-s-major-polluters-went-green/. This contrasted with the Blezard Valley, twenty-one kilometres north of Sudbury, where farming was thriving. Cf Peter Krats, "'A Commodity So Closely Aligned to Armageddon': The Sudbury Region in Wartime and Aftermath," *The Northern Review* 44 (2017): 371–414.

180 Mark Kuhlberg, "Pulp and Paper Industry," *The Canadian Encyclopedia*, accessed 22 September 2021, www.thecanadianencyclopedia.ca/en/article/pulp-and-paper-industry/.

181 Hearst, "Red-Haired Boy," 40.

182 Bacher, *Two Billion Trees*, 40. Zavitz is sometimes referred to as the Ontario government's first forester. He was actually the second. The first had been Dr Judson Clark, who joined the Crown Lands Department in 1904 but resigned after disagreements over forest management procedures in 1907. Bruce W. Hodgins et al., "The Ontario and Quebec Experiments in Forest Reserves 1883–1930," *Journal of Forest History* 26, no. 1 (1982): 28.

183 Ibid.

184 Ibid, 93.
185 Ibid, 101–7.
186 Whitney fonds. Hearst to Whitney, 4 September 1913; *The Globe*, 13 September 1913.

**Chapter 3**

1 Hearst speech, Sault Ste. Marie, 4 December 1914, quoted in in J. Castell Hopkins, *The Province of Ontario in the War* (Toronto, 1919), 4.
2 *Sault Daily Star*, 8 January 1914. He and his wife were staying in the Manhattan Hotel.
3 Ibid, 12 January 1914. That was true but he was also 67 years old and not in good health.
4 Ibid, 18 February 1914.
5 D.M. LeBourdais, *Canada and the Atomic Revolution* (Toronto, 1959), 84–5.
6 *The Globe*, 27 March 1914; *Bills Presented to the Legislative Assembly* (1914): #37.
7 *The Mail and Empire*, 1 April 1914.
8 *Statutes of Ontario*, 1914, 4 Geo. V. c.6.
9 Ibid. 4 Geo. V. c.5.
10 *The Mail and Empire*, 12 March 1914.
11 *Journal of the Legislative Assembly* (1914): 67.
12 The Laurier government did create the first Department of Labour in 1900, but it came under the jurisdiction of the Postmaster General until 1909 when W.L. Mackenzie King became the first full-time Minister of Labour.
13 *Final Report on Laws Relating to the Liability of Employers to Make Compensation to Their Employees for Injuries Received in the Course of Their Employment Which Are in Force in Other Countries* (Toronto: King's Printer, 1913). On the background to the Act, see R.C.B. Risk, "'This Nuisance of Litigation': The Origins of Workers' Compensation in Ontario," in *Essays in the History of Canadian Law*, vol. 2, ed. David H. Flaherty (Toronto, 2012): 418–91.
14 Quoted in Humphries, "Whitney, Sir James Pliny," in *Dictionary of Canadian Biography*, vol. 14 (University of Toronto/Université Laval, 2003–), accessed 13 June 2019, www.biographi.ca/en/bio/whitney_james_pliny_14E.html/. *Canadian Annual Review* (1914): 391.
15 *The Globe*, 2 May 1914.
16 Ibid, 7 May 1914, quoted in the *Sault Daily Star*, 17 May 1914.
17 The *Globe*, apparently unaware that Cochrane was away, assumed that Hearst and Lucas had met with him. *The Globe*, 11 May 1914. Borden diary, 5 May 1914. Borden's diary entry is just a terse note saying that he had written to them.
18 LAC. Borden fonds. Diary, 10 May 1914, 13 May 1914.

19 Ibid, 5 May 1914.
20 Cf. David Zeni, *Forgotten Empress: The Empress of Ireland Story* (Wellington, 1998).
21 Whitney fonds. Rev. Ben Spence to Whitney, 19 June 1914; Whitney to Rev. W. Philip, 22 July 1914; *The Globe*, 9 May 1914, 27 May 1914.
22 Ibid, 28 May 1914.
23 Borden diary, 27 March 1912.
24 Quoted in Prang, *Rowell*, 139.
25 Whitney fonds. Reuben Millichamp to Whitney, 1 April 1912. *The Globe*, 13 February 1913.
26 *The Globe*, 30 May 1913.
27 Ibid, also 26 November 1913 and 24 June 1914.
28 Whitney fonds; Whitney to Rev W. Philip, 22 July 1914.
29 F.W. Merchant, *Report on the Condition of English-French Schools in the Province of Ontario* (Toronto, 1912), 69.
30 Ibid, 15–16.
31 Whitney to Bishop W.A. Macdonell, 14 November 1912, quoted in Humphries, *Honest Enough*, 203.
32 Whitney fonds. Bishop Fallon to Whitney, 28 December 1912; Whitney to Bishop Charles Gauthier, 28 December 1912. AO. Ferguson fonds. Ferguson to D'Arcy Scott, 22 November 1916. Scott was a prominent Irish Catholic Ottawa lawyer, former mayor, and the son of Sir Richard Scott, author of the Scott Act, which established the local-option temperance policy. AO, Cody fonds. Hearst to Rev H.J. Cody, 29 April 1919; cf. *The Globe*, 28 December 1912; *The Mail and Empire*, 11 March 1916; *Ottawa Free Press*, 12 May 1916.
33 For many years the Ontario public school system used the British term "form" instead of "grade." There were four forms in elementary schools, each equivalent to two grades.
34 For the full text, see *Report of the Minister of Education, 1912* (Toronto, 1913), 211–3; cf. C.B. Sissons, *Bi-lingual Schools in Canada* (London, 1917), 103–5.
35 For the full text, see the *Report of the Minister of Education, 1912* (Toronto, 1913), 213–5.
36 For the full text, see *Report of the Minister of Education, 1913* (Toronto, 1914), 211–3; cf. C.B. Sissons, *Bi-lingual* Schools, 218–21.
37 Whitney fonds. Central Committee of L'Action catholique de la jeunesse canadienne to Whitney, 15 January 1912; *Cf The Truth, Nothing but the Truth* (Montreal, 1915); *The Juridical and Pedagogical Position of English-French Schools in Ontario*, (Ottawa, 1915). LAC, Gouin fonds 2661, *Observations des Evèques de la Province écclésiastique de Québec sur le Règlement XVII* (n.d.); *Bi-lingualism in Ontario* (Ottawa, January 1912).
38 *Observations des Evèques.*

39 A century later some people, including historians, are still confused about the issue. Tim Cook wrote in 2011 that Regulation 17 "sought to remove the teaching of [the French] language from schools." Tim Cook, "'Our First Duty Is to Win, at Any Cost': Sir Robert Borden during the Great War," *Journal of Military and Strategic Studies* 13, no. 3 (Spring 2011): 14. Seven years later Patrice Dutil and David Mackenzie referred to "the stripping of French-Canadian rights" in *Embattled Nation: Canada's Wartime Election of 1917* (Toronto, 2017), 42.
40 Whitney fonds. Mgr. J.O. Routhier to Whitney, 20 September 1912; cf. *Observations des Evèques*; *Canadian Annual Review* (1915): 564.
41 Senator Landry to Bishop Charles Gauthier, 15 May 1915, quoted in Rumilly, *Histoire de Quebec, XX*, 54–5; cf. *The Juridical and Pedagogical Position, Observations des Evèques.* Gouin fonds 2617. Gouin to Hearst, 3 February 1915; cf. Elizabeth H. Armstrong, *The Crisis of Quebec, 1914–1918* (New York, 1937), 36.
42 *The Catholic Record,* 15 November 1913; *The Daily Star,* 30 August 1915.
43 University of Toronto Library. *Correspondence Between the Ontario Department of Education and the Roman Catholic Authorities Concerning the Bi-lingual Schools Issue in Ontario*; John Seath to Sir William Meredith, 17 February 1910; Whitney to the Ontario archbishops, 9 March 1910; Memorandum of Bishop M.F. Fallon to the Ontario bishops, 24 January 1917.
44 Barber, "Bilingual Schools," 236. Cf. Robert Sellar, *The Tragedy of Quebec* (Huntingdon, 1907).
45 Sissons, *Bi-lingual Schools,* 72.
46 Rowell fonds 8761. Copy of resolution.
47 *The Globe,* 28 December 1912; cf. Whitney fonds; Whitney to Sam Genest, 9 January 1913.
48 *Canadian Annual Review* (1913): 428.
49 Rumilly, *Histoire de Québec,* XVIII, 57; Mason Wade, *The French Canadians* (Toronto, 1956), 634.
50 *Canadian Annual Review* (1913): 429.
51 *The Globe,* 2 May 1916.
52 *The Mail and Empire,* 24 October 1913; *Canadian Annual Review* (1913): 430.
53 *The Globe,* 24 June 1914.
54 Ibid, 20 June 1914; *The Evening Telegram,* 20, 26, 27 June 1914.
55 *The Globe,* 27 June 1914; *Canadian Annual Review* (1914): 448.
56 See *The Globe,* 24 October 1913 and 22 June 1914; *Canadian Annual Review* (1914): 447–8.
57 *The Globe,* 17 June 1914.
58 Brockville, Dufferin, Durham East, Frontenac, Grenville, Hamilton East, Hastings West, Manitoulin, Norfolk South, Parkdale, Simcoe West, Victoria

North, Waterloo North, and Welland. By contrast, the Conservatives only conceded one, Norfolk North.

59 Quoted in Humphries, *Honest Enough*, 212.

60 *The Globe*, 6 May, 6 June 1914; Cf. Whitney fonds; A.E.H. Creswicke to Whitney, 19 June 1914; Whitney to Creswicke, 20 June 1914. Creswicke was a prominent Conservative lawyer and former mayor of Barrie.

61 *The Globe*, 6 June 1914.

62 Ibid, 12, 13 June 1914.

63 Spence, *Prohibition in Canada*, 397. *The Star Weekly* reported that he did not tolerate the least indication of intemperance in those working under him. *The Star Weekly*, 17 October 1914.

64 *The Globe*, 12 June 1914.

65 Ibid, 27 May 1914.

66 W.R. Plewman, *Adam Beck and the Ontario Hydro* (Toronto, 1947), 154. Mark Sholdice cites this reference in a rather confused interpretation of Reaume's defeat in the election. See Mark Sholdice, "The Ontario Experiment: Hydroelectricity, Public Ownership, and Transnational Progressivism, 1906–1939" (unpublished PhD diss., University of Guelph, 2019), 154.

67 On McNaught's promotion of public power, see Hector Charlesworth, *The Canadian Scene: Sketches: Political and Historical* (Toronto, 1927), 214–5.

68 *Windsor Evening Record*, 24 April 1914, quoted in Cecillon, *Prayers*, 95.

69 Cecillon, *Prayers*, 96.

70 Tolmie was able to win because the Conservative vote was divided. He served overseas as a chaplain, then ran against Hartley Dewart for the Liberal leadership in 1919 and lost by only thirty-seven votes. He was re-elected in the 1919 election, then ran again for the party leadership in 1922, and again was unsuccessful.

71 *Sault Daily Star*, 9 June 1914.

72 Ibid, 23 June 1914.

73 Ibid.

74 Ibid, 24 June 1914.

75 *The Globe*, 25 June 1914.

76 Michel Dupuis, "A Unique Career in Canadian Journalism: William R. Plewman of the Toronto Daily Star," *Canadian Journal of Media Studies* 2, no. 1 (April 2007): 111.

77 Hearst, "Red-Haired Boy," 116–18.

78 Ibid.

79 The labour candidate, Allan Studholme, was re-elected in Hamilton East.

80 Ibid, 30 June 1914.

81 Whitney to S.T. Loucks, 2 July 1914, quoted in Humphries, *Honest Enough*, 213.

82 Whitney fonds; Whitney to Sir Hugh John Macdonald, 6 July 1914.

83 Ibid. Whitney to Rev. A.E. Burke, 3 July 1914; *Cf* Whitney statement in *The Mail and Empire*, 1 July 1914. Burke was director of the Toronto-based Catholic Church Extension Society of Canada and an outspoken opponent of bilingual schools. He was also a Conservative and when he went overseas as a chaplain in 1915 he was appointed a lieutenant colonel, after which he claimed to be the senior Catholic chaplain in the Canadian Expeditionary Force. That led to a revolt among the Catholic chaplains, and he resigned in September 1917 and returned home. *Cf* Mark G. McGowan, "Burke, Alfred Edward," in *Dictionary of Canadian Biography*, vol. 15 (University of Toronto/Université Laval, 2003–), accessed 13 May 2019, www.biographi.ca/en/bio/burke_alfred_edward_15E.html/.

84 Schull describes him as "a loyal subordinate" who was "always close to the Premier," had few public enemies, and "had maintained a neutral image." Schull, *Ontario*, 212.

85 *The Daily Star*, 24 September 1914.

86 *The Globe*, 26 September 1914.

87 Ibid.

88 Plewman, *Adam Beck*, 158. Hearst fonds. R.A. Pyne to Hearst, 13 September 1918, statement re the succession attached. Publicly, he "distinctly" let it be known "that he would refuse absolutely to assume the responsibility." Quoted in the *World*, 2 October 1914. Pyne also knew that Whitney wanted Hearst to succeed him.

89 Ibid, 28 September 1914; 30 September 1914.

90 *The Globe*, 29 September 1914.

91 Ibid.

92 Ibid, 29 September 1914; *The World*, 30 September 1914.

93 Ibid, 1 October 1914.

94 A former journalist and newspaper editor, Wallis was appointed secretary to the office of the Prime Minister of Ontario in 1905. When Hearst became Premier in 1914, he created the Department of the President of the Privy Council with Wallis as deputy minister. He had long been "active ... in the establishment of Temperance organizations, and in the promotion of the Prohibition movement." Charlesworth, *Cyclopedia*, 116.

95 Scott and Astrid Young cautiously suggest that "it would not be unreasonable to assume" that the succession was one of the topics they discussed and Cochrane "might even have seen [the memo] at the time. Young and Young, *Cochrane*, 180.

96 Hearst fonds. Whitney letter, 13 May 1914.

97 Borden diary, 23 September 1914, 25 September 1914. Sir John Gibson's term was up. In the unlikely event that Cochrane was offered and accepted the leadership of the provincial party, J.D. Reid suggested to Borden that

he invite Hearst to replace him in the federal cabinet. Borden diary, 26 September 1914.

98 Charlesworth, *Candid Chronicles,* 189. *The Globe,* 2 October 1914.

99 *The Globe,* 2 October 1914.

100 Plewman, *Adam Beck,* 158. He later joined Imperial Oil's board of directors and in February 1918 became president. *Imperial Oil Review* 2, no. 3 (March 1918): 2.

101 *The Evening News,* quoted in the *World,* 2 October 1914.

102 For a detailed account of the evolution of what became the Hydro-Electric Power Commission, see Plewman, *Adam Beck,* and Neil B. Freeman, *The Politics of Power: Ontario Hydro and Its Government, 1906–1995* (Toronto, 1996), 10–29.

103 For a detailed account of the evolution of what became the Hydro-Electric Power Commission, see Plewman, *Adam Beck,* and Freeman, *The Politics of Power,* 10–29, 158. One wonders if Plewman was forgetting about Lucas's strong support of Beck or if he understood that supporting Beck as chairman of the hydro commission and supporting him as Premier were two very different things.

104 *The Evening Telegram,* quoted in *The World,* 3 October 1914.

105 Nelles, "Beck," *Dictionary of Canadian Biography.*

106 *The Daily Star,* 28 September 1914.

107 *The Globe,* 29 September 1914.

108 Pendarves was an Italianate villa-style mansion built at 33 St. George Street, near College Street, in 1860 by Frederic Cumberland, a prominent Toronto architect, facing east towards the new University of Toronto campus. When the government closed the old government house on Simcoe Street in 1912, it leased Pendarves as a temporary official residence for the lieutenant governor while a new vice-regal resident was being built in Rosedale. It was first occupied by Sir John Gibson until 1914 and then by Sir John Hendrie until Chorley Park was completed in 1915, and then was acquired by the University of Toronto in 1923. It is now known as Cumberland House and houses the university's Centre for International Experience.

109 Ibid, 30 September 1914.

110 *The Globe,* 30 September 1914, 1 October 1914, 2 October 1914.

111 Ibid, 3 October 1914. It also described Hearst as "aggressive" and "in manner … brusque and retiring, in disposition kindly but firm."

112 *The World,* 2 October 1914.

113 *The Globe,* 25 December 1913.

114 Ibid, 30 May 1914.

115 Ibid, 3 October 1914.

116 Schull, *Ontario,* 212.

117 *The Globe*, 2 October 1914.

118 Ibid, 3 October 1914. J.D. Reid was the Conservative MP for Grenville, "a shrewd political practitioner and notorious manipulator" who was fast becoming one of the most powerful figures in the Borden government. Peter Oliver, *G. Howard Ferguson: Ontario Tory* (Toronto, 1977), 31.

119 All quotations from the *Sault Daily Star*, 2 October 1914. Dr. James McLurg, a physician from Woodstock, had moved to Sault Ste. Marie in 1901. Described as "a staunch Liberal," he was president of the Algoma West Liberal Association "for a number of years." Anon, *History of the Medical Profession* (Sault Ste. Marie, 1922), 38, accessed 15 February 2020, https://archive.org/details/historyofmedical00sauluoft/page/n17/mode/2up/.

120 *The Globe*, 3 October 1914. It's not clear why A.E. Ames was present. A prominent Toronto financier, Methodist, and Liberal, he and Hearst may have become friends when both were young men in Owen Sound in the 1880s.

121 Ibid; *Sudbury Star*, 3 October 1914.

122 Ibid, 7 October 1914.

**Chapter 4**

1 Hearst speech, Sault Ste. Marie, 4 December 1914; quoted in J. Castell Hopkins, *The Province of Ontario in the War* (Toronto, 1919), 4.

2 Comeau, "Hanna."

3 *The Daily Star*, 18 September 1914.

4 Morel was a prosperous butcher in Mattawa. First elected in 1908, he held the seat until being defeated in 1919. He regained it in 1923 and held it until 1930, when he resigned to run in the federal election. Defeated, he was appointed superintendent of the Trans-Canada Highway construction program in the area.

5 Young and Young, *Cochrane*, 182.

6 *The Daily Star*, 28 September 1914. Typically, Beck regarded Hendrie's "insistence on a critical examination of many early projects … as personal animosity rather than a concern for diligence." Thomas H. Ferns, "Hendrie, Sir John Strathearn," in *Dictionary of Canadian Biography*, vol. 15 (University of Toronto/Université Laval, 2003–), accessed 19 January 2019, www.biographi.ca/en/bio/hendrie_john_strathearn_15E.html/.

7 *The Evening Telegram* editorial, reprinted in *The World*, 3 October 1914.

8 Hearst kept McNaught on the commission until 1919. E.B. Biggar, *Hydro-Electric Development in Ontario* (Toronto, 1920), 61. On McNaught's promotion of public power, see Hector Charlesworth, *The Canadian Scene: Sketches: Political and Historical* (Toronto, 1927), 214–5.

9 *The World*, 2 October 1914.

10 Quoted in Nelles, *Politics of Development*, 388.
11 Nelles, *Politics of Development*, 376; Gillis and Roach, *Lost Initiatives*, 99.
12 Bacher, *Two Billion Trees*, 95.
13 Kuhlberg, "Pulpwood," 78–80.
14 Quoted in *The Globe*, 5 August 1914; Hopkins, *Ontario*, 2.
15 Quoted in Hopkins, *Ontario*, 4. His thinking did not evolve over the years. Asked in February 1939 if Canada was automatically at war when Britain went to war, he replied: "I have never considered that matter from a constitutional standpoint – but as a matter of fact, how could we help it?" *The Daily Star*, 16 February 1939.
16 *Sault Daily Star*, 5 August 1914.
17 *The Globe*, 17 October 1914. The first contingent had sailed for England on 3 October.
18 Hearst fonds. Ms of speech to Fort William Canadian Club, September 1912. Ms of speech to Toronto Empire Club, 28 November 1912.
19 Ibid. Fort William speech.
20 Ibid.
21 Ibid. Ms of speech in legislature on war resolution, 1917.
22 Ibid. Ms of speech at University of Toronto Convocation Hall, 27 April 1917.
23 Ibid. War resolution speech.
24 Ibid. Convocation Hall speech.
25 Ibid. Fort William speech.
26 Quoted in Robert Rutherdale, *Hometown Horizons: Local Responses to Canada's Great War* (Vancouver, 2004), 138–9.
27 Ibid. Ms of speech to New York City Canadian Club, 12 January 1915.
28 Miller, *Our Glory and Our Grief*, 31–2.
29 P. Whitney Lackenbauer and Nikolas Gardner, "Citizen Soldiers as 'Liminaries': The CEF Soldier Riots of 1916 Reconsidered," in *Canadian Military History Since the 17th Century*, ed. Yves Tremblay (Ottawa, 2013), 159–62.
30 Hearst to Falconer, 9 October 1914; Falconer to Hearst, 10 October 1914; Hearst to Falconer, 15 October 1914. Quoted in James Greenlee, *Robert Falconer: A Biography* (Toronto 1988), 203.
31 Greenlee, *Falconer*, 201–11.
32 Richard Franklin Preston was a physician in Carleton Place who represented Lanark North in the legislature from 1894 to 1898 and 1905 to 1919 and then served in the House of Commons from 1922 to 1929. For a time during the Whitney years he was the Conservative Party whip in the legislature. Thomas Hook was a Toronto real estate agent in Toronto and very active in the Conservative Party before being elected to the legislature in 1914. According to Charlesworth, he was "untiring in his recruiting

efforts" during the war. Charlesworth, *Cyclopaedia*, 300. *The Daily Star*, 7 December 1914; *The Globe*, 8 December 1914 and 9 December 1914, all quoted in Greenlee, *Falconer*, 211.

33 Greenlee, *Falconer*, 211.

34 *The Globe*, 16 December 1914, quoted in ibid, 212. It should be noted that German professors at other universities such as Queen's, McMaster, and Western Ontario continued to be employed with harassment, presumably because they were less dependent on public financial support than the University of Toronto. Adam Crerar, "Ontario and the Great War," in *Canada and the First World War*, ed. David Mackenzie (Toronto, 2005), 754.

35 Canadian War Museum, "The Internment of Ukrainian Canadians," accessed 8 August 2019, www.warmuseum.ca/firstworldwar/history/life-at-home-during-the-war/enemy-aliens/the-internment-of-ukrainian-canadians/. On the federal government's struggle to develop a response to the fact that thousands of enemy aliens throughout the country, who had been encouraged to immigrate to Canada, were being dismissed from their jobs and were unable to support themselves, see Bohdan S. Kordan, "'They Will Be Dangerous': Security and the Control of Enemy Aliens in Canada, 1914," in *Canadian State Trials*, vol. 4, ed. Barry Wright, Eric Tucker and Susan Binnie (Toronto, 2018), 42–70.

36 The six "camps" were at Kapuskasing (December 1914 to February 1920), Fort Henry, Kingston (August 1914 to November 1917), Niagara Falls armoury (December 1914 to August 1918), Camp Petawawa (December 1914 to May 1916), Sault Ste. Marie armoury (January 1915 to January 1918), and Stanley Barracks, Toronto (December 1914 to October 1916). Technically, the camps at Niagara Falls, Toronto, and Sault Ste. Marie were receiving stations that only held prisoners until they were sent to a permanent camp.

37 Watson Kirkconnell, "Kapuskasing: An Historical Sketch," *Bulletin of the Departments of History and Political and Economic Science in Queen's University* 38 (January 1921): 5, accessed 31 May 2019, https://archive.org/details/kapuskasinghisto00kirkuoft/page/14/.

38 *Sault Daily Star*, 11 December 1914.

39 According to Edmund Newcombe, the Deputy Minister of Justice, the purpose of internment was to afford "some occupation for people who must necessarily, in the interest of humanity, be maintained at the public expense." In other words, they were not being mistreated; they were being protected and given employment" with the status of prisoners of war. Needless to say, the internees rejected this position, arguing that they had left their former homes to live in Canada and had committed no crimes. Bohdan S. Kordan, "First World Internment in Canada: Enemy Aliens and the Blurring of the Military/Civilian Distinction," *Canadian Military History*

29, no. 2 (2020): 6–11. On the cooperation by the federal and provincial governments on this project, see Hearst fonds. "Memorandum Relating to the Soldier Settlement and Suggestions Relating to Agricultural Training for Returned Soldiers" (unpublished manuscript, 1918); *Canadian Annual Review* (1918): 605–6.

40 This policy was legitimate because internees were classified as prisoners of war, entitled under the Hague Convention to the same pay and the same standard of food, clothing and shelter as privates in the Canadian army not engaged in military duties. "How the Sault was Involved in the Internment of 'Enemy Aliens' during the First World War," *SooToday.com,* 19 August 2018, www.sootoday.com/columns/remember-this/how-the-sault-was-involved-in-the-internment-of-enemy-aliens-during-the-first-world-war-1018841/. Cf. *Kapuskasing Internment Camp,* accessed 15 September 2019, www.cdli.ca/monuments/on/kapplaq.htm/.

41 Kirkconnell, "Kapuskasing," 7, 11.

42 Ibid, 11.

43 *The Globe,* 10 January 1914.

44 *The Daily Star,* 22 December 1914.

45 Ibid, 13 January 1915.

46 *Canadian Annual Review* (1914): 239.

47 *The Globe,* 8 January 1915. Its members were W.F. Gundy, Archbishop Neil McNeil, Archdeacon H.J. Cody, Rev Dr Daniel Strachan, Professor A.T. DeLury, G. Frank Beer, W.K. McNaught, W.L. Best, Joseph Gibbons, Marjorie MacMurchy, and G.E. Jackson as secretary.

48 *The Daily Star,* 23 January 1915.

49 Prang, "Rowell," 206.

50 *Ontario Commission on Unemployment Interim Report* (Toronto, 20 July 1915); Cf. *The Daily Star,* 21 July 1915.

51 *The Daily Star,* 5 June 1915, 23 July 1915, 23 October 1915; *Cf* ibid, 17 November 1915, 2 December 1915, 6 December 1915.

52 *The Daily Star,* 2 December 1915.

53 *Speech of Hon. W.H. Hearst on The Ontario Temperance Act* (Toronto, n.d.).

54 Craig Heron, "Baillie, Sir Frank Wilton," in *Dictionary of Canadian Biography,* vol. 15 (University of Toronto/Université Laval, 2003–), accessed 5 August 2019, www.biographi.ca/en/bio/baillie_frank_wilton_15E.html/.

55 My calculation, based on figures in Chris Sharpe, "Enlistment in the Canadian Expeditionary Force 1914–1918: A Re-Evaluation," *Canadian Military History* 24, no. 1 (Spring 2015): 5–6.

56 F. Douglas Reville, *History of the County of Brant* (Brantford, 1920), 378.

57 "Effects of WW1 on Welland Industry," accessed 27 August 2019, www.welland.library.on.ca/industry/War/Effects%20of%20WWI%20on%20Welland%20Industry.htm/.

58 "Town of Renfrew," accessed 3 August 2019, www.renfrew.ca/history-of-renfrew.cfm/.

59 "Imperial War Museum," accessed 3 August 2019, www.iwm.org.uk/collections/item/object/205220663/.

60 "Brief History of Nobel," accessed 3 August 2019, www.gumptioninc.org/2017/06/02/brief-history-nobel/.

61 David Carnegie, *The History of Munitions Supply in Canada 1914–1918* (Toronto, 1925), lx.

62 Remarkably, no one was killed because the event took place on the evening of 14 October, the Thanksgiving Day holiday. Cf. John Melady, *Explosion: Trenton* (Belleville, 1980).

63 Heron, "Baillie."

64 The IMB had discovered that nearly half of a shell casing's initial composition was removed as the casing was hollowed out during machining and that about 350,000 tons of this "waste" was being generated annually in Canada. The turnings could be melted down and recast into ingots, but there were no furnaces in Canada capable of doing such work, so the steel turnings were being sold to American manufacturers for little more than the cost of handling. The British Forgings plant recycled the turnings into ingots, then produced the shell casings. Michael Moir, "Toronto's Waterfront at War, 1914–1918," *Archivaria* 28 (Summer 1989): 130–2.

65 Crerar, "Ontario and the Great War," 677.

66 *The Mail and Empire*, 2 March 1917. He was speaking on the royal commission report.

67 The most thorough account of this episode is Daryl White, "Managing a War Metal: The International Nickel Company's First World War," in *Smart Globalization: The Canadian Business and Economic History Experience*, ed. Andrew Smith and Dimitry Anastakis (Toronto, 2014), 92–107. Cf. Peter Krats, "'A Commodity So Closely Aligned to Armageddon': The Sudbury Region in Wartime and Aftermath," *The Northern Review* 44 (2017): 371–414.

68 Ferguson to Borden, 27 January 1916, quoted in Oliver, *Ferguson*, 83. Hammermill did establish a permanent office in the province, however.

69 *The Mail and Empire*, 23 February 1915. Meanwhile, when some people expressed concerns over the Hammermill Paper Company, an American company owned by German interests, being allowed to continue exporting pulpwood for its paper mill in Erie, Pennsylvania, as it had been doing since 1908, the government ignored them. Paper, of course, was not as controversial as nickel in wartime.

70 *Munition Resources Commission, First Report* (Ottawa, 1918), 9.

71 Ibid.

72 *Glengarry News*, 29 August 1919, accessed 23 October 2019, www.glengarrycountyarchives.ca/Glengarry_pdf/The-Glengarry-News/1911-1920/1919/Aug/08-29-1919.pdf/.

73 Nelles, *Politics of Development*, 350.

74 Oliver, *Ferguson*, 84–5.

75 Nelles, *Politics of Development*, 359. Construction of the refinery didn't actually begin until 1918. The government sweetened the deal with International Nickel by declining to offer any financial support to the British American Nickel Corporation, a small Canadian-based rival that had acquired a mine and built a smelter at Sudbury and a refinery at Deschenes, Quebec, whose assets International Nickel soon acquired.

76 "Discovery of the Orford Process for Nickel Extraction," 23 November 1999, accessed 16 October 2021, https://uwaterloo.ca/wat-on-earth/news/discovery-orford-process-nickel-extraction/.

77 "Inco One of the Biggest Stories in in Port Colborne's History," *Welland Tribune*, 30 October 2013, accessed 11 June 2022, www.pressreader.com/canada/the-welland-tribune/20131030/281616713117517/; *Environmental Justice Atlas: Port Colborne Class Action Lawsuit Against Vale, Canada*, accessed 11 June 2022, https://ejatlas.org/conflict/port-colborne-class-action-lawsuit-against-vale/.

78 Schull, *Ontario*, 216. Cf. Hopkins, *Ontario*, 7–9.

79 Gertrude E.M. Vaughan, "The Ontario Model Hospital at Orpington," *The World's Work Magazine*, July 1916, accessed 14 December 2018, www.scarletfinders.co.uk/162.html/.

80 John Pateman, *The Ontario Military Hospital Orpington Kent* (Sleaford, 2012), 17.

81 Thomas McGarry, speaking in the legislature on 7 March 1916. *Financial Statement of the Hon T.W. McGarry, Treasurer of the Province of Ontario Delivered on the 7th March 1916* (Toronto, 1916), 6.

82 David William McPherson was born in Toronto in 1871, attended the University of Toronto, was a surgeon in Toronto, and was active in the militia, when he volunteered in September 1914. He was assigned to command No 2 Field Ambulance with the rank of lieutenant colonel and served at the Front until November 1915 when he was transferred to England. He died in 1923 at the age of fifty-two. Margaret Heggie Smith was born in Ottawa in 1872 and was a nurse in the Canadian Army Medical Corps before the war. She served initially in No 2 Canadian Stationary Hospital before being transferred to Orpington.

83 George Kendal Lucas, a son of I.B. Lucas, served on its administrative staff from February 1916 until December 1917, when he joined the Royal Naval Air Service and became a pilot.

84 A modern hospital now occupies the site, but there is a memorial cross at All Saints' Church commemorating both the hospital and the 182 men who died in it. Unveiled in 1921, it was the first Canadian war memorial in Britain. For an account of the experiences of Roberta MacAdams, a nurse who worked there, see Debbie Marshall, *Give Your Other Vote to the Sister: A Woman's Journey into the Great War* (Calgary, 2007).
85 On the Speedwell Hospital, see Brook Durham, "'The Place is a Prison, and You Can't Change It': Rehabilitation, Retraining, and Soldiers' Re-establishment at Speedwell Military Hospital, Guelph, 1911–1921," *Ontario History* 109, no. 2 (Fall 2017): 184–212.
86 Rowell fonds 8498 and 8505. Hearst to Rowell, 28 March 1916 and 10 April 1916. *The Mail and Empire*, 29 March 1916.
87 The seven MPPs were T.W. McGarry, W.D. McPherson, Howard Ferguson, and Forbes Godfrey, representing the Conservative Party and C.M. Bowman, G.A Gillespie, and Severin Ducharme, representing the Liberal Party Dr. A.H. Abbott, a former professor of psychology at the University of Toronto, was executive secretary. Rowell fonds 8507; Hearst to Rowell, 14 April 1916. Ibid 8530; Hearst to Rowell, 19 May 1916.
88 *Journals of the Legislative Assembly* (1916): 108; Cf. Hopkins, *Ontario*, 18.
89 Rowell fonds 8531. Hearst to Rowell, 25 May 1916; Ibid 8532; Rowell to Hearst, 5 June 1916. Cf. Prang, *Rowell*, 167.
90 Rowell fonds 8533. Rowell to Hearst, 26 June 1916.
91 *Canadian Annual Review* (1916): 541. They included H.W. Richardson, W.J. Bell, W.H. Shapley, Norman Sommerville, J.W. Woods, M.J Haney, W.A. Riddell, W.E. Rundle, N.W. Woollatt, F. Cook, A. Little, William Dryden, Walter Rollo and G.C. Creelman. Most were prominent businessmen, although Dryden and Creelman represented agriculture and Rollo represented labour. Richardson was a Conservative and Shapley, an engineer, had built the Sault Ste. Marie canal.
92 Rowell fonds 8568. Rowell to Hearst, 27 January 1917. Ibid 8577. Hearst to Rowell, 30 January 1917. Ibid 8591. Rowell to Hearst, 1 February 1917.
93 Hopkins, *Ontario*, 57–9. *Canadian Annual Review* (1916): 541.
94 H.V. Nelles, "Beck, Sir Adam," in *Dictionary of Canadian Biography*, vol 15 (University of Toronto/Université Laval, 2003–), accessed 21 November 2018, www.biographi.ca/en/bio/beck_adam_15E.html/.
95 Nelles, *Politics of Development*, 363.
96 James Mavor, *Niagara in Politics* (New York, 1925), 193. Mavor originally expressed his opinions in a series of articles in Toronto's *Financial Post* in 1916.
97 *The Ministry of Transportation 1916–2016: A History*, accessed 28 December 2018, www.mto.gov.on.ca/english/about/mto-100/index.shtml/; Dimitry

Anastakis, "Car Nation," *Canada's History* 101, no. 6 (December 2021/ January 2022): 25.

98 *Report of the Public Roads and Highways Commission of Ontario* (Toronto, 1914), 9, 35, accessed 9 June 2022, https://archive.org/details/reportofpubroads1914onta/page/34/mode/1up?ref=ol&_autoReadAloud=show&view=theater/.

99 Hearst, "Red-Haired Boy," 87.

100 "City of Mississauga," accessed 7 January 2019, www.mississauga.ca/file/COM/8147_ClarksonBook_PartThree/.

101 Hearst, "Red-Haired Boy," 106.

102 Andrew Scott McEwen, "'Maintaining the Mobility of the Corps:' Horses, Mules, and the Canadian Army Veterinary Corps in the Great War (unpublished PhD diss., University of Calgary, 2016), 183, 179.

103 Ibid, 184.

104 W.J. Lowe, the Liberal candidate, naturally framed the contest as a test of public opinion on "profiteering and graft." *The Daily Star*, 22 February 1916, quoted in Ryan Targa, "From Governors to Grocers: How Profiteering Changed English-Canadian Perceptions of Liberalism in the Great War of 1914–1918" (unpublished MA diss., Queen's University, 2013), 39.

105 Targa, "From Governors," 39. *Cf Report of the Royal Commission on Purchase of Horses in Nova Scotia for First Canadian Contingent* (Ottawa, 1917). Borden subsequently appointed Foster superintendent of the new Canadian National Railway's colonization department, a position that presumably did not require much in the way of administrative and financial supervisory skills. That conveniently made the Kings County seat available for Borden in the 1917 election.

106 Quoted in McEwen, "Maintaining the Mobility," 187.

107 H.V. Nelles, "Sir Adam Beck," in *Canada's Entrepreneurs From the Fur Trade to the 1929 Stock Market Crash*, eds. J. Andrew Ross and Andrew D. Smith (Toronto, 2011), 389.

108 Nelles, "Sir Adam Beck," in *Dictionary of Canadian Biography*. Clancy was a former businessman and local politician who had represented Kent West as a Conservative in the legislature from 1883 to 1894 and Bothwell in the House of Commons from 1896 to 1904. Whitney appointed him provincial auditor after he ran again for the Kent West seat in the 1905 provincial election but was defeated.

109 Ibid.

110 Nelles, *Politics of Development*, 407.

111 Joseph Atkinson to C.M. Goddard, 26 August 1916, quoted in Oliver, *Ferguson*, 81. Cf. Ross Harkness, J.E. Atkinson of the Star 81–4.

112 Freeman, *Politics*, 46.

113 Hearst to Falconer, 2 November 1916, quoted in Michiel Horn, *Academic Freedom in Canada: A History* (Toronto, 1999), 38.

114 Ibid.

115 Hearst to Falconer, 9 October 1914; Falconer to Hearst, 10 October 1914; Hearst to Falconer, 15 October 1914. Quoted in Greenlee, *Falconer*, 203.

116 Mavor to Falconer, 9 November 1916, quoted in Horn, *Academic Freedom*, 38.

117 Hearst to Falconer, 26 November and 30 November 1916, quoted in ibid, 49.

118 James Mavor, *Public Ownership and the Hydro-Electric Commission of Ontario* (Toronto, 1917). It was published by J.B. Maclean, publisher of the *Financial Post* and *Maclean's* magazine. For Mavor's career, see E. Lisa Panayotidis, "Mavor, James," in *Dictionary of Canadian Biography*, vol. 15 (University of Toronto/Université Laval, 2003–), accessed 23 January 2019, www.biographi.ca/en/bio/mavor_james_15E.html/.

119 Plewman, Beck, 193–5, quoted in Oliver, *Ferguson*, 81.

120 Bureau of Municipal Affairs Act, RSO 1927, c232, accessed 30 September 2019, https://digitalcommons.osgoode.yorku.ca/cgi/viewcontent.cgi?article=4558&context=rso/. Cf. Peter H. Howden, *The Ontario Municipal Board* (Victoria, 2017), 2.

121 Freeman, *Politics of Power*, 47.

122 Nelles, *Politics of Development*, 363, 365.

123 Barbara M. Wilson, ed., *Ontario and the First World War 1914–1918: A Collection of Documents* (Toronto, 1977), lxii.

124 J.B. Maclean, "Germany Must Pay Canada's War Bill," *Maclean's Magazine* (November 1918), 74A.

125 See *Report on Export of Electricity from Canada and Report of the Power Controller* (Ottawa, 1917).

126 Nelles, *Politics of Development*, 369.

127 The Hydro Commission also purchased the Toronto Power Company in 1921 for $27 million.

128 Hopkins, *Ontario*, 10

129 Quoted in *The Chesley Enterprise*, 8 June 1916, accessed 14 February 2021, https://bruceremembers.org/battalion/160th-battalion/. The 160th was commanded by Adam Weir, a fifty-three-year-old businessman who had lengthy militia experience and took the battalion to England in October 1916. He was replaced six months later by Donald Sutherland, who ran in the 1917 federal election as a Laurier Liberal and was replaced by Andrew McLean Moffatt, but in February 1918 the battalion was broken up to provide reinforcements for battalions already in France. After the war Sutherland was elected to

parliament as a Conservative in 1925, was defeated in 1926, but re-elected in 1930 and served as Minister of National Defence and then Minister of Pensions and National Health but was defeated and retired in 1935.

130 *Financial Statement of the Hon T.W. McGarry, Treasurer of the Province of Ontario Delivered on the 7th March, 1916* (Toronto, 1916), 4. Nickle also reported in September 1916 that Hearst was ill. Borden diary, 13 September 1916.

131 Reid's appointment was, of course, political. He had run unsuccessfully against Mackenzie King in North Waterloo in 1908. He proved to be an effective representative of the province, assisting Canadian and particularly Ontario soldiers when they were in London, and assisted with the creation of the Ontario hospital at Orpington. When he died unexpectedly at the age of 54 in October 1918, a guard of honour and a firing party made up of Ontario recovered casualties represented the province at the funeral service in St. James Anglican Church at Hampton Hill, and Henry Cody, who happened to be in England, performed the service. *News Record and Milverton Sun*, undated, cited in Waterloo Historical Society, *Sixth Annual Report* (Kitchener, 1918), 51.

132 Hearst, "The Red-Haired Boy," 123.

133 Lady Drummond had moved to London to head the Canadian Red Cross Information Bureau, which provided information to families of missing and wounded soldiers, an experience that made her realize the need for facilities in the city for Canadian servicemen on leave.

134 Guy Drummond had married Mary Hendrie Braithwaite, a niece of J.S. Hendrie, Ontario's lieutenant governor.

135 Cozzie, "A Long, Long Way from Home," 55.

136 Ibid, 57.

137 Ibid, 56.

138 Belcher fonds. Hearst to Belcher, 19 March 1917. Vernon Hearst interview.

139 Vernon Hearst interview.

140 *Canadian Annual Review* (1917): 646.

141 When the 74th Battalion was broken up to provide reinforcements for other battalions, Vernon served in the 52nd (New Ontario) Battalion until September 1916 when he received a serious wound in his left arm. He returned home in December but re-enlisted in the 259th Battalion and served in the Siberian expedition from October 1918 to June 1919. Irving served briefly in the 5th Battalion until being transferred to the Ordinance Corps depot at Ashford, England, and Canadian Corps Headquarters in France. For their service records, see LAC, Personnel Records of the First World War. "Howard Vernon Hearst," accessed 8 May 2021, https://central.bac-lac.gc.ca/.item/?op=pdf&app=CEF&id=B4215-S006, and "William Irving Hearst," accessed 15 January 2021, https://central.bac-lac.gc.ca/.item/?op=pdf&app=CEF&id=B4215-S010/.

142 Gouin fonds 2626. Hearst to Gouin, 19 February 1915. Cody fonds; Hearst to Cody, 29 April 1919.

143 D.J. Scollard to Hearst, 6 October 1914, quoted in Robert Choquette, *Language and Religion: A History of English-French Conflict in Ontario* (Ottawa, 1975), 183.

144 Hearst to the Rockland separate school board, quoted in Patrice A. Dutil, "Against Isolationism: Napoléon Belcourt, French Canada, and 'La Grande Guerre," in *Canada and the First World War*, ed. David Mackenzie (Toronto, 2005), 346.

145 Ferguson openly blamed the Liberals for the bilingual schools controversy because they had stirred up discontent among the Franco-Ontarians. Ferguson fonds. Ferguson to W.J. Brown, 18 February 1916; Ferguson to Robert Borden, 25 February 1916; Ferguson to R.H. McElroy, 1 May 1916; Ferguson to D'Arcy Scott, 22 November 1916. Borden fonds, RLB 98573; Ferguson to Borden, 10 April 1916; *Cf The Mail and Empire*, 11 March 1916; *The Evening News*, 13 April 1916.

146 Quoted in Oliver, *Ferguson*, 250.

147 Rumilly, *Histoire de Québec*, XIX, 104.

148 Ibid, 82, 134–7; *The Daily Star*, 12 January 1915.

149 Canada, *Senate Debates* (1915): 62.

150 Choquette, *English-French Relations*, 200.

151 Michael Power, "The Mitred Warrior: A Critical Reassessment of Bishop Michael Francis Fallon, 1867–1931," *Catholic Insight* 8, no. 3 (2000): 18.

152 Michael Fallon to T.W. McGarry, 16 February 1915, quoted in Choquette, *English-French Relations*, 188. Cf. R. Mackell, J.F Lanigan et al. to Hearst and Pyne, 20 February 1915. Ibid.

153 *The Daily Star*, 12 January 1915; *Hamilton Herald*, 12 January 1915; *Brockville Times*, 13 January 1915; *Belleville Intelligencer*, 21 January 1915; *Peterborough Review*, 25 January 1915; Cf. Rumilly, *Histoire de Québec*, XIX, 141.

154 Rumilly, *Histoire de Québec*, XIX, 82, 84, 92.

155 Landry to Hearst, 4 June 1915, quoted in Dutil, "Against Isolation," in *Canada and the First World War*, ed. David Mackenzie (Toronto, 2005), 379.

156 Quoted in *The Globe*, 2 April 1915.

157 "Orangiste lui-même, [il] aurait declaré qu'il voyait les choses différement depuis son entrée dans le cabinet et qu'il sympathisait beaucoup avec les Canadiens-français."Bruchési, "Pourparlers de sa Grandeur Monseigneur Bruchési avec MM les Curés, MM les Commissaires d'Ecoles et les Officiers de l'Association d'Education, 1915," quoted in Oliver, *Ferguson*, 76–7.

158 Ferguson, speaking in the legislature, 14 April 1916, quoted in Oliver, *Ferguson*, 73.

159 Ibid. Ferguson told W.J. Brown that "the purpose of the Regulation is not to obliterate the French language but to promote the teaching of the

English language." Ferguson to W.J. Brown, 25 February 1916, quoted in Choquette, *English-French Relations,* 199. W.J. Brown was the fire chief of Belleville.

160 Bruchési, "Pourparlers," quoted in Oliver, *Ferguson,* 77.

161 *The Daily Star,* 24, 30, 31 August 1915.

162 Ibid, 24 July 1915.

163 Ibid, 28, 30 July 1915.

164 Ibid, 1 September 1915.

165 Rumilly, *Histoire de Québec,* XX, 112.

166 *The Daily Star,* 18 October 1915.

167 Ibid, 6 October 1915 and 3 February 1916; *Canadian Annual Review* (1916): 527.

168 Rumilly, *Histoire de Québec,* XX, 112.

169 For an account of Belcourt's significant role in the controversy, see Dutil, "Against Isolationism," in *Canada and the First World War,* ed. David Mackenzie (Toronto, 2005), 343–450.

170 Laurier fonds 191322; Laurier to Rowell, 4 March 1916.

171 Belcourt had assured Hearst that Rowell had promised Laurier that he would "consider the matter fully and even sympathetically." Laurier fonds 191321. Rowell to Laurier, 7 March 1916. Cf. ibid, 191310; Stewart Lyon to Laurier, 6 March 1916. Rumilly, *Histoire de Québec,* XXI, 74.

172 Laurier to M.K. Cowan, 11 April 1916, quoted in Prang, "Bilingual Schools," 299. The phrase quoted was originally Cowan's.

173 Quoted in the *Canadian Annual Review* (1916): 530.

174 Quoted (in translation) in the *Canadian Annual Review* (1916): 530.

175 Rumilly, *Histoire de Québec,* XXI, 180.

176 Ibid, XX, 127–8.

177 Choquette, *English-French Relations,* 199.

178 Borden diary, 8 March 1916.

179 Ibid, 8 March 1916; Rumilly, *Histoire de Québec,* XX, 127–8.

180 Ibid, 11 March 1916.

181 Ferguson returned five days later for another "long conf[eren]ce" with Borden as well. Ibid, 13 March 1916, 18 March 1916, 21 March 1916.

182 Borden diary, 7 April 1916.

183 Ibid, 8 April 1916.

184 Ibid, 11 April 1916.

185 Borden fonds, RLB 98582. Blondin, Casgrain and Patenaude to Borden, 20 April 1916; Ibid, 98597; same to same, 22 April 1916.

186 Ibid. Blondin, Casgrain and Patenaude to Borden, 25 April 1916.

187 Borden diary, 8 May 1916.

188 *Canada, House of Commons Debates* (1916): 3618, 3681–97.

189 Ibid, 3826.

190 Borden diary, 11 May 1916.

191 Laurier to Stewart Lyon, 29 February 1916; quoted in Dutil, "Against Isolationism," 384. Laurier to Rowell, 11 May 1916, quoted in Oscar Douglas Skelton, *Life and Letters of Sir Wilfrid Laurier*, vol. 2 (Toronto, 1921), 477.

192 Rumilly, *Histoire de Québec*, XX, 130.

**Chapter 5**

1 *The Mail and Empire*, 5 April 1916; *Speech of Hon W.H. Hearst on The Ontario Temperance Act* (Toronto?: s.n., 1916?).

2 Richard Allen, *Beyond the Noise of Solemn Assemblies: The Protestant Ethic and the Quest for Social Justice in Canada* (Montreal/Kingston, 2018), 104.

3 Hopkins, *Ontario*, 87.

4 Tim Cook, "'More a Medicine than a Beverage': 'Demon Rum' and the Canadian Trench Soldier of the First World War," *Canadian Military History* 9, no. 1 (Winter 2000): 6–22.

5 Augustus Bridle, *The Masques of Ottawa* (Toronto, 1921), 278.

6 *The Daily Star*, 1 December 1914, 7 December 1914.

7 Ibid, 5 March 1915.

8 Quoted in *The Mail and Empire*, 24 March 1915.

9 "John Almayne Ayearst," accessed 19 December 2018, www.wikitree.com/wiki/Ayearst-9/. The date of the *Globe* article is not known.

10 He has been described as "the driving force behind the Canadian Unionist League," established as a fund-raising body for the Unionists in Northern Ireland in October 1913. William Jenkins, "Homeland Crisis and Local Ethnicity: The Toronto Irish and the Cartoons of the Evening Telegram 1910–1914," *Urban History Review* 38, no. 2 (Spring 2010): 57.

11 Among other things, Frank Cochrane's Mines Act of 1906 had authorized the appointment of regional mining recorders and Smith was the first man appointed to the position in Haileybury. Little is known about Smith. He was born in Quebec but lived in Renfrew for some time, working as an accountant for Charles McCool, a lumber merchant who also served in the House of Commons as a Liberal from 1900 to 1908. McCool was an Irish Catholic, as was Smith, so he was probably a Liberal as well. If so, it seems slightly surprising that he was given this patronage appointment, although that is probably a tribute to Cochrane.

12 *The Daily Star*, 29 May 1915.

13 Report of Rowell speech to Lincoln Liberal Association; *Toronto Daily Star*, 4 June 1915.

14 Hearst also thought it would create "a difficult situation with reference to the accommodation of the travelling public." Willison fonds 15073. Hearst to Sir John Willison, 9 December 1915, Private and Confidential.

15 *The Daily Star*, 10 June 1915.
16 *The Globe*, 11 September 1915.
17 Ibid, 21 December 1915. I have found no evidence to support this claim and it did not name him but it must have been referring to John because he was then living in Sault Ste. Marie. Hearst's other brother, Robert, lived in North Dakota.
18 Willison fonds 15073. Hearst to Sir John Willison, 9 December 1915, Private and Confidential.
19 Ibid.
20 Rowell fonds. Warburton to Rowell, 27 January 1917.
21 *The Daily Star*, 24 September 1915.
22 Ibid, 6 October 1915.
23 Ibid, 4 October 1915.
24 Ibid, 7 October 1915. Cosgrave Brewery survived until 1921 when it was absorbed by Canadian Breweries Limited.
25 Ibid, 8 October 1915.
26 W.L. Mackenzie King fonds. Diary, 15 November 1916.
27 *The Daily Star*, 14 October 1915, 16 October 1915, 19 October 1915. Prang, "Rowell," 214.
28 *The Daily Star*, 26 November 1915.
29 Ibid, 5 January 1916.
30 Ibid, 21 January 1916.
31 Ibid, 5 February 1916.
32 Rowell fonds 8571. Warburton to Rowell, 27 January 1917.
33 *The Globe*, 1 March 1916. Hopkins, *Ontario*, 88. Rowell fonds 8571. Warburton to Rowell, 27 January 1917.
34 Spence, *Prohibition in Canada*, 402. Craig Heron, *Booze: A Distilled History* (Toronto, 2003), 180. Ontario's population in the 1911 census was 2,527,292.
35 Willison fonds 15079. Hearst to Willison, 10 April 1916, Private.
36 *The Mail and Empire*, 3 March 1916.
37 Belcher fonds. F18, MS 93. Belcher to Hearst, 10 March 1916. Hearst shared this letter with Hanna and Lucas. Hanna seems not to have responded but Lucas told Belcher, "[P]ersonally, I think there are very substantial reasons for the line of action you suggest. Ibid, Lucas to Belcher, 13 March 1916, Private.
38 *The Mail and Empire*, 20, 21, 25, 25, 27, 27 January 1919.
39 *Canadian Annual Review* (1916): 518–20.
40 *The Globe*, 2 March 1916.
41 Rowell fonds 8558. Rowell to Warburton, 24 January 1917; *The Daily Star*, 13 September 1919; *The Evening Telegram*, 21 October 1929, quoted in Oliver, *Ferguson*, 82.

42 *Address Delivered by Lieut-Colonel H.A.C. Machin, MPP, Kenora, in the Ontario Legislature, Tuesday, March 4, 1919, during the Debate on the Address in Reply to the Speech from the Throne* (Toronto: s.n., 1919).

43 Rowell did publicly oppose compensation. *The Mail and Empire, The Globe,* 28 March 1916.

44 Hearst fonds. Ms of speech to Conservative caucus, n.d. [1916].

45 Hearst made this revelation when introducing the referendum bill on 7 April 1919. *The Referendum Ballot* (Toronto: s.n., 1919), text of Hearst speech, accessed 4 May 2020, www.canadiana.ca/view/oocihm.79168/25?r=0&s=1/. Although passed by the legislature, the so-called Macdonald Act was not proclaimed until June 1916.

46 *Bills Presented to the Legislative Assembly* (1916): #100. Spence, *Prohibition in Canada,* 609–12.

47 *The Globe,* 23 March 1916.

48 *The Mail and Empire,* 5 April 1916.

49 Hopkins, *Ontario,* 90.

50 *The Mail and Empire,* 5 April 1916; *Speech of Hon W.H. Hearst on the Ontario Temperance Act* (S.l., n.d.).

51 Rowell fonds 8558. Rowell to Warburton, 24 January 1917.

52 Nor did the government have any control over the fact that the troops overseas, including Hearst's own two sons, were offered rum daily in the field. When Hearst visited England in 1916, he asked Irving if he drank the rum ration, and Irving admitted that he did. Hearst's response was, "You know the conditions, Son, and are the one best able to decide what you should do." Hearst, "Red-Haired Boy," 123.

53 Ibid. Hearst to W.I. Hearst, 31 October 1916.

54 Hearst, "Red-Haired Boy," 126.

55 Sharon Anne Cook, *"Through Sunshine and Shadow:" The Women's Christian Temperance Union, Evangelicalism, and Reform in Ontario, 1874–1930* (Montreal/Kingston, 1995), 41. The OTA did not constitute prohibition, of course, just strict temperance.

56 *Canadian Annual Review* (1918): 625.

57 Matthew J. Bellamy, "The Canadian Brewing Industry's Response to Prohibition, 1874–1920," *Journal of the Brewery History Society* 132 (2009): 7. Heron, *Booze,* 181.

58 Wallace, *Foster,* 190. An effort in 1919 to extend the order in council by means of an act of parliament failed.

59 According to Charlesworth, the orders in council were promoted by C.J. Doherty, Newton Rowell and Sir George Foster. Charlesworth, *More Candid Chronicles,* 193. Foster was certainly a long-time advocate of prohibition but his biographer says only that "he derived perhaps the greatest gratification" from its triumph. Wallace, *Foster,* 190.

60 Hearst fonds F6MU1307. Hearst to Irving Hearst, 23 December 1917.
61 See, for example, his comments in *The Mail and Empire*, 16 February 1917.
62 Hearst fonds. Ms of speech to Toronto Northeast Conservative Association, 10 June 1918.
63 Rowell fonds, 8551. Rowell to J.G. Cane, 12 January 1917. Cane was a lumberman whose son ran unsuccessfully as a Liberal in Toronto Northwest in the 1919 election.
64 Laurier fonds 192894. Laurier to H.F. Gadsby, 24 August 1916. Gadsby was a Toronto journalist and art critic.
65 George Ecclestone held the seat until 1934.
66 *The Globe*, 30 June 1916. Prang, *Rowell*, 180.
67 *Canadian Annual Review* (1916): 501–2.
68 *The Globe*, 11 July 1916.
69 Carolyn Strange, "Dewart, Herbert Hartley," in *Dictionary of Canadian Biography*, vol. 15 (University of Toronto/Université Laval, 2003–), accessed 21 July 2019, www.biographi.ca/en/bio/dewart_herbert_hartley_15E.html/.
70 One reason for Dewart's popularity was that just a few months earlier he had successfully defended a young housemaid accused of the murder of Charles Massey, a member of the wealthy Massey family. He then successfully sued the *Daily Star* because it had carelessly run a headline referring to the young housemaid as a "murderess." Cf. Charlotte Gray, *The Massey Murder* (Toronto, 2013), 279.
71 Even so, Ferguson described Dewart's victory as "a revengeful victory of the liquor interests." Quoted in the *Canadian Annual Review* (1916): 503. *Cf* Oliver, *Ferguson*, 78.
72 J.E. Atkinson to C.M. Goddard, 26 August 1916, quoted in Peter Oliver, "Sir William Hearst and the Collapse of the Conservative Party," *Canadian Historical Review* (March 1972): 31.
73 O.D. Skelton to W.L. Grant, 19 March 1917; quoted in Oliver, "Ferguson," 33.
74 Oliver, "Sir William Hearst," 31.
75 He made the comment in a speech in Sault Ste. Marie. *The Globe*, 26 July 1916, cited in Oliver "Sir William Hearst," 30.
76 J.E. Atkinson to C.M. Goddard, 26 August 1916, quoted in Oliver, "Sir William Hearst," 31.
77 Borden diary, 21 August 1916, 31 August 1916.
78 Ibid, 13 September 1916.
79 Charlesworth, *More Candid Chronicles*, 193.
80 C.L. Cleverdon, *The Woman Suffrage Movement in Canada* (Toronto, 1950), 21.
81 Tarah Brookfield, "Women's Suffrage in Ontario," *The Canadian Encyclopedia*, accessed 5 March 2020, www.thecanadianencyclopedia.ca/en/

article/womens-suffrage-in-ontario/. Whitney, cited in Charlotte Gray, *The Massey Murder* (Toronto, 2013), 270.

82 Quoted in the *Canadian Annual Review* (1913): 374.
83 *Canadian Annual Review* (1912): 328.
84 Quoted in *The Globe*, 17 October 1914.
85 Ibid.
86 Brookfield, "Women's Suffrage in Ontario."
87 Hearst fonds. Ms of Speech to Woman's Suffrage Delegation, n.d. [24 February 1915]. His italics.
88 Quoted in the *Canadian Annual Review 1915* (Toronto, 1916), 483.
89 *Canadian Annual Review* (1915): 483.
90 Ibid (1916): 480.
91 Ibid, 498.
92 Tarah Brookfield, *Our Voices Must Be Heard: Women and the Vote in Ontario* (Vancouver, 2018), 163–4.
93 Cleverdon, *Woman Suffrage*, 41.
94 *The Mail and Empire*, 16 February 1917.
95 Prang, *Rowell*, 184. In the absence of any evidence, Prang appears to have borrowed this idea from Cleverdon, *Woman Suffrage*, 40–3.
96 Ibid.
97 Carol Lee Bacchi, *Liberation Deferred? The Ideas of the English-Canadian Suffragettes, 1877–1918* (Toronto, 1983), 138.
98 Ibid.
99 Ibid. Printed circular of the Association Opposed to Woman Suffrage in Canada (n.d.); cf. *How Women May Best Serve the State* (Toronto, 1913). A leading figure in the movement was Clementina Trenholme Fessenden of Hamilton. Cf. Molly Pulver Ungar, "Trenholme, Clementina," in *Dictionary of Canadian Biography*, vol. 14 (University of Toronto/Université Laval, 2003–), accessed 3 June 2020, www.biographi.ca/en/bio/trenholme_clementina_14E.html/.
100 According to the 1911 census, there were 802,000 males and 742,000 females in Ontario over 20 years of age. Many of the men were, of course, overseas during the war.
101 Hearst fonds. Woman Suffrage Delegation Speech.
102 Ibid. Hearst to Irving Hearst, 4 March 1917.
103 Ibid. Sir Hugh John Macdonald to Hearst, n.d. [March 1917]; copy.
104 Johnson's bills addressed the municipal and provincial franchise separately. John Wesley Johnson was principal of the Ontario Business College in Belleville and served four terms as mayor before being elected in 1908 to the legislature, in which he served until his death in March 1919.
105 *The Mail and Empire*, 16 February 1917.
106 Brookfield, *Our Voices*, 166.

107 Ibid, 28 February 1917.

108 Ibid; *The Globe*, 8 March 1917.

109 Schull, *Ontario*, 222.

110 *Canadian Annual Review 1916*, 480.

**Chapter 6**

1 Hearst fonds. "Address to Women's Canadian Club of Brockville," 14 December 1916.

2 *The Globe*, 22 January 1915, 23 January 1915.

3 Gray, *Massey Murder*, 160.

4 Leslie M. Frost, *Fighting Men* (Toronto, 1967), 44, 46. Frost went on to become Premier of Ontario from 1949 to 1961.

5 A fifth division was formed but only served in England before being broken up to provide reinforcements for the four divisions in France.

6 *The Globe*, 12 July 1915.

7 Ian Hugh Maclean Miller, *Our Glory and Our Grief: Torontonians and the Great War* (Toronto, 2002), 83–4.

8 Willison fonds 15078. Hearst to Willison, 3 March 1916, Private; Hopkins, *Ontario*, 11.

9 Martha Hanna, *Anxious Days and Tearful Nights: Canadian War Wives During the Great War* (Montreal/Kingston, 2020), 50.

10 *The Daily Star*, 20 March 1916.

11 Hanna, *Anxious Days*, 51.

12 Miller, *Our Glory*, 92.

13 *The World*, 1 May 1916. Unusually, there were no politicians present.

14 *The Globe*, 12 July 1915.

15 Butts, *Wartime*, 89.

16 Hearst fonds. "Address to Recruiting Meeting, Massey Hall, 29 October 1916."

17 *The Daily Star*, 30 January 1917.

18 *The World*, 14 April 1917. *The World* was owned by W.F. "Billy" Maclean. Although a Conservative, he was a highly independent populist. No doubt for that reason he was able to get elected to parliament in 1892 and held the seat until 1926. Cf. Minko Sotiron, "Maclean, William Findlay," in *Dictionary of Canadian Biography*, vol. 15 (University of Toronto/Université Laval, 2003–), accessed 15 February 2019, www.biographi.ca/en/bio/maclean_william_findlay_15E.html/.

19 Miller, *Our Glory*, 64. Curiously, Nathan Smith has a different version of this episode, claiming that it took place at the White City Café and "there was no violence." Nathan Smith, "Fighting the Alien Problem in a British Country: Returned Soldiers and Anti-Alien Activism in Wartime Canada, 1916–19," in

*Other Combatants, Other Fronts: Competing Histories of the First World War*, ed. James Kitchen, Alisa Miller and Laura Rowe (Newcastle, 2011), 294.

20 Quoted in Miller, *Our Glory*, 65.

21 Miller, *Our Glory*, 65–6.

22 *Canadian Annual Review* (1916): 542.

23 Hopkins, *Ontario*, 10.

24 Hearst fonds. "Address to Women's Canadian Club."

25 Ibid. War resolution speech.

26 G.F. Gadsby, "The Inside Story of the Union," *Maclean's Magazine*, 1 December 1917, 41.

27 Sir George Foster diary, 1 August 1917; quoted in John R. Witham, "Opposition to Conscription in Ontario 1917" (Unpublished MA diss., University of Ottawa, 1970), 37.

28 Born in England, Cecil Grosvenor Hamilton Williams (1874–1948) immigrated to Canada around the turn of the century. He settled in Lindsay, Ontario, and became involved in the local militia. In April 1916 he joined the 109th Battalion as chaplain but was sent home when it was broken up. He subsequently joined the Military District 3 (Eastern Ontario) Forestry Depot, with the astonishing promotion to lieutenant colonel but shortly afterward was appointed the recruiting officer for Military District 2 (Toronto).

29 "Address to Methodist Ministers Assembled at Carlton Street Methodist Church Toronto," quoted in Paterson, "Loyalty," 135.

30 Hearst fonds. Ms of speech in legislature on war resolution, 1917.

31 C.P. Stacey, ed., *Historical Documents of Canada: The Arts of War and Peace 1914–1945*, vol. 5 (London, 1972), 568. The Canadian Manufacturing Association's Special Committee on the Co-ordinating of Recruiting and Production reported to the Association's annual meeting in June 1916 that, of the 334,209 men who had enlisted by 31 May 1916, Ontario had reached 75 per cent of its quota, the Western provinces 114 per cent, and the Maritimes 48 per cent. Quebec's figure was 25 per cent and predominantly English-speaking. Overall, 60 per cent of recruits were British-born, 13 per cent were Canadian-born anglophones, 6 per cent were foreign-born, and 3 per cent were Canadian-born francophones. *Report of the Special Committee on the Co-Ordination of Recruiting and Production to the Annual Meeting* (Toronto, 1916), 5. These statistics were provided to the committee by Cecil Williams. By the end of the war, Ontario had provided 242,655 men and women, or 38.7 per cent, of the national total of 626,557, and more than 68,000 of them had been killed or wounded. Schull, *Ontario*, 214; Crerar, "Ontario," 233. Hearst fonds. "Report of Lt. Col. (Rev) C.G. Williams, Chief Recruiting Officer for Canada, to Sir William H. Hearst" (unpublished manuscript, 1917).

32 *The Sentinel*, 31 May 1917, 22 September 1917, both quoted in Paterson, "Loyalty," 133.

33 Both quotations from Oliver, *Ferguson*, 77, 78. Ferguson repeated this conspiracy theory in Toronto on 17 September 1916. Ibid, 78.

34 Oliver, *Ferguson*, 78.

35 Quoted in the *Ottawa Journal*, 21 June 1916; cited in Oliver, *Ferguson*, 78.

36 *The Globe*, 27 October 1916; Full text in Sissons, *Bi-lingual Schools*, 226–7.

37 University of Toronto Library, *Correspondence*; Memorandum of Bishop Fallon, 24 January 1917; *The Globe*, 5 February 1917; Rumilly, *Histoire de Québec*, XXI, 189–97.

38 Sissons, *Church and State*, 228–37.

39 Ibid, 237–42.

40 Armstrong, *Crisis in Quebec*, 157.

41 *The Globe*, 3 November 1916.

42 *Canadian Annual Review* (1916): 532.

43 Rumilly, *Histoire de Québec*, XXI, 221.

44 *Canadian Annual Review* (1917): 502.

45 *The Mail and Empire*, 20, 23 March 1917; *The Globe*, 30, 31 March 1917. The constitutionality of this act was upheld by the Ontario Supreme Court in December 1917.

46 Rowell fonds 8745. Rowell to Laurier, 29 March 1917.

47 Belcourt to W.H. Moore, 27 July 1921, quoted in Oliver, *Ferguson*, 79. Moore was a prominent Liberal lawyer in Toronto and, unusually, a strong defender of French language rights in Canada. In 1918 he published *The Clash: A Study in Nationalities* (London, 1918). He was also a member of parliament from 1930 to 1945.

48 Oliver, *Ferguson*, 79.

49 *The Globe*, *The Mail and Empire*, 4 April 1917.

50 Sissons, *Church and State*, 91.

51 Marilyn Barber, "The Ontario Schools Issue: Sources of Conflict," in *Minorities, Schools and Politics*, ed. Ramsay Cook, Craig Brown, and Carl Berger (Toronto, 1969) 74.

52 F.W. Merchant, *Report of the Committee Appointed to Enquire into the Condition of the Schools Attended by French-Speaking Pupils* (Toronto, 1927).

53 Françoise Noël, "The Impact of Regulation 17 on the Study of District Schools: Some Methodological Considerations," *Historical Studies in Education/Revue de l'éducation* 24, no. 1 (Spring 2012): 75

54 Cf. Peter Oliver, "The Resolution of the Ontario Bilingual Schools Crisis, 1916–1929," *Journal of Canadian Studies* 7, no. 1 (February 1972): 22–45.

55 *Canadian Annual Review* (1917): 644.

56 Rowell to A.E. MacLean, 18 May 1917, quoted in Oliver, "Ferguson," 33. Alfred MacLean was a farmer and businessman in Summerside, Prince

Edward Island. He served in the provincial legislature as a Liberal from 1915 to 1921 and succeeded Mackenzie King as MP for Prince County in 1921.

57 *The Globe,* 12 June 1917.

58 Borden, *Memoirs,* 730, 732. Among them were Rowell, Willison and Frederick Pardee, a Sarnia lawyer who had served in the legislature from 1898 to 1905, then in the House of Commons, and was re-elected in 1917 as a Liberal Unionist.

59 Gayle Comeau says that Hanna resigned because of ill health but this is inconsistent with Borden's diary entries, and a few months later Hanna was appointed president of the Imperial Oil Company. On Hanna's term as food controller, see Mourad Djebabla, "'Fight the Huns with Food': Mobilizing Canadian Civilians for the War Effort during the Great War, 1914–1918," in *World War 1 and Propaganda,* ed. Troy Paddock (London, 2014), 68–88. Three weeks after Hanna's resignation in January 1918 the government replaced his office with the Canada Food Board, which operated under the authority of the Department of Agriculture.

60 J.D. Reid told Borden in August that Cochrane was "entirely incapable of attending to the business of a heavy department." Borden diary, 12 August 1917. Borden tentatively offered him the presidency of Canadian National Railways with a seat in the cabinet. Cochrane agreed but he never got the CNR presidency.

61 Borden and Reid discussed the possibility of Hearst replacing Cochrane in the cabinet in September 1914. Borden diary, 26 September 1914. Rowell fonds 8706. Hearst to Rowell, 28 August 1919, Private and Confidential.

62 Quoted in *The Globe,* 3 August 1917. Hopkins, *Ontario,* 19–20. Miller, *Our Glory,* 139–40. The next day a mass meeting of women presided over by Florence Gooderham Huestis, a prominent social activist and president of the Toronto Council of Women, also called for conscription.

63 Hearst fonds F6MU 1307. Hearst to Irving Hearst, 10 August 1917.

64 Borden diary, 31 August 1917.

65 Prang, "Rowell," 448. Harkness, *Atkinson,* 108.

66 Miller, *Our Glory,* 141–2.

67 Cf. Martha, Hanna, Martha. *Anxious Days and Tearful Nights: Canadian War Wives during the Great War* (Montreal/Kingston, 2020).

68 Hearst fonds. Ms of speech at Massey Hall, 21 November 1917.

69 Quoted in Hopkins, *Union Government,* 75. Cf. Hearst's speech at Georgetown, Ontario, reported in *The Globe,* 13 December 1917.

70 Quoted in *The Daily Star,* 15 December 1917.

71 Robert Craig Brown, "Reid, John Dowsley," in *Dictionary of Canadian Biography*, vol. 15 (University of Toronto/Université Laval, 2003–), accessed 14 February 2019, www.biographi.ca/en/bio/reid_john_dowsley_15E.html/.

Reid had been the Conservative regional leader in Eastern Ontario for years and, as Robert Craig Brown says, was "one of Borden's closest confidants." Brown implies that Reid only became responsible for the Ontario campaign because of Cochrane's failing health but a careful reading of Borden's unedited diary suggests that Reid had replaced Cochrane in charge of Ontario as early as 1912. Brown, "Reid, John Dowsley," Wallace claims that Sir George Foster "took charge of Ontario, and the success of the Unionists at the polls in Ontario was a reflection of the tact and adroitness which he used in reconciling the conflicting claims of Conservative and Liberal-Unionists." Wallace, *Foster*, 188. It's more likely that Foster was responsible for the Toronto area.

72 Augustus Bridle, *The Masques of Ottawa* (Toronto, 1921), 119; Dutil and Mackenzie, *Embattled Nation*, 189. It appears that historians have just assumed that Thornton was rewarded for his cooperation but never bothered to confirm that he was appointed to the Senate. He wasn't. The truth appears to be that he had held the seat since 1908 and, at sixty-seven years of age, was prepared to retire.

73 Sutherland won the seat in 1925 and later served as Minister of Defence in R.B. Bennett's government. *Cf* Matthew Barrett, "The Undeterred: Lieutenant Colonel Donald Sutherland," accessed 27 January 2020, https://matthewkbarrett.com/2014/12/01/the-undeterred/.

74 See Jennifer Arthur-Lackenbauer, Peter Kikkert, and P. Whitney Lackenbauer, *Familiar Fields to Foreign Soil Three Rural Townships at War, 1914–1918* (Otterville, 2018), 273–86.

75 *Sault Express*, 23 June 1916, reprinted in Wilson, *Ontario*, 36–7.

76 It responded by publishing in English until merging with the *News Record* in 1919.

77 Wilson, *Ontario*, xlix.

78 Quoted in the *Sault Daily Star*, 6 December 1917.

79 *The Evening Telegram*, undated, quoted in Anon, "Charles Napier Smith: Anti-Censorship Crusader or 'An Ass'?," *Sootoday*, 23 February 2020, accessed 25 February 2020, www.sootoday.com/columns/remember-this/charles-napier-smith-anti-censorship-crusader-or-an-ass-2112535/. Smith was neither charged with treason nor sent to jail but the *Sault Express* did not reopen after the war. Smith did, however, have the satisfaction before he died relatively young at fifty-three, of seeing Hearst defeated in the 1919 election.

80 Hearst fonds F6MU1307. Hearst to Irving Hearst, 28 October 1917.

81 Ibid.

82 Hearst fonds FMU1307. Hearst to Irving Hearst, 11 October 1917.
83 Ibid. Hearst to Irving Hearst, 16 November 1917.
84 Ibid.
85 Main Johnson diary, quoted in Hall, *Sifton*, vol. 2, 291.
86 Sifton to J.M. Godfrey, 8 November 1917, quoted in ibid, 290.
87 Borden diary, 30 November 1917.
88 Hall, *Sifton*, vol 2, 290.
89 Ibid, 291.
90 Borden diary, 2 December 1917.
91 Hall, *Sifton*, 291.
92 Main Johnson diary, quoted in ibid.
93 Quoted in Hall, *Sifton*, 291. On John Godfrey's role in trying to improve English-French relations, see R. Matthew Bray, "'Fighting as an Ally': The English-Canadian Patriotic Response to the Great War," *Canadian Historical Review* 61, no. 2 (1980): 141–68.
94 Rowell had been advocating for months that conscription should exempt "any men now in agriculture who cannot be replaced" because "we must keep up our agricultural production" and there was already a shortage of farm labour. Quoted in the Woodstock *Daily Sentinel-Review*, 13 February 1917; cited in Arthur-Lackenbauer et al, *Familiar Fields*, 179.
95 Quoted in Hall, *Sifton*, 291. What Godfrey actually said was that "Tory farmers were placated," but so too, presumably, were Liberal and independent farmers.
96 *Sault Daily Star*, 30 November 1917.
97 Ibid, 6 December 1917.
98 Ibid.
99 Ibid, 5 December 1917, 6 December 1917.
100 Ibid, 6 December 1917.
101 Ibid.
102 Ibid.
103 Matt Bray, "1910–1920," in *Sudbury: Rail Town to Regional Capital*, eds. C.M. Wallace and Ashley Thomson (Toronto, 1993), 89. Lapierre was a Sudbury businessman. Although he lost in 1917, he won the seat in 1921, held it until 1930, and then served in the legislature from 1934 to 1937.
104 Quoted in *The Globe*, 7 December 1917.
105 Ibid.
106 Hearst fonds F6MU 1307. Hearst to Irving Hearst, 23 December 1917. Dutil and Mackenzcie incorrectly state that this letter was addressed to H.V. Hearst. Dutil and Mackenzie, *Embattled Nation*, 253.
107 Anderson, "This Typical," 69.
108 This account is based on Brian F. Hogan, "The Guelph Novitiate Raid: Conscription, Censorship and Bigotry During the Great War," Canadian

Catholic Historical Association *Study Sessions* 45(1978): 57–80; Mark Reynolds, "The Guelph Raid," *The Beaver* 82, no. 1 (February/March 2002): 25–30; and Debra Nash-Chambers, "Sectarianism and Scandal: The 1918 Novitiate Raid in Guelph Township," *Wellington County History* 19 (2006): 4–16.

109 Butts, *Wartime*, 130. Eventually a royal commission chaired by two judges in 1919 concluded that the Jesuit students had been exempt, and Captain A.C. Macauley, Assistant Deputy Provost Marshall, who had led the raid was fully to blame.

110 Quoted in Butts, *Wartime*, 130.

111 Quoted in *Canadian Annual Review* (1917): 605.

112 Belcher fonds. Borden to Belcher, 21 December 1917. It is seldom mentioned but the brothers and sons of men already serving overseas were also exempted.

113 Hearst fonds F6MU 1307. Hearst to Irving Hearst, 23 December 1917.

114 The popular vote was 515,000 Unionist to 269,000 Liberal, including the overseas soldiers' vote of 95,000 Unionist and 6,000 Liberal. The ten constituencies that the Liberal Unionists won were Brant (John Harold), Durham (Rowell), Fort William, Glengarry (Jack McMartin), Hamilton East (Sydney Mewburn), Lambton West (F.F. Pardee), Norfolk (William Charlton), Oxford North (Edward Nesbitt), Parkdale (Herbert Mowat), and Wellington South (Hugh Guthrie). Charlton, Guthrie, Nesbitt and Pardee retained seats they already held, while seats had been found for Mewburn and Rowell. The Liberal Unionist elected by acclamation was John McMartin, the Liberal incumbent in Glengarry-Stormont. Rather oddly, Sydney Mewburn was not elected by acclamation but apparently won 100 per cent of the votes cast, which meant that George Halcrow won none, which seems incredible.

115 The other two were Albert Sévigny and P.E. Blondin, in Quebec.

116 Candidates were allowed to run in more than one constituency and if successful in both they chose which one to represent. Ottawa was a two-member constituency, and Laurier was probably trying to divide the vote in 1917. The Conservative candidates won both seats.

117 Various slightly different numbers are given for the election results. This depends on how one classifies some of the candidates. The figures given here are based on an examination of all eighty-two constituencies.

118 According to the *Daily Star*, some people in Bruce South and Kent regarded Truax and McCoig as Unionists posing as Liberals. *The Daily Star*, 18 December 1917.

119 Michael Power, "Kennedy, William Costello," in *Dictionary of Canadian Biography*, vol. 15 (University of Toronto/Université Laval, 2003–), accessed 11 February 2020, www.biographi.ca/en/bio/kennedy_william_costello_15E.html/.

120 Algoma West, Fort William, Hamilton East, Hamilton West, Toronto Centre, Toronto North, Toronto South, Toronto West, Waterloo North, Waterloo South, Welland, Wellington South, Wentworth, York East, and York South.

121 He ran against Michael Steele, who had won the seat in 1911 as a Conservative. Forrester defeated him in 1921.

122 J.E. Rea, *T.A. Crerar: A Political Life* (Montreal/Kingston, 1997), 37. The criticism of Mowat for not going overseas was hardly fair given that he was fifty-four years old.

123 *Soldier-Candidates and the 1917 Wartime Election,* accessed 16 September 2019, www.greatwaralbum.ca/Great-War-Album/About-the-Great-War/Unrest-on-the-homefront/Soldier-Candidates-and-the-1917-Wartime-Election/.

124 *Canadian Annual Review* (1918): 618.

125 This did not mean that the government could not call by-elections but only that it was not required to do so. *The Mail and Empire,* 6 April 1917; *The Globe,* 7 April 1917.

126 Hearst fonds F61307. Hearst to Irving Hearst, 10 February 1918.

127 Ibid.

128 *The Mail and Empire,* 8 February 1918; *The Globe,* 8 February 1918, *The Mail and Empire,* 6 March 1918; *Cf* Hearst fonds. Hearst to Proudfoot, n.d. [1918].

129 Quoted in the *Goderich Signal Star,* 17 January 2020; David Yates, "Senator William Proudfoot: 'Country over Party'," accessed 15 January 2020, www.nugget.ca/opinion/columnists/senator-william-proudfoot-country-over-party/wcm/019a4c99-ac10-475e-ba03-dd21c8cdc1ae/.

130 Hearst fonds. Hearst to Irving Hearst, 24 March 1918.

131 *The Mail and Empire,* 6 March 1918.

132 Hearst fonds. Hearst to Irving Hearst, 24 March 1918. A close political ally of Newton Rowell, Proudfoot supported conscription and Union government, fully sharing Hearst's belief that all other issues were secondary to winning the war. He told a Toronto newspaper that he was "strongly in favour of the Provincial Government, during the term of the war and afterwards, doing everything that will prove of beneficial assistance to the soldiers." Quoted in David Yates, "Senator William Proudfoot: 'Country over Party,'" *Goderich Signal Star,* 17 January 2020, www.nugget.ca/opinion/columnists/senator-william-proudfoot-country-over-party/wcm/019a4c99-ac10-475e-ba03-dd21c8cdc1ae/.

133 Quoted in Yates, "Senator Proudfoot."

134 A year later Borden rewarded Proudfoot with a seat in the Senate.

135 Quoted in the London *Advertiser,* 16 July 1919. Hartt was a lumberman from Orillia who had been elected to the legislature in 1911. He joined the 177th Battalion in February 1916 and went overseas in May 1917. When it was disbanded he was transferred into the Canadian Forestry Corps and served briefly in France and England before being sent home in January 1918, apparently to resume his duties in the legislature. He returned to France in May 1918 but was again sent home in August 1918 because of an ear infection. He lost his seat in the 1919 election.

136 Hearst fonds. Hearst to Irving Hearst, 24 March 1918.

137 Ibid. MS of speech to Toronto Northeast Conservative Association, 10 June 1918.

138 *The Globe,* 17 August 1918, 19 August 1918.

139 J.B. Maclean, "Now That the War Is Won," *Maclean's Magazine,* 31, no. 14 (December 1918): 125.

140 Hopkins, *Ontario,* 31. Cody had served as a member of the Royal Commission on the University of Toronto in 1906 and was appointed a member of the university's Board of Governors in 1917. He went on to chair the Royal Commission on University Finances in 1921, served as chairman of the Board of Governors from 1923 to 1932, then president of the university, and finally its chancellor in 1944.

141 Charlesworth, *Cyclopedia,* 109. Varley may have been popular and he had served overseas, but he had not distinguished himself, although neither Charlesworth nor anyone else would have known that. He had served in France for only one year, all but one week of it in a pioneer battalion, and it was during that final week that he received what the battalion medical officer described as a "slight" wound that broke one toe on his left foot. After being sent to hospital he complained of damage to his eardrums caused when a box of ammunition had exploded nearby, pain in his legs from myalgia, and a sinus problem. After being hospitalized in England, he was sent home in November 1917 and discharged in April 1918. LAC, Personnel Records of the First World War. "William Varley," accessed 25 August 2020, https://central.bac-lac.gc.ca/.item/?op=pdf&app=CEF&id=B9914-S041.

142 James Naylor, *The New Democracy:Challenging the Social Order in Industrial Ontario, 1914–1925* (Toronto, 1991), 104.

143 "The Military Hospitals Commission replaced Whitby Hospital in February 1917 with a Convalescent Hospital for wounded WWI veterans. The hospital was temporarily renamed the Ontario Military Hospital to reflect its current patient intake. Following WW1, in July 1919, the veterans left Whitby to return to civilian life. That same year, on 23 October, Whitby reopened as a psychiatric facility, and was renamed the Ontario Hospital for the Insane." Accessed 5 September 2019, www.ontarioshores.ca/UserFiles/Servers/Server_6/File/BriefHistory_December2018.pdf/.

144 The only military hospitals in Kingston were the temporary wartime hospitals in Grant Hall and Kingston Hall at Queen's University, and the Sir Oliver Mowat Sanatorium, the largest tuberculosis hospital in Canada. If Varley was ever a patient at the Whitby hospital, therefore, it must have been after the war.
145 *The Globe*, 17 August 1918.
146 Quoted in Naylor, *Democracy*, 105.
147 *The Globe*, 20 August 1918.
148 Cf. Dan Mowat, *One-Two-Three: The Story of the 123rd Overseas Battalion, Royal Grenadiers CEF* (Ottawa, 2015). His wife, Laura Ryerson, was a daughter of George Ryerson, the founder of the Canadian Red Cross. She and her mother were passengers on the *Lusitania* when it was torpedoed on 7 May 1915, killing 1,198 of the passengers and crew. They survived, however, and Laura distinguished herself by taking charge of a lifeboat and assisting other passengers until they were rescued three hours later. *The Lusitania Resource*, accessed 10 December 2019, www.rmslusitania.info/people/saloon/laura-ryerson/. Galbraith's brother, Robert Galbraith, also served overseas in the 127th Battalion and was awarded the Military Cross in March 1918.
149 He retained the seat until 1943, serving in Howard Ferguson's cabinet during the 1920s and succeeding him as Premier in 1930.
150 *The Globe*, 20 August 1918.
151 Quoted in ibid, 20 August 1918.

## Chapter 7

1 R.H. Halbert, quoted in the *Canadian Annual Review* (1917): 669.
2 McHenry, *Third Force*, 7.
3 C.R.W. Biggar, *Sir Oliver Mowat*, vol. 2 (Toronto, 1905), 499–500.
4 On the Grange and Patrons, see Darren Ferry, "'Severing the Connections in a Complex Community': The Grange, the Patrons of Industry, and the Construction/Contestation of a Late 19th-Century Agrarian Identity in Ontario," *Labour/Le Travail* 54 (2004): 9–47.
5 Private letter, E.C. Drury to J.W. Foster, 19 February 1963. I am deeply indebted to Dr Foster for permission to make use of this personal letter. Drury's father, Charles Drury, had also been a prominent agrarian activist and served as the province's first Minister of Agriculture from 1885 to 1890. See Charles M. Johnston, "Drury, Charles Alfred," in *Dictionary of Canadian Biography*, vol. 13 (University of Toronto/Université Laval, 2003–), accessed 12 January 2019, www.biographi.ca/en/bio/drury_charles_alfred_13E.html/.
6 McHenry, *Third Force*, 12.
7 Ibid. *Cf* George Fisher Chipman, *The Siege of Ottawa* (Winnipeg, 1910).

8 E.C. Drury, *Farmer Premier*, 66.

9 Ibid, 83.

10 Drury letter.

11 LAC, Good fonds. Ms of speech to the Dominion Grange, 1913.

12 *Canadian Annual Review* (1909): 253.

13 Jacob Spelt, *The Urban Development of South Central Ontario* (Assen, 1955), 139.

14 Ibid, 142.

15 *The Daily Star*, 31 October 1919.

16 Ibid, 18 November 1919.

17 Ibid, 26 February 1915; *Cf* 15 April 1915.

18 *The Mail and Empire*, 16 February and 14 March 1917.

19 *The Globe*, 20 February and 14 March 1917.

20 Spanner, "Henry," 84.

21 See Spanner, "Henry," 89–91.

22 Ibid, 68–9.

23 United Co-operatives of Ontario. UFO Minute Books, I, 66–7.

24 Don Spanner, "'The Strait Furrow': The Life of George S. Henry, Ontario's Unknown Premier" (unpublished PhD diss., University of Western Ontario, 1993) 96.

25 United Co-operatives of Ontario. UFO Minute Books, I, 66–7.

26 Doherty to Henry, 25 May 1918; Burnaby to Henry, 1 August 1918; both quoted in Spanner, "Henry," 97. Doherty had also attended both Upper Canada College and the OAC as well as Cornell University, and succeeded Henry as Minister of Agriculture in the Drury government. A former Conservative, he supported Arthur Meighen's Conservatives in the 1925 federal election, then went into business and was a founder of Doherty, Roadhouse and Company, a Toronto brokerage. He became secretary of the Toronto Stock Exchange in 1936 and was its vice-president when he died in 1938. Burnaby was a cattle farmer at Richmond Hill.

27 Johnston, *Drury*, 69. Cf. Kechnie, *Organizing Rural Women*, 71.

28 York East consisted of the townships of Markham, Scarborough, and Toronto east of Yonge Street.

29 Staples, *Challenge of Agriculture*, 184; Jean MacLeod, "The United Farmer Movement in Ontario, 1914–1943" (Unpublished MA diss., Queen's University, 1958), 42.

30 *The UFO Is Built on You* (Toronto, 1925).

31 Nancy Christie and Michael Gauvreau, *A Full-Orbed Christianity: The Protestant Churches and Social Welfare in Canada, 1900–1940* (Montreal/Kingston, 1996), 168. On MacDougall's ideas, see James Murton, *Creating a Modern Countryside: Liberalism and Land Resettlement in British Columbia* (Vancouver, 2007), 54.

32 Christie and Gauvreau, *A Full-Orbed Christianity*, 169.
33 Ibid, 170.
34 P.J. Smith, "Commission of Conservation," in *Canadian Encyclopedia*, 2015, accessed 6 December 2019, www.thecanadianencyclopedia.ca/en/article/commission-of-conservation/.
35 Jonathan Vance, *A Township at War* (Waterloo, 2018), 46.
36 MacLeod, "United Farmer Movement," 34.
37 Vance, *Township*, 46.
38 Quoted in Adam Crerar, "Ties that Bind: Agrarian Ideals and Life in Ontario, 1890–1930" (unpublished PhD diss., University of Toronto, 1999), 243. Otter had commanded the Canadian troops in South Africa and was the first Canadian-born Chief of the General Staff in the Department of Militia and Defence. He came out of retirement in 1914 to command the internment camps established for enemy aliens. Cf. Desmond Morton, *The Canadian General: Sir William Otter* (Toronto, 1974).
39 *Canadian Annual Review* (1914): 460.
40 Quoted in Hopkins, *Ontario*, 48.
41 Hopkins, *Ontario*, 48.
42 Crerar, "Ties that Bind," 241.
43 Adam Crerar, "Ontario and the Great War," in *Canada and the First World War*, ed. David Mackenzie (Toronto, 2005), 684.
44 Hopkins, *Ontario*, 54, 56, 57. Cf. Margaret Evans and R.W. Irwin, "Government Tractors in Ontario, 1917 and 1918," *Ontario History* 61, no. 2 (June 1969): 99–109. McGarry, *Financial Statement*, 44.
45 Badgley, *Common Love*, 145–6.
46 Hopkins, *Ontario*, 53, 57.
47 *Perth Courier*, 17 October 1919; Badgley, *Common Love*, 146–7.
48 Ibid; Badgley, *Common Love*, 148. Needless to say, the Drury government continued the encouragement of co-op marketing.
49 Quoted in Crerar, "Ties that Bind," 243.
50 Quoted in ibid, 247.
51 Speech by R.H. Halbert, quoted in *Canadian Annual Review* (1916): 553. On the efforts of the Ontario Department of Agriculture to increase farm production, see ibid, 51–5 and ibid (1918): 509.
52 Morrison, "Memoirs," 32. For the attitude of the urban press, see the *Mail and Empire*, cited in the *Weekly Sun*, 29 May 1918.
53 The average subscriptions to the Victory Loan campaigns were $38.26 per rural capita compared to $110.87 per urban capita. *Canadian Annual Review* (1918): 510.
54 UFO Minute Books, I, 87–8.
55 E.C. Drury, speaking to the Toronto Methodist Conference, quoted in Spanner, "The Strait Furrow," 95.

56 Quoted in Hopkins, *Ontario*, 65.
57 *Journals of the Legislative Assembly of the Province of Ontario 1918* (Toronto, 1918), 159.
58 Quoted in Hopkins, *Ontario*, 65.
59 Morrison, "Memoirs," 28. MacLeod, "United Farmer Movement," 44.
60 Ibid.
61 Quoted in *The Globe*, 12 April 1919; cited in Spanner, "Henry," 98.
62 Quoted in *Canadian Annual Review* (1918): 466.
63 *The Globe*, 7 January 1918; 9 April 1918.
64 Morrison, "Memoirs," 33.
65 He did later meet with them at the Russell Theatre.
66 Peter McArthur, "The Farmers' Delegation," *Farmer's Magazine* (1 June 1918): 7, quoted in W.R. Young, "Conscription, Rural Depopulation, and the Farmers of Ontario, 1917–1919," *Canadian Historical Review* 53, no. 3 (September 1972): 312.
67 Staples, *Challenge of Agriculture*, 184.
68 UFO Minute Books, I, 33, 70.
69 Quoted in *Canadian Annual Review* (1917): 669; Cf. William Irvine, *The Farmers in Politics* (Toronto, 1920), 202; *The Daily Star*, 10 September 1919; *Canadian Annual Review* (1918): 624. There were other important issues about which farmers were frustrated. One was daylight saving, which the federal government introduced in March 1918 over their opposition. Another was Hearst's highways program, which many thought would only benefit the automobile interests and urban people, although it was intended to benefit farmers, who were replacing horse-drawn wagons with more efficient trucks but also buying cars in large numbers as well. R.A. Farquharson, "When Sir Adam Beck Tried to Be Premier," *Saturday Night* 67 (14 June 1952): 20. At the same time many opposed Beck's electric railway scheme, believing it would involve the expenditure of millions merely to duplicate existing railway lines. To be fair, the Hearst government and many urban people shared those concerns.
70 *The Globe*, 27 June 1919.
71 *The Farmers' Sun*, 10 September 1919; quoted in W.L. Morton, *The Progressive Party in Canada*, 75.
72 Morrison, "Memoirs," 15.
73 H.H. Hannam, *Pulling Together for 25 Years* (Toronto, 1940), 17; *Canadian Annual Review* (1918): 624; MacLeod, "United Farmer Movement," 34.
74 Hannam, *Pulling Together*, 36.
75 Ibid, 37. For the official report of the case, see "Supreme Court of Canada In Re George Edwin Gray, (1918) 57 S.C.R. 150," accessed 7 September 2019, https://scc-csc.lexum.com/scc-csc/scc-csc/en/item/9496/index.do/. To be fair, E.L. Newcombe, the Deputy Minister of Justice, provided

a lawyer to defend Gray, and his prison sentence was later reduced to ten years. Philip Girard, "That's History: State Trials During Turbulent Times," *Law Times News*, 21 December 2015, www.lawtimesnews.com/archive/thats-history-state-trials-during-turbulent-times/261983/. Cf. Patricia McMahon, "Conscription and the Courts: The Case of George Edwin Gray, 1918," in *Security, Dissent, and the Limits of Toleration in War and Peace, 1914–1939*, ed. Barry Wright, Eric Tucker and Susan Binnie (Toronto, 2015), 132–71.

76 Jonathan Swinger, "Erroneous and Detestable: Seditious Language and the Great War in Western Canada," in *Security, Dissent, and the Limits of Toleration in War and Peace, 1914–1939*, ed. Barry Wright, Eric Ticker, and Susan Binnie (Toronto, 2015), 99. Cf. Brock Millman, *Polarity, Patriotism, and Dissent in Great War Canada, 1914–1919* (Toronto, 2016).

77 F.J.K. Griezic, "'Power to the People': The Beginning of Agrarian Revolt in Ontario, the Manitoulin By-Election, October 24, 1918," *Ontario History* 69, no. 1 (March 1977): 38.

78 Cf. Ian Milligan, "Sedition in Wartime Ontario: The Trials and Imprisonment of Isaac Bainbridge, 1917–1918," *Ontario History* 100, no. 2 (Autumn 2008): 150–77.

79 Hearst fonds. Speech to Toronto Northeast Conservative Association.

80 *The Weekly Sun*, 18 September 1918, quoted in Griezic, "Power," 39.

81 J.D. McColeman to Hearst, 16 August 1918; Hearst to McColeman, 20 August 1918; *The Globe*, 11 September 1918, cited in Griezic, "Power," 45.

82 Morrison, "Memoirs," 46.

83 Quoted in Jamie Bradburn, "The Year the UFOs Came to Power in Ontario," *TVO Current Affairs*, 3 May 2018, accessed 9 January 2019, www.tvo.org/article/current-affairs/the-year-the-ufos-came-to-power-in-ontario/.

84 *The Sentinel*, 10 October 1918, cited in Griezic, "Power to the People," 47–8.

85 Morrison, "Memoirs," 51.

86 Ibid, 50. Cf. Johnston, *Drury*, 53–4.

87 Irving Hearst interview.

88 By comparison, Gamey had been re-elected in 1914 with a majority of only 226.

89 *The Globe*, *Sault Daily Star* and the *Daily Star*, all cited in Griezic, "Power," 52–3; Morrison, "Memoirs," 52.

90 Griezic, "Power," 52.

91 Morrison, "Memoirs," 52.

92 Margaret Kechnie, *Organizing Rural Women: The Federated Women's Institutes of Ontario, 1897–1919* (Montreal/Kingston, 2003), 104.

93 *The Farmers' Sun*, 9 July 1919, 13 August 1919. The Drury government appointed a five-person royal commission to examine the problem of civil

service appointments. Ironically, three of the new members had ties to the UFO or ILP, which naturally aroused accusations of political patronage! For more on this issue, see J.E. Hodgetts and O.P. Dwivedi, *Provincial Governments as Employers:A Survey of Public Personnel Administration in Canada's Provinces* (Montreal/Kingston, 1976), 17–20, and M. Sholdice, "'Patronage, like Hamlet's Ghost Will Not Down!': Ontario's Farmer-Labour Government and Political Patronage, 1919–1923," *Ontario History* 106, no. 2 (Fall 2014): 191–213.

94 Quoted in *The World*, 3 December 1918. Spotton won the federal seat in 1927 and held it until 1935.

95 Drury, *Farmer Premier*, 83.

96 *The World*, 7 February 1919.

97 Ibid.

98 Quoted in ibid, 20 February 1919.

99 *The World*, 7 February 1919.

100 *Cf* Gregory S. Kealey and Bryan D. Palmer, *Dreaming of What Might Be: The Knights of Labor in Ontario, 1880–1900* (London, 1982).

101 Hodgetts and Dwivedi, *Provincial Governments*, 22. Cf. J.F. Cahan, "A Survey of the Political Activities of the Ontario Labour Movement, 1850–1935" (unpublished MA diss., University of Toronto, 1945).

102 *The Daily Star*, 6 March 1915. The editor was referring specifically to labour but his argument applied equally to farmers.

103 Wilson, *Ontario*, lxiii.

104 Quoted in Craig Heron and Myer Siematycki, "The Great War, the State, and Working-Class Canada," in Heron, *The Workers' Revolt in Canada 1917–1925*, ed. Craig Heron (Toronto 1998), 25.

105 D.J. Bercuson, "Organized Labour and the Imperial Munitions Board," *Relations Industrielles/Industrial Relations* 28, no. 3 (1973): 602. Ironically, Borden, his Minister of Labour (T.W. Crothers), and Mark Irish supported labour's request for fair wage clauses in all contracts but yielded to the adamant refusal of J.W. Flavelle, the IMB's chairman, who opposed labour unions in principle.

106 Desmond Morton, *Fight or Pay: Soldiers' Families in the Great War* (Vancouver, 2005), xi. Cf. Nic Clarke, *Unwanted Warriors: The Rejected Volunteers of the Canadian Expeditionary Force* (Vancouver, 20015).

107 Mark Osborne Humphries, "In Death's Shadow: The 1918–19 Influence Pandemic and War in Canada," in *Canada 1919: A Nation Shaped by War*, eds. Tim Cook and J.L. Granatstein (Vancouver, 2020), 142.

108 Some might argue that Daniel O'Donoghue was the first labour MPP, both in Ontario and in Canada. Remembered as the father of the Canadian labour movement, he represented Ottawa from 1874 to 1879, but as a Liberal. Cf. John G. O'Donoghue, "Daniel John O'Donoghue Father of

the Canadian Labour Movement," *Canadian Catholic Historical Association Report* (1942–3): 87–96. On Studholme, see Craig Heron, "Studholme, Allan," *Dictionary of Canadian Biography*, vol. 14 (University of Toronto/ Université Laval, 2003–), accessed 11 January 2019, www.biographi.ca/en/ bio/studholme_allan_14E.html/.

109 *Cf* Martin Robin, "Registration, Conscription and Independent Labour Politics 1916–1917," *Canadian Historical Review* 47, no. 2 (June 1966): 101–18.

110 Cahan, "A Survey," 43–4.

111 Ibid, 42.

112 The nineteen constituencies contested in Ontario by the ILP, Social Democratic Party or independent labour candidates were Algoma West, Brantford, Fort William and Rainy River, Hamilton East, Hamilton West, Port Arthur and Kenora, Toronto East, Toronto North, Toronto South, Toronto West, Waterloo North, Waterloo South, Welland, Wellington South, Wentworth, York East, and York South. Martin Robin claims that Charles Harrison "received the ILP nomination but ran unopposed by the Unionists" in Nipissing but that is not quite correct. He was endorsed by the ILP but ran (and won) as a Unionist. Robin, "Registration," 115. For an excellent account of how complex some contests were, see Michael Beaulieu, "The Lakehead and Canada's First Social Democratic Party: The Search for Socialist Unity," *Thunder Bay Historical Museum Society Papers & Records* 39 (2011): 29–54, accessed 2 July 2019, www.academia. edu/1202377/_The_Lakehead_and_Canadas_First_Social_Democratic_ Party_The_Search_for_Socialist_Unity/.

113 Michael Bliss, *A Canadian Millionaire: The Life and Business Times of Sir Joseph Flavelle, Bart, 1858–1939* (Toronto, 1978), 379.

114 Craig Heron, "National Contours, Solidarity and Fragmentation," in *The Workers' Revolt in Canada 1917–1925*, ed. Craig Heron (Toronto 1998), 270. Paterson gives the 1918 figure as 378,000. Paterson, "Loyalty," 170.

115 James Naylor, "Southern Ontario: Striking at the Ballot Box," in Heron, *The Workers' Revolt in Canada 1917–1925*, ed. Craig Heron (Toronto 1998), 147.

116 Ibid, 11; Jamie Bradburn, "'Don't Worry and Don't Work': When Toronto Workers Went on Strike in 1919," *TVO*, accessed 20 March 2021, www.tvo.org/article/ dont-worry-and-dont-work-when-toronto-workers-went-on-strike-in-1919/.

117 Gregory S. Kealey, "1919: The Canadian Labour Revolt," *Labour/Le Travail*, 13 (Spring 1984): 17.

118 Peter Krats, "'A Commodity So Closely Aligned to Armageddon': The Sudbury Region in Wartime and Aftermath," *The Northern Review* 44 (2017): 381.

119 Kealey, "1919," 12.

120 Quoted in ibid, 13.

121 Piva, "Workers and Tories: The Collapse of the Conservative Party in Urban Ontario, 1908–1919," *Urban History Review* 3, no. 76 (1977): 38.

122 Mourad Djebabla, "Fight the Huns With Food: Mobilizing Canadian Civilians for the Great War Effort During the Great War, 1914–1918," in *World War 1 and Propaganda*, ed. Troy Paddock (London, 2014), 73. The Department of Labour calculated in 1919 that the average price of farm products rose between 1913 and 1918 by 80 per cent and that of industrial products by 170 per cent. *Canadian Annual Review 1919* (Toronto, 1920), 341.

123 Longden had enlisted in the 58th Battalion in July 1915 but was found unfit for France and was assigned to the Service Corps in England. In 1917 he was diagnosed with tuberculosis and was invalided home in February 1918.

124 *The World*, 7 February 1919; *The Daily Star*, 11 February 1919.

125 Peter Campbell, *Rose Henderson: A Woman for the People* (Montreal/Kingston, 2010), 63. No doubt to the surprise of some, Longden was also supported by Angus Cockburn, a wealthy Toronto merchant who had raised and briefly commanded the 182nd Battalion in the spring of 1917. It is not known why Cockburn publicly supported Longden, not having any apparent connection to St. Catharines, and there is no reason to think he had any impact.

126 Campbell, *Henderson*, 62.

127 Quoted in *The World*, 7 February 1919; Campbell, *Henderson*, 62.

128 Joseph Marks editor to the letter, *The World*, 10 February 1919.

129 Quoted in Naylor, *The New Democracy*, 114.

130 *The World*, 17 February 1919.

## Chapter 8

1 Onusko, *Ontario's Soldiers' Aid Commission*, 16.

2 *The Globe*, 12 November 1918.

3 Miller, *Glory and Grief*, 192.

4 *The Daily Star*, 12 November 1918.

5 On the Canadian Siberian expedition, see Benjamin Isitt, *From Victoria to Vladivostok: Canada's Siberian Expedition 1917–19* (Vancouver, 2010).

6 Stephen Leacock, "Social Control for Equal Opportunity," *New York Times*, 12 October 1919, 89; reprinted in *The Unsolved Riddle of Social Justice* (New York, 1920), 127–8.

7 Quoted in Jonathan Scotland, "And the Men Returned: Canadian Veterans and the Aftermath of the Great War" (unpublished PhD diss., University of Western Ontario, 2016), 209.

8 Desmond Morton and Glenn Wright, *Winning the Second Battle: Canadian Veterans and the Return to Civilian Life 1915–1930* (Toronto, 1987), 18.

9 Shortly after his appointment, Laidlaw found himself leading the defence of the Canadian Fire Underwriters Association in an inquiry established by Hearst to investigate charges that it constituted a monopoly that fixed premiums at unnecessarily high rates. Ontario Supreme Court Justice C.A. Masten, who carried out the inquiry, eventually concluded that the CFUA did exercise "considerable monopoly power" but "functioned in the best interests of the general public." *Report on the Insurance Commission* (Toronto, 1915), quoted in "History of the Fire Underwriters Survey," accessed 11 July 2020, https://fireunderwriters.ca/about.html#:~:text=Insured%20fire%20losses%20were%20staggering,fire%20conditions%20in%20major%20cities/.

10 Onusko, *Ontario's Soldiers' Aid Commission*, 16; Morton and Wright, *Winning the Second Battle*, 40.

11 On the work of the commission, see Hopkins, *Ontario*, 42–7.

12 Onusko, *Ontario's Soldiers' Aid Commission*, 15, 16.

13 Quoted in ibid, 16. The Soldiers' Aid Commission did not shut down after the war. Its work continued through the 1920s and 1930s, then through the Second World War. It celebrated its centennial in 2015 and is still aiding veterans and their families today. Its historian claims that, while "relatively little" has been published about the commission, "it has made a vital difference to thousands of Veterans and their families over the past century ... with very little public fanfare and with limited expense to Ontarians." Onusko, *Ontario's Soldiers' Aid Commission*, xi.

14 Quoted in Scotland, "And the Men Returned," 210.

15 Speech to the annual meeting of the Liberal-Conservative Association of West Algoma and Sault Ste. Marie on 14 July 1916, quoted in the *Sault Daily Star*, 15 July 1916.

16 Sir Robert Borden, "To the People of Canada," *Sydney Post*, 12 November 1917.

17 Quoted in Scotland, "And the Men Returned," 188.

18 *Canadian Annual Review* (1919): 634.

19 Jeff Keshen, "A Timid Transformation," in *Canada 1919: A Nation Shaped by War*, ed. Tim Cook and J.L. Granatstein (Vancouver, 2020), 213; Struthers, *No Fault of Their Own*, 18.

20 Peter Neary, *The Origins and Evolution of Veterans Benefits in Canada 1914–2004* (Ottawa, 2004), 2.

21 It did, however, very controversially, give into political pressure between 1912 and 1914 and paid a $100 bounty to each of the more than 17,000 surviving men who claimed to have served in the militia during the 1866 Fenian crisis.

22 Cf. Nic Clarke, *Unwanted Warriors: The Rejected Volunteers of the Canadian Expeditionary Force* (Vancouver, 2015).

23 Riddell's father, who was a physician, died in 1905. Walter Riddell left the government in 1920 to become chief of agricultural service in the International Labour Office of the League of Nations, then in 1925 joined the Department of External Affairs. B.M. Greene, ed., *Who's Who in Canada* (Toronto, 1927), 424.

24 Nancy Christie, *Engendering the State: Family, Work, and Welfare in Canada* (Toronto, 2000), 131.

25 James Struthers, "'In the Interests of the Children': Mothers' Allowances and the Origins of Income Security in Ontario, 117–1930," in *Social Fabric or Patchwork Quilt: The Development of Social Policy in Canada*, eds. Raymond B. Blake and Jeffrey A. Keshen (Peterborough, 2006), 65, 66.

26 Margaret E. McCallum, "Keeping Women in Their Place: The Minimum Wage in Canada, 1910–25," *Labour/Le Travail* 17, no. 1 (Spring 1986): 34.

27 Ibid, 35.

28 Ibid, 33–9.

29 *The Farmers' Sun*, 8 January 1919.

30 McCallum, "Keeping Women," 42.

31 Oliver, *Ferguson*, 216.

32 Drury's Minimum Wage Act excluded large numbers of workers because it applied mainly to industrial occupations and did not include farm workers, domestic workers, or pieceworkers in the garment industry.

33 John Bacher, *Keeping to the Marketplace: The Evolution of Canadian Housing Policy* (Montreal/Kingston, 1993), 56.

34 Ibid.

35 Hearst fonds. Hearst to Willison, 29 May 1918, Personal.

36 The key members were Frank Beer, a Toronto clothing manufacturer who had spearheaded the creation in 1913 of Sumach Street Terraces, later known as Spruce Court, Toronto's first experiment in social housing; Rev. Peter Bryce, a Methodist clergyman in Toronto who had spent his career working among the poor and disadvantaged; Joseph Gibbons, a Toronto streetcar driver and active unionist who became an alderman; F.H. Marani, a Toronto architect; and C.B. Sissons, a progressive Methodist professor (and friend of E.C. Drury) at the University of Toronto, who served as secretary.

37 Bacher, *Keeping*, 57.

38 Hearst to Willison, 17 July 1918, quoted in ibid.

39 Quoted in ibid, *Keeping*, 56.

40 Beer to Hearst, 4 September 1918, quoted in ibid, 57.

41 Quoted in Bacher, *Keeping*, 60.

42 J.A. Ellis, "Memorandum re Progress of the Housing Scheme," n.d. [1919], cited in Bacher, *Keeping*, 60; Matt Sendbueuhler and Jason Gilliland, "'to

Produce the Highest Type of Manhood and Womanhood': The Ontario Housing Act, 1919, and a New Suburban Ideal," *Urban History Review* 26, no. 2 (March 1998): 42.

43 Sendbueuhler and Gilliland, "Housing," 42.

44 Bacher, *Keeping*, 60.

45 It was designed by Francis Heakes, the chief architect of the Department of Public Works.

46 The cost of maintaining the building was also enormous and in 1937 the government closed it, leaving the province's lieutenant governors without an official residence. Since then they have lived in their own homes or been provided a rented residence, and have an office and suite of rooms for entertainment in the Ontario Legislative Building. Chorley Park served as a military hospital during the Second World War, then was torn down in 1959. For a brief history of Chorley Park, see Jamie Bradburn, "The Saga of Chorley Park," *Torontoist*, 9 August 2008, accessed 19 February 2020, https://torontoist.com/2008/08/historicist/.

47 Understandably, "no other reward could have given him the same satisfaction as the approval of his sovereign." Hearst, "Red-Haired Boy," 125. Borden made this possible when he requested in March 1917 that the names of Canadians being considered for knighthoods or other honours be vetted by his office. Two years later the practice of recommending honours was abandoned by a resolution approved by the House of Commons. That resolution was not passed by the Senate, however, and a few knighthoods were awarded on the recommendation of the R.B. Bennett government between 1933 and 1935.

48 Bacher, *Keeping*, 58.

49 Ibid, 59.

50 Ibid. Hearst fonds. Hearst to Willison, 23 November 1918; Hearst to J.A. Ellis, 23 November 1918; Hearst to W.E. Turley, 28 November 1918, Private & Confidential.

51 Shirley Spragge, "A Confluence of Interests: Housing Reform in Toronto, 1900–1920," in *The Usable Urban Past: Planning and Politics in the Modern Canadian City*, ed. Alan F.R. Artibise and Gilbert A. Stelter (Montreal/Kingston, 1979), 259–60.

52 Bacher, *Keeping*, 61.

53 Sendbueuhler and Gilliland, "Housing," 43.

54 Ibid.

55 *The Mail and Empire*, 17 February 1917; *The Globe*, 27 February 1917. On the cooperation by the federal and provincial governments, see *Canadian Annual Review* (1918): 605–6; Cf. Hearst fonds. "Memorandum Relating to the Soldier Settlement and Suggestions Relating to Agricultural Training for Returned Soldiers" (unpublished manuscript, 1918).

56 Hopkins, Ontario, 40. For a brief history of the Kapuskasing internment camp and the soldiers' settlement colony by an officer who was stationed there, see Watson Kirkconnell, "Kapuskasing: An Historical Sketch," *Bulletin of the Departments of History and Political and Economic Science in Queen's University* 38 (January 1921), accessed 31 May 2019, https://archive.org/details/kapuskasinghisto00kirkuoft/page/14/mode/2up/. Kirkconnell served as paymaster of the troops at the camp for two years. He subsequently pursued an academic career at Acadia University, serving as president from 1948 to 1964. Cf. Kirkconnell, "When We Locked Up Fritz," *Maclean's Magazine* 33, no. 16 (1 September 1920): 20–1, 57–63.

57 Scotland, "And the Men Returned," 193, 197.

58 Hopkins, *Ontario*, 40–1.

59 Kirkconnell, "Kapuskasing," 13.

60 An experienced farmer, he was appointed to Kapuskasing in June 1917 but resigned in the spring of 1918 and was one of the few Conservatives elected to the legislature in 1919. He served as Minister of Agriculture in the Henry, Drew and Frost governments and was briefly Premier in 1948–9.

61 Scotland, "And the Men Returned," 200. Scotland incorrectly refers to "a series of superintendents," but there were only two: Kennedy and Innes.

62 Drury, *Farmer Premier*, 96–7. *Cf* the report of the *Commission of Enquiry Kapuskasing Colony, 1920* (Toronto, 1920). Nickle was a very independent Conservative MP for Kingston from 1911 to 1919, when he resigned because he thought the government should have followed Hearst's lead in seeking a post-war mandate. In 1922 he was elected to the legislature in a by-election and served as Attorney General in Ferguson's government until 1926 when Ferguson announced his plan to modify the Ontario Temperance Act to allow the sale of liquor through government outlets.

63 Canadian Public Health Association, "The Development of Public Health in Ontario," *Canadian Public Health Journal* 26, no. 3 (March 1935): 111–2.

64 Ibid.

65 John W.S. McCullough, "The Ontario Public Health Act," *The Public Health Journal* 3, no. 10 (October 1912): 553–4; Canadian Public Health Association, "The Development of Public Health in Ontario," *Canadian Public Health Journal* 26, no. 3 (March 1935): 110–23.

66 Patricia R. Comacchio, *Nations Are Built of Babies: Saving Ontario's Mothers and Children, 1900–1940* (Montreal/Kingston, 1998), 45–6.

67 Quoted in Rutty and Sullivan, *This Is Public Health*, 2.7.

68 In fact, the act proved to be "a continual source of controversy for successive Ontario governments," despite its limitations and the support of "public health reformers, organized medicine, health departments, and the Canadian Council on Child and Family Welfare." The result was that pasteurization was not made mandatory until 1938. If that

seems unnecessarily conservative, even then Ontario was only the second province to require pasteurization of milk until 1950. As Cynthia Comacchio observes, "governments could only do so much to reduce death and disease transmitted by impure milk" until "public ignorance and carelessness" was remedied through education. Comacchio, *Nations Are Built of Babies*, 46.

69 Brian Douglas Tennyson, *Nova Scotia at War 1914–1919* (Halifax, 2017), 241. Cf. Mark Osborne Humphries, *The Last Plague: Spanish Influenza and the Politics of Public Health in Canada* (Toronto, 2013).

70 Quoted in *The World*, 1 October 1918.

71 John W.S. McCullough, "The Control of Influenza in Ontario," *Canadian Medical Association Journal* 8, no. 12 (December 1918): 1084. Humphries, *The Last Plague*, 118. Cf. Magda Fahrni and Esyllt W. Jones, eds., *Epidemic Encounters: Influenza, Society and Culture in Canada, 1918–20* (Vancouver, 2012).

72 This paragraph is based on Linda J. Quiney, "'Rendering Valuable Service': The Politics of Nursing During the 1918–19 Influenza Crisis," in *Epidemic Encounters: Influenza, Society, and Culture in Canada, 1918–20*, ed. Magda Fahrni and Esyllt W. Jones (Vancouver, 2012), 48–69.

73 *Belleville Intelligencer*, 4 October 1918, accessed 16 July 2020, https://firstworldwarbelleville.ca/2018/10/04/100-years-ago-bugle-band-parades-toronto-civilians-get-spanish-flu-ontario-raises-war-tax-at-theatres-spanish-flu-hits-renfrew-how-to-dodge-flu-letter-of-sympathy-for-georges-thibaults-wife-p/.

74 Linda J. Quiney, "'Filling the Gaps': Canadian Voluntary Nurses, the 1917 Halifax Explosion, and the Influenza Epidemic of 1918," *Canadian Bulletin of Medical History*, 29, no. 2 (2003): 362.

75 Karen Black, "How Ontarians Came Together to Fight the Spanish Flu," *TVO*, 3 April 2020, www.tvo.org/article/how-ontarians-came-together-to-fight-the-spanish-flu/.

76 Quiney, "Rendering Valuable Service," 62.

77 *The World*, 22 October 1918. Laura Frances (Thornhill) Duff (1862–1930) was the wife of Thomas Alexander Duff (1869–1924), a Toronto businessman. Their son, Percy Alexander Duff, served in the war.

78 Jamie Bradburn, "When the Spanish Flu Came to Ontario," accessed 10 June 2019, https://m.tvokids.com/article/when-the-spanish-flu-came-to-ontario/; and Andrew Belyea, "The Reality of the Flu: Kingston's United Effort Against the Spanish Influenza," accessed 10 June 2019, https://museumofhealthcare.blog/the-reality-of-the-flu-kingstons-united-effort-against-the-spanish-influenza/.

79 Marble, "Halifax," 26.

80 Susan R. Fisher, *Boys and Girls in No Man's Land* (Toronto, 2011), 5.

81 *Canada, House of Commons Debates* (29 March 1919), 843. The first deputy minister was Dr. John Amyot, a highly respected Toronto bacteriologist who was one the first proponents in North America of preventive medicine. He created the first postgraduate course in public health at the University of Toronto, developed the first diphtheria antitoxin in Canada and was involved in the development of typhoid and smallpox vaccines. He was among the first to direct attention to the pasteurization of milk and to the filtration and chlorination of the water supplies. During the war he had served as Adviser on Sanitation, Canadian Corps and, later, Consultant on Sanitation, Canadian Overseas Forces.

82 *Canada City Population History: Montreal, Ottawa, Toronto & Vancouver,* accessed 25 May 2022, http://demographia.com/db-cancityhist.htm/.

83 Kathleen Yolande Sharman and Larry Glassford, "The Appeal of Technical Education in Tough Times: A Comparison of the Toronto and Windsor Experiences, 1890–1930," *Historical Studies in Education* 23, no. 2 (Fall 2011): 55.

84 Quoted in Robert M. Stamp, "Technical Education, National Policy, and Federal-Provincial Relations in Canadian Education, 1899–1919," *Canadian Historical Review* 52, no. 4 (December 1971): 409.

85 *The Globe,* 5 November 1909; cited in Stamp, "Technical Education," 413.

86 Sharman and Glassford, "The Appeal," 60, 61.

87 Ibid, 62.

88 Cody speech in Toronto, quoted in *The World,* 27 August 1919.

89 Ibid. Cf. Bruce Curtis, D.W. Livingstone and Harry Smaller, *Stacking the Deck: The Streaming of Working-Class Kids in Ontario Schools* (Toronto, 1992), 41–2.

90 Quoted in Christopher Rutty, PhD, and Sue C. Sullivan, *This Is Public Health: A Canadian History* (Ottawa, 2010), 2.8.

91 Quoted in *The World,* 27 August 1919.

92 David W. Monaghan, "Canada's 'New Main Street:' The Trans-Canada Highway as Idea and Reality, 1912–1956" (unpublished MA diss., University of Ottawa, 1996), 9–10, accessed 9 June 2022, https://ruor.uottawa.ca/bitstream/10393/4179/1/MQ20980.PDF/.

93 Ibid, 19, 22.

94 Robert Craig Brown, "Campbell, Archibald William," in *Dictionary of Canadian Biography,* vol. 15 (University of Toronto/Université Laval, 2003–), accessed 9 June 2022, www.biographi.ca/en/bio/campbell_archibald_william_15E.html/.

95 Monaghan, "Canada's New Main Street," 22. Monaghan states that "the Department of Northern Development had responsibility for highways" in Northern Ontario." Ibid. The Department of Northern Development was not created until 1972.

96 Merrill Denison, *The People's Power* (Toronto, 1960), 125.

97 Ontario Hydro Archives 15–154. Hearst to Beck, 12 October 1917; Beck to Hearst, 24 October 1917, Personal.

98 *Canadian Annual Review* (1916): 511. The Hydro Commission subsequently bought the Toronto Power Company in 1921, at a cost of $32 million, making it the largest producer of electrical power in the world.

99 Denison, *Power*, 129.

100 *Canadian Annual Review* (1919): 672.

101 Quoted in Denison, *Power*, 135. Cf. Freeman, *Politics of Power*, 55–6. The Royal Commission Appointed to Inquire into Hydro-Electric Railways was chaired by W.D. Gregory, a prominent Liberal lawyer in Toronto. Cf. Dawna Petsche-Wark and Catherine Johnson, eds., *Royal Commissions and Commissions of Inquiry for the Provinces of Upper Canada, Canada and Ontario 1792 to 1991: A Checklist of Reports* (Toronto, 1992), 59–60.

102 *The Evening Telegram*, 22 November 1922.

103 A. Brady, "The Ontario Hydro-Electric Power Commission," *Canadian Journal of Economics and Political Science* 2, no. 3 (August 1936): 336fn.

104 Quoted in Plewman, *Adam Beck*, 451. Robinson was editor of *The Evening Telegram* and an outspoken supporter of Adam Beck and public power.

105 *The Daily Star*, 16 February 1939.

106 Howard Hampton with Bill Reno, *Public Power: The Fight for Publicly Owned Electricity* (Toronto, 2003), 72. Ontario Hydro subsequently acquired the Kaministiquia Power Company in 1949.

107 Ibid.

108 On the hostility of veterans to immigrants, especially those from the former enemy countries, see James Eayrs, *In Defence of Canada: From the Great War to the Great Depression* (Toronto, 1964), 46–9.

109 Williams, quoted in *The Daily Star*, 5 February 1918. Hearst speech, 4 February 1918, quoted in Hopkins, *Ontario*, 19.

110 European immigrants, whether from the German and Austrian empires or other countries were, of course, white, but it was common at the time for xenophobic extremists to refer to anyone who was not British or at least of north-western European ethnicity as non-white.

111 This paragraph is based on Butts, *Wartime*, 261–4.

112 Greg Marquis, "Grasset, Henry James," *Dictionary of Canadian Biography*, vol. 15 (University of Toronto/Université Laval, 2003–), accessed 1 June 2022, www.biographi.ca/en/bio/grasett_henry_james_1847_1930_15E.html/.

113 Smith, "Fighting the Alien," 302–3. *Cf The Evening Telegram*, 3 August 1918. For a fuller account of this episode, see Thomas Gallant et al., *The 1918 Anti-Greek Riot in Toronto* (Toronto, 2005).

114 Marquis, "Grasset, Henry James."

115 Quoted in the *Kemptville Advance*, 30 January 1919; Oliver, "Ferguson," 42.

116 *The Daily Star*, 18 July 1919, quoted in Jamie Bradburn, "The Violence and Racism of Peace Day, 1919," *TVO*, 19 July 1919, accessed 16 February 2020, www.tvo.org/article/the-violence-and-racism-of-peace-day-1919/.

117 Ibid.

118 *The World*, 21 July 1919, quoted in ibid.

119 Bradburn, "The Violence."

120 *Hamilton Herald*, 21 July 1919, quoted in ibid. London *Advertiser*, 15 July 1919.

121 Michael J. Piva, "Workers and Tories: The Collapse of the Conservative Party in Urban Ontario, 1908–1919," *Urban History Review* 3, no. 76 (1977): 40; Mourad Djebabla, "Fight the Huns With Food: Mobilizing Canadian Civilians for the Great War Effort During the Great War, 1914–1918," in *World War 1 and Propaganda*, ed. Troy Paddock (London, 2014), 73. The federal Department of Labour calculated in 1919 that the cost of an average family for food rose by 50 per cent between 1913 and 1918. *Canadian Annual Review 1919* (Toronto, 1920), 341.

122 Ontario Heritage Foundation, "The Warriors Day Parade," accessed 25 March 2020, www.thewarriorsdayparade.ca/Parade%20History-Historical%20Plaque/. The Grand Army of Canada was a veterans' association founded in October 1918 largely to serve the needs of men discharged before they made it overseas, a group not represented by the GWVA. By the middle of 1919 it had nearly 5,000 members, "most of them belonging to its several Toronto branches and virtually all of them in industrial Ontario." Nathan Smith, "Comrades and Citizens: Great War Veterans in Toronto, 1915–1919" (PhD diss, University of Toronto, 2012), 206.

123 Valerie Knowles, *Strangers at Our Gates: Canadian Immigration and Immigration Policy, 1540–1997* (Toronto, 1997), 106. The permanent residence requirement for citizenship was also raised from three to five years.

124 Donald Creighton, *Dominion of the North* (Toronto, 1957), 456.

125 *Canadian Annual Review* (1918): 618.

126 This did not mean that the government could not call by-elections but only that it was not required to do so. *The Mail and Empire*, 6 April 1917; *The Globe*, 7 April 1917.

127 Proudfoot claimed that he had made the offer "without previous consultation with Premier Hearst." *The World*, 20 February 1919.

128 Hearst fonds F61307. Hearst to Irving Hearst, 10 February 1918.

129 T.W. McGarry, *Financial Statement of the Hon. T.W. McGarry, Treasurer of the Province of Ontario Delivered on the 6th March, 1919 in the Legislative Assembly of Ontario* (Toronto, 1919), 9, 10, 11, 14. Cf. Hearst statement on 23 September 1919, cited in *The World*, 24 September 1919.

130 Hopkins, *Province of Ontario*, 67–70.
131 Ibid, 15.
132 Ibid, 33.
133 Ibid, 6–7.
134 Henry fonds. A.C. Pratt to Sir Adam Beck, 21 January 1919, copy.
135 McGarry, *Financial Statement*, 33, 34, 36.

## Chapter 9

1 Hearst fonds. Ms of speech at Eugenia Falls, 26 June 1919.
2 Quoted in *The World*, 20 February 1919.
3 Hearst fonds. Wallis to Davison, 19 September 1919.
4 Hearst speech in the legislature, 7 April 1919, published as *The Referendum Ballot* (Toronto: s.n., 1919), 19, 20, accessed 15 May 2020, www.canadiana.ca/view/oocihm.79168/25/. Before the OTA was passed the strength of beer was 9 per cent by volume. Today it is generally around 5 per cent.
5 Rowell fonds. Proudfoot to Rowell, 8 July 1919.
6 *The World*, 9 September 1919.
7 Ibid.
8 Two pro-temperance referendum campaign committees urged Hearst to hold the referendum separately from the election so as not to distract attention from the main issue. Hearst fonds. Gordon Finlay (Haldimand) to Hearst, 11 September 1919, telegram; A.B. Cunningham (Peterborough) to Hearst, 24 September 1919, telegram.
9 Hearst fonds. Alex Ferguson to Hearst, 2 September 1919; G.C. Wilson to Hearst, 12 September 1919. Wilson was the Conservative/Unionist MP for Wentworth from 1911 to 1935.
10 Ibid. R. Davison to Hearst, 12 September 1919. This correspondent appears to have been Robert Davison, who operated a cheese factory near Picton.
11 Ibid. T.E. Simpson to Hearst, 6 May 1919.
12 Quoted in *The World*, 10 September 1919 and 24 September 1919.
13 Ibid. Horace Wallis to Robert Davison, 19 September 1919. Wallis was secretary of the Department of the Prime Minister. Cf. Neil Watson to Hearst, 9 September 1919; Hearst to Watson, 12 September 1919. Toronto's Liberal alderman, George Ramsden, had publicly declared on 9 September that that, even "if the Premier does not desire to announce the date we already know what is going to happen." Quoted in the *The World*, 10 September 1919.
14 Johnston, *Drury*, 57.
15 Willison fonds 15118. Hearst to Willison, 30 December 1918.
16 Brown, "Reid, John Dowsley."

17 The *Windsor Star* described Clysdale, an electrician in Windsor, as the party's provincial organizer on 5 August 1919. According to Larry Glassford, he "ran the [provincial party] machine on a day-to-day basis" and in the 1930 federal election was "a key person in both federal and provincial wings" of the party. By 1932 he was the permanent secretary of the party. Larry A. Glassford, *Reaction and Reform: The Politics of the Conservative Party Under R.B. Bennett, 1927–1938* (Toronto, 1992), 66, 67, 132. *Cf* the *Windsor Star*, 31 December 1928 and 16 December 1936.

18 Quoted in *The World*, 16 July 1919.

19 Rowell speech, quoted in the London *Advertiser*, 16 July 1919.

20 Lewis Wigle, a seventy-four-year-old former Conservative MPP and MP, ran as an independent in Essex South, and the Conservatives backed Proudfoot in Huron Centre and Hugh Stevenson, the Labour candidate in London.

21 Johnston, *Drury*, 56.

22 There were three candidates in fifty ridings, four in six and six in one.

23 R. McGregor Dawson, *William Lyon Mackenzie King: A Political Biography* (Toronto, 1958), 316.

24 No Liberal candidates ran in Carleton, Dufferin, Dundas, Durham East, Elgin East, Elgin West, Essex North, Frontenac, Grenville, Grey Centre, Grey North, Grey South, Haldimand, Hamilton East, Hastings East, Hastings North, Huron Centre, Kent East, Kingston, Lambton West, Lanark South, London, Manitoulin, Middlesex West, Norfolk North, Norfolk South, Northumberland East, Parkdale, Perth South, Peterborough East, Renfrew South, Sault Ste. Marie, Simcoe Centre, Simcoe East, Simcoe South, Simcoe West, Toronto Northeast A, Toronto Riverdale, Victoria North, Victoria South, Wellington West, Wentworth North, and York West. The UFO won twenty-nine of them, the ILP and Conservatives four each, and Liberal-UFO and Soldier candidates won one each. In the eight constituencies where the Liberals did run against UFO candidates, the UFO won seven. Grey North was a special case because the contest there was between a Conservative and a Liberal-UFO candidate, who won.

25 Quoted in *The World*, 22 September 1919; *Canadian Annual Review* (1919): 651. Pratt was speaking at the Norfolk South Conservative Association's nominating convention on 21 September 1919, where he received an "icy" reception.

26 The twenty-one Conservative incumbents who did not reoffer in 1919 were Charles McKeown (Dufferin), Charles Brower (Elgin East), Colin Cameron (Grey North), John Allan (Hamilton West), J.W. Johnson (Hastings West), Henry Eilber (Huron South), George Sulman (Kent West), W.J. Hanna (Lambton West), F.W. Hall (Lanark South), John Dargavel (Leeds), John MacFarlan (Middlesex East), Samuel Nesbitt (Northumberland

West), James Ellis (Ottawa West), John Gennewies (Perth South), Alfred Thompson (Simcoe Centre), Robert Shearer (Stormont), Joseph Russell (Toronto Riverdale), Edward Owens (Toronto Southeast A), Thomas Hook (Toronto Southeast B), John Carew (Victoria South), and Arthur Rykert (Wentworth North). Mark Irish (Toronto Northeast B) ran in Toronto Southwest B. The four Conservatives who ran as Independents were Lewis Wigle (Essex South), Harold Machin (Kenora), Adam Beck (London) and Arthur Pratt (Norfolk South). Pratt was rejected by the local Conservatives but not necessarily because of his anti-Hearst campaign. He had only won by 168 votes in 1914 and had been overseas for much of the war. The Norfolk South Conservative nominating convention chose John Martin, a respected local farmer who fully supported Hearst, especially his agricultural policies, and the Liberals did not offer a candidate. When Joseph Cridland ran for the UFO, Martin withdrew, so it was a two-way contest between Cridland and Pratt, running as an independent. *The World*, 22 September 1919. Cridland won handily, but Martin took it in 1923 and served as Minister of Agriculture in the Ferguson government until 1931.

27 *The Daily Star*, 13 September 1919.

28 Machin speech to the legislature, 4 March 1919. *Address Delivered by Lieut-Colonel H.A.C. Machin, MPP, Kenora, in the Ontario Legislature, Tuesday, March 4, 1919, during the Debate on the Address in Reply to the Speech from the Throne* (S.l.: s.n, 1919).

29 Hearst fonds. Gooderham to Hearst, 11 September 1919.

30 Machin speech.

31 Ibid.

32 Heron, *Booze*, 193. A meeting of veterans in Windsor bluntly warned Hearst that unless provision was made to enable all Ontario soldiers still overseas to vote in the referendum "a telegram would be sent to every [legion] command in the province, asking that it use its best endeavours to secure the defeat of the Government at the election." London *Advertiser*, 16 October 1919.

33 Quoted in Heron, *Booze*, 193.

34 *The World*, 21 October 1919.

35 Ibid, 192. For Leacock's views at the time, see *The Truth About Prohibition from the Viewpoint of an Eminent Professor* (S.l.: s.n., 1915?) and "The Tyranny of Prohibition," *The Living Age* (2 August 1919): 301–6. On Fallon, see John K.A. Farrell, "Michael Francis Fallon Bishop of London Ontario, Canada 1909–1931: The Man and His Controversies," *Canadian Catholic Historical Association Study Sessions* 35 (1968): 73–90.

36 *The Daily Star*, 17 October 1919, reprinted in *Sault Daily Star*, 18 October 1919.

37 *The World*, 21 October 1919.

38 "Cannot Support Mr. G.H. Ferguson Says Col. Pratt." *The Daily Star*, n.d., reprinted in the *Canadian Statesman* (Bowmanville), 21 June 1923, 7, accessed 15 October 2019, https://vitacollections.ca/claringtonnews/2501483/1923-06-21/issue/. Although this interview took place four years later, it certainly represented Pratt's views in 1919. Pratt wasn't referring to Ferguson, presumably, because he had been elected at a party convention in 1920.

39 "Cannot Support Mr. G.H. Ferguson."

40 Hearst, "Red-Haired Boy," 90. The position went to R.F. Manley Sims, a former British army officer who had served in South Africa before moving to Port Arthur, where he was an associate of J.J. Carrick, the real estate developer and Conservative politician. When Sam Hughes attached Carrick to the First Division as "Official Recorder" with the rank of honorary lieutenant colonel in March 1915, Manley Sims accompanied him and in January 1917 succeeded Max Aitken as the Canadian representative at the British army's general headquarters in France. Desmond Morton claims that "Sim's liaison role was essentially limited to serving as a travel agent for visiting Canadian celebrities," but G.W.L. Nicholson says that he represented the overseas minister "in all matters" and was the liaison "between the Minister, the War Office and the Canadian Corps" and was also the "channel of direct communication on domestic matters" between the overseas ministry in London and the Canadian Corps." Desmond Morton, "'Junior But Sovereign Allies': The Transformation of the Canadian Expeditionary Force, 1914–1918," *Journal of Imperial and Commonwealth Studies* 8, no. 1 (October 1979): 62; G.W.L. Nicholson, *Canadian Expeditionary Force 1914–1919* (Ottawa, 1964), 356. Sims also appears to have played a significant role in the troubled relationship between Sir Richard Turner, who commanded Canadian forces in England, and General Arthur Currie. Sir George Perley, the overseas minister, believed that Sims "was liked by Byng, the other commanders, and the authorities at GHQ" but Currie "disliked Sims, regarding him as a meddler and wanted him removed. William F. Stewart, *The Embattled General: Sir Richard Turner and the First World War* (Montreal/Kingston, 2015), 203, 247. Along with "members of Turner's staff and others" such as Lord Beaverbrook (Max Aitken) and D.M. Hogarth, another Ontario Conservative MPP and associate of Carrick, Sims also "worked diligently for the Government" in the 1917 election campaign. Ibid, 242. Sims was rewarded for his services with promotion to brigadier general in December 1917 and received the Distinguished Service Order in December 1918. "Thunder Bay Canadians Who Won Decorations for Bravery on the Battlefields of Europe," *Fort William Daily Times Journal*, 14 December 1918. When E.C. Drury became Premier he replaced Manley

Sims as Ontario's agent general with George Creelman, the president of the Ontario Agricultural College.

41 *The World*, 21 October 1919.

42 Oliver, *Ferguson*, 85.

43 *The World*, 21 October 1919.

44 Hearst fonds. Ms of speech at Sault Ste. Marie, n.d. [1920]. Manitoba and Prince Edward Island held elections in 1915; British Columbia, Nova Scotia, and Quebec in 1916; and Alberta, New Brunswick, and Saskatchewan in 1917.

45 Quoted in *The Star Weekly*, 11 December 1920; cited in Oliver, "Sir William Hearst," 47.

46 Exactly what Pratt meant by Hearst's "following of lawyers" is not clear. Of the ten members of the cabinet in the summer of 1919, five were lawyers, two were physicians and two were farmers, not including George Henry, who did have a law degree but was a farmer/businessman. Whitney's cabinet in 1914 had had six lawyers, two doctors, one businessman, and one farmer.

47 Henry fonds. A.C. Pratt to Sir Adam Beck, 21 January 1919, copy.

48 *London Free Press*, 28 February 1919.

49 Hearst fonds. Beck to Hearst, 17 April 1919.

50 Ibid. Hearst to Beck, 24 April 1919.

51 Ibid. Cf. Beck to Hearst, 30 April 1919; Hearst to Beck, 8 May 1919. Nelles, "Beck." Elliott, *Politics Is Funny*, 71.

52 Hearst, "Red-Haired Boy," 127. Herbert Lennox was Conservative MPP for York North from 1905 to 1923 and MP from 1925 to 1934. He had the distinction of defeating Mackenzie King in the 1925 election.

53 *The Globe*, 20 March 1919.

54 Hearst fonds. Reid to Hearst, 20 May 1919.

55 *Stratford Beacon*, reprinted in the *Glengarry News*, 29 August 1919, accessed 15 October 2023, www.glengarrycountyarchives.ca/Glengarry_pdf/The-Glengarry-News/1911-1920/1919/Aug/08-08-1919.pdf.

56 Quoted in *The World*, 22 September 1919.

57 The twenty-two Conservative incumbents who did not reoffer in 1919 were Charles McKeown (Dufferin), Charles Brower (Elgin East), Colin Cameron (Grey North), John Allan (Hamilton West), J.W. Johnson (Hastings West), Henry Eilber (Huron South), George Sulman (Kent West), W.J. Hanna (Lambton West), F.W. Hall (Lanark South), John Dargavel (Leeds), John MacFarlan (Middlesex East), Arthur Pratt (Norfolk South), Samuel Nesbitt (Northumberland West), James Ellis (Ottawa West), John Gennewies (Perth South), Alfred Thompson (Simcoe Centre), Robert Shearer (Stormont), Joseph Russell (Toronto Riverdale), Edward Owens (Toronto Southeast A), Thomas Hook (Toronto Southeast B), John Carew (Victoria

South), and Arthur Rykert (Wentworth North). Mark Irish (Toronto Northeast B) ran in Toronto Southwest B. We should not automatically assume that all of the members who did not reoffer did so because they did not support Hearst or opposed the OTA. Sufficient research has not been done, but it is reasonable to assume that some who had been in office for several years simply retired, while others just didn't think they could get re-elected. This was George Sulman's decision (Kent West) because he only won by only thirteen votes in 1914.

58 J.W. Dafoe to Sir Clifford Sifton, 21 July 1919; quoted in Ramsey Cook, ed, *The Dafoe-Sifton Correspondence 1919–1927* (Winnipeg, 1966), 7.

59 *The Daily Star*, 20 September 1919.

60 Ibid, 23 September 1933. Cf. Fergus Cronin, "Adam Beck's Fight for Public Hydro," *Maclean's Magazine* (15 June 1954): 51.

61 Morrison, "Memoirs," 59–62.

62 Farquharson, "When Sir Adam Beck Tried to Be Premier," 13.

63 *The World*, 22 September 1919.

64 Quoted in Plewman, *Adam Beck*, 235–6.

65 Elliott, *Politics Is Funny*, 71.

66 According to *The World*, Proudfoot claimed that he had made the offer "without previous consultation with Premier Hearst." *The World*, 20 February 1919. Proudfoot was the first leader of the opposition in Ontario to be granted a stipend or budget in addition to his sessional allowance to cover office and other expenses. According to Dewart, always on the alert for a scandal, the legislature approved the payment in the last ten minutes of the session and "had been promptly drawn." Quoted in *The World*, 19 September 1919. Joseph Pinard, the Liberal MPP for Ottawa East, supported Dewart's opposition to the extension but did not vote against it.

67 The percentage figures were 42 per cent of the Liberal MPPs and 31 per cent of the Conservatives The nine Liberals who retired were Thomas Davidson (Brant North), Joseph Ham (Brant South), C.M. Bowman (Bruce West), Robert McElroy (Carleton), Severin Ducharme (Essex North), Hugh Munro (Glengarry), Walter Ferguson (Kent East), J.C. Elliott (Middlesex West), and Thomas Atkinson (Norfolk North). William Proudfoot lost the nomination in Huron Centre and ran as an Independent.

68 Willison fonds 1514. Hearst to Willison, 14 February 1919, Private and Confidential.

69 For a brief summary of Dewart's career, see Carolyn Strange, "Dewart, Herbert Hartley," in *Dictionary of Canadian Biography* , vol. 15 (University of Toronto/Université Laval, 2003–), accessed 26 April 2024, accessed 6 November 2019, www.biographi.ca/en/bio/dewart_herbert_hartley_15E.html.

70 Hearst fonds. Eugenia Falls speech, 26 June 1919.

71 Ibid.

72 Ibid.

73 The quotation is taken from a letter that Hearst wrote to Willison but he repeated this declaration frequently throughout 1919. Willison fonds 15141; Hearst to Willison, 14 February 1919, Private and Confidential.

74 Quoted in *The Globe*, 17 April 1919. Cf. Elliott, *Politics Is Funny*, 28.

75 They were Alfred Nixon (Halton), H.A.C. Machin (Kenora), A.E. Ross (Kingston), A.C. Pratt (Norfolk South), W.H. Price (Toronto Parkdale), D.M. Hogarth (Port Arthur), James Hartt (Simcoe East), Thomas Magladery (Temiskaming), Donald Sharpe (Welland), A.F. Rykert (Wentworth North), and T.H. Lennox (York North). By comparison, only two Liberal MPPs – Malcolm Lang (Cochrane) and J.C. Tolmie (Windsor) – had served overseas.

76 The Disqualification Act, 1919. Statutes of Ontario, 1919, c6.

77 Oliver, "Sir William Hearst," 36.

78 The Department of Labour was created in April 1919 and was placed temporarily under Finlay MacDiarmid. Hearst intended to appoint W.D. Robbins its minister after the election. He was a popular union leader and municipal politician in Toronto who was contesting Riverdale for the Conservatives. Hearst also intended to appoint Brigadier General A.E. Ross, the Conservative MPP for Kingston who had served as the CEF's Director of Medical Services, Minister of Health, and representative of veterans in the cabinet. Because the legislation creating the department was not passed before the election, he was brought into the cabinet temporarily as a minister without portfolio.

79 The Drury government passed the bill, which included "every female person in any trade or occupation ... who works for wages," in 1920.

80 *Canadian Annual Review* (1919): 649–50.

81 *The Daily Star*, 17 October 1919.

82 *The Daily Star* agreed with this calculation. *The Daily Star*, 14 October 1919.

83 *The World*, 24 September 1919; *The Globe*, 5 March 1919; *The Mail and Empire*, 20 March 1919.

84 Hearst fonds. Unsigned letter to Ferguson, 25 September 1919, quoted in Oliver, *Ferguson*, 88.

85 Oliver, *Ferguson*, 88.

86 Quoted in *Sault Daily Star*, 27 September 1919.

87 *Sault Daily Star*, 30 September 1919.

88 Anon, "Remember This? The Story of F.J. Davey," *Sootoday*, 31 July 2016, www.sootoday.com/columns/remember-this/remember-this-the-story-of-fj-davey-346198/.

89 *Sault Daily Star*, 30 September 1919.

90 Ibid, 3 October 1919.

91 The *Sault Daily Star* shared his optimism, if no other reason than that "it would be politic on the part of the riding to accord an acclamation to Sir William." Even if there were a contest, it argued that an isolated community that depended on government interest and support would be irresponsible to elect a millworker to represent it when it could have the Premier. *Sault Daily Star*, 24 September 1919.

92 Information provided by Cunningham. *Sault Daily Star*, 18 October 1919.

93 Quoted in the *Daily Star* (11 October 1919), which thought Hearst had the support of the local UFO clubs. William Wesley Lethbridge was a farmer in the rural municipality of Korah.

94 *Sault Daily Star*, 2 October 1919.

95 Ibid, 10 October 1919.

96 Ibid. What Cunningham was advocating was corporatism, a philosophy that offered a liberal alternative to socialism and communism. It was embraced by the Catholic Church as well as by some Social Gospel leaders and the eminent British philosopher, John Stuart Mill. Economic democracy meant that companies should not just focus on making profits but also recognize the needs of their employees. *Cf* Alexander Hicks, "Social Democratic Corporatism and Economic Growth," *The Journal of Politics* 50, no. 3 (1988): 677–704.

97 *Sault Daily Star*, 14 October 1919.

98 Gerald Killan, *Protected Places: A History of Ontario's Provincial Parks System* (Toronto, 1993), 43.

99 Cf. "Shevlin-Clarke Co Ltd Ends 32 Years of Lumbering Operations in Fort Frances," Fort Frances Times and Rainy Lake Herald, 23 April 1942; "James A. Mathieu," ibid, 23 November 1966, accessed 1 April 2020, www.fftimes.com/100-years-100-stories/mathieu.html/.

100 Johnston, *Drury*, 57–8.

101 Quoted in *The Daily Star*, 8 October 1919.

102 Drury, *Farmer Premier*, 84. Ferguson vigorously denied everything, of course, and survived the election, albeit by a narrow majority. But the UFO did form the next government and Drury appointed a royal commission chaired by W.R. Riddell and F.R. Latchford to investigate the matter. William Riddell was a Toronto lawyer and legal historian who had been appointed to the Supreme Court of Ontario in 1906. Francis Latchford was a Renfrew lawyer who had served in Liberal governments from 1899 to 1905 before being appointed to the Supreme Court of Ontario in 1908. Their report documented the rampant corruption in the department and made clear that it reached up to – or more likely down from – the minister who, in historian Charles Johnston's words, "had breezily abused his powers and defied timber regulations." Johnston, *Drury*, 172. For a summary of the report's findings, see Nelles, *Politics of Development*, 377–9.

Shevlin-Clarke was charged with fraud and paid a fine of $1.5 million. Mathieu left Shevlin-Clarke in 1921 and founded J.A. Mathieu Limited, which established a mill at Rainy Lake. *Cf* "Lumber Company Is Charged with Fraud," *The World*, 2 November 1920, "Fort Frances: Where Manufacturing of Lumber, Paper, Machinery Produces Wealth," and *Fort Frances Times and Rainy Lake Herald*, 10 December 1925. When Mathieu died in 1966, the same newspaper reported that he later became "a leader in many present day conservation practices." *Fort Frances Times and Rainy Lake Herald*, 23 November 1966. All three of these newspaper stories were available online but are not today.

103 Quoted in the *Sault Daily Star*, 14 October 1919.
104 *Sault Daily Star*, 16 October 1919.
105 Quoted in ibid, 14 October 1919.
106 Ibid.
107 Ibid, 16 October 1919.
108 Ibid.
109 Ibid.
110 Ibid, 17 October 1919.
111 Ibid.
112 Ibid, 18 October 1919.
113 *The World*, 18 October 1919.
114 Ibid.
115 Ibid, 21 October 1919.
116 Ibid. Rowell fonds 8703. Hearst to Rowell, 19 August 1919; Ibid 8706; Hearst to Rowell, 29 August 1919; Ibid 8708; Rowell to Hearst, 29 August 1919.
117 Nelles, *Politics of Development*, 359.
118 Harkness, *Atkinson*, 218.
119 UFO Minute Books, I, 65.
120 *The Mail and Empire*, 12 April 1919.
121 Morrison, "Memoirs," 56. W.L. Morton claims that they hoped to win thirty-one seats, in which case they might hold the balance of power in the next legislature. Morton, *The Progressive Party*, 85.
122 Quoted in MacLeod, *The United Farmer Movement*, 49; *Cf* Halbert statement in *The Globe*, 25 August 1919.
123 Quoted in the *Sault Daily Star*, 17 October 1919.
124 UFO Minute Books, I, 6; Cf. Staples, *Challenge of Agriculture*, 147–50.
125 Ibid, I, 61, 65, 88. Rhodes, "The *Star*," 74.
126 Willison fonds 15152. Willison to Hearst, 19 February 1919; Ibid 15170, same to same, 7 August 1919.
127 Plewman, *Adam Beck*, 81.
128 UFO Minute Books, I, 61, 65, 88. Rhodes, "The *Star*," 74.
129 *Canadian Annual Review* (1919): 655.

130 Ibid, 656.

131 Morrison, "Memoirs," 66–7.

132 Statements quoted in *The Daily Star*, 27 September 1919 and Dawson, *Mackenzie King*, 325.

133 *The Daily Star*, 1 October 1919 and 14 October 1919. He later said that 55 per cent of those elected were former Conservatives. Morrison, "Memoirs," 67.

134 *The Daily Star* agreed with Hearst on this. *The Daily Star*, 14 October 1919.

135 *The Farmers Sun*', quoted in MacLeod, *The United Farmer Movement*, 49; cf. Halbert statement in *The Globe*, 25 August 1919.

136 MacLeod, *The United Farmer Movement*, 53. Parliament was re-elected and served as speaker of the legislature under the Drury government.

137 James Naylor, "Southern Ontario: Striking at the Ballot Box," in Heron, *The Workers' Revolt in Canada, 1917–1925* (Toronto, 1998), 161.

138 *Canadian Annual Review* (1919): 657–8.

139 Willison fonds 15141. Hearst to Willison, 14 February 1919, Private & Confidential.

140 Morrison McBride, although a businessman, was a labour politician in Brantford. John Vanier was president of the Pulp and Sulphite Union at the pulp mill in Cochrane. Henry Mills was a locomotive engineer and union activist and chairman of the Board of Education in Fort William. George Halcrow was an alderman and had run against Mewburn in the 1917 election. Sam Landers, a prominent labour journalist in Hamilton, ran as a Soldier-Labour candidate. Walter Rollo was secretary of the Hamilton Trades and Labour Council and editor of the *Labor News*. Peter Heenan was a CPR locomotive engineer active in the labour movement who served on town council and as chairman of the local public utilities commission. Hugh Stevenson wasn't a labour leader but he was a popular pro-labour physician who had served two years on city council and two years as mayor from 1915 to 1917. Thomas Tooms was president of the local Building Trades Council. Frank Greenlaw, was a member of the Trades and Labour Council. James Cunningham was a union leader and labour activist. John Macdonald was a radical member of the Toronto District Labour Council. James Simpson was a prominent union leader who had won election to Toronto's Board of Control in January 1919 with the largest majority in history.

141 The other two were William Black (Addington) and J.R. Cooke (Hastings North).

142 *The Daily Star*, reprinted in *Sault Daily Star*, 17 October 1919. Belcher fonds. I.B. Lucas to Belcher, 22 September 1919. Hearst fonds. E.C. Drury to Hearst, 25 September 1919; Senator E.D. Smith to Hearst, 7 October 1919. Smith was the founder and owner of the food company best known

for its jams. He had also been the Conservative MP for Wentworth from 1900 to 1913, when he was appointed to the Senate. *The Daily Star*, 20, 25 September, 18 October 1919.

143 *The Daily Star*, 18 October 1919.

144 Quoted in ibid, 17 October 1919.

145 Drury, *Farmer Premier*, 84.

146 *Sault Daily Star*, 20 October 1919; *Glengarry News*, 24 October 1919.

147 Drury, *Farmer Premier*, 84. Cf.

148 The percentage for the 1914 election is not available, but in the 1911 provincial election it was only 53 per cent, accessed 10 October 2021, http://canadianelectionsdatabase.ca/PHASE5/?p=0&type=election&ID=658/.

149 *The World*, 21 October 1919.

150 In the 1914 election the Conservatives had won eighty-six seats, the Liberals twenty-four, and labour one. Since then the Conservatives had lost four seats to the Liberals and two to the UFO in by-elections.

151 The Conservatives received 391,278 votes, the Liberals 333,550, the UFO 258,090 and the ILP 131,394. Another 56,256 people voted for independent candidates.

152 Ibid. "Spectator" was probably Billy Maclean, the paper's outspoken owner.

153 J.W. Curry to W.L. Mackenzie King, 24 October 1919; cited in Oliver, "Sir William Hearst," 48.

154 W.D. Gregory to W.L. Mackenzie King, 21 October 919; W.K. Murphy to W.L. Mackenzie King, 21 October 1919; both cited in ibid.

155 King Fonds. Diary, 20 October 1919.

156 *Sault Daily Star*, 21 October 1919.

157 Ibid, 24 September 1919.

158 Quoted in ibid, 21 October 1919.

159 James Eayrs, *In Defence of Canada: From the Great War to the Great Depression* (Toronto, 1964), 41.

160 Ibid, 43.

161 Quoted in ibid, 52.

162 Ibid, 55–7. While the committee's report rejected cash gratuities, it recommended further support for education and occupational training. Undeterred, the GWVA pressed the matter when it met with the government in March 1920 but it was adamant, convinced that the GWVA had been taken over by extremists. "Ne'er do wells and English rads and roustabouts will persist and give trouble," Sir George Foster wrote, "but in the end come to naught." Sir George Foster diary, 3 April 1920; cited in Eayrs, *In Defence of Canada*, 58.

163 Most calculations include an eighth incumbent Conservative MPP, J.R. Cooke (Hastings North), but he wasn't actually a veteran. He did volunteer

but was very quickly rejected because he had lied about his age and was too old for military service. Even so, he was re-elected by acclamation.

164 More precisely, Kelly Evans opposed bars and liquor but thought men should have their beer. *The World*, 7 October 1919.

165 Naylor describes Landers as a "Conservative-labour" candidate. Naylor, *New Democracy*, 217.

166 Wilkinson was only technically a veteran because he had enlisted in the 186th Battalion at the age of seventeen but was discharged two months as unfit for health reasons. RG 150, Accession 1992–93/166. His brief service record can be found in the Library and Archives records, accessed 4 July 2022, https://central.bac-lac.gc.ca/.item/?op=pdf&app=CEF&id=B10372-S005.

167 Ibid.

168 *The Western Independent* (Calgary) 1, no. 1 (1 October 1919), 11.

169 Smith, *Comrades and Citizens*, 206. He served as a minister without portfolio in Drury's government, was re-elected in 1923, and then ran unsuccessfully in the 1925 federal election. In 1930, he was appointed to the War Veterans Allowance Board.

170 Cf. Frederick Brent Scollie, "The Woman Candidate for the Ontario Legislative Assembly, 1919–1929," *Ontario History* 104, no. 2 (Fall 2012): 1–27, accessed 26 August 2023, www.erudit.org/en/journals/onhistory/2012-v104-n2-onhistory04937/1065435ar/.

171 *The World*, 18 October 1919 and 21 October 1919.

172 James Hylands to E.C. Drury, 25 November 1919 and 29 November 1919, quoted in Johnston, *Drury*, 166.

173 Prang, "Clerics, Politicians," 286. The two predominantly Franco-Ontarian constituencies were Prescott and Russell. Prang does not name the others that had a significant francophone population but seventeen of them were probably Algoma, Bruce South, Cochrane, Essex North, Essex South, Fort William, Glengarry, Kent East, Kent West, Nipissing, Ottawa East, Parry Sound, Port Arthur, Renfrew South, Sturgeon Falls, Sudbury, and Temiskaming. The Conservatives ran candidates in all but two (Glengarry and Russell) of these constituencies and won only two (Sudbury and Temiskaming).

174 The Liberals did almost as badly. Having won all four constituencies in 1914, they held onto only one of them (Ottawa East) in 1919. The UFO won the other three (Essex South, Essex North, and Glengarry).

175 The claim that Alphonse Tisdelle was supported by the Liberals is from Francis X. Chauvin, *Men of Achievement Essex County* (Windsor, 1927), 29.

176 He was appointed the first mayor of Tecumseh in 1921, then was elected in Essex North by acclamation in the 1926 election, and served as a minister without portfolio in George Henry's government.

177 Quoted in *The World*, 24 September 1919.

178 Scholfield had represented Wellington South from 1911 to 1919 and Toronto St. George's from 1929 to 1934.
179 Hearst fonds. Ms of speech on the OTA referendum.
180 Willison fonds 15178. Hearst to Willison, 29 October 1919.
181 Meighen fonds 4139. Hearst to Meighen, 24 October 1919, Private & Confidential.
182 Ibid.
183 These figures are not precisely accurate because several candidates ran under other labels, such as Independent Conservatives, Independent Liberals, Liberal-UFO, and Soldiers, among others, accounting for 9.2 per cent of the popular vote.
184 Quoted in *The World*, 21 October 1919. *The Daily Star*, 22 October 1919. Willison fonds 15178. Hearst to Willison, 29 October 1919. *Canadian Annual Review* (1919): 666.
185 LAC. George Foster fonds. Diary, 25 October 1919.
186 Cf. Charles W. Humphries, "The Sources of Ontario 'Progressive' Conservatism, 1900–1914," *Canadian Historical Association Historical Papers* 2, no. 1 (1967): 118–29.
187 J.W. Dafoe to Sir Clifford Sifton, 21 July 1919; quoted in Cook, *Dafoe-Sifton Correspondence*, 3.
188 Willison to G.M. Wrong, 28 November 1919, quoted in A.H.U. Colquhoun, *Press, Politics and People* (Toronto, 1935), 254–5.
189 J.K. Munro, "Ottawa Is Ready for the Worst," *Maclean's Magazine* (1 December 1919), 25.
190 Meighen fonds 4137. Meighen to Hearst, 21 October 1919.
191 *The Daily Star*, 23 October 1919.
192 Oliver, *Ferguson*, 87.
193 Munro, "Ottawa Is Ready," 24.
194 Oliver, "Sir William Hearst," 48–9.
195 Howard Ferguson to Sir Thomas White, 28 December 1927; quoted in Glassford, *Reaction & Reform*, 51.
196 Hearst fonds. Ms of speech at Sault Ste. Marie, n.d. [1920]. Whitney called elections every three years.

**Chapter 10**

1 Hector Charlesworth, speaking in 1919, quoted in Charlesworth, *More Candid Chronicles*, 193.
2 Belcher fonds. Cody to Belcher, 28 October 1919.
3 London *Advertiser*, 23 October 1919.
4 Johnston, *Drury*, 48–9. He was also the son of Charles Drury, who had served in the Mowat government as Ontario's first Minister of Agriculture from

1882 to 1890. Drury and George Burgess were the only prominen members of the UFO who ran in the 1917 election, in Simcoe North and Lanark.

5 Drury, *Farmer Premier*, 88.

6 Doherty got elected in a by-election in 1920 and served as Minister of Agriculture in the Drury government. He led the party briefly from 1923 to 1925, when he supported Arthur Meighen's Conservatives in the federal election, then founded a stock brokerage firm in Toronto.

7 Smith served as Provincial Treasurer in the Drury government until 1924, when he and Aemilius Jarvis, a prominent Toronto financier, were convicted of conspiracy to defraud the government. Smith was sentenced to three years in prison, Jarvis to six months, and they were jointly fined $600,000. Drury publicly described Jarvis as Canada's Dreyfus, however, and he was later exonerated of any wrongdoing. Cf. David Ricardo Williams, *Call in Pinkerton's: American Detectives at Work for Canada* (Toronto, 1998), 211–5.

8 Drury, *Farmer Premier*, 86.

9 Morrison, "Memoirs," 69; Cf. Plewman, *Adam Beck*, 237–8.

10 Drury, *Farmer Premier*, 117, 118.

11 Johnston, *Drury*, 61–2.

12 *The Daily Star*, 24 October 1919; Drury, *Farmer Premier*, 85, 87.

13 *The Daily Star*, 27 October 1919. Cf. Good, *Farmer Citizen*, 121.

14 Good, *Farmer Citizen*, 120.

15 Hearst letter, published in *The Daily Star*, 27 September 1933. Drury, *Farmer Premier*, 88.

16 *The Globe*, 2 December 1920.

17 *The Mail and Empire*, 6 October 1927. Cf. John C. Courtney, *Do Conventions Matter? Choosing National Party Leaders in Canada* (Montreal/Kingston, 1995), 11.

18 Oliver, "Sir William Hearst," 47.

19 *The Globe*, 1 December 1920.

20 The vote count was not revealed. A Toronto lawyer, Earl Lawson, was elected to the House of Commons in a by-election in 1928 and served briefly as Minister of National Revenue in R.B. Bennett's government in 1935. In 1938 he ran unsuccessfully for the leadership of both the federal and provincial parties.

21 Masters, *Cody*, 124.

22 Hearst, "Red-Haired Boy," 141.

23 Ferguson fonds. Hearst to Ferguson, 27 October 1924. Sherbourne Street Methodist Church became Sherbourne United Church in 1925. In 1959 it joined with Carlton United Church to become Saint Luke's United Church.

24 *The Evening Telegram*, 21 October 1929; *Globe*, 22 October 1929; Elliott, *Politics Is Funny*, 27–8.

25 Vernon Hearst interview.

26 Ibid. *The Globe* reported in 1939 that during his twenty years as a member of the IJC, Hearst scrupulously avoided politics because he felt very strongly that his position was a quasi-judicial one and that he therefore was obliged to avoid public controversy. *The Globe*, 22 October 1929, 16 February 1939.
27 *The Daily Star*, 3 November 1919.
28 Meighen fonds 4141. Hearst to Meighen, 25 October 1919, Confidential. Ibid 4144; Meighen to Hearst, 28 October 1919.
29 Hearst, "Red-Haired Boy," 138. Cf. "The Late Mr. Justice Orde," *Canadian Bar Review* (September 1932): 456–7.
30 Vernon and Irving Hearst interviews. Hearst, "Red-Haired Boy," 138–9. The only apparent justification for this belief was that Reid's wife was a member of the Labatt brewing family.
31 Borden diary, 31 December 1919, in Henry Borden, ed., *Borden Memoirs*, vol 2, 1019. His appointment took effect on 23 February 1920.
32 International Joint Commission, "Role of the IJC," accessed 18 July 2022, www.ijc.org/en/who/role/.
33 Willison fonds 15187. Hearst to Willison, 5 January 1920, Confidential. IJC Files. Hearst Correspondence. Hearst to J. Ross Stewart, 28 March 1932. Hearst to J.E. Atkinson, 21 July 1934, Personal.
34 There are three major publications on the functions and history of the International Joint Commission but none of them refer to the commissioners aside from noting their appointments. See Joseph Chacko, *The International Joint Commission* (New York, 1932), L.M. Bloomfield and G.F. Fitzgerald, *Boundary Waters Problems of Canada and the United States (The International Joint Commission 1912–1958)* (Toronto, 1958), and D. Macfarlane and M. Clamen, *The First Century of the International Joint Commission* (Calgary, 2000).
35 All Ontario MPPs received a sessional allowance of $20 per day or $30 per day if the session lasted more than thirty days. Cabinet ministers were also paid $6,000 and the Premier received an additional $3,000, a total of approximately $10,000. *Revised Statutes of Ontario 1914* (Toronto, 1914), 290, 296. I am indebted to Laura Syms, Business & Data Services Librarian, Cape Breton University Library, for finding this information for me. The salary of members of the IJC was reported in United Kingdom, *The Dominions Office and Colonial Office List 1936* (London, 1936), 109.
36 Hearst, "Red-Haired Boy," 142. Willison Papers 15187. Hearst to Willison, 5 January 1920, Confidential.
37 Hearst, "Red-Haired Boy," 142, 143; Vernon Hearst interview.
38 The offer was made through James Mitchell, president of Imperial Trust. Hearst fonds F6MU 1307. James H. Mitchell to Hearst, 4 December 1919. Hearst's response is not in the file, but he did not accept the offer. One of

Sir Robert Borden's last acts before his retirement in 1920 was to appoint Webster to the Senate in 1920.

39 Hearst, "Red-Haired Boy," 144, 146. *The Globe and Mail*, 30 September 1941.

40 *Report of the Secretary of State of Canada, for the Year Ended March 31, 1924* (Ottawa, 1924), 101, accessed 28 June 2020, https://archive.org/details/1925v61i4p22_1768/mode/2up/.

41 Greene, *Who's Who in Canada 1927*, 605.

42 City council approved the idea but the project proved to be highly controversial and was abandoned in 1930. Cf. Harkness, *Atkinson*, 143–6.

43 William Dana Archbold's obituary refers to his having spent "youthful summers at his Canadian grandparents' cottage on Lake Simcoe." *The Globe and Mail*, 8 October 2005.

44 Irving Hearst interview.

45 Vernon Hearst interview.

46 Lady Drummond, *Women of Canada* (Montreal, 1930), 120.

47 Hearst, "Red-Haired Boy," 143–4.

48 Barry E.C. Boothman, *Corporate Capitalism: Abitibi Power & Paper and the Collapse of the Newsprint Industry, 1912–1946* (Toronto, 2020), 219.

49 Ontario Land Registry Records, Algoma Land Registry Office (001), Book 7–8 2nd, Folio 401 & 405; www.onland.ca/ui/1/books/76136/viewer/957023163?page=1/. I am grateful to Matthew Shoemaker for providing this information.

50 Information from *The Torontonian Society Blue Book and Club Membership Register* (Toronto, 1935).

51 "Thayer Lindsley," accessed 7 April 2021, www.mininghalloffame.ca/thayer-lindsley/.

52 Hearst, "Red-Haired Boy," 152–4. Irving records that he used his share to buy a sailboat, "and for the next ten of the happiest years of my life I sailed her under the name of 'Josephine.'" He presumably had already owned a boat, perhaps a smaller one, because he had been a member of the Royal Canadian Yacht Club since 1935.

53 Willison fonds 15187. Hearst to Willison, 5 January 1920, Confidential. IJC Files. Hearst Correspondence. Hearst to J. Ross Stewart, 28 March 1932. Hearst to J.E. Atkinson, 21 July 1934, Personal. On the functions of the International Joint Commission, see Joseph Chacko, *The International Joint Commission* (New York, 1932) and L.M. Bloomfield and G.P. Fitzgerald, *Boundary Waters Problems of Canada and the United States (The International Joint Commission 1912–1958)* (Toronto, 1958).

54 LAC, Magrath fonds. "Mr King's Attitude towards the Members of the International Joint Commission," 3 February 1922.

55 Ibid. Magrath to King, 28 January 1922.

56 Ibid. "Meeting of the Canadian Section on Monday, 6 February 1922."

57 Ibid. Hearst to King, 25 February 1922, copy; Cf. Hearst to Magrath, 22 February 1922. IJC Files, Hearst Correspondence. Hearst to Magrath, 16 February 1932. Cf. Hearst statements in *The Globe*, 22 October 1929 and 16 February 1939.

58 Ibid. Hearst to Magrath, 20 February 1922.

59 King fonds. King to Mulock, 6 January 1923, Private and Confidential.

60 Borden fonds. OC 489, 52047; Sir Thomas White to Borden, 28 October 1918.

61 *The Daily Star*, 3 February 1922.

62 Ibid.

63 Magrath fonds. Hearst to Magrath, 9 February 1922, Personal. LAC, King fonds. Diary, 16 February 1922.

64 Magrath fonds. Hearst to Magrath, 17 February 1922, Private. Ibid, same to same, 25 February 1922, Personal.

65 Reginald Whitaker, *The Government Party: Organizing and Financing the Liberal Party of Canada* (Toronto, 1977), 11; T.D. Regehr, "Haydon, Andrew," in *Dictionary of Canadian Biography*, vol. 16 (University of Toronto/Université Laval, 2003–22), accessed 22 June, www.biographi.ca/en/bio/haydon_andrew_16E.html/.

66 King fonds. Diary, 16 February 1922. Unlike King and Hearst, Mulock enjoyed his whiskey and had acquired a large supply long before Hearst passed the OTA. Charlotte Gray, *The Massey Murder*, 163.

67 Magrath fonds. Hearst to Magrath, 17 February 1922, Private. Ibid, same to same, 25 February 1922, Personal.

68 Hearst did write a long letter to King outlining his position and explaining why he declined to tender his resignation but he did not send it. Magrath fonds. Hearst to King, 25 February 1922, copy.

69 King fonds. King to Mulock, 6 January 1923, Private and Confidential.

70 Ibid. As bizarre as this suggestion may seem, it was not unique. In 1929 King told Sir Robert Borden that he would be pleased to appoint him to the Senate if he could get one of the younger Conservative senators to resign in his favour. Borden responded coolly that "he did not think he would be interested." King fonds. Diary, 12 January 1929.

71 Richard Meredith had been appointed in 1905, and Sir Ralph Meredith, who had led the Ontario Conservative Party from 1878 to 1894, had been appointed chief justice in 1913.

72 King fonds. Mulock to King, n.d. [January 1923].

73 Magrath fonds. Hearst to Magrath, 7 November 1924, Confidential.

74 *The Evening Telegram*, 30 September 1925. Beck had died in August.

75 Magrath fonds. Diary notes, 24 February 1928.

76 Ibid, 27 February 1928.

77 Ibid, 1 March 1928.

78 Ibid. Hearst to Magrath, 8 November 1935, Personal.
79 King fonds. Diary, 14 November 1935. Magrath fonds. Magrath to Dr W.H. Smith, 15 November 1935; Magrath to Hearst, 16 November 1935, Private; Hearst to Magrath, 20 November 1935, Confidential; Magrath to Hearst, 22 November 1935, Confidential.
80 IJC Files, Hearst Correspondence. Irving Hearst to Magrath, 25 March 1935; Hearst to Magrath, 16 May 1935.
81 Ibid. Personnel File. Hearst to Stewart, 15 April 1940, Confidential; King to Stewart, 16 April 1940, Private and Confidential; King to Hearst, 27 September 1940. *The Daily Star*, 29 September 1941. After twenty years of frustration, King now finally got to appoint a Liberal from Quebec. Joseph-Eduard Perrault was a lawyer from Arthabaska and Liberal member of the Quebec legislature and provincial cabinet minister from 1929 to 1936 when he was defeated by a Union Nationale candidate.
82 In 1959 Sherbourne United Church merged with Carlton United Church to become Saint Luke's United Church.
83 Claude Bissell, *The Young Vincent Massey* (Toronto, 1981), 3.
84 When Bella died on 9 April 1942, she was buried with him. Their two sons and Evelyn are also buried with their spouses at Mount Pleasant.
85 Isabelle was buried in Sherman, Connecticut, where she had lived for several years with her husband, Sherman Archbold.
86 *Sault Daily Star*, 29 September 1941. *The Globe and Mail*, 30 September 1941.
87 *The Daily Star*, 30 September 1941.
88 Hector Charlesworth, speaking in 1919, quoted in Charlesworth, *More Candid Chronicles*, 193.
89 Bridle, *Masques of Ottawa*, 115, 118.
90 Ibid.
91 Ibid.
92 Quoted in ibid.
93 Quoted in *The Mail and Empire*, 5 April 1916.
94 *The Star Weekly*, 13 January 1917.

# Bibliography

## Primary Sources

### *Library and Archives Canada (LAC)*

Sir Robert Borden fonds.
J.W. Dafoe fonds.
W.C. Good fonds.
Sir Lomer Gouin fonds.
George F. Graham fonds.
Ernest Lapointe fonds.
Sir Wilfrid Laurier fonds.
W.L. Mackenzie King fonds.
Charles A. Magrath fonds.
Arthur Meighen fonds.
J.J. Morrison Memoirs.
Newton W. Rowell fonds.
Sir Clifford Sifton fonds.
Sir John Willison fonds.

### *Personnel Records of the First World War*

"Howard Vernon Hearst," LAC. RG 150, Accession 1992–93/166, Box B4215-S006/, accessed 24 June 2022.

"William Irving Hearst," LAC. RG 150, Accession 1992–93/166, Box B4215-S010/, accessed 24 June 2022.

"William Edward Longden," LAC. RG 150, Accession 1992–93/166, Box B5730-S054/, accessed 24 June 2022.

"William Varley," LAC. RG 150, Accession 1992–93/166, Box B9914-S041/, accessed 20 November 2020.

### Other

"British Army and Canadian Militia Muster Rolls and Pay Lists, 1795–1850." *Ancestry.com Database.* Accessed 25 September 2019.

"Immigrants Sponsored by the Montreal Emigrant Society, 1832." RG7 G18, Vol 46, 12 October 1832, ticket #1827, Item #1339. Mfm H-962. Accessed 4 January 2020. www.bac-lac.gc.ca/eng/discover/immigration/immigration-records/immigrants-montreal-emigrant-society/Pages/introduction.aspx/.

United Kingdom. *The Dominions Office and Colonial Office List 1936.* London: Waterlow & Sons Limited, 1936.

### Ontario Archives (OA)

A.E. Belcher fonds.

Rev. H.J. Cody fonds.

G. Howard Ferguson fonds.

Sir William Hearst fonds.

George S. Henry fonds.

Wallace Family fonds.

Sir James Whitney fonds.

### Other

Anon. "Memorandum Relating to the Soldier Settlement and Suggestions Relating to Agricultural Training for Returned Soldiers." Unpublished Manuscript, 1918. Hearst Papers.

Hearst, William I. *The Red-Haired Boy.* Unpublished Manuscript, Toronto, undated [1982]. Ontario Archives, W.H. Hearst Papers.

Hydro One, Toronto. Correspondence Between the Hydro-Electric Commission and the Prime Minister of Ontario, 1914–1919.

International Joint Commission, Ottawa. Hearst Correspondence. Personnel File, 1940–1948. Staff, Classification, Salaries, Etc File, 1918–1920.

Ontario Department of Education Records, Toronto.

United Co-operatives of Ontario, Minute Books. Toronto.

University of Toronto Library. Correspondence between the Ontario Department of Education and the Roman Catholic Authorities Concerning the Bi-lingual School Issue in Ontario.

### Newspapers

*The Daily Star* (Toronto)

*The Globe* (Toronto)

*The Mail and Empire* (Toronto)
*The Sault Daily Star* (Sault Ste. Marie)
*The Star Weekly* (Toronto)
*The World* (Toronto)

## Government of Canada Publications

Anon. *Functions, Powers and Duties of the International Joint Commission and of the International Boards Operating Under Its Jurisdiction.* Ottawa: King's Printer, 1935.

Canada, House of Commons Debates.

Canada, Senate Debates.

Commission on Export of Electricity from Canada. *Report on Export of Electricity from Canada, and Report of the Power Controller.* Ottawa: King's Printer, 1917.

Commissioner on Purchase of Horses in Nova Scotia for First Canadian Contingent. *Report.* Ottawa: King's Printer, 1917.

Kyte, George W. *Organization and Work of the International Joint Commission.* Ottawa: King's Printer, 1937.

Munition Resources Commission. *First Report of the Work of the Commission, November, 1915, to February, 1918 Inclusive.* Ottawa: Mortimer Co, 1918.

Royal Commission on Pulpwood. *Report.* Ottawa: King's Printer, 1924.

Supreme Court of Canada. "Supreme Court of Canada in Re George Edwin Gray, (1918) 57 S.C.R. 150." Accessed 7 September 2019. https://decisions.scc-csc.ca/scc-csc/scc-csc/en/item/9496/index.do/.

## Government of Ontario Publications

*Bills Presented to the Legislative Assembly of the Province of Ontario.* Toronto: King's Printer, 1910–1919.

– "Minutes and Evidence before the Committee on Privileges and Elections in the Matter of Certain Charges Made by William Proudfoot, Esquire, Member for the Centre Riding of Huron." *Journal of the Legislative Assembly,* Appendix 2 (1913).

Department of Education. *Reports of the Minister of Education.* Toronto: King's Printer, 1911–9.

Department of Transportation. "The Ministry of Transportation 1916–2016: A History." Accessed 28 December 2018. www.mto.gov.on.ca/english/about/mto-100/index.shtml/.

Johnston, Larry, and Rick Sage. *Referendums in Ontario: An Historical Summary.* Toronto: Legislative Assembly of Ontario, 2007.

*Journals of the Legislative Assembly of the Province of Ontario.* Toronto: King's Printer, 1910–9.

Lewis, Roderick, comp. *A Statistical History of All the Electoral Districts of the Province of Ontario Since 1867.* Toronto: Queen's Printer, n.d. [1960].

Machin, H.A.C. *Address Delivered by Lieut-Colonel H.A.C. Machin, MPP, Kenora, in the Ontario Legislature, Tuesday, March 4, 1919, During the Debate on the Address in Reply to the Speech from the Throne. S.l.: s.n.*, 1919.

McGarry, T.W. *Financial Statement of the Hon. T.W. McGarry, Treasurer of the Province of Ontario Delivered on the 6th March, 1919 in the Legislative Assembly of Ontario.* Toronto: Legislative Assembly of Ontario, 1919. Accessed 25 September 2019. www.archives.gov.on.ca/en/historical_documents_project/1908-1922/1919.pdf/.

Merchant, F.W. *Report on English-French Schools.* Toronto: King's Printer, 1909.

– *Report on the Condition of English-French Schools in the Province of Ontario.* Toronto: King's Printer, 1912.

– *Report of the Committee Appointed to Enquire into the Condition of the Schools Attended by French-Speaking Pupils.* Toronto: King's Printer, 1927.

Ontario Commission on Unemployment. *Interim Report.* Toronto: King's Printer, 20 July 1915.

Petsche-Wark, Dawna, and Catherine Johnson, eds. *Royal Commissions and Commissions of Inquiry for the Provinces of Upper Canada, Canada and Ontario 1792 to 1991: A Checklist of Reports.* Toronto: Ontario Legislative Library, 1992.

*Return of Documents in Connection with the Bill Respecting Aid to the Algoma Central and Hudson Bay Railway.* Toronto: King's Printer, 1904.

*Return of Documents re Boundary Dispute.* Ontario Sessional Papers, 1912, #54.

*Return of Documents re Keewatin Power Company Case.* Ontario Sessional Papers, 1912, #70.

*Statutes of the Province of Ontario.* Toronto: King's Printer, 1910–1919.

Williams, C.G. "Report of Lieut Col (Rev) C.G. Williams, Chief Recruiting Officer for Canada to Sir William H. Hearst." Unpublished Manuscript, Hearst Papers.

### *Pamphlets*

Anon. *Answer to Hon. Mr Foy.* Ottawa: L'Association canadienne-française d'Education d'Ontario, November 1911a.

– *New Measures and a New Leader.* Toronto: The Reform Association for Ontario, 1911b.

– *Seven Years of the Square Deal.* Toronto: Liberal-Conservative Association of Ontario, 1911c.

– *Bi-lingualism in Ontario.* Ottawa: L'Association canadienne-française d'Education d'Ontario, January 1912.

– *How Women May Best Serve the State.* S.l.: The Association Opposed to Woman Suffrage in Canada, 1913.
– *Nine Years of the Square Deal.* Toronto: Liberal-Conservative Association of Ontario, 1914.
– *The Truth, Nothing But the Truth.* Montreal: Le Devoir, 1915a.
– *The Juridical and Pedagogical Position of English-French Schools in Ontario.* Ottawa: Le Droit, 1915b.
– *The Ottawa Separate School Case.* Ottawa: Ottawa Roman Catholic Separate School Board, February 1916.
– *The UFO Is Built on You.* Toronto: United Farmers of Ontario, 1925.
– *Observations des Evèques de la Province ecclésiastique de Québec sur le Règlement XVII,* n.d.
Belcourt, N.A. "Bilingualism." Text of speech by Senator N.A. Belcourt to the Quebec City Canadian Club, 28 March 1916. Accessed 30 September 1919. https://gutenberg.ca/ebooks/belcourt-bilingualism/belcourt-bilingualism-00-h-dir/belcourt-bilingualism-00-h.html/.
Hearst, W.H. *Speech of Hon. W.H. Hearst on The Ontario Temperance Act.* Toronto: s.n., [1916?].
– *The Referendum Ballot.* Toronto: s.n., [1919]. Accessed 12 May 2021. www.canadiana.ca/view/oocihm.79168/25?r=0/.
Machin, H.A.C. *Address Delivered by Lieut-Colonel H.A.C. Machin, MPP, Kenora, in the Ontario Legislature, Tuesday, March 4, 1919, during the Debate on the Address in Reply to the Speech from the Throne.* S.l: s.n. [1919?].
Rowell, N.W. *Address to the Electors of N.W. Rowell.* Toronto: The Reform Association of Ontario, November 1911.

## Secondary Sources

### *Unpublished Dissertations*

Anderson Kevin P. "'This Typical Old Canadian Form of Racial and Religious Hate': Anti-Catholicism and English Canadian Nationalism, 1905–1965." PhD diss., McMaster University, 2013. Accessed 15 November 2022. https://macsphere.mcmaster.ca/handle/11375/13205.
Barter, Hillary C. "Slaughterhouse Rules: Declining Abattoirs and the Politics of Food Safety Regulation in Ontario." MA diss., University of Toronto, 2014. Accessed 25 September 2022. https://tspace.library.utoronto.ca/bitstream/1807/68573/1/Barter_Hillary_C_201411_MA_thesis.pdf/.
Bristow, D.A. "Agrarian Interests in the Politics of Ontario: A Study with Special Reference to the Period 1919–1949." MA diss., University of Toronto, 1950.

Cahan, J.F. "A Survey of the Political Activities of the Ontario Labour Movement, 1850–1935." MA diss., University of Toronto, 1945.

Cecillon, Jack D. "Language, Schools and Religious Conflict in the Windsor Borden Region: A Case Study of Francophone Resistance to the Ontario Government's Imposition of Regulation XVII, 1910–1928." PhD diss., York University, 2007. Accessed 10 June 2022. www.collectionscanada.gc.ca/obj/thesescanada/vol2/002/NR38993.PDF/.

Crerar, Adam. "Ties That Bind: Farming, Agrarian Ideals and Life in Ontario 1890–1938." PhD diss., University of Toronto, 1999. Accessed 15 June 2022. www.collectionscanada.ca/obj/s4/f2/dsk1/tape9/PQDD_0012/N105.pdf/.

Farraro, Patrick. "English Canada and the Election of 1917." MA diss., McGill University, 1972. Accessed 23 September 2023. https://escholarship.mcgill.ca/concern/theses/xs55md387/.

Hoffman, J.D. "Farmer-Labour Government in Ontario, 1919–23." MA diss., University of Toronto, 1959.

Keelan, Geoff. "Bourassa's War: Henri Bourassa and the First World War." PhD diss., University of Waterloo, 2015.

Lang, Dave. "The Log Export Question in British Columbia, 1865–1930." Hons BA diss., University of Victoria, 2019. Accessed 4 March 2022. www.uvic.ca/humanities/history/assets/docs/honours-thesis---dave-lang-2019.pdf.

MacLeod, Jean. "The United Farmer Movement in Ontario, 1914–1943." MA diss., Queen's University, 1958.

MacMartin, D.G. "Intergovernmental Conflict and Ontario's Treaty 9 Role." Unpublished MA diss., University of Calgary, 2015. Accessed 15 January 2023. https://prism.ucalgary.ca/bitstreams/ecdf0c9a-8e9c-454f-918f-17dc5c04d7cd/download.

McEwen, Andrew. "'Maintaining the Mobility of the Corps': Horses, Mules, and the Canadian Army Veterinary Corps in the Great War." Unpublished PhD thesis, 2016. Accessed 28 July 2023. https://prism.ucalgary.ca/server/api/core/bitstreams/f3304197-ad70-4caa-a017-524c9849c037/content/.

Monaghan, David W. "Canada's "New Main Street:" The Trans-Canada Highway as Idea and Reality, 1912–1956." Unpublished MA diss., University of Ottawa, 1996. Accessed 9 June 2022. https://ruor.uottawa.ca/bitstream/10393/4179/1/M980.PDF/.

Neatby, H. Blair. "Laurier and a Liberal Quebec." Unpublished PhD diss., University of Toronto, 1959.

Nelson, V.M. "The Orange Order in Canadian Politics." Unpublished MA diss., Queen's University, 1950.

Paterson, David W. "Loyalty, Ontario and the First World War." Unpublished MA diss., McGill University, 1986. Accessed 15 February 2022. https://escholarship.mcgill.ca/concern/theses/vx021g20j/.

Prang, Margaret E. "The Political Career of N.W. Rowell." Unpublished PhD diss., University of Toronto, 1959.

Rhodes, D.B. "The *Star* and the New Radicalism: 1917–1926." Unpublished MA diss., University of Toronto, 1955.

Scotland, Jonathan. "And the Men Returned: Canadian Veterans and the Aftermath of the Great War." Unpublished PhD diss., University of Western Ontario, 2016. Accessed 25 October 2022. https://ir.lib.uwo.ca/cgi/viewcontent.cgi?article=5142&context=etd/.

Shouldice, Mark. "The Ontario Experiment: Hydroelectricity, Public Ownership, and Transnational Progressivism, 1906–1939." Unpublished PhD diss., University of Guelph, 2019. Accessed 20 May 2022. http://handel.net/10214/15239.

Spanner, Don. "'The Strait Furrow': The Life of George S. Henry, Ontario's Unknown Premier." Unpublished PhD diss., University of Western Ontario, 1993. Accessed 20 February 2023. https://ir.lib.uwo.ca/digitizedtheses/2332/.

Talbot, Robert. "Moving Beyond Two Solitudes: Constructing a Dynamic and Unifying Francophone/Anglophone Relationship, 1916–1940." Unpublished PhD diss., University of Ottawa, 2014. Accessed 15 March 2022. https://ruor.uottawa.ca/server/api/core/bitstreams/cee11f46-b6d2-4941-a59a-bc766df0e0fe/content/.

Targa, Ryan. "From Governors to Grocers: How Profiteering Changed English-Canadian Perceptions of Liberalism in the Great War of 1914–1918." Unpublished MA diss., Queen's University, 2013. Accessed 26 April 2023. https://qspace.library.queensu.ca/server/api/core/bitstreams/6f0cbbb8-55f8-4900-ba66-7d7ead86ddd4/content.

Witham, John R. "Opposition to Conscription in Ontario 1917." Unpublished MA diss., University of Ottawa, 1970. Accessed 15 June 2022. https://ruor.uottawa.ca/server/api/core/bitstreams/1d3d8863-29a9-439b-9d1f-14baa00eebeb/content.

### *Books*

Abel, Kerry. *Changing Places: History, Community, and Identity in Northeastern Ontario.* Montreal and Kingston: McGill-Queen's University Press, 2006.

Allen, Ralph. *Ordeal by Fire.* Toronto: Doubleday, 1961.

Allen, Richard. *Beyond the Noise of Solemn Assemblies: The Protestant Ethic and the Quest for Social Justice in Canada.* Montreal and Kingston: McGill-Queen's University Press, 2018.

Anon. *The Society Blue Book Toronto 1913: A Social Directory.* New York: Dau Publishing Company, 1913.

Armstrong, Christopher. *The Politics of Federalism: Ontario's Relations with the Federal Government, 1867–1942.* Toronto: University of Toronto Press, 1981.

Armstrong, Elizabeth H. *The Crisis of Quebec, 1914–1918.* New York: Columbia University Press, 1937.

Arthur-Lackenbauer, Jennifer, Peter Kikkert, and P. Whitney Lackenbauer. *Familiar Fields to Foreign Soil: Three Rural Townships at War, 1914–1918.* Otterville: South Norwich Historical Society, 2018.

Bacchi, Carol. *Liberation Deferred? The Ideas of the English-Canadian Suffragettes, 1877–1918.* Toronto: University of Toronto Press, 1983.

Bacher, John. *Keeping to the Marketplace: The Evolution of Canadian Housing Policy.* Montreal and Kingston: McGill-Queen's University Press, 1993.

– *Two Billion Trees and Counting: The Legacy of Edmund Zavitz.* Toronto: Dundurn, 2011.

Badgley, Kerry A. *Ringing in the Common Love of Good: The United Farmers of Ontario, 1914–1926.* Montreal and Kingston: McGill-Queen's University Press, 2000.

Beaverbrook, Lord. *Courage: The Story of Sir James Dunn.* Fredericton: Brunswick Press, 1961.

Benedickson, Jamie. *Levelling the Lake: Transboundary Resource Management in the Lake of the Woods Watershed.* Vancouver: UBC Press, 2019.

Biggar, C.R.W. *Sir Oliver Mowat.* Toronto: Warwick, 1905.

Biggar, E.B. *Hydro-Electric Development in Ontario.* Toronto: Ryerson, 1920.

Bissell, Claude. *The Young Vincent Massey.* Toronto: University of Toronto Press, 1981.

Blake, Raymond B., and Jeffrey A. Keshen, eds. *Social Fabric or Patchwork Quilt: The Development of Social Policy in Canada.* Peterborough: Broadview Press, 2006.

Bloomfield, L.M., and G.P. Fitzgerald. *Boundary Waters Problems of Canada and the United States: The International Joint Commission 1912–1958.* Toronto: Carswell, 1958.

Borden, Robert. *Robert Laird Borden: His Memoirs.* Edited by Henry Borden. Toronto: Macmillan, 1938.

Borg, Ronald, ed. *Peterborough: Land of Shining Waters.* Peterborough: Centennial Publications Committee, 1967.

Boyer, J. Patrick. *A Passion for Justice: The Legacy of James Chalmers McRuer.* Toronto: Osgoode Society for Canadian Legal History, 1994.

Bridle, Augustus. *The Masques of Ottawa.* Toronto: Macmillan, 1921.

Brookfield, Tarah. *Our Voices Must Be Heard: Women and the Vote in Ontario.* Vancouver: UBC Press, 2018.

Bull, W.P. *From the Boyne to Brampton.* Toronto: McLeod, 1936.

Butts, Edward. *Wartime: The First World War in a Canadian Town.* Toronto: James Lorimer, 2017.

Campbell, Peter. *Canadian Marxists and the Search for a Third Way.* Montreal and Kingston: McGill-Queen's University Press, 2000.

– *Rose Henderson: A Woman for the People.* Montreal and Kingston: McGill-Queen's University Press, 2010.

Capp, Edward H. *The Story of Baw-a-Ting, Being the Annals of Sault Sainte Marie.* Sault Ste Marie: Privately Published, 1904.

Carnegie, David. *The History of Munitions Supply in Canada 1914–1918.* Toronto: Longmans Green, 1925.

Cecillon, Jack D. *Prayers, Petitions, and Protests: The Catholic Church and the Ontario Schools Crisis in the Windsor Border Region, 1910–1928.* Montreal and Kingston: McGill-Queen's University Press, 2013.

Chacko, Joseph. *The International Joint Commission.* New York: Columbia University Press, 1932.

Chambers, Ernest J. *The Canadian Militia.* Montreal: L.M. Fresco, 1907.

–, ed. *The Canadian Parliamentary Guide.* Toronto: Mortimer, 1919.

Charlesworth, Hector, ed. *A Cyclopedia of Canadian Biography.* Toronto: Hunter-Rose, 1919.

– *Candid Chronicles: Leaves from the Note Book of a Canadian Journalist.* Toronto: Macmillan, 1925.

– *More Candid Chronicles: Further Leaves from the Note Book of a Canadian Journalist.* Toronto: Macmillan, 1928.

Chauvin, Francis X. *Men of Achievement Essex County.* Windsor: Windsor & Region Publications, 1927.

Chipman, George Fisher. *The Siege of Ottawa*: Winnipeg: Grain Growers Guide, 1910.

Choquette, Robert. *Language and Religion: A History of English-French Conflict in Ontario.* Ottawa: Editions de l'Université d'Ottawa, 1975.

Christie, Nancy. *Engendering the State: Family, Work, and Welfare in Canada.* Toronto: University of Toronto Press, 2000.

Christie, Nancy, and Michael Gauvreau. *A Full-Orbed Christianity: The Protestant Churches and Social Welfare in Canada, 1900–1940.* Montreal and Kingston: McGill-Queen's University Press, 1996.

Cleverdon, C.L. *The Women Suffrage Movement in Canada.* Toronto: University of Toronto Press, 1950.

Clippingdale, Richard T. *The Power of the Pen: The Politics, Nationalism and Influence of Sir John Willison.* Toronto: Dundurn, 2012.

Colquhoun, A.H.U. *Press, Politics and People.* Toronto: Macmillan, 1935.

Comacchio, Patricia R. *Nations Are Built of Babies: Saving Ontario's Mothers and Children, 1900–1940.* Montreal and Kingston: McGill-Queen's University Press, 1998.

Cook, Ramsay, ed. *The Dafoe-Sifton Correspondence 1919–1927.* Winnipeg: Manitoba Record Society Publications, 1966.

Cook, Sharon Anne. *"Through Sunshine and Shadow:" The Women's Christian Temperance Union, Evangelicalism, and Reform in Ontario, 1874–1930.* Montreal and Kingston: McGill-Queen's University Press, 1995.

Cook, Tim. *At the Sharp End: Canadians Fighting the Great War, 1914–1916*. Toronto: Viking, 2007.

Cook, Tim, and J.L. Granatstein, eds. *Canada 1919: A Nation Shaped by War.* Vancouver: UBC Press, 2020.

Corbett, P.E. *The Settlement of Canadian-American Disputes.* New Haven: Yale University Press, 1937.

Courtney, John C. *Do Conventions Matter? Choosing National Party Leaders in Canada.* Montreal and Kingston: McGill-Queen's University Press, 1995.

Creighton, Donald. *Dominion of the North.* Toronto: Macmillan, 1957.

Curtis, Bruce, D.W. Livingstone, and Harry Smaller. *Stacking the Deck: The Streaming of Working-Class Kids in Ontario Schools.* Toronto: Our Schools/Our Selves Education Foundation, 1992.

Dafoe, J.W. *Laurier: A Study in Canadian Politics.* Toronto: Allen, 1922.

Dawson, R. McGregor. *William Lyon Mackenzie King: A Political Biography.* Toronto: University of Toronto Press, 1958.

Denison, Merrill. *The People's Power: The History of Ontario Hydro.* Toronto: McClelland & Stewart, 1960.

Dickason, Olive Patricia. *Canada's First Nations: A History of Founding Peoples from Earliest Times.* Don Mills: Oxford, 2002.

Donald, W.J.A. *The Canadian Iron and Steel Industry.* New York: Houghton Mifflin, 1915.

Drummond, Lady. *Women of Canada.* Montreal: Women of Canada Publishing Company, 1930. Accessed 10 May 2021. https://numerique.banq.qc.ca/patrimoine/details/52327/2749205?docref=hk1gjyiC-EI-jkxBrAEDxA/.

Drury, E.C. *Farmer Premier: Memoirs of the Honourable E.C. Drury.* Toronto: McClelland and Stewart, 1966.

Duguid, A.F. *Official History of the Canadian Forces in the Great War 1914–1919*, Vol. 1. Ottawa: King's Printer, 1938.

Dutil, Patrice, and David MacKenzie. *Canada 1911: The Decisive Election that Shaped the Country.* Toronto: Dundurn, 2011.

– *Embattled Nation: Canada's Wartime Election of 1917.* Toronto: Dundurn, 2017.

Eayrs, James. *In Defence of Canada: From the Great War to the Great Depression.* Toronto: University of Toronto Press, 1964.

Elliott, W.E. *Politics Is Funny.* Toronto: Burns and MacEachern, 1952.

Emery, George. *Principles and Gerrymanders: Parliamentary Redistribution of Ridings in Ontario, 1840–1954.* Montreal/Kingston: McGill-Queen's University Press, 2016.

English, John. *The Decline of Politics: The Conservatives and the Party System, 1901–20.* Toronto: University of Toronto Press, 1977.

Evans, A. Margaret. *Sir Oliver Mowat.* Toronto: University of Toronto Press, 1992.

Fahrni, Magda, and Esyllt W. Jones, eds. *Epidemic Encounters: Influenza, Society, and Culture in Canada, 1918–20.* Vancouver: UBC Press, 2012.

Falconer, Sir Robert. *The United States as a Neighbour.* London: Cambridge University Press, 1925.

Ferns, H.S., and Bernard Ostry. *The Age of Mackenzie King.* Toronto: James Lorimer, 1976.

Fisher, Susan R. *Boys and Girls in No Man's Land.* Toronto: University of Toronto Press, 2011.

Flaherty, David H., ed. *Essays in the History of Canadian Law,* Vol. 2. Toronto: Osgoode Society for Canadian Legal History, 2012.

Foster, J.G. *Foster's Sault Ste Marie, Ont. Directory 1901–1902.* Toronto: J.G. Foster, 1901.

Freeman, Neil B. *The Politics of Power: Ontario Hydro and Its Government, 1906–1995.* Toronto: University of Toronto Press, 1996.

Frost, Leslie M. *Fighting Men.* Toronto: Clarke, Irwin & Company, 1967.

Gallant, Thomas, Michael Vitopoulos, and George Treheles. *The 1918 Anti-Greek Riot in Toronto.* Toronto: Thessalonikeans Society of Metro Toronto and the Canadian Hellenic Historical Society, 2005.

Getty, Ian A.L., and Antoine S. Lussier, eds. *As Long as the Sun Shines and the Water Flows: A Reader in Canadian Native Studies.* Vancouver: UBC Press, 1983.

Gillis, R. Peter, and Thomas R. Roach. *Lost Initiatives: Canada's Forest Industries, Forest Policy and Forest Conservation.* New York: Praeger, 1986.

Glassford, Larry. *Reaction and Reform: The Politics of the Conservative Party under R.B. Bennett, 1927–1938.* Toronto: University of Toronto Press, 1992.

Glassford, Sarah, and Amy Shaw. *Sisterhood of Suffering and Service: Women and Girls of Canada and Newfoundland During the First World War.* Vancouver: UBC Press, 2012.

Good, W.C. *Farmer Citizen, My Fifty Years in the Canadian Farmers' Movement.* Toronto: Ryerson, 1958.

Graham, Roger. *Arthur Meighen: Door of Opportunity.* Toronto: Clarke Irwin, 1960.

Gray, Charlotte. *Mrs. King: The Life & Times of Isabel Mackenzie King.* Toronto: Viking, 1997.

– *The Massey Murder: A Maid, Her Master and the Trial that Shocked a Country.* Toronto: HarperCollins, 2013.

Greene, B.M., ed. *Who's Who in Canada.* Toronto: International Press, 1927.

Greenlee, James G. *Sir Robert Falconer: A Biography.* Toronto: University of Toronto Press, 1988.

Guillet, Edwin C. *The Lives and Times of the Patriots: An Account of the Rebellion in Upper Canada 1837–1838, and the Patriot Agitation in the United States, 1837–1842.* Toronto: University of Toronto Press, 1963.

Hall, D.J. *Clifford Sifton: A Lonely Eminence,* Vol. 2. Vancouver: UBC Press, 1985.

Hall, Roger, William Westfall, and Laurel Sefton MacDowell, eds. *Patterns of the Past: Interpreting Ontario's History.* Toronto: Dundurn, 1988.

Hampton, Howard, and Bill Reno. *Public Power: The Fight for Publicly Owned Electricity.* Toronto: Insomniac Press, 2003.

Hanna, Martha. *Anxious Days and Tearful Nights: Canadian War Wives During the Great War.* Montreal/Kingston: McGill-Queen's University Press, 2020.

Hannam, H.H. *Pulling Together for 25 Years.* Toronto: United Farmers of Ontario, 1940.

Harkness, Ross. *J.E. Atkinson of the Star.* Toronto: University of Toronto Press, 1963.

Hartley, L.P. *The Go-Between.* New York: New York Review of Books, 2002. 1st published London: Hamish Hamilton, 1953.

Heron, Craig, ed. *The Workers' Revolt in Canada 1917–1925.* Toronto: University of Toronto Press, 1998.

– *Booze: A Distilled History.* Toronto: Between the Lines, 2003.

Hodgetts, J.E., and O.P. Dwivedi. *Provincial Governments as Employers: A Survey of Public Personnel Administration in Canada's Provinces.* Montreal/Kingston: McGill-Queen's University Press, 1976.

Hopkins, J. Castell. *The Book of the Union Government.* Toronto: Canadian Annual Review Publishing Company, 1918.

– *The Canadian Annual Review of Public Affairs.* Toronto: Canadian Annual Review Publishing Company, 1909–1919a.

– *The Province of Ontario in the War.* Toronto: Canadian Annual Review Publishing Company, 1919b.

Horn, Michiel. *Academic Freedom in Canada: A History.* Toronto: University of Toronto Press, 1999.

Howden, Peter H. *The Ontario Municipal Board.* Victoria: Friesen Press, 2017.

Humphries, Charles W. *"Honest Enough to be Bold": The Life and Times of James Pliny Whitney.* Toronto: University of Toronto Press, 1985.

Humphries, Mark Osborne. *The Last Plague: Spanish Influenza and the Politics of Public Health in Canada.* Toronto: University of Toronto Press, 2013.

Irvine, William. *The Farmers in Politics.* Toronto: McClelland & Stewart, 1920.

– *Co-Operative Government.* Ottawa: Mutual, 1929.

Johnston, Charles M. *E.C. Drury: Agrarian Idealist.* Toronto: University of Toronto Press, 1986.

Kealey, Gregory S., and Bryan D. Palmer. *Dreaming of What Might Be: The Knights of Labor in Ontario, 1880–1900.* Cambridge: Cambridge University Press, 1982.

Kechnie, Margaret. *Organizing Rural Women: The Federated Women's Institutes of Ontario, 1897–1919.* Montreal/Kingston: McGill-Queen's University Press, 2003.

Keenleyside, Hugh L. *Canada and the United States.* New York: Knopf, 1929.

Killan, Gerald. *Protected Places: A History of Ontario's Provincial Parks System.* Toronto: Dundurn, 1993.

Kitchen, James, Alisa Miller, and Laura Rowe, eds. *Other Combatants, Other Fronts: Competing Histories of the First World War.* Newcastle: Cambridge Scholars Publishing, 2011. Accessed 24 November 2021. www.academia.edu/7203300/Fighting_the_Alien_Problem_in_a_British_Country_Returned_Soldiers_and_Anti_Alien_Activism_in_Wartime_Canada_1916_1919/.

Knowles, Valerie. *Strangers at Our Gates: Canadian Immigration and Immigration Policy, 1540–1997.* Toronto: Dundurn, 1997.

Kuhlberg, Mark. *In the Power of the Government: The Rise and Fall of Newsprint in Ontario, 1894–1932.* Toronto: University of Toronto Press, 2015.

Lambert, Richard S., and Paul Pross. *Renewing Nature's Wealth: A Centennial History of the Public Management of Lands, Forests & Wildlife in Ontario 1763–1967.* Toronto: Queen's Printer, 1967.

Leacock, Stephen. *The Unsolved Riddle of Social Justice.* New York: John Lane, 1920.

LeBourdais, D.M. *Sudbury Basin.* Toronto: Ryerson, 1953.

MacKay, R.A., and E.B. Rogers. *Canada Looks Abroad.* Toronto: Oxford University Press, 1938.

MacKaye, Benton. *Employment and Natural Resources.* Washington: Department of Labor, 1919.

Mackenzie, David, ed. *Canada and the First World War.* Toronto: University of Toronto Press, 2018.

Main, O.W. *The Canadian Nickel Industry.* Toronto: University of Toronto Press, 1955.

Marshall, Debbie. *Give Your Other Vote to the Sister: A Woman's Journey into the Great War.* Calgary: University of Calgary Press, 2007.

Masten, C.A. *Report on the Insurance Commission.* Toronto, 1915, quoted in "History of the Fire Underwriters Survey." Accessed 11 July 2020. www.google.com/search?q=https%3A+fireunderwriters.ca&oq=https%3A+fireunderwriters.ca&gs_lcrp=EgZjaHJvbWUyBggAEEUYOTIGCAEQRRg8MgYIAhBFGDwyBggDEEUYOjIGCAQQBRgs0gEIMTMyN2owajeoAgiwAgE&sourceid=chrome&ie=UTF-8/.

Masters, D.C. *Henry John Cody: An Outstanding Life.* Toronto: Dundurn, 1995.

Mavor, James. *Public Ownership and the Hydro-Electric Commission of Ontario.* Toronto: Maclean, 1917.

– *Niagara in Politics: A Critical Account of the Ontario Hydro-Electric Commission.* New York: E.P. Dutton, 1925.

McDowall, Duncan. *Steel at the Sault: Francis H. Clergue, Sir James Dunn, and the Algoma Steel Corporation 1901–1956.* Toronto: University of Toronto Press, 1984.

McGregor, F.A. *The Fall and Rise of Mackenzie King.* Toronto: Macmillan, 1962.

McHenry, Dean E. *The Third Force in Canada.* Toronto: Oxford University Press, 1950.

McMillan, Alan D., and Eldon Yellowhorn. *First Peoples in Canada.* Vancouver: Douglas & McIntyre, 2004.

Melady, John. *Explosion: Trenton.* Belleville: Mika, 1980.

Middleton, J.E. *The Municipality of Toronto: A History.* Toronto: Dominion Publishing Company, 1923.

Miller, Ian Hugh Maclean. *Our Glory and Our Grief: Torontonians and the Great War.* Toronto: University of Toronto Press, 2002.

Miller, J.R. *Skyscrapers Hide the Heavens: A History of Indian-White Relations in Canada.* 3rd ed. Toronto: University of Toronto Press, 2000.

Moore, E.S. *American Influence in Canadian Mining.* Toronto: University of Toronto Press, 1941.

Morgan, H.J., ed. *The Canadian Men and Women of the Time.* Toronto: Briggs, 1898.

– *The Canadian Men and Women of the Time.* Toronto: Briggs, 1912.

Morton, Desmond. *Fight or Pay: Soldiers' Families in the Great War.* Vancouver: UBC Press, 2005.

Morton, Desmond, and Glenn Wright. *Winning the Second Battle*: Canadian Veterans and the Return to Civilian *Life 1915–1930.* Toronto: University of Toronto Press, 1987.

Morton, W.L. *The Progressive Party in Canada.* Toronto: University of Toronto Press, 1950.

– *Manitoba: A History.* Toronto: University of Toronto Press, 1961.

Mowat, Dan. *One-Two-Three: The Story of the 123rd Overseas Battalion, Royal Grenadiers CEF.* Ottawa: Servant Publications, 2015.

Murton, James. *Creating a Modern Countryside: Liberalism and Land Resettlement in British Columbia.* Vancouver: UBC Press, 2007.

Naylor, James. *The New Democracy: Challenging the Social Order in Industrial Ontario, 1914–1925.* Toronto: University of Toronto Press, 1991.

Neary, Peter. *The Origins and Evolution of Veterans Benefits in Canada 1914–2004.* Ottawa: Veterans Affairs Canada – Canadian Forces Advisory Council, 2004.

Nelles, H.V. *The Politics of Development: Forests, Mines & Hydro-Electric Power in Ontario, 1849–1941.* Montreal/Kingston: McGill-Queen's University Press, 2005.

Oliver, Peter. *Public & Private Persons.* Toronto: Clarke, Irwin & Company, 1975.

– *G. Howard Ferguson: Ontario Tory.* Toronto: University of Toronto Press, 1977.

Onusko, James A. *Ontario's Soldiers' Aid Commission: 100 Years of Assistance to Veterans in Need 1915–2015.* Toronto: Ontario Soldiers' Aid Commission, 2015.

Oreopoulos, Philip. *Canadian Compulsory School Laws and their Impact on Educational Attainment and Future Earnings.* Ottawa: Minister of Industry,

2005. Accessed 1 July 2019. https://www.publications.gc.ca/site/eng/274387/publication.html.

Pateman, John. *The Ontario Military Hospital Orpington Kent.* Sleaford: The Pateran Press, 2012.

Patrias, Carmela, and Larry Savage. *Union Power: Solidarity and Struggle in Niagara.* Edmonton: Athabasca University Press, 2012.

Plewman, W.R. *Adam Beck and the Ontario Hydro.* Toronto: Ryerson, 1947.

Poole, Thomas W. Poole. *A Sketch of the Early Settlement and Subsequent Progress of the Town of Peterborough, and of Each Township in the County of Peterborough.* Peterborough: Peterborough Review, 1867.

Prang, Margaret. *N.W. Rowell: Ontario Nationalist.* Toronto: University of Toronto Press, 1975.

Preston, W.T.R. *My Generation of Politics and Politicians.* Toronto: D.A. Rose, 1927.

Rea, J.E. *T.A. Crerar: A Political Life.* Montreal/Kingston: McGill-Queen's University Press, 1997.

Reville, F. Douglas. *History of the County of Brant.* Brantford: Brantford Historical Society, 1920.

Ridley, Hilda. *A Synopsis of Woman Suffrage in Canada.* Toronto: s.n., n.d.

Robertson, Norman. *History of the County of Bruce, Ontario, Canada.* Toronto: Briggs, 1906.

Ross, Sir George W. *Getting into Parliament and After.* Toronto: Briggs, 1913.

Ross, J. Andrew, and Andrew D. Smith, eds. *Canada's Entrepreneurs from the Fur Trade to the 1929 Stock Market Crash.* Toronto: University of Toronto Press, 2011.

Ross, Margaret. *Life of Sir George W. Ross.* Toronto: Ryerson, 1923.

Rumilly, Robert. *Histoire de la Province de Québec,* Vols. 16–21. Montréal: Montréal-Edition, 1940–60.

Rutherdale, Robert. *Hometown Horizons: Local Responses to Canada's Great War.* Vancouver: UBC Press, 2004.

Rutty, Christopher, and Sue C. Sullivan. *This is Public Health: A Canadian History.* Ottawa: Canadian Public Health Association, 2010.

Sarkka, Timo, Miquel Gutierrez-Poch, and Mark Kuhlberg, eds. *Technological Transformation in the Global Pulp and Paper Industry 1800–2018: Comparative Perspectives.* Cham, Switzerland: Springer, 2018.

Schull, Joseph. *Ontario Since 1867.* Toronto: McClelland and Stewart, 1978.

Searle, R. Newell. *Saving Quetico-Superior: A Land Set Apart.* St Paul: Minnesota Historical Society Press, 1977.

Sellar, Robert. *The Tragedy of Quebec.* Toronto: Ontario Press, 1916.

Shannon, Fred A. *American Farmers' Movements.* New York: Van Nostrand, 1957.

Shaw, S. Bernard. *Lake Opeongo: Untold Stories of Algonquin Park's Largest Lake.* Burnstown: General Store Publishing House, 1998.

Siegfried, André. *The Race Question in Canada.* London: Eveleigh Nash, 1907.

Sissons, C.B. *Bi-lingual Schools in Canada.* London: Dent, 1917.

– *Church and State in Canadian Education.* Toronto: Ryerson, 1959.

– *Nil Alienum: The Memoirs of C.B. Sissons.* Toronto: University of Toronto Press, 1964.

Skelton, O.D. *Life and Letters of Sir Wilfrid Laurier,* Vol. 2. Toronto: Oxford University Press, 1921.

Smith, Andrew, and Dimitry Anastakis, eds. *Smart Globalization: The Canadian Business and Economic History Experience.* Toronto: University of Toronto Press, 2014.

Sotiron, Minko. *From Politics to Profit: The Commercialization of Canadian Daily Newspapers, 1890–1920.* Montreal/Kingston: McGill-Queen's University Press, 1997.

Soward, F.H., J.F. Parkinson, N.A.M. MacKenzie, and T.W.L. MacDermot. *Canada in World Affairs: The Pre-War Years.* Toronto: Oxford University Press, 1941.

Spelt, Jacob. *The Urban Development of South Central Ontario.* Assen: Van Gorcum, 1955.

Spence, R.E. *Prohibition in Canada.* Toronto: Ontario Branch of the Dominion Alliance, 1919.

Stacey, C.P, ed. *Historical Documents of Canada: The Arts of War and Peace 1914–1945.* London: St Martin's Press, 1972.

Staples, M.H. *The Challenge of Agriculture.* Toronto: Morang, 1921.

Stewart, William Frederick. *The Embattled General: Sir Richard Turner and the First World War.* Montreal/Kingston: McGill-Queen's University Press, 2015.

Struthers, James. *No Fault of Their Own: Unemployment and the Canadian Welfare State, 1914–41.* Toronto: University of Toronto Press, 1983.

Tennyson, Brian Douglas. *Nova Scotia at War 1914–1919.* Halifax: Nimbus, 2017.

Tremblay, Yves, ed. *Canadian Military History Since the 17th Century.* Ottawa: Department of National Defence, 2013.

*Vernon's 1917 Sault Ste Marie and Steelton Directory.* Hamilton: Henry Vernon & Son, 1917.

Wade, Mason. *The French Canadians.* Toronto: Macmillan, 1956.

Wallace, C.M., and Ashley Thomson, eds. *Sudbury: Rail Town to Regional Capital.* Toronto: Dundurn, 1993.

Wallace, W.S. *The Memoirs of the Rt Hon Sir George Foster.* Toronto: Macmillan, 1933.

Warsh, Cheryl Krasnick, ed. *Drink in Canada: Historical Essays.* Montreal/Kingston: McGill-Queen's University Press, 1993.

Weir, G.M. *The Separate School Question in Canada.* Toronto: Ryerson, 1934.

Whitaker, Reginald. *The Government Party: Organizing and Financing the Liberal Party of Canada.* Toronto: University of Toronto Press, 1977.

Williams, David Ricardo. *Call in Pinkerton's: American Detectives at Work for Canada*. Toronto: Dundurn, 1998.

Willison, Sir John. *Reminiscences, Political and Personal.* Toronto: McClelland & Stewart, 1919.

– *Sir Wilfrid Laurier.* London: Oxford University Press, 1926.

Wilson, Barbara M., ed. *Ontario and the First World War 1914–1918: A Collection of Documents.* Toronto: The Champlain Society, 1977.

Wright, Barry, Eric Tucker, and Susan Binnie, eds. *Security, Dissent, and the Limits of Toleration in War and Peace, 1914–1939.* Toronto: University of Toronto Press, 2015.

Young, Scott, and Astrid Young. *Silent Frank Cochrane: The North's First Great Politician.* Toronto: Macmillan, 1973.

Zaslow, Morris. *The Opening of the Canadian North 1870–1914*. Toronto: McClelland and Stewart, 1971.

Zeni, David. *Forgotten Empress: The Empress of Ireland Story.* Wellington: Halsgrove, 1998.

## Articles

Adams, Tom. "Century of Mayhem." *National Post,* 8 June 2006. Accessed 20 January 2019. https://ep.probeinternational.org/2007/11/14/century-mayhem-tom-adams/.

Allen, Richard. "The Social Gospel and the Reform Tradition in Canada, 1890–1928." *Canadian Historical Review* 49, no. 4 (December 1968): 381–99.

Anastakis, Dimitry. "Car Nation." *Canada's History* 101, no. 6 (December 2021–January 2022): 20–9.

Anon. "Brief History of Nobel." Accessed 7 January 2019. www.gumptioninc.org/2017/06/02/brief-history-nobel/.

– "Charles Napier Smith: Anti-Censorship Crusader or 'An Ass'?" *Sootoday.com,* 23 February 2020. Accessed 25 February 2020. www.sootoday.com/columns/remember-this/charles-napier-smith-anti-censorship-crusader-or-an-ass-2112535/.

– "City of Mississauga." Accessed 7 January 2019. www.mississauga.ca/file/COM/8147_ClarksonBook_PartThree/.

– "Discovery of the Orford Process for Nickel Extraction." 23 November 1999. Accessed 16 October 2021. https://uwaterloo.ca/wat-on-earth/news/discovery-orford-process-nickel-extraction/.

– "Effects of WW1 on Welland Industry." Accessed 27 August 2019. www.welland.library.on.ca/industry/War/Effects%20of%20WWI%20on%20Welland%20Iindustry.htm/.

– "Environmental Justice Atlas: Port Colborne Class Action Lawsuit Against Vale, Canada." Accessed 11 June 2022. https://ejatlas.org/conflict/port-colborne-class-action-lawsuit-against-vale/.

– "How the Sault Was Involved in the Internment of 'Enemy Aliens' During the First World War." *Sootoday.com*, 19 August 2018. Accessed 7 August 2019. www.sootoday.com/columns/remember-this/how-the-sault-was-involved-in-the-internment-of-enemy-aliens-during-the-first-world-war-1018841/.

– "John Almayne Ayearst." Accessed 19 December 2018. www.wikitree.com/wiki/Ayearst-9/.

– "Keystone Lodge No 412 History." Accessed 10 May 2020. https://algomaeastmasons.com/keystone-lodge-history/.

– "Kapuskasing Internment Camp." Accessed 15 September 2019. www.cdli.ca/monuments/on/kapplaq.htm.

– "The Late Mr. Justice Orde." *Canadian Bar Review* (September 1932): 456–7.

– "The Lusitania Resource." Accessed 10 December 2019. www.rmslusitania.info/people/saloon/laura-ryerson/.

– "Ontario Shores Centre for Mental Health Sciences." Accessed 5 September 2019. www.ontarioshores.ca/UserFiles/Servers/Server_6/File/BriefHistory_December2018.pdf/.

– "Remember This? Home is Where the Hearst Is." *Sootoday.com*, 27 March 2016. Accessed 14 January 2019. www.sootoday.com/columns/remember-this/remember-this-home-is-where-the-hearst-is-270513/.

– "Remember This? Pointe Aux Pins." *Sootoday*, 27 November 2016. Accessed 7 January 2020. www.sootoday.com/columns/remember-this/remember-this-pointe-aux-pins-474834/.

– "Remember This? The Saultite Who Became Premier." *Sootoday.com*, 13 March 2016. Accessed 28 November 2018. www.sootoday.com/columns/remember-this/remember-this-the-saultite-who-became-premiere-265098.

– "Remember This? The Story of F.J. Davey." *Sootoday*, 31 July 2016. Anon. www.sootoday.com/columns/remember-this/remember-this-the-story-of-fj-davey-346198/.

– "The Sault Ste Marie Bridge." *Engineering News* 24, no. 42 (18 October 1890): 334–5.

– "Soldier-Candidates and the 1917 Wartime Election." Accessed 16 September 2019. www.greatwaralbum.ca/Great-War-Album/About-the-Great-War/Unrest-on-the-homefront/Soldier-Candidates-and-the-1917-Wartime-Election/.

– "Town of Renfrew." Accessed 3 August 2019. www.renfrew.ca/history-of-renfrew.cfm/.

Baehre, Rainer. "Pauper Emigration to Upper Canada in the 1830s." *Histoire sociale/Social History* 14, no. 28 (November 1981): 339–67.

Barber, Marilyn. "The Ontario Bilingual Schools Issue: Sources of Conflict." *Canadian Historical Review* 47, no. 3 (September 1966): 227–48.

Barranger, Chelsea V. "Shifting Attitudes: Torontonians and their Response to the Great War." *The Graduate History Review* 6, no. 1 (2017): 1–28.

Barrett, Matthew. "Soldier-Candidates and the 1917 Wartime Election." *Active History*, 13 October 2015. Accessed 5 July 2019. http://activehistory.ca/2015/10/soldier-candidates-and-the-1917-wartime-election/#9/.

– "The Undeterred: Lieutenant Colonel Donald Sutherland." Accessed 27 January 2020. https://matthewkbarrett.com/2014/12/01/the-undeterred/.

– "The United Farmer: Lieutenant Colonel Doug Carmichael, DSO, MC, 116th (Ontario County) Battalion," 29 May 2015. Accessed 27 November 2019. https://matthewkbarrett.com/2015/05/29/the-united-farmer/#more-1639/.

Beaulieu, Michael. "The Lakehead and Canada's First Social Democratic Party: The Search for Socialist Unity." *Thunder Bay Historical Museum Society Papers & Records* 39 (2011): 29–54. Accessed 2 July 2019. www.academia.edu/1202377/_The_Lakehead_and_Canadas_First_Social_Democratic_Party_The_Search_for_Socialist_Unity/.

Belcourt, N.A. "French Canada Under Confederation." *Canadian Historical Association Annual Report* 6, no. 1 (1927): 29–38.

Bellamy, Matthew J. "The Canadian Brewing Industry's Response to Prohibition, 1874–1920." *Journal of the Brewery History Society* 132 (2009): 2–17.

Belyea, Andrew. "The Reality of the Flu: Kingston's United Effort Against the Spanish Influenza." Accessed 10 June 2019; https://museumofhealthcare.blog/the-reality-of-the-flu-kingstons-united-effort-against-the-spanish-influenza/

Bercuson, D.J. "Organized Labour and the Imperial Munitions Board." *Relations Industrielles/Industrial Relations* 28, no. 3 (1973): 601–16.

Black, Karen. "How Ontarians Came Together to Fight the Spanish Flu." *TVO*, 3 April 2020. Accessed 17 July 2020. www.tvo.org/article/how-ontarians-came-together-to-fight-the-spanish-flu/.

Bliss, Michael. "Flavelle, Sir Joseph Wesley." In *Dictionary of Canadian Biography*, Vol. 16. University of Toronto/Université Laval, 2003. Accessed 22 December 2018. www.biographi.ca/en/bio/flavelle_joseph_wesley_16E.html/.

Bogdanski, Bryan E.C. "The Rise and Fall of the Canadian Pulp and Paper Sector." *The Forestry Chronicle* 90, no. 6 (November/December 2014): 786–7. Accessed 2 April 2019. https://pubs.cif-ifc.org/doi/pdf/10.5558/tfc2014-151/.

Bowley, Patricia. "Farm Forestry in Agricultural Southern Ontario, ca. 1850–1940: Evolving Strategies in the Management and Conservation of Forests, Soils and Water on Private Lands." *Scientia Canadensis* 38, no. 1 (2015): 22–49. Accessed 20 April 2020. https://www.erudit.org/en/journals/scientia/2015-v38-n1-scientia02451/1036041ar/.

Bradburn, Jamie. "'Don't Worry and Don't Work': When Toronto Workers Went on Strike in 1919." *TVO*. Accessed 20 March 2021. www.tvo.org/article/dont-worry-and-dont-work-when-toronto-workers-went-on-strike-in-1919.

– "The Saga of Chorley Park." *Torontoist*, 9 August 2008. Accessed 19 February 2020. https://torontoist.com/2008/08/historicist/.

– "The Violence and Racism of Peace Day, 1919." *TVO Current Affairs*, 19 July 1919. Accessed 16 February 2020. www.tvo.org/article/the-violence-and-racism-of-peace-day-1919/.

– "When the Spanish Flu Came to Ontario." Accessed 10 June 2019. www.tvo.org/article/when-the-spanish-flu-came-to-ontario/.

– "The Year the UFOs Came to Power in Ontario." *TVO Current Affairs*, 3 May 2018. Accessed 9 January 2019. www.tvo.org/article/the-year-the-ufos-came-to-power-in-ontario/.

Brady, A. "The Ontario Hydro-Electric Power Commission." *Canadian Journal of Economics and Political Science* 2, no. 3 (August 1936): 331–53.

Bray, R. Matthew. "Cochrane, Francis." In *Dictionary of Canadian Biography*, Vol. 14. University of Toronto/Université Laval, 2003. Accessed 2 December 2018. www.biographi.ca/en/bio/cochrane_francis_14E.html/.

– "'Fighting as an Ally': The English-Canadian Patriotic Response to the Great War." *Canadian Historical Review* 61, no. 2 (1980): 141–68.

– "Lyon, Robert Adam." In *Dictionary of Canadian Biography*, Vol. 13. University of Toronto/ Université Laval, 2003. Accessed 3 December 2018. www.biographi.ca/en/bio/lyon_robert_adam_13E.html/.

– "1910–1920." In *Sudbury: Rail Town to Regional Capital*, edited by C.M. Wallace and Ashley Thomson, 86–112. Toronto, 1993.

Brookfield, Tarah. "Women's Suffrage in Ontario." *The Canadian Encyclopedia*. Accessed 5 March 2020. www.thecanadianencyclopedia.ca/en/article/womens-suffrage-in-ontario/.

Brown, Robert Craig. "Campbell, Archibald William." In *Dictionary of Canadian Biography*, Vol. 15. University of Toronto/Université Laval, 2003a. Accessed 9 June 2022. www.biographi.ca/en/bio/campbell_archibald_william_15E.html/.

– "Reid, John Dowsley." In *Dictionary of Canadian Biography*, Vol. 15. University of Toronto/Université Laval, 2003b. Accessed 14 February 2019. www.biographi.ca/en/bio/reid_john_dowsley_15E.html/.

Canadian War Museum. "The Internment of Ukrainian Canadians." Accessed 8 August 2019. www.warmuseum.ca/firstworldwar/history/life-at-home-during-the-war/enemy-aliens/the-internment-of-ukrainian-canadians/.

Carter-Edwards, Dennis. "Promoting a 'Unity of Feeling': The Rebellions of 1837/1838 and the Peterborough Region." *Ontario History* 101, no. 2 (Autumn 2009): 165–86.

Cecillon, Jack D. "Early Struggles for Bilingual Schools and the French Language in the Windsor Border Region 1851–1910." *Historical Studies in Education* 21, no. 1 (2009): 66–84.

– "Turbulent Times in the Diocese of London: Bishop Fallon and the French-Language Controversy, 1910–18." *Ontario History* 87, no. 4 (1995): 369–95.

Champniss, Kim Clarke. "Interned in Niagara Falls." Accessed 8 August 2019. https://kimchampniss.wordpress.com/2017/11/07/interned-in-niagara-falls/.

Clippingdale, Richard T. "Willison, Sir John Stephen." In *Dictionary of Canadian Biography*, Vol. 15. University of Toronto/Université Laval, 2003. Accessed 11 February 2019. www.biographi.ca/en/bio/willison_john_stephen_15E.html/.

Comeau, Gayle M. "Hanna, William John." In *Dictionary of Canadian Biography*, Vol. 14. University of Toronto/Université Laval, 2003. Accessed 24 December 2018. www.biographi.ca/en/bio/hanna_william_john_14E.html/.

Cook, Ramsay. "Dafoe, Laurier and the Formation of Union Government." *Canadian Historical Review* 42, no. 3 (September 1961): 185–208.

Cook, Tim. "'More a Medicine than a Beverage': 'Demon Rum' and the Canadian Trench Soldier of the First World War." *Canadian Military History* 9, no. 1 (Winter 2000): 6–22.

– "Documenting War and Forging Reputations: Sir Max Aitken and the Canadian War Records Office in the First World War 1." *War in History* 10, no. 3 (2003): 265–95.

– "'Our First Duty is to Win, at Any Cost': Sir Robert Borden during the Great War." *Journal of Military and Strategic Studies* 13, no. 3 (Spring 2011): 1–24.

Cozzi, Sarah. "'When You're a Long, Long Way from Home:' The Establishment of Canadian-Only Social Clubs for CEF Soldiers in London, 1915–1919." *Canadian Military History* 20, no. 1 (Winter 2011): 45–60.

Crerar, Adam. "Ontario in the Great War." In *Canada and the First World War*, edited by David Mackenzie, 230–71. Toronto, 2018.

Cronin, Fergus. "Adam Beck's Fight for Public Hydro." *Maclean's*, 15 June 1954, 29–30, 32, 35–6, 51–9.

Cross, Michael S. "The Shiners' War: Social Violence in the Ottawa Valley in the 1830s." *Canadian Historical Review* 54, no. 1 (March 1973): 1–26.

Cuff, Robert. "The Conservative Party Machine and the Election of 1911 in Ontario." *Ontario History* 57, no. 3 (September 1965): 149–56.

Cummings, Don, Serge Occhietti, and Maude-Emmanuelle Lambert. "Grosse Île and the Irish Memorial National Historic Site." *The Canadian Encyclopedia*. Accessed 12 June 2021. www.thecanadianencyclopedia.ca/en/article/la-grosse-ile.

Dirks, Patricia. "Warburton, George Augustus." In *Dictionary of Canadian Biography*, Vol. 15. University of Toronto/Université Laval, 2003. Accessed 22 December 2018. https://www.biographi.ca/en/bio/warburton_george_augustus_15E.html

Djebabla, Mourad. "Fight the Huns with Food: Mobilizing Canadian Civilians for the War Effort During the Great War, 1914–1918." In *World War 1 and Propaganda*, edited by Troy Paddock, 68–88. London: Brill, 2014.

Dupuis, Michel. "A Unique Career in Canadian Journalism: William R. Plewman of the Toronto Daily Star." *Canadian Journal of Media Studies* 2, no. 1 (April 2007): 109–29.

Durham, Brook. "'The Place is a Prison, and You Can't Change It': Rehabilitation, Retraining, and Soldiers' Re-Establishment at Speedwell Military Hospital, Guelph, 1911–1921." *Ontario History* 109, no. 2 (Fall 2017): 184–212.

Dutil, Patrice A. "Against Isolationism: Napoléon Belcourt, French Canada, and 'La Grande Guerre'." In *Canada and the First World War*, edited by David Mackenzie, 96–137. Toronto, 2018.

Evans, Margaret, and R.W. Irwin. "Government Tractors in Ontario, 1917 and 1918." *Ontario History* 61, no. 2 (June 1969): 99–109.

Farquharson, R.A. "The Rise and Fall of the UFO." *Saturday Night* 67 (21 June 1952): 14.

– "When Sir Adam Beck Tried to be Premier." *Saturday Night* 67 (14 June 1952): 36.

Farrell, John K.A. "Michael Francis Fallon Bishop of London Ontario, Canada 1909–1931: The Man and His Controversies." *Canadian Catholic Historical Association Study Sessions* 35 (1968): 73–90.

Ferns, Thomas H. "Hendrie, Sir John Strathearn." In *Dictionary of Canadian Biography*, Vol. 15. University of Toronto/Université Laval, 2003. Accessed 19 January 2019. www.biographi.ca/en/bio/hendrie_john_strathearn_15E.html/.

Ferry, Darren. "'Severing the Connections in a Complex Community': The Grange, the Patrons of Industry, and the Construction/Contestation of a Late 19th-Century Agrarian Identity in Ontario." *Labour/Le Travail* 54 (2004): 9–47.

Fine, Sean. "Crown Broke 1850 Land Treaties with First Nations, Ontario Court of Appeals Rules." *The Globe and Mail*, 8 November 2021. Accessed 25 May 2022. www.theglobeandmail.com/canada/article-crown-broke-1850-land-treaties-with-first-nations-ontario-court-of/#:~:text=Ontario's%20highest%20court%20has%20ruled,northern%20part%20of%20the%20province/.

– "First Nations Seek Billions for Broken Treaty, But Ontario Says It Owes No Money." *The Globe and Mail*, 2 February 2023. Accessed 15 May 2023. www.theglobeandmail.com/canada/article-ontario-judge-weighs-how-many-billions-governments-owe-over-173-year/.

Finn, Billy. "Bram Stoker's Donegal Roots." *Donegal Annual: Journal of the Donegal Historical Society* 57 (2005): 66. Accessed 13 June 2021. http://www.coolfinbooks.ie/Periodicals/Donegal%20Annual/6072.html

Freeman, Neil B. "Turn-of-the Century Intervention: Ontario Hydro and Its Government: Creating the Hydro-Electric Power Commission of Ontario, 1906." *Ontario History* 84, no. 3 (September 1992): 171–94.

Gadsby, H.F. "The Inside Story of the Union." *Maclean's Magazine* (1 December 1917): 41–3, 80–1.

Girard, Philip. "That's History: State Trials During Turbulent Times." *Lawtimesnews*, 21 December 2015. Accessed 12 March 2020. www.lawtimesnews.com/archive/thats-history-state-trials-during-turbulent-times/261983/.

Grant, John Webster. "Hunter, John Edwin." In *Dictionary of Canadian Biography*, vol. 14, University of Toronto/Université Laval, 2003. Accessed 11 January 2020. www.biographi.ca/en/bio/hunter_john_edwin_14E.html/.

Griezic, F.J.K. "Power to the People: The Beginning of Agrarian Revolt in Ontario, the Manitoulin By-Election, October 24, 1918." *Ontario History* 69, no. 1 (March 1977): 33–54.

Grundy, John. "The Employment Service in Early Twentieth Century Ontario." Unpublished Paper, Undated: 3. Accessed 2 January 2019. https://cpsa-acsp.ca/papers-2008/Grundy.pdf/.

Hall, David J. "Sifton, Sir Clifford." In *Dictionary of Canadian Biography*, Vol. 15. University of Toronto/Université Laval, 2003. Accessed 22 April 2019. www.biographi.ca/en/bio/sifton_clifford_15E.html/.

Heron, Craig. "Baillie, Sir Frank Wilton." In *Dictionary of Canadian Biography*, Vol. 15. University of Toronto/Université Laval, 2003. Accessed 5 August 2019. www.biographi.ca/en/bio/baillie_frank_wilton_15E.html.

– "National Contours, Solidarity and Fragmentation." In *The Workers' Revolt in Canada 1917–1925*, edited by Craig Heron, 268–304. Toronto: University of Toronto Press, 1998.

– "Studholme, Allan." In *Dictionary of Canadian Biography*, Vol. 14. University of Toronto/Université Laval, 2003. Accessed 11 January 2019. www.biographi.ca/en/bio/studholme_allan_14E.html/.

Heron, Craig, and Myer Siemiatycki. "The Great War, the State, and Working-Class Canada." In *The Workers' Revolt in Canada 1917–1925*, edited by Craig Heron, 11–42. Toronto: University of Toronto Press, 1998.

Hicks. Alexander Hicks. "Social Democratic Corporatism and Economic Growth." *The Journal of Politics* 50, no. 3 (August 1988): 677–704. Accessed 25 January 2020. https://doi.org/10.2307/2131463/.

Hodgins, Bruce W., Jamie Benidickson, and Peter Gillis. "The Ontario and Quebec Experiments In Forest Reserves 1883–1930." *Journal of Forest History* 26, no. 1 (January 1982): 20–33. Accessed 9 April 2019. https://www.jstor.org/stable/4004566/.

Hoffman, David. "Intra-Party Democracy: A Case Study." *Canadian Journal of Economics and Political Science* 27, no. 2 (May 1961): 223–35.

Hogan, Brian F. "The Guelph Novitiate Raid: Conscription, Censorship and Bigotry During the Great War." *Canadian Catholic Historical Association Study Sessions* 45 (1978): 57–80.

Humphries, Charles W. "Mackenzie King Looks at Two Elections." *Ontario History* 56, no. 3 (September 1964): 203–6.

– "The Gamey Affair." *Ontario History* 59, no. 2 (June 1967a): 101–9.

– "The Sources of Ontario 'Progressive' Conservatism, 1900–1914." *Canadian Historical Association Historical Papers* 2, no. 1 (1967b): 118–29.

– "Whitney, Sir James Pliny." In *Dictionary of Canadian Biography*, Vol. 14. University of Toronto/Université Laval, 2003. Accessed 13 June 2019. www.biographi.ca/en/bio/whitney_james_pliny_14E.html/.

Humphries, Mark Osborneff. "In Death's Shadow: The 1918–19 Influence Pandemic and War in Canada." In *Canada 1919: A Nation Shaped by War*, edited by Tim Cook and J.L. Granatstein, 135–47. Vancouver, 2020.

Imperial War Museum. "Energite Explosives Company Ltd." Accessed 3 August 2019. www.iwm.org.uk/collections/item/object/205220663/.

Jenkins, William. "Homeland Crisis and Local Ethnicity: The Toronto Irish and the Cartoons of the *Evening Telegram* 1910–1914." *Urban History Review* 38, no. 2 (Spring 2010): 48–63.

Johnston, Charles M. "Drury, Charles Alfred." In *Dictionary of Canadian Biography*, Vol. 13. University of Toronto/Université Laval, 2003. Accessed 12 January 2019. www.biographi.ca/en/bio/drury_charles_alfred_13E.html/.

Johnston, Richard, and Michael B. Percy. "Reciprocity, Imperial Sentiment, and Party Politics in the 1911 Election." *Canadian Journal of Political Science* 13, no. 4 (December 1980): 711–29.

Karn, Sara. "'The Town's Gone Wild': Sounds of Victory in Toronto, 11 November 1918." *Active History*, 9 November 2018. Accessed 25 March 2020. http://activehistory.ca/2018/11/the-towns-gone-wild-sounds-of-victory-in-toronto-11-november-1918/.

Kealey, Gregory S. "1919: The Canadian Labour Revolt." *Labour/Le Travail* 13 (Spring 1984): 11–44.

Kerr, Janet B. "Mowat's 1894 Campaign." *Ontario History* 55, no. 1 (March 1963): 1–13.

Keshen, Jeff. "A Timid Transformation: The First World War's Legacy on Canada's Federal Government." In *Canada 1919: A Nation Shaped by War*, edited by Tim Cook and J.L. Granatstein, 204–19. Vancouver: UBC Press, 2020.

Kirkconnell, Watson. "When We Locked Up Fritz." *Maclean's Magazine* 33, no. 16 (1 September 1920): 20–1, 57–63.

– "Kapuskasing: An Historical Sketch." *Bulletin of the Departments of History and Political and Economic Science in Queen's University* 38 (January 1921): 1–15.

Accessed 31 May 2019. https://archive.org/details/kapuskasinghisto00kirkuoft/page/14/.

Kordan, Bohdan, and S. Kordan. "'They Will Be Dangerous': Security and the Control of Enemy Aliens in Canada, 1914." In *Canadian State Trials*, edited by Barry Wright, Eric Tucker, and Susan Binnie, Vol. 4, 42–70. Toronto, 2018.

– "First World Internment in Canada: Enemy Aliens and the Blurring of the Mililtary/Civilian Distinction." *Canadian Military History* 29, no. 2 (2020): 6–11.

Krats, Peter. "'A Commodity So Closely Aligned to Armageddon': The Sudbury Region in Wartime and Aftermath." *The Northern Review* 44 (2017): 371–414.

Kuhlberg, Mark. "Little, James Arthur." In *Dictionary of Canadian Biography*, Vol. 16. University of Toronto/Université Laval, 2003. Accessed 28 March 2019. www.biographi.ca/en/bio/little_james_arthur_16E.html/.

– "'Eyes Wide Open': E. W. Backus and the Pitfalls of Investing in Ontario's Pulp and Paper Industry, 1902–1932." *Journal of the Canadian Historical Association* 16, no. 1 (2005): 201–33.

– "'Deliberately and Properly Framed': The Origins and Early History of the Port Arthur Pulp Company, 1916–1921." *Thunder Bay Historical Museum Society Papers and Records* 44 (2016): 29–41.

– "Natural Potential, Artificial Restraint: The Dryden Paper Company and the Fetters on Adopting Technological Innovation in a Canadian Pulp and Paper Sector, 1900–1950." In *Technological Transformation in the Global Pulp and Paper Industry 1800–2018: Comparative Perspectives*, edited by Timo Sarkka, Miquel Gutierrez-Poch, and Mark Kuhlberg, 138–60. Cham, 2018.

Lackenbauer, P. Whitney, and Nikolas Gardner. "Citizen-Soldiers as 'Liminaries': The CEF Soldier Riots of 1916 Reconsidered." In *Canadian Military History Since the 17th Century*, edited by Yves Tremblay, 155–65. Ottawa, 2013.

Leacock, Stephen. "Social Control for Equal Opportunity." *New York Times*, 12 October 1919, 89–90; reprinted in Stephen Leacock. *The Unsolved Riddle of Social Justice*, 127–8. New York, 1920.

Maclean, J.B. "Germany Must Pay Canada's War Bill." *Maclean's Magazine* 31, no. 13 (November 1918a): 46–7, 72–47A.

– "Now That the War is Over." *Maclean's Magazine* 31, no. 14 (December 1918b): 7, 124–5.

Marble, Allan. "Halifax Was Plunged into Gloom: The Impact of the Spanish Influenza Pandemic on Nova Scotia." *Royal Nova Scotia Historical Society Journal* 22 (2019): 8–31.

McCallum, Margaret E. "Keeping Women in Their Place: The Minimum Wage in Canada, 1910–25." *Labour/Le Travail* 17, no. 1 (Spring 1986): 29–56.

McClure, Shirley McClure. "Sir William Hearst." In *The Bruce County Historical Society Yearbook 1999*, edited by Shirley McClure, 24. Southampton, 1999.

McCullough, John W.S. "The Control of Influenza in Ontario." *Canadian Medical Association Journal* 8, no. 12 (December 1918): 1084–6.

McDowell, Duncan. "Clergue, Francis Hector." In *Dictionary of Canadian Biography*, Vol. 16. University of Toronto/Université Laval, 2003. Accessed 21 November 2018. www.biographi.ca/en/bio/clergue_francis_hector_16E.html/.

McMahon, Patricia. "Conscription and the Courts: The Case of George Edwin Gray, 1918." In *Security, Dissent, and the Limits of Toleration in War and Peace, 1914–1939*, edited by Barry Wright, Eric Tucker and Susan Binnie, 132–71. Toronto, 2015.

McNab, David T. "The Administration of Treaty 3: The Location of the Boundaries of Treaty 3 Indian Reserves in Ontario, 1873–1916." In *As Long as the Sun Shines and the Water Flows: A Reader in Canadian Native Studies*, edited by Ian A.L. Getty and Antoine S. Lussier, 145–57. Vancouver: UBC Press, 1983.

Mentzer, Marc S. "Irrational Optimism in a Declining Industry: Sir Adam Beck's Interurban Railway Proposal." *Management & Organizational History* 1, no. 4 (2006): 371–84.

Miller, J.R. *Skyscrapers Hide the Heavens: A History of Indian-White Relations in Canada*. Toronto: University of Toronto Press, 1989.

Milligan, Ian. "Sedition in Wartime Ontario: The Trials and Imprisonment of Isaac Bainbridge, 1917–1918." *Ontario History* 100, no. 2 (Autumn 2008): 150–77.

Moir, John S. "Canadian Protestant Reaction to the *Ne Temere Decree*." *Canadian Catholic Historical Association Study Sessions* 48 (1981): 78–90.

Moir, Michael. "Toronto's Waterfront at War, 1914–1918." *Archivaria* 28 (Summer 1989): 126–40.

Molinaro, Dennis G. "Section 98: The Trial of Rex v. Buck et al and the 'State of Exception' in Canada, 1919–36." In *Security, Dissent, and the Limits of Toleration in War and Peace, 1914–1939*, edited by Barry Wright, Eric Tucker, and Susan Binnie, 324–63. Toronto: University of Toronto Press, 2015.

Morton, Desmond. "'Junior But Sovereign Allies': The Transformation of the Canadian Expeditionary Force, 1914–1918." *Journal of Imperial and Commonwealth Studies* 8, no. 1 (1979): 56–67.

Morton, Desmond, and Glenn Wright. "The Bonus Campaign, 1919–1921: Veterans and the Campaign for Re-Establishment." *Canadian Historical Review* 64, no. 2 (June 1983): 147–67.

Munro, J.K. "Ottawa is Ready for the Worst." *Maclean's*, 1 December 1919, 24–5, 108.

Nash-Chambers, Debra. "Sectarianism and Scandal: The 1918 Novitiate Raid in Guelph Township." *Wellington County History* 19 (2006): 4–16.

Naylor, James. “Ontario Workers and the Decline of Labourism.” In *Patterns of the Past: Interpreting Ontario's History*, edited by Roger Hall, William Westfall, and Laurel Sefton MacDowell, 278–300. Toronto: Dundurn, 1988.

– “Southern Ontario: Striking at the Ballot Box.” In *The Workers' Revolt in Canada 1917–1925*, edited by Craig Heron, 144–75. Toronto: University of Toronto Press, 1998.

Nelles, H.V. “Beck, Sir Adam Beck.” In *Dictionary of Canadian Biography*, Vol. 15. University of Toronto/Université Laval, 2003. Accessed 21 November 2018. www.biographi.ca/en/bio/beck_adam_15E.html/.

– “Sir Adam Beck.” In *Canada's Entrepreneurs From the Fur Trade to the 1929 Stock Market Crash*, edited by J. Andrew Ross and Andrew D. Smith, 371–406. Toronto: University of Toronto Press, 2011.

Nicholson, Karen. “Rogers, Robert.” In *Dictionary of Canadian Biography*, Vol. 16. University of Toronto/Université Laval, 2003. Accessed 25 February 2019. www.biographi.ca/en/bio/rogers_robert_16E.html/.

Oliver, Peter. “Tory Hatchet Man: Howard Ferguson on the Whitney Backbenches.” *Ontario History* 61, no. 3 (September 1969): 121–35.

– “Howard Ferguson, the Timber Scandal and the Leadership of the Ontario Conservative Party.” *Ontario History* 62, no. 3 (September 1970): 163–78. Revised version in Peter Oliver, *Public & Private Persons*, 44–63. Toronto: Clarke, Irwin & Company, 1975.

– “Sir William Hearst and the Collapse of the Ontario Conservative Party.” *Canadian Historical Review* 53, no. 1 (March 1972a): 21–50. Revised version in Peter Oliver. *Public & Private Persons*, 16–43. Toronto: Clarke, Irwin & Company, 1975.

– “The Resolution of the Ontario Bilingual Schools Crisis, 1919–1929.” *Journal of Canadian Studies* 7, no. 1 (February 1972b): 22–45. Revised version in Peter Oliver. *Public & Private Persons*, 92–124. Toronto: Clarke, Irwin & Company, 1975.

Ontario Heritage Foundation. “The Warriors Day Parade.” Accessed 25 March 2020. http://www.thewarriorsdayparade.ca/Parade%20History-Historical%20Background.htm/.

Panayotidis, E. Lisa. “Mavor, James.” In *Dictionary of Canadian Biography*, Vol. 15. University of Toronto/Université Laval, 2003. Accessed 23 January 2019. www.biographi.ca/en/bio/mavor_james_15E.html/.

Piva, Michael J. “Workers and Tories: The Collapse of the Conservative Party in Urban Ontario, 1908–1919.” *Urban History Review* 3, no. 76 (February 1977): 23–39.

– “The Toronto District Labour Council and Independent Political Action: Factionalism and Frustration, 1900–192.” *Labour/Le Travailleur* 4 (1979): 115–30.

Power, Michael. "The Mitred Warrior: A Critical Reassessment of Bishop Michael Francis Fallon, 1867–1931." *Catholic Insight* 8, no. 3 (2000): 18–26.

– "Kennedy, William Costello." In *Dictionary of Canadian Biography*, Vol. 15. University of Toronto/Université Laval, 2003. Accessed 11 February 2020. www.biographi.ca/en/bio/kennedy_william_costello_15E.html/.

Prang, Margaret E. "Clerics, Politicians, and the Bilingual Schools Issue in Ontario: 1910–1917." *Canadian Historical Review* 41, no. 4 (December 1960): 281–307.

– "Rowell, Newton Wesley." In *Dictionary of Canadian Biography*, Vol. 17. University of Toronto/Université Laval, 2003. Accessed 15 February 2019. www.biographi.ca/en/bio/rowell_newton_wesley_17E.html/.

Quiney, Linda J. "'Filling the Gaps': Canadian Voluntary Nurses, the 1917 Halifax Explosion, and the Influenza Epidemic of 1918." *Canadian Bulletin of Medical History* 29, no. 2 (2003): 351–74.

– "'Rendering Valuable Service': The Politics of Nursing During the 1918–19 influenza Crisis." In *Epidemic Encounters: Influenza, Society, and Culture in Canada, 1918–20*, edited by Magda Fahrni and Esyllt W. Jones, 48–69. Vancouver, 2012.

Reynolds, Mark. "The Guelph Raid: When Police Routed Alleged World War I Draft Dodgers – Including a Cabinet Minister's Son – In a Catholic Seminary in the Heart of Orange Ontario, a National Scandal Erupted." *The Beaver*, 1 February 2002, 25–30.

Risk, R.C.B. "'This Nuisance of Litigation': The Origins of Workers' Compensation in Ontario." In *Essays in the History of Canadian Law*, edited by David H. Flaherty, Vol. 2, 418–91. Toronto, 2012.

Roberston, J.S. "The Canadian Lumber Industry." *The Engineering Magazine* 10, no. 1 (October 1895): 17–32.

Robin, Martin. "Registration, Conscription and Independent Labour Politics 1916–1917." *Canadian Historical Review* 47, no. 2 (June 1966): 101–18.

Sautter, Udo. "The Origin of the Employment Service of Canada, 1900–1920." *Labour/Le Travailleur* 6 (Autumn 1980): 89–112.

Scollie, Frederick Brent. "Conmee, James." In *Dictionary of Canadian Biography*, Vol. 14. University of Toronto/Université Laval, 2003. Accessed 3 December 2018. www.biographi.ca/en/bio/conmee_james_14E.html/.

– "The Woman Candidate for the Ontario Legislative Assembly, 1919–1929." *Ontario History* 104, no. 2 (Fall 2012): 1–27.

Sendbueuhler, Matt, and Jason Gilliland. "'… To Produce the Highest Type of Manhood and Womanhood': The Ontario Housing Act, 1919, and a New Suburban Ideal." *Urban History Review* 26, no. 2 (March 1998): 42–55.

Sharman, Kathleen Yolande, and Larry Glassford. "The Appeal of Technical Education in Tough Times: A Comparison of the Toronto and Windsor Experiences, 1890–1930." *Historical Studies in Education* 23, no. 2 (Fall 2011): 54–71.

Sharpe, Chris. "Enlistment in the Canadian Expeditionary Force 1914–1918: A Re-Evaluation." *Canadian Military History* 24, no. 1 (Spring 2015): 17–60.

Sholdice, M. "'Patronage, Like Hamlet's Ghost will not Down!': Ontario's Farmer-Labour Government and Political Patronage, 1919–1923." *Ontario History* 106, no. 2 (Fall 2014): 191–213.

Skelton, O.D. "The Language Issue in Canada." *Queen's Quarterly* 24, no. 4 (April 1917): 460–3.

Smith, Nathan. "Fighting the Alien Problem in a British Country: Returned Soldiers and Anti-Alien Activism in Wartime Canada, 1916–19." In *Other Combatants, Other Fronts: Competing Histories of the First World War*, edited by James Kitchen, Alisa Miller and Laura Rowe, 285–310. Newcastle: Cambridge Scholars Publishing, 2011. Accessed 7 June 2020. www.academia.edu/7203300/Fighting_the_Alien_Problem_in_a_British_Country_Returned_Soldiers_and_Anti_Alien_Activism_in_Wartime_Canada_1916_1919/.

Smith, P.J. "Commission of Conservation." *Canadian Encyclopedia*, 2015. Accessed 6 December 2019. www.thecanadianencyclopedia.ca/en/article/commission-of-conservation/.

Sotiron, Minko. "Maclean, William Findlay." In *Dictionary of Canadian Biography*, Vol. 15. University of Toronto/Université Laval, 2003. Accessed 15 February 2019. www.biographi.ca/en/bio/maclean_william_findlay_15E.html/.

Spragge, Shirley. "A Confluence of Interests: Housing Reform in Toronto, 1900–1920." In *The Usable Urban Past: Planning and Politics in the Modern Canadian City*, edited by Alan F.R. Artibise and Gilbert A. Stelter, 247–67. Montreal/Kingston: McGill-Queen's University Press, 1979.

Stamp, Robert M. "Cody, Henry John." *Canadian Encyclopedia.* Accessed 5 January 2019. www.thecanadianencyclopedia.ca/en/article/henry-john-cody/.

– "Technical Education, the National Policy, and Federal-Provincial Relations in Canadian Education, 1899–1919." *Canadian Historical Review* 52, no. 4 (December 1971): 404–23.

Strange, Carolyn. "Dewart, Hebert Hartley." In *Dictionary of Canadian Biography*, Vol. 15. University of Toronto/Université Laval, 2003. Accessed 21 July 2019. www.biographi.ca/en/bio/dewart_herbert_hartley_15E.html/.

Strong-Boag, Veronica. "Canada's Early Experience with Income Supplements: The Introduction of Mothers' Allowances." *Atlantis: A Women's Studies Journal* 4, no. 2 (Spring 1979): 35–43.

Struthers, James. "'In the Interests of the Children': Mothers' Allowances and the Origins of Income Security in Ontario." In *Social Fabric or Patchwork Quilt: The Development of Social Policy in Canada*, edited by Raymond B. Blake and Jeffrey A. Keshen, 59–87. Toronto: University of Toronto Press, 2006.

Swinger, Jonathan. "Erroneous and Detestable: Seditious Language and the Great War in Western Canada." In *Security, Dissent, and the Limits of*

*Toleration in War and Peace, 1914–1939*, edited by Barry Wright, Eric Ticker, and Susan Binnie, 97–131. Toronto: University of Toronto Press, 2015.

Turley-Ewart, John A., and Robert Craig Brown. "Kemp, Sir Albert Edward." In *Dictionary of Canadian Biography*, Vol. 15. University of Toronto/Université Laval, 2003. Accessed 19 April 2020. www.biographi.ca/en/bio/kemp _albert_edward_15E.html/.

Ungar, Molly Pulver. "Trenholme, Clementina." In *Dictionary of Canadian Biography*, Vol. 14. University of Toronto/Université Laval, 2003. Accessed 3 June 2020. www.biographi.ca/en/bio/trenholme_clementina_14E.html/.

Van Every, Margaret. "Francis Hector Clergue and the Rise of Sault Ste Marie as an Industrial Centre." *Ontario History* 56, no. 3 (September 1964): 191–202.

Vaughan, Gertrude E.M. "The Ontario Model Hospital at Orpington." *The World's Work Magazine*, July 1916. Accessed 15 November 2019. www .scarletfinders.co.uk/162.html.

Wallace, W.S. "L'Avenir de la Race Canadienne-Francais." *Review of Historical Publications Relating to Canada* 15, no. 1 (January 1911a): 100–1.

– "The Future of the French Canadian Race." *The Canadian Magazine* 37, no. 2 (May 1911b): 11–17.

Warsh, Cheryl Krasnick, ed. "'John Barleycorn Must Die': An Introduction to the Social History of Alcohol." In *Drink in Canada: Historical Essays*, edited by Cheryl Krasnick Warsh, 3–26. Montreal, Kingston: McGill-Queen's University Press, 1993.

White, Daryl. "Managing a War Metal: The International Nickel Company's First World War." In *Smart Globalization: The Canadian Business and Economic History Experience*, edited by Andrew Smith and Dimitry Anastakis, 92–107. Toronto: University of Toronto Press, 2014.

Yates, David. "Senator William Proudfoot: 'Country Over Party'." *Goderich Signal Star*, 17 January 2020. Accessed 15 January 2020. www.nugget.ca /opinion/columnists/senator-william-proudfoot-country-over-party/wcm /019a4c99-ac10-475e-ba03-dd21c8cdc1ae/.

Young, W.R. "Conscription, Rural Depopulation, and the Farmers of Ontario, 1917–1919." *Canadian Historical Review* 53, no. 3 (September 1972): 289–320.

### *Miscellaneous*

Interview with Howard Vernon Hearst, 14 January 1963.

Interview with William Irving Hearst, 4 June 1963.

Private Hearst family correspondence, copied to the author by William Irving Hearst.

Private letter from E.C. Drury to Dr. John W. Foster, 19 February 1963.

# Index